CRIC

M000027696

FOREWORD

With events moving so swiftly in the days leading up to my copy deadline, I have had to rewrite some of this Foreword because of the Coronavirus, which, over the last weekend – in sporting terms – accounted for the abandonment of the Formula One Grand Prix in Australia, the domestic football programme and England's tour of Sri Lanka. Things are expected to get worse before they get any better, so I fear that the fixture lists at the back of the book could prove to be a case of wishful thinking, rather than reality. Instead of looking forward, therefore, perhaps this is an opportunity to look back – and happily last summer was undoubtedly one of the greatest for any cricket fan. England's World Cup final Super Over win against New Zealand and their astonishing Ashes Test triumph by one wicket at Headingley will never be forgotten.

This year's cover star, Sussex's Jofra Archer, earns his place after a series of superb performances in both red- and white-ball cricket for England during last summer, and was at the centre of so much of that drama. It is hard to remember the last time a debutant had such an instant impact. The fact that he is the quickest bowler England have possessed in years, that he is unspoiled enough to tie his sweater round his waist and he has a quirky social media presence all add to the sense of real excitement around him. I was fortunate to be at The Oval for his domestic 50-over debut on 8 May, against Pakistan. He may have bowled only four overs before the weather caused the match to be abandoned, but the response from the crowd was palpable. On the field, his team-mates saw what a potent weapon they had; his opponents simply tried to get to the non-striker's end.

And yet that first period of his career – which also featured a stunning spell against Steve Smith and the highest pressure to perform in that Super Over – ended with him suffering a stress fracture to his elbow, and he is currently out of action. This led to some accusations that he had been over-bowled: he sent down slightly more than 400 overs in 22 England appearances in 2019. These criticisms have been dismissed by the England camp, but clearly – if we are to continue to see the best of him in the years ahead (he turns 25 the day before the Annual is published) – he needs to be sensibly managed. And there may be a lesson to be had in how the Australians rotated their pacemen during the Ashes.

But it is not just about him. England travelled to Sri Lanka this month missing not only Archer but also Mark Wood and James Anderson through injury. Had this series gone ahead, England would have played Test cricket on five continents between February 2019 and March 2020. During this summer, England's men should not only face Test series against West Indies and Pakistan, but also white-ball series against Australia and Ireland. The international programme is obviously a highlight, but the players can't be expected to cope with so much of it, and nor – perhaps – can the fans' wallets and purses.

And yet, into that crowded field of international cricket comes a major new domestic commitment, The Hundred. The counties have been given plenty of money to compensate them for this competition. But the Royal London One-Day Cup takes place at the same time, so the format in which we are now world champions will be deprived of some 120 top cricketers who will be finding their way round a format that is played nowhere else. And as for bringing in players that fans wouldn't normally be able to see, the register I have supplied for the teams reveals that just 11 of them are not already playing for a county. Superstar cricketers such as Steve Smith, Mitchell Starc, David Warner and Kane Williamson are welcome arrivals, as is Nepal's Sandeep Lamichhane, but when 90 per cent of these players can be seen in county action anyway, you sense it is not quite the revolution some hoped for.

Ian Marshall
Eastbourne, 16 March 2020

GUIDE TO USING PLAYFAIR

The basic layout of *Playfair* has remained the same for this edition. The Annual is divided into five sections, as follows: Test match cricket, county cricket (including The Hundred), international limited-overs cricket (including the ICC World Cup and Twenty20), other cricket (IPL, Big Bash, Kia Super League, Ireland and women's international cricket), and fixtures for the coming season. Each section, where applicable, begins with a preview of forthcoming events, followed by events during the previous year, then come the player records, and finally the records sections.

Within the players' register, there has been some debate with the county scorers over those who are defined as 'Released/Retired', pointing out that some players are drafted in for a game or two, and may re-appear in the current season, despite not having a contract as the book goes to press. What I try to do is to ensure that everyone who appeared in last season's games is included somewhere – this way, at least, if they do play in 2020 their details are available to readers. Players' Second XI Championship debuts and their England Under-19 Test appearances are given for those under the age of 25.

In the county limited-overs records in the Register, those records denoted by '50ov' cover any limited-overs game of 50 or more overs – in the early days, each team could have as many as 65 overs per innings. The '40ov' section refers to games of 40 or 45 overs per innings.

For both men's and women's IT20 records sections, I have taken the decision to limit the records listed to those games that feature at least one side that has appeared in an official LOI. While I welcome the ICC's efforts to broaden the game's profile, when Uganda's women can beat Mali's by 304 runs (after scoring 314 for two – including a run out), you wonder who really benefits here. Or when Turkey's men set the three lowest scores on record on successive days, do they deserve to be shamed three times over?

ACKNOWLEDGEMENTS AND THANKS

As ever, this book could not have been compiled without the assistance of many people giving so generously of their time and expertise, so I must thank the following for all they have done to help ensure this edition of *Playfair Cricket Annual* could be written:

At the counties, I would like to thank the following for their help over the last year: Derbyshire – Stephen Martin and John Brown; Durham – Sam Blacklock and William Dobson; Essex – George Haberman and Tony Choat; Glamorgan – Andrew Hignell; Gloucestershire – Lizzie Allen and Adrian Bull; Hampshire – Tim Tremlett and Kevin Baker; Kent – Becca Smith and Lorne Hart; Lancashire – Diana Lloyd and Chris Rimmer; Leicestershire – Dan Nice and Paul Rogers; Middlesex – Steven Fletcher and Don Shelley; Northamptonshire – Tony Kingston; Nottinghamshire – Helen Palmer and Roger Marshall; Somerset – Polly Rhodes; Surrey – Steve Howes and Phil Makepeace; Sussex – Colin Bowley and Graham Irwin; Warwickshire – Keith Cook and Mel Smith; Worcestershire – Carrie Lloyd and Sue Drinkwater; Yorkshire – Cecilia Allen and John Potter.

Thanks to Alan Fordham for the Principal and Second XI Fixtures, Chris Kelly for the first-class umpires and Philip August for the National Counties fixtures. I am very grateful as always to Philip Bailey for providing the first-class and List A career records, and his help in compiling the book.

At Headline, my thanks as ever go to Jonathan Taylor for his support and enthusiasm; Louise Rothwell does a great job in ensuring that finished copies are ready only a few days after I write these words; Rob Chilver kindly looked after the *Playfair* website throughout last summer so it was as up-to-date as possible. John Skermer did a thorough and extremely efficient job in checking the proofs. At Letterpart, the *Playfair* typesetter since 1994, Chris Leggett and Caroline Leggett play a largely unsung but crucial part in the process.

Finally, my thanks go to my family for their patience and support. Daughters Kiri and Sophia have now both reached the age where the attractions of their phones and iPads mean they rarely want to disturb me as the deadline draws close – except for providing a parental taxi service, of course. My wife Sugra made sure I could focus as much as possible on finishing the book as deadline day approached, which was an enormous help. Thank you all.

ENGLAND v WEST INDIES

SERIES RECORDS 1928 to 2018-19

HIGHEST INNINGS TOTALS

England	in England	619-6d		Nottingham	1957
	in West Indies	849		Kingston	1929-30
West Indies	in England	692-8d		The Oval	1995
	in West Indies	751-5d		St John's	2003-04

LOWEST INNINGS TOTALS

England	in England	71		Manchester	1976
	in West Indies	46		Port-of-Spain	1993-94
West Indies	in England	54		Lord's	2000
	in West Indies	47		Kingston	2003-04

HIGHEST MATCH AGGREGATE   1815 for 34 wickets   Kingston   1929-30

LOWEST MATCH AGGREGATE   309 for 29 wickets   Bridgetown   1934-35

HIGHEST INDIVIDUAL INNINGS

England	in England	285*	P.B.H.May	Birmingham	1957
	in West Indies	325	A.Sandham	Kingston	1929-30
West Indies	in England	291	I.V.A.Richards	The Oval	1976
	in West Indies	400*	B.C.Lara	St John's	2003-04

HIGHEST AGGREGATE OF RUNS IN A SERIES

England	in England	506	(av 42.16)	G.P.Thorpe (6 Tests)	1995
	in West Indies	693	(av 115.50)	E.H.Hendren	1929-30
West Indies	in England	829	(av 118.42)	I.V.A.Richards	1976
	in West Indies	798	(av 99.75)	B.C.Lara	1993-94

RECORD WICKET PARTNERSHIPS – ENGLAND

1st	229	A.J.Strauss (142)/A.N.Cook (94)	Bridgetown	2008-09
2nd	291	A.J.Strauss (137)/R.W.T.Key (221)	Lord's	2004
3rd	303	M.A.Atherton (135)/R.A.Smith (175)	St John's	1993-94
4th	411	P.B.H.May (285*)/M.C.Cowdrey (154)	Birmingham	1957
5th	218	P.D.Collingwood (161)/M.J.Prior (131*)	Port-of-Spain	2008-09
6th	205	M.R.Ramprakash (154)/G.P.Thorpe (103)	Bridgetown	1997-98
7th	197	M.J.K.Smith (96)/J.M.Parks (101*)	Port-of-Spain	1959-60
8th	217	T.W.Graveney (165)/J.T.Murray (112)	The Oval	1966
9th	109	G.A.R.Lock (89)/P.I.Pocock (13)	Georgetown	1967-68
10th	128	K.Higgs (63)/J.A.Snow (59*)	The Oval	1966

RECORD WICKET PARTNERSHIPS – WEST INDIES

1st	298	C.G.Greenidge (149)/D.L.Haynes (167)	St John's	1989-90
2nd	287*	C.G.Greenidge (214*)/H.A.Gomes (92*)	Lord's	1984
3rd	338	E.de C.Weekes (206)/F.M.M.Worrell (167)	Port-of-Spain	1953-54
4th	399	G.St A.Sobers (226)/F.M.M.Worrell (197*)	Bridgetown	1959-60
5th	265	S.M.Nurse (137)/G.St A.Sobers (174)	Leeds	1966
6th	282*	B.C.Lara (400*)/R.D.Jacobs (107*)	St John's	2003-04
7th	295*	S.O.Dowrich (116*)/J.O.Holder (202*)	Bridgetown	2018-19
8th	99	C.A.McWatt (54)/J.K.Holt (48*)	Georgetown	1953-54
9th	150	E.A.E.Baptiste (87*)/M.A.Holding (69)	Birmingham	1984
10th	143	D.Ramdin (107*)/T.L.Best (95)	Birmingham	2012

BEST INNINGS BOWLING ANALYSIS

England	in England	8-103	I.T.Botham	Lord's	1984
	in West Indies	8- 53	A.R.C.Fraser	Port-of-Spain	1997-98
West Indies	in England	8- 92	M.A.Holding	The Oval	1976
	in West Indies	8- 45	C.E.L.Ambrose	Bridgetown	1989-90

BEST MATCH BOWLING ANALYSIS

England	in England	12-119	F.S.Trueman	Birmingham	1963
	in West Indies	13-156	A.W.Greig	Port-of-Spain	1973-74
West Indies	in England	14-149	M.A.Holding	The Oval	1976
	in West Indies	11- 84	C.E.L.Ambrose	Port-of-Spain	1993-94

HIGHEST AGGREGATE OF WICKETS IN A SERIES

England	in England	34	(av 17.47)	F.S.Trueman	1963
	in West Indies	27	(av 18.66)	J.A.Snow	1967-68
		27	(av 18.22)	A.R.C.Fraser	1997-98
West Indies	in England	35	(av 12.65)	M.D.Marshall	1988
	in West Indies	30	(av 14.26)	C.E.L.Ambrose	1997-98

RESULTS SUMMARY – ENGLAND v WEST INDIES – IN ENGLAND

	Tests	Series			Lord's			Manchester			The Oval			Nottingham			Birmingham			Leeds			Chester-le-St		
		E	WI	D	E	WI	D	E	WI	D	E	WI	D	E	WI	D	E	WI	D	E	WI	D	E	WI	D
1928	3	3	–	–	1			1			1														
1933	3	2	–	1	1					1	1														
1939	3	1	–	2	1					1			1												
1950	4	1	3	–		1		1				1			1										
1957	5	3	–	2	1						1					1			1	1					
1963	5	1	3	1			1		1			1					1				1				
1966	5	1	3	1			1		1		1				1						1				
1969	3	2	–	1			1	1												1					
1973	3	–	2	1		1						1						1							
1976	5	–	3	2			1		1			1				1					1				
1980	5	–	1	4			1			1			1		1							1			
1984	5	–	5	–		1			1			1						1			1				
1988	5	–	4	1		1			1			1				1					1				
1991	5	2	2	1			1				1				1			1		1					
1995	6	2	2	2	1			1					1			1		1			1				
2000	5	3	1	1	1					1	1							1		1					
2004	4	4	–	–	1			1			1						1								
2007	4	3	–	1			1	1												1			1		
2009	2	2	–	–	1																		1		
2012	3	2	–	1	1									1					1						
2017	3	2	1	–	1												1				1				
86		**34**	**30**	**22**	**10**	**4**	**7**	**6**	**5**	**4**	**7**	**6**	**3**	**1**	**4**	**4**	**3**	**4**	**3**	**5**	**7**	**1**	**2**	**–**	**–**

ENGLAND v WEST INDIES – IN WEST INDIES

	Tests	Series			Bridgetown			Port-of-Spain			Georgetown			Kingston			Antigua*			St George			Gros Islet		
		E	WI	D	E	WI	D	E	WI	D	E	WI	D	E	WI	D	E	WI	D	E	WI	D	E	WI	D
1929-30	4	1	1	2			1	1				1				1									
1934-35	4	1	2	1	1				1				1		1										
1947-48	4	–	2	2			1			1		1			1										
1953-54	5	2	2	1		1				1	1			1	1										
1959-60	5	1	–	4			1	1		1			1			1									
1967-68	5	1	–	4			1	1		1			1			1									
1973-74	5	1	1	3			1	1	1				1			1									
1980-81	4	–	2	2		1			1							1			1						
1985-86	5	–	5	–		1			2						1			1							
1989-90	4	1	2	1		1				1				1				1							
1993-94	5	1	3	1	1				1			1			1				1						
1997-98	6	1	3	2			1	1	1			1				1		1							
2003-04	4	3	–	1	1			1						1					1						
2008-09	5	–	1	4			1			1					1				2						
2015	3	1	1	1		1													1	1					
2018-19	3	1	2	–		1												1					1		
71		**15**	**27**	**29**	**3**	**6**	**7**	**6**	**7**	**6**	**1**	**4**	**4**	**3**	**6**	**6**	**–**	**4**	**6**	**1**	**–**	**–**	**1**	**–**	**–**
Totals	**157**	**49**	**57**	**51**																					

Antigua venues: St John's 1980-81 to 2008-09; Sir Vivian Richards Stadium, North Sound, 2008-09 to date.

ENGLAND v PAKISTAN

SERIES RECORDS 1954 to 2018
HIGHEST INNINGS TOTALS

England	in England	589-8d		Manchester	2016
	in Pakistan	546-8d		Faisalabad	1983-84
	in UAE	598-9d		Abu Dhabi	2015-16
Pakistan	in England	708		The Oval	1987
	in Pakistan	636-8d		Lahore	2005-06
	in UAE	523-8d		Abu Dhabi	2015-16

LOWEST INNINGS TOTALS

England	in England	130		The Oval	1954
	in Pakistan	130		Lahore	1987-88
	in UAE	72		Abu Dhabi	2011-12
Pakistan	in England	72		Birmingham	2010
	in Pakistan	158		Karachi	2000-01
	in UAE	99		Dubai	2011-12

HIGHEST INDIVIDUAL INNINGS

England	in England	278	D.C.S.Compton	Nottingham	1954
	in Pakistan	205	E.R.Dexter	Karachi	1961-62
	in UAE	263	A.N.Cook	Abu Dhabi	2015-16
Pakistan	in England	274	Zaheer Abbas	Birmingham	1971
	in Pakistan	223	Mohammad Yousuf	Lahore	2005-06
	in UAE	245	Shoaib Malik	Abu Dhabi	2015-16

HIGHEST AGGREGATE OF RUNS IN A SERIES

England	in England	512	(av 73.14)	J.E.Root	2016
	in Pakistan	449	(av 112.25)	D.I.Gower	1983-84
	in UAE	450	(av 90.00)	A.N.Cook	2015-16
Pakistan	in England	631	(av 90.14)	Mohammad Yousuf	2006
	in Pakistan	431	(av 107.75)	Inzamam-ul-Haq	2005-06
	in UAE	380	(av 63.33)	Mohammad Hafeez	2015-16

RECORD WICKET PARTNERSHIPS – ENGLAND

1st	198	G.Pullar (165)/R.W.Barber (86)	Dacca	1961-62
2nd	248	M.C.Cowdrey (182)/E.R.Dexter (172)	The Oval	1962
3rd	267	M.P.Vaughan (120)/G.P.Thorpe (138)	Manchester	2001
4th	233	A.N.Cook (105)/P.D.Collingwood (186)	Lord's	2006
5th	219	P.D.Collingwood (82)/E.J.G.Morgan (130)	Nottingham	2010
6th	166	G.P.Thorpe (118)/C.White (93)	Lahore	2000-01
7th	167	D.I.Gower (152)/V.J.Marks (83)	Faisalabad	1983-84
8th	332	I.J.L.Trott (184)/S.C.J.Broad (169)	Lord's	2010
9th	76	T.W.Graveney (153)/F.S.Trueman (29)	Lord's	1962
10th	79	R.W.Taylor (54)/R.G.D.Willis (28*)	Birmingham	1982

RECORD WICKET PARTNERSHIPS – PAKISTAN

1st	173	Mohsin Khan (104)/Shoaib Mohammad (80)	Lahore	1983-84
2nd	291	Zaheer Abbas (274)/Mushtaq Mohammad (100)	Birmingham	1971
3rd	363	Younus Khan (173)/Mohammad Yousuf (192)	Leeds	2006
4th	322	Javed Miandad (153*)/Salim Malik (165)	Birmingham	1992
5th	248	Shoaib Malik (245)/Asad Shafiq (107)	Abu Dhabi	2015-16
6th	269	Mohammad Yousuf (223)/Kamran Akmal (154)	Lahore	2005-06
7th	112	Asif Mujtaba (51)/Moin Khan (105)	Leeds	1996
8th	130	Hanif Mohammad (187*)/Asif Iqbal (76)	Lord's	1967
9th	190	Asif Iqbal (146)/Intikhab Alam (51)	The Oval	1967
10th	62	Sarfraz Nawaz (53)/Asif Mahmood (4*)	Leeds	1974

BEST INNINGS BOWLING ANALYSIS

England	in England	8-34	I.T.Botham	Lord's	1978
	in Pakistan	7-66	P.H.Edmonds	Karachi	1977-78
	in UAE	6-62	M.S.Panesar	Abu Dhabi	2011-12
Pakistan	in England	7-40	Imran Khan	Leeds	1987
	in Pakistan	9-56	Abdul Qadir	Lahore	1987-88
	in UAE	7-55	Saeed Ajmal	Dubai	2011-12

BEST MATCH BOWLING ANALYSIS

England	in England	13- 71	D.L.Underwood	Lord's	1974
	in Pakistan	11- 83	N.G.B.Cook	Karachi	1983-84
	in UAE	7-149	M.S.Panesar	Dubai	2011-12
Pakistan	in England	12- 99	Fazal Mahmood	The Oval	1954
	in Pakistan	13-101	Abdul Qadir	Lahore	1987-88
	in UAE	10- 97	Saeed Ajmal	Dubai	2011-12

HIGHEST AGGREGATE OF WICKETS IN A SERIES

England	in England	26	(av 16.73)	C.R.Woakes	2016
	in Pakistan	17	(av 24.11)	A.F.Giles	2000-01
	in UAE	14	(av 21.57)	M.S.Panesar	2011-12
Pakistan	in England	22	(av 25.31)	Waqar Younis	1992
	in Pakistan	30	(av 14.56)	Abdul Qadir	1987-88
	in UAE	24	(av 14.70)	Saeed Ajmal	2011-12

RESULTS SUMMARY – ENGLAND v PAKISTAN – IN ENGLAND

	Tests	Series E	P	D	Lord's E	P	D	Nottingham E	P	D	Manchester E	P	D	The Oval E	P	D	Birmingham E	P	D	Leeds E	P	D
1954	4	1	1	2	–	–	1	1	–	–	–	1	–	1	–	–	–	–	–	–	–	–
1962	5	4	–	1	1	–	–	1	–	–	1	–	–	1	–	–	–	–	–	–	–
1967	3	2	–	1	–	–	1	1	–	–	–	–	–	1	–	–	1	–	–	–	–
1971	3	1	–	2	–	–	1	–	–	–	–	–	1	–	–	–	–	–	1	–	–
1974	3	–	–	3	–	–	1	–	–	–	–	–	–	–	–	–	–	1	–	–	1
1978	3	2	–	1	1	–	–	–	–	–	–	–	–	–	–	1	–	–	1	–	–
1982	3	2	1	–	1	–	–	–	–	–	1	–	–	–	–	–	–	–	1	–	–
1987	5	–	1	4	–	–	1	–	–	1	–	–	1	–	1	–	–	–	1	–	–
1992	5	1	2	2	–	1	–	–	–	1	–	1	–	–	–	1	1	–	–	1	–
1996	3	–	2	1	–	1	–	–	–	–	–	–	1	–	1	–	–	–	1	–	–
2001	2	1	1	–	1	–	–	–	–	–	–	–	–	–	1	–	–	–	1	–	–
2006	4	3	–	1	–	–	1	–	–	–	1	–	–	1	–	–	–	–	1	–	–
2010	4	3	1	–	1	–	–	–	–	–	–	–	–	1	–	–	–	–	1	1	–
2016	4	2	2	–	–	1	–	1	–	–	–	–	–	1	–	–	–	–	–	–	1
2018	2	1	1	–	1	–	–	–	–	–	–	–	–	–	–	–	–	–	1	–	–
	53	23	12	18	4	5	6	3	–	1	2	1	3	3	5	2	5	–	3	6	1	3

ENGLAND v PAKISTAN – IN PAKISTAN

	Tests	Series E	P	D	Lahore E	P	D	Dacca E	P	D	Karachi E	P	D	Hyderabad E	P	D	Faisalabad E	P	D	Multan E	P	D
1961-62	3	1	–	2	1	–	–	–	–	1	–	–	1	–	–	–	–	–	–	–	–	–
1968-69	3	–	–	3	–	1	–	1	–	–	1	–	–	–	–	–	–	–	–	–	–
1972-73	3	–	–	3	–	–	1	–	–	1	–	–	1	–	–	–	–	–	–	–	–
1977-78	3	–	–	3	–	–	1	–	–	1	–	–	1	–	–	–	–	–	–	–	–
1983-84	3	–	1	2	–	–	1	–	–	–	–	1	–	–	–	–	–	1	–	–	–
1987-88	3	–	1	2	1	–	–	–	–	–	–	–	1	–	–	–	–	1	–	–	–
2000-01	3	1	–	2	–	–	1	–	–	1	–	–	1	–	–	–	–	–	–	–	–
2005-06	3	–	2	1	–	1	–	–	–	–	–	–	1	–	–	–	–	1	–	–	–
	24	2	4	18	2	1	5	1	–	5	1	1	5	–	–	2	–	–	4	–	1	–

ENGLAND v PAKISTAN – IN UNITED ARAB EMIRATES

	Tests	Series E	P	D	Dubai E	P	D	Abu Dhabi (SZ) E	P	D	Sharjah E	P	D
2011-12	3	–	3	–	–	2	–	–	1	–	–	–	–
2015-16	3	–	2	1	–	1	–	–	–	1	–	1	–
	6	–	5	1	–	3	–	–	1	1	–	1	–
Totals	83	25	21	37									

TOURING TEAMS REGISTER 2020

Neither West Indies nor Pakistan had selected their 2020 touring teams at the time of going to press. The following players, who had represented those teams in Test matches since 6 December 2018, were still available for selection:

WEST INDIES

Full Names	Birthdate	Birthplace	Team	Type	F-C Debut
BLACKWOOD, Jermaine	20.11.91	St Elizabeth	Jamaica	RHB/OB	2011-12
BRATHWAITE, Kraigg Clairmonte	01.12.92	St Michael	Barbados	RHB/OB	2008-09
BRAVO, Darren Michael	06.02.89	Santa Cruz	Trinidad & T	LHB/RM	2006-07
BROOKS, Shamarh Shaqad Joshua	01.10.98	St Michael	Barbados	RHB/LB	2006-07
CAMPBELL, John Dillon	21.09.93	St James	Jamaica	LHB/OB	2013-14
CHASE, Roston Lamar	22.03.92	Christ Church	Barbados	RHB/OB	2010-11
CORNWALL, Rahkeem Rashawn Shane	01.02.93	Antigua	Leeward Is	RHB/OB	2014-15
DOWRICH, Shane Omari	30.10.91	St James	Barbados	RHB/WK	2009-10
GABRIEL, Shannon Terry	28.04.88	Trinidad	Trinidad	RHB/RFM	2009-10
HAMILTON, Jahmar Neville	22.09.90	Anguilla	Leeward Is	RHB/WK	2007-08
HETMYER, Shimron Odilon	26.12.96	Georgetown	Guyana	LHB/WK	2013-14
HOLDER, Jason Omar	05.11.91	St George	Barbados	RHB/RMF	2008-09
HOPE, Shai Diego	10.11.93	Barbados	Barbados	RHB/WK	2012-13
JOSEPH, Alzarri Shaheim	20.11.96	Antigua	Leeward Is	RHB/RFM	2014-15
PAUL, Keemo Mandela Angus	21.02.98	Guyana	Guyana	RHB/RFM	2016-17
ROACH, Kemar Andre Jamal	30.06.88	St Lucy	Barbados	RHB/RF	2007-08
WARRICAN, Jomel Andrel	20.05.92	Richmond Hill	Barbados	RHB/SLA	2011-12

PAKISTAN

Full Names	Birthdate	Birthplace	Team	Type	F-C Debut
ABID ALI	16.10.87	Lahore	Sindh	RHB/LB	2007-08
ASAD SHAFIQ	28.01.86	Karachi	Sindh	RHB/LB	2007-08
AZHAR ALI	19.02.85	Lahore	Central Punjab	RHB/OB	2001-02
BABAR AZAM	15.10.94	Lahore	Central Punjab	RHB/OB	2010-11
BILAL ASIF	24.09.85	Sialkot	Central Punjab	RHB/OB	2011-12
FAHEEM ASHRAF	16.01.94	Kasur	Central Punjab	RHB/RFM	2013-14
FAKHAR ZAMAN	10.04.90	Mardan	Khyber Pakhtun	LHB/SLA	2012-13
HARIS SOHAIL	09.01.89	Sialkot	Baluchistan	LHB/LM	2007-08
HASAN ALI	07.02.94	Punjab	Central Punjab	RHB/RFM	2013-14
IFTIKHAR AHMED	03.09.90	Peshawar	Baluchistan	RHB/OB	2011-12
IMAM-UL-HAQ	12.12.95	Lahore	Habib Bank	LHB/LB	2012-13
IMRAN KHAN	15.07.87	Lower Dir	Khyber Pakhtun	RHB/RMF	2007-08
MOHAMMAD ABBAS	10.03.90	Sialkot	Southern Punjab	RHB/RMF	2008-09
MOHAMMAD AMIR	13.04.92	Gujar Khan	Sui Southern	LHB/LFM	2008-09
MOHAMMAD HAFEEZ	17.10.90	Sargodha	Sui Northern	RHB/OB	1998-99
MOHAMMAD RIZWAN	01.06.92	Peshawar	Khyber Pakhtun	RHB/RM	2008-09
MUSA KHAN	20.08.00	Islamabad	Sui Northern	RHB/RMF	2018-19
NASEEM SHAH	15.02.03		Central Punjab	RHB/RF	2018-19
SARFRAZ AHMED	22.05.87	Karachi	Sindh	RHB/WK	2005-06
SHADAB KHAN	04.10.98	Mianwali	Sui Northern	RHB/LBG	2016-17
SHAHEEN SHAH AFRIDI	06.04.00	Khyber Agency	Northerrn	LHB/LMF	2017-18
SHAN MASOOD	14.10.89	Kuwait	Southern Punjab	LHB/RMF	2007-08
USMAN SHINWARI	01.05.94	Khyber Agency	Khyber Pakhtun	RHB/LMF	2013-14
YASIR SHAH	02.05.86	Swabi	Baluchistan	RHB/LBG	2001-02

STATISTICAL HIGHLIGHTS IN 2019 TESTS

Including Tests from No. 2335 (Australia v India, 4th Test) and No. 2339 (South Africa v Pakistan, 2nd Test) to No. 2375 (Australia v New Zealand, 2nd Test) and No. 2377 (South Africa v England, 1st Test).

   † = National record

TEAM HIGHLIGHTS
HIGHEST INNINGS TOTALS

715-6d†	New Zealand v Bangladesh	Hamilton
622-7d	India v Australia	Sydney
615-9d	New Zealand v England	Mount Maunganui
601-5d	India v South Africa	Pune

HIGHEST FOURTH INNINGS TOTAL

362-9	England (set 359) v Australia	Leeds

LOWEST INNINGS TOTALS

38†	Ireland v England	Lord's
67	England v Australia	Leeds
77	England v West Indies	Bridgetown
85	England v Ireland	Lord's

HIGHEST MATCH AGGREGATE

1447-31	India (502-7d & 323-4d) v South Africa (431 & 191)	Visakhapatnam

LARGE MARGINS OF VICTORY

Inns & 202 runs	India (497-9d) beat South Africa (162 & 133)	Ranchi
381 runs	West Indies (289 & 415-6d) beat England (77 & 246)	Bridgetown
366 runs	Australia (534-5d & 196-3d) beat Sri Lanka (215 & 149)	Canberra
318 runs	India (297 & 343-7d) beat West Indies (222 & 100)	North Sound

NARROW MARGINS OF VICTORY

1 wkt	Sri Lanka (191 & 304-9) beat South Africa (235 & 259)	Durban

World record 10th-wkt partnership in 4th innings of 78 between M.D.K.J.Perera (153*) and M.V.T.Fernando (6*) to win any f-c match.

1 wkt	England (67 & 362-9) beat Australia (179 & 246)	Leeds

FOUR HUNDREDS IN AN INNINGS

Pakistan (555-3d) v Sri Lanka		Karachi

MOST EXTRAS IN AN INNINGS

	B	LB	W	NB		
54	22	9	21	2	New Zealand (615-9d) v England	Mount Maunganui

BATTING HIGHLIGHTS
TREBLE HUNDREDS

D.A.Warner	335*	Australia v Pakistan	Adelaide

DOUBLE HUNDREDS

M.A.Agarwal (2)	215	India v South Africa	Visakhapatnam
	243	India v Bangladesh	Indore

J.O.Holder	202*	West Indies v England	Bridgetown
V.Kohli	254*	India v South Africa	Pune
J.E.Root	226	England v New Zealand	Hamilton
R.G.Sharma	212	India v South Africa	Ranchi
S.P.D.Smith	211	Australia v England	Manchester
L.R.P.L.Taylor	200	New Zealand v Bangladesh	Wellington
B.J.Watling	205	New Zealand v England	Mount Maunganui
K.S.Williamson	200*	New Zealand v Bangladesh	Hamilton

HUNDRED IN EACH INNINGS OF A MATCH

| R.G.Sharma | 176 | 127 | India v South Africa | Visakhapatnam |
| S.P.D.Smith | 144 | 142 | Australia v England | Birmingham |

MOST SIXES IN AN INNINGS

8	M.A.Agarwal (243)	India v Bangladesh	Indore
8	J.O.Holder (202*)	West Indies v England	Bridgetown
8	B.A.Stokes (135*)	England v Australia	Leeds

150 RUNS OR MORE IN BOUNDARIES IN AN INNINGS

Runs	6s	4s			
162	1	39	D.A.Warner	Australia v Pakistan	Adelaide
160	8	28	M.A.Agarwal	India v Bangladesh	Indore

200 RUNS IN A DAY

| M.A.Agarwal (37*-243) | India v Bangladesh | Indore |

LONG INNINGS (Qualification: 600 mins and/or 400 balls)

Mins	Balls			
636	441	J.E.Root (226)	England v New Zealand	Hamilton
554	418	D.A.Warner (335*)	Australia v Pakistan	Adelaide
667	473	B.J.Watling (205)	New Zealand v England	Mount Maunganui

NOTABLE PARTNERSHIPS

Qualifications: 1st-4th wkts: 250 runs; 5th-6th: 225; 7th: 200; 8th: 175; 9th: 150; 10th: 100.

First Wicket

317	M.A.Agarwal/R.G.Sharma	India v South Africa	Visakhapatnam
278	Shan Masood/Abid Ali	Pakistan v Sri Lanka	Karachi
254	J.A.Raval/T.W.M.Latham	New Zealand v Bangladesh	Hamilton

Second Wicket

| 361 | D.A.Warner/M.Labuschagne | Australia v Pakistan | Adelaide |

Fourth Wicket

| 308 | J.A.Burns/T.M.Head | Australia v Sri Lanka | Canberra |
| 267 | R.G.Sharma/A.M.Rahane | India v South Africa | Ranchi |

Fifth Wicket

| 235 | Soumya Sarkar/Mahmudullah | Bangladesh v New Zealand | Hamilton |
| 225 | V.Kohli/R.A.Jadeja | India v South Africa | Pune |

Seventh Wicket

295*	S.O.Dowrich/J.O.Holder	West Indies v England	Bridgetown
261†	B.J.Watling/M.J.Santner	New Zealand v England	Mount Maunganui
204	R.R.Pant/R.A.Jadeja	India v Australia	Sydney

BOWLING HIGHLIGHTS
EIGHT WICKETS IN AN INNINGS

R.L.Chase	8-60	West Indies v England	Bridgetown

TEN WICKETS IN A MATCH

R.R.S.Cornwall	10-121	West Indies v Afghanistan	Lucknow
P.J.Cummins	10- 62	Australia v Sri Lanka	Brisbane
Rashid Khan †	11-104	Afghanistan v Bangladesh	Chittagong
M.A.Starc	10-100	Australia v Sri Lanka	Canberra

FIVE WICKETS IN AN INNINGS ON DEBUT

L.Ambuldeniya	5-61	Sri Lanka v South Africa	Durban
Hamza Hotak	5-74	Afghanistan v West Indies	Lucknow

HAT-TRICK

J.J.Bumrah	India v West Indies	Kingston

BOWLING UNCHANGED THROUGHOUT AN INNINGS

S.C.J.Broad (8-3-19-4)/C.R.Woakes (7.4-2-17-6)	England v Ireland	Lord's

MOST OVERS IN AN INNINGS

N.M.Lyon	57.2-8-178-4	Australia v India	Sydney

200 RUNS CONCEDED IN AN INNINGS

Mehedi Hasan	49-2-246-2†	Bangladesh v New Zealand	Hamilton
Yasir Shah	48.4-1-205-4	Pakistan v Australia	Brisbane

WICKET-KEEPING HIGHLIGHTS
SIX WICKET-KEEPING DISMISSALS IN AN INNINGS

Q.de Kock	6ct	South Africa v England	Centurion

NINE OR MORE WICKET-KEEPING DISMISSALS IN A MATCH

Sarfraz Ahmed	10ct	Pakistan v South Africa	Johannesburg

NO BYES CONCEDED IN AN INNINGS OF 600

715-6d	Liton Das	Bangladesh v New Zealand	Hamilton
601-5d	Q.de Kock	South Africa v India	Pune

FIELDING HIGHLIGHTS
FOUR CATCHES IN AN INNINGS IN THE FIELD

J.E.Root	4ct	England v Ireland	Lord's
S.P.D.Smith	4ct	Australia v England	The Oval
D.A.Warner	4ct	Australia v England	Leeds

SIX CATCHES IN A MATCH IN THE FIELD

S.P.D.Smith	6ct	Australia v England	The Oval
D.A.Warner	6ct	Australia v England	Leeds

LEADING TEST AGGREGATES IN 2019

1000 RUNS IN 2019

	M	I	NO	HS	Runs	Avge	100	50
M.Labuschagne (A)	11	17	–	185	**1104**	64.94	3	7

RECORD CALENDAR YEAR RUNS AGGREGATE

	M	I	NO	HS	Runs	Avge	100	50
M.Yousuf (P) (2006)	11	19	1	202	**1788**	99.33	9	3

RECORD CALENDAR YEAR RUNS AVERAGE

	M	I	NO	HS	Runs	Avge	100	50
G.St A.Sobers (WI) (1958)	7	12	3	365*	1193	**132.55**	5	3

1000 RUNS IN DEBUT CALENDAR YEAR

	M	I	NO	HS	Runs	Avge	100	50
M.A.Taylor (A) (1989)	11	20	1	219	**1219**	64.15	4	5
A.C.Voges (A) (2015)	12	18	6	269*	**1028**	85.66	4	3
A.N.Cook (E) (2006)	13	24	2	127	**1013**	46.04	4	3

50 WICKETS IN 2019

	M	O	R	W	Avge	Best	5wI	10wM
P.J.Cummins (A)	12	440.0	1188	**59**	20.13	6-23	2	1

RECORD CALENDAR YEAR WICKETS AGGREGATE

	M	O	R	W	Avge	Best	5wI	10wM
M.Muralitharan (SL) (2006)	11	588.4	1521	**90**	16.90	8-70	9	5
S.K.Warne (A) (2005)	14	691.4	2043	**90**	22.70	6-46	6	2

50 WICKET-KEEPING DISMISSALS IN 2019

	M	Dis	Ct	St
T.D.Paine (A)	12	58	56	2

RECORD CALENDAR YEAR DISMISSALS AGGREGATE

	M	Dis	Ct	St
J.M.Bairstow (E) (2016)	17	70	66	4

20 CATCHES BY FIELDERS IN 2019

	M	Ct
J.E.Root (E)	12	25
S.P.D.Smith (A)	8	21

RECORD CALENDAR YEAR FIELDER'S AGGREGATE

	M	Ct
G.C.Smith (SA) (2008)	15	30

TEST MATCH SCORES
NEW ZEALAND v BANGLADESH (1st Test)

At Seddon Park, Hamilton, on 28 February, 1, 2, 3 March 2019.
Toss: New Zealand. Result: **NEW ZEALAND** won by an innings and 12 runs.
Debut: Bangladesh – Ebadat Hossain.

BANGLADESH

Tamim Iqbal	c Williamson b de Grandhomme	126	c Watling b Southee		74
Shadman Islam	b Boult	24	c Boult b Wagner		37
Mominul Haque	c Watling b Wagner	12	c Taylor b Boult		8
Mithun Ali	c Latham b Wagner	8	c Williamson b Boult		0
Soumya Sarkar	c Watling b Southee	1	b Boult		149
*Mahmudullah	c Boult b Wagner	22	c Boult b Southee		146
†Liton Das	c Boult b Wagner	29	b Boult		1
Mehedi Hasan	c Nicholls b Wagner	10	c Raval b Wagner		1
Abu Jayed	c Watling b Southee	2	b Boult		3
Khaled Ahmed	b Southee	0	not out		4
Ebadat Hossain	not out	0	c Williamson b Southee		0
Extras		–	(W 6)		6
Total	**(59.2 overs; 253 mins)**	**234**	**(103 overs; 451 mins)**		**429**

NEW ZEALAND

J.A.Raval	c Khaled b Mahmudullah	132
T.W.M.Latham	c Mithun b Soumya	161
*K.S.Williamson	not out	200
L.R.P.L.Taylor	lbw b Soumya	4
H.M.Nicholls	b Mehedi	53
N.Wagner	c Liton b Ebadat	47
†B.J.Watling	c Liton b Mehedi	31
C.de Grandhomme	not out	76
T.D.Astle		
T.G.Southee		
T.A.Boult		
Extras	(LB 7, NB 2, W 2)	11
Total	**(6 wkts dec; 163 overs; 690 mins)**	**715**

NEW ZEALAND	O	M	R	W	O	M	R	W
Boult	13	1	62	1	28	3	123	5
Southee	14	2	76	3	24	4	98	3
De Grandhomme	11	0	39	1	10	1	33	0
Wagner	16.2	4	47	5	24	4	104	2
Astle	5	1	10	0	15	3	58	0
Williamson					2	0	13	0

BANGLADESH	O	M	R	W
Abu Jayed	30	5	103	0
Ebadat Hossain	27	4	107	1
Khaled Ahmed	30	6	149	0
Soumya Sarkar	21	1	68	2
Mehedi Hasan	49	2	246	2
Mahmudullah	1	0	3	1
Mominul Haque	5	0	32	0

FALL OF WICKETS

	B	NZ	B
Wkt	1st	1st	2nd
1st	57	254	88
2nd	121	333	100
3rd	147	349	110
4th	149	449	126
5th	180	509	361
6th	207	605	379
7th	217	–	380
8th	226	–	413
9th	234	–	429
10th	234	–	429

Umpires: N.J.Llong (*England*) (56) and P.R.Reiffel (*Australia*) (42).
Referee: D.C.Boon (*Australia*) (54).   **Test No. 2348/14 (NZ432/B113)**

NEW ZEALAND v BANGLADESH (2nd Test)

At Basin Reserve, Wellington, on 8 (*no play*), 9 (*no play*), 10, 11, 12 March 2019.
Toss: New Zealand. Result: **NEW ZEALAND** won by an innings and 12 runs.
Debuts: None.

BANGLADESH

Tamim Iqbal	c Southee b Wagner	74	b Boult		4
Shadman Islam	c Taylor b de Grandhomme	27	c Watling b Henry		29
Mominul Haque	c Watling b Wagner	15	c Southee b Boult		10
Mithun Ali	c Watling b Wagner	3	c Southee b Wagner		47
Soumya Sarkar	c Watling b Henry	20	c Taylor b Boult		28
*Mahmudullah	c de Grandhomme b Wagner	13	c Boult b Wagner		67
†Liton Das	c Williamson b Southee	33	c Boult b Wagner		1
Taijul Islam	lbw b Boult	8	c Latham b Wagner		0
Mustafizur Rahman	b Boult	0	b Boult		16
Abu Jayed	b Boult	4	not out		0
Ebadat Hossain	not out	0	b Wagner		0
Extras	(B 4, LB 7, NB 1, W 2)	14	(LB 4, W 3)		7
Total	**(61 overs; 273 mins)**	**211**	**(56 overs; 255 mins)**		**209**

NEW ZEALAND

J.A.Raval	c Soumya b Abu	3
T.W.M.Latham	c Liton b Abu	4
*K.S.Williamson	c and b Taijul	74
L.R.P.L.Taylor	c Liton b Mustafizur	200
H.M.Nicholls	b Taijul	107
C.de Grandhomme	not out	23
†B.J.Watling	c Soumya b Abu	8
N.Wagner		
M.J.Henry		
T.G.Southee		
T.A.Boult		
Extras	(LB 5, NB 1, W 7)	13
Total	**(6 wkts dec; 84.5 overs; 370 mins)**	**432**

NEW ZEALAND	O	M	R	W		O	M	R	W		FALL OF WICKETS		
Boult	11	3	38	0		16	5	52	4			B	NZ	B
Southee	15	2	51	1		12	1	57	0		*Wkt*	*1st*	*1st*	*2nd*
De Grandhomme	7	0	15	1	(4)	4	0	11	0		1st	75	5	4
Henry	15	0	67	1	(3)	9	3	40	1		2nd	119	8	20
Wagner	13	4	28	4		14	4	45	5		3rd	127	180	55
											4th	134	396	112
BANGLADESH											5th	152	421	152
Abu Jayed	18.5	2	94	3							6th	168	432	158
Ebadat Hossain	16	2	84	0							7th	206	–	170
Mustafizur Rahman	14	2	74	1							8th	206	–	203
Soumya Sarkar	6	0	35	0							9th	207	–	209
Taijul Islam	21	0	99	2							10th	211	–	209
Mominul Haque	9	0	41	0										

Umpires: R.S.A.Palliyaguruge (*Sri Lanka*) (2) and P.R.Reiffel (*Australia*) (43).
Referee: D.C.Boon (*Australia*) (55). **Test No. 2349/15 (NZ433/B114)**
The third Test, scheduled for 16-20 March at Hagley Oval, Christchurch, was abandoned without a ball being bowled.

AFGHANISTAN v IRELAND (Only Test)

At Rajiv Gandhi International Cricket Stadium, Dehra Dun, on 15, 16, 17, 18 March 2019.
Toss: Ireland. Result: **AFGHANISTAN** won by seven wickets.
Debuts: Afghanistan – Ihsanullah Janat, Ikram Alikhil, Waqar Salamkheil; Ireland –
J.Cameron-Dow, G.H.Dockrell, A.R.McBrine, J.A.McCollum, S.W.Poynter.

IRELAND

*W.T.S.Porterfield	lbw b Nabi	9	c Alikhil b Ahmadzai		0
P.R.Stirling	c Alikhil b Ahmadzai	26	lbw b Ahmadzai		14
A.Balbirnie	b Ahmadzai	4	c Alikhil b Salamkheil		82
J.A.McCollum	b Khan	4	lbw b Khan		39
K.J.O'Brien	lbw b Nabi	12	lbw b Khan		56
†S.W.Poynter	lbw b Khan	0	c Janat b Salamkheil		1
S.R.Thompson	c Shahidi b Nabi	3	c Janat b Khan		1
G.H.Dockrell	c Alikhil b Ahmadzai	39	lbw b Khan		25
A.R.McBrine	b Salamkheil	3	st Alikhil b Khan		4
J.Cameron-Dow	lbw b Salamkheil	9	not out		32
T.J.Murtagh	not out	54	c Shah b Ahmadzai		27
Extras	(B 4, LB 5)	9	(B 4, LB 2, W 1)		7
Total	**(60 overs)**	**172**	**(93 overs)**		**288**

AFGHANISTAN

Mohammad Shahzad	c and b Cameron-Dow	40	c Poynter b McBrine		2
Ihsanullah Janat	lbw b Cameron-Dow	7	not out		65
Rahmat Shah	b Murtagh	98	st Poynter b Cameron-Dow		76
Hashmatullah Shahidi	lbw b McBrine	61	(5) not out		4
*Asghar Stanikzai	c Poynter b Thompson	67			
Mohammad Nabi	c Cameron-Dow b Thompson	0	(4) run out		1
†Ikram Alikhil	b McBrine	7			
Rashid Khan	lbw b Dockrell	10			
Yamin Ahmadzai	lbw b Dockrell	2			
Wafadar Momand	c Balbirnie b Thompson	6			
Waqar Salamkheil	not out	0			
Extras	(B 5, LB 3, NB 3, W 4)	15	(W 1)		1
Total	**(106.3 overs)**	**314**	**(3 wkts; 47.5 overs)**		**149**

AFGHANISTAN	O	M	R	W		O	M	R	W	FALL OF WICKETS				
											Ire	Afg	Ire	Afg
Yamin Ahmadzai	12	2	41	3		14	1	52	3	*Wkt*	*1st*	*1st*	*2nd*	*2nd*
Wafadar Momand	8	3	31	0	(5)	8	0	24	0	1st	37	27	0	5
Mohammad Nabi	14	5	36	3	(2)	20	1	58	0	2nd	41	68	33	144
Rashid Khan	12	5	20	2	(3)	34	7	82	5	3rd	41	198	137	145
Waqar Salamkheil	14	4	35	2	(4)	17	2	66	2	4th	55	226	141	–
										5th	55	227	150	–
IRELAND										6th	59	255	157	–
Murtagh	22	9	33	1	(4)	5	3	15	0	7th	62	272	220	–
McBrine	27	4	77	2		13	5	35	1	8th	69	280	229	–
Cameron-Dow	18	0	94	2		5.5	0	24	1	9th	85	311	230	–
Thompson	17.3	5	28	3	(5)	1	0	9	0	10th	172	314	288	–
Dockrell	18	4	63	2	(1)	22	7	58	0					
O'Brien	4	1	11	0										
Balbirnie					(6)	1	0	8	0					

Umpires: R.K.Illingworth (*England*) (42) and S.Ravi (*India*) (33).
Referee: J.Srinath (*India*) (46).   Test No. 2350/1 (Afg2/Ire2)

ENGLAND v IRELAND (Only Test)

At Lord's, London, on 24, 25, 26 July 2019.
Toss: England. Result: **ENGLAND** won by 143 runs.
Debuts: England – J.J.Roy, O.P.Stone; Ireland – M.R.Adair.

ENGLAND

R.J.Burns	c Wilson b Murtagh	6	(2) c Wilson b Rankin		6
J.J.Roy	c Stirling b Murtagh	5	(3) b Thompson		72
J.L.Denly	lbw b Adair	23	(4) run out		10
*J.E.Root	lbw b Adair	2	(5) c Wilson b Adair		31
†J.M.Bairstow	b Murtagh	0	(6) lbw b Adair		0
M.M.Ali	c Wilson b Murtagh	0	(7) c Wilson b Rankin		9
C.R.Woakes	lbw b Murtagh	0	(8) c Balbirnie b Adair		13
S.M.Curran	c McCollum b Rankin	18	(9) c McCollum b Thompson		37
S.C.J.Broad	c Wilson b Rankin	3	(10) not out		21
O.P.Stone	b Adair	19	(11) b Thompson		0
M.J.Leach	not out	1	(1) c Adair b Murtagh		92
Extras	(LB 5, NB 2, W 1)	8	(B 1, LB 7, NB 4)		12
Total	**(23.4 overs)**	**85**	**(77.5 overs)**		**303**

IRELAND

*W.T.S.Porterfield	c Leach b Curran	14	c Bairstow b Woakes		2
J.A.McCollum	b Curran	19	c Root b Woakes		11
A.Balbirnie	b Stone	55	c Root b Broad		5
P.R.Stirling	lbw b Broad	36	b Woakes		0
K.J.O'Brien	not out	28	lbw b Broad		4
†G.C.Wilson	c Root b Stone	0	lbw b Woakes		0
S.R.Thompson	b Broad	4	c Root b Woakes		4
M.R.Adair	b Curran	3	b Broad		8
A.R.McBrine	b Broad	11	c Root b Broad		0
T.J.Murtagh	c Burns b Stone	16	b Woakes		2
W.B.Rankin	b Ali	7	not out		0
Extras	(B 10, LB 6, W 2)	18	(B 1, LB 1)		2
Total	**(58.2 overs)**	**207**	**(15.4 overs)**		**38**

IRELAND	O	M	R	W		O	M	R	W	FALL OF WICKETS				
											E	Ire	E	Ire
Murtagh	9	2	13	5		18	3	52	1	*Wkt*	*1st*	*1st*	*2nd*	*2nd*
Adair	7.4	1	32	3		20	7	66	3	1st	8	32	26	11
Thompson	4	1	30	0	(4)	12.5	0	44	3	2nd	36	45	171	18
Rankin	3	1	5	2	(3)	17	1	86	2	3rd	36	132	182	19
McBrine						10	1	47	0	4th	42	138	194	24
										5th	42	138	194	24
ENGLAND										6th	42	141	219	24
Broad	19	5	60	3		8	3	19	4	7th	43	149	239	32
Woakes	10	2	34	0		7.4	2	17	6	8th	58	174	248	36
Stone	12	3	29	3						9th	67	195	293	36
Curran	10	3	28	3						10th	85	207	303	38
Leach	3	0	26	0										
Ali	4.2	1	14	1										

Umpires: Alim Dar (*Pakistan*) (126) and R.S.A.Palliyaguruge (*Sri Lanka*) (3).
Referee: A.J.Pycroft (*Zimbabwe*) (69).   **Test No. 2351/1 (E1011/Ire3)**

ENGLAND v AUSTRALIA (1st Test)

At Edgbaston, Birmingham, on 1, 2, 3, 4, 5 August 2019.
Toss: Australia. Result: **AUSTRALIA** won by 251 runs.
Debuts: None.

AUSTRALIA

C.T.Bancroft	c Root b Broad	8	c Buttler b Ali	7
D.A.Warner	lbw b Broad	2	c Bairstow b Broad	8
U.T.Khawaja	c Bairstow b Woakes	13	c Bairstow b Stokes	40
S.P.D.Smith	b Broad	144	c Bairstow b Woakes	142
T.M.Head	lbw b Woakes	35	c Bairstow b Stokes	51
M.S.Wade	lbw b Woakes	1	c Denly b Stokes	110
*†T.D.Paine	c Burns b Broad	5	b Ali	34
J.L.Pattinson	lbw b Broad	0	not out	47
P.J.Cummins	lbw b Stokes	5	not out	26
P.M.Siddle	c Burns b Stone	44		
N.M.Lyon	c Buttler b Ali	12		
Extras	(LB 13, W 2)	15	(B 11, LB 2, NB 6, W 3)	22
Total	(80.4 overs)	284	(7 wkts dec; 112 overs)	487

ENGLAND

R.J.Burns	c Paine b Lyon	133	c Lyon b Cummins	11
J.J.Roy	c Smith b Pattinson	10	b Lyon	28
*J.E.Root	c and b Siddle	57	c Bancroft b Lyon	28
J.L.Denly	lbw b Pattinson	18	c Bancroft b Lyon	11
J.C.Buttler	c Bancroft b Cummins	5	b Cummins	1
B.A.Stokes	c Paine b Cummins	50	c Paine b Lyon	6
†J.M.Bairstow	c Warner b Siddle	8	c Bancroft b Cummins	6
M.M.Ali	b Lyon	0	c Warner b Lyon	4
C.R.Woakes	not out	37	c Smith b Cummins	37
S.C.J.Broad	c Pattinson b Cummins	29	c Smith b Lyon	0
J.M.Anderson	c Cummins b Lyon	3	not out	4
Extras	(B 10, LB 11, NB 1, W 2)	24	(B 4, LB 4, NB 2)	10
Total	(135.5 overs)	374	(52.3 overs)	146

ENGLAND	O	M	R	W		O	M	R	W
Anderson	4	3	1	0					
Broad	22.4	4	86	5	(1)	22	3	91	1
Woakes	21	2	58	3	(2)	13	1	46	1
Stokes	18	1	77	1	(5)	22	5	85	3
Ali	13	3	42	1	(3)	29	1	130	2
Denly	2	1	7	0		14	1	72	0
Root					(4)	12	1	50	0

AUSTRALIA	O	M	R	W		O	M	R	W
Cummins	33	9	84	3	(4)	11.3	3	32	4
Pattinson	27	3	82	2	(3)	8	1	29	0
Siddle	27	8	52	2	(1)	12	2	28	0
Lyon	43.5	8	112	3	(2)	20	5	49	6
Wade	1	0	7	0					
Head	2	1	7	0					
Smith	2	0	9	0	(5)	1	1	0	0

FALL OF WICKETS

	A	E	A	E
Wkt	1st	1st	2nd	2nd
1st	2	22	13	19
2nd	17	154	27	60
3rd	35	189	75	80
4th	99	194	205	85
5th	105	282	331	85
6th	112	296	407	97
7th	112	300	409	97
8th	122	300	–	136
9th	210	365	–	136
10th	284	374	–	146

Umpires: Alim Dar (*Pakistan*) (127) and J.S.Wilson (*West Indies*) (14).
Referee: R.S.Madugalle (*Sri Lanka*) (188).   Test No. 2352/347 (E1012/A821)

17

ENGLAND v AUSTRALIA (2nd Test)

At Lord's, London, on 14 (*no play*), 15, 16, 17, 18 August 2019.
Toss: Australia. Result: **MATCH DRAWN**.
Debut: England – J.C.Archer.

ENGLAND

R.J.Burns	c Bancroft b Cummins	53		c Paine b Siddle	29
J.J.Roy	c Paine b Hazlewood	0		c and b Cummins	2
*J.E.Root	lbw b Hazlewood	14		c Paine b Cummins	0
J.L.Denly	c Paine b Hazlewood	30		c and b Siddle	26
J.C.Buttler	c Paine b Siddle	12	(6)	c Hazlewood b Cummins	31
B.A.Stokes	lbw b Lyon	13	(5)	not out	115
†J.M.Bairstow	c Khawaja b Lyon	52		not out	30
C.R.Woakes	c Paine b Cummins	32			
J.C.Archer	c Khawaja b Cummins	12			
S.C.J.Broad	b Lyon	11			
M.J.Leach	not out	6			
Extras	(B 12, LB 5, W 6)	23		(B 5, LB 19, NB 1)	25
Total	**(77.1 overs)**	**258**		**(5 wkts dec; 71 overs)**	**258**

AUSTRALIA

C.T.Bancroft	lbw b Archer	13		lbw b Leach	16
D.A.Warner	b Broad	3		c Burns b Archer	5
U.T.Khawaja	c Bairstow b Woakes	36		c Bairstow b Archer	2
S.P.D.Smith	lbw b Woakes	92			
T.M.Head	lbw b Broad	7		not out	42
M.S.Wade	c Burns b Broad	6		c Buttler b Leach	1
*†T.D.Paine	c Buttler b Archer	23		c Denly b Archer	4
P.J.Cummins	c Bairstow b Broad	20		not out	1
P.M.Siddle	c Bairstow b Woakes	9			
N.M.Lyon	lbw b Leach	6			
J.R.Hazlewood	not out	3			
M.Labuschagne			(4)	c Root b Leach	59
Extras	(B 17, LB 12, NB 1, W 2)	32		(B 4, LB 18, NB 1, W 1)	24
Total	**(94.3 overs)**	**250**		**(6 wkts; 47.3 overs)**	**154**

AUSTRALIA	O	M	R	W		O	M	R	W
Cummins	21	8	61	3		17	6	35	3
Hazlewood	22	6	58	3		13	1	43	0
Siddle	13	2	48	1		15	4	54	2
Lyon	19.1	2	68	3		26	3	102	0
Smith	2	0	6	0					

ENGLAND	O	M	R	W		O	M	R	W
Broad	27.3	7	65	4		7	0	29	0
Archer	29	11	59	2		15	2	32	3
Woakes	19	6	61	3		3	0	11	0
Stokes	8	1	17	0	(5)	3	1	16	0
Leach	11	3	19	1	(4)	16.3	5	37	3
Root						1	0	7	0
Denly						2	2	0	0

FALL OF WICKETS				
	E	A	E	A
Wkt	*1st*	*1st*	*2nd*	*2nd*
1st	0	11	9	13
2nd	26	60	9	19
3rd	92	60	64	47
4th	116	71	71	132
5th	138	102	161	138
6th	138	162	–	149
7th	210	218	–	–
8th	230	234	–	–
9th	251	246	–	–
10th	258	250	–	–

Umpires: Alim Dar (*Pakistan*) (128) and C.B.Gaffaney (*New Zealand*) (28).
Referee: R.S.Madugalle (*Sri Lanka*) (189).   **Test No. 2353/348 (E1013/A822)**
S.P.D.Smith retired hurt at 203-6 and resumed at 218-7. M.Labuschagne replaced him in the second innings as the first concussion replacement in Test history.

ENGLAND v AUSTRALIA (3rd Test)

At Headingley, Leeds, on 22, 23, 24, 25 August 2019.
Toss: England. Result: **ENGLAND** won by one wicket.
Debuts: None.

AUSTRALIA

D.A.Warner	c Bairstow b Archer	61	(2)	lbw b Broad	0
M.S.Harris	c Bairstow b Archer	8	(1)	b Leach	19
U.T.Khawaja	c Bairstow b Broad	8		c Roy b Woakes	23
M.Labuschagne	lbw b Stokes	74		run out	80
T.M.Head	b Broad	0		b Stokes	25
M.S.Wade	b Archer	0		c Bairstow b Stokes	33
*†T.D.Paine	lbw b Woakes	11		c Denly b Broad	0
J.L.Pattinson	c Root b Archer	2		c Root b Archer	20
P.J.Cummins	c Bairstow b Archer	0		c Burns b Stokes	6
N.M.Lyon	lbw b Archer	1		b Archer	9
J.R.Hazlewood	not out	1		not out	4
Extras	(B 4, LB 2, NB 2, W 5)	13		(B 5, LB 13, NB 7, W 2)	27
Total	**(52.1 overs)**	**179**		**(75.2 overs)**	**246**

ENGLAND

R.J.Burns	c Paine b Cummins	9		c Warner b Hazlewood	7
J.J.Roy	c Warner b Hazlewood	9		b Cummins	8
*J.E.Root	c Warner b Hazlewood	0		c Warner b Lyon	77
J.L.Denly	c Paine b Pattinson	12		c Paine b Hazlewood	50
B.A.Stokes	c Warner b Pattinson	8		not out	135
†J.M.Bairstow	c Warner b Hazlewood	4		c Labuschagne b Hazlewood	36
J.C.Buttler	c Khawaja b Hazlewood	5		run out	1
C.R.Woakes	c Paine b Cummins	5		c Wade b Hazlewood	1
J.C.Archer	c Paine b Cummins	7		c Head b Lyon	15
S.C.J.Broad	not out	4		lbw b Pattinson	0
M.J.Leach	b Hazlewood	1		not out	1
Extras	(LB 3)	3		(B 5, LB 15, NB 1, W 10)	31
Total	**(27.5 overs)**	**67**		**(9 wkts; 125.4 overs)**	**362**

ENGLAND	O	M	R	W		O	M	R	W
Broad	14	4	32	2	(2)	16	2	52	2
Archer	17.1	3	45	6	(1)	14	2	40	2
Woakes	12	4	51	0		10	1	34	1
Stokes	9	0	45	1	(5)	24.2	7	56	3
Leach					(4)	11	0	46	1

AUSTRALIA	O	M	R	W	O	M	R	W
Cummins	9	4	23	3	24.4	5	80	1
Hazlewood	12.5	2	30	5	31	11	85	4
Lyon	1	0	2	0	39	5	114	2
Pattinson	5	2	9	2	25	9	47	1
Labuschagne					6	0	16	0

FALL OF WICKETS

	A	E	A	E
Wkt	1st	1st	2nd	2nd
1st	12	10	10	15
2nd	25	10	36	15
3rd	136	20	52	141
4th	138	34	97	159
5th	139	45	163	245
6th	162	45	164	253
7th	173	54	215	261
8th	174	56	226	286
9th	177	66	237	286
10th	179	67	246	–

Umpires: C.B.Gaffaney (*New Zealand*) (29) and J.S.Wilson (*West Indies*) (15).
Referee: J.Srinath (*India*) (47).   **Test No. 2354/349 (E1014/A823)**

ENGLAND v AUSTRALIA (4th Test)

At Old Trafford, Manchester, on 4, 5, 6, 7, 8 September 2019.
Toss: Australia. Result: **AUSTRALIA** won by 185 runs.
Debuts: None.

AUSTRALIA

M.S.Harris	lbw b Broad	13	(2)	lbw b Broad	6
D.A.Warner	c Bairstow b Broad	0	(1)	lbw b Broad	0
M.Labuschagne	b Overton	67		lbw b Archer	11
S.P.D.Smith	c Denly b Root	211		c Stokes b Leach	82
T.M.Head	lbw b Broad	19		b Archer	12
M.S.Wade	c Root b Leach	16		c Bairstow b Archer	34
*†T.D.Paine	c Bairstow b Overton	58		not out	23
P.J.Cummins	c Stokes b Leach	4			
M.A.Starc	not out	54	(8)	not out	3
N.M.Lyon	not out	26			
J.R.Hazlewood					
Extras	(B 8, LB 14, NB 4, W 3)	29		(B 5, LB 2, NB 1, W 7)	15
Total	**(8 wkts dec; 126 overs)**	**497**		**(6 wkts dec; 42.5 overs)**	**186**

ENGLAND

R.J.Burns	c Smith b Hazlewood	81		c Head b Cummins	0
J.L.Denly	c Wade b Cummins	4		c Labuschagne b Lyon	53
C.Overton	c Smith b Hazlewood	5	(8)	lbw b Hazlewood	21
*J.E.Root	lbw b Hazlewood	71	(3)	b Cummins	0
J.J.Roy	b Hazlewood	22	(4)	b Cummins	31
B.A.Stokes	c Smith b Starc	26	(5)	c Paine b Cummins	1
†J.M.Bairstow	b Starc	17	(6)	lbw b Starc	25
J.C.Buttler	b Cummins	41	(7)	b Hazlewood	34
J.C.Archer	c Paine b Cummins	1		lbw b Lyon	1
S.C.J.Broad	b Starc	5	(11)	not out	0
M.J.Leach	not out	24	(10)	c Wade b Labuschagne	12
Extras	(B 4, LB 11, NB 4, W 5)	24		(B 9, LB 8, NB 2)	19
Total	**(107 overs)**	**301**		**(91.3 overs)**	**197**

ENGLAND	O	M	R	W		O	M	R	W		FALL OF WICKETS				
												A	E	A	E
Broad	25	2	97	3		14	4	54	2		Wkt	1st	1st	2nd	2nd
Archer	27	3	97	0		14	2	45	3		1st	1	10	0	0
Stokes	10.5	0	66	0							2nd	28	25	16	0
Leach	26.1	3	83	2	(4)	9	0	58	1		3rd	144	166	24	66
Overton	28	3	85	2	(3)	5.5	1	22	0		4th	183	175	44	74
Denly	3	1	8	0							5th	224	196	149	93
Root	6	0	39	1							6th	369	228	158	138
											7th	387	243	–	172
AUSTRALIA											8th	438	256	–	173
Starc	22	7	80	3	(4)	16	2	46	1		9th	–	283	–	196
Hazlewood	25	6	57	4		17.3	5	31	2		10th	–	301	–	197
Cummins	24	6	60	3	(1)	24	9	43	4						
Lyon	36	4	89	0	(3)	29	12	51	2						
Labuschagne						4	1	9	1						
Head						1	1	0	0						

Umpires: H.D.P.K.Dharmasena (*Sri Lanka*) (61) and M.Erasmus (*South Africa*) (56).
Referee: J.Srinath (*India*) (48).   Test No. 2355/350 (E1015/A824)

ENGLAND v AUSTRALIA (5th Test)

At The Oval, London, on 12, 13, 14, 15 September 2019.
Toss: Australia. Result: **ENGLAND** won by 135 runs.
Debuts: None.

ENGLAND

R.J.Burns	c Marsh b Hazlewood	47	c Paine b Lyon		20
J.L.Denly	c Smith b Cummins	14	c Smith b Siddle		94
*J.E.Root	b Cummins	57	c Smith b Lyon		21
B.A.Stokes	c Lyon b Marsh	20	b Lyon		67
†J.M.Bairstow	lbw b Marsh	22	c Smith b Marsh		14
J.C.Buttler	b Cummins	70	c Labuschagne b Siddle		47
S.M.Curran	c Smith b Marsh	15	c Paine b Cummins		17
C.R.Woakes	lbw b Marsh	2	c Smith b Marsh		6
J.C.Archer	c Paine b Hazlewood	9	c Paine b Cummins		3
M.J.Leach	b Marsh	21	c Hazlewood b Lyon		9
S.C.J.Broad	not out	0	not out		12
Extras	(B 3, LB 7, NB 2, W 5)	17	(B 7, LB 11, NB 1)		19
Total	**(87.1 overs)**	**294**	**(95.3 overs)**		**329**

AUSTRALIA

D.A.Warner	c Bairstow b Archer	5	(2) c Burns b Broad		11
M.S.Harris	c Stokes b Archer	3	(1) b Broad		9
M.Labuschagne	lbw b Archer	48	st Bairstow b Leach		14
S.P.D.Smith	lbw b Woakes	80	c Stokes b Broad		23
M.S.Wade	lbw b Curran	19	st Bairstow b Root		117
M.R.Marsh	c Leach b Archer	17	c Buttler b Root		24
*†T.D.Paine	c Bairstow b Curran	1	lbw b Leach		21
P.J.Cummins	lbw b Curran	0	c Bairstow b Broad		9
P.M.Siddle	c Burns b Archer	18	not out		13
N.M.Lyon	b Archer	25	c Root b Leach		1
J.R.Hazlewood	not out	1	c Root b Leach		0
Extras	(B 1, LB 2, W 5)	8	(B 2, LB 12, NB 2, Pen 5)		21
Total	**(68.5 overs)**	**225**	**(77 overs)**		**263**

AUSTRALIA	O	M	R	W		O	M	R	W
Cummins	25.5	6	84	3		21	5	67	2
Hazlewood	21	7	76	2		19	5	57	0
Siddle	17	1	61	0	(4)	13	4	52	2
Marsh	18.2	4	46	5	(5)	11	1	40	2
Lyon	4	0	12	0	(3)	24.3	5	69	4
Labuschagne	1	0	3	0		1	1	26	0

ENGLAND	O	M	R	W		O	M	R	W
Broad	12	3	45	0		15	1	62	4
Archer	23.5	9	62	6		16	2	66	0
Curran	17	6	46	3		8	3	22	0
Woakes	10	2	51	1	(5)	7	1	19	0
Leach	6	1	18	0	(4)	22	8	49	4
Root						9	1	26	2

FALL OF WICKETS

	E	A	E	A
Wkt	1st	1st	2nd	2nd
1st	27	5	54	18
2nd	103	14	87	29
3rd	130	83	214	56
4th	170	118	222	85
5th	176	160	249	148
6th	199	166	279	200
7th	205	166	305	244
8th	226	187	305	260
9th	294	224	317	263
10th	294	225	329	263

Umpires: H.D.P.K.Dharmasena (*Sri Lanka*) (62) and M.Erasmus (*South Africa*) (57).
Referee: J.Srinath (*India*) (49).   **Test No. 2356/351 (E1016/A825)**

SRI LANKA v NEW ZEALAND (1st Test)

At Galle International Stadium, on 14, 15, 16, 17, 18 August 2019.
Toss: New Zealand. Result: **SRI LANKA** won by six wickets.
Debuts: None.

NEW ZEALAND

Batsman	1st innings		2nd innings	
J.A.Raval	c de Silva b M.K.P.A.D.Perera	33	c Karunaratne b de Silva	4
T.W.M.Latham	c Dickwella b M.K.P.A.D.Perera	30	c Thirimanne b M.K.P.A.D.Perera	45
*K.S.Williamson	c Karunaratne b M.K.P.A.D.Perera	0	c M.D.K.J.Perera b Ambuldeniya	4
L.R.P.L.Taylor	c Dickwella b Lakmal	86	c de Silva b Ambuldeniya	3
H.M.Nicholls	lbw b M.K.P.A.D.Perera	42	c Mendis b de Silva	26
†B.J.Watling	lbw b M.K.P.A.D.Perera	1	c Dickwella b Kumara	77
M.J.Santner	lbw b Lakmal	13	c Lakmal b Ambuldeniya	12
T.G.Southee	run out	14	st Dickwella b Ambuldeniya	23
W.E.R.Somerville	not out	9	not out	40
T.A.Boult	c M.D.K.J.Perera b Lakmal	18	c de Silva b Kumara	26
A.Y.Patel	lbw b Lakmal	0	lbw b de Silva	14
Extras	(LB 2, NB 1)	3	(B 4, LB 5, NB 2)	11
Total	**(83.2 overs; 329 mins)**	**249**	**(106 overs)**	**285**

SRI LANKA

Batsman	1st innings		2nd innings	
*F.D.M.Karunaratne	lbw b Patel	39	c Watling b Southee	122
H.D.R.L.Thirimanne	st Watling b Patel	10	lbw b Somerville	64
B.K.G.Mendis	c Taylor b Patel	53	c Raval b Patel	10
A.D.Mathews	c Taylor b Patel	50	not out	28
M.D.K.J.Perera	c Santner b Boult	1	c Santner b Boult	23
D.M.de Silva	c and b Patel	5	not out	14
†D.P.D.N.Dickwella	c Williamson b Somerville	61		
M.K.P.A.D.Perera	c Taylor b Somerville	0		
R.A.S.Lakmal	b Boult	40		
L.Ambuldeniya	lbw b Somerville	5		
C.B.R.L.S.Kumara	not out	0		
Extras	(B 1, LB 1, W 1)	3	(B 6, LB 1)	7
Total	**(93.2 overs; 397 mins)**	**267**	**(4 wkts; 86.1 overs; 362 mins)**	**268**

SRI LANKA	O	M	R	W		O	M	R	W
Lakmal	15.2	5	29	4		15	2	37	0
Kumara	10	1	37	0	(5)	10	0	31	2
M.K.P.A.D.Perera	30	3	80	5	(2)	32	4	84	1
De Silva	6	0	20	0	(3)	12	3	25	3
Ambuldeniya	22	1	81	0	(4)	37	4	99	4

NEW ZEALAND	O	M	R	W		O	M	R	W
Boult	20	4	45	2		9.1	1	34	1
Southee	7	3	17	0		12	2	33	1
Somerville	22.2	3	83	3		31	6	73	1
Patel	33	6	89	5		18	0	74	1
Santner	11	0	31	0		13	2	38	0
Williamson						3	0	9	0

FALL OF WICKETS

Wkt	NZ 1st	SL 1st	NZ 2nd	SL 2nd
1st	64	27	8	161
2nd	64	66	20	174
3rd	71	143	25	218
4th	171	144	81	250
5th	179	155	98	–
6th	205	158	124	–
7th	216	161	178	–
8th	222	242	224	–
9th	249	262	260	–
10th	249	267	285	–

Umpires: M.A.Gough (*England*) (10) and R.K.Illingworth (*England*) (43).
Referee: A.J.Pycroft (*Zimbabwe*) (70). **Test No. 2357/35 (SL284/NZ434)**

SRI LANKA v NEW ZEALAND (2nd Test)

At P Sara Oval, Colombo, on 22, 23, 24, 25, 26 August 2019.
Toss: Sri Lanka. Result: **NEW ZEALAND** won by an innings and 65 runs.
Debuts: None.

SRI LANKA

*F.D.M.Karunaratne	c Watling b Southee	65	(7) lbw b Southee		21
H.D.R.L.Thirimanne	c Williamson b Somerville	2	(1) run out		0
B.K.G.Mendis	c Watling b de Grandhomme	32	b Somerville		20
A.D.Mathews	c Watling b Boult	2	c Taylor b de Grandhomme		7
M.D.K.J.Perera	lbw b Boult	0	(2) c Watling b Boult		0
D.M.de Silva	b Boult	109	(5) c Southee b Patel		1
†D.P.D.N.Dickwella	c Watling b Southee	0	(6) c Latham b Patel		51
M.D.K.Perera	lbw b Patel	13	c Taylor b Southee		0
R.A.S.Lakmal	c Watling b Southee	10	c Latham b Somerville		14
L.Ambuldeniya	lbw b Southee	0	c Williamson b Boult		5
C.B.R.L.S.Kumara	not out	5	not out		0
Extras	(B 1, LB 2, NB 3)	6	(LB 2, W 1)		3
Total	**(90.2 overs; 410 mins)**	**244**	**(70.2 overs; 297 mins)**		**122**

NEW ZEALAND

J.A.Raval	c de Silva b M.D.K.Perera	0
T.W.M.Latham	lbw b M.D.K.Perera	154
*K.S.Williamson	c Mendis b Kumara	20
L.R.P.L.Taylor	c de Silva b Ambuldeniya	23
H.M.Nicholls	c de Silva b M.D.K.Perera	15
†B.J.Watling	not out	105
C.de Grandhomme	c Kumara b Ambuldeniya	83
T.G.Southee	not out	24
W.E.R.Somerville		
T.A.Boult		
A.Y.Patel		
Extras	(LB 4, W 3)	7
Total	**(6 wkts dec; 115 overs; 490 mins)**	**431**

NEW ZEALAND	O	M	R	W		O	M	R	W		FALL OF WICKETS
Boult	22.2	6	75	3		14.2	8	17	2		SL NZ SL
Southee	29	7	63	4		12	6	15	2		*Wkt 1st 1st 2nd*
De Grandhomme	17	3	35	1	(4)	4	1	8	1		1st 29 1 0
Somerville	6	3	20	1	(5)	21	6	49	2		2nd 79 34 4
Patel	16	4	48	1	(3)	19	3	31	2		3rd 93 84 11
SRI LANKA											4th 93 126 22
M.D.K.Perera	37	4	114	3							5th 130 269 32
De Silva	5	1	10	0							6th 130 382 73
Lakmal	11	2	32	0							7th 171 – 75
Kumara	25	0	115	1							8th 214 – 118
Ambuldeniya	37	4	156	2							9th 224 – 118
											10th 244 – 122

Umpires: M.A.Gough (*England*) (11) and B.N.J.Oxenford (*Australia*) (56).
Referee: A.J.Pycroft (*Zimbabwe*) (71).   **Test No. 2358/36 (SL285/NZ435)**

WEST INDIES v INDIA (1st Test)

At Sir Vivian Richards Stadium, North Sound, Antigua, on 22, 23, 24, 25 August 2019.
Toss: West Indies. Result: **INDIA** won by 318 runs.
Debut: West Indies – S.S.J.Brooks.

INDIA

K.L.Rahul	c Hope b Chase	44	b Chase		38
M.A.Agarwal	c Hope b Roach	5	lbw b Chase		16
C.A.Pujara	c Hope b Roach	2	b Roach		25
*V.Kohli	c Brooks b Gabriel	9	c Campbell b Chase		51
A.M.Rahane	b Gabriel	81	c Holder b Gabriel		102
G.H.Vihari	c Hope b Roach	32	c Hope b Holder		93
†R.R.Pant	c Holder b Roach	24	c sub (K.M.A.Paul) b Chase		7
R.A.Jadeja	c Hope b Holder	58	not out		1
I.Sharma	b Gabriel	19			
Mohammed Shami	c and b Chase	0			
J.J.Bumrah	not out	4			
Extras	(B 9, LB 8, NB 2)	19	(B 6, LB 4)		10
Total	**(96.4 overs)**	297	**(7 wkts dec; 112.3 overs)**		343

WEST INDIES

K.C.Brathwaite	c and b Sharma	14	c Pant b Bumrah		1
J.D.Campbell	b Shami	23	b Bumrah		7
S.S.J.Brooks	c Rahane b Jadeja	11	lbw b Sharma		2
D.M.Bravo	lbw b Bumrah	18	b Bumrah		2
R.L.Chase	c Rahul b Sharma	48	(6) b Shami		12
†S.D.Hope	c Pant b Sharma	24	(7) b Bumrah		2
S.O.Hetmyer	c and b Sharma	35	(5) c Rahane b Sharma		1
*J.O.Holder	c Pant b Shami	39	b Bumrah		8
K.A.J.Roach	c Kohli b Sharma	0	c Pant b Sharma		38
M.L.Cummins	b Jadeja	0	c Pant b Shami		0
S.T.Gabriel	not out	2	not out		19
Extras	(B 4, LB 1, NB 2, W 1)	8	(LB 7, NB 1)		8
Total	**(74.2 overs)**	222	**(26.5 overs)**		100

WEST INDIES	O	M	R	W		O	M	R	W	FALL OF WICKETS				
											I	WI	I	WI
Roach	25	6	66	4		20	8	29	1	Wkt	1st	1st	2nd	2nd
Gabriel	22	5	71	3		16	3	63	1	1st	5	36	30	7
Holder	20.4	11	36	1	(4) 18.3	4	45	1	2nd	7	48	73	10
Cummins	13	1	49	0	(5) 7	1	20	0	3rd	25	50	81	10
Chase	16	3	58	2	(3) 38	5	132	4	4th	93	88	187	13
Campbell					6	0	20	0	5th	175	130	322	15
Brathwaite					7	0	24	0	6th	189	174	336	27
										7th	207	179	343	37
INDIA										8th	267	179	–	50
Sharma	17	5	43	5	9.5	1	31	3	9th	268	220	–	50
Bumrah	18	4	55	1	8	4	7	5	10th	297	222	–	100
Mohammed Shami	17	3	48	2	(4) 5	3	13	2					
Jadeja	20.2	4	64	2	(3) 4	0	42	0					
Vihari	2	0	7	0									

Umpires: R.A.Kettleborough (*England*) (59) and R.J.Tucker (*Australia*) (68).
Referee: D.C.Boon (*Australia*) (56).   Test No. 2359/97 (WI1543/1534)

WEST INDIES v INDIA (2nd Test)

At Sabina Park, Kingston, Jamaica, on 30, 31 August, 1, 2 September 2019.
Toss: West Indies. Result: **INDIA** won by 257 runs.
Debuts: West Indies – R.R.S.Cornwall, J.N.Hamilton.

INDIA

K.L.Rahul	c Cornwall b Holder	13	c Hamilton b Roach		6
M.A.Agarwal	c Cornwall b Holder	55	lbw b Roach		4
C.A.Pujara	c Brooks b Cornwall	6	c Brooks b Holder		27
*V.Kohli	c Hamilton b Holder	76	c Hamilton b Roach		0
A.M.Rahane	c Hamilton b Roach	24	not out		64
G.H.Vihari	c Roach b Holder	111	not out		53
†R.R.Pant	b Holder	27			
R.A.Jadeja	c Bravo b Cornwall	16			
I.Sharma	c Hetmyer b Brathwaite	57			
Mohammed Shami	c Hamilton b Cornwall	0			
J.J.Bumrah	not out	0			
Extras	(B 11, LB 19, W 1)	31	(B 8, LB 4, NB 2)		14
Total	**(140.1 overs)**	**416**	**(4 wkts dec; 54.4 overs)**		**168**

WEST INDIES

K.C.Brathwaite	c Pant b Bumrah	10	(2) c Pant b I.Sharma		3
J.D.Campbell	c Pant b Bumrah	2	(1) c Kohli b Shami		16
D.M.Bravo	c Rahul b Bumrah	4	retired hurt		23
S.S.J.Brooks	lbw b Bumrah	0	run out		50
R.L.Chase	lbw b Bumrah	0	lbw b Jadeja		12
S.O.Hetmyer	b Shami	34	c Agarwal b I.Sharma		1
*J.O.Holder	c sub (R.G.Sharma) b Bumrah	18	(8) b Jadeja		39
†J.N.Hamilton	c Kohli b I.Sharma	5	(9) c Rahul b Jadeja		0
R.R.S.Cornwall	c Rahane b Shami	14	(10) c Pant b Shami		1
K.A.J.Roach	c Agarwal b Jadeja	17	(11) c Pant b Shami		5
S.T.Gabriel	not out	0	(12) not out		0
J.Blackwood			(7) c Pant b Bumrah		38
Extras	(B 8, LB 5)	13	(B 14, LB 2, NB 1, W 5)		22
Total	**(47.1 overs)**	**117**	**(59.5 overs)**		**210**

WEST INDIES	O	M	R	W		O	M	R	W
Roach	30	9	77	1		10	3	28	3
Gabriel	21	4	74	0	(4)	7	3	18	0
Holder	32.1	9	77	5	(2)	11.4	5	20	1
Cornwall	41	10	105	3	(3)	23	7	68	0
Chase	14	4	45	0		3	0	22	0
Brathwaite	2	0	8	1					

INDIA	O	M	R	W		O	M	R	W
I.Sharma	10.5	3	24	1		12	3	37	2
Bumrah	12.1	3	27	6		11	4	31	1
Mohammed Shami	13	4	34	2		16	2	65	3
Jadeja	11.1	7	19	1		19.5	4	58	3
Vihari						1	0	3	0

FALL OF WICKETS				
	I	WI	I	WI
Wkt	1st	1st	2nd	2nd
1st	32	9	9	9
2nd	46	13	36	37
3rd	115	13	36	97
4th	164	13	57	98
5th	202	22	–	159
6th	264	67	–	177
7th	302	78	–	177
8th	414	97	–	180
9th	416	117	–	206
10th	416	117	–	210

Umpires: R.A.Kettleborough (*England*) (60) and P.R.Reiffel (*Australia*) (44).
Referee: D.C.Boon (*Australia*) (57). **Test No. 2360/98 (WI544/I535)**
D.M.Bravo retired hurt at 55-2 and was replaced by J.Blackwood.

BANGLADESH v AFGHANISTAN (Only Test)

At Zahur Ahmed Chowdhury Stadium, Chittagong, on 5, 6, 7, 8, 9 September 2019.
Toss: Afghanistan. Result: **AFGHANISTAN** won by 224 runs.
Debuts: Afghanistan – Ibrahim Zadran, Qais Ahmad, Zahir Khan.

AFGHANISTAN

Ibrahim Zadran	c Mahmudullah b Taijul	21	(2) c Mominul b Nayeem		87
Ihsanullah Janat	b Taijul	9	(1) lbw b Shakib		4
Rahmat Shah	c Soumya b Nayeem	102	c and b Shakib		0
Hashmatullah Shahidi	c Soumya b Mahmudullah	14	c Soumya b Nayeem		12
Asghar Stanikzai	c Mushfiqur b Taijul	92	c Shakib b Taijul		50
Mohammad Nabi	b Nayeem	0	(7) c Mominul b Mehedi		8
†Afsar Zazai	b Taijul	41	(6) not out		48
*Rashid Khan	c and b Mehedi	51	b Taijul		24
Qais Ahmad	c Mominul b Shakib	9	lbw b Shakib		14
Yamin Ahmadzai	c Soumya b Shakib	0	run out		9
Zahir Khan	not out	0	c Mominul b Mehedi		0
Extras	(LB 1, NB 2)	3	(B 4)		4
Total	**(117 overs; 452 mins)**	**342**	**(90.1 overs; 336 mins)**		**260**

BANGLADESH

Shadman Islam	c Zazai b Ahmadzai	0	(2) lbw b Nabi		41
Soumya Sarkar	lbw b Rashid	17	(8) c Zadran b Rashid		15
Liton Das	b Rashid	33	(1) lbw b Zahir		9
Mominul Haque	c Stanikzai b Nabi	52	(5) lbw b Rashid		3
*Shakib Al Hasan	lbw b Rashid	11	(6) c Zazai b Zahir		44
†Mushfiqur Rahim	c Zadran b Rashid	14	(4) lbw b Rashid		23
Mahmudullah	b Rashid	7	c Zadran b Rashid		7
Mosaddek Hossain	not out	48	(3) c Stanikzai b Zahir		12
Mehedi Hasan	b Ahmad	11	lbw b Rashid		12
Taijul Islam	b Nabi	14	lbw b Rashid		0
Nayeem Hasan	lbw b Rashid	5	not out		0
Extras	(B 4, LB 1)	5	(B 4, LB 2)		6
Total	**(70.5 overs; 295 mins)**	**205**	**(61.4 overs; 231 mins)**		**173**

BANGLADESH	O	M	R	W		O	M	R	W		FALL OF WICKETS			
												Afg	B	Afg	B
Taijul Islam	41	5	116	4	(3)	28	6	86	2		*Wkt*	*1st*	*1st*	*2nd*	*2nd*
Shakib Al Hasan	22	1	64	2	(1)	19	3	58	3		1st	19	0	4	30
Mehedi Hasan	28	5	73	1	(2)	12.1	3	35	2		2nd	48	38	4	52
Nayeem Hasan	13	0	43	2		17	2	61	2		3rd	77	54	28	78
Mahmudullah	4	0	9	1							4th	197	88	136	82
Soumya Sarkar	4	0	26	0							5th	197	88	171	106
Mominul Haque	4	0	9	0	(5)	10	6	13	0		6th	278	104	180	125
Mosaddek Hossain	1	0	1	0	(6)	4	1	0	0		7th	299	130	210	143
											8th	322	146	235	166
AFGHANISTAN											9th	327	194	260	166
Yamin Ahmadzai	10	2	21	1		4	1	14	0		10th	342	205	260	173
Mohammad Nabi	24	6	56	3		20	5	39	1						
Zahir Khan	9	1	46	0	(4)	15	0	59	3						
Rashid Khan	19.5	3	55	5	(3)	21.4	6	49	6						
Qais Ahmad	8	2	22	1		1	0	6	0						

Umpires: N.J.Llong (*England*) (57) and P.Wilson (*Australia*) (1).
Referee: B.C.Broad (*England*) (99).   Test No. 2361/1 (B115/Afg3)

INDIA v SOUTH AFRICA (1st Test)

At Dr Y.S.Rajasekhara Reddy ACA-VDCA Stadium, Visakhapatnam, on 2, 3, 4, 5, 6 October 2019.
Toss: India. Result: **INDIA** won by 203 runs.
Debut: South Africa – S.Muthusamy.

INDIA

M.A.Agarwal	c Piedt b Elgar	215	c du Plessis b Maharaj	7
R.G.Sharma	st de Kock b Maharaj	176	st de Kock b Maharaj	127
C.A.Pujara	b Philander	6	lbw b Philander	81
*V.Kohli	c and b Muthusamy	20	(5) not out	31
A.M.Rahane	c Bavuma b Maharaj	15	(6) not out	27
R.A.Jadeja	not out	30	(4) b Rabada	40
G.H.Vihari	c Elgar b Maharaj	10		
†W.P.Saha	c Muthusamy b Piedt	21		
R.Ashwin	not out	1		
I.Sharma				
Mohammed Shami				
Extras	(B 4, LB 1, NB 2, W 1)	8	(B 8, LB 2)	10
Total	**(7 wkts dec; 136 overs)**	**502**	**(4 wkts dec; 67 overs)**	**323**

SOUTH AFRICA

D.Elgar	c Pujara b Jadeja	160	(2) lbw b Jadeja	2
A.K.Markram	b Ashwin	5	(1) c and b Jadeja	39
T.B.de Bruyn	c Saha b Ashwin	4	b Ashwin	10
D.L.Piedt	b Jadeja	0	(10) b Shami	56
T.Bavuma	lbw b I.Sharma	18	(4) b Shami	0
*F.du Plessis	c Pujara b Ashwin	55	(5) b Shami	13
†Q.de Kock	b Ashwin	111	(6) b Shami	0
S.Muthusamy	not out	33	(7) not out	49
V.D.Philander	b Ashwin	0	(8) lbw b Jadeja	0
K.A.Maharaj	c Agarwal b Ashwin	9	(9) lbw b Jadeja	0
K.Rabada	lbw b Ashwin	15	c Saha b Shami	18
Extras	(B 12, LB 4, NB 5)	21	(B 2, LB 2)	4
Total	**(131.2 overs)**	**431**	**(63.5 overs)**	**191**

SOUTH AFRICA	O	M	R	W	O	M	R	W
Philander	22	4	68	1	12	5	21	1
Rabada	24	7	66	0	(3) 13	3	41	1
Maharaj	55	6	189	3	(2) 22	0	129	2
Piedt	19	1	107	1	17	3	102	0
Muthusamy	15	1	63	1	3	0	20	0
Elgar	1	0	4	1				

INDIA	O	M	R	W	O	M	R	W
I.Sharma	16	2	54	1	(4) 7	2	18	0
Mohammed Shami	18	4	47	0	(3) 10.5	2	35	5
Ashwin	46.2	11	145	7	(1) 20	5	44	1
Jadeja	40	5	124	2	(2) 25	6	87	4
Vihari	9	1	38	0				
R.G.Sharma	2	1	7	0	(5) 1	0	3	0

FALL OF WICKETS

	I	SA	I	SA
Wkt	1st	1st	2nd	2nd
1st	317	14	21	4
2nd	324	31	190	19
3rd	377	34	239	20
4th	431	63	286	52
5th	436	178	–	60
6th	457	342	–	70
7th	494	370	–	70
8th	–	376	–	70
9th	–	396	–	161
10th	–	431	–	191

Umpires: C.B.Gaffaney (*New Zealand*) (30) and R.K.Illingworth (*England*) (44).
Referee: Sir R.B.Richardson (*West Indies*) (23).   Test No. 2362/37 (I536/SA433)

INDIA v SOUTH AFRICA (2nd Test)

At Maharashtra CA Stadium, Pune, on 10, 11, 12, 13 October 2019.
Toss: India. Result: **INDIA** won by an innings and 137 runs.
Debut: South Africa – A.A.Nortje.

INDIA

M.A.Agarwal	c du Plessis b Rabada	108			
R.G.Sharma	c de Kock b Rabada	14			
C.A.Pujara	c du Plessis b Rabada	58			
*V.Kohli	not out	254			
A.M.Rahane	c de Kock b Maharaj	59			
R.A.Jadeja	c de Bruyn b Muthusamy	91			
†W.P.Saha					
R.Ashwin					
I.Sharma					
Mohammed Shami					
U.T.Yadav					
Extras	(LB 6, NB 11)	17			
Total	**(5 wkts dec; 156.3 overs)**	**601**			

SOUTH AFRICA

D.Elgar	b Yadav	6	(2)	c Yadav b Ashwin	48
A.K.Markram	lbw b Yadav	0	(1)	lbw b I.Sharma	0
T.B.de Bruyn	c Saha b Yadav	30		c Saha b Yadav	8
T.Bavuma	c Saha b Shami	8	(5)	c Rahane b Jadeja	38
A.A.Nortje	c Kohli b Shami	3	(11)	not out	0
*F.du Plessis	c Rahane b Ashwin	64	(4)	b Shami	5
†Q.de Kock	b Ashwin	31	(6)	b Jadeja	5
S.Muthusamy	lbw b Jadeja	7	(7)	c R.G.Sharma b Shami	9
V.D.Philander	not out	44	(8)	c Saha b Yadav	37
K.A.Maharaj	c R.G.Sharma b Ashwin	72	(9)	lbw b Jadeja	22
K.Rabada	lbw b Ashwin	8	(10)	c R.G.Sharma b Yadav	4
Extras	(LB 8)	8		(B 8, LB 3, W 2)	13
Total	**(105.4 overs)**	**275**		**(67.2 overs)**	**189**

SOUTH AFRICA	O	M	R	W	O	M	R	W
Philander	26	6	66	0				
Rabada	30	3	93	3				
Nortje	25	5	100	0				
Maharaj	50	10	196	1				
Muthusamy	19.3	1	97	1				
Elgar	4	0	26	0				
Markram	2	0	17	0				

INDIA	O	M	R	W	O	M	R	W
I.Sharma	10	1	36	0	5	2	17	1
Yadav	13	2	37	3	8	3	22	3
Jadeja	36	15	81	1	21.2	4	52	3
Mohammed Shami	17	3	44	2	(3) 9	2	34	1
Ashwin	28.4	9	69	4	(4) 21	6	45	2
R.G.Sharma	1	1	0	0	2	0	4	0
Kohli					1	0	4	0

FALL OF WICKETS			
	I	SA	SA
Wkt	1st	1st	2nd
1st	25	2	0
2nd	163	13	21
3rd	198	33	70
4th	376	41	71
5th	601	53	79
6th	–	128	125
7th	–	139	129
8th	–	162	185
9th	–	271	189
10th	–	275	189

Umpires: C.B.Gaffaney (*New Zealand*) (31) and N.J.Llong (*England*) (58).
Referee: Sir R.B.Richardson (*West Indies*) (24).   **Test No. 2363/38 (I537/SA434)**

INDIA v SOUTH AFRICA (3rd Test)

At JSCA International Stadium Complex, Ranchi, on 19, 20, 21, 22 October 2019.
Toss: India. Result: **INDIA** won by an innings and 202 runs.
Debuts: India – S.Nadeem; South Africa – H.Klaasen, G.F.Linde.

INDIA

M.A.Agarwal	c Elgar b Rabada	10
R.G.Sharma	c Ngidi b Rabada	212
C.A.Pujara	lbw b Rabada	0
*V.Kohli	lbw b Nortje	12
A.M.Rahane	c Klaasen b Linde	115
R.A.Jadeja	c Klaasen b Linde	51
†W.P.Saha	b Linde	24
R.Ashwin	st Klaasen b Linde	14
U.T.Yadav	c Klaasen b Linde	31
S.Nadeem	not out	1
Mohammed Shami	not out	10
Extras	(B 10, LB 6, NB 1)	17
Total	**(9 wkts dec; 116.3 overs)**	**497**

SOUTH AFRICA

D.Elgar	c Saha b Shami	0	(2) retired hurt		16
Q.de Kock	c Saha b Yadav	4	(1) b Yadav		5
M.Z.Hamza	b Jadeja	62	b Shami		0
*F.du Plessis	b Yadav	1	lbw b Shami		4
T.Bavuma	st Saha b Nadeem	32	c Saha b Shami		0
†H.Klaasen	b Jadeja	6	lbw b Yadav		5
G.F.Linde	c Sharma b Yadav	37	run out		27
D.L.Piedt	lbw b Shami	4	b Jadeja		23
K.Rabada	run out	0	(10) c Jadeja b Ashwin		12
A.A.Nortje	lbw b Nadeem	4	(11) not out		5
L.T.Ngidi	not out	0	(12) c and b Nadeem		0
T.B.de Bruyn			(9) c Saha b Nadeem		30
Extras	(B 8, LB 3, NB 1)	12	(B 5, LB 1)		6
Total	**(56.2 overs)**	**162**	**(48 overs)**		**133**

SOUTH AFRICA	O	M	R	W	O	M	R	W
Rabada	23	7	85	3				
Ngidi	20	5	83	0				
Nortje	24.3	5	79	1				
Linde	31	2	133	4				
Piedt	18	3	101	1				

INDIA	O	M	R	W	O	M	R	W
Mohammed Shami	10	4	22	2	10	6	10	3
Yadav	9	1	40	3	9	1	35	2
Nadeem	11.2	4	22	2	(4) 6	1	18	2
Jadeja	14	3	19	2	(3) 13	5	36	1
Ashwin	12	1	48	0	10	3	28	1

FALL OF WICKETS			
	I	SA	SA
Wkt	1st	1st	2nd
1st	12	4	5
2nd	16	8	10
3rd	39	16	18
4th	306	107	22
5th	370	107	36
6th	417	119	67
7th	450	129	98
8th	464	130	121
9th	482	162	133
10th	–	162	133

Umpires: R.K.Illingworth (*England*) (45) and N.J.Llong (*England*) (59).
Referee: Sir R.B.Richardson (*West Indies*) (25).   **Test No. 2364/39 (I538/SA435)**
D.Elgar retired hurt at 26-4 and was replaced by T.B.de Bruyn.

INDIA v BANGLADESH (1st Test)

At Holkar Cricket Stadium, Indore, on 14, 15, 16 November 2019.
Toss: Bangladesh. Result: **INDIA** won by an innings and 130 runs.
Debuts: None.

BANGLADESH

Shadman Islam	c Saha b I.Sharma	6	b I.Sharma		6
Imrul Kayes	c Rahane b Yadav	6	b Yadav		6
*Mominul Haque	b Ashwin	37	lbw b Shami		7
Mithun Ali	lbw b Shami	13	c Agarwal b Shami		18
Mushfiqur Rahim	b Shami	43	c Pujara b Ashwin		64
Mahmudullah	b Ashwin	10	c R.G.Sharma b Shami		15
†Liton Das	c Kohli b I.Sharma	21	c and b Ashwin		35
Mehedi Hasan	lbw b Shami	0	b Yadav		38
Taijul Islam	run out	1	c Saha b Shami		6
Abu Jayed	not out	7	not out		4
Ebadat Hossain	b Yadav	2	c Yadav b Ashwin		1
Extras	(LB 3, W 1)	4	(B 2, LB 9, NB 1, W 1)		13
Total	**(58.3 overs)**	**150**	**(69.2 overs)**		**213**

INDIA

M.A.Agarwal	c Abu b Mehedi	243
R.G.Sharma	c Liton b Abu	6
C.A.Pujara	c sub (Saif Hasan) b Abu	54
*V.Kohli	lbw b Abu	0
A.M.Rahane	c Taijul b Abu	86
R.A.Jadeja	not out	60
†W.P.Saha	b Ebadat	12
U.T.Yadav	not out	25
R.Ashwin		
I.Sharma		
Mohammed Shami		
Extras	(LB 1, NB 3, W 3)	7
Total	**(6 wkts dec; 114 overs)**	**493**

INDIA	O	M	R	W		O	M	R	W
I.Sharma	12	6	20	2		11	3	31	1
Yadav	14.3	3	47	2		14	1	51	2
Mohammed Shami	13	5	27	3		16	7	31	4
Ashwin	16	1	43	2	(5)	14.2	6	42	3
Jadeja	3	0	10	0	(4)	14	2	47	0

BANGLADESH	O	M	R	W
Ebadat Hossain	31	5	115	1
Abu Jayed	25	3	108	4
Taijul Islam	28	4	120	0
Mehedi Hasan	27	0	125	1
Mahmudullah	3	0	24	0

FALL OF WICKETS

	B	I	B
Wkt	1st	1st	2nd
1st	12	14	10
2nd	12	105	16
3rd	31	119	37
4th	99	309	44
5th	115	432	72
6th	140	454	135
7th	140	–	194
8th	140	–	208
9th	148	–	208
10th	150	–	213

Umpires: M.Erasmus (*South Africa*) (58) and R.J.Tucker (*Australia*) (69).
Referee: R.S.Madugalle (*Sri Lanka*) (190).　　　　Test No. 2365/10 (I539/B116)

INDIA v BANGLADESH (2nd Test)

At Eden Gardens, Kolkata, on 22, 23, 24 November 2019 (day/night).
Toss: Bangladesh. Result: **INDIA** won by an innings and 46 runs.
Debuts: None.

BANGLADESH

Shadman Islam	c Saha b Yadav	29	lbw b I.Sharma		0
Imrul Kayes	lbw b I.Sharma	4	c Kohli b I.Sharma		5
*Mominul Haque	c R.G.Sharma b Yadav	0	c Saha b I.Sharma		0
Mithun Ali	b Yadav	0	c Shami b Yadav		6
Mushfiqur Rahim	b Shami	0	c Jadeja b Yadav		74
Mahmudullah	c Saha b I.Sharma	6	retired hurt		39
†Liton Das	retired hurt	24			
Nayeem Hasan	b I.Sharma	19			
Ebadat Hossain	b I.Sharma	1	c Kohli b Yadav		0
Mehedi Hasan	c Pujara b I.Sharma	8	(7) c Kohli b I.Sharma		15
Al-Amin Hossain	not out	1	(10) c Saha b Yadav		21
Abu Jayed	c Pujara b Shami	0	(11) not out		2
Taijul Islam			(8) c Rahane b Yadav		11
Extras	(B 8, LB 6)	14	(B 8, LB 9, W 5)		22
Total	**(30.3 overs)**	**106**	**(41.1 overs)**		**195**

INDIA

M.A.Agarwal	c Mehedi b Al-Amin	14
R.G.Sharma	lbw b Ebadat	21
C.A.Pujara	c Shadman b Ebadat	55
*V.Kohli	c Taijul b Ebadat	136
A.M.Rahane	c Ebadat b Taijul	51
R.A.Jadeja	b Abu	12
†W.P.Saha	not out	17
R.Ashwin	lbw b Al-Amin	9
U.T.Yadav	c Shadman b Abu	0
I.Sharma	lbw b Al-Amin	0
Mohammed Shami	not out	10
Extras	(B 12, LB 2, W 8)	22
Total	**(9 wkts dec; 89.4 overs)**	**347**

INDIA	O	M	R	W		O	M	R	W
I.Sharma	12	4	22	5		13	2	56	4
Yadav	7	2	29	3		14.1	1	53	5
Mohammed Shami	10.3	2	36	2		8	0	42	0
Jadeja	1	0	5	0	(5)	1	0	8	0
Ashwin					(4)	5	0	19	0

BANGLADESH	O	M	R	W
Al-Amin Hossain	22.4	3	85	3
Abu Jayed	21	6	77	2
Ebadat Hossain	21	3	91	3
Taijul Islam	25	2	80	1

FALL OF WICKETS			
	B	I	B
Wkt	1st	1st	2nd
1st	15	26	0
2nd	17	43	2
3rd	17	137	9
4th	26	236	13
5th	38	289	133
6th	60	308	152
7th	82	329	152
8th	98	330	184
9th	105	331	195
10th	106	–	–

Umpires: M.Erasmus (*South Africa*) (59) and J.S.Wilson (*West Indies*) (16).
Referee: R.S.Madugalle (*Sri Lanka*) (191). **Test No. 2366/11 (I540/B117)**
Mehedi Hasan replaced Liton Das at 73-6 (1st innings); Taijul Islam replaced Nayeem
Hasan (India 1st innings, 6.6 overs); Mahmudullah retired hurt at 82-4 (2nd innings).

31

NEW ZEALAND v ENGLAND (1st Test)

At Bay Oval, Mount Maunganui, on 21, 22, 23, 24, 25 November 2019.
Toss: England. Result: **NEW ZEALAND** won by an innings and 65 runs.
Debut: England – D.P.Sibley.

ENGLAND

R.J.Burns	c Watling b de Grandhomme	52		c de Grandhomme b Santner	31
D.P.Sibley	c Taylor b de Grandhomme	22		c Watling b Santner	12
J.L.Denly	c Watling b Southee	74		c Watling b Wagner	35
*J.E.Root	c Southee b Wagner	2	(5)	c Latham b de Grandhomme	11
B.A.Stokes	c Taylor b Southee	91	(6)	b Southee	28
O.J.D.Pope	c Watling b Southee	29	(7)	c Santner b Wagner	6
†J.C.Buttler	c Santner b Wagner	43	(8)	b Wagner	0
S.M.Curran	lbw b Southee	0	(9)	not out	29
J.C.Archer	c Southee b Boult	4	(10)	c sub (M.J.Henry) b Wagner	30
M.J.Leach	not out	18	(4)	c Latham b Santner	0
S.C.J.Broad	b Wagner	1		lbw b Wagner	0
Extras	(B 2, LB 11, NB 1, W 3)	17		(B 12, LB 1, NB 1, W 1)	15
Total	(124 overs; 539 mins)	353		(96.2 overs; 408 mins)	197

NEW ZEALAND

J.A.Raval	c Denly b Leach	19
T.W.M.Latham	lbw b Curran	8
*K.S.Williamson	c Stokes b Curran	51
L.R.P.L.Taylor	c Pope b Stokes	25
H.M.Nicholls	lbw b Root	41
†B.J.Watling	c Buttler b Archer	205
C.de Grandhomme	c Sibley b Stokes	65
M.J.Santner	c Pope b Curran	126
T.G.Southee	c and b Leach	9
N.Wagner	not out	11
T.A.Boult	not out	1
Extras	(B 22, LB 9, NB 2, W 21)	54
Total	(9 wkts dec; 201 overs; 845 mins)	615

NEW ZEALAND	O	M	R	W		O	M	R	W
Boult	31	6	97	1	(2)	6	4	6	0
Southee	32	7	88	4	(1)	20	4	60	1
De Grandhomme	23	5	41	2		10	3	15	1
Wagner	32	7	90	3	(5)	19.2	6	44	5
Santner	6	1	24	0	(4)	40	19	53	3
Williamson						1	0	6	0

ENGLAND	O	M	R	W
Broad	33	13	64	0
Archer	42	15	107	1
Curran	35	7	119	3
Leach	47	7	153	2
Stokes	26	5	74	2
Root	18	3	67	1

FALL OF WICKETS

Wkt	E 1st	NZ 1st	E 2nd
1st	52	-18	48
2nd	113	72	53
3rd	120	106	55
4th	203	127	69
5th	277	197	121
6th	286	316	132
7th	286	577	133
8th	295	598	138
9th	347	603	197
10th	353	–	197

Umpires: H.D.P.K.Dharmasena (*Sri Lanka*) (63) and B.N.J.Oxenford (*Australia*) (57).
Referee: J.Srinath (*India*) (50).   Test No. 2367/104 (E1017/NZ436)

32

NEW ZEALAND v ENGLAND (2nd Test)

At Seddon Park, Hamilton, on 29, 30 November, 1, 2, 3 December 2019.
Toss: England. Result: **MATCH DRAWN**.
Debuts: New Zealand – D.J.Mitchell; England – Z.Crawley.

NEW ZEALAND

J.A.Raval	c Root b Broad	5	(2) lbw b Curran		0
T.W.M.Latham	b Broad	105	(1) c Root b Woakes		18
*K.S.Williamson	c Root b Woakes	4	not out		104
L.R.P.L.Taylor	c Root b Woakes	53	not out		105
H.M.Nicholls	c Broad b Curran	16			
†B.J.Watling	c Burns b Broad	55			
D.J.Mitchell	c Archer b Broad	73			
M.J.Santner	c Woakes b Archer	23			
T.G.Southee	c Pope b Woakes	18			
M.J.Henry	not out	5			
N.Wagner	c Sibley b Curran	0			
Extras	(B 15, LB 3)	18	(B 2, LB 3, NB 1, W 3, Pen 5)		14
Total	**(129.1 overs; 572 mins)**	**375**	**(2 wkts; 75 overs; 318 mins)**		**241**

ENGLAND

R.J.Burns	run out	101
D.P.Sibley	lbw b Southee	4
J.L.Denly	c Watling b Henry	4
*J.E.Root	c Nicholls b Santner	226
B.A.Stokes	c Taylor b Southee	26
Z.Crawley	c Watling b Wagner	1
†O.J.D.Pope	c Raval b Wagner	75
S.M.Curran	not out	11
C.R.Woakes	c Watling b Wagner	0
J.C.Archer	b Wagner	8
S.C.J.Broad	b Wagner	0
Extras	(B 4, LB 14, NB 1, W 1)	20
Total	**(162.5 overs; 706 mins)**	**476**

ENGLAND	O	M	R	W		O	M	R	W
Broad	28	7	73	4		9	0	28	0
Archer	28	8	75	1	(3)	12	1	27	0
Woakes	31	6	83	3	(4)	11	4	12	1
Curran	23.1	7	63	2	(2)	16	2	56	1
Root	3	0	14	0	(7)	4	1	23	0
Stokes	13	5	36	0	(5)	14	1	58	0
Denly	3	0	13	0	(6)	9	1	27	0

NEW ZEALAND	O	M	R	W
Southee	37	4	90	2
Henry	33	6	87	1
Wagner	35.5	3	124	5
Mitchell	22	5	69	0
Santner	35	4	88	1

FALL OF WICKETS

	NZ	E	NZ
Wkt	1st	1st	2nd
1st	16	11	2
2nd	39	24	28
3rd	155	201	
4th	182	245	
5th	191	262	
6th	315	455	
7th	330	458	
8th	357	460	
9th	375	476	
10th	375	476	

Umpires: H.D.P.K.Dharmasena (*Sri Lanka*) (64) and P.Wilson (*Australia*) (2).
Referee: J.Srinath (*India*) (51).

Test No. 2368/105 (E1018/NZ437)

AUSTRALIA v PAKISTAN (1st Test)

At Woolloongabba, Brisbane, on 21, 22, 23, 24 November 2019.
Toss: Pakistan. Result: **AUSTRALIA** won by an innings and 5 runs.
Debut: Pakistan – Naseem Shah.

PAKISTAN

Shan Masood	c Smith b Cummins	27	c Paine b Cummins		42
*Azhar Ali	c Burns b Hazlewood	39	lbw b Starc		5
Haris Sohail	c Paine b Starc	1	c Paine b Starc		8
Asad Shafiq	b Cummins	76	c Smith b Cummins		0
Babar Azam	c Burns b Hazlewood	1	c Paine b Lyon		104
Iftikhar Ahmed	c Labuschagne b Lyon	7	c Paine b Hazlewood		0
†Mohammad Rizwan	c Paine b Cummins	37	c Lyon b Hazlewood		95
Yasir Shah	b Starc	26	c Wade b Hazlewood		42
Shaheen Shah Afridi	c Paine b Starc	0	c Cummins b Hazlewood		10
Naseem Shah	c and b Starc	7	(11) not out		0
Imran Khan	not out	5	(10) c Wade b Starc		5
Extras	(B 4, LB 8, NB 1, W 1)	14	(B 9, LB 9, NB 1, W 5)		24
Total	(86.2 overs)	240	(84.2 overs)		335

AUSTRALIA

D.A.Warner	c Rizwan b Naseem	154
J.A.Burns	b Yasir	97
M.Labuschagne	c Azam b Afridi	185
S.P.D.Smith	b Yasir	4
M.S.Wade	c Rizwan b Sohail	60
T.M.Head	c Rizwan b Sohail	24
*†T.D.Paine	c Shafiq b Afridi	13
P.J.Cummins	c Rizwan b Khan	7
M.A.Starc	lbw b Shah	5
N.M.Lyon	not out	13
J.R.Hazlewood	lbw b Shah	5
Extras	(B 6, LB 4, NB 3)	13
Total	(157.4 overs)	580

AUSTRALIA	O	M	R	W	O	M	R	W
Starc	18.2	5	52	4	16.2	1	73	3
Hazlewood	20	6	46	2	(3) 21	3	63	4
Cummins	22	7	60	3	(2) 21	6	69	2
Lyon	17	3	40	1	21	3	74	1
Labuschagne	8	0	24	0	5	0	38	0
Smith	1	0	6	0				

PAKISTAN	O	M	R	W
Shaheen Shah Afridi	34	7	96	2
Imran Khan	24	3	73	1
Naseem Shah	20	1	68	1
Iftikhar Ahmed	12	0	53	0
Yasir Shah	48.4	1	205	4
Haris Sohail	19	1	75	2

FALL OF WICKETS			
	P	A	P
Wkt	1st	1st	2nd
1st	75	222	13
2nd	75	351	25
3rd	77	358	25
4th	78	468	93
5th	94	506	94
6th	143	545	226
7th	227	546	305
8th	227	559	324
9th	227	567	331
10th	240	580	335

Umpires: R.K.Illingworth (*England*) (46) and R.A.Kettleborough (*England*) (61).
Referee: J.J.Crowe (*New Zealand*) (96).   **Test No. 2369/65 (A826/P424)**

AUSTRALIA v PAKISTAN (2nd Test)

At Adelaide Oval, on 29, 30 November, 1, 2 December 2019 (day/night).
Toss: Australia. Result: **AUSTRALIA** won by an innings and 48 runs.
Debut: Pakistan – Musa Khan.

AUSTRALIA

D.A.Warner	not out	335
J.A.Burns	c Rizwan b Afridi	4
M.Labuschagne	b Afridi	162
S.P.D.Smith	c Rizwan b Afridi	36
M.S.Wade	not out	38
T.M.Head		
*†T.D.Paine		
P.J.Cummins		
M.A.Starc		
N.M.Lyon		
J.R.Hazlewood		
Extras	(LB 6, NB 7, W 1)	14
Total	**(3 wkts dec; 127 overs)**	**589**

PAKISTAN

Shan Masood	c Paine b Hazlewood	19	c Starc b Lyon		68
Imam-ul-Haq	c Warner b Starc	2	lbw b Hazlewood		0
*Azhar Ali	c Smith b Cummins	9	c Smith b Starc		9
Babar Azam	c Paine b Starc	97	c Paine b Hazlewood		8
Asad Shafiq	c Paine b Starc	9	c Warner b Lyon		57
Iftikhar Ahmed	c Paine b Starc	10	c Labuschagne b Lyon		27
†Mohammad Rizwan	c Paine b Starc	0	b Hazlewood		45
Yasir Shah	c Lyon b Cummins	113	lbw b Lyon		13
Shaheen Shah Afridi	lbw b Starc	0	c Hazlewood b Lyon		1
Mohammad Abbas	c Warner b Cummins	29	run out		1
Musa Khan	not out	12	not out		4
Extras	(LB 2)	2	(LB 6)		6
Total	**(94.4 overs)**	**302**	**(82 overs)**		**239**

PAKISTAN	O	M	R	W		O	M	R	W
Mohammad Abbas	29	7	100	0					
Shaheen Shah Afridi	30	5	88	3					
Musa Khan	20	1	114	0					
Yasir Shah	32	1	197	0					
Iftikhar Ahmed	15	0	75	0					
Azhar Ali	1	0	9	0					

AUSTRALIA	O	M	R	W		O	M	R	W
Starc	25	6	66	6		16	3	47	1
Cummins	22.4	2	83	3	(3)	15	4	45	0
Hazlewood	14	2	48	1	(2)	23	4	63	3
Lyon	22	3	65	0		25	7	69	5
Labuschagne	10	2	32	0		3	0	9	0
Smith	1	0	6	0					

FALL OF WICKETS

	A	P	P
Wkt	1st	1st	2nd
1st	8	3	2
2nd	369	22	11
3rd	490	38	20
4th	–	69	123
5th	–	89	154
6th	–	89	201
7th	–	194	221
8th	–	194	229
9th	–	281	235
10th	–	302	239

Umpires: M.A.Gough (*England*) (12) and R.K.Illingworth (*England*) (47).
Referee: J.J.Crowe (*New Zealand*) (97).   **Test No. 2370/66 (A827/P425)**

AFGHANISTAN v WEST INDIES (Only Test)

At Ekana International Cricket Stadium, Lucknow, on 27, 28, 29 November 2019.
Toss: West Indies. Result: **WEST INDIES** won by nine wickets.
Debuts: Afghanistan – Nasir Ahmadzai, Hamza Hotak.

AFGHANISTAN

Batsman	1st innings		2nd innings	
Ibrahim Zadran	c Holder b Cornwall	17	lbw b Cornwall	23
Javed Ahmadi	c Brooks b Warrican	39	c Cornwall b Chase	62
Ihsanullah Janat	c Hope b Cornwall	24	run out	1
Rahmat Shah	c Holder b Cornwall	4	c Brooks b Cornwall	0
Asghar Stanikzai	c Dowrich b Cornwall	4	c Brooks b Cornwall	0
Nasir Ahmadzai	c Hope b Cornwall	2	b Chase	15
†Afsar Zazai	lbw b Cornwall	32	(8) c Dowrich b Holder	7
*Rashid Khan	c Cornwall b Holder	1	(9) c Dowrich b Holder	1
Hamza Hotak	c Dowrich b Holder	34	(7) c Cornwall b Chase	1
Yamin Ahmadzai	c Warrican b Cornwall	18	b Holder	1
Zahir Khan	not out	0	not out	1
Extras	(B 7, LB 5)	12	(B 4, LB 4, NB 1)	9
Total	(68.3 overs; 263 mins)	187	(43.1 overs; 160 mins)	120

WEST INDIES

Batsman	1st innings		2nd innings	
K.C.Brathwaite	lbw b Hotak	11	c Zazai b Hotak	8
J.D.Campbell	c Janat b Hotak	55	not out	19
S.D.Hope	c Janat b Rashid	7	not out	6
S.S.J.Brooks	b Hotak	111		
S.O.Hetmyer	lbw b Rashid	13		
†R.L.Chase	c Zadran b Zahir	2		
S.O.Dowrich	lbw b Zahir	42		
*J.O.Holder	st Zazai b Hotak	11		
R.R.S.Cornwall	lbw b Hotak	5		
K.A.J.Roach	lbw b Hotak	3		
J.A.Warrican	not out	4		
Extras	(LB 12, NB 1)	13		
Total	(83.3 overs; 311 mins)	277	(1 wkt; 6.2 overs; 23 mins)	33

WEST INDIES	O	M	R	W		O	M	R	W
Roach	8	1	33	0		4	2	5	0
Holder	17	10	22	2		6.1	2	20	3
Cornwall	25.3	5	75	7	(4)	18	3	46	3
Warrican	13	1	35	1	(3)	12	3	31	0
Chase	5	0	10	0		3	1	10	3

AFGHANISTAN	O	M	R	W		O	M	R	W
Yamin Ahmadzai	10	3	24	0		1	0	8	0
Hamza Hotak	28.3	4	74	5	(3)	2.2	1	5	1
Rashid Khan	32	5	114	3	(4)	2	0	11	0
Zahir Khan	13	2	53	2					
Javed Ahmadi					(2)	1	0	9	0

FALL OF WICKETS

Wkt	Afg 1st	WI 1st	Afg 2nd	WI 2nd
1st	28	27	53	22
2nd	84	34	55	
3rd	90	116	55	
4th	91	137	59	
5th	95	150	96	
6th	98	224	98	
7th	111	243	109	
8th	165	260	111	
9th	187	270	119	
10th	187	277	120	

Umpires: N.N.Menon (*India*) (1) and P.R.Reiffel (*Australia*) (45).
Referee: B.C.Broad (*England*) (100).

Test No. 2371/1 (Afg4/WI545)

PAKISTAN v SRI LANKA (1st Test)

At Rawalpindi Cricket Stadium, on 11, 12, 13, 14 (*no play*), 15 December 2019.
Toss: Sri Lanka. Result: **MATCH DRAWN**.
Debuts: Pakistan – Abid Ali, Usman Shinwari.

SRI LANKA

*F.D.M.Karunaratne	lbw b Afridi	59
B.O.P.Fernando	c Sohail b Shah	40
B.K.G.Mendis	c Rizwan b Shinwari	10
A.D.Mathews	c Shafiq b Shah	31
L.D.Chandimal	b Abbas	2
D.M.de Silva	not out	102
†D.P.D.N.Dickwella	c Azam b Afridi	33
M.D.K.Perera	not out	16
M.V.T.Fernando		
C.A.K.Rajitha		
C.B.R.L.S.Kumara		
Extras	(B 5, LB 7, NB 3)	15
Total	**(6 wkts dec; 97 overs)**	**308**

PAKISTAN

Shan Masood	c Chandimal b Rajitha	0
Abid Ali	not out	109
*Azhar Ali	c Karunaratne b Kumara	36
Babar Azam	not out	102
Haris Sohail		
Asad Shafiq		
†Mohammad Rizwan		
Usman Shinwari		
Mohammad Abbas		
Naseem Shah		
Shaheen Shah Afridi		
Extras	(B 2, NB 2, W 1)	5
Total	**(2 wkts; 70 overs)**	**252**

PAKISTAN	O	M	R	W	O	M	R	W
Mohammad Abbas	27	9	72	1				
Shaheen Shah Afridi	22	7	58	2				
Usman Shinwari	15	4	54	1				
Naseem Shah	27	5	92	2				
Haris Sohail	3	0	12	0				
Shan Masood	1	1	0	0				
Asad Shafiq	2	0	8	0				

SRI LANKA	O	M	R	W
Rajitha	6	2	5	1
M.V.T.Fernando	13	1	49	0
Kumara	14	4	46	1
Perera	24	0	85	0
De Silva	11	0	48	0
B.O.P.Fernando	1	0	3	0
Mendis	1	0	14	0

FALL OF WICKETS		
	P	A
Wkt	1st	1st
1st	96	3
2nd	109	90
3rd	120	–
4th	127	–
5th	189	–
6th	256	–
7th	–	–
8th	–	–
9th	–	–
10th	–	–

Umpires: M.A.Gough (*England*) (13) and R.A.Kettleborough (*England*) (62).
Referee: A.J.Pycroft (*Zimbabwe*) (72). **Test No. 2372/54 (P426/SL286)**

PAKISTAN v SRI LANKA (2nd Test)

At National Stadium, Karachi, on 19, 20, 21, 22, 23 December 2019.
Toss: Pakistan. Result: **PAKISTAN** won by 263 runs.
Debuts: None.

PAKISTAN

Shan Masood	b M.V.T.Fernando	5	c B.O.P.Fernando b Kumara	135
Abid Ali	lbw b Kumara	38	lbw b Kumara	174
*Azhar Ali	b M.V.T.Fernando	0	st Dickwella b Ambuldeniya	118
Babar Azam	st Dickwella b Ambuldeniya	60	not out	100
Asad Shafiq	c M.V.T.Fernando b Kumara	63		
Haris Sohail	lbw b Ambuldeniya	9		
†Mohammad Rizwan	b Kumara	4	(5) not out	21
Yasir Shah	b Kumara	0		
Mohammad Abbas	c de Silva b Ambuldeniya	0		
Shaheen Shah Afridi	c Mathews b Ambuldeniya	5		
Naseem Shah	not out	1		
Extras	(B 4, LB 2)	6	(LB 5, W 2)	7
Total	(59.3 overs)	191	(3 wkts dec; 131 overs)	555

SRI LANKA

B.O.P.Fernando	c Rizwan b Afridi	4	(2) c Shafiq b Yasir	102
*F.D.M.Karunaratne	b Abbas	25	(1) c Rizwan b Abbas	16
B.K.G.Mendis	c Sohail b Abbas	13	c Azam b Naseem	0
A.D.Mathews	c Rizwan b Afridi	13	c Rizwan b Afridi	19
L.Ambuldeniya	c Shafiq b Abbas	13	(9) c Rizwan b Naseem	0
L.D.Chandimal	c Masood b Sohail	74	(5) lbw b Naseem	2
D.M.de Silva	c Abbas b Afridi	32	(6) b Yasir	0
†D.P.D.N.Dickwella	b Abbas	21	(7) b Sohail	65
M.D.K.Perera	lbw b Afridi	48	(8) c Rizwan b Naseem	5
M.V.T.Fernando	not out	5	lbw b Naseem	0
C.B.R.L.S.Kumara	b Afridi	0	not out	0
Extras	(B 4, LB 10, NB 3, W 6)	23	(LB 3)	3
Total	(85.5 overs)	271	(62.5 overs)	212

SRI LANKA	O	M	R	W	O	M	R	W
M.V.T.Fernando	13	3	31	2	24	2	105	0
Kumara	18	5	49	4	29	5	139	2
Karunaratne	1	0	11	0				
Ambuldeniya	20.3	3	71	4	(3) 50	4	193	1
Perera	7	0	23	0	(4) 21	1	94	0
De Silva					(5) 7	0	19	0

PAKISTAN	O	M	R	W	O	M	R	W
Shaheen Shah Afridi	26.5	5	77	5	14	3	51	1
Mohammad Abbas	27	9	55	4	12	2	33	1
Naseem Shah	16	1	71	0	12.5	4	31	5
Yasir Shah	13	0	43	0	20	3	84	2
Haris Sohail	3	0	11	1	4	0	10	1

FALL OF WICKETS

	P	A	P	A
Wkt	1st	1st	2nd	2nd
1st	10	28	278	39
2nd	10	39	355	40
3rd	65	61	503	70
4th	127	78	–	96
5th	167	80	–	97
6th	172	147	–	201
7th	172	184	–	212
8th	179	235	–	212
9th	185	271	–	212
10th	191	271	–	212

Umpires: B.N.J.Oxenford (*Australia*) (58) and J.S.Wilson (*West Indies*) (17).
Referee: J.J.Crowe (*New Zealand*) (98).   **Test No. 2373/55 (P427/SL287)**

AUSTRALIA v NEW ZEALAND (1st Test)

At Perth Stadium, on 12, 13, 14, 15 December 2019 (day/night).
Toss: Australia. Result: **AUSTRALIA** won by 296 runs.
Debut: New Zealand – L.H.Ferguson.

AUSTRALIA

D.A.Warner	c and b Wagner	43	c sub (T.A.Blundell) b Southee		19
J.A.Burns	lbw b de Grandhomme	9	c Nicholls b Southee		53
M.Labuschagne	b Wagner	143	c Santner b Wagner		50
S.P.D.Smith	c Southee b Wagner	43	c Raval b Wagner		16
M.S.Wade	b Southee	12	c Raval b de Grandhomme		17
T.M.Head	c Santner b Southee	56	c de Grandhomme b Southee		5
*†T.D.Paine	c Watling b Southee	39	b Southee		0
P.J.Cummins	b Raval	20	c Watling b Wagner		13
M.A.Starc	c Williamson b Southee	30	c Taylor b Southee		23
N.M.Lyon	c de Grandhomme b Wagner	8	not out		0
J.R.Hazlewood	not out	0			
Extras	(B 2, LB 1, NB 2, W 8)	13	(LB 7, NB 6, W 8)		21
Total	**(146.2 overs)**	**416**	**(9 wkts dec; 69.1 overs)**		**217**

NEW ZEALAND

J.A.Raval	b Hazlewood	1	c Lyon b Starc		1
T.W.M.Latham	c and b Starc	0	lbw b Lyon		18
*K.S.Williamson	c Smith b Starc	34	c Wade b Lyon		14
L.R.P.L.Taylor	c Smith b Lyon	80	c Paine b Starc		22
H.M.Nicholls	c Paine b Starc	7	c Head b Lyon		21
N.Wagner	b Starc	0	(10) c Paine b Starc		8
†B.J.Watling	b Cummins	8	(6) c Paine b Starc		40
C.de Grandhomme	c Smith b Starc	23	(7) c Smith b Cummins		33
M.J.Santner	b Labuschagne	2	(8) c Head b Cummins		0
T.G.Southee	c sub (M.G.Neser) b Lyon	8	(9) c Smith b Lyon		4
L.H.Ferguson	not out	0	not out		1
Extras	(B 1, LB 2)	3	(LB 6, NB 1, W 2)		9
Total	**(55.2 overs)**	**166**	**(65.3 overs)**		**171**

NEW ZEALAND	O	M	R	W		O	M	R	W
Southee	30.2	7	93	4		21.1	6	69	5
Ferguson	11	1	47	0					
Wagner	37	7	92	4		23	4	59	3
De Grandhomme	22	8	37	1	(2)	17	2	47	1
Santner	33	5	111	0	(4)	8	0	35	0
Raval	13	1	33	1					

AUSTRALIA	O	M	R	W		O	M	R	W
Starc	18	2	52	5		14	5	45	4
Hazlewood	1.2	1	0	1					
Cummins	14.4	3	46	1	(2)	19	6	31	2
Wade	2	0	8	0					
Lyon	14.2	2	48	2	(3)	22.3	3	63	4
Labuschagne	5	1	9	1	(5)	5	0	13	0
Head					(4)	5	1	13	0

FALL OF WICKETS

	A	NZ	A	NZ
Wkt	1st	1st	2nd	2nd
1st	40	1	44	6
2nd	75	1	131	21
3rd	207	77	148	57
4th	225	97	154	57
5th	301	97	160	98
6th	325	120	160	154
7th	363	147	180	154
8th	408	155	189	154
9th	416	166	217	163
10th	416	166	–	171

Umpires: Alim Dar (*Pakistan*) (129) and N.J.Llong (*England*) (60).
Referee: Sir R.B.Richardson (*West Indies*) (26).   Test No. 2374/58 (A828/NZ438)

39

AUSTRALIA v NEW ZEALAND (2nd Test)

At Melbourne Cricket Ground, on 26, 27, 28, 29 December 2019.
Toss: New Zealand. Result: **AUSTRALIA** won by 247 runs.
Debuts: None.

AUSTRALIA

D.A.Warner	c Southee b Wagner	41	c Blundell b Wagner		38
J.A.Burns	b Boult	0	c Watling b Santner		35
M.Labuschagne	b de Grandhomme	63	run out		19
S.P.D.Smith	c Nicholls b Wagner	85	c Southee b Wagner		7
M.S.Wade	c Watling b de Grandhomme	38	not out		30
T.M.Head	c Santner b Wagner	114	b Wagner		28
*†T.D.Paine	lbw b Wagner	79			
M.A.Starc	c Williamson b Southee	1			
J.L.Pattinson	not out	14			
P.J.Cummins	c Latham b Southee	0			
N.M.Lyon	c Wagner b Southee	1			
Extras	(B 5, LB 22, W 4)	31	(B 4, LB 4, NB 1, W 2)		11
Total	(155.1 overs; 671 mins)	467	(5 wkts dec; 54.2 overs; 234 mins)		168

NEW ZEALAND

T.W.M.Latham	c Paine b Cummins	50	c Paine b Pattinson		8
T.A.Blundell	c Paine b Cummins	15	c Lyon b Labuschagne		121
*K.S.Williamson	c Paine b Pattinson	9	lbw b Pattinson		0
L.R.P.L.Taylor	c Burns b Cummins	4	b Pattinson		2
H.M.Nicholls	lbw b Pattinson	0	st Paine b Lyon		33
†B.J.Watling	c Burns b Pattinson	7	c Warner b Lyon		22
C.de Grandhomme	c Warner b Starc	11	c Warner b Lyon		9
M.J.Santner	c Paine b Pattinson	3	c Paine b Lyon		27
T.G.Southee	c Paine b Cummins	10	run out		2
N.Wagner	not out	18	not out		6
T.A.Boult	b Starc	8	absent hurt		
Extras	(B 4, LB 4, NB 3, W 2)	13	(LB 7, NB 1, W 2)		10
Total	(54.5 overs; 278 mins)	148	(71 overs; 321 mins)		240

NEW ZEALAND	O	M	R	W	O	M	R	W		FALL OF WICKETS			
Boult	31	3	91	1	9	0	30	0			A	NZ	A	NZ
Southee	33.1	6	103	3	15	3	44	0	*Wkt*	*1st*	*1st*	*2nd*	*2nd*
De Grandhomme	30	5	68	2	5	0	14	0	1st	1	23	62	32
Wagner	38	11	83	4	17.2	1	50	3	2nd	61	39	100	33
Santner	20	1	82	0	8	0	22	1	3rd	144	46	110	35
Blundell	3	0	13	0					4th	216	46	110	89
									5th	284	58	168	161
AUSTRALIA									6th	434	97	–	172
Starc	12.5	4	30	2	15	3	59	0	7th	435	112	–	212
Cummins	17	5	28	5	18	4	47	0	8th	458	116	–	214
Pattinson	15	2	34	3	12	3	35	3	9th	463	124	–	240
Lyon	9	1	35	0	23	4	81	4	10th	467	148	–	–
Wade	1	0	13	0									
Labuschagne					(5)	3	1	11	1					

Umpires: M.Erasmus (*South Africa*) (60) and N.J.Llong (*England*) (61).
Referee: Sir R.B.Richardson (*West Indies*) (27).   Test No. 2375/59 (A829/NZ439)

AUSTRALIA v NEW ZEALAND (3rd Test)

At Sydney Cricket Ground, on 3, 4, 5, 6 January 2020.
Toss: Australia. Result: **AUSTRALIA** won by 279 runs.
Debuts: New Zealand – G.D.Phillips.

AUSTRALIA

D.A.Warner	c de Grandhomme b Wagner	45	not out		111
J.A.Burns	c Taylor b de Grandhomme	18	lbw b Astle		40
M.Labuschagne	c and b Astle	215	c Latham b Henry		59
S.P.D.Smith	c Taylor b de Grandhomme	63			
M.S.Wade	b Somerville	22			
T.M.Head	c Watling b Henry	10			
*†T.D.Paine	b de Grandhomme	35			
J.L.Pattinson	b Wagner	2			
P.J.Cummins	c Phillips b Astle	8			
M.A.Starc	b Wagner	22			
N.M.Lyon	not out	6			
Extras	(LB 6, NB 1, W 1)	8	(B 3, LB 3, W 1)		7
Total	**(150.1 overs; 623 mins)**	**454**	**(2 wkts dec; 52 overs; 225 mins)**		**217**

NEW ZEALAND

*T.W.M.Latham	c Starc b Cummins	49	lbw b Starc		1
T.A.Blundell	b Lyon	34	c Lyon b Starc		2
J.A.Raval	lbw b Lyon	31	c Paine b Henry		12
L.R.P.L.Taylor	lbw b Cummins	22	b Cummins		22
G.D.Phillips	b Cummins	52	c Paine b Lyon		0
†B.J.Watling	b Starc	9	c Cummins b Lyon		19
C.de Grandhomme	run out	20	c Burns b Lyon		52
T.D.Astle	not out	25	c Pattinson b Lyon		17
W.E.R.Somerville	b Lyon	0	b Starc		7
N.Wagner	b Lyon	0	not out		0
M.J.Henry	st Paine b Lyon	3	absent hurt		
Extras	(B 1, LB 4, NB 1, Pen 5)	11	(B 3, LB 1)		4
Total	**(95.4 overs; 440 mins)**	**256**	**(47.5 overs; 211 mins)**		**136**

NEW ZEALAND	O	M	R	W	O	M	R	W
Henry	32	3	94	1	12	2	54	1
De Grandhomme	24	1	78	3	13	1	43	0
Wagner	33.1	9	66	3	9	1	37	0
Somerville	29	2	99	1	10	0	36	0
Astle	32	0	111	2	8	1	41	0

AUSTRALIA	O	M	R	W	O	M	R	W
Starc	21	1	57	0	9	3	25	2
Cummins	22	6	44	3	11	3	29	1
Pattinson	16	3	58	0	6	3	8	0
Lyon	30.4	10	68	5	16.5	4	50	5
Labuschagne	4	0	8	0	5	0	20	0
Head	2	0	11	0				

FALL OF WICKETS

	A	NZ	A	NZ
Wkt	1st	1st	2nd	2nd
1st	39	68	107	3
2nd	95	117	217	4
3rd	251	117	–	22
4th	288	145	–	22
5th	331	163	–	38
6th	410	195	–	107
7th	416	235	–	128
8th	426	237	–	136
9th	430	237	–	136
10th	454	256	–	–

Umpires: Alim Dar (*Pakistan*) (130) and M.Erasmus (*South Africa*) (61).
Referee: Sir R.B.Richardson (*West Indies*) (28).   **Test No. 2376/60 (A830/NZ440)**

SOUTH AFRICA v ENGLAND (1st Test)

At SuperSport Park, Centurion, on 26, 27, 28, 29 December 2019.
Toss: England. Result: **SOUTH AFRICA** won by 107 runs.
Debuts: South Africa – D.Pretorius, H.E.van der Dussen.

SOUTH AFRICA

D.Elgar	c Buttler b Anderson	0	(2) c Buttler b Archer		22
A.K.Markram	c Bairstow b Curran	20	(1) lbw b Anderson		2
M.Z.Hamza	c Stokes b Broad	39	c Buttler b Broad		4
*F.du Plessis	c Root b Broad	29	c Curran b Archer		20
H.E.van der Dussen	c Root b Curran	6	lbw b Archer		51
†Q.de Kock	c Buttler b Curran	95	(7) c Bairstow b Stokes		34
D.Pretorius	c Root b Curran	33	(8) c Sibley b Stokes		7
V.D.Philander	c Buttler b Broad	35	(9) c Bairstow b Curran		46
K.A.Maharaj	c Stokes b Archer	6	(10) c Curran b Archer		11
K.Rabada	b Broad	12	(11) not out		16
A.A.Nortje	not out	0	(6) c sub (Z.Crawley) b Archer		40
Extras	(LB 4, NB 2, W 3)	9	(B 5, LB 3, NB 2, W 9)		19
Total	(84.3 overs; 388 mins)	284	(61.4 overs; 310 mins)		272

ENGLAND

R.J.Burns	c de Kock b Philander	9	c Rabada b Nortje		84
D.P.Sibley	c de Kock b Rabada	4	c and b Maharaj		29
J.L.Denly	c de Kock b Pretorius	50	lbw b Pretorius		31
*J.E.Root	c de Kock b Philander	29	c de Kock b Nortje		48
B.A.Stokes	c de Kock b Nortje	35	b Maharaj		14
J.M.Bairstow	b Nortje	1	c Hamza b Rabada		9
†J.C.Buttler	c de Kock b Philander	12	c Pretorius b Rabada		22
S.M.Curran	c Hamza b Rabada	20	c de Kock b Rabada		9
J.C.Archer	b Philander	3	c van der Dussen b Nortje		4
S.C.J.Broad	c Elgar b Rabada	2	b Rabada		6
J.M.Anderson	not out	0	not out		0
Extras	(B 4, LB 5, NB 2, W 5)	16	(B 8, LB 3, W 1)		12
Total	(53.2 overs; 259 mins)	181	(93 overs; 417 mins)		268

ENGLAND	O	M	R	W	O	M	R	W		FALL OF WICKETS			
											SA	E	SA	E
Anderson	20	4	69	1	13	1	47	1		Wkt	1st	1st	2nd	2nd
Broad	18.3	4	58	4	11	2	42	1		1st	0	11	2	92
Curran	20	5	58	4	(4) 12.4	3	51	1		2nd	32	15	25	139
Archer	19	4	65	1	(3) 17	1	102	5		3rd	71	70	29	158
Root	4	0	26	0						4th	97	142	62	204
Denly	3	0	4	0						5th	111	143	153	222
Stokes					(5) 8	1	22	2		6th	198	150	170	232
										7th	245	176	177	251
SOUTH AFRICA										8th	252	176	220	256
Rabada	15	1	68	3	24	3	103	4		9th	277	181	250	262
Philander	14.2	8	16	4	20	8	35	0		10th	284	181	272	268
Pretorius	8	2	23	1	(4) 16	6	26	1						
Nortje	12	2	47	2	(3) 17	4	56	3						
Maharaj	4	1	18	0	16	3	37	2						

Umpires: C.B.Gaffaney (*New Zealand*) (32) and P.R.Reiffel (*Australia*) (46).
Referee: A.J.Pycroft (*Zimbabwe*) (73).   Test No. 2377/150 (SA436/E1019)

SOUTH AFRICA v ENGLAND (2nd Test)

At Newlands, Cape Town, on 3, 4, 5, 6, 7 January 2020.
Toss: England. Result: **ENGLAND** won by 189 runs.
Debut: South Africa – P.J.Malan.

ENGLAND

Z.Crawley	c de Kock b Philander	4		c de Kock b Rabada	25
D.P.Sibley	c de Kock b Rabada	34		not out	133
J.L.Denly	b Maharaj	38		c Pretorius b Nortje	31
*J.E.Root	c de Kock b Nortje	35		c du Plessis b Pretorius	61
B.A.Stokes	c Elgar b Nortje	47	(6)	c van der Dussen b Maharaj	72
O.J.D.Pope	not out	61	(7)	b Rabada	3
†J.C.Buttler	c de Kock b Pretorius	29	(8)	c de Kock b Nortje	23
S.M.Curran	b Pretorius	9	(9)	c Hamza b Maharaj	13
D.M.Bess	c de Kock b Philander	5	(5)	c de Kock b Nortje	0
S.C.J.Broad	b Rabada	1		not out	8
J.M.Anderson	c van der Dussen b Rabada	4			
Extras	(B 4, LB 1, NB 1, W 1)	7		(B 18, LB 3, W 1)	22
Total	(91.5 overs; 399 mins)	269		(8 wkts dec; 111 overs; 497 mins)	391

SOUTH AFRICA

D.Elgar	c Root b Bess	88	(2)	c Buttler b Denly	34
P.J.Malan	c Root b Broad	5	(1)	c Stokes b Curran	84
M.Z.Hamza	c Stokes b Broad	5		c Buttler b Anderson	18
*F.du Plessis	c Stokes b Anderson	1	(5)	c Denly b Bess	19
H.E.van der Dussen	c Stokes b Curran	68	(6)	c Anderson b Broad	17
†Q.de Kock	c Anderson b Curran	20	(7)	c Crawley b Denly	50
V.D.Philander	not out	17	(8)	c Pope b Stokes	8
D.Pretorius	c Stokes b Anderson	4	(9)	c Root b Stokes	0
K.A.Maharaj	c Sibley b Anderson	4	(4)	lbw b Anderson	2
K.Rabada	c Buttler b Anderson	0	(11)	not out	3
A.A.Nortje	c Stokes b Anderson	4	(10)	c Crawley b Stokes	0
Extras	(B 4, LB 2, NB 1)	7		(B 4, LB 2, NB 5, W 2)	13
Total	(89 overs; 373 mins)	223		(137.4 overs; 565 mins)	248

SOUTH AFRICA	O	M	R	W		O	M	R	W
Philander	16	3	46	2	(2)	4	7	24	0
Rabada	19.5	4	68	3	(1)	20	3	69	2
Nortje	18	2	56	2		18	2	61	3
Maharaj	27	6	68	1	(5)	43	9	160	2
Pretorius	11	5	26	2	(4)	16	4	56	1

ENGLAND	O	M	R	W		O	M	R	W
Anderson	19	6	40	5		18	9	23	2
Broad	18	6	38	2		23	8	37	1
Curran	13	3	39	2	(4)	16	4	37	1
Bess	27	3	62	1	(3)	33	14	57	1
Stokes	9	0	34	0	(7)	23.4	8	35	3
Root	3	1	4	0		6	0	11	0
Denly					(5)	18	4	42	2

FALL OF WICKETS				
	E	SA	E	SA
Wkt	1st	1st	2nd	2nd
1st	8	26	28	71
2nd	63	38	101	123
3rd	105	40	217	129
4th	127	157	218	164
5th	185	191	310	171
6th	221	200	315	237
7th	231	207	356	237
8th	231	215	375	241
9th	234	215	–	241
10th	269	223	–	248

Umpires: H.D.P.K.Dharmasena (*Sri Lanka*) (65) and P.R.Reiffel (*Australia*) (47).
Referee: A.J.Pycroft (*Zimbabwe*) (74).   Test No. 2378/151 (SA437/E1020)

SOUTH AFRICA v ENGLAND (3rd Test)

At St George's Park, Port Elizabeth, on 16, 17, 18, 19, 20 January 2020.
Toss: England. Result: **ENGLAND** won by an innings and 53 runs.
Debut: South Africa – D.Paterson.

ENGLAND

Z.Crawley	c van der Dussen b Nortje	44
D.P.Sibley	c Elgar b Rabada	36
J.L.Denly	lbw b Maharaj	25
*J.E.Root	b Rabada	27
B.A.Stokes	c Elgar b Paterson	120
O.J.D.Pope	not out	135
†J.C.Buttler	c and b Maharaj	1
S.M.Curran	c Elgar b Maharaj	44
D.M.Bess	c Malan b Maharaj	1
M.A.Wood	c Nortje b Maharaj	42
S.C.J.Broad		
Extras	(B 2, LB 14, NB 4, W 4)	24
Total	**(9 wkts dec; 152 overs; 655 mins)**	**499**

SOUTH AFRICA

D.Elgar	c Pope b Bess	35	(2) b Wood		15
P.J.Malan	c and b Bess	18	(1) lbw b Root		12
M.Z.Hamza	c Pope b Bess	10	c Buttler b Wood		2
A.A.Nortje	c Root b Stokes	18	(10) b Bess		5
*F.du Plessis	c Pope b Bess	8	(4) c Pope b Root		36
H.E.van der Dussen	b Bess	24	(5) c Pope b Root		10
†Q.de Kock	b Curran	63	(6) c Wood b Root		3
V.D.Philander	b Broad	27	(7) c Pope b Broad		13
K.A.Maharaj	b Broad	0	(8) run out		71
K.Rabada	c Wood b Broad	1	(9) c Broad b Wood		16
D.Paterson	not out	0	not out		39
Extras	(B 4, W 1)	5	(B 12, LB 1, NB 1, W 1)		15
Total	**(86.4 overs; 360 mins)**	**209**	**(88.5 overs; 348 mins)**		**237**

SOUTH AFRICA	O	M	R	W		O	M	R	W
Philander	16	5	41	0					
Paterson	24	3	62	1					
Rabada	28	6	97	2					
Nortje	25	4	97	1					
Maharaj	58	15	180	5					
Elgar	1	0	6	0					
ENGLAND									
Broad	13.4	6	30	3		10	5	14	1
Curran	11	2	32	1		6	0	46	0
Bess	31	12	51	5	(4)	22	11	36	1
Wood	11	4	31	0	(3)	16.5	6	32	3
Denly	4	1	10	0					
Root	11	4	25	0		29	13	87	4
Stokes	5	1	26	1	(5)	5	2	9	0

FALL OF WICKETS

	E	SA	SA
Wkt	1st	1st	2nd
1st	70	50	18
2nd	103	60	22
3rd	134	63	44
4th	148	71	66
5th	351	109	74
6th	354	154	83
7th	413	208	102
8th	426	208	128
9th	499	208	138
10th	–	209	237

Umpires: B.N.J.Oxenford (*Australia*) (59) and R.J.Tucker (*Australia*) (70).
Referee: A.J.Pycroft (*Zimbabwe*) (75).   Test No. 2379/152 (SA438/E1021)

SOUTH AFRICA v ENGLAND (4th Test)

At New Wanderers Stadium, Johannesburg, on 24, 25, 26, 27 January 2020.
Toss: England. Result: **ENGLAND** won by 191 runs.
Debut: South Africa – B.E.Hendricks.

ENGLAND

Z.Crawley	c van der Dussen b Philander	66	c de Kock b Pretorius	24
D.P.Sibley	c de Kock b Hendricks	44	c Malan b Hendricks	44
J.L.Denly	c van der Dussen b Paterson	27	b Paterson	8
*J.E.Root	c de Kock b Nortje	59	c du Plessis b Hendricks	58
B.A.Stokes	c van der Dussen b Nortje	2	c van der Dussen b Hendricks	28
O.J.D.Pope	b Nortje	56	c de Kock b Nortje	11
†J.C.Buttler	c Elgar b Philander	20	c de Kock b Nortje	8
S.M.Curran	c de Kock b Nortje	0	c Paterson b Hendricks	35
C.R.Woakes	c du Plessis b Nortje	32	c de Kock b Hendricks	0
M.A.Wood	not out	35	b Pretorius	18
S.C.J.Broad	c Malan b Paterson	43	not out	1
Extras	(LB 9, NB 3, W 4)	16	(B 4, LB 8, W 1)	13
Total	**(98.2 overs; 454 mins)**	**400**	**(61.3 overs; 289 mins)**	**248**

SOUTH AFRICA

D.Elgar	c Woakes b Stokes	26	(2) c and b Stokes	24
P.J.Malan	c Buttler b Wood	15	(1) c Stokes b Woakes	22
H.E.van der Dussen	c Stokes b Curran	6	c Broad b Wood	98
*F.du Plessis	lbw b Woakes	3	b Stokes	35
†Q.de Kock	b Wood	76	c Woakes b Wood	39
T.Bavuma	c Stokes b Wood	6	c Buttler b Broad	27
A.A.Nortje	c Denly b Wood	6	(9) c Buttler b Wood	4
V.D.Philander	c Broad b Woakes	4	c Buttler b Wood	10
D.Pretorius	c Crawley b Stokes	37	(7) c Curran b Broad	2
B.E.Hendricks	not out	5	run out	4
D.Paterson	c Buttler b Wood	4	not out	0
Extras	(W 1)	1	(B 4, LB 2, W 3)	9
Total	**(68.3 overs; 323 mins)**	**183**	**(77.1 overs)**	**274**

SOUTH AFRICA	O	M	R	W	O	M	R	W
Philander	20	2	50	2	1.3	1	1	0
Hendricks	23	3	111	1	(4) 15.3	2	64	5
Nortje	24	1	110	5	(2) 11	1	61	2
Paterson	20.2	3	86	2	(3) 13.3	5	18	1
Pretorius	11	3	34	0	18	2	87	2
Malan					2	0	5	0

ENGLAND	O	M	R	W	O	M	R	W
Broad	14	3	27	0	10	1	26	2
Curran	12	4	25	1	11	2	38	0
Woakes	17	7	38	2	(4) 14	3	47	1
Wood	14.3	2	46	5	(3) 16.1	3	54	4
Stokes	11	1	47	2	16	4	47	2
Root					7	1	37	0
Denly					3	0	19	0

FALL OF WICKETS

	E	SA	E	SA
Wkt	1st	1st	2nd	2nd
1st	107	29	56	39
2nd	116	37	75	89
3rd	150	43	92	181
4th	157	60	136	187
5th	258	74	150	235
6th	269	88	160	239
7th	269	93	206	260
8th	309	172	206	267
9th	318	174	240	273
10th	400	183	248	274

Umpires: R.J.Tucker (*Australia*) (71) and J.S.Wilson (*West Indies*) (18).
Referee: A.J.Pycroft (*Zimbabwe*) (76).   Test No. 2380/153 (SA439/E1022)

ZIMBABWE v SRI LANKA (1st Test)

At Harare Sports Club, on 19, 20, 21, 22, 23 January 2020.
Toss: Zimbabwe. Result: **SRI LANKA** won by ten wickets.
Debuts: Zimbabwe – K.T.Kasuza, B.S.Mudzinganyama, A.Ndlovu, V.M.Nyauchi.
‡(P.A.D.L.R.Sandakan)

ZIMBABWE

P.S.Masvaure	c Karunaratne b Ambuldeniya	55	c Dickwella b Lakmal		17
K.T.Kasuza	lbw b Kumara	63			
C.R.Ervine	b Lakmal	85	c Karunaratne b Lakmal		7
B.R.M.Taylor	lbw b Lakmal	21	c Mendis b Lakmal		38
*S.C.Williams	c Dickwella b Ambuldeniya	18	c Dickwella b Rajitha		39
Sikandar Raza	st Dickwella b Ambuldeniya	41	st Dickwella b Ambuldeniya		17
†R.W.Chakabva	c Mathews b Ambuldeniya	8	b Ambuldeniya		26
D.T.Tiripano	not out	44	lbw b Kumara		6
K.M.Jarvis	b Ambuldeniya	1	b Kumara		1
A.Ndlovu	c Mendis b Kumara	5	b Kumara		0
V.M.Nyauchi	c sub‡ b Lakmal	11	not out		0
B.S.Mudzinganyama			(2) lbw b Lakmal		16
Extras	(LB 4, NB 2)	6	(B 2, NB 1)		3
Total	(148 overs; 647 mins)	358	(92 overs; 392 mins)		170

SRI LANKA

*F.D.M.Karunaratne	c Ndlovu b Nyauchi	37	(2) not out		10
B.O.P.Fernando	b Tiripano	21	(1) not out		4
B.K.G.Mendis	c Taylor b Nyauchi	80			
A.D.Mathews	not out	200			
L.D.Chandimal	c and b Williams	12			
D.M.de Silva	c Masvaure b Nyauchi	63			
†D.P.D.N.Dickwella	lbw b Raza	63			
R.A.S.Lakmal	st Chakabva b Raza	27			
L.Ambuldeniya	b Raza	0			
C.A.K.Rajitha	lbw b Williams	1			
C.B.R.L.S.Kumara					
Extras	(B 2, LB 5, NB 4)	11			
Total	(9 wkts dec; 176.2 overs; 733 mins)	515	(0 wkts; 3 overs; 12 mins)		14

SRI LANKA	O	M	R	W		O	M	R	W
Lakmal	27	10	53	3		20	8	27	4
Rajitha	29	9	55	0		14	6	23	1
Ambuldeniya	42	12	114	5	(5)	26	8	74	2
Kumara	29	8	82	2		21	8	32	3
De Silva	21	8	50	0	(3)	11	6	12	0

ZIMBABWE	O	M	R	W		O	M	R	W
Jarvis	37	12	84	0					
Nyauchi	32	7	69	3		1	0	6	0
Tiripano	31	3	82	1	(1)	2	0	8	0
Ndlovu	28	3	107	0					
Williams	32.2	3	104	2					
Sikandar Raza	16	0	62	3					

FALL OF WICKETS

	Z	SL	Z	SL
Wkt	1st	1st	2nd	2nd
1st	96	32	33	–
2nd	164	92	36	–
3rd	208	184	41	–
4th	247	227	120	–
5th	247	325	120	–
6th	266	461	148	–
7th	307	510	159	–
8th	309	510	163	–
9th	328	515	165	–
10th	358	–	170	–

Umpires: M.Erasmus (*South Africa*) (62) and N.M.Menon (*India*) (2).
Referee: J.Srinath (*India*) (52).　　　　　　　**Test No. 2381/19 (Z108/SL288)**
B.S.Mudzinganyama replaced K.T.Kasuza, Sri Lanka 1st innings, 43.1 overs.

ZIMBABWE v SRI LANKA (2nd Test)

At Harare Sports Club, on 27, 28, 29, 30, 31 January 2020.
Toss: Zimbabwe. Result: **MATCH DRAWN**.
Debut: Zimbabwe – C.T.Mutombodzi.

‡(B.S.Mudzinganyama)

ZIMBABWE

Batsman	1st innings		2nd innings	
P.S.Masvaure	c Dickwella b Kumara	9	run out	35
K.T.Kasuza	b Lakmal	38		
C.R.Ervine	c B.O.P.Fernando b de Silva	12	(2) c Dickwella b M.V.T.Fernando	13
B.R.M.Taylor	lbw b Lakmal	62	lbw b Kumara	67
*S.C.Williams	b de Silva	107	(7) not out	53
Sikandar Raza	c Mathews b Ambuldeniya	72	lbw b M.V.T.Fernando	34
†R.W.Chakabva	c Dickwella b Ambuldeniya	31	(3) c de Silva b Ambuldeniya	15
C.T.Mutombodzi	lbw b de Silva	33	b Lakmal	8
D.T.Tiripano	c Lakmal b Ambuldeniya	13	not out	1
C.T.Mumba	not out	11		
V.M.Nyauchi	c de Silva b Ambuldeniya	6		
T.Maruma			(5) st Dickwella b Ambuldeniya	0
Extras	(B 8, LB 3, NB 1)	12	(B 4, LB 15, NB 1, W 1)	21
Total	(115.3 overs; 495 mins)	406	(7 wkts dec; 75 overs; 333 mins)	247

SRI LANKA

Batsman	1st innings		2nd innings	
*F.D.M.Karunaratne	lbw b Raza	44	(2) c Chakabva b Mumba	12
B.O.P.Fernando	c Chakabva b Tiripano	44	(1) lbw b Raza	47
B.K.G.Mendis	c Mumba b Raza	22	not out	116
A.D.Mathews	c Chakabva b Mumba	64	c Ervine b Nyauchi	13
L.D.Chandimal	c and b Raza	6	not out	13
D.M.de Silva	b Raza	42		
†D.P.D.N.Dickwella	lbw b Raza	1		
R.A.S.Lakmal	c Mutombodzi b Raza	5		
L.Ambuldeniya	c sub‡ b Raza	5		
M.V.T.Fernanado	c Chakabva b Nyauchi	38		
C.B.R.L.S.Kumara	not out	3		
Extras	(B 9, LB 10)	19	(B 1, LB 1, NB 1)	3
Total	(119.5 overs; 490 mins)	293	(3 wkts; 87 overs; 360 mins)	204

SRI LANKA	O	M	R	W		O	M	R	W
Lakmal	22	9	37	2		18	5	34	1
M.V.T.Fernando	14	1	45	0	(3)	20	5	43	2
Kumara	20	5	60	1	(4)	10	2	38	1
Ambuldeniya	42.3	8	182	4	(5)	20	0	81	2
De Silva	17	1	71	3	(2)	7	2	32	0

ZIMBABWE	O	M	R	W		O	M	R	W
Mumba	18	4	43	1	(3)	4	1	13	1
Sikandar Raza	43	8	113	7	(1)	32	10	63	1
Tiripano	24	12	30	1	(2)	16	10	15	0
Nyauchi	22.5	7	40	1	(5)	12	3	43	1
Mutombodzi	12	1	48	0	(6)	7	2	19	0
Williams					(4)	16	0	49	0

FALL OF WICKETS

	Z	SL	Z	SL
Wkt	1st	1st	2nd	2nd
1st	21	94	32	26
2nd	49	104	64	107
3rd	114	134	111	140
4th	133	142	124	
5th	292	226	151	
6th	324	228	221	
7th	362	242	240	
8th	386	244		
9th	394	268		
10th	406	293		

Umpires: Alim Dar (*Pakistan*) (131) and N.M.Menon (*India*) (3).
Referee: J.Srinath (*India*) (53). **Test No. 2382/20 (Z109/SL289)**
T.Maruma replaced K.T.Kasuza, Zimbabwe 2nd innings, 0.1 overs.

PAKISTAN v BANGLADESH (1st Test)

At Rawalpindi Cricket Stadium, on 7, 8, 9, 10 February 2020.
Toss: Pakistan. Result: **PAKISTAN** won by an innings and 44 runs.
Debut: Bangladesh – Saif Hasan.

BANGLADESH

Tamim Iqbal	lbw b Abbas	3	lbw b Yasir		34
Saif Hasan	c Shafiq b Afridi	0	b Naseem		16
Nazmul Hossain	c Rizwan b Abbas	44	lbw b Naseem		38
*Mominul Haque	c Rizwan b Afridi	30	lbw b Afridi		41
Mahmudullah	c Shafiq b Afridi	25	(6) c Sohail b Naseem		0
Mithun Ali	c Rizwan b Naseem	63	(7) b Yasir		0
†Liton Das	lbw b Sohail	33	(8) lbw b Yasir		29
Taijul Islam	c Yasir b Sohail	24	(5) lbw b Naseem		0
Rubel Hossain	b Afridi	1	lbw b Abbas		5
Abu Jayed	run out	0	c Shafiq b Yasir		3
Ebadat Hossain	not out	0	not out		0
Extras	(B 6, NB 3, W 1)	10	(W 2)		2
Total	**(82.5 overs)**	**233**	**(62.2 overs)**		**168**

PAKISTAN

Shan Masood	b Taijul	100
Abid Ali	c Liton b Abu	0
*Azhar Ali	c Nazmul b Abu	34
Babar Azam	c Mithun b Abu	143
Asad Shafiq	c Liton b Ebadat	65
Haris Sohail	c Tamim b Taijul	75
†Mohammad Rizwan	c Mahmudullah b Rubel	10
Yasir Shah	lbw b Rubel	5
Shaheen Shah Afridi	lbw b Rubel	3
Mohammad Abbas	not out	1
Naseem Shah	run out	2
Extras	(B 1, LB 2, NB 2, W 1)	7
Total	**(122.5 overs)**	**445**

PAKISTAN	O	M	R	W	O	M	R	W
Shaheen Shah Afridi	21.5	3	53	4	16	6	39	1
Mohammad Abbas	17	9	19	2	17.4	6	33	1
Naseem Shah	16	0	61	1	8.2	2	26	4
Yasir Shah	22	3	83	0	17.2	3	58	4
Haris Sohail	6	2	11	2				
Asad Shafiq					(5) 3	0	12	0

BANGLADESH	O	M	R	W
Ebadat Hossain	25	6	97	1
Abu Jayed	29	4	86	3
Rubel Hossain	25.5	3	113	3
Taijul Islam	41	6	139	2
Mahmudullah	2	0	6	0

FALL OF WICKETS

	B	P	B
Wkt	1st	1st	2nd
1st	3	2	39
2nd	3	93	53
3rd	62	205	124
4th	95	342	124
5th	107	353	124
6th	161	374	126
7th	214	415	130
8th	229	422	156
9th	233	442	165
10th	233	445	168

Umpires: C.B.Gaffaney (*New Zealand*) (33) and N.J.Llong (*England*) (62).
Referee: Sir R.B.Richardson (*West Indies*) (29).   **Test No. 2383/11 (P428/B118)**
The second Test of the series was originally scheduled for 5–9 April, in Karachi, but
postponed due to the Coronavirus.

BANGLADESH v ZIMBABWE (Only Test)

At Shere Bangla National Stadium, Mirpur, Dhaka, on 22, 23, 24, 25 February 2020.
Toss: Zimbabwe. Result: **BANGLADESH** won by an innings and 106 runs.
Debut: Zimbabwe – C.K.Tshuma.

ZIMBABWE

P.S.Masvaure	c and b Nayeem	64		b Nayeem	0
K.T.Kasuza	c Nayeem b Abu	2		c Mithun b Taijul	10
*C.R.Ervine	b Nayeem	107	(5)	run out	43
B.R.M.Taylor	b Nayeem	10		c Taijul b Nayeem	16
Sikandar Raza	c Liton b Nayeem	18	(6)	c Mushfiqur b Taijul	37
T.Maruma	lbw b Abu	7	(7)	c Tamim b Nayeem	41
†R.W.Chakabva	c Nayeem b Taijul	30	(8)	c Tamim b Taijul	18
D.T.Tiripano	c Liton b Abu	8	(3)	c Liton b Nayeem	0
A.Ndlovu	lbw b Abu	0		lbw b Nayeem	4
C.K.Tshuma	lbw b Taijul	0		lbw b Taijul	3
V.M.Nyauchi	not out	6		not out	7
Extras	(B 4, LB 4, W 5)	13		(B 9)	9
Total	**(106.3 overs)**	**265**		**(57.3 overs)**	**189**

BANGLADESH

Tamim Iqbal	c Chakabva b Tiripano	41
Saif Hasan	c Chakabva b Nyauchi	8
Nazmul Hossain	c Chakabva b Tshuma	71
*Mominul Haque	c and b Ndlovu	132
Mushfiqur Rahim	not out	203
Mithun Ali	c Chakabva b Ndlovu	17
†Liton Das	c Chakabva b Raza	53
Taijul Islam	not out	14
Nayeem Hasan		
Ebadat Hossain		
Abu Jayed		
Extras	(B 8, LB 3, NB 5, W 5)	21
Total	**(6 wkts dec; 154 overs)**	**560**

BANGLADESH	O	M	R	W		O	M	R	W
Ebadat Hossain	17	8	26	0	(4)	5	1	16	0
Abu Jayed	24	6	71	4	(3)	4	3	4	0
Nayeem Hasan	38	9	70	4	(1)	24	6	82	5
Taijul Islam	27.3	1	90	2	(2)	24.3	7	78	4

ZIMBABWE	O	M	R	W
Tiripano	30	6	96	1
Nyauchi	27	3	87	1
Sikandar Raza	30	2	111	1
Tshuma	25	2	85	1
Ndlovu	42	4	170	2

FALL OF WICKETS

	Z	B	Z
Wkt	1st	1st	2nd
1st	7	18	0
2nd	118	96	0
3rd	134	172	15
4th	174	394	44
5th	199	421	104
6th	226	532	121
7th	240	–	165
8th	244	–	170
9th	245	–	181
10th	265	–	189

Umpires: P.R.Reiffel (*Australia*) (48) and J.S.Wilson (*West Indies*) (19).
Referee: J.J.Crowe (*New Zealand*) (99).

Test No. 2387/17 (B119/Z110)

NEW ZEALAND v INDIA (1st Test)

At Basin Reserve, Wellington, on 21, 22, 23, 24 February 2020.
Toss: New Zealand. Result: **NEW ZEALAND** won by ten wickets.
Debut: New Zealand – K.A.Jamieson.

INDIA

P.P.Shaw	b Southee	16	c Latham b Boult		14
M.A.Agarwal	c Jamieson b Boult	34	c Watling b Southee		58
C.A.Pujara	c Watling b Jamieson	11	b Boult		11
*V.Kohli	c Taylor b Jamieson	2	c Watling b Boult		19
A.M.Rahane	c Watling b Southee	46	c Watling b Boult		29
G.H.Vihari	c Watling b Jamieson	7	b Southee		15
†R.R.Pant	run out	19	c Boult b Southee		25
R.Ashwin	b Southee	0	lbw b Southee		4
I.Sharma	c Watling b Jamieson	5	lbw b de Grandhomme		12
Mohammed Shami	c Blundell b Southee	21	not out		2
J.J.Bumrah	not out	0	c sub (D.J.Mitchell) b Southee		0
Extras	(B 1, W 3)	4	(W 2)		2
Total	**(68.1 overs; 309 mins)**	**165**	**(81 overs; 372 mins)**		**191**

NEW ZEALAND

T.W.M.Latham	c Pant b Sharma	11	not out	7
T.A.Blundell	b Sharma	30	not out	2
*K.S.Williamson	c sub (R.A.Jadeja) b Shami	89		
L.R.P.L.Taylor	c Pujara b Sharma	44		
H.M.Nicholls	c Kohli b Ashwin	17		
†B.J.Watling	c Pant b Bumrah	14		
C.de Grandhomme	c Pant b Ashwin	43		
T.G.Southee	c Shami b Sharma	6		
K.A.Jamieson	c Vihari b Ashwin	44		
A.Y.Patel	not out	4		
T.A.Boult	c Patel b Sharma	38		
Extras	(B 1, LB 1, W 6)	8		–
Total	**(100.2 overs; 458 mins)**	**348**	**(0 wkts; 1.4 overs; 7 mins)**	**9**

NEW ZEALAND	O	M	R	W		O	M	R	W
Southee	20.1	5	49	4		21	6	61	5
Boult	18	2	57	1		22	8	39	4
De Grandhomme	11	5	12	0		16	5	28	1
Jamieson	16	3	39	4		19	7	45	0
Patel	3	2	7	0		3	0	18	0
INDIA									
Bumrah	26	5	88	1	(2)	0.4	0	1	0
Sharma	22.2	6	68	5	(1)	1	0	8	0
Mohammed Shami	23	2	91	1					
Ashwin	29	1	99	3					

FALL OF WICKETS

	I	NZ	I	NZ
Wkt	1st	1st	2nd	2nd
1st	16	26	27	–
2nd	35	73	78	–
3rd	40	166	96	–
4th	88	185	113	–
5th	101	207	148	–
6th	132	216	148	–
7th	132	225	162	–
8th	165	296	189	–
9th	165	310	191	–
10th	165	348	191	–

Umpires: Alim Dar (*Pakistan*) (132) and R.A.Kettleborough (*England*) (63).
Referee: R.S.Madugalle (*Sri Lanka*) (192).   **Test No. 2385/58 (NZ441/I541)**

NEW ZEALAND v INDIA (2nd Test)

At Hagley Oval, Christchurch, on 29 February, 1, 2 March 2020.
Toss: New Zealand. Result: **NEW ZEALAND** won by seven wickets.
Debuts: None.

INDIA

P.P.Shaw	c Latham b Jamieson	54		c Latham b Southee	14
M.A.Agarwal	lbw b Boult	7		lbw b Boult	3
C.A.Pujara	c Watling b Jamieson	54		b Boult	24
*V.Kohli	lbw b Southee	3		lbw b de Grandhomme	14
A.M.Rahane	c Taylor b Southee	7		b Wagner	9
G.H.Vihari	c Watling b Wagner	55	(7)	c Watling b Southee	9
†R.R.Pant	b Jamieson	12	(8)	c Watling b Boult	4
R.A.Jadeja	c Boult b Jamieson	9	(9)	not out	16
U.T.Yadav	c Watling b Jamieson	0	(6)	b Boult	1
Mohammed Shami	b Boult	16		c Blundell b Southee	5
J.J.Bumrah	not out	10		run out	4
Extras	(B 4, LB 6, W 5)	15		(B 9, LB 12)	21
Total	**(63 overs; 286 mins)**	**242**		**(46 overs; 207 mins)**	**124**

NEW ZEALAND

T.W.M.Latham	b Shami	52		c Pant b Yadav	52
T.A.Blundell	lbw b Yadav	30		b Bumrah	55
*K.S.Williamson	c Pant b Bumrah	3		c Rahane b Bumrah	5
L.R.P.L.Taylor	c Yadav b Jadeja	15		not out	5
H.M.Nicholls	c Kohli b Shami	14		not out	5
†B.J.Watling	c Jadeja b Bumrah	0			
C.de Grandhomme	b Jadeja	26			
T.G.Southee	c Pant b Bumrah	0			
K.A.Jamieson	c Pant b Shami	49			
N.Wagner	c Jadeja b Shami	21			
T.A.Boult	not out	1			
Extras	(B 20, LB 4)	24		(B 1, LB 8, NB 1)	10
Total	**(73.1 overs; 330 mins)**	**235**		**(3 wkts; 36 overs; 157 mins)**	**132**

NEW ZEALAND	O	M	R	W		O	M	R	W
Southee	13	5	38	2		11	2	36	3
Boult	17	2	89	2		14	4	28	4
De Grandhomme	9	2	31	0	(4)	5	3	3	1
Jamieson	14	3	45	4	(3)	8	4	18	0
Wagner	10	2	29	1		8	1	18	1
INDIA									
Bumrah	22	6	62	3		13	2	39	2
Yadav	18	2	46	1		14	3	45	1
Mohammed Shami	23.1	3	81	4		3	1	11	0
Jadeja	10	2	22	2		5	0	24	0
Kohli						1	0	4	0

FALL OF WICKETS

	I	NZ	I	NZ
Wkt	1st	1st	2nd	2nd
1st	30	66	8	103
2nd	80	69	26	112
3rd	85	109	51	121
4th	113	130	72	–
5th	194	133	84	–
6th	197	153	89	–
7th	207	153	97	–
8th	207	177	97	–
9th	216	228	108	–
10th	242	235	124	–

Umpires: M.A.Gough (*England*) (14) and R.A.Kettleborough (*England*) (64).
Referee: R.S.Madugalle (*Sri Lanka*) (193).

Test No. 2386/59 (NZ442/1542)

INTERNATIONAL UMPIRES AND REFEREES 2020

ELITE PANEL OF UMPIRES 2020

The Elite Panel of ICC Umpires and Referees was introduced in April 2002 to raise standards and guarantee impartial adjudication. Two umpires from this panel stand in Test matches while one officiates with a home umpire from the Supplementary International Panel in limited-overs internationals.

Full Names	Birthdate	Birthplace	Tests	Debut	LOI	Debut
ALIM Sarwar DAR	06.06.68	Jhang, Pakistan	132	2003-04	208	1999-00
DHARMASENA, H.D.P.Kumar	24.04.71	Colombo, Sri Lanka	65	2010-11	105	2008-09
ERASMUS, Marais	27.02.64	George, South Africa	62	2009-10	91	2007-08
GAFFANEY, Christopher Blair	30.11.75	Dunedin, New Zealand	33	2014	68	2010
GOUGH, Michael Andrew	18.12.79	Hartlepool, England	14	2016	62	2013
ILLINGWORTH, Richard Keith	23.08.63	Bradford, England	47	2012-13	68	2010
KETTLEBOROUGH, Richard Allan	15.03.73	Sheffield, England	64	2010-11	89	2009
LLONG, Nigel James	11.02.69	Ashford, England	62	2007-08	130	2006
OXENFORD, Bruce Nicholas James	05.03.60	Southport, Australia	59	2010-11	96	2007-08
REIFFEL, Paul Ronald	19.04.66	Box Hill, Australia	48	2012	70	2008-09
TUCKER, Rodney James	28.08.64	Sydney, Australia	71	2009-10	48	2008-09
WILSON, Joel Sheldon	30.12.66	Trinidad, West Indies	19	2015	66	2011

ELITE PANEL OF REFEREES 2020

Full Names	Birthdate	Birthplace	Tests	Debut	LOI	Debut
BOON, David Clarence	29.12.60	Launceston, Australia	57	2011	143	2011
BROAD, Brian Christopher	29.09.57	Bristol, England	100	2003-04	323	2003-04
CROWE, Jeffrey John	14.09.58	Auckland, New Zealand	99	2004-05	298	2003-04
MADUGALLE, Ranjan Senerath	22.04.59	Kandy, Sri Lanka	193	1993-94	362	1993-94
PYCROFT, Andrew John	06.06.56	Harare, Zimbabwe	76	2009	178	2009
RICHARDSON, Sir Richard Benjamin	12.01.62	Five Islands, Antigua	29	2016	54	2016
SRINATH, Javagal	31.08.69	Mysore, India	53	2006	223	2006-07

INTERNATIONAL UMPIRES PANEL 2020

Nominated by their respective cricket boards, members from this panel officiate in home LOIs and supplement the Elite panel for Test matches. The number of Test matches/LOI in which they have stood is shown in brackets.

Afghanistan	Ahmed Shah Pakteen (-/12)	Ahmed Shah Durrani (-/4)	Bismallah Jan Shinwari (-/5)
			Izafullah Safi (-/-)
Australia	S.A.J.Craig (-/-)	P.Wilson (2/30)	S.J.Nogajski (-/5)
			G.A.Abood (-/1)
Bangladesh	Tanvir Ahmed (-/-)	Sharfuddoula (-/42)	Masudur Rahman (-/8)
			Gazi Sohel (-/-)
England	A.G.Wharf (-/3)	D.J.Millns (-/-)	M.Burns (-/-)
			M.J.Saggers (-/-)
India	C.Shamshuddin (-/43)	A.K.Chaudhary (-/20)	V.K.Sharma (-/2)
			N.N.Menon (3/24)
Ireland	M.Hawthorne (-/31)	R.E.Black (-/14)	A.J.Neill (-/8)
			P.A.Reynolds (-/3)
New Zealand	W.R.Knights (-/15)	C.M.Brown (-/18)	S.B.Haig (-/6)
Pakistan	Shozab Raza (-/24)	Ahsan Raza (-/38)	Asif Yaqoob (-/1)
			Rashid Riaz (-/1)
South Africa	A.T.Holdstock (-/23)	S.George (-/54)	B.P.Jele (-/10)
			A.Paleker (-/2)
Sri Lanka	R.M.P.J.Rambukwella (-/-)	R.S.A.Palliyaguruge (3/79)	R.R.Wimalasiri (-/14)
			L.E.Hannibal (-/9)
West Indies	G.O.Brathwaite (-/44)	L.S.Reifer (-/4)	P.A.Gustard (-/-)
			N.Duguid (-/7)
Zimbabwe	L.Rusere (-/14)	I.Chabi (-/1)	C.Phiri (-/-)
			F.Mutizwa (-/-)

Test Match and LOI statistics to 11 March 2020.

TEST MATCH CAREER RECORDS

These records, complete to 18 March 2020, contain all players registered for county cricket or The Hundred in 2020 at the time of going to press, plus those who have played Test cricket since 6 December 2018 (Test No. 2332).

ENGLAND – BATTING AND FIELDING

	M	I	NO	HS	Runs	Avge	100	50	Ct/St
M.M.Ali	60	104	8	155*	2782	28.97	5	14	32
T.R.Ambrose	11	16	1	102	447	29.80	1	3	31
J.M.Anderson	151	212	89	81	1185	9.63	–	1	93
J.C.Archer	7	12	–	30	97	8.08	–	–	1
J.M.Bairstow	70	123	7	167*	4030	34.74	6	21	184/13
J.T.Ball	4	8	–	31	67	8.37	–	–	1
G.S.Ballance	23	42	2	156	1498	37.45	4	7	22
G.J.Batty	9	12	2	38	149	14.90	–	–	3
I.R.Bell	118	205	24	235	7727	42.69	22	46	100
D.M.Bess	4	6	–	57	112	18.66	–	1	2
R.S.Bopara	13	19	1	143	575	31.94	3	–	6
S.G.Borthwick	1	2	–	4	5	2.50	–	–	2
T.T.Bresnan	23	26	4	91	575	26.13	–	3	8
S.C.J.Broad	138	203	31	169	3211	18.66	1	12	46
R.J.Burns	15	29	–	133	979	33.75	2	6	12
J.C.Buttler	41	73	6	106	2127	31.74	1	15	88
R.Clarke	2	3	–	55	96	32.00	–	1	1
A.N.Cook	161	291	16	294	12472	45.35	33	57	175
M.S.Crane	1	2	–	4	6	3.00	–	–	–
Z.Crawley	4	6	–	66	164	27.33	–	1	3
S.M.Curran	17	30	4	78	711	27.34	–	3	3
T.K.Curran	2	3	1	39	66	33.00	–	–	–
L.A.Dawson	3	6	2	66*	84	21.00	–	1	2
J.L.Denly	14	26	–	94	780	30.00	–	6	7
B.M.Duckett	4	7	–	56	110	15.71	–	1	–
S.T.Finn	36	47	22	56	279	11.16	–	1	8
B.T.Foakes	5	10	2	107	332	41.50	1	1	10/2
A.D.Hales	11	21	–	94	573	27.28	–	5	8
H.Hameed	3	6	1	82	219	43.80	–	2	4
K.K.Jennings	17	32	1	146*	781	25.19	2	1	17
C.J.Jordan	8	11	1	35	180	18.00	–	–	14
M.J.Leach	10	18	6	92	220	18.33	–	1	5
A.Lyth	7	13	–	107	265	20.38	1	–	8
D.J.Malan	15	26	–	140	724	27.84	1	6	11
E.J.G.Morgan	16	24	1	130	700	30.43	2	3	11
G.Onions	9	10	7	17*	30	10.00	–	–	–
C.Overton	4	8	2	41*	124	20.66	–	–	1
S.R.Patel	6	9	–	42	151	16.77	–	–	3
L.E.Plunkett	13	20	5	55*	238	15.86	–	1	3
O.J.D.Pope	7	11	2	135*	430	47.77	1	3	12
A.U.Rashid	19	33	5	61	540	19.28	–	1	3
S.D.Robson	7	11	–	127	336	30.54	1	1	5
T.S.Roland-Jones	4	6	2	25	82	20.50	–	–	–
J.E.Root	92	169	12	254	7599	48.40	17	48	114
J.J.Roy	5	10	–	72	187	18.70	–	1	1
D.P.Sibley	6	10	1	133*	362	40.22	1	–	4
B.A.Stokes	63	115	4	258	4056	36.54	9	21	72
O.P.Stone	1	2	–	19	19	9.50	–	–	–
M.D.Stoneman	11	20	1	60	526	27.68	–	5	1
J.M.Vince	13	22	–	83	548	24.90	–	3	8
T.Westley	5	9	1	59	193	24.12	–	1	1
C.R.Woakes	33	55	11	137*	1177	26.75	1	4	15
M.A.Wood	15	26	6	52	392	19.60	–	1	7

ENGLAND – BOWLING

TESTS

	O	M	R	W	Avge	Best	5wI	10wM
M.M.Ali	1828.4	265	6624	181	36.59	6- 53	5	1
J.M.Anderson	5463.1	1388	15670	584	26.83	7- 42	28	3
J.C.Archer	274	63	822	30	27.40	6- 45	3	–
J.T.Ball	102	23	343	3	114.33	1- 47	–	–
G.S.Ballance	2	1	5	0	–	–	–	–
G.J.Batty	285.4	38	914	15	60.93	3- 55	–	–
I.R.Bell	18	3	76	1	76.00	1- 33	–	–
D.M.Bess	144.4	41	327	11	29.72	5- 51	1	–
R.S.Bopara	72.2	10	290	1	290.00	1- 39	–	–
S.G.Borthwick	13	0	82	4	20.50	3- 33	–	–
T.T.Bresnan	779	185	2357	72	32.73	5- 48	1	–
S.C.J.Broad	4679.5	1096	13827	485	28.50	8- 15	17	2
R.Clarke	29	11	60	4	15.00	2- 7	–	–
A.N.Cook	3	0	7	1	7.00	1- 6	–	–
M.S.Crane	48	3	193	1	193.00	1-193	–	–
S.M.Curran	359.4	70	1173	37	31.70	4- 58	–	–
T.K.Curran	66	14	200	2	100.00	1- 65	–	–
L.A.Dawson	87.4	12	298	7	42.57	4-101	–	–
J.L.Denly	65	11	219	2	109.50	2- 42	–	–
S.T.Finn	1068.4	190	3800	125	30.40	6- 79	5	–
A.D.Hales	3	1	2	0	–	–	–	–
K.K.Jennings	12.1	1	55	0	–	–	–	–
C.J.Jordan	255	74	752	21	35.80	4- 18	–	–
M.J.Leach	345.2	61	987	34	29.02	5- 83	1	–
A.Lyth		1	0	0	–	–	–	–
D.J.Malan	26	4	70	0	–	–	–	–
G.Onions	267.4	50	957	32	29.90	5- 38	1	–
C.Overton	117.5	15	403	9	44.77	3-105	–	–
S.R.Patel	143	23	421	7	60.14	2- 27	–	–
L.E.Plunkett	443.1	71	1536	41	37.46	5- 64	1	–
A.U.Rashid	636	50	2390	60	39.83	5- 49	2	–
T.S.Roland-Jones	89.2	23	334	17	19.64	5- 57	1	–
J.E.Root	441	92	1402	28	50.07	4- 87	–	–
B.A.Stokes	1447.1	264	4804	147	32.68	6- 22	4	–
O.P.Stone	12	3	29	3	9.66	3- 29	–	–
J.M.Vince	4	1	13	0	–	–	–	–
T.Westley	4	0	12	0	–	–	–	–
C.R.Woakes	952.2	211	2934	95	30.88	6- 17	3	1
M.A.Wood	459.5	110	1508	48	31.41	5- 41	2	–

AUSTRALIA – BATTING AND FIELDING

	M	I	NO	HS	Runs	Avge	100	50	Ct/St
C.T.Bancroft	10	18	1	82*	446	26.23	–	3	16
J.A.Burns	21	36	–	180	1379	38.30	4	6	23
P.J.Cummins	30	44	6	63	647	17.02	–	2	13
J.P.Faulkner	1	2	–	23	45	22.50	–	–	–
A.J.Finch	5	10	–	62	278	27.80	–	2	7
P.S.P.Handscomb	16	29	5	110	934	38.91	2	4	28
M.S.Harris	9	17	1	79	385	24.06	–	2	7
J.R.Hazlewood	51	62	29	39	402	12.18	–	–	18
T.M.Head	17	28	2	161	1091	41.96	2	7	10
M.C.Henriques	4	8	1	81*	164	23.42	–	2	1
U.T.Khawaja	44	77	6	174	2887	40.66	8	14	35
M.Labuschagne	14	23	–	215	1459	63.43	4	8	13
N.M.Lyon	96	123	39	47	1031	12.27	–	–	48
M.R.Marsh	32	55	5	181	1260	25.20	2	3	16
S.E.Marsh	38	68	2	182	2265	34.31	6	10	23

AUSTRALIA – BATTING AND FIELDING (continued)

	M	I	NO	HS	Runs	Avge	100	50	Ct/St
G.J.Maxwell	7	14	1	104	339	26.07	1	–	5
T.D.Paine	31	50	8	92	1330	31.66	–	7	133/7
K.R.Patterson	2	2	1	114*	144	144.00	1	–	6
J.L.Pattinson	21	25	9	47*	417	26.06	–	–	6
J.A.Richardson	2	1	–	1	1	1.00	–	–	–
P.M.Siddle	67	94	15	51	1164	14.73	–	2	19
S.P.D.Smith	73	131	16	239	7227	62.84	26	29	117
M.A.Starc	71	85	17	99	1515	22.27	–	10	29
M.S.Wade	32	55	9	117	1440	31.30	4	5	69/11
D.A.Warner	84	155	7	335*	7244	48.94	24	30	68

AUSTRALIA – BOWLING

	O	M	R	W	Avge	Best	5wI	10wM
P.J.Cummins	1126.5	267	3121	143	21.82	6- 23	5	1
J.P.Faulkner	27.4	4	98	6	16.33	4- 51	–	–
A.J.Finch	2	0	8	0	–	–	–	–
J.R.Hazlewood	1836.3	466	5109	195	26.20	6- 67	7	–
T.M.Head	21	4	76	0	–	–	–	–
M.C.Henriques	55	12	164	2	82.00	1- 48	–	–
U.T.Khawaja	2	0	5	0	–	–	–	–
M.Labuschagne	126	11	464	12	38.66	3- 45	–	–
N.M.Lyon	4094.4	768	12320	390	31.58	8- 50	18	3
M.R.Marsh	475.3	83	1623	42	38.64	5- 46	1	–
G.J.Maxwell	77	4	341	8	42.62	4-127	–	–
J.L.Pattinson	660.3	142	2133	81	26.33	5- 27	4	–
J.A.Richardson	51	15	123	6	20.50	3- 26	–	–
P.M.Siddle	2317.5	615	6777	221	30.66	6- 54	8	–
S.P.D.Smith	230.1	25	960	17	56.47	3- 18	–	–
M.A.Starc	1958.5	386	6583	244	26.97	6- 50	13	2
M.S.Wade	5	1	28	0	–	–	–	–
D.A.Warner	57	1	269	4	67.25	2- 45	–	–

SOUTH AFRICA – BATTING AND FIELDING

	M	I	NO	HS	Runs	Avge	100	50	Ct/St
K.J.Abbott	11	14	–	17	95	6.78	–	–	4
H.M.Amla	124	215	16	311*	9282	46.64	28	41	108
T.Bavuma	40	67	7	102*	1845	30.75	1	13	17
T.B.de Bruyn	12	23	1	101	428	19.45	1	–	11
Q.de Kock	47	80	5	129*	2934	39.12	5	21	191/11
M.de Lange	2	2	–	9	9	4.50	–	–	1
F.du Plessis	65	112	14	137	3901	39.80	9	21	59
D.Elgar	63	110	9	199	3888	38.49	12	14	67
M.Z.Hamza	5	10	–	62	181	18.10	–	1	5
S.R.Harmer	5	6	1	13	58	11.60	–	1	5
B.E.Hendricks	1	2	1	5*	9	9.00	–	–	1
H.Klaasen	1	2	–	6	11	5.50	–	–	3/1
H.G.Kuhn	4	8	–	34	113	14.12	–	–	1
G.F.Linde	1	2	–	37	64	32.00	–	–	–
K.A.Maharaj	30	48	6	72	643	15.30	–	2	8
P.J.Malan	3	6	–	84	156	26.00	–	1	3
A.K.Markram	20	37	–	152	1424	38.48	4	6	15
M.Morkel	86	104	23	40	944	11.65	–	–	25
P.W.A.Mulder	1	2	–	9	14	7.00	–	–	–
S.Muthusamy	2	4	2	49*	98	49.00	–	–	2
L.T.Ngidi	5	9	4	5	15	3.00	–	–	3
A.A.Nortje	6	12	3	40	89	9.88	–	–	1
D.Olivier	10	12	5	10*	26	3.71	–	–	2
W.D.Parnell	6	4	–	23	67	16.75	–	–	3
D.Paterson	2	4	3	39*	43	43.00	–	–	1

TESTS   SOUTH AFRICA – BATTING AND FIELDING (continued)

	M	I	NO	HS	Runs	Avge	100	50	Ct/St
V.D.Philander	64	94	20	74	1779	24.04	–	8	17
D.L.Piedt	9	12	1	56	131	11.90	–	1	5
D.Pretorius	3	6	–	37	83	13.83	–	–	2
K.Rabada	43	64	11	34	606	11.43	–	–	22
D.W.Steyn	93	119	27	76	1251	13.59	–	2	26
H.E.van der Dussen	4	8	–	98	274	34.25	–	3	8
S.van Zyl	12	17	2	101*	395	26.33	1	–	6
D.J.Vilas	6	9	–	26	94	10.44	–	–	13

SOUTH AFRICA – BOWLING

	O	M	R	W	Avge	Best	5wI	10wM
K.J.Abbott	346.5	95	886	39	22.71	7- 29	3	–
H.M.Amla	9	0	37	0	–	–	–	–
T.Bavuma	16	1	61	1	61.00	1- 29	–	–
T.B.de Bruyn	17	1	74	0	–	–	–	–
M.de Lange	74.4	10	277	9	30.77	7- 81	1	–
F.du Plessis	13	0	69	0	–	–	–	–
D.Elgar	170.3	12	659	15	43.93	4- 22	–	–
S.R.Harmer	191.2	34	588	20	29.40	4- 61	–	–
B.E.Hendricks	38.3	5	175	6	29.16	5- 64	1	–
G.F.Linde	31	2	133	4	33.25	4-133	–	–
K.A.Maharaj	1113	204	3651	110	33.19	9-129	6	1
P.J.Malan	2	0	5	0	–	–	–	–
A.K.Markram	27.2	3	87	0	–	–	–	–
M.Morkel	2749.4	605	8550	309	27.66	6- 23	8	–
P.W.A.Mulder	7	3	12	1	12.00	1- 6	–	–
S.Muthusamy	37.3	2	180	2	90.00	1- 63	–	–
L.T.Ngidi	123.1	33	376	15	25.06	6- 39	1	–
A.A.Nortje	174.3	26	667	19	35.10	5-110	1	–
D.Olivier	240	43	924	48	19.25	6- 37	3	1
W.D.Parnell	92.4	11	414	15	27.60	4- 51	–	–
D.Paterson	57.5	11	166	4	41.50	2- 86	–	–
V.D.Philander	1898.3	507	5000	224	22.32	6- 21	13	2
D.L.Piedt	304	46	1175	26	45.19	5-153	1	–
D.Pretorius	80	22	252	7	36.00	2- 26	–	–
K.Rabada	1335.1	270	4523	197	22.95	7-112	9	4
D.W.Steyn	3101.2	660	10077	439	22.95	7- 51	26	5
S.van Zyl	67.1	15	148	6	24.66	3- 20	–	–

WEST INDIES – BATTING AND FIELDING

	M	I	NO	HS	Runs	Avge	100	50	Ct/St
J.Blackwood	28	49	4	112*	1362	30.26	1	10	24
K.C.Brathwaite	59	112	7	212	3496	33.29	8	17	26
D.M.Bravo	54	98	5	218	3506	37.69	8	17	51
S.S.J.Brooks	3	5	–	111	174	34.80	1	1	6
J.D.Campbell	6	12	2	55	298	29.80	–	1	4
R.L.Chase	32	58	4	137*	1695	31.38	5	7	14
R.R.S.Cornwall	2	3	–	14	20	6.66	–	–	5
M.L.Cummins	14	22	7	24*	114	7.60	–	–	4
S.O.Dowrich	31	56	8	125*	1444	30.08	3	8	78/5
F.H.Edwards	55	88	28	30	394	6.56	–	–	10
S.T.Gabriel	45	66	24	20*	200	4.76	–	–	16
J.N.Hamilton	1	2	–	5	5	2.50	–	–	5
S.O.Hetmyer	16	30	–	93	838	27.93	–	5	7
J.O.Holder	40	69	11	202*	1898	32.72	3	8	33
S.D.Hope	31	58	3	147	1498	27.23	2	5	44/1
A.S.Joseph	9	15	–	34	84	5.60	–	–	6
S.P.Narine	6	7	2	22*	40	8.00	–	–	2

WEST INDIES – BATTING AND FIELDING (continued)

	M	I	NO	HS	Runs	Avge	100	50	Ct/St
K.M.A.Paul	3	6	–	47	96	16.00	–	–	2
R.Rampaul	18	31	8	40*	335	14.56	–	–	3
K.A.J.Roach	56	90	17	41	890	12.19	–	–	13
J.E.Taylor	46	73	7	106	856	12.96	1	1	8
J.A.Warrican	8	14	9	41	142	28.40	–	–	3

WEST INDIES – BOWLING

	O	M	R	W	Avge	Best	5wI	10wM
J.Blackwood	54	9	194	2	97.00	2-14	–	–
K.C.Brathwaite	316.3	26	1025	18	56.94	6-29	1	–
D.M.Bravo	1	0	2	0	–	–	–	–
J.D.Campbell	10.1	0	30	0	–	–	–	–
R.L.Chase	726.2	81	2500	59	42.37	8-60	2	–
R.R.S.Cornwall	107.3	25	294	13	22.61	7-75	1	1
M.L.Cummins	329.2	60	1084	27	40.14	6-48	1	–
F.H.Edwards	1600.2	183	6249	165	37.87	7-87	12	–
S.T.Gabriel	1205.4	216	4075	133	30.63	8-62	5	1
J.O.Holder	1090.1	294	2796	106	26.37	6-59	6	1
A.S.Joseph	254.1	60	821	25	32.84	3-53	–	–
S.P.Narine	275	60	851	21	40.52	6-91	2	–
K.M.A.Paul	57	11	189	6	31.50	2-25	–	–
R.Rampaul	573.2	111	1705	49	34.75	4-48	–	–
K.A.J.Roach	1670	370	5238	193	27.13	6-48	9	1
J.E.Taylor	1292.5	258	4480	130	34.46	6-47	4	–
J.A.Warrican	257.4	32	872	22	39.63	4-62	–	–

NEW ZEALAND – BATTING AND FIELDING

	M	I	NO	HS	Runs	Avge	100	50	Ct/St
C.J.Anderson	13	22	1	116	683	32.52	1	4	7
T.D.Astle	5	6	1	35	98	19.60	–	–	3
T.A.Blundell	6	11	2	121	425	47.22	2	1	5
T.A.Boult	67	82	39	52*	654	15.20	–	1	38
C.de Grandhomme	24	36	4	105	1185	37.03	1	8	15
L.H.Ferguson	1	2	2	1*	1	–	–	–	–
M.J.Henry	12	16	4	66	224	18.66	–	1	5
K.A.Jamieson	2	2	–	49	93	46.50	–	–	1
T.W.M.Latham	52	92	4	264*	3726	42.34	11	18	52
D.J.Mitchell	1	1	–	73	73	73.00	–	1	–
H.M.Nicholls	33	50	6	162*	1747	39.70	5	9	21
A.Y.Patel	8	10	3	14	53	7.57	–	–	4
J.S.Patel	24	38	8	47	381	12.70	–	–	13
G.D.Phillips	1	2	–	52	52	26.00	–	1	1
J.A.Raval	24	39	1	132	1143	30.07	1	7	21
H.D.Rutherford	16	29	1	171	755	26.96	1	1	11
M.J.Santner	22	29	–	126	741	25.55	1	2	14
W.E.R.Somerville	4	6	2	40*	72	18.00	–	–	1
T.G.Southee	73	106	10	77*	1668	17.37	–	5	52
L.R.P.L.Taylor	101	178	21	290	7238	46.10	19	33	147
N.Wagner	48	63	17	47	575	12.50	–	–	12
B.J.Watling	70	110	15	205	3658	38.50	8	18	241/8
K.S.Williamson	80	140	13	242*	6476	50.99	21	32	71

NEW ZEALAND – BOWLING

	O	M	R	W	Avge	Best	5wI	10wM
C.J.Anderson	217	34	659	16	41.18	3-47	–	–
T.D.Astle	111.1	16	368	7	52.57	3-39	–	–
T.A.Blundell	3	0	13	0	–	–	–	–
T.A.Boult	2479	561	7384	267	27.65	6-30	8	1

NEW ZEALAND – BOWLING (continued)

	O	M	R	W	Avge	Best	5wI	10wM
C.de Grandhomme	613.5	140	1487	47	31.63	6- 41	1	–
L.H.Ferguson	11	1	47	0	–	–	–	–
M.J.Henry	460.1	79	1505	30	50.16	4- 93	–	–
K.A.Jamieson	57	17	147	9	16.33	5- 45	1	–
D.J.Mitchell	22	5	69	0	–	–	–	–
A.Y.Patel	270.5	56	733	22	33.31	5- 59	2	–
J.S.Patel	972.1	202	3078	65	47.35	5-110	1	–
J.A.Raval	14	1	34	1	34.00	1- 33	–	–
H.D.Rutherford	1	0	2	0	–	–	–	–
M.J.Santner	624.2	128	1744	39	44.71	3- 53	–	–
W.E.R.Somerville	175.2	30	487	15	32.46	4- 75	–	–
T.G.Southee	2732.1	618	8237	284	29.00	7- 64	10	1
L.R.P.L.Taylor	16	3	48	2	24.00	2- 4	–	–
N.Wagner	1790.3	374	5480	206	26.60	7- 39	9	–
K.S.Williamson	350.3	47	1178	29	40.62	4- 44	–	–

INDIA – BATTING AND FIELDING

	M	I	NO	HS	Runs	Avge	100	50	Ct/St
M.A.Agarwal	11	17	–	243	974	57.29	3	4	7
R.Ashwin	71	98	13	124	2389	28.10	4	11	24
J.J.Bumrah	14	21	10	10*	32	2.90	–	–	3
R.A.Jadeja	49	71	18	100*	1869	35.26	1	14	36
V.Kohli	86	145	10	254*	7240	53.62	27	22	82
Kuldeep Yadav	6	6	–	26	51	8.50	–	–	3
Mohammed Shami	49	64	20	51*	497	11.29	–	1	11
S.Nadeem	1	1	1	1*	1	–	–	–	1
R.R.Pant	13	22	1	159*	814	38.76	2	2	59/2
C.A.Pujara	77	128	8	206*	5840	48.66	18	25	51
A.M.Rahane	65	109	11	188	4203	42.88	11	22	81
K.L.Rahul	36	60	2	199	2006	34.58	5	11	46
W.P.Saha	37	50	9	117	1238	30.19	3	5	92/11
I.Sharma	97	129	43	57	720	8.37	–	1	21
R.G.Sharma	32	53	7	212	2141	46.54	6	10	31
P.P.Shaw	4	7	1	134	335	55.83	1	2	2
G.H.Vihari	9	16	1	111	552	36.80	1	4	2
M.Vijay	61	105	1	167	3982	38.28	12	15	49
U.T.Yadav	46	52	22	31	340	11.33	–	–	17

INDIA – BOWLING

	O	M	R	W	Avge	Best	5wI	10wM
R.Ashwin	3264.2	672	9282	365	25.43	7-59	27	7
J.J.Bumrah	513.3	122	1383	68	20.33	6-27	5	–
R.A.Jadeja	2152	544	5246	213	24.62	7-48	9	1
V.Kohli	29.1	2	84	0	–	–	–	–
Kuldeep Yadav	164.5	22	579	24	24.12	5-57	2	–
Mohammed Shami	1482.5	271	4925	180	27.36	6-56	5	–
S.Nadeem	17.2	5	40	4	10.00	2-18	–	–
C.A.Pujara	1	0	2	0	–	–	–	–
I.Sharma	3025	601	9620	297	32.39	7-74	11	1
R.G.Sharma	61.4	5	216	2	108.00	1-26	–	–
G.H.Vihari	57.3	10	180	5	36.00	3-37	–	–
M.Vijay	64	6	198	1	198.00	1-12	–	–
U.T.Yadav	1230.3	205	4388	144	30.47	6-88	3	1

PAKISTAN – BATTING AND FIELDING

	M	I	NO	HS	Runs	Avge	100	50	Ct/St
Abid Ali	3	4	1	174	321	107.00	2	–	–
Asad Shafiq	74	123	6	137	4593	39.25	12	27	74

PAKISTAN – BATTING AND FIELDING (continued)

	M	I	NO	HS	Runs	Avge	100	50	Ct/St
Azhar Ali	78	147	8	302*	5919	42.58	16	31	61
Babar Azam	26	48	7	143	1850	45.12	5	13	19
Bilal Asif	5	8	–	15	73	9.12	–	–	2
Faheem Ashraf	4	6	–	83	138	23.00	–	1	–
Fakhar Zaman	3	6	–	94	192	32.00	–	2	3
Haris Sohail	14	23	1	147	819	37.22	2	3	11
Hasan Ali	9	15	5	29	155	15.50	–	–	4
Iftikhar Ahmed	3	5	–	27	48	9.60	–	–	1
Imam-ul-Haq	11	21	2	76	485	25.52	–	3	7
Imran Khan	10	10	3	6	16	2.28	–	–	–
Mohammad Abbas	18	25	12	29	94	7.23	–	–	5
Mohammad Amir	36	67	11	48	751	13.41	–	–	5
Mohammad Hafeez	55	105	8	224	3652	37.64	10	12	45
Mohammad Rizwan	6	9	2	95	225	32.14	–	1	17
Musa Khan	1	2	2	12*	16	–	–	–	–
Naseem Shah	4	4	2	7	10	5.00	–	–	–
Sarfraz Ahmed	49	86	13	112	2657	36.39	3	18	146/21
Shadab Khan	5	9	2	56	240	34.28	–	3	1
Shaheen Shah Afridi	8	12	2	14	42	4.20	–	–	–
Shan Masood	20	38	–	135	1189	31.28	3	6	11
Usman Shinwari	1	–	–	–	–	–	–	–	–
Yasir Shah	39	58	6	113	707	13.59	1	–	20

PAKISTAN – BOWLING

	O	M	R	W	Avge	Best	5wI	10wM
Asad Shafiq	49.4	1	172	2	86.00	1- 7	–	–
Azhar Ali	142.2	8	611	8	76.37	2-35	–	–
Bilal Asif	195.4	40	424	16	26.50	6-36	2	–
Faheem Ashraf	90	18	287	11	26.09	3-42	–	–
Haris Sohail	99	12	275	13	21.15	3- 1	–	–
Hasan Ali	289.3	72	896	31	28.90	5-45	1	–
Iftikhar Ahmed	31.2	1	141	1	141.00	1- 1	–	–
Imran Khan	272.4	50	917	29	31.62	5-58	1	–
Mohammad Abbas	635.4	188	1557	75	20.76	5-33	4	1
Mohammad Amir	1269.5	292	3627	119	30.47	6-44	4	–
Mohammad Hafeez	677.5	118	1808	53	34.11	4-16	–	–
Musa Khan	20	1	114	0	–	–	–	–
Naseem Shah	100.1	13	349	13	26.84	5-31	1	–
Shadab Khan	147.3	19	466	12	38.83	3-31	–	–
Shaheen Shah Afridi	267.5	52	839	30	27.96	5-77	1	–
Shan Masood	13	4	44	2	22.00	1- 6	–	–
Usman Shinwari	15	4	54	1	54.00	1-54	–	–
Yasir Shah	2035.1	315	6502	213	30.52	8-41	16	3

SRI LANKA – BATTING AND FIELDING

	M	I	NO	HS	Runs	Avge	100	50	Ct/St
L.Ambuldeniya	7	9	–	24	56	6.22	–	–	1
P.V.D.Chameera	8	15	2	19	69	5.30	–	–	4
L.D.Chandimal	57	103	8	164	3877	40.81	11	18	77/10
D.M.de Silva	31	57	4	173	1863	35.15	6	6	34
D.P.D.N.Dickwella	37	66	4	83	1921	30.98	–	15	87/23
B.O.P.Fernando	6	11	2	102	393	43.66	1	1	4
M.V.T.Fernando	8	12	6	38	54	9.00	–	–	2
M.D.Gunathilleke	8	16	–	61	299	18.68	–	2	6
C.Karanuratne	1	2	–	22	22	11.00	–	–	1
F.D.M.Karunaratne	66	128	5	196	4524	36.78	9	24	52
C.B.R.L.S.Kumara	21	28	14	10	52	3.71	–	–	4
R.A.S.Lakmal	61	95	23	42	836	11.61	–	–	18
A.D.Mathews	86	154	22	200*	5981	45.31	10	35	68

TESTS   SRI LANKA – BATTING AND FIELDING (continued)

	M	I	NO	HS	Runs	Avge	100	50	Ct/St
B.K.G.Mendis	44	85	4	196	2995	36.97	7	11	65
M.D.K.Perera	41	73	8	95	1208	18.58	–	6	19
M.D.K.J.Perera	18	33	3	153*	934	31.13	2	4	19/8
M.K.P.A.D.Perera	6	10	2	43*	135	16.87	–	–	1
C.A.K.Rajitha	8	10	2	12	23	2.87	–	–	4
A.R.S.Silva	12	23	3	109	702	35.10	1	5	2
H.D.R.L.Thirimanne	35	68	6	155*	1404	22.64	1	6	209

SRI LANKA – BOWLING

	O	M	R	W	Avge	Best	5wI	10wM
L.Ambuldeniya	338.3	48	1194	30	39.80	5-66	2	–
P.V.D.Chameera	231.5	19	984	24	41.00	5-47	1	–
D.M.de Silva	326.1	39	1091	21	51.95	3-25	–	–
B.O.P.Fernando	3	0	19	0	–	–	–	–
M.V.T.Fernando	215.3	25	772	23	33.56	4-62	–	–
M.D.Gunathilleke	33	3	111	1	111.00	1-16	–	–
C.Karunaratne	26	1	148	1	148.00	1-130	–	–
F.D.M.Karunaratne	39.3	4	149	2	74.50	1-12	–	–
C.B.R.L.S.Kumara	650.5	93	2451	67	36.58	6-122	1	–
R.A.S.Lakmal	1849.5	371	5651	151	37.42	5-54	3	–
A.D.Mathews	646	158	1745	33	52.87	4-44	–	–
B.K.G.Mendis	14	1	69	1	69.00	1-10	–	–
M.D.K.Perera	1707.4	230	5512	156	35.33	6-32	8	2
M.K.P.A.D.Perera	230.5	33	819	33	24.81	6-115	4	–
C.A.K.Rajitha	233.4	44	763	25	30.52	3-20	–	–
H.D.R.L.Thirimanne	14	1	51	0	–	–	–	–

M.K.P.A.D.Perera is also known as A.Dananjaya.

ZIMBABWE – BATTING AND FIELDING

	M	I	NO	HS	Runs	Avge	100	50	Ct/St
R.W.Chakabva	17	34	2	101	806	25.18	1	4	34/4
C.R.Ervine	18	36	2	160	1208	35.52	3	4	16
K.M.Jarvis	13	24	10	25*	128	9.14	–	–	3
K.T.Kasuza	3	4	–	63	113	28.25	–	1	–
T.Maruma	3	5	–	41	68	13.60	–	–	1
P.S.Masvaure	5	10	–	64	235	23.50	–	2	1
B.S.Mudzinganyama	1	1	–	16	16	16.00	–	–	–
C.T.Mumba	3	5	2	11*	25	8.33	–	–	2
C.T.Mutombodzi	2	3	–	33	41	20.50	–	–	1
B.Muzarabani	1	2	1	10	14	14.00	–	–	–
A.Ndlovu	2	4	–	5	9	2.25	–	–	2
V.M.Nyauchi	3	5	3	11	30	15.00	–	–	–
Sikandar Raza	15	30	–	127	1037	34.56	1	7	3
B.R.M.Taylor	31	62	4	171	2055	35.43	6	10	28
D.T.Tiripano	10	20	5	49*	299	19.93	–	–	2
C.K.Tshuma	1	2	–	3	3	1.50	–	–	–
S.C.Williams	12	24	1	119	770	33.47	2	3	10

ZIMBABWE – BOWLING

	O	M	R	W	Avge	Best	5wI	10wM
K.M.Jarvis	418.3	79	1354	46	29.43	5-54	3	–
P.S.Masvaure	14	0	61	0	–	–	–	–
C.T.Mumba	99.5	17	354	10	35.40	4-50	–	–
C.T.Mutombodzi	19	3	67	0	–	–	–	–
B.Muzarabani	13	2	48	0	–	–	–	–
A.Ndlovu	70	7	277	2	138.50	2-170	–	–
V.M.Nyauchi	94.5	20	245	6	40.83	3-69	–	–
Sikandar Raza	404.5	52	1338	32	41.81	7-113	2	–

TESTS

ZIMBABWE – BOWLING (continued)

	O	M	R	W	Avge	Best	5wI	10wM
B.R.M.Taylor	7	0	38	0	–	–	–	–
D.T.Tiripano	310.4	71	837	16	52.31	3-91	–	–
C.K.Tshuma	25	2	85	1	85.00	1-85	–	–
S.C.Williams	295.3	33	925	19	48.68	3-20	–	–

BANGLADESH – BATTING AND FIELDING

	M	I	NO	HS	Runs	Avge	100	50	Ct/St
Abu Jayed	9	16	6	7*	27	2.70	–	–	1
Al-Amin Hossain	7	11	7	32*	90	22.50	–	–	1
Ebadat Hossain	6	10	4	2	4	0.66	–	–	1
Imrul Kayes	39	76	2	150	1797	24.28	3	4	35
Khaled Ahmed	2	2	1	4*	4	4.00	–	–	2
Liton Das	20	34	1	94	859	26.03	–	5	32/2
Mahmudullah	49	93	6	146	2764	31.77	4	16	38/1
Mehedi Hasan	22	42	6	68*	638	17.72	–	2	19
Mithun Ali	9	16	–	67	308	19.25	–	2	4
Mominul Haque	40	74	4	181	2860	40.85	9	13	29
Mosaddek Hossain	3	6	2	75	164	41.00	–	1	2
Mushfiqur Rahim	70	130	10	219*	4143	36.77	7	21	104/15
Mustafizur Rahman	13	19	6	16	56	4.30	–	–	4
Nayeem Hasan	5	6	2	26	70	17.50	–	–	4
Nazmul Hossain	4	7	–	71	201	28.71	–	1	3
Rubel Hossain	27	47	19	45*	265	9.46	–	–	11
Saif Hasan	2	3	–	16	24	8.00	–	–	–
Shadman Islam	6	11	–	76	275	25.00	–	1	3
Shakib Al Hasan	56	105	7	217	3862	39.40	5	24	24
Soumya Sarkar	15	28	–	149	818	29.21	1	4	21
Taijul Islam	29	48	7	39*	412	10.04	–	–	16
Tamim Iqbal	60	115	1	206	4405	38.64	9	27	17

BANGLADESH – BOWLING

	O	M	R	W	Avge	Best	5wI	10wM
Abu Jayed	232.2	48	779	24	32.45	4- 71	–	–
Al-Amin Hossain	169.2	35	545	9	60.55	3- 80	–	–
Ebadat Hossain	142	29	536	6	89.33	3- 91	–	–
Imrul Kayes	4	0	12	0	–	–	–	–
Khaled Ahmed	60	17	242	0	–	–	–	–
Mahmudullah	566.3	56	1949	43	45.32	5- 51	1	–
Mehedi Hasan	884.2	107	2981	90	33.12	7- 58	7	2
Mominul Haque	100.1	8	376	4	94.00	3- 27	–	–
Mosaddek Hossain	15	1	49	0	–	–	–	–
Mustafizur Rahman	307.3	63	985	28	35.17	4- 37	–	–
Nayeem Hasan	130	22	389	19	20.47	5- 61	2	–
Nazmul Hossain	0.4	0	13	0	–	–	–	–
Rubel Hossain	703.5	73	2764	36	76.77	5-166	1	–
Shakib Al Hasan	2170	393	6537	210	31.12	7- 36	18	2
Soumya Sarkar	73.4	2	288	3	96.00	2- 68	–	–
Taijul Islam	1174.4	173	3782	114	33.17	8- 39	7	1
Tamim Iqbal	5	0	20	0	–	–	–	–

IRELAND – BATTING AND FIELDING

	M	I	NO	HS	Runs	Avge	100	50	Ct/St
M.R.Adair	1	2	–	8	11	5.50	–	–	1
A.Balbirnie	3	6	–	82	146	24.33	–	2	3
J.Cameron-Dow	1	2	–	82	146	24.33	–	2	3
G.H.Dockrell	1	2	1	32*	41	41.00	–	–	2
A.R.McBrine	1	2	–	39	64	32.00	–	–	–
J.A.McCollum	2	4	–	11	18	4.50	–	–	–
	2	4	–	39	73	18.25	–	–	2

61

TESTS   **IRELAND – BATTING AND FIELDING (continued)**

	M	I	NO	HS	Runs	Avge	100	50	Ct/St
T.J.Murtagh	3	6	2	54*	109	27.25	–	1	–
K.J.O'Brien	3	6	–	118	258	51.60	1	1	–
W.T.S.Porterfield	3	6	–	32	58	9.66	–	–	2
S.W.Poynter	1	2	–	1	1	0.50	–	–	2/1
W.B.Rankin †	3	6	1	17	43	8.60	–	–	–
P.R.Stirling	3	6	–	36	104	17.33	–	1	4
S.R.Thompson	3	6	–	53	64	10.66	–	1	–
G.C.Wilson	2	4	1	33*	45	15.00	–	–	6

IRELAND – BOWLING

	O	M	R	W	Avge	Best	5wI	10wM
M.R.Adair	27.4	8	98	6	16.33	3-32	–	–
A.Balbirnie	1	0	8	0	–	–	–	–
J.Cameron-Dow	23.5	0	118	3	39.33	2-94	–	–
G.H.Dockrell	40	11	121	2	60.50	2-63	–	–
A.R.McBrine	50	10	159	3	53.00	2-77	–	–
T.J.Murtagh	95	25	213	13	16.38	5-13	1	–
K.J.O'Brien	10	2	31	0	–	–	–	–
W.B.Rankin	73.5	6	304	8	38.00	2- 5	–	–
P.R.Stirling	2	0	11	0	–	–	–	–
S.R.Thompson	68.2	14	204	10	20.40	3-28	–	–

† *W.B.Rankin made one Test appearance for England, v A in Jan 2014, scoring 13 and 0, with bowling figures of 0-34 and 1-47.*

AFGHANISTAN – BATTING AND FIELDING

	M	I	NO	HS	Runs	Avge	100	50	Ct/St
Afsar Zazai	3	6	1	48*	135	27.00	–	–	5/1
Asghar Stanikzai	4	7	–	92	249	35.57	–	3	2
Hamza Hotak	1	2	–	34	35	17.50	–	–	–
Hashmatullah Shahidi	3	6	2	61	138	34.50	–	1	1
Ibrahim Zadran	2	4	–	87	148	37.00	–	1	4
Ihsanullah Janat	3	6	1	65*	110	22.00	–	1	4
Ikram Alikhil	1	1	–	7	7	7.00	–	–	4/1
Javed Ahmadi	2	4	–	62	105	26.25	–	1	–
Mohammad Nabi	3	6	–	24	33	5.50	–	–	2
Mohammad Shahzad	2	4	–	40	69	17.25	–	–	–
Mujeeb Zadran	1	2	–	15	18	9.00	–	–	–
Nasir Ahmadzai	1	2	–	15	17	8.50	–	–	–
Qais Ahmad	1	2	–	14	23	11.50	–	–	–
Rahmat Shah	4	8	–	102	298	37.25	1	2	2
Rashid Khan	4	7	–	51	106	15.14	–	1	1
Wafadar Momand	2	3	1	6*	12	6.00	–	–	–
Waqar Salamkheil	1	1	1	1*	1	–	–	–	–
Yamin Ahmadzai	4	7	–	18	31	4.42	–	–	–
Zahir Khan	2	4	3	0*	0	0.00	–	–	–

AFGHANISTAN – BOWLING

	O	M	R	W	Avge	Best	5wI	10wM
Asghar Stanikzai	2	0	16	0	–	–	–	–
Hamza Hotak	30.5	5	79	6	13.16	5- 74	1	–
Javed Ahmadi	1	0	9	0	–	–	–	–
Mohammad Nabi	91	17	254	8	31.75	3- 36	–	–
Mujeeb Zadran	15	1	75	1	75.00	1- 75	–	–
Qais Ahmad	1	0	28	1	28.00	1- 22	–	–
Rashid Khan	156.2	28	485	23	21.08	6- 49	3	1
Wafadar Momand	37	8	155	2	77.50	2-100	–	–
Waqar Salamkheil	31	6	101	4	25.25	2- 35	–	–
Yamin Ahmadzai	70	16	211	10	21.10	3- 41	–	–
Zahir Khan	37	3	158	5	31.60	3- 59	–	–

INTERNATIONAL TEST MATCH RESULTS

Complete to 18 March 2020.

Team	Opponents	Tests	E	A	SA	WI	NZ	I	P	SL	Z	B	Ire	Afg	Tied	Drawn
England	Australia	351	110	146	–	–	–	–	–	–	–	–	–	–	–	95
	South Africa	153	64	–	34	–	–	–	–	–	–	–	–	–	–	55
	West Indies	157	49	–	–	57	–	–	–	–	–	–	–	–	–	51
	New Zealand	105	48	–	–	–	11	–	–	–	–	–	–	–	–	46
	India	122	47	–	–	–	–	26	–	–	–	–	–	–	–	49
	Pakistan	83	25	–	–	–	–	–	21	–	–	–	–	–	–	37
	Sri Lanka	34	15	–	–	–	–	–	–	8	–	–	–	–	–	11
	Zimbabwe	6	3	–	–	–	–	–	–	–	0	–	–	–	–	3
	Bangladesh	10	9	–	–	–	–	–	–	–	–	1	–	–	–	0
	Ireland	1	1	–	–	–	–	–	–	–	–	–	0	–	–	0
Australia	South Africa	98	–	52	26	–	–	–	–	–	–	–	–	–	–	20
	West Indies	116	–	58	–	32	–	–	–	–	–	–	–	–	1	25
	New Zealand	60	–	34	–	–	8	–	–	–	–	–	–	–	–	18
	India	98	–	42	–	–	–	28	–	–	–	–	–	–	1	27
	Pakistan	66	–	33	–	–	–	–	15	–	–	–	–	–	–	18
	Sri Lanka	31	–	19	–	–	–	–	–	4	–	–	–	–	–	8
	Zimbabwe	3	–	3	–	–	–	–	–	–	0	–	–	–	–	0
	Bangladesh	6	–	5	–	–	–	–	–	–	–	1	–	–	–	0
S Africa	West Indies	28	–	–	18	3	–	–	–	–	–	–	–	–	–	7
	New Zealand	45	–	–	25	–	4	–	–	–	–	–	–	–	–	16
	India	39	–	–	15	–	–	14	–	–	–	–	–	–	–	10
	Pakistan	26	–	–	15	–	–	–	4	–	–	–	–	–	–	7
	Sri Lanka	29	–	–	14	–	–	–	–	9	–	–	–	–	–	6
	Zimbabwe	9	–	–	8	–	–	–	–	–	0	–	–	–	–	1
	Bangladesh	12	–	–	10	–	–	–	–	–	–	0	–	–	–	2
W Indies	New Zealand	47	–	–	–	13	15	–	–	–	–	–	–	–	–	19
	India	98	–	–	–	30	–	22	–	–	–	–	–	–	–	46
	Pakistan	52	–	–	–	17	–	–	20	–	–	–	–	–	–	15
	Sri Lanka	20	–	–	–	4	–	–	–	9	–	–	–	–	–	7
	Zimbabwe	10	–	–	–	7	–	–	–	–	0	–	–	–	–	3
	Bangladesh	16	–	–	–	10	–	–	–	–	–	4	–	–	–	2
	Afghanistan	1	–	–	–	1	–	–	–	–	–	–	–	0	–	0
N Zealand	India	59	–	–	–	–	12	21	–	–	–	–	–	–	–	26
	Pakistan	58	–	–	–	–	12	–	25	–	–	–	–	–	–	21
	Sri Lanka	36	–	–	–	–	16	–	–	9	–	–	–	–	–	11
	Zimbabwe	17	–	–	–	–	11	–	–	–	0	–	–	–	–	6
	Bangladesh	15	–	–	–	–	12	–	–	–	–	0	–	–	–	3
India	Pakistan	59	–	–	–	–	–	9	12	–	–	–	–	–	–	38
	Sri Lanka	44	–	–	–	–	–	20	–	7	–	–	–	–	–	17
	Zimbabwe	11	–	–	–	–	–	7	–	–	2	–	–	–	–	2
	Bangladesh	11	–	–	–	–	–	9	–	–	–	0	–	–	–	2
	Afghanistan	1	–	–	–	–	–	1	–	–	–	–	–	0	–	0
Pakistan	Sri Lanka	55	–	–	–	–	–	–	20	16	–	–	–	–	–	19
	Zimbabwe	17	–	–	–	–	–	–	10	–	3	–	–	–	–	4
	Bangladesh	11	–	–	–	–	–	–	10	–	–	0	–	–	–	1
	Ireland	1	–	–	–	–	–	–	1	–	–	–	–	–	–	0
Sri Lanka	Zimbabwe	20	–	–	–	–	–	–	–	14	0	0	–	–	–	6
	Bangladesh	20	–	–	–	–	–	–	–	16	–	1	–	–	–	3
Zimbabwe	Bangladesh	17	–	–	–	–	–	–	–	–	7	7	–	–	–	3
Bangladesh	Afghanistan	1	–	–	–	–	–	–	–	–	–	0	–	1	–	0
Ireland	Afghanistan	1	–	–	–	–	–	–	–	–	–	–	0	1	–	0
		2386	371	392	165	174	101	157	138	92	12	14	0	2	2	766

	Tests	Won	Lost	Drawn	Tied	Toss Won
England	1022	371	304	347	–	500
Australia	830†	393†	224	211	2	415†
South Africa	437	165	150	124	–	209
West Indies	545	174	195	175	1	285
New Zealand	442	101	175	166	–	221
India	542	157	167	217	1	272
Pakistan	428	138	130	160	–	203
Sri Lanka	289	92	109	88	–	155
Zimbabwe	110	12	70	28	–	63
Bangladesh	119	14	89	16	–	61
Ireland	3	–	3	–	–	2
Afghanistan	4	2	2	–	–	1

† total includes Australia's victory against the ICC World XI.

INTERNATIONAL TEST CRICKET RECORDS

(To 18 March 2020)

TEAM RECORDS

HIGHEST INNINGS TOTALS

952-6d	Sri Lanka v India	Colombo (RPS)	1997-98
903-7d	England v Australia	The Oval	1938
849	England v West Indies	Kingston	1929-30
790-3d	West Indies v Pakistan	Kingston	1957-58
765-6d	Pakistan v Sri Lanka	Karachi	2008-09
760-7d	Sri Lanka v India	Ahmedabad	2009-10
759-7d	India v England	Chennai	2016-17
758-8d	Australia v West Indies	Kingston	1954-55
756-5d	Sri Lanka v South Africa	Colombo (SSC)	2006
751-5d	West Indies v England	St John's	2003-04
749-9d	West Indies v England	Bridgetown	2008-09
747	West Indies v South Africa	St John's	2004-05
735-6d	Australia v Zimbabwe	Perth	2003-04
730-6d	Sri Lanka v Bangladesh	Dhaka	2013-14
729-6d	Australia v England	Lord's	1930
726-9d	India v Sri Lanka	Mumbai	2009-10
715-6d	New Zealand v Bangladesh	Hamilton	2018-19
713-3d	Sri Lanka v Zimbabwe	Bulawayo	2003-04
713-9d	Sri Lanka v Bangladesh	Chittagong	2017-18
710-7d	England v India	Birmingham	2011
708	Pakistan v England	The Oval	1987
707	India v Sri Lanka	Colombo (SSC)	2010
705-7d	India v Australia	Sydney	2003-04
701	Australia v England	The Oval	1934
699-5	Pakistan v India	Lahore	1989-90
695	Australia v England	The Oval	1930
692-8d	West Indies v England	The Oval	1995
690	New Zealand v Pakistan	Sharjah	2014-15
687-8d	West Indies v England	The Oval	1976
687-6d	India v Bangladesh	Hyderabad	2016-17
682-6d	South Africa v England	Lord's	2003
681-8d	West Indies v England	Port-of-Spain	1953-54
680-8d	New Zealand v India	Wellington	2013-14
679-7d	Pakistan v India	Lahore	2005-06

676-7	India v Sri Lanka	Kanpur	1986-87
675-5d	India v Pakistan	Multan	2003-04
674	Australia v India	Adelaide	1947-48
674-6	Pakistan v India	Faisalabad	1984-85
674-6d	Australia v England	Cardiff	2009
671-4	New Zealand v Sri Lanka	Wellington	1990-91
668	Australia v West Indies	Bridgetown	1954-55
664	India v England	The Oval	2007
662-9d	Australia v England	Perth	2017-18
660-5d	West Indies v New Zealand	Wellington	1994-95
659-8d	Australia v England	Sydney	1946-47
659-4d	Australia v India	Sydney	2011-12
658-8d	England v Australia	Nottingham	1938
658-9d	South Africa v West Indies	Durban	2003-04
657-8d	Pakistan v West Indies	Bridgetown	1957-58
657-7d	India v Australia	Calcutta	2000-01
656-8d	Australia v England	Manchester	1964
654-5	England v South Africa	Durban	1938-39
653-4d	England v India	Lord's	1990
653-4d	Australia v England	Leeds	1993
652-8d	West Indies v England	Lord's	1973
652	Pakistan v India	Faisalabad	1982-83
652-7d	England v India	Madras	1984-85
652-7d	Australia v South Africa	Johannesburg	2001-02
651	South Africa v Australia	Cape Town	2008-09
650-6d	Australia v West Indies	Bridgetown	1964-65

The highest for Zimbabwe is 563-9d (v WI, Harare, 2001), and for Bangladesh 638 (v SL, Galle, 2012-13).

LOWEST INNINGS TOTALS

† One batsman absent

26	New Zealand v England	Auckland	1954-55
30	South Africa v England	Port Elizabeth	1895-96
30	South Africa v England	Birmingham	1924
35	South Africa v England	Cape Town	1898-99
36	Australia v England	Birmingham	1902
36	South Africa v Australia	Melbourne	1931-32
38	Ireland v England	Lord's	2019
42	Australia v England	Sydney	1887-88
42	New Zealand v Australia	Wellington	1945-46
42†	India v England	Lord's	1974
43	South Africa v England	Cape Town	1888-89
43	Bangladesh v West Indies	North Sound	2018
44	Australia v England	The Oval	1896
45	England v Australia	Sydney	1886-87
45	South Africa v Australia	Melbourne	1931-32
45	New Zealand v South Africa	Cape Town	2012-13
46	England v West Indies	Port-of-Spain	1993-94
47	South Africa v England	Cape Town	1888-89
47	New Zealand v England	Lord's	1958
47	West Indies v England	Kingston	2003-04
47	Australia v South Africa	Cape Town	2011-12
49	Pakistan v South Africa	Johannesburg	2012-13

The lowest for Sri Lanka is 71 (v P, Kandy, 1994-95) and for Zimbabwe 51 (v NZ, Napier, 2011-12).

BATTING RECORDS
5000 RUNS IN TESTS

Runs			M	I	NO	HS	Avge	100	50
15921	S.R.Tendulkar	I	200	329	33	248*	53.78	51	68
13378	R.T.Ponting	A	168	287	29	257	51.85	41	62
13289	J.H.Kallis	SA/ICC	166	280	40	224	55.37	45	58
13288	R.S.Dravid	I/ICC	164	286	32	270	52.31	36	63
12472	A.N.Cook	E	161	291	16	294	45.35	33	57
12400	K.C.Sangakkara	SL	134	233	17	319	57.40	38	52
11953	B.C.Lara	WI/ICC	131	232	6	400*	52.88	34	48
11867	S.Chanderpaul	WI	164	280	49	203*	51.37	30	66
11814	D.P.M.D.Jayawardena	SL	149	252	15	374	49.84	34	50
11174	A.R.Border	A	156	265	44	205	50.56	27	63
10927	S.R.Waugh	A	168	260	46	200	51.06	32	50
10122	S.M.Gavaskar	I	125	214	16	236*	51.12	34	45
10099	Younus Khan	P	118	213	19	313	52.05	34	33
9282	H.M.Amla	SA	124	215	16	311*	46.64	28	41
9265	G.C.Smith	SA/ICC	117	205	13	277	48.25	27	38
8900	G.A.Gooch	E	118	215	6	333	42.58	20	46
8832	Javed Miandad	P	124	189	21	280*	52.57	23	43
8830	Inzamam-ul-Haq	P/ICC	120	200	22	329	49.60	25	46
8781	V.V.S.Laxman	I	134	225	34	281	45.97	17	56
8765	A.B.de Villiers	SA	114	191	18	278*	50.66	22	46
8643	M.J.Clarke	A	115	198	22	329*	49.10	28	27
8625	M.L.Hayden	A	103	184	14	380	50.73	30	29
8586	V.Sehwag	I/ICC	104	180	6	319	49.34	23	32
8540	I.V.A.Richards	WI	121	182	12	291	50.23	24	45
8463	A.J.Stewart	E	133	235	21	190	39.54	15	45
8231	D.I.Gower	E	117	204	18	215	44.25	18	39
8181	K.P.Pietersen	E	104	181	8	227	47.28	23	35
8114	G.Boycott	E	108	193	23	246*	47.72	22	42
8032	G.St A.Sobers	WI	93	160	21	365*	57.78	26	30
8029	M.E.Waugh	A	128	209	17	153*	41.81	20	47
7728	M.A.Atherton	E	115	212	7	185*	37.70	16	46
7727	I.R.Bell	E	118	205	24	235	42.69	22	46
7696	J.L.Langer	A	105	182	12	250	45.27	23	30
7624	M.C.Cowdrey	E	114	188	15	182	44.06	22	38
7599	J.E.Root	E	92	169	12	254	48.40	17	48
7558	C.G.Greenidge	WI	108	185	16	226	44.72	19	34
7530	Mohammad Yousuf	P	90	156	12	223	52.29	24	33
7525	M.A.Taylor	A	104	186	13	334*	43.49	19	40
7515	C.H.Lloyd	WI	110	175	14	242*	46.67	19	39
7487	D.L.Haynes	WI	116	202	25	184	42.29	18	39
7422	D.C.Boon	A	107	190	20	200	43.65	21	32
7289	G.Kirsten	SA	101	176	15	275	45.27	21	34
7249	W.R.Hammond	E	85	140	16	336*	58.45	22	24
7244	D.A.Warner	A	84	155	7	335*	48.94	24	30
7240	V.Kohli	I	86	145	10	254*	53.62	27	22
7238	L.R.P.L.Taylor	NZ	101	178	21	290	46.10	19	33
7227	S.P.D.Smith	A	73	131	16	239	62.84	26	29
7214	C.H.Gayle	WI	103	182	11	333	42.18	15	37
7212	S.C.Ganguly	I	113	188	17	239	42.17	16	35
7172	S.P.Fleming	NZ	111	189	10	274*	40.06	9	46
7110	G.S.Chappell	A	87	151	19	247*	53.86	24	31
7037	A.J.Strauss	E	100	178	6	177	40.91	21	27
6996	D.G.Bradman	A	52	80	10	334	99.94	29	13

66

Runs			M	I	NO	HS	Avge	100	50
6973	S.T.Jayasuriya	SL	110	188	14	340	40.07	14	31
6971	L.Hutton	E	79	138	15	364	56.67	19	33
6868	D.B.Vengsarkar	I	116	185	22	166	42.13	17	35
6806	K.F.Barrington	E	82	131	15	256	58.67	20	35
6744	G.P.Thorpe	E	100	179	28	200*	44.66	16	39
6476	K.S.Williamson	NZ	80	140	13	242*	50.99	21	32
6453	B.B.McCullum	NZ	101	176	9	302	38.64	12	31
6361	P.A.de Silva	SL	93	159	11	267	42.97	20	22
6235	M.E.K.Hussey	A	79	137	16	195	51.52	19	29
6227	R.B.Kanhai	WI	79	137	6	256	47.53	15	28
6215	M.Azharuddin	I	99	147	9	199	45.03	22	21
6167	H.H.Gibbs	SA	90	154	7	228	41.95	14	26
6149	R.N.Harvey	A	79	137	10	205	48.41	21	24
6080	G.R.Viswanath	I	91	155	10	222	41.93	14	35
5981	A.D.Mathews	SL	86	154	22	200*	45.31	10	35
5949	R.B.Richardson	WI	86	146	12	194	44.39	16	27
5919	Azhar Ali	P	78	147	8	302*	42.58	16	31
5842	R.R.Sarwan	WI	87	154	8	291	40.01	15	31
5840	C.A.Pujara	I	77	128	3	206*	48.66	18	25
5825	M.E.Trescothick	E	76	143	10	219	43.79	14	29
5807	D.C.S.Compton	E	78	131	15	278	50.06	17	28
5768	Salim Malik	P	103	154	22	237	43.69	15	29
5764	N.Hussain	E	96	171	16	207	37.19	14	33
5762	C.L.Hooper	WI	102	173	15	233	36.46	13	27
5719	M.P.Vaughan	E	82	147	9	197	41.44	18	18
5570	A.C.Gilchrist	A	96	137	20	204*	47.60	17	26
5515	M.V.Boucher	SA/ICC	147	206	24	125	30.30	5	35
5502	M.S.Atapattu	SL	90	156	15	249	39.02	16	17
5492	T.M.Dilshan	SL	87	145	11	193	40.98	16	23
5462	T.T.Samaraweera	SL	81	132	20	231	48.76	14	30
5444	M.D.Crowe	NZ	77	131	11	299	45.36	17	18
5410	J.B.Hobbs	E	61	102	7	211	56.94	15	28
5357	K.D.Walters	A	74	125	14	250	48.26	15	33
5345	I.M.Chappell	A	75	136	10	196	42.42	14	26
5334	J.G.Wright	NZ	82	148	7	185	37.82	12	23
5312	M.J.Slater	A	74	131	7	219	42.84	14	21
5248	Kapil Dev	I	131	184	15	163	31.05	8	27
5234	W.M.Lawry	A	67	123	12	210	47.15	13	27
5222	Misbah-ul-Haq	P	75	132	20	161*	46.62	10	39
5200	I.T.Botham	E	102	161	6	208	33.54	14	22
5138	J.H.Edrich	E	77	127	9	310*	43.54	12	24
5105	A.Ranatunga	SL	93	155	12	135*	35.69	4	38
5062	Zaheer Abbas	P	78	124	11	274	44.79	12	20

The most for Zimbabwe is 4794 by A.Flower (112 innings), and for Bangladesh 4405 by Tamim Iqbal (115 innings).

750 RUNS IN A SERIES

Runs			Series	M	I	NO	HS	Avge	100	50
974	D.G.Bradman	A v E	1930	5	7	–	334	139.14	4	–
905	W.R.Hammond	E v A	1928-29	5	9	1	251	113.12	4	–
839	M.A.Taylor	A v E	1989	6	11	1	219	83.90	2	5
834	R.N.Harvey	A v SA	1952-53	5	9	–	205	92.66	4	3
829	I.V.A.Richards	WI v E	1976	4	7	–	291	118.42	3	2
827	C.L.Walcott	WI v A	1954-55	5	10	–	155	82.70	5	2
824	G.St A.Sobers	WI v P	1957-58	5	8	2	365*	137.33	3	3

Runs		Series	M	I	NO	HS	Avge	100	50
810	D.G.Bradman	A v E	1936-37	5	9	–	270	90.00	3	1
806	D.G.Bradman	A v SA	1931-32	5	5	1	299*	201.50	4	–
798	B.C.Lara	WI v E	1993-94	5	8	–	375	99.75	2	2
779	E.de C.Weekes	WI v I	1948-49	5	7	–	194	111.28	4	2
774	S.M.Gavaskar	I v WI	1970-71	4	8	3	220	154.80	4	3
774	S.P.D.Smith	A v E	2019	4	7	–	211	110.57	3	3
769	S.P.D.Smith	A v I	2014-15	4	8	2	192	128.16	4	2
766	A.N.Cook	E v A	2010-11	5	7	1	235*	127.66	3	2
765	B.C.Lara	WI v E	1995	6	10	1	179	85.00	3	3
761	Mudassar Nazar	P v I	1982-83	6	8	2	231	126.83	4	1
758	D.G.Bradman	A v E	1934	5	8	–	304	94.75	2	1
753	D.C.S.Compton	E v SA	1947	5	8	–	208	94.12	4	1
752	G.A.Gooch	E v I	1990	3	6	–	333	125.33	3	2

HIGHEST INDIVIDUAL INNINGS

400*	B.C.Lara	WI v E	St John's	2003-04
380	M.L.Hayden	A v Z	Perth	2003-04
375	B.C.Lara	WI v E	St John's	1993-94
374	D.P.M.D.Jayawardena	SL v SA	Colombo (SSC)	2006
365*	G.St A.Sobers	WI v P	Kingston	1957-58
364	L.Hutton	E v A	The Oval	1938
340	S.T.Jayasuriya	SL v I	Colombo (RPS)	1997-98
337	Hanif Mohammed	P v WI	Bridgetown	1957-58
336*	W.R.Hammond	E v NZ	Auckland	1932-33
335*	D.A.Warner	A v P	Adelaide	2019-20
334*	M.A.Taylor	A v P	Peshawar	1998-99
334	D.G.Bradman	A v E	Leeds	1930
333	G.A.Gooch	E v I	Lord's	1990
333	C.H.Gayle	WI v SL	Galle	2010-11
329*	M.J.Clarke	A v I	Sydney	2011-12
329	Inzamam-ul-Haq	P v NZ	Lahore	2001-02
325	A.Sandham	E v WI	Kingston	1929-30
319	V.Sehwag	I v SA	Chennai	2007-08
319	K.C.Sangakkara	SL v B	Chittagong	2013-14
317	C.H.Gayle	WI v SA	St John's	2004-05
313	Younus Khan	P v SL	Karachi	2008-09
311*	H.M.Amla	SA v E	The Oval	2012
311	R.B.Simpson	A v E	Manchester	1964
310*	J.H.Edrich	E v NZ	Leeds	1965
309	V.Sehwag	I v P	Multan	2003-04
307	R.M.Cowper	A v E	Melbourne	1965-66
304	D.G.Bradman	A v E	Leeds	1934
303*	K.K.Nair	I v E	Chennai	2016-17
302*	Azhar Ali	P v WI	Dubai (DSC)	2016-17
302	L.G.Rowe	WI v E	Bridgetown	1973-74
302	B.B.McCullum	NZ v I	Wellington	2013-14
299*	D.G.Bradman	A v SA	Adelaide	1931-32
299	M.D.Crowe	NZ v SL	Wellington	1990-91
294	A.N.Cook	E v I	Birmingham	2011
293	V.Sehwag	I v SL	Mumbai	2009-10
291	I.V.A.Richards	WI v E	The Oval	1976
291	R.R.Sarwan	WI v E	Bridgetown	2008-09
290	L.R.P.L.Taylor	NZ v A	Perth	2015-16
287	R.E.Foster	E v A	Sydney	1903-04
287	K.C.Sangakkara	SL v SA	Colombo (SSC)	2006

285*	P.B.H.May	E v WI	Birmingham	1957
281	V.V.S.Laxman	I v A	Calcutta	2000-01
280*	Javed Miandad	P v I	Hyderabad	1982-83
278*	A.B.de Villiers	SA v P	Abu Dhabi	2010-11
278	D.C.S.Compton	E v P	Nottingham	1954
277	B.C.Lara	WI v A	Sydney	1992-93
277	G.C.Smith	SA v E	Birmingham	2003
275*	D.J.Cullinan	SA v NZ	Auckland	1998-99
275	G.Kirsten	SA v E	Durban	1999-00
275	D.P.M.D.Jayawardena	SL v I	Ahmedabad	2009-10
274*	S.P.Fleming	NZ v SL	Colombo (SSC)	2002-03
274	R.G.Pollock	SA v A	Durban	1969-70
274	Zaheer Abbas	P v E	Birmingham	1971
271	Javed Miandad	P v NZ	Auckland	1988-89
270*	G.A.Headley	WI v E	Kingston	1934-35
270	D.G.Bradman	A v E	Melbourne	1936-37
270	R.S.Dravid	I v P	Rawalpindi	2003-04
270	K.C.Sangakkara	SL v Z	Bulawayo	2004
269*	A.C.Voges	A v WI	Hobart	2015-16
268	G.N.Yallop	A v P	Melbourne	1983-84
267*	B.A.Young	NZ v SL	Dunedin	1996-97
267	P.A.de Silva	SL v NZ	Wellington	1990-91
267	Younus Khan	P v I	Bangalore	2004-05
266	W.H.Ponsford	A v E	The Oval	1934
266	D.L.Houghton	Z v SL	Bulawayo	1994-95
264*	T.W.M.Latham	NZ v SL	Wellington	2018-19
263	A.N.Cook	E v P	Abu Dhabi	2015-16
262*	D.L.Amiss	E v WI	Kingston	1973-74
262	S.P.Fleming	NZ v SA	Cape Town	2005-06
261*	R.R.Sarwan	WI v B	Kingston	2004
261	F.M.M.Worrell	WI v E	Nottingham	1950
260	C.C.Hunte	WI v P	Kingston	1957-58
260	Javed Miandad	P v E	The Oval	1987
260	M.N.Samuels	WI v B	Khulna	2012-13
259*	M.J.Clarke	A v SA	Brisbane	2012-13
259	G.M.Turner	NZ v WI	Georgetown	1971-72
259	G.C.Smith	SA v E	Lord's	2003
258	T.W.Graveney	E v WI	Nottingham	1957
258	S.M.Nurse	WI v NZ	Christchurch	1968-69
258	B.A.Stokes	E v SA	Cape Town	2015-16
257*	Wasim Akram	P v Z	Sheikhupura	1996-97
257	R.T.Ponting	A v I	Melbourne	2003-04
256	R.B.Kanhai	WI v I	Calcutta	1958-59
256	K.F.Barrington	E v A	Manchester	1964
255*	D.J.McGlew	SA v NZ	Wellington	1952-53
254*	V.Kohli	I v SA	Pune	2019-20
254	D.G.Bradman	A v E	Lord's	1930
254	V.Sehwag	I v P	Lahore	2005-06
254	J.E.Root	E v P	Manchester	2016
253*	H.M.Amla	SA v I	Nagpur	2009-10
253	S.T.Jayasuriya	SL v P	Faisalabad	2004-05
253	D.A.Warner	A v NZ	Perth	2015-16
251	W.R.Hammond	E v A	Sydney	1928-29
250	K.D.Walters	A v NZ	Christchurch	1976-77
250	S.F.A.F.Bacchus	WI v I	Kanpur	1978-79
250	J.L.Langer	A v E	Melbourne	2002-03

The highest for Bangladesh is 219* by Mushfiqur Rahim (v Z, Dhaka, 2018-19).

20 HUNDREDS

								Opponents					
		200	Inn	E	A	SA	WI	NZ	I	P	SL	Z	B
51	S.R.Tendulkar	I	6	329	7	11	7	3	4	–	2	9	3	5
45	J.H.Kallis	SA	2	280	8	5	–	8	6	7	6	1	3	1
41	R.T.Ponting	A	6	287	8	–	8	7	2	8	5	1	1	1
38	K.C.Sangakkara	SL	11	233	1	3	3	4	5	10	–	2		7
36	R.S.Dravid	I	5	286	7	2	2	5	6	–	5	3	3	3
34	Younus Khan	P	6	213	4	4	4	3	2	5	–	8	1	3
34	S.M.Gavaskar	I	4	214	4	8	–	13	2	–	5	2	–	
34	B.C.Lara	WI	9	232	7	9	4	–	1	2	4	5	1	1
34	D.P.M.D.Jayawardena	SL	7	252	8	2	6	1	3	6	2	–	1	5
33	A.N.Cook	E	5	291	–	5	2	6	3	7	5	3	–	2
32	S.R.Waugh	A	1	260	10	–	2	7	2	2	3	3	1	2
30	M.L.Hayden †	A	2	184	5	–	6	5	1	6	1	3	2	
30	S.Chanderpaul	WI	2	280	5	5	5	–	2	7	1	–	1	4
29	D.G.Bradman	A	12	80	19	–	4	2	–	4				
28	M.J.Clarke	A	4	198	7	–	5	1	4	7	1	3	–	
28	H.M.Amla	SA	4	215	6	5	–	1	4	5	2	2	–	3
27	V.Kohli	I	7	145	5	7	3	2	3	–	–	5	–	2
27	G.C.Smith	SA	5	205	7	3	–	7	2	–	4	–	1	3
27	A.R.Border	A	2	265	8	–	3	5	4	6	1	–		
26	S.P.D.Smith	A	3	131	11	–	1	2	2	7	2	1	–	
26	G.St A.Sobers	WI	2	160	10	4	–	1	8	3	–			
25	Inzamam-ul-Haq	P	2	200	5	1	4	3	3	1	6	–	5	2	2
24	G.S.Chappell	A	4	151	9	–	5	3	1	6	–			
24	D.A.Warner	A	2	155	3	–	4	1	5	4	5	–	2	
24	Mohammad Yousuf	P	4	156	6	1	–	7	1	4	–	1	2	2
24	I.V.A.Richards	WI	3	182	8	5	–	1	8	2	–			
23	V.Sehwag	I	6	180	3	5	2	2	–	4	5	–		
23	K.P.Pietersen	E	3	181	–	4	3	5	2	6	2	3	–	
23	J.L.Langer	A	3	182	5	–	2	3	4	3	4	2	–	
23	Javed Miandad	P	6	189	2	5	–	2	6	5	2	1	–	
22	W.R.Hammond	E	7	140	–	9	6	1	4	2	–			
22	M.Azharuddin	I	–	147	6	2	4	–	2	–	3	5	–	
22	M.C.Cowdrey	E	–	188	–	5	3	6	2	3	3	–		
22	A.B.de Villiers	SA	2	191	2	6	–	6	–	3	4	1	–	
22	G.Boycott	E	1	193	–	7	1	5	2	4	3	–		
22	I.R.Bell	E	1	205	–	4	2	2	1	4	4	3	–	
21	R.N.Harvey	A	2	137	6	–	8	3	–	4				
21	K.S.Williamson	NZ	2	140	3	2	3	2	–	2	3	1	3	
21	G.Kirsten	SA	3	176	5	2	–	3	2	3	2	1	1	2
21	A.J.Strauss	E	–	178	–	4	4	3	3	1	4	–		
21	D.C.Boon	A	2	190	7	–	5	2	3	6	1	1	–	
20	K.F.Barrington	E	1	131	–	5	2	3	3	6	1			
20	P.A.de Silva	SL	2	159	2	1	–	2	5	8	–	1	1	
20	M.E.Waugh	A	–	209	6	–	4	4	1	1	3	1		
20	G.A.Gooch	E	2	215	–	4	5	4	5	1	1	–		

† Includes century scored for Australia v ICC in 2005-06.

The most for Zimbabwe 12 by A.Flower (112), and for Bangladesh 9 by Mominul Haque (74) and Tamim Iqbal (115).

The most double hundreds by batsmen not included above are 6 by M.S.Atapattu (16 hundreds for Sri Lanka), 4 by L.Hutton (19 for England), 4 by C.G.Greenidge (19 for West Indies), 4 by Zaheer Abbas (12 for Pakistan), and 4 by B.B.McCullum (12 for New Zealand).

HIGHEST PARTNERSHIP FOR EACH WICKET

1st	415	N.D.McKenzie/G.C.Smith	SA v B	Chittagong	2007-08
2nd	576	S.T.Jayasuriya/R.S.Mahanama	SL v I	Colombo (RPS)	1997-98
3rd	624	K.C.Sangakkara/D.P.M.D.Jayawardena	SL v SA	Colombo (SSC)	2006
4th	449	A.C.Voges/S.E.Marsh	A v WI	Hobart	2015-16
5th	405	S.G.Barnes/D.G.Bradman	A v E	Sydney	1946-47
6th	399	B.A.Stokes/J.M.Bairstow	E v SA	Cape Town	2015-16
7th	347	D.St E.Atkinson/C.C.Depeiza	WI v A	Bridgetown	1954-55
8th	332	I.J.L.Trott/S.C.J.Broad	E v P	Lord's	2010
9th	195	M.V.Boucher/P.L.Symcox	SA v P	Johannesburg	1997-98
10th	198	J.E.Root/J.M.Anderson	E v I	Nottingham	2014

BOWLING RECORDS
200 WICKETS IN TESTS

Wkts			M	Balls	Runs	Avge	5 wI	10 wM
800	M.Muralitharan	SL/ICC	133	44039	18180	22.72	67	22
708	S.K.Warne	A	145	40705	17995	25.41	37	10
619	A.Kumble	I	132	40850	18355	29.65	35	8
584	J.M.Anderson	E	125	32779	15670	26.83	28	3
563	G.D.McGrath	A	124	29248	12186	21.64	29	3
519	C.A.Walsh	WI	132	30019	12688	24.44	22	3
485	S.C.J.Broad	E	138	28079	13827	28.50	17	2
439	D.W.Steyn	SA	93	18608	10077	22.95	26	5
434	Kapil Dev	I	131	27740	12867	29.64	23	2
433	H.M.R.K.B.Herath	SL	93	25993	12157	28.07	34	9
431	R.J.Hadlee	NZ	86	21918	9612	22.30	36	9
421	S.M.Pollock	SA	108	24453	9733	23.11	16	1
417	Harbhajan Singh	I	103	28580	13537	32.46	25	5
414	Wasim Akram	P	104	22627	9779	23.62	25	5
405	C.E.L.Ambrose	WI	98	22104	8500	23.62	25	3
390	M.Ntini	SA	101	20834	11242	20.98	22	4
390	N.M.Lyon	A	96	24568	12320	28.82	18	3
383	I.T.Botham	E	102	21815	10878	31.58	18	4
376	M.D.Marshall	WI	81	17584	7876	28.40	27	4
373	Waqar Younis	P	87	16224	8788	20.94	22	5
365	R.Ashwin	I	71	19586	9282	23.56	27	7
362	Imran Khan	P	88	19458	8258	25.43	23	6
362	D.L.Vettori	NZ/ICC	113	28814	12441	22.81	20	3
355	D.K.Lillee	A	70	18467	8493	34.36	23	7
355	W.P.J.U.C.Vaas	SL	111	23438	10501	23.92	12	2
330	A.A.Donald	SA	72	15519	7344	29.58	20	3
325	R.G.D.Willis	E	90	17357	8190	22.25	16	0
313	M.G.Johnson	A	73	16001	8891	25.20	12	3
311	Z.Khan	I	92	18785	10247	28.40	11	1
310	B.Lee	A	76	16531	9554	32.94	10	—
309	M.Morkel	SA	86	16498	8550	30.81	8	—
309	L.R.Gibbs	WI	79	27115	8989	27.66	18	2
307	F.S.Trueman	E	67	15178	6625	29.09	17	3
297	D.L.Underwood	E	86	21862	6625	21.57	17	6
297	I.Sharma	I	97	18150	7674	25.83	11	1
292	J.H.Kallis	SA/ICC	166	20232	9620	32.39	5	—
291	C.J.McDermott	A	71	16586	9535	32.65	14	2
284	T.G.Southee	NZ	73	16393	8332	28.63	10	1
267	T.A.Boult	NZ	67	14874	8237	29.00	8	1
266	B.S.Bedi	I	67	21364	7384	27.65	14	1
261	Danish Kaneria	P	61	17697	7637	28.71	15	2
259	J.Garner	WI	58	13169	9082	34.79	15	2
259	J.N.Gillespie	A	71	14234	5433	20.97	7	—
255	G.P.Swann	E	60	15349	6770	26.13	8	—
252	J.B.Statham	E	70	16056	7642	29.96	17	3
					6261	24.84	9	1

Wkts			M	Balls	Runs	Avge	5 wI	10 wM
249	M.A.Holding	WI	60	12680	5898	23.68	13	2
248	R.Benaud	A	63	19108	6704	27.03	16	1
248	M.J.Hoggard	E	67	13909	7564	30.50	7	1
246	G.D.McKenzie	A	60	17681	7328	29.78	16	3
244	M.A.Starc	A	57	11753	6583	26.97	13	2
242	B.S.Chandrasekhar	I	58	15963	7199	29.74	16	2
236	A.V.Bedser	E	51	15918	5876	24.89	15	5
236	J.Srinath	I	67	15104	7196	30.49	10	1
236	Abdul Qadir	P	67	17126	7742	32.80	15	5
235	G.St A.Sobers	WI	93	21599	7999	34.03	6	
234	A.R.Caddick	E	62	13558	6999	29.91	13	1
233	C.S.Martin	NZ	71	14026	7878	33.81	10	1
229	D.Gough	E	58	11821	6503	28.39	9	
228	R.R.Lindwall	A	61	13650	5251	23.03	12	
228	S.J.Harmison	E/ICC	63	13375	7192	31.82	8	1
226	A.Flintoff	E/ICC	79	14951	7410	32.78	3	
224	V.D.Philander	SA	64	11391	5000	22.32	13	2
221	P.M.Siddle	A	67	13907	6777	30.66	8	
218	C.L.Cairns	NZ	62	11698	6410	29.40	13	1
216	C.V.Grimmett	A	37	14513	5231	24.21	21	7
216	H.H.Streak	Z	65	13559	6079	28.14	7	
213	R.A.Jadeja	I	49	12912	5246	24.62	9	1
213	Yasir Shah	P	39	12211	6502	30.52	16	3
212	M.G.Hughes	A	53	12285	6017	28.38	7	1
210	Shakib Al Hasan	B	56	13020	6537	31.12	18	2
208	S.C.G.MacGill	A	44	11237	6038	29.02	12	2
208	Saqlain Mushtaq	P	49	14070	6206	29.83	13	3
206	N.Wagner	NZ	48	10743	5480	26.60	9	
202	A.M.E.Roberts	WI	47	11136	5174	25.61	11	2
202	J.A.Snow	E	49	12021	5387	26.66	8	1
200	J.R.Thomson	A	51	10535	5601	28.00	8	

35 OR MORE WICKETS IN A SERIES

Wkts		Series	M	Balls	Runs	Avge	5 wI	10 wM
49	S.F.Barnes	E v SA	1913-14	4	1356	536	10.93	7	3
46	J.C.Laker	E v A	1956	5	1703	442	9.60	4	2
44	C.V.Grimmett	A v SA	1935-36	5	2077	642	14.59	5	3
42	T.M.Alderman	A v E	1981	6	1950	893	21.26	4	
41	R.M.Hogg	A v E	1978-79	6	1740	527	12.85	5	2
41	T.M.Alderman	A v E	1989	6	1616	712	17.36	6	1
40	Imran Khan	P v I	1982-83	6	1339	558	13.95	4	2
40	S.K.Warne	A v E	2005	5	1517	797	19.92	3	2
39	A.V.Bedser	E v A	1953	5	1591	682	17.48	5	1
39	D.K.Lillee	A v E	1981	6	1870	870	22.30	2	1
38	M.W.Tate	A v E	1924-25	5	2528	881	23.18	5	1
37	W.J.Whitty	A v SA	1910-11	5	1395	632	17.08	2	
37	H.J.Tayfield	SA v E	1956-57	5	2280	636	17.18	4	1
37	M.G.Johnson	A v E	2013-14	5	1132	517	13.97	3	
36	A.E.E.Vogler	SA v E	1909-10	5	1349	783	21.75	4	1
36	A.A.Mailey	A v E	1920-21	5	1465	946	26.27	4	2
36	G.D.McGrath	A v E	1997	6	1499	701	19.47	2	
36	G.A.Lohmann	E v SA	1895-96	3	520	203	5.80	4	2
35	B.S.Chandrasekhar	I v E	1972-73	5	1747	662	18.91	4	
35	M.D.Marshall	WI v E	1988	5	1219	443	12.65	3	1

The most for New Zealand is 33 by R.J.Hadlee (3 Tests v A, 1985-86), for Sri Lanka 30 by M.Muralitharan (3 Tests v Z, 2001-02), for Zimbabwe 22 by H.H.Streak (3 Tests v P, 1994-95), and for Bangladesh 19 by Mehedi Hasan (2 Tests v E, 2016-17).

15 OR MORE WICKETS IN A TEST († *On debut*)

19- 90	J.C.Laker	E v A	Manchester	1956
17-159	S.F.Barnes	E v SA	Johannesburg	1913-14
16-136†	N.D.Hirwani	I v WI	Madras	1987-88
16-137†	R.A.L.Massie	A v E	Lord's	1972
16-220	M.Muralitharan	SL v E	The Oval	1998
15- 28	J.Briggs	E v SA	Cape Town	1888-89
15- 45	G.A.Lohmann	E v SA	Port Elizabeth	1895-96
15- 99	C.Blythe	E v SA	Leeds	1907
15-104	H.Verity	E v A	Lord's	1934
15-123	R.J.Hadlee	NZ v A	Brisbane	1985-86
15-124	W.Rhodes	E v A	Melbourne	1903-04
15-217	Harbhajan Singh	I v A	Madras	2000-01

The best analysis for South Africa is 13-132 by M.Ntini (v WI, Port-of-Spain, 2004-05), for West Indies 14-149 by M.A.Holding (v E, The Oval, 1976), for Pakistan 14-116 by Imran Khan (v SL, Lahore, 1981-82), for Zimbabwe 11-257 by A.G.Huckle (v NZ, Bulawayo, 1997-98), and for Bangladesh 12-117 by Mehedi Hasan (v WI, Dhaka, 2018-19).

NINE OR MORE WICKETS IN AN INNINGS

10- 53	J.C.Laker	E v A	Manchester	1956
10- 74	A.Kumble	I v P	Delhi	1998-99
9- 28	G.A.Lohmann	E v SA	Johannesburg	1895-96
9- 37	J.C.Laker	E v A	Manchester	1956
9- 51	M.Muralitharan	SL v Z	Kandy	2001-02
9- 52	R.J.Hadlee	NZ v A	Brisbane	1985-86
9- 56	Abdul Qadir	P v E	Lahore	1987-88
9- 57	D.E.Malcolm	E v SA	The Oval	1994
9- 65	M.Muralitharan	SL v E	The Oval	1998
9- 69	J.M.Patel	I v A	Kanpur	1959-60
9- 83	Kapil Dev	I v WI	Ahmedabad	1983-84
9- 86	Sarfraz Nawaz	P v A	Melbourne	1978-79
9- 95	J.M.Noreiga	WI v I	Port-of-Spain	1970-71
9-102	S.P.Gupte	I v WI	Kanpur	1958-59
9-103	S.F.Barnes	E v SA	Johannesburg	1913-14
9-113	H.J.Tayfield	SA v E	Johannesburg	1956-57
9-121	A.A.Mailey	A v E	Melbourne	1920-21
9-127	H.M.R.K.B.Herath	SL v P	Colombo (SSC)	2014
9-129	K.A.Maharaj	SA v SL	Colombo (SSC)	2018

The best analysis for Zimbabwe is 8-109 by P.A.Strang (v NZ, Bulawayo, 2000-01), and for Bangladesh 8-39 by Taijul Islam (v Z, Dhaka, 2014-15).

HAT-TRICKS

F.R.Spofforth	Australia v England	Melbourne	1878-79
W.Bates[7]	England v Australia	Melbourne	1882-83
J.Briggs[7]	England v Australia	Sydney	1891-92
G.A.Lohmann	England v South Africa	Port Elizabeth	1895-96
J.T.Hearne	England v Australia	Leeds	1899
H.Trumble	Australia v England	Melbourne	1901-02
H.Trumble	Australia v England	Melbourne	1903-04
T.J.Matthews (2)[2]	Australia v South Africa	Manchester	1912
M.J.C.Allom[1]	England v New Zealand	Christchurch	1929-30
T.W.J.Goddard	England v South Africa	Johannesburg	1938-39
P.J.Loader	England v West Indies	Leeds	1957
L.F.Kline	Australia v South Africa	Cape Town	1957-58
W.W.Hall	West Indies v Pakistan	Lahore	1958-59

G.M.Griffin[7]	South Africa v England	Lord's	1960
L.R.Gibbs	West Indies v Australia	Adelaide	1960-61
P.J.Petherick[1/7]	New Zealand v Pakistan	Lahore	1976-77
C.A.Walsh[3]	West Indies v Australia	Brisbane	1988-89
M.G.Hughes[3/7]	Australia v West Indies	Perth	1988-89
D.W.Fleming[1]	Australia v Pakistan	Rawalpindi	1994-95
S.K.Warne	Australia v England	Melbourne	1994-95
D.G.Cork	England v West Indies	Manchester	1995
D.Gough[7]	England v Australia	Sydney	1998-99
Wasim Akram[4]	Pakistan v Sri Lanka	Lahore	1998-99
Wasim Akram[4]	Pakistan v Sri Lanka	Dhaka	1998-99
D.N.T.Zoysa[5]	Sri Lanka v Zimbabwe	Harare	1999-00
Abdul Razzaq	Pakistan v Sri Lanka	Galle	2000-01
G.D.McGrath	Australia v West Indies	Perth	2000-01
Harbhajan Singh	India v Australia	Calcutta	2000-01
Mohammad Sami	Pakistan v Sri Lanka	Lahore	2001-02
J.J.C.Lawson[7]	West Indies v Australia	Bridgetown	2002-03
Alok Kapali[7]	Bangladesh v Pakistan	Peshawar	2003
A.M.Blignaut	Zimbabwe v Bangladesh	Harare	2003-04
M.J.Hoggard	England v West Indies	Bridgetown	2003-04
J.E.C.Franklin	New Zealand v Bangladesh	Dhaka	2004-05
I.K.Pathan[6/7]	India v Pakistan	Karachi	2005-06
R.J.Sidebottom[7]	England v New Zealand	Hamilton	2007-08
P.M.Siddle	Australia v England	Brisbane	2010-11
S.C.J.Broad	England v India	Nottingham	2011
Sohag Gazi	Bangladesh v New Zealand	Chittagong	2013-14
S.C.J.Broad[7]	England v Sri Lanka	Leeds	2014
H.M.R.K.B.Herath	Sri Lanka v Australia	Galle	2016
M.M.Ali	England v South Africa	The Oval	2017
J.J.Bumrah	India v West Indies	Kingston	2019
Naseem Shah	Pakistan v Bangladesh	Rawalpindi	2019-20

[1] On debut. [2] Hat-trick in each innings. [3] Involving both innings. [4] In successive Tests.
[5] His first 3 balls (second over of the match). [6] The fourth, fifth and sixth balls of the match.
[7] On losing side.

WICKET-KEEPING RECORDS
150 DISMISSALS IN TESTS†

Total			Tests	Ct	St
555	M.V.Boucher	South Africa/ICC	147	532	23
416	A.C.Gilchrist	Australia	96	379	37
395	I.A.Healy	Australia	119	366	29
355	R.W.Marsh	Australia	96	343	12
294	M.S.Dhoni	India	90	256	38
270	B.J.Haddin	Australia	66	262	8
270†	P.J.L.Dujon	West Indies	81	265	5
269	A.P.E.Knott	England	95	250	19
256	M.J.Prior	England	79	243	13
241†	A.J.Stewart	England	133	227	14
239	B.J.Watling	New Zealand	70	231	8
228	Wasim Bari	Pakistan	81	201	27
219	R.D.Jacobs	West Indies	65	207	12
219	T.G.Evans	England	91	173	46
217	D.Ramdin	West Indies	74	205	12
206	Kamran Akmal	Pakistan	53	184	22
202	Q.de Kock	South Africa	47	191	11
201†	A.C.Parore	New Zealand	78	194	7

Total			Tests	Ct	St
198	S.M.H.Kirmani	India	88	160	38
189	D.L.Murray	West Indies	62	181	8
187	A.T.W.Grout	Australia	51	163	24
186†	J.M.Bairstow	England	70	173	13
179†	B.B.McCullum	New Zealand	101	168	11
176	I.D.S.Smith	New Zealand	63	168	8
174	R.W.Taylor	England	57	167	7
167	Sarfraz Ahmed	Pakistan	49	146	21
165	R.C.Russell	England	54	153	12
156	H.A.P.W.Jayawardena	Sri Lanka	58	124	32
152	D.J.Richardson	South Africa	42	150	2
151†	K.C.Sangakkara	Sri Lanka	134	131	20
151†	A.Flower	Zimbabwe	63	142	9

The most for Bangladesh is 113 (98 ct, 15 st) by Mushfiqur Rahim in 70 Tests.
† *Excluding catches taken in the field.*

25 OR MORE DISMISSALS IN A SERIES

29	B.J.Haddin	Australia v England		2013
28	R.W.Marsh	Australia v England		1982-83
27 (inc 2st)	R.C.Russell	England v South Africa		1995-96
27 (inc 2st)	I.A.Healy	Australia v England (6 Tests)		1997
26 (inc 3st)	J.H.B.Waite	South Africa v New Zealand		1961-62
26	R.W.Marsh	Australia v West Indies (6 Tests)		1975-76
26 (inc 5st)	I.A.Healy	Australia v England (6 Tests)		1993
26 (inc 1st)	M.V.Boucher	South Africa v England		1998
26 (inc 2st)	A.C.Gilchrist	Australia v England		2001
26 (inc 2st)	A.C.Gilchrist	Australia v England		2006-07
26 (inc 1st)	T.D.Paine	Australia v England		2017-18
25 (inc 2st)	I.A.Healy	Australia v England		1994-95
25 (inc 2st)	A.C.Gilchrist	Australia v England		2002-03
25	A.C.Gilchrist	Australia v India		2007-08

TEN OR MORE DISMISSALS IN A TEST

11	R.C.Russell	England v South Africa	Johannesburg	1995-96
11	A.B.de Villiers	South Africa v Pakistan	Johannesburg	2012-13
11	R.R.Pant	India v Australia	Adelaide	2018-19
10	R.W.Taylor	England v India	Bombay	1979-80
10	A.C.Gilchrist	Australia v New Zealand	Hamilton	1999-00
10	W.P.Saha	India v South Africa	Cape Town	2017-18
10	Sarfraz Ahmed	Pakistan v South Africa	Johannesburg	2018-19

SEVEN DISMISSALS IN AN INNINGS

7	Wasim Bari	Pakistan v New Zealand	Auckland	1978-79
7	R.W.Taylor	England v India	Bombay	1979-80
7	I.D.S.Smith	New Zealand v Sri Lanka	Hamilton	1990-91
7	R.D.Jacobs	West Indies v Australia	Melbourne	2000-01

FIVE STUMPINGS IN AN INNINGS

5	K.S.More	India v West Indies	Madras	1987-88

FIELDING RECORDS
100 CATCHES IN TESTS

Total			Tests		Total			Tests
210	R.S.Dravid	India/ICC	164		121†	A.B.de Villiers	South Africa	114
205	D.P.M.D.Jayawardena	Sri Lanka	149		121	A.J.Strauss	England	100
200	J.H.Kallis	South Africa/ICC	166		120	I.T.Botham	England	102
196	R.T.Ponting	Australia	168		120	M.C.Cowdrey	England	114
181	M.E.Waugh	Australia	128		117	S.P.D.Smith	Australia	73
175	A.N.Cook	England	161		115	C.L.Hooper	West Indies	102
171	S.P.Fleming	New Zealand	111		115	S.R.Tendulkar	India	200
169	G.C.Smith	South Africa/ICC	117		114	J.E.Root	England	92
164	B.C.Lara	West Indies/ICC	131		112	S.R.Waugh	Australia	168
157	M.A.Taylor	Australia	104		110	R.B.Simpson	Australia	62
156	A.R.Border	Australia	156		110	W.R.Hammond	England	85
147	L.R.P.L.Taylor	New Zealand	101		109	G.St A.Sobers	West Indies	93
139	Younus Khan	Pakistan	118		108	H.M.Amla	South Africa	124
135	V.V.S.Laxman	India	134		108	S.M.Gavaskar	India	125
134	M.J.Clarke	Australia	115		105	I.M.Chappell	Australia	75
128	M.L.Hayden	Australia	103		105	M.Azharuddin	India	99
125	S.K.Warne	Australia	145		105	G.P.Thorpe	England	100
122	G.S.Chappell	Australia	87		103	G.A.Gooch	England	118
122	I.V.A.Richards	West Indies	121		102	I.R.Bell	England	118

The most for Zimbabwe is 60 by A.D.R.Campbell (60) and for Bangladesh 38 by Mahmudullah (49). † *Excluding catches taken when wicket-keeping.*

15 CATCHES IN A SERIES

15	J.M.Gregory	Australia v England		1920-21

SEVEN OR MORE CATCHES IN A TEST

8	A.M.Rahane	India v Sri Lanka	Galle	2015
7	G.S.Chappell	Australia v England	Perth	1974-75
7	Yajurvindra Singh	India v England	Bangalore	1976-77
7	H.P.Tillekeratne	Sri Lanka v New Zealand	Colombo (SSC)	1992-93
7	S.P.Fleming	New Zealand v Zimbabwe	Harare	1997-98
7	M.L.Hayden	Australia v Sri Lanka	Galle	2003-04
7	K.L.Rahul	India v England	Nottingham	2018

FIVE CATCHES IN AN INNINGS

5	V.Y.Richardson	Australia v South Africa	Durban	1935-36
5	Yajurvindra Singh	India v England	Bangalore	1976-77
5	M.Azharuddin	India v Pakistan	Karachi	1989-90
5	K.Srikkanth	India v Australia	Perth	1991-92
5	S.P.Fleming	New Zealand v Zimbabwe	Harare	1997-98
5	G.C.Smith	South Africa v Australia	Perth	2012-13
5	D.J.G.Sammy	West Indies v India	Mumbai	2013-14
5	D.M.Bravo	West Indies v Bangladesh	Kingstown	2014
5	A.M.Rahane	India v Sri Lanka	Galle	2015
5	J.Blackwood	West Indies v Sri Lanka	Colombo (PSS)	2015-16
5	S.P.D.Smith	Australia v South Africa	Cape Town	2017-18
5	B.A.Stokes	England v South Africa	Cape Town	2019-20

APPEARANCE RECORDS
100 TEST MATCH APPEARANCES

			Opponents											
			E	A	SA	WI	NZ	I	P	SL	Z	B	Ire	Afg
200	S.R.Tendulkar	India	32	39	25	21	24	–	18	25	9	7	–	–
168†	R.T.Ponting	Australia	35	–	26	24	17	29	15	14	3	4	–	–
168	S.R.Waugh	Australia	46	–	16	32	23	18	20	8	3	2	–	–

	Player	Team	E	A	SA	WI	NZ	I	P	SL	Z	B	Ire	Afg
166†	J.H.Kallis	South Africa/ICC	31	28	–	24	18	18	19	15	6	6	–	–
164	S.Chanderpaul	West Indies	35	20	24	–	21	25	14	7	8	10	–	–
164†	R.S.Dravid	India/ICC	21	32	21	23	15	–	15	20	9	7	–	–
161	A.N.Cook	England	–	35	19	20	15	30	20	16	–	6	–	–
156	A.R.Border	Australia	47	–	6	31	23	20	22	7	–	–		
151	J.M.Anderson	England	–	32	26	20	14	27	15	13	2	2	–	–
149	D.P.M.D.Jayawardena	Sri Lanka	23	16	18	11	13	18	29	–	8	13	–	–
147†	M.V.Boucher	South Africa/ICC	25	20	–	24	17	14	15	17	6	8	–	–
145†	S.K.Warne	Australia	36	–	24	19	20	14	15	13	1	2	–	–
138	S.C.J.Broad	England	–	32	22	17	16	20	16	11	–	3	1	–
134	V.V.S.Laxman	India	17	29	19	22	10	–	15	13	6	3	–	–
134	K.C.Sangakkara	Sri Lanka	22	11	17	12	12	17	23	–	5	15	–	–
133†	M.Muralitharan	Sri Lanka/ICC	16	12	15	12	14	22	16	–	14	11	–	–
133	A.J.Stewart	England	–	33	23	24	16	9	13	9	6	–	–	
132	A.Kumble	India	19	20	21	17	11	–	15	18	7	4	–	–
132	C.A.Walsh	West Indies	36	38	10	–	10	15	18	3	2	–	–	
131	Kapil Dev	India	27	20	4	25	10	–	29	14	2	–	–	
131†	B.C.Lara	West Indies/ICC	30	30	18	–	11	17	12	8	2	2	–	–
128	M.E.Waugh	Australia	29	–	18	28	14	14	15	9	1	–	–	
125	S.M.Gavaskar	India	38	20	–	27	9	–	24	7	–	–		
124	H.M.Amla	South Africa	21	21	–	9	14	21	14	14	2	8	–	–
124	Javed Miandad	Pakistan	22	24	–	17	18	28	–	12	3	–	–	
124†	G.D.McGrath	Australia	30	–	17	23	14	11	17	8	1	2	–	–
121	I.V.A.Richards	West Indies	36	34	–	–	7	28	16	–	–	–		
120†	Inzamam-ul-Haq	Pakistan/ICC	19	13	13	15	12	10	–	20	11	6	–	–
119	I.A.Healy	Australia	33	–	12	28	11	9	14	11	1	–	–	
118	I.R.Bell	England	–	33	11	12	13	20	13	10	–	6	–	–
118	G.A.Gooch	England	–	42	3	26	15	19	10	3	–	–		
118	Younus Khan	Pakistan	17	11	14	15	11	9	–	29	5	7	–	–
117	D.I.Gower	England	–	42	–	19	13	24	17	2	–	–		
117†	G.C.Smith	South Africa/ICC	21	21	–	14	13	15	16	7	2	8	–	–
116	D.L.Haynes	West Indies	36	33	1	–	10	19	16	1	–	–		
116	D.B.Vengsarkar	India	26	24	–	25	11	–	22	8	–	–		
115	M.A.Atherton	England	–	33	18	27	11	7	11	4	4	–	–	
115†	M.J.Clarke	Australia	35	–	14	12	11	22	10	8	–	2	–	–
114	M.C.Cowdrey	England	–	43	14	21	18	8	10	–	–			
114	A.B.de Villiers	South Africa	20	24	–	13	10	20	12	7	4	4	–	–
113	S.C.Ganguly	India	12	24	17	12	8	–	12	14	9	5	–	–
113†	D.L.Vettori	New Zealand/ICC	17	18	14	10	–	15	9	11	9	9	–	–
111	S.P.Fleming	New Zealand	19	14	15	11	–	13	9	13	11	6	–	–
111	W.P.J.U.C.Vaas	Sri Lanka	15	12	11	9	10	14	18	–	15	7	–	–
110	S.T.Jayasuriya	Sri Lanka	14	13	15	10	13	10	17	–	13	5	–	–
110	C.H.Lloyd	West Indies	34	29	–	–	8	28	11	–	–			
108	G.Boycott	England	–	38	7	29	15	13	6	–	–			
108	C.G.Greenidge	West Indies	29	32	–	–	10	23	14	–	–			
108	S.M.Pollock	South Africa	23	13	–	16	11	12	12	13	5	3	–	–
107	D.C.Boon	Australia	31	–	6	22	17	11	11	9	–	–		
105†	J.L.Langer	Australia	21	–	11	18	14	14	13	8	3	2	–	–
104	K.P.Pietersen	England	–	27	10	14	8	16	14	11	–	4	–	–
104†	V.Sehwag	India/ICC	17	23	15	10	12	–	9	11	3	4	–	–
104	M.A.Taylor	Australia	33	–	11	20	11	9	12	8	–	–		
104	Wasim Akram	Pakistan	18	13	4	17	9	12	–	19	10	2	–	–
103	C.H.Gayle	West Indies	20	8	16	–	12	14	8	10	8	7	–	–
103	Harbhajan Singh	India	14	18	11	11	13	–	9	16	7	4	–	–
103†	M.L.Hayden	Australia	20	–	19	15	11	18	6	7	2	4	–	–
103	Salim Malik	Pakistan	19	15	1	7	18	22	–	15	6	–	–	

		Opponents												
			E	A	SA	WI	NZ	I	P	SL	Z	B	Ire	Afg
102	I.T.Botham	England	–	36	–	20	15	14	14	3	–	–	–	–
102	C.L.Hooper	West Indies	24	25	10	–	2	19	14	6	2	–	–	–
101	G.Kirsten	South Africa	22	18	–	13	13	10	11	9	3	2	–	–
101	B.B.McCullum	New Zealand	16	16	13	13	–	10	8	12	4	9	–	–
101	M.Ntini	South Africa	18	15	–	15	11	10	9	12	3	8	–	–
101	L.R.P.L.Taylor	New Zealand	17	12	8	12	–	14	13	12	4	9	–	–
100	A.J.Strauss	England	–	20	16	18	9	12	13	8	–	4	–	–
100	G.P.Thorpe	England	–	16	16	27	13	5	8	9	2	4	–	–

† Includes appearance in the Australia v ICC 'Test' in 2005-06. The most for Zimbabwe is 67 by G.W.Flower, and for Bangladesh 70 by Mushfiqur Rahim.

100 CONSECUTIVE TEST APPEARANCES

159	A.N.Cook	England	May 2006 to September 2018
153	A.R.Border	Australia	March 1979 to March 1994
107	M.E.Waugh	Australia	June 1993 to October 2002
106	S.M.Gavaskar	India	January 1975 to February 1987
101	B.B.McCullum	New Zealand	March 2004 to February 2016

50 TESTS AS CAPTAIN

			Won	Lost	Drawn	Tied
109	G.C.Smith	South Africa	53	29	27	–
93	A.R.Border	Australia	32	22	38	1
80	S.P.Fleming	New Zealand	28	27	25	–
77	R.T.Ponting	Australia	48	16	13	–
74	C.H.Lloyd	West Indies	36	12	26	–
60	M.S.Dhoni	India	27	18	15	–
59	A.N.Cook	England	24	22	13	–
57	S.R.Waugh	Australia	41	9	7	–
56	Misbah-ul-Haq	Pakistan	26	19	11	–
56	A.Ranatunga	Sri Lanka	12	19	25	–
55	V.Kohli	India	33	12	10	–
54	M.A.Atherton	England	13	21	20	–
53	W.J.Cronje	South Africa	27	11	15	–
51	M.P.Vaughan	England	26	11	14	–
50	I.V.A.Richards	West Indies	27	8	15	–
50	M.A.Taylor	Australia	26	13	11	–
50	A.J.Strauss	England	24	11	15	–

The most for Zimbabwe is 21 by A.D.R.Campbell and H.H.Streak, and for Bangladesh 34 by Mushfiqur Rahim.

65 TEST UMPIRING APPEARANCES

132	Alim Dar	(Pakistan)	21.10.2003 to 24.02.2020
128	S.A.Bucknor	(West Indies)	28.04.1989 to 22.03.2009
108	R.E.Koertzen	(South Africa)	26.12.1992 to 24.07.2010
95	D.J.Harper	(Australia)	28.11.1998 to 23.06.2011
92	D.R.Shepherd	(England)	01.08.1985 to 07.06.2005
84	B.F.Bowden	(New Zealand)	11.03.2000 to 03.05.2015
78	D.B.Hair	(Australia)	25.01.1992 to 08.06.2008
74	I.J.Gould	(England)	19.11.2008 to 23.02.2019
74	S.J.A.Taufel	(Australia)	26.12.2000 to 20.08.2012
73	S.Venkataraghavan	(India)	29.01.1993 to 20.01.2004
71	R.J.Tucker	(Australia)	15.02.2010 to 27.01.2020
66	H.D.Bird	(England)	05.07.1973 to 24.06.1996
65	H.D.P.K.Dharmasena	(Sri Lanka)	04.11.2010 to 07.01.2020

THE FIRST-CLASS COUNTIES REGISTER, RECORDS AND 2019 AVERAGES

All statistics are to 11 March 2020.

ABBREVIATIONS – General

*	not out/unbroken partnership	IT20	International Twenty20
b	born	l-o	limited-overs
BB	Best innings bowling analysis	LOI	Limited-Overs Internationals
Cap	Awarded 1st XI County Cap	Tests	International Test Matches
f-c	first-class	F-c Tours	Overseas tours involving first-class
HS	Highest Score		appearances

Awards

PCA 2019   Professional Cricketers' Association Player of 2019
Wisden 2018   One of *Wisden Cricketers' Almanack's* Five Cricketers of 2018
YC 2019   Cricket Writers' Club Young Cricketer of 2019

ECB Competitions

CB40	Clydesdale Bank 40 (2010-12)	EP	Eastern Province
CC	County Championship	GL	Gujarat Lions
CGT	Cheltenham & Gloucester Trophy (2001-06)	GW	Griqualand West
		HB	Habib Bank Limited
FPT	Friends Provident Trophy (2007-09)	HH	Hobart Hurricanes
NL	National League (1999-2005)	KD	Karachi Dolphins
P40	NatWest PRO 40 League (2006-09)	KP	Khyber Pakhtunkhwa
RLC	Royal London One-Day Cup (2014-18)	KKR	Kolkata Knight Riders
		KRL	Khan Research Laboratories
T20	Twenty20 Competition	KXIP	Kings XI Punjab
Y40	Yorkshire Bank 40 (2013)	KZN	KwaZulu-Natal Inland
		ME	Mashonaland Eagles

Education

Ac	Academy	MI	Mumbai Indians
BHS	Boys' High School	MR	Melbourne Renegades
C	College	MS	Melbourne Stars
CS	Comprehensive School	MSC	Mohammedan Sporting Club
GS	Grammar School	MT	Matabeleland Tuskers
HS	High School	MWR	Mid West Rhinos
I	Institute	NBP	National Bank of Pakistan
S	School	ND	Northern Districts
SFC	Sixth Form College	NSW	New South Wales
SS	Secondary School	NT	Northern Transvaal
TC	Technical College	NW	North West
U	University	(O)FS	(Orange) Free State

Playing Categories

LBG	Bowls right-arm leg-breaks and googlies	PIA	Pakistan International Airlines
		PDSC	Prime Doleshwar Sporting Club
LF	Bowls left-arm fast	PS	Perth Scorchers
LFM	Bowls left-arm fast-medium	PW	Pune Warriors
LHB	Bats left-handed	Q	Queensland
LM	Bowls left-arm medium pace	RCB	Royal Challengers Bangalore
LMF	Bowls left-arm medium fast	RPS	Rising Pune Supergiant
OB	Bowls right-arm off-breaks	RR	Rajasthan Royals
RF	Bowls right-arm fast	RS	Rising Stars
RFM	Bowls right-arm fast-medium	SA	South Australia
RHB	Bats right-handed	SGR	Speen Ghar Region
RM	Bowls right-arm medium pace	SH	Sunrisers Hyderabad
RMF	Bowls right-arm medium-fast	SJD	Sheikh Jamal Dhanmondi
SLA	Bowls left-arm leg-breaks	SNGPL	Sui Northern Gas Pipelines Limited
SLC	Bowls left-arm 'Chinamen'	SR	Southern Rocks
WK	Wicket-keeper	SS	Sydney Sixers
		SGC	Sui Southern Gas Corporation

Teams (see also p 226)

AS	Adelaide Strikers	ST	Sydney Thunder
BH	Brisbane Heat	Tas	Tasmania
BMT	Bulawayo Metropolitan Tuskers	T&T	Trinidad & Tobago
CC&C	Combined Campuses & Colleges	TU	Tamil Union
CD	Central Districts	UB	United Bank Limited
CSK	Chennai Super Kings	Vic	Victoria
DC	Deccan Chargers	WA	Western Australia
DCa	Delhi Capitals	WAPDA	Water & Power Development Authority
DD	Delhi Daredevils	WP	Western Province
EL	England Lions	ZT	Zarai Taraqiati Bank Limited

DERBYSHIRE

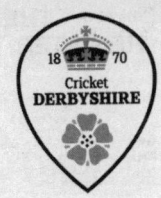

Formation of Present Club: 4 November 1870
Inaugural First-Class Match: 1871
Colours: Chocolate, Amber and Pale Blue
Badge: Rose and Crown
County Champions: (1) 1936
NatWest Trophy Winners: (1) 1981
Benson and Hedges Cup Winners: (1) 1993
Sunday League Winners: (1) 1990
Twenty20 Cup Winners: (0) best – Semi-Finalist 2019

Chief Executive: Ryan Duckett, Derbyshire County Cricket Club, The Pattonair County Ground, Nottingham Road, Derby, DE21 6DA • Tel: 01332 388101 • Email: info@derbyshireccc.com • Web: www. derbyshireccc.com • Twitter: @DerbyshireCCC (61,984 followers)

Head of Cricket: David Houghton. **Assistant Coaches:** Steve Kirby (bowling) and Mal Loye (batting). **T20 Head Coach:** Dominic Cork. **Captain:** B.A.Godleman. **Overseas Players:** S.A.Abbott and B.R.McDermott (white ball only). **2020 Testimonial:** None. **Head Groundsman:** Neil Godrich. **Scorer:** John Brown. **Blast Team Name:** Derbyshire Falcons. ‡ New registration. ᴺᑫ Not qualified for England.

‡**ᴺᑫABBOTT, Sean** Anthony, b Windsor, NSW, Australia 29 Feb 1992. RHB, RMF. Squad No 23. New South Wales 2011-12 to date. IPL: RCB 2015. Big Bash: ST 2011-12 to 2012-13. SS 2013-14 to date. **LOI** (A): 1 (2014-15); HS 3 and BB 1-25 v P (Sharjah) 2014-15. **IT20** (A): 4 (2014-15 to 2019-20); HS 5 v SA (Sydney) 2014-15; BB 2-14 v P (Perth) 2019-20. F-c Tour (Aus A): I 2015. HS 86 NSW v Q (Sydney) 2019-20. BB 7-45 NSW v Tas (Hobart) 2018-19. LO HS 50 NSW v SA (Sydney, DO) 2013-14. LO BB 5-43 NSW v Tas (Sydney, NS) 2018-19. T20 HS 39. T20 BB 5-16.

‡**ᴺᑫCOHEN, Michael** Alexander Robert (Reddam House C), b Cape Town, South Africa 4 Aug 1998. LHB, LFM. Squad No 8. Western Province 2017-18 to 2018-19. Cape Cobras 2017-18. EU qualified. Nottinghamshire 2nd XI 2019. HS 23* WP v Northern Cape (Kimberley) 2017-18. BB 5-40 WP v SW Districts (Rondebosch) 2017-18. LO HS 16 WP v Northerns (Rondebosch) 2017-18. LO BB 1-17 WP v SW Districts (Rondebosch) 2017-18. T20 HS 1*. T20 BB 2-17.

CONNERS, Samuel (George Spencer Ac), b Nottingham 13 Feb 1999. 6'0". RHB, RM. Squad No 59. Debut (Derbyshire) 2019. Derbyshire 2nd XI debut 2016. England U19 2018. HS 14 and CC BB 1-36 v Lancs (Derby) 2019. BB 2-13 v Leeds/Brad MCCU (Derby) 2019. LO HS 4 and LO BB 1-45 v Durham (Chester-le-St) 2019 (RLC).

CRITCHLEY, Matthew James John (St Michael's HS, Chorley), b Preston, Lancs 13 Aug 1996. 6'2". RHB, LB. Squad No 20. Debut (Derbyshire) 2015; cap 2019. Derbyshire 2nd XI debut 2014. HS 137* v Northants (Derby) 2015. BB 6-106 (10-194 match) v Northants (Chesterfield) 2018. LO HS 64* v Northants (Derby) 2019 (RLC). LO BB 4-48 v Northants (Derby) 2015 (RLC). T20 HS 72*. T20 BB 4-36.

DAL, Anuj Kailash (Durban HS; Nottingham HS), b Newcastle-upon-Tyne, Northumb 8 Jul 1996. 5'9". RHB, RM. Squad No 65. Debut (Derbyshire) 2018. Nottinghamshire 2nd XI 2013-17. HS 92 v Middx (Derby) 2019. BB 3-11 v Sussex (Derby) 2019. LO HS 52 v Lancs (Manchester) 2019 (RLC). T20 HS 35.

NQDu PLOOY, Jacobus Leus, b Pretoria, South Africa 12 Jan 1995. LHB, SLA. Squad No 76. Free State 2014-15 to 2017-18. Knights 2015-16. Northerns 2018-19. Titans 2018-19. Derbyshire debut 2013 (Kolpak signing). HS 181 FS v Namibia (Windhoek) 2015-16. De HS 118 v Middx (Derby) 2019. BB 3-76 Northerns v WP (Pretoria, TU) 2018-19. De BB 2-24 v Glamorgan (Swansea) 2019. LO HS 155 Northerns v WP (Pretoria, TU) 2018-19. LO BB 3-19 Northerns v KZN (Pretoria, TU) 2018-19. T20 HS 70. T20 BB 4-15.

GODLEMAN, Billy Ashley (Islington Green S), b Islington, London 11 Feb 1989. 6'3". LHB, LB. Squad No 1. Middlesex 2005-09. Essex 2010-12. Derbyshire debut 2013; cap 2015; captain 2016 to date. F-c Tour (MCC): Nepal 2019-20. 1000 runs (2); most – 1087 (2019). HS 227 v Glamorgan (Swansea) 2016. BB – . LO HS 137 v Warwks (Birmingham) 2018 (RLC). T20 HS 92.

HOSEIN, Harvey Richard (Denstone C), b Chesterfield 12 Aug 1996. 5'10". RHB, WK. Squad No 16. Debut (Derbyshire) 2014, taking seven catches in an innings and UK record-equalling 11 in match v Surrey (Oval). Derbyshire 2nd XI debut 2010, aged 13y 287d. HS 138* v Leeds/Brad MCCU (Derby) 2019. CC HS 108 v Worcs (Worcester) 2016. LO HS 41* v Lancs (Manchester) 2019 (RLC). T20 HS 0*.

HUDSON-PRENTICE, Fynn Jake (Warden Park S, Cuckfield; Bede's S, Upper Dicker), b Haywards Heath, Sussex 12 Jan 1996. RHB, RMF. Squad No 33. Sussex 2015-16. Sussex 2nd XI 2012-16. MCC YC 2017-19. HS 99 v Middx (Derby) 2019. BB 3-27 v Worcs (Kidderminster) 2019. LO HS 48 Sx v Kent (Hove) 2016 (RLC). LO BB – . T20 HS 31*. T20 BB 2-2.

HUGHES, Alex Lloyd (Ounsdale HS, Wolverhampton), b Wordsley, Staffs 29 Sep 1991. 5'10". RHB, RM. Squad No 18. Debut (Derbyshire) 2013; cap 2017. HS 142 v Glos (Bristol) 2017. BB 4-46 v Glamorgan (Derby) 2014. LO HS 96* v Leics (Leicester) 2016 (RLC). LO BB 4-44 v Northants (Derby) 2019 (RLC). T20 HS 43*. T20 BB 4-42.

‡NQMcDERMOTT, Benjamin Reginald, b Caboolture, Queensland, Australia 12 Dec 1994. Son of C.J.McDermott (Queensland and Australia 1983-84 to 1995-96); younger brother of A.C.McDermott (Queensland 2009-10 to 2014-15). RHB, WK, occ RM. Squad No 47. Queensland 2014-15. Tasmania 2015-16 to date. Big Bash: BH 2013-14. MR 2015-16. HH 2016-17 to date. Joins Derbyshire for white-ball season. **IT20** (A): 12 (2018-19 to 2019-20); HS 32* v I (Melbourne) 2018-19. HS 104 Tas v SA (Hobart) 2016-17. BB – . LO HS 117 Tas v Q (Townsville) 2018-19. T20 HS 114.

McKIERNAN, Matthew Harry (**'Mattie'**) (Lowton HS; St John Rigby C, Wigan), b Billinge, Lancs 14 Jun 1994. 6'0". RHB, LB. Squad No 21. Debut (Derbyshire) 2019. Cumberland 2016-17. HS 7 v Sussex (Derby) 2019. T20 HS 1*. T20 BB – .

MADSEN, Wayne Lee (Kearsney C, Durban; U of South Africa), b Durban, South Africa 2 Jan 1984. Nephew of M.B.Madsen (Natal 1967-68 to 1978-79), T.R.Madsen (Natal 1976-77 to 1989-90) and H.R.Fotheringham (Natal, Transvaal 1971-72 to 1989-90), cousin of G.S.Fotheringham (KwaZulu-Natal 2008-09 to 2009-10). 5'11". RHB, OB. Squad No 77. KwaZulu-Natal 2003-04 to 2007-08. Dolphins 2006-07 to 2007-08. Derbyshire debut 2009, scoring 170 v Glos (Cheltenham); cap 2011; captain 2012-15; testimonial 2017. Qualified for England by residence in February 2015. 1000 runs (5); most – 1292 (2016). HS 231* v Northants (Northampton) 2012. BB 3-45 KZN v EP (Pt Elizabeth) 2007-08. De BB 2-9 v Sussex (Hove) 2013. LO HS 138 v Hants (Derby) 2014 (RLC). LO BB 3-27 v Durham (Derby) 2013 (Y40). T20 HS 86*. T20 BB 2-20.

MELTON, Dustin Renton (Pretoria Boys HS; U of Pretoria), b Harare, Zimbabwe 11 Apr 1995. RHB, RFM. Squad No 30. Debut (Derbyshire) 2019. Leicestershire 2nd XI 2016. Essex 2nd XI 2017. HS 1* and BB 1-24 v Sussex (Derby) 2019.

PALLADINO, Antonio Paul (Cardinal Pole SS; Anglia Polytechnic U), b Tower Hamlets, London 29 Jun 1983. 6'0". RHB, RMF. Squad No 28. Cambridge UCCE 2003-05. Essex 2003-10. Namibia 2009-10. Derbyshire debut 2011; cap 2012; testimonial 2018. HS 106 v Australia A (Derby) 2012. CC HS 68 v Warwks (Birmingham) 2013. 50 wkts (3); most – 56 (2012). BB 7-53 v Kent (Derby) 2012. Hat-trick v Leics (Leicester) 2012. LO HS 31 Namibia v Boland (Windhoek) 2009-10. LO BB 5-49 v Lancs (Derby) 2014 (RLC). T20 HS 14*. T20 BB 4-21.

PRIESTLEY, Nils Oscar (Blessed Robert Sutton S; Abbotsholme SFC), b Sutton Coldfield, Warwks 18 Sep 2000. LHB, RM. Squad No 53. Derbyshire 2nd XI debut 2017. Awaiting 1st XI debut.

^NO^**RAMPAUL, Ravi**, b Preysal, Trinidad 15 Oct 1984. 6'1". LHB, RFM. Squad No 14. Trinidad & Tobago 2001-02 to date. Surrey 2016-17. Derbyshire debut 2018; cap 2019. IPL: RCB 2013-14. **Tests** (WI): 18 (2009-10 to 2012-13); HS 40* v A (Adelaide) 2009-10; BB 4-48 v P (Providence) 2011. **LOI** (WI): 92 (2003-04 to 2015-16); HS 86* v I (Visakhapatnam) 2011-12; BB 5-49 v B (Khulna) 2012-13. **IT20** (WI): 23 (2007 to 2015-16); HS 8 v Ire (Providence) 2010; BB 3-16 v A (Colombo, RPS) 2012-13. F-c Tours (WI): E 2007, 2012; A 2009-10; SA 2003-04 (WI A); I 2011-12; B 2011-12, 2012-13. HS 64* WI A v SL A (Basseterre) 2006-07. De HS 30 v Glamorgan (Derby) 2019. BB 7-51 T&T v Barbados (Pointe-a-Pierre) 2006-07. De BB 5-77 v Durham (Chester-le-St) 2019. LO HS 86* (*see LOI*). LO BB 5-48 v Yorks (Derby) 2018 (RLC). T20 HS 23*. T20 BB 5-9.

REECE, Luis Michael (St Michael's HS, Chorley; Leeds Met U), b Taunton, Somerset 4 Aug 1990. 6'1". LHB, LM. Squad No 10. Leeds/Bradford MCCU 2012-13. Lancashire 2013-15, no f-c appearances in 2016. Derbyshire debut 2017; cap 2019. MCC 2014. Unicorns 2011-12. HS 184 v Sussex (Derby) 2019. 50 wkts (1): 55 (2019). BB 7-20 v Glos (Derby) 2019. LO HS 128 v Worcs (Derby) 2019 (RLC). LO BB 4-35 Unicorns v Glos (Exmouth) 2011 (CB40). T20 HS 97*. T20 BB 3-33.

RELEASED/RETIRED

(Having made a County 1st XI appearance in 2019)

GLEADALL, Alfie Frank (Westfield Sports C, Sheffield), b Chesterfield 28 May 2000. 5'10". RHB, RMF. Derbyshire 2018-19. Derbyshire 2nd XI debut 2017. England U19 2018. HS 27* and BB 1-20 v Durham (Chester-le-St) 2018. LO HS – . LO BB 3-43 v Notts (Derby) 2019 (RLC).

HAMIDULLAH QADRI – *see KENT*.

LACE, T.C. – *see MIDDLESEX*.

RANKIN, W.B. – *see IRELAND*.

^NO^**SMIT, Daryn** (Northwood S; U of SA), b Durban, South Africa 28 Jan 1984. 5'11". RHB, LB, occ WK. KwaZulu Natal 2004-05 to 2016-17. Dolphins 2005-06 to 2016-17. Derbyshire 2017-18 (non-overseas player). 1000 runs (0+1): 1081 (2015-16). HS 156* KZN v NW (Durban) 2015-16. De HS 45* v Durham (Derby) 2017. BB 7-27 KZN v SW Districts (Durban) 2013-14. De BB – . LO HS 109 Dolphins v Warriors (East London) 2011-12. LO BB 4-39 KZN v GW (Kimberley) 2013-14. T20 HS 57. T20 BB 3-19.

TAYLOR, J.P.A. – *see SURREY*.

[NQ]**VAN BEEK, Logan** Verjus, b Christchurch, New Zealand 7 Sep 1990. Grandson of S.C.Guillen (Trinidad, Canterbury, West Indies and New Zealand 1947-48 to 1960-61). 6'1". RHB, RMF. Canterbury 2009-10 to 2016-17. Netherlands 2017. Wellington 2017-18 to date. Derbyshire 2019. **IT20** (Neth): 8 (2013-14 to 2015-16); HS 4* v B (Dharamsala) 2015-16; BB 3-9 v E (Chattogram) 2013-14. F-c Tour (NZA): UAE 2018-19 (v P A). HS 111* Cant v Otago (Christchurch) 2015-16. De HS 34* v Glos (Derby) 2019. BB 6-46 Well v Auckland (Auckland) 2017-18. De BB 3-20 v Leics (Leicester) 2019. LO HS 64* Neth v Z (Amstelveen) 2017. LO BB 6-18 Neth v UAE (Voorburg) 2017. T20 HS 24*. T20 BB 4-17.

[NQ]**WATT, Mark** Robert James, b Edinburgh, Scotland 29 Jul 1996. LHB, SLA. Scotland 2016 to 2017-18. Lancashire 2018 (T20 only). Derbyshire 2019 (l-o and T20 only). **LOI** (Scot): 27 (2016 to 2019-20); HS 31* v Ire (Harare) 2017-18; BB 4-42 v USA (Sharjah) 2019-20. **IT20** (Scot): 35 (2015 to 2019-20); HS 14* v Ire (Dublin) 2019; BB 5-27 v Netherlands (Dubai, ICCA) 2015-16. HS 81* Scot v PNG (Port Moresby) 2017-18. BB 3-60 Scot v Ire (Dubai, DSC) 2017-18. LO HS 36 Scot v Oman (Al Amerat) 2018-19. LO BB 4-42 (*see LOI*). T20 HS 14*. T20 BB 5-27.

COUNTY CAPS AWARDED IN 2019

Derbyshire	M.J.J.Critchley, R.Rampaul, L.M.Reece
Durham	–
Essex	–
Glamorgan	M.de Lange, M.Labuschagne, D.L.Lloyd
Gloucestershire	B.M.J.Allison, E.R.Bamber, S.T.Gabriel, H.J.Hankins, C.J.Sayers
Hampshire	S.A.Northeast
Kent	Z.Crawley, A.F.Milne, H.W.Podmore
Lancashire	J.P.Faulkner, M.W.Parkinson
Leicestershire	C.N.Ackermann
Middlesex	T.G.Helm
Northamptonshire	R.I.Keogh, A.M.Rossington
Nottinghamshire	R.Ashwin
Somerset	Azhar Ali, J.Overton
Surrey	–
Sussex	O.E.Robinson, S.van Zyl
Warwickshire	O.J.Hannon-Dalby, D.P.Sibley
Worcestershire (colours)	J.J.Dell, C.J.Ferguson, A.W.Finch, J.A.Haynes, H.D.Rutherford, M.H.Wessels
Yorkshire	T.Kohler-Cadmore

Durham abolished their capping system after 2005. Gloucestershire award caps on first-class debut. Worcestershire award club colours on Championship debut. Glamorgan's capping system is now based on a player's number of appearances and not on his performances.

DERBYSHIRE 2019

RESULTS SUMMARY

	Place	Won	Lost	Drew	NR	Tied
Specsavers County Champ (2nd Division)	7th	4	6	4		
All First-Class Matches		5	7	4		
Royal London One-Day Cup (North Group)	5th	3	4			1
Vitality Blast (North Group)	SF	8	6		2	

SPECSAVERS COUNTY CHAMPIONSHIP AVERAGES
BATTING AND FIELDING

Cap		M	I	NO	HS	Runs	Avge	100	50	Ct/St
	T.C.Lace	10	19	1	143	780	43.33	3	3	10
	J.L.du Plooy	10	17	3	118	554	39.57	2	2	9
2015	B.A.Godleman	14	26	–	227	1008	38.76	4	2	2
2011	W.L.Madsen	13	24	1	204*	794	34.52	1	3	21
	F.J.Hudson-Prentice	7	12	2	99	342	34.20	–	2	1
2019	L.M.Reece	14	26	–	184	785	30.19	2	1	5
	H.R.Hosein	14	25	3	91*	618	28.09	–	5	30/2
2017	A.L.Hughes	11	20	1	109*	510	26.84	1	1	11
2019	M.J.J.Critchley	14	23	2	79*	461	21.95	–	3	14
	A.K.Dal	9	16	3	92	278	21.38	–	2	5
	L.V.van Beek	9	12	3	34*	127	14.11	–	–	5
2019	R.Rampaul	12	19	5	30	186	13.28	–	–	2
	Hamidullah Qadri	2	4	2	17*	23	11.50	–	–	–
2012	A.P.Palladino	10	15	3	58	134	11.16	–	1	4

Also batted: S.Conners (2 matches) 14, 6*; M.H.McKiernan (1) 0, 7 (3 ct); D.R.Melton (2) 1*, 0 (1 ct).

BOWLING

	O	M	R	W	Avge	Best	5wI	10wM
L.M.Reece	371	105	1022	52	19.65	6- 58	3	–
F.J.Hudson-Prentice	148	38	465	20	23.25	3- 27	–	–
A.P.Palladino	282.5	99	652	27	24.14	5- 29	1	–
R.Rampaul	374	79	1139	44	25.88	5- 77	2	–
L.V.van Beek	219.2	34	726	19	38.21	3- 20	–	–
M.J.J.Critchley	229.1	26	841	19	44.26	4-107	–	–

Also bowled:
| Hamidullah Qadri | 31.3 | 3 | 140 | 5 | 28.00 | 2- 24 | – | – |
| A.K.Dal | 45.4 | 8 | 142 | 7 | 20.28 | 3- 11 | – | – |

S.Conners 23-3-77-2; J.L.du Plooy 46.3-2-182-4; A.L.Hughes 81-14-219-3; W.L.Madsen 59-12-188-4; D.R.Melton 17.5-1-94-2.

The First-Class Averages (pp 226–241) give the records of Derbyshire players in all first-class county matches (Derbyshire's other opponents being Leeds/Bradford MCCU and the Australians), with the exception of:
T.C.Lace 11-21-1-143-810-40.50-3-3-11ct. Did not bowl.

DERBYSHIRE RECORDS

FIRST-CLASS CRICKET

Highest Total	For 801-8d			v	Somerset	Taunton	2007
	V 677-7d			by	Yorkshire	Leeds	2013
Lowest Total	For 16			v	Notts	Nottingham	1879
	V 23			by	Hampshire	Burton upon T	1958
Highest Innings	For 274	G.A.Davidson		v	Lancashire	Manchester	1896
	V 343*	P.A.Perrin		for	Essex	Chesterfield	1904

Highest Partnership for each Wicket

1st	333	L.M.Reece/B.A.Godleman	v	Northants	Derby	2017
2nd	417	K.J.Barnett/T.A.Tweats	v	Yorkshire	Derby	1997
3rd	316*	A.S.Rollins/K.J.Barnett	v	Leics	Leicester	1997
4th	328	P.Vaulkhard/D.Smith	v	Notts	Nottingham	1946
5th	302*†	J.E.Morris/D.G.Cork	v	Glos	Cheltenham	1993
6th	212	G.M.Lee/T.S.Worthington	v	Essex	Chesterfield	1932
7th	258	M.P.Dowman/D.G.Cork	v	Durham	Derby	2000
8th	198	K.M.Krikken/D.G.Cork	v	Lancashire	Manchester	1996
9th	283	A.Warren/J.Chapman	v	Warwicks	Blackwell	1910
10th	132	A.Hill/M.Jean-Jacques	v	Yorkshire	Sheffield	1986

† *346 runs were added for this wicket in two separate partnerships*

Best Bowling	For 10- 40	W.Bestwick		v	Glamorgan	Cardiff	1921
(Innings)	V 10- 45	R.L.Johnson		for	Middlesex	Derby	1994
Best Bowling	For 17-103	W.Mycroft		v	Hampshire	Southampton	1876
(Match)	V 16-101	G.Giffen		for	Australians	Derby	1886

Most Runs – Season		2165	D.B.Carr	(av 48.11)	1959
Most Runs – Career		23854	K.J.Barnett	(av 41.12)	1979-98
Most 100s – Season		8	P.N.Kirsten		1982
Most 100s – Career		53	K.J.Barnett		1979-98
Most Wkts – Season		168	T.B.Mitchell	(av 19.55)	1935
Most Wkts – Career		1670	H.L.Jackson	(av 17.11)	1947-63
Most Career W-K Dismissals		1304	R.W.Taylor	(1157 ct; 147 st)	1961-84
Most Career Catches in the Field		563	D.C.Morgan		1950-69

LIMITED-OVERS CRICKET

Highest Total	50ov	366-4		v	Comb Univs	Oxford	1991
	40ov	321-5		v	Essex	Leek	2013
	T20	222-5		v	Yorkshire	Leeds	2010
		222-5		v	Notts	Nottingham	2017
Lowest Total	50ov	73		v	Lancashire	Derby	1993
	40ov	60		v	Kent	Canterbury	2008
	T20	72		v	Leics	Derby	2013
Highest Innings	50ov	173*	M.J.Di Venuto	v	Derbys CB	Derby	2000
	40ov	141*	C.J.Adams	v	Kent	Chesterfield	1992
	T20	111	W.J.Durston	v	Notts	Nottingham	2010
Best Bowling	50ov	8-21	M.A.Holding	v	Sussex	Hove	1988
	40ov	6- 7	M.Hendrick	v	Notts	Nottingham	1972
	T20	5-27	T.Lungley	v	Leics	Leicester	2009

DURHAM

Formation of Present Club: 23 May 1882
Inaugural First-Class Match: 1992
Colours: Navy Blue, Yellow and Maroon
Badge: Coat of Arms of the County of Durham
County Champions: (3) 2008, 2009, 2013
Friends Provident Trophy Winners: (1) 2007
Royal London One-Day Cup Winners: (1) 2014
Twenty20 Cup Winners: (0); best – Finalist 2016

Chief Executive: Tim Bostock, Emirates Riverside, Chester-le-Street, Co Durham DH3
3QR • Tel: 0191 387 1717 • Email: marcoms@durhamcricket.co.uk • Web:
www.durhamcricket.co.uk • Twitter: @DurhamCricket (75,721 followers)

Director of Cricket: Marcus North. **Lead High Performance Coach**: James Franklin.
Bowling Coach: Neil Killeen. **Assistant Coach**: Alan Walker. **Captain**: tba. **Overseas
Player**: C.T.Bancroft. **2020 Testimonial**: None. **Head Groundsman**: Vic Demain. **Scorer**:
William Dobson. ‡ New registration. NQ Not qualified for England.

*Durham initially awarded caps immediately after their players joined the staff but revised
this policy in 1998, capping players on merit, past 'awards' having been nullified. Durham
abolished both their capping and 'awards' systems after the 2005 season.*

ADAIR, Harry Robert David (Shrewsbury S; Oxford Brookes U), b Chesterfield, Derbys
14 Dec 1997. RHB, LB. Oxford MCCU 2018-19. Durham (T20 only) 2019. Northamptonshire
2nd XI 2016-17. HS 6 Oxford MCCU v Middx (Northwood) 2019. T20 HS 32.

^{NQ}**BANCROFT, Cameron** Timothy (Aquinas C, Perth), b Attadale, Perth, Australia 19 Nov
1992. 6'0". RHB, RM, occ WK. Squad No 4. W Australia 2013-14 to date. Gloucestershire
2016-17; cap 2016. Durham debut 2019; captain 2019. Big Bash: PS 2014-15 to date. **Tests**
(A): 10 (2017-18 to 2019); HS 82* v E (Brisbane) 2017-18. **IT20** (A): 1 (2015-16); HS 0*
v I (Sydney) 2015-16. F-c Tours (A): E 2019; SA 2017-18; I 2015 (Aus A). HS 228* WA v
SA (Perth) 2017-18. CC HS 206* Gs v Kent (Bristol) 2017. Du HS 158 v Sussex (Hove)
2019, sharing Du record 6th wkt partnership of 282 with E.J.H.Eckersley. BB 1-10 WA v Q
(Brisbane) 2019-20. LO HS 176 WA v SA (Sydney, HO) 2015-16. T20 HS 87*.

‡^{NQ}**BEDINGHAM, David** Guy, b George, Cape Province, South Africa 22 Apr 1994. 5'9".
RHB, OB, occ WK. Squad No 5. Western Province 2012-13 to date. Boland 2015-16 to
2018-19. Cape Cobras 2018-19 to date. HS 147 Boland v Easterns (Paarl) 2017-18. BB – .
LO HS 104* Boland v Border (East London) 2017-18. LO BB – . T20 HS 73.

‡^{NQ}**BEHARDIEN, Farhaan**, b Johannesburg, South Africa 9 Oct 1983. 5'8". RHB, RFM.
Squad No 36. W Province 2004-05. Titans 2006-07 to 2008-09. Northerns 2007-08 to 2008-09.
IPL: KXIP 2016. Leicestershire (T20 only) 2016. Joins Durham in 2020 on a Kolpak deal.
LOI (SA): 59 (2012-13 to 2017-18); HS 70 v NZ (Potchefstroom) 2015; BB 3-19 v SL
(Pallekele) 2013. **IT20** (SA): 38 (2011-12 to 2018-19); HS 64* v E (Southampton) 2017;
BB 2-15 v SL (Delhi) 2015-16. F-c Tours (SA): A 2014; Ire 2012 (v SL A). HS 150*
Titans v Eagles (Benoni) 2008-09. BB 3-48 WP v E Province (Pt Elizabeth) 2004-05 – on
debut. LO HS 113* Titans v Lions (Centurion) 2013-14. LO BB 3-16 Northerns v KZN
(Pretoria) 2008-09. T20 HS 72*. T20 BB 2-15.

BELL, Solomon Jack David (Durham S), b Newcastle upon Tyne 27 Feb 2001. RHB, LB.
Debut (Durham) 2019. Durham 2nd XI debut 2017. HS 1 v Glamorgan (Chester-le-St) 2019.

BURNHAM, Jack Tony Arthur (Deerness Valley CS, Durham), b Durham 18 Jan 1997. 6'1". RHB, RM. Squad No 8. Debut (Durham) 2015. Durham 2nd XI debut 2014. Northumberland 2015. HS 135 v Surrey (Oval) 2016. LO HS 45 v Derbys (Chester-le-St) 2019 (RLC). T20 HS 53*.

CAMPBELL, Jack Oliver Ian (Churcher's C, Petersfield; Durham U), b Portsmouth, Hants 11 Nov 1999. 6'7". RHB, LMF. Squad No 21. Durham MCCU 2019. Durham debut 2019. Hampshire 2nd XI 2017. Kent 2nd XI 2018. Durham 2nd XI debut 2018. HS 2 Durham MCCU v Durham (Chester-le-St) 2019. Du HS 0* and BB 1-43 v Leics (Leicester) 2019.

CARSE, Brydon Alexander (Pearson HS, Pt Elizabeth), b Port Elizabeth, South Africa 31 Jul 1995. Son of J.A.Carse (Rhodesia, W Province, E Province, Northants, Border, Griqualand W 1977-78 to 1992-93). 6'1½". RHB, RF. Squad No 99. Debut (Durham) 2016. Durham 2nd XI debut 2015. F-c Tour (EL): A 2019-20. HS 77* v Northants (Chester-le-St) 2019, sharing Du record 8th wkt partnership of 154 with B.A.Raine. BB 6-26 v Middx (Lord's) 2019. LO HS 2 v Derbys (Chester-le-St) 2019 (RLC). LO BB 3-52 v Warwks (Birmingham) 2019 (RLC). T20 HS 14. T20 BB 1-11.

CLARK, Graham (St Benedict's Catholic HS, Whitehaven), b Whitehaven, Cumbria 16 Mar 1993. Younger brother of J.Clark (*see SURREY*). 6'1". RHB, LB. Squad No 7. Debut (Durham) 2015. HS 109 v Glamorgan (Chester-le-St) 2017. BB 1-10 v Sussex (Arundel) 2018. LO HS 114 v Worcs (Worcester) 2017 (RLC). LO BB 3-18 v Leics (Leicester) 2018 (RLC). T20 HS 91*. T20 BB – .

COUGHLIN, Josh (St Robert of Newminster Catholic CS, Washington), b Sunderland 29 Sep 1997. Younger brother of P.Coughlin (*see below*); nephew of T.Harland (Durham 1974-78). 6'4". LHB, RM. Squad No 29. Debut (Durham) 2016. Durham 2nd XI debut 2015. England U19 2016. HS 24 v Durham MCCU (Chester-le-St) 2019. CC HS 19 and BB 2-31 v Derbys (Chester-le-St) 2018.

COUGHLIN, Paul (St Robert of Newminster Catholic CS, Washington), b Sunderland 23 Oct 1992. Elder brother of J.Coughlin (*see above*); nephew of T.Harland (Durham 1974-78). 6'3". RHB, RM. Squad No 23. Debut (Durham) 2012. Nottinghamshire in 2019. Northumberland 2011. F-c Tour (EL): WI 2017-18. HS 85 v Lancs (Chester-le-St) 2014, sharing Du record 9th wkt partnership of 150 with P.Mustard. BB 5-49 (10-133 match) v Northants (Chester-le-St) 2017. LO HS 22 v Notts (Nottingham) 2017 (RLC) and 22 v Lancs (Chester-le-St) 2017 (RLC). LO BB 3-36 v Worcs (Worcester) 2017 (RLC). T20 HS 53. T20 BB 5-42.

ECKERSLEY, Edmund John Holden ('**Ned**') (St Benedict's GS, Ealing), b Oxford 9 Aug 1989. 6'0". RHB, WK, occ OB. Squad No 66. Leicestershire 2011-18; cap 2013. Mountaineers 2011-12. Durham debut 2019. MCC 2013. 1000 runs (1): 1302 (2013). HS 158 Le v Derbys (Derby) 2017. Du HS 118 v Sussex (Hove) 2019, sharing Du record 6th wkt partnership of 282 with C.T.Bancroft. BB 2-29 Le v Lancs (Manchester) 2013. LO HS 108 Le v Yorks (Leicester) 2013 (Y40). T20 HS 43.

HARTE, Gareth Jason (King Edward VII S), b Johannesburg, South Africa 15 Mar 1993. 5'9". RHB, RM. Squad No 93. Debut (Durham) 2018. HS 114 v Derbys (Chester-le-St) 2018. BB 4-15 v Derbys (Chester-le-St) 2019. LO HS 51* v Warwks (Birmingham) 2019 (RLC). LO BB 2-35 v Notts (Chester-le-St) 2018 (RLC). T20 HS 11. T20 BB 1-11.

^(NQ)**JONES, Michael** Alexander (Ormskirk S; Myerscough C), b Ormskirk, Lancs 5 Jan 1998. 6'2". RHB, OB. Debut (Durham) 2018. Durham 2nd XI 2017. Derbyshire 2nd XI 2017. Leicestershire 2nd XI 2017. **LOI** (Scot): 8 (2017-18 to 2019-20); HS 87 v Ire (Dubai, ICCA) 2017-18. HS 10 v Derbys (Chester-le-St) 2018. LO HS 87 (*see LOI*).

LEES, Alexander Zak (Holy Trinity SS, Halifax), b Halifax, Yorks 14 Apr 1993. 6'3". LHB, LB. Squad No 19. Yorkshire 2010-18; cap 2014; captain (l-o) 2016. Durham debut 2018. MCC 2017. YC 2014. 1000 runs (2); most – 1199 (2016). HS 275* Y v Derbys (Chesterfield) 2013. Du HS 181 v Leics (Chester-le-St) 2019. BB 2-51 Y v Middx (Lord's) 2016. LO HS 115 v Lancs (Gosforth) 2019 (RLC). T20 HS 67*.

POTTS, Matthew ('Matty') James (St Robert of Newminster Catholic S), b Sunderland 29 Oct 1998. 6'0". RHB, RM. Squad No 35. Debut (Durham) 2017. Durham 2nd XI debut 2016. England U19 2017. HS 53* v Derbys (Chester-le-St) 2017. BB 3-48 v Glamorgan (Chester-le-St) 2017. LO HS 30 v Yorks (Chester-le-St) 2018 (RLC). LO BB 4-62 v Northants (Chester-le-St) 2019 (RLC). T20 HS 3*. T20 BB 3-22.

NQPOYNTER, Stuart William (Teddington S), b Hammersmith, London 18 Oct 1990. Younger brother of A.D.Poynter (Middlesex and Ireland 2005-11). 5'9". RHB, WK. Squad No 90. Middlesex 2010. Ireland 2011 to date. Warwickshire 2013. Durham debut 2018. **Tests** (Ire): 1 (2018-19); HS 1 v Afg (Dehradun) 2018-19. **LOI** (Ire): 21 (2014 to 2018-19); HS 36 v SL (Dublin) 2016. **IT20** (Ire): 25 (2015 to 2018-19); HS 39 v Scotland (Dubai, DSC) 2016-17. F-c Tour (Ire): Z 2015-16. HS 170 v Derbys (Derby) 2018. LO HS 109 Ire v Sri Lanka A (Belfast) 2014. T20 HS 61*.

RAINE, Benjamin Alexander (St Aidan's RC SS, Sunderland) b Sunderland, 14 Sep 1991. 6'0". LHB, RMF. Squad No 44. Debut (Durham) 2011 – one game only. Leicestershire 2013-18; cap 2018. HS 82 v Northants (Chester-le-St) 2019, sharing Du record 8th wkt partnership of 154 with B.A.Carse. 50 wkts (2); most – 61 (2015). BB 6-27 v Sussex (Hove) 2019. LO HS 83 Le v Worcs (Worcester) 2018 (RLC). LO BB 3-31 Le v Northants (Northampton) 2018 (RLC). T20 HS 113 v Warwks (Birmingham) 2018 – Le record. T20 BB 3-7.

NQRIMMINGTON, Nathan John (Wellington C), b Redcliffe, Queensland, Australia 11 Nov 1982. 5'10". RHB, RFM. Squad No 11. Queensland 2005-06 to 2017-18 W Australia 2011-12 to 2016-17. Hampshire 2014. Durham debut 2018. Derbyshire 2015 (T20 only). IPL: KXIP 2011. Big Bash: PS 2011-12 to 2012-13. MR 2012-13 to 2016-17. HS 102* WA v NSW (Sydney) 2011-12. CC HS 92 v Leics (Leicester) 2019. BB 5-27 WA v Q (Perth) 2014-15. CC BB 4-42 v Lancs (Sedbergh) 2019. LO HS 55 WA v Tas (Sydney) 2014-15. LO BB 4-34 WA v SA (Perth) 2016-17 T20 HS 26. T20 BB 5-27.

RUSHWORTH, Christopher (Castle View CS, Sunderland), b Sunderland 11 Jul 1986. Cousin of P.Mustard (Durham, Mountaineers, Auckland, Lancashire and Gloucestershire 2002-17). 6'2". RHB, RMF. Squad No 22. Debut (Durham) 2010; testimonial 2019. MCC 2013, 2015. Northumberland 2004-05. PCA 2015. HS 57 v Kent (Canterbury) 2017. 50 wkts (5); most – 88 (2015) – Du record. BB 9-52 (15-95 match – Du record) v Northants (Chester-le-St) 2014. Hat-trick v Hants (Southampton) 2015. LO HS 38* v Derbys (Chester-le-St) 2015 (RLC). LO BB 5-31 v Notts (Chester-le-St) 2010 (CB40). T20 HS 5. T20 BB 3-14.

SALISBURY, Matthew Edward Thomas (Shenfield HS; Anglia Ruskin U), b Chelmsford, Essex 18 Apr 1993. 6'0½". RHB, RMF. Squad No 32. Cambridge MCCU 2012-13. Essex 2014-15. Hampshire 2017. Durham debut 2018. Suffolk 2016. HS 37 v Warwks (Birmingham) 2018. BB 6-37 v Middx (Chester-le-St) 2018. LO HS 5* Ex v Leics (Chelmsford) 2014 (RLC). LO BB 4-55 Ex v Lancs (Chelmsford) 2014 (RLC). T20 HS 1*. T20 BB 2-19.

STEEL, Cameron Tate (Scotch C, Perth, Australia; Millfield S; Durham U), b San Francisco, USA 13 Sep 1995. 5'10". RHB, LB. Squad No 14. Durham MCCU 2014-16. Durham debut 2017. Middlesex 2nd XI 2013-16. Somerset 2nd XI 2013. Durham 2nd XI debut 2016. HS 224 v Leics (Leicester) 2017. BB 2-7 v Glamorgan (Cardiff) 2018. LO HS 77 v Notts (Nottingham) 2017 (RLC). LO BB – . T20 HS 37. T20 BB 2-60.

STEEL, Scott (Belmont Community S), b Durham 20 Apr 1999. RHB, OB. Squad No 55. Debut (Durham) 2019. Durham 2nd XI debut 2016. Northumberland 2017. HS 39 v Middx (Lord's) 2019. BB – . LO HS 68 v Northants (Chester-le-St) 2019 (RLC) and 68 v Yorks (Leeds) 2019 (RLC). T20 HS 70.

STOKES, Benjamin Andrew (Cockermouth S), b Christchurch, Canterbury, New Zealand 4 Jun 1991. 6'1". LHB, RFM. Squad No 38. Debut (Durham) 2010. IPL: RPS 2017. RR 2018 to date. Big Bash: MR 2014-15. YC 2013. *Wisden* 2015. BBC Sports Personality of the Year 2019. OBE 2020. **ECB Test & LO Central Contract 2019-20. Tests**: 63 (2013-14 to 2019-20); HS 258 v SA (Cape Town) 2015-16, setting E record fastest double century in 163 balls; BB 6-22 v WI (Lord's) 2017. **LOI**: 95 (2011 to 2019); HS 102* v A (Birmingham) 2017; BB 5-61 v A (Southampton) 2013. **IT20**: 26 (2011 to 2019-20); HS 47* v SA (Durban) 2019-20; BB 3-26 v NZ (Delhi) 2015-16. F-c Tours: A 2013-14; SA 2015-16, 2019-20; WI 2010-11 (EL), 2014-15, 2018-19; NZ 2017-18, 2019-20; I 2016-17; SL 2018-19; B 2016-17; UAE 2015-16 (v P). HS 258 (*see Tests*). Du HS 185 v Lancs (Chester-le-St) 2011, sharing Du record 4th wkt partnership of 331 with D.M.Benkenstein. BB 7-67 (10-121 match) v Sussex (Chester-le-St) 2014. LO HS 164 v Notts (Chester-le-St) 2014 (RLC) – Du record. LO BB 5-61 (*see LOI*). T20 HS 103*. T20 BB 4-16.

TREVASKIS, Liam (Q Elizabeth GS, Penrith), b Carlisle, Cumberland 18 Apr 1999. 5'8". LHB, SLA. Squad No 80. Debut (Durham) 2017. Durham 2nd XI debut 2015. HS 64 v Leics (Leicester) 2019. BB 2-96 v Leics (Chester-le-St) 2019. LO HS 16 v Lancs (Gosforth) 2019 (RLC). LO BB 2-37 v Leics (Chester-le-St) 2019 (RLC). T20 HS 26. T20 BB 4-16.

WEIGHELL, William James (Stokesley S), b Middlesbrough, Yorks 28 Jan 1994. 6'4". LHB, RMF. Squad No 28. Debut (Durham) 2015. Northumberland 2012-15. HS 84 v Kent (Chester-le-St) 2018. BB 7-32 v Leics (Chester-le-St) 2018. LO HS 23 v Lancs (Manchester) 2018 (RLC). LO BB 5-57 v Warwks (Birmingham) 2017 (RLC). T20 HS 28. T20 BB 3-28.

WHITEHEAD, Benjamin Guy (Hetton S), b Sunderland 28 Apr 1997. 6'0". RHB, LBG. Squad No 97. Awaiting f-c debut. Durham 2nd XI debut 2014. Northumberland 2015-16. T20 HS 2*. T20 BB 2-23.

WOOD, Mark Andrew (Ashington HS; Newcastle C), b Ashington 11 Jan 1990. 5'11". RHB, RF. Squad No 33. Debut (Durham) 2011. IPL: CSK 2018. Northumberland 2008-10. **ECB L-O Central Contract 2019-20. Tests**: 15 (2015 to 2019-20); HS 52 v NZ (Christchurch) 2017-18; BB 5-41 v WI (Gros Islet) 2018-19. **LOI**: 51 (2015 to 2019); HS 13 v A (Manchester) 2015; BB 4-33 v A (Birmingham) 2017. **IT20**: 8 (2015 to 2019-20); HS 5* v A (Hobart) 2017-18 and 5* v NZ (Wellington) 2017-18; BB 3-9 v WI (Basseterre) 2018-19. F-c Tours: SA 2014-15 (EL), 2019-20; WI 2018-19; NZ 2017-18; SL 2013-14 (EL); UAE 2015-16 (v P), 2018-19 (EL v P A). HS 72* v Kent (Chester-le-St) 2017. BB 6-46 v Derbys (Derby) 2018. LO HS 24 EL v Pakistan A (Abu Dhabi) 2018-19. LO BB 4-33 (*see LOI*). T20 HS 27*. T20 BB 4-25.

RELEASED/RETIRED

(Having made a County 1st XI appearance in 2019)

HANDSCOMB, P.S.P. – *see MIDDLESEX.*

HARDING, George Harvey Idris (Brine Leas HS, Nantwich; Myerscough C), b Poole, Dorset 12 Oct 1996. 6'6". RHB, SLA. Durham 2017-19. Durham 2nd XI debut 2015. Northumberland 2016. HS 36 v Durham MCCU (Chester-le-St) 2019. LO HS 7 v Glos (Cheltenham) 2018. BB 4-111 v Glamorgan (Swansea) 2017. LO HS 18* v Lancs (Chester-le-St) 2017 (RLC). LO BB 2-52 v Worcs (Worcester) 2017 (RLC).

PRINGLE, Ryan David (Durham SFC), b Sunderland 17 Apr 1992. 6'0". RHB, OB. Durham 2014-19. Northumberland 2011-12. HS 99 v Hants (Chester-le-St) 2015. BB 7-107 (10-260 match) v Hants (Southampton) 2016. LO HS 125 v Derbys (Derby) 2016 (RLC). LO BB 2-39 v Northants (Northampton) 2016 (RLC) and 2-39 v Notts (Chester-le-St) 2018 (RLC). T20 HS 35. T20 BB 3-30.

RICHARDSON, Michael John (Rondebosch HS; Stonyhurst C, Nottingham U), b Pt Elizabeth, South Africa 4 Oct 1986. Son of D.J.Richardson (South Africa, EP and NT 1977-78 to 1997-98), grandson of J.H.Richardson (NE Transvaal and Transvaal B 1952-53 to 1960-61), nephew of R.P.Richardson (WP 1984-85 to 1988-89). 5'10". RHB, WK. Durham 2010-19. Colombo CC 2014-15. **IT20** (Germany): 5 (2019 to 2019-20); HS 42 v Spain (Almeria) 2019-20. 1000 runs (1): 1007 (2015). HS 148 v Yorks (Chester-le-St) 2014. LO HS 111 v Warwks (Chester-le-St) 2017 (RLC). T20 HS 53.

ROBSON, Angus James (Marcellin C, Randwick; Australian C of PE), b Darlinghurst, Sydney, Australia 19 Feb 1992. Younger brother of S.D.Robson (*see MIDDLESEX*). 5'9". RHB, LB. Leicestershire 2013-16. Sussex 2017. Durham 2019. 1000 runs (2); most – 1086 (2014). HS 120 Le v Essex (Chelmsford) 2015. Du HS 64 v Middx (Lord's) 2015. BB – . LO HS 90 Le v Yorks (Leeds) 2015 (RLC).

SHORT, D.J.M. – *see SURREY*.

SMITH, William Rew (Bedford S; Collingwood C, Durham U), b Luton, Beds 28 Sep 1982. 5'9". RHB, OB. Nottinghamshire 2002-06. Durham UCCE 2003-05; captain 2004-05. British U 2004-05. Durham 2007-19; captain 2009-10 (*part*). Hampshire 2014-17; cap 2015. Bedfordshire 1999-2002. 1000 runs (1): 1187 (2014). HS 210 H v Lancs (Southampton) 2016. Du HS 201* v Surrey (Guildford) 2008. BB 3-34 DU v Leics (Leicester) 2005. CC BB 2-27 H v Kent (Southampton) 2014. Du BB 2-30 v Durham MCCU (Chester-le-St) 2013. LO HS 120* v Surrey (Chester-le-St) 2013 (Y40). LO BB 2-19 Du v Derbys (Derby) 2013 (Y40). T20 HS 55. T20 BB 3-15.

WATLING, B.J. – *see LANCASHIRE*.

G.T.Main left the staff without making a County 1st XI appearance in 2019.

DURHAM 2019

RESULTS SUMMARY

	Place	Won	Lost	Drew	NR
Specsavers County Champ (2nd Division)	5th	5	5	4	
All First-Class Matches		6	5	4	
Royal London One-Day Cup (North Group)	4th	4	2		2
Vitality Blast (North Group)	6th	5	7		2

SPECSAVERS COUNTY CHAMPIONSHIP AVERAGES
BATTING AND FIELDING

Cap		M	I	NO	HS	Runs	Avge	100	50	Ct/St
	C.T.Bancroft	9	17	1	158	726	45.37	2	3	16
	E.J.H.Eckersley	13	22	4	118	720	40.00	1	4	42
	A.Z.Lees	14	25	1	181	899	37.45	3	3	10
	N.J.Rimmington	6	9	2	92	210	30.00	–	2	3
	J.T.A.Burnham	13	23	1	86	598	27.18	–	4	4
	L.Trevaskis	10	17	1	64	392	24.50	–	2	2
	G.J.Harte	11	21	1	77	459	22.95	–	3	2
	B.A.Raine	14	23	2	82	464	22.09	–	2	2
	B.A.Carse	10	15	3	77*	246	20.50	–	1	1
	A.J.Robson	4	6	–	64	97	16.16	–	1	6
	C.T.Steel	6	10	–	39	133	13.30	–	–	2
	S.Steel	2	4	–	39	48	12.00	–	–	1
	M.J.Potts	3	5	1	20	46	11.50	–	–	1
	G.Clark	4	8	1	26	79	11.28	–	–	4
	R.D.Pringle	2	4	–	30	41	10.25	–	–	1
	M.E.T.Salisbury	5	10	1	23	76	8.44	–	–	1
	W.J.Weighell	3	5	–	24	37	7.40	–	–	1
	C.Rushworth	14	19	8	12*	56	5.09	–	–	3

Also batted: S.J.D.Bell (1 match) J; J.O.I.Campbell (1) 0*; P.S.P.Handscomb (2) 29, 54, 3 (4 ct); M.A.Jones (2) 0, 9, 0; S.W.Poynter (1) 8, 7 (3 ct); M.J.Richardson (1) 7, 5 (5 ct); W.R.Smith (1) 4, 0 (1 ct); B.J.Watling (2) 0, 35, 104* (1 ct).

BOWLING

	O	M	R	W	Avge	Best	5wI	10wM
C.Rushworth	486.4	127	1271	69	18.42	6-39	4	1
B.A.Raine	463.4	122	1179	54	21.83	6-27	3	–
M.E.T.Salisbury	137.1	27	448	19	23.57	4-67	–	–
N.J.Rimmington	140.2	29	392	16	24.50	4-42	–	–
G.J.Harte	91	23	256	10	25.60	4-15	–	–
B.A.Carse	250.4	42	940	35	26.85	6-26	3	–
Also bowled:								
W.J.Weighell	75.1	17	222	9	24.66	3-41	–	–
L.Trevaskis	149.3	36	410	6	68.33	2-96	–	–

J.T.A.Burnham 10.1-2-17-0; J.O.I.Campbell 28-3-87-1; G.Clark 2-0-7-0; A.Z.Lees 0.1-0-0-0; M.J.Potts 68-13-213-2; R.D.Pringle 2-0-6-0; W.R.Smith 2-1-10-0; C.T.Steel 10-1-35-2; S.Steel 7-3-16-0.

The First-Class Averages (pp 226–241) give the records of Durham players in all first-class county matches (Durham's other opponents being Durham MCCU), with the exception of C.T.Bancroft and J.O.I.Campbell, whose first-class figures for Durham are as above.

DURHAM RECORDS

FIRST-CLASS CRICKET

Highest Total	For 648-5d		v	Notts	Chester-le-St[2]	2009
	V 810-4d		by	Warwicks	Birmingham	1994
Lowest Total	For 61		v	Leics	Leicester	2018
	V 18		by	Durham MCCU	Chester-le-St[2]	2012
Highest Innings	For 273	M.L.Love	v	Hampshire	Chester-le-St[2]	2003
	V 501*	B.C.Lara	for	Warwicks	Birmingham	1994

Highest Partnership for each Wicket

1st	334*	S.Hutton/M.A.Roseberry	v	Oxford U	Oxford	1996
2nd	274	M.D.Stoneman/S.G.Borthwick	v	Middlesex	Chester-le-St[2]	2014
3rd	212	M.J.Di Venuto/D.M.Benkenstein	v	Essex	Chester-le-St[2]	2010
4th	331	B.A.Stokes/D.M.Benkenstein	v	Lancashire	Chester-le-St[2]	2011
5th	247	G.J.Muchall/I.D.Blackwell	v	Worcs	Worcester	2011
6th	282	C.T.Bancroft/E.J.H.Eckersley	v	Sussex	Hove	2019
7th	315	D.M.Benkenstein/O.D.Gibson	v	Yorkshire	Leeds	2006
8th	154	B.A.Raine/B.A.Carse	v	Yorkshire	Chester-le-St[2]	2019
9th	150	P.Mustard/P.Coughlin	v	Northants	Chester-le-St[2]	2014
10th	103	M.M.Betts/D.M.Cox	v	Sussex	Hove	1996

Best Bowling	For	10- 47	O.D.Gibson	v	Hampshire	Chester-le-St[2]	2007
(Innings)	V	9- 34	J.A.R.Harris	for	Middlesex	Lord's	2015
Best Bowling	For	15- 95	C.Rushworth	v	Northants	Chester-le-St[2]	2014
(Match)	V	13-103	J.A.R.Harris	for	Middlesex	Lord's	2015

Most Runs – Season	1654	M.J.Di Venuto	(av 78.76)		2009
Most Runs – Career	12030	P.D.Collingwood	(av 33.98)		1996-2018
Most 100s – Season	7	K.K.Jennings			2016
Most 100s – Career	25	P.D.Collingwood			1996-2018
Most Wkts – Season	80	O.D.Gibson	(av 20.75)		2007
Most Wkts – Career	527	G.Onions	(av 25.58)		2004-17
Most Career W-K Dismissals	638	P.Mustard	(619 ct; 19 st)		2002-16
Most Career Catches in the Field	246	P.D.Collingwood			1996-2018

LIMITED-OVERS CRICKET

Highest Total	50ov	353-8		v	Notts	Chester-le-St[2]	2014
	40ov	325-9		v	Surrey	The Oval	2011
	T20	225-2		v	Leics	Chester-le-St[2]	2010
Lowest Total	50ov	82		v	Worcs	Chester-le-St[1]	1968
	40ov	72		v	Warwicks	Birmingham	2002
	T20	78		v	Lancashire	Chester-le-St[2]	2009
Highest Innings	50ov	164	B.A.Stokes	v	Notts	Chester-le-St[2]	2014
	40ov	150*	B.A.Stokes	v	Warwicks	Birmingham	2011
	T20	108*	P.D.Collingwood	v	Worcs	Worcester	2017
Best Bowling	50ov	7-32	S.P.Davis	v	Lancashire	Chester-le-St[1]	1983
	40ov	6-31	N.Killeen	v	Derbyshire	Derby	2000
	T20	5- 6	P.D.Collingwood	v	Northants	Chester-le-St[2]	2011

[1] Chester-le-Street CC (Ropery Lane) [2] Emirates Riverside

ESSEX

Formation of Present Club: 14 January 1876
Inaugural First-Class Match: 1894
Colours: Blue, Gold and Red
Badge: Three Seaxes above Scroll bearing 'Essex'
County Champions: (8) 1979, 1983, 1984, 1986, 1991, 1992, 2017, 2019
NatWest/Friends Prov Trophy Winners: (3) 1985, 1997, 2008
Benson and Hedges Cup Winners: (2) 1979, 1998
Pro 40/National League (Div 1) Winners: (2) 2005, 2006
Sunday League Winners: (3) 1981, 1984, 1985
Twenty20 Cup Winners: (1) 2019

Chief Executive: Derek Bowden, The Cloudfm County Ground, New Writtle Street, Chelmsford CM2 0PG • Tel: 01245 252420 • Email: administration@essexcricket.org.uk • Web: www.essexcricket.org.uk • Twitter: @EssexCricket (103,240 followers)

Head Coach: Anthony McGrath. **Assistant Head Coach:** Andre Nel. **Captains:** T.Westley (f-c and 50 ov) and S.R.Harmer (T20). **Overseas Players:** M.C.Henriques (T20 only), P.M.Siddle and A.Zampa (T20 only). **2020 Testimonial:** None. **Head Groundsman:** Stuart Kerrison. **Scorer:** Tony Choat. **Blast Team Name:** Essex Eagles. ‡ New registration. NQ Not qualified for England.

ALLISON, Benjamin Michael John (New Hall S; Chelmsford C), b 18 Dec 1999. RHB, RFM. Squad No 65. Gloucestershire 2019; cap 2019. Essex 2nd XI debut 2017. Awaiting Essex 1st XI debut. Bedfordshire 2018. Cambridgeshire 2019. HS 0 and BB 3-109 Gs v Derbys (Derby) 2019.

BEARD, Aaron Paul (Boswells S, Chelmsford), b Chelmsford 15 Oct 1997. LHB, RFM. Squad No 14. Debut (Essex) 2016. England U19 2016 to 2016-17. HS 58* v Durham MCCU (Chelmsford) 2017. CC HS 41 v Yorks (Chelmsford) 2019. BB 4-23 v Somerset (Chelmsford) 2019. LO HS 22* v Kent (Beckenham) 2019 (RLC). LO BB 3-51 v Glos (Chelmsford) 2019 (RLC). T20 HS 13. T20 BB 2-31.

BROWNE, Nicholas Lawrence Joseph (Trinity Catholic HS, Woodford Green), b Leytonstone 24 Mar 1991. 6'3½". LHB, LB. Squad No 10. Debut (Essex) 2013; cap 2015. MCC 2016. 1000 runs (3); most – 1262 (2016). HS 255 v Derbys (Chelmsford) 2016. BB – . LO HS 99 v Glamorgan (Chelmsford) 2016 (RLC). T20 HS 38.

BUTTLEMAN, William Edward Lewis (Felsted S), b Chelmsford 20 Apr 2000. Younger brother of J.E.L.Buttleman (Durham UCCE 2007-09). RHB, WK, occ OB. Squad No 9. Debut (Essex) 2019. Essex 2nd XI debut 2017. HS 0 v Yorks (Leeds) 2019 – only 1st XI appearance.

CHOPRA, Varun (Ilford County HS), b Barking 21 Jun 1987. 6'1". RHB, LB. Squad No 6. Debut (Essex) 2006, scoring 106 v Glos (Chelmsford) on CC debut; cap 2018. Warwickshire 2010-16; cap 2012; captain 2015. Tamil Union 2011-12. Sussex 2019. F-c Tour (EL): SL 2013-14. 1000 runs (3); most – 1203 (2011). HS 233* TU v Sinhalese (Colombo, PSS) 2011-12. CC HS 228 Wa v Worcs (Worcester) 2011 (in 2nd CC game of season, having scored 210 v Somerset in 1st). Ex HS 155 v Glos (Bristol) 2008. BB – . LO HS 160 v Somerset (Chelmsford) 2018 (RLC). T20 HS 116.

COOK, Sir Alastair Nathan (Bedford S), b Gloucester 25 Dec 1984. 6'3". LHB, OB. Squad No 26. Debut (Essex) 2003; cap 2005; benefit 2014. MCC 2004-07, 2015. YC 2005. *Wisden* 2011. Knighted in 2019 New Year's honours list. **Tests**: 161 (2005-06 to 2018, 59 as captain); 1000 runs (5); most – 1364 (2015); HS 294 v I (Birmingham) 2011. Scored 60 and 104* v I (Nagpur) 2005-06 on debut, and 71 and 147 in final Test v I (Oval) 2018. Second, after M.A.Taylor, to score 1000 runs in the calendar year of his debut. Finished career after appearing in world record 159 consecutive Tests. **LOI**: 92 (2006 to 2014-15, 69 as captain); HS 137 v P (Abu Dhabi) 2011-12. **IT20**: 4 (2007 to 2009-10); HS 26 v SA (Centurion) 2009-10. F-c Tours (C=Captain): A 2006-07, 2010-11, 2013-14C, 2017-18; SA 2009-10, 2015-16C; WI 2005-06 (Eng A), 2008-09, 2014-15C; NZ 2007-08, 2012-13C, 2017-18; I 2005-06, 2008-09, 2012-13C, 2016-17C; SL 2004-05 (Eng A), 2007-08, 2011-12; B 2009-10C, 2016-17C; UAE 2011-12 (v P), 2015-16C (v P). 1000 runs (8+1); most – 1466 (2005). HS 294 (*see Tests*). CC HS 195 v Northants (Northampton) 2005. BB 3-13 v Northants (Chelmsford) 2005. LO HS 137 (*see LOI*). BB – . T20 HS 100*.

COOK, Samuel James (Great Baddow HS & SFC; Loughborough U), b Chelmsford 4 Aug 1997. RHB, RFM. Squad No 16. Loughborough MCCU 2016-17. Essex debut 2017. MCC 2019. Essex 2nd XI debut 2014. HS 37* v Yorks (Leeds) 2019. BB 7-23 (12-65 match) v Kent (Canterbury) 2019. LO HS 6 v Middx (Chelmsford) 2019 (RLC). LO BB 3-37 v Surrey (Oval) 2019 (RLC). T20 HS 0*. T20 BB 1-27.

^{NQ}**DELPORT, Cameron** Scott (Kloof Senior S, Durban; Westville BHS), b Durban, South Africa 12 May 1989. 5'10". LHB, RM. Squad No 89. UK ancestry visa. KwaZulu-Natal 2008-09 to 2016-17. Dolphins 2008-09 to 2011-12. Leicestershire 2017 (white ball 2016-18). Essex debut 2019 (T20 only). Big Bash: ST 2014-15. Won Walter Lawrence Trophy in 2019 for 38-ball hundred v Surrey in T20. HS 163 KZN v Northerns (Centurion) 2010-11. CC HS 20 Le v Glamorgan (Leicester) 2017. BB 2-10 KZN v Northern Cape (Chatsworth) 2016-17. LO HS 169* Dolphins v Knights (Bloemfontein) 2014-15. LO BB 4-42 Dolphins v Titans (Durban) 2011-12. T20 HS 129. T20 BB 4-17.

^{NQ}**HARMER, Simon** Ross, b Pretoria, South Africa 10 Feb 1993. RHB, OB. Squad No 11. Eastern Province 2009-10 to 2011-12. Warriors 2010-11 to 2018-19. Essex debut 2017 (Kolpak signing); cap 2018; captain 2020 (T20 only). **Tests** (SA): 5 (2014-15 to 2015-16); HS 13 v I (Nagpur) 2015-16; BB 4-61 v I (Mohali) 2015-16. F-c Tours (SA): A 2014 (SA A); I 2015-16; B 2015; Ire 2012 (SA A). HS 102* v Surrey (Oval) 2018. 50 wkts (3+1); most – 86 (2019). BB 9-95 (14-172 match) v Middx (Chelmsford) 2017. LO HS 44* v Surrey (Oval) 2017 (RLC). LO BB 4-42 Warriors v Lions (Potchefstroom) 2011-12. T20 HS 43. T20 BB 4-19.

‡^{NQ}**HENRIQUES, Moises** Constantino, b Funchal, Madeira, Portugal 1 Feb 1987. 6'1½". RHB, RFM. New South Wales 2006-07 to date. Glamorgan 2012. Surrey 2015-17 (T20 only). IPL: KKR 2009. DD 2009-10. RCB 2013. SH 2014-17. Big Bash: SS 2011-12 to date. **Tests** (A): 4 (2012-13 to 2016); HS 81* and BB 1-48 v I (Chennai) 2012-13. **LOI** (A): 11 (2009-10 to 2017); HS 18 v NZ (Birmingham) 2017; BB 3-32 v SL (Hobart) 2012-13. **IT20** (A): 11 (2009-10 to 2017-18); HS 62* v I (Guwahati) 2017-18; BB 2-35 v E (Hobart) 2013-14. F-c Tours (A): SA/Z 2013 (Aus A); I 2012-13; SL 2016; Scot/Ire 2013 (Aus A). HS 265 NSW v Q (Sydney) 2016-17. BB 5-17 NSW v Q (Brisbane) 2006-07. LO HS 164* NSW v Cricket Aus (Sydney) 2016-17. LO BB 4-17 NSW v Tas (Sydney) 2013-14. T20 HS 77. T20 BB 3-11.

KHUSHI, Feroze Isa Nazir (Kelmscott S, Walthamstow; Leyton SFC), b Whipps Cross 23 Jun 1999. RHB. OB. Squad No 23. Essex 2nd XI debut 2015. Suffolk 2019. Awaiting 1st XI debut.

LAWRENCE, Daniel William (Trinity Catholic HS, Woodford Green), b Whipps Cross 12 Jul 1997. 6'2". RHB, LB. Squad No 28. Debut (Essex) 2015; cap 2017. MCC 2019. Essex 2nd XI debut 2013, aged 15y 321d. England U19 2015. F-c Tour (EL): A 2019-20. 1000 runs (1): 1070 (2016). HS 161 v Surrey (Oval) 2015. BB 2-63 v MCC (Bridgetown) 2017-18. CC BB 1-5 v Kent (Chelmsford) 2016. LO HS 115 v Kent (Chelmsford) 2018 (RLC). LO BB 3-35 v Middx (Lord's) 2016 (RLC). T20 HS 86. T20 BB 3-21.

NIJJAR, Aron Stuart Singh (Ilford County HS), b Goodmayes 24 Sep 1994. LHB, SLA. Squad No 24. Debut (Essex) 2015. Suffolk 2014. HS 53 v Northants (Chelmsford) 2015. BB 2-28 v Cambridge MCCU (Cambridge) 2019. CC BB2 2-33 v Lancs (Chelmsford) 2015. LO HS 21 v Yorks (Chelmsford) 2015 (RLC). LO BB 1-39 v Sussex (Hove) 2015 (RLC). T20 BB 3-26.

PATEL, Rishi Ketan (Brentwood S), b Chigwell 26 Jul 1998. RHB, LB. Squad No 12. Cambridge MCCU 2019. Essex debut 2019. Essex 2nd XI debut 2015. Hertfordshire 2019. HS 35 v Yorks (Chelmsford) 2019. LO HS 35 v Hants (Chelmsford) 2019 (RLC).

PEPPER, Michael-Kyle Steven (The Perse S), b Harlow 25 Jun 1998. Younger brother of C.A.Pepper (Cambridgeshire 2013-16). RHB, WK. Squad No 19. Debut (Essex) 2018. Essex 2nd XI debut 2017. Cambridgeshire 2014-19. HS 42 v Somerset (Chelmsford) 2018. T20 HS 27.

PLOM, Jack Henry (Gable Hall S; S Essex C), b Basildon 27 Aug 1999. LHB, RFM. Squad No 77. Debut (Essex) 2018 – did not bat or bowl. Essex 2nd XI debut 2016. No 1st XI appearances in 2019.

PORTER, James Alexander (Oak Park HS, Newbury Park; Epping Forest C), b Leytonstone 25 May 1993. 5'11½". RHB, RFM. Squad No 44. Debut (Essex) 2014, taking a wkt with his 5th ball; *Wisden* 2017. F-c Tours (EL): UAE 2017-18 to date; UAE 2018-19 (v P A). HS 34 v Glamorgan (Cardiff) 2015. 50 wkts (5); most – 85 (2017). BB 7-41 (11-98 match) v Worcs (Chelmsford) 2018. LO HS 7* v Middx (Chelmsford) 2019 (RLC). LO BB 4-29 v Glamorgan (Chelmsford) 2018 (RLC). T20 HS 1*. T20 BB 4-20.

QUINN, Matthew Richard, b Auckland, New Zealand 28 Feb 1993. RHB, RMF. Squad No 94. Auckland 2012-13 to 2015-16. Essex debut 2016. UK passport. HS 50 Auckland v Canterbury (Auckland) 2013-14. Ex HS 16 v Notts (Chelmsford) 2018. BB 7-76 (11-163 match) v Glos (Cheltenham) 2016. LO HS 36 Auckland v CD (Auckland) 2013-14. LO BB 4-71 v Sussex (Hove) 2016 (RLC). T20 HS 8*. T20 BB 4-20.

RYMELL, Joshua Sean (Ipswich S; Colchester SFC), b Ipswich, Suffolk 4 Apr 2001. RHB. Essex 2nd XI debut 2017. Awaiting 1st XI debut.

^{NQ}**SIDDLE, Peter** Matthew, b Traralgon, Victoria, Australia 25 Nov 1984. 6'1½". RHB, RFM. Squad No 64. Victoria 2005-06 to date. Nottinghamshire 2014; cap 2014. Lancashire 2015. Essex debut 2018. Big Bash: MR 2013-14 to 2014-15. AS 2017-18 to date. **Tests** (A): 67 (2008-09 to 2019); HS 51 v I (Delhi) 2012-13; BB 6-54 v E (Brisbane) 2010-11. **LOI** (A): 20 (2008-09 to 2018-19); HS 10* v I (Melbourne) 2019. BB 3-55 v E (Centurion) 2009-10. **IT20** (A): 2 (2008-09 to 2010-11); HS 1* and BB 2-24 v NZ (Sydney) 2008-09. F-c Tours (A): E 2009, 2013, 2015, 2019; SA 2008-09, 2011-12, 2013-14; WI 2011-12; NZ 2015-16; I 2008-09 (Aus A), 2008-09, 2012-13; SL 2011; Z 2011 (Aus A); UAE 2014-15 (v P), 2018-19 (v P). HS 103* Aus A v Scotland (Edinburgh) 2013. CC HS 89 La v Northants (Northampton) 2015. Ex HS 60 v Yorks (Leeds) 2019. 50 wkts (0+1): 54 (2011-12). BB 8-54 Vic v S Aus (Adelaide) 2014-15. CC BB 6-104 v Surrey (Oval) 2019. LO HS 62 Vic v Q (N Sydney) 2017-18. LO BB 4-27 Vic v Tas (Hobart) 2008-09. T20 HS 11. T20 BB 4-29.

NQSNATER, Shane (St John's C, Harare), b Harare, Zimbabwe 24 Mar 1996. RHB, RM. Squad No 29. Netherlands 2016 to date. Awaiting Essex f-c debut. Essex 2nd XI debut 2017. **LOI** (Neth): 2 (2018); HS 12 and BB 1-41 v Nepal (Amstelveen) 2018. **IT20** (Neth): 13 (2018 to 2019-20); HS 10 and BB 3-42 v Scotland (Dublin) 2019. HS 50* and BB 5-88 Neth v Namibia (Dubai, ICCA) 2017-18. LO HS 23* Neth v Nepal (Kwekwe) 2017-18. LO BB 5-60 v Somerset (Chelmsford) 2018 (RLC). T20 HS 10. T20 BB 3-42.

NQTen DOESCHATE, Ryan Neil (Fairbairn C; Cape Town U), b Port Elizabeth, South Africa 30 Jun 1980. 5'10½". RHB, RMF. Squad No 27. Debut (Essex) 2003; cap 2006; captain (l-o) 2014-15; captain 2016-19. EU passport – Dutch ancestry. Netherlands 2005 to 2009-10. Otago 2012-13. IPL: KKR 2011-15. Big Bash: AS 2014-15. **LOI** (Neth): 33 (2006 to 2010-11); HS 119 v E (Nagpur) 2010-11; BB 4-31 v Canada (Nairobi) 2006-07. **IT20** (Neth): 22 (2008 to 2019-20); HS 59 v Namibia (Dubai, ICCA) 2019-20; BB 3-23 v Scotland (Belfast) 2008. F-c Tours (Ne): SA 2006-07, 2007-08; K 2005-06, 2009-10; Ireland 2005. 1000 runs (1): 1226 (2016). HS 259* and BB 6-20 Neth v Canada (Pretoria) 2006. Ex HS 173* v Somerset (Chelmsford) 2018. Ex BB 6-57 v New Zealanders (Chelmsford) 2008. CC BB 5-13 v Hants (Chelmsford) 2010. LO HS 180 v Scotland (Chelmsford) 2013 (Y40) – Ex 40-over record, inc 15 sixes. LO BB 5-50 v Glos (Bristol) 2007 (FPT). T20 HS 121*. T20 BB 4-24.

WALTER, Paul Ian (Billericay S), b Basildon 28 May 1994. LHB, LMF. Squad No 22. Debut (Essex) 2016. HS 68* v West Indians (Chelmsford) 2017. CC HS 47 and BB 3-44 v Derbys (Derby) 2016. LO HS 25 v Surrey (Oval) 2019 (RLC). LO BB 4-37 v Middx (Chelmsford) 2017 (RLC). T20 HS 40. T20 BB 3-24.

WESTLEY, Thomas (Linton Village C; Hills Road SFC), b Cambridge 13 March 1989. 6'2". RHB, OB. Squad No 21. Debut (Essex) 2007; cap 2013; captain 2020. MCC 2007, 2009, 2016, 2019. Durham MCCU 2010-11. Cambridgeshire 2005. **Tests**: 5 (2017); HS 59 v SA (Oval) 2017. F-c Tours: SL 2016-17 (EL); Nepal 2019-20 (MCC). 1000 runs (1): 1435 (2016). HS 254 v Worcs (Chelmsford) 2016. BB 4-55 DU v Durham (Durham) 2010. CC BB 4-75 v Surrey (Colchester) 2015. LO HS 134 v Middx (Radlett) 2019 (RLC). LO BB 4-60 v Northants (Northampton) 2014 (RLC). T20 HS 109*. T20 BB 2-27.

WHEATER, Adam Jack Aubrey (Millfield S), b Whipps Cross 13 Feb 1990. 5'6". RHB, WK. Squad No 31. Debut (Essex) 2008. Cambridge MCCU 2010. Matabeleland Tuskers 2010-11 to 2012-13. Badureliya Sports Club 2011-12. Northern Districts 2012-13. Hampshire 2013-16; cap 2016. HS 204* H v Warwks (Birmingham) 2016. Ex HS 164 v Northants (Chelmsford) 2011, sharing Ex record 6th wkt partnership of 253 with J.S.Foster. BB 1-86 v Leics (Leicester) 2012 – in contrived circumstances. LO HS 135 v Essex (Chelmsford) 2014 (RLC). T20 HS 78.

NQZAMPA, Adam, b Shellharbour, NSW, Australia 31 Mar 1992. RHB, LB. Squad No 88. New South Wales 2012-13. S Australia 2013-14 to date. Essex debut 2018 (T20 only). IPL: RPS 2016-17. Big Bash: ST 2012-13. AS 2013-14 to 2014-15. MS 2015-16 to date. **LOI** (A): 54 (2015-16 to 2019-20); HS 22 v SA (Adelaide) 2018-19; BB 4-43 v P (Abu Dhabi) 2018-19. **IT20** (A): 30 (2015-16 to 2019-20); HS 9 v P (Dubai, DSC) 2018-19; BB 3-14 v SL (Adelaide) 2019-20. HS 74 SA v WA (Adelaide) 2014-15. BB 6-62 (10-119 match) SA v Q (Adelaide) 2016-17. LO HS 66 SA v Q (N Sydney) 2013-14. LO BB 4-18 SA v WA (Brisbane) 2014-15. T20 HS 17*. T20 BB 6-19.

RELEASED/RETIRED continued on p 123

ESSEX 2019

RESULTS SUMMARY

	Place	Won	Lost	Drew	Tied	NR
Specsavers County Champ (1st Division)	**1st**	9	1	4		
All First-Class Matches		10	1	4		
Royal London One-Day Cup (South Group)	8th	2	6			
Vitality Blast (South Group)	Winners	8	4		1	4

SPECSAVERS COUNTY CHAMPIONSHIP AVERAGES
BATTING AND FIELDING

Cap		M	I	NO	HS	Runs	Avge	100	50	Ct/St
2005	A.N.Cook	14	24	4	125	913	45.65	1	7	15
2005	R.S.Bopara	10	14	1	135	514	39.53	2	2	9
2017	D.W.Lawrence	14	22	3	147	725	38.15	1	5	9
2013	T.Westley	14	23	1	141	794	36.09	1	3	11
	P.M.Siddle	8	11	4	60	227	32.42	–	1	2
2015	N.L.J.Browne	14	23	1	163	604	27.45	1	2	11
2006	R.N.ten Doeschate	14	19	1	130	483	26.83	2	1	8
	A.P.Beard	7	9	4	41	112	22.40	–	–	3
2018	S.R.Harmer	14	19	2	62	340	20.00	–	2	15
	R.K.Patel	4	5	–	35	87	17.40	–	–	1
	A.J.A.Wheater	10	12	1	30*	177	16.09	–	–	26/3
	M.R.Quinn	3	5	2	10	23	7.66	–	–	–
	S.J.Cook	9	10	2	37*	54	6.75	–	–	2
2015	J.A.Porter	13	15	5	17	31	3.10	–	–	3

Also batted: W.E.L.Buttleman (1 match) 0 (3 ct); Mohammad Amir (1) 28, 4*; A.S.S.Nijjar (1) 2; M.S.Pepper (1) 1, 7 (6 ct); R.G.White (2) 39, 2 (4 ct, 2 st).

BOWLING

	O	M	R	W	Avge	Best	5wI	10wM
S.R.Harmer	595.5	175	1518	83	18.28	8- 98	10	2
P.M.Siddle	263.4	72	683	34	20.08	6-104	2	–
S.J.Cook	235.5	61	673	32	21.03	7- 23	3	1
A.P.Beard	114	18	406	17	23.88	4- 23	–	–
J.A.Porter	391.2	83	1234	48	25.70	5- 51	2	–
Also bowled:								
Mohammad Amir	30	8	64	6	10.66	4- 48	–	–
R.S.Bopara	69	12	222	6	37.00	2- 54	–	–
M.R.Quinn	89	12	327	5	65.40	3-104	–	–

D.W.Lawrence 23-4-52-0; A.S.S.Nijjar 4.4-0-18-1; R.N.ten Doeschate 7-0-21-0; T.Westley 15-2-58-0.

The First-Class Averages (pp 226–241) give the records of Essex players in all first-class county matches (Essex's other opponents being Cambridge MCCU), with the exception of R.K.Patel, P.M.Siddle and R.G.White, whose first-class figures for Essex are as above, and: J.A.Porter 14-15-5-17-31-3.10-0-0-3ct. 415.1-90-1294-51-25.37-5/51-2-0.

ESSEX RECORDS

FIRST-CLASS CRICKET

Highest Total	For	761-6d		v	Leics	Chelmsford	1990
	V	803-4d		by	Kent	Brentwood	1934
Lowest Total	For	20		v	Lancashire	Chelmsford	2013
	V	14		by	Surrey	Chelmsford	1983
Highest Innings	For	343*	P.A.Perrin	v	Derbyshire	Chesterfield	1904
	V	332	W.H.Ashdown	for	Kent	Brentwood	1934

Highest Partnership for each Wicket

1st	373	N.L.J.Browne/A.N.Cook	v	Middlesex	Chelmsford	2017
2nd	403	G.A.Gooch/P.J.Prichard	v	Leics	Chelmsford	1990
3rd	347*	M.E.Waugh/N.Hussain	v	Lancashire	Ilford	1992
4th	314	Salim Malik/N.Hussain	v	Surrey	The Oval	1991
5th	339	J.C.Mickleburgh/J.S.Foster	v	Durham	Chester-le-St[2]	2010
6th	253	A.J.A.Wheater/J.S.Foster	v	Northants	Chelmsford	2011
7th	261	J.W.H.T.Douglas/J.Freeman	v	Lancashire	Leyton	1914
8th	263	D.R.Wilcox/R.M.Taylor	v	Warwicks	Southend	1946
9th	251	J.W.H.T.Douglas/S.N.Hare	v	Derbyshire	Leyton	1921
10th	218	F.H.Vigar/T.P.B.Smith	v	Derbyshire	Chesterfield	1947

Best Bowling	For	10- 32	H.Pickett	v	Leics	Leyton	1895
(Innings)	V	10- 40	E.G.Dennett	for	Glos	Bristol	1906
Best Bowling	For	17-119	W.Mead	v	Hampshire	Southampton[1]	1895
(Match)	V	17- 56	C.W.L.Parker	for	Glos	Gloucester	1925

Most Runs – Season	2559	G.A.Gooch	(av 67.34)		1984
Most Runs – Career	30701	G.A.Gooch	(av 51.77)		1973-97
Most 100s – Season	9	J.O'Connor			1929, 1934
	9	D.J.Insole			1955
Most 100s – Career	94	G.A.Gooch			1973-97
Most Wkts – Season	172	T.P.B Smith	(av 27.13)		1947
Most Wkts – Career	1610	T.P.B.Smith	(av 26.68)		1929-51
Most Career W-K Dismissals	1231	B.Taylor	(1040 ct; 191 st)		1949-73
Most Career Catches in the Field	519	K.W.R.Fletcher			1962-88

LIMITED-OVERS CRICKET

Highest Total	50ov	391-5		v	Surrey	The Oval	2008
	40ov	368-7		v	Scotland	Chelmsford	2013
	T20	242-3		v	Sussex	Chelmsford	2008
Lowest Total	50ov	57		v	Lancashire	Lord's	1996
	40ov	69		v	Derbyshire	Chesterfield	1974
	T20	74		v	Middlesex	Chelmsford	2013
Highest Innings	50ov	201*	R.S.Bopara	v	Leics	Leicester	2008
	40ov	180	R.N.ten Doeschate	v	Scotland	Chelmsford	2013
	T20	152*	G.R.Napier	v	Sussex	Chelmsford	2008
Best Bowling	50ov	5- 8	J.K.Lever	v	Middlesex	Westcliff	1972
		5- 8	G.A.Gooch	v	Cheshire	Chester	1995
	40ov	8-26	K.D.Boyce	v	Lancashire	Manchester	1971
	T20	6-16	T.G.Southee	v	Glamorgan	Chelmsford	2011

GLAMORGAN

GLAMORGAN

Formation of Present Club: 6 July 1888
Inaugural First-Class Match: 1921
Colours: Blue and Gold
Badge: Gold Daffodil
County Champions: (3) 1948, 1969, 1997
Pro 40/National League (Div 1) Winners: (2) 2002, 2004
Sunday League Winners: (1) 1993
Twenty20 Cup Winners: (0); best – Semi-Finalist 2004, 2017

Chief Executive: Hugh Morris, Sophia Gardens, Cardiff, CF11 9XR • Tel: 02920 409380 • email: info@glamorgancricket.co.uk • Web: www.glamorgancricket.com • Twitter: @GlamCricket (70,217 followers)

Director of Cricket: Mark Wallace. **Head Coach**: Matthew Maynard. **2nd XI Coach**: Steve Watkin. **Player Development Manager**: Richard Almond. **Captain**: C.B.Cooke (f-c and T20) and D.L.Lloyd (l-o). **Overseas Player**: M.Labuschagne. **2020 Testimonial**: M.G.Hogan. **Head Groundsman**: Robin Saxton. **Scorer**: Andrew K.Hignell. ‡ New registration. NQ Not qualified for England.

BROWN, Connor Rhys (Y Pant CS; Cardiff U), b Caerphilly 28 Apr 1997. RHB, OB. Squad No 28. Cardiff MCCU 2017. Glamorgan debut 2017. Glamorgan 2nd XI debut 2014. Wales MC 2014 to date. HS 35 v Glos (Cardiff) 2017. BB – . LO HS 98 v Surrey (Oval) 2018 (RLC).

BULL, Kieran Andrew (Q Elizabeth HS, Haverfordwest; Cardiff Met U), b Haverfordwest 5 Apr 1995. 6'2". RHB, OB. Squad No 11. Debut (Glamorgan) 2014. Cardiff MCCU 2015. Wales MC 2012-13. HS 31 v Glos (Swansea) 2015. BB 4-62 v Kent (Canterbury) 2014. LO HS – . LO BB 1-40 v Middx (Lord's) 2015 (RLC).

CAREY, Lukas John (Pontarddulais CS; Gower SFC), b Carmarthen 17 Jul 1997. 6'0". RHB, RFM. Squad No 17. Debut (Glamorgan) 2016. Glamorgan 2nd XI debut 2014. Wales MC 2016. HS 62* v Derbys (Swansea) 2019. BB 4-54 v Middx (Cardiff) 2019. LO HS 39 v Somerset (Cardiff) 2019 (RLC). LO BB 2-57 v Somerset (Taunton) 2018 (RLC). T20 HS 5. T20 BB 1-15.

CARLSON, Kiran Shah (Whitchurch HS; Cardiff U), b Cardiff 16 May 1998. 5'8". RHB, OB. Squad No 5. Debut (Glamorgan) 2016. Cardiff MCCU 2019. Glamorgan 2nd XI debut 2015. Wales MC 2014. HS 191 v Glos (Cardiff) 2017. BB 5-28 v Northants (Northampton) 2016 – on debut. Youngest ever to score a century & take five wkts in an innings in a f-c career, aged 18y 119d. LO HS 63 v Somerset (Cardiff) 2017 (RLC). LO BB 1-30 v Middx (Radlett) 2017 (RLC). T20 HS 58.

COOKE, Christopher Barry (Bishops S, Cape Town; U of Cape Town), b Johannesburg, South Africa 30 May 1986. 5'11". RHB, WK. Squad No 46. W Province 2009-10. Glamorgan debut 2013; cap 2016; captain 2019 to date. HS 171 v Kent (Canterbury) 2014. LO HS 161 v Glos (Bristol) 2019 (RLC). T20 HS 65*.

CULLEN, Thomas Nicholas (Aquinas C, Stockport; Cardiff Met U), b Perth, Australia 4 Jan 1992. RHB, WK. Squad No 54. Cardiff MCCU 2015-17. Glamorgan debut 2017. HS 63 v Northants (Northampton) 2019.

NQDe LANGE, Marchant, b Tzaneen, South Africa 13 Oct 1990. RHB, RF. Squad No 90. Easterns 2010-11 to 2015-16. Titans 2010-11 to 2015-16. Knights 2016-17 to 2018-19. Free State 2016-17. Glamorgan debut 2017; cap 2019. IPL: KKR 2012. MI 2014-15. Not overseas due to wife's UK passport. **Tests** (SA): 2 (2011-12); HS 9 and BB 7-81 v SL (Durban) 2011-12 – on debut. **LOI** (SA): 4 (2011-12 to 2015-16); HS – ; BB 4-46 v NZ (Auckland) 2011-12. **IT20** (SA): 6 (2011-12 to 2015-16); HS – ; BB 2-26 v WI (Durban) 2014-15. F-c Tours (SA): A 2014 (SA A); NZ 2011-12. HS 90 v Leics (Leicester) 2018. BB 7-23 Knights v Titans (Centurion) 2016-17. Gm BB 5-62 v Glos (Bristol) 2018. LO HS 58* v Surrey (Cardiff) 2019 (RLC). LO BB 5-49 v Hants (Southampton) 2017 (RLC). T20 HS 27*. T20 BB 4-23.

DOUTHWAITE, Daniel Alexander (Reed's S, Cobham), b Kingston-upon-Thames, Surrey 8 Feb 1997. RHB, RMF. Squad No 88. Cardiff MCCU 2019. Glamorgan debut 2019. Warwickshire 2018 (l-o only). Surrey 2nd XI 2015-16. Sussex 2nd XI 2016. HS 100* Cardiff MCCU v Sussex (Hove) 2019. Gm HS 63 v Sussex (Hove) 2019. BB 4-48 v Derbys (Derby) 2019. LO HS 52* v Sussex (Hove) 2019 (RLC). LO BB 3-43 Wa v West Indies A (Birmingham) 2018. T20 HS 24. T20 BB 1-7.

HEMPHREY, Charles Richard (Harvey GS, Folkestone), b Doncaster, Yorks 31 Aug 1990. RHB, OB. Squad No 22. Queensland 2014-15 to date. Glamorgan debut 2019. HS 118 Q v SA (Brisbane) 2014-15. Gm HS 75 v Derbys (Derby) 2019. BB 2-56 Q v SA (Adelaide) 2015-16. Gm BB 1-17 v Middx (Cardiff) 2019. LO HS 87 v Middx (Lord's) 2019 (RLC). LO BB 1-18 Q v Cricket Australia (Sydney, DO) 2015-16.

HOGAN, Michael Garry, b Newcastle, New South Wales, Australia 31 May 1981. British passport. 6'5". RHB, RFM. Squad No 31. W Australia 2009-10 to 2015-16. Glamorgan debut/cap 2013; captain 2018; testimonial 2020. Big Bash: HH 2011-12 to 2012-13. HS 57 v Lancs (Colwyn Bay) 2015. 50 wkts (3); most – 67 (2013). BB 7-92 v Glos (Bristol) 2013. LO HS 27 WA v Vic (Melbourne) 2011-12. LO BB 5-44 WA v Vic (Melbourne) 2010-11. T20 HS 17*. T20 BB 5-17.

NQINGRAM, Colin Alexander, b Port Elizabeth, South Africa 3 Jul 1985. LHB, LB. Squad No 41. Free State 2004-05 to 2005-06. Eastern Province 2005-06 to 2008-09. Warriors 2006-07 to 2016-17. Somerset 2014. Glamorgan debut 2015 (Kolpak signing); cap 2017; captain 2018-19 (T20 only). IPL: DD 2011. Big Bash: AS 2017-18 to 2018-19. **LOI** (SA): 31 (2010-11 to 2013-14); HS 124 v Z (Bloemfontein) 2010-11 – on debut; BB – . **IT20** (SA): 9 (2010-11 to 2011-12); HS 78 v I (Johannesburg) 2011-12. HS 190 EP v KZN (Port Elizabeth) 2008-09. Gm HS 155* v Notts (Cardiff) 2017. BB 4-16 EP v Boland (Port Elizabeth) 2005-06. Gm BB 3-49 v Essex (Chelmsford) 2015. LO HS 142 v Essex (Cardiff) 2017 (RLC). LO BB 4-39 v Middx (Radlett) 2017 (RLC). T20 HS 127*. T20 BB 4-32.

NQLABUSCHAGNE, Marnus, b Klerksdorp, South Africa 22 Jun 1994. RHB, LB/RM. Squad No 99. Queensland 2014-15 to date. Glamorgan 2019; cap 2019. Big Bash: BH 2016-17 to date. **Tests** (A): 14 (2018-19 to 2019-20); 1000 runs (1): 1104 (2019); HS 215 v NZ (Sydney) 2019-20; BB 3-45 v P (Abu Dhabi) 2018-19. **LOI** (A): 6 (2019-20); HS 108 v SA (Potchefstroom) 2019-20; BB – . F-c Tours (A): E 2019; I 2018-19 (Aus A); UAE 2018-19 (v P). 1000 runs (1+1); most – 1530 (2019). HS 215 (see Tests). Gm HS 182 v Sussex (Hove) 2019, sharing Gm record 2nd wkt partnership of 291 with N.J.Selman. BB 3-45 (see Tests). Gm BB 3-52 v Middx (Radlett) 2019. LO HS 135 Q v SA (Brisbane) 2019-20. LO BB 3-46 v Somerset (Cardiff) 2019 (RLC). T20 HS 28. T20 BB 1-25.

LLOYD, David Liam (Darland HS; Shrewsbury S), b St Asaph, Denbighs 15 May 1992. 5'9". RHB, RM. Squad No 73. Debut (Glamorgan) 2012; cap 2019; captain 2020 (50 ov only). Wales MC 2010-11. HS 119 v Glos (Bristol) 2018. BB 3-36 v Northants (Swansea) 2016. LO HS 92 v Middx (Cardiff) 2018 (RLC). LO BB 5-53 v Kent (Swansea) 2017 (RLC). T20 HS 97*. T20 BB 2-13.

McILROY, Jamie Peter (Builth Wells HS), b Hereford 19 Jun 1994. RHB, LFM. Squad No 35. Glamorgan 2nd XI debut 2017. MCC YC 2018-19. Worcestershire 2nd XI 2018. Gloucestershire 2nd XI 2018. Herefordshire 2014-18. Awaiting 1st XI debut.

MESCHEDE, Craig Anthony Joseph (King's C, Taunton), b Johannesburg, South Africa 21 Nov 1991. 6'1''. RHB, RMF. Squad No 44. Somerset 2011-14. Glamorgan debut 2015. **IT20** (Germ): 5 (2019); HS 67 v Denmark (Castel) 2019; BB 2-11 v Norway (St Peter Port) 2019. HS 107 v Northants (Cardiff) 2015. BB 5-84 v Essex (Chelmsford) 2016. LO HS 45 v Hants (Swansea) 2016 (RLC). LO BB 4-5 Sm v Leics (Taunton) 2013 (Y40). T20 HS 77*. T20 BB 3-9.

MORGAN, Alan Owen (Ysgol Gyfun yr Strade, Llanelli; Cardiff U), b Swansea 14 Apr 1994. 5'11''. RHB, SLA. Squad No 29. Cardiff MCCU 2014. Glamorgan debut 2016. Wales MC 2012-16. HS 103* v Worcs (Worcester) 2016. BB 2-37 v Northants (Northampton) 2016. LO HS 29 and LO BB 2-49 v Pakistan A (Newport) 2016. T20 HS 11. T20 BB – .

ROOT, William ('Billy') Thomas (Worksop C; Leeds Beckett U), b Sheffield, Yorks 5 Aug 1992. Younger brother of J.E.Root (*see YORKSHIRE*). LHB, OB. Squad No 66. Leeds/Bradford MCCU 2015-16. Nottinghamshire 2015-18. Glamorgan debut 2019. Suffolk 2014. HS 229 v Northants (Northampton) 2019. BB 3-29 Nt v Sussex (Hove) 2017. Gm BB 2-63 v Northants (Cardiff) 2019. LO HS 113* v Surrey (Cardiff) 2019 (RLC). LO BB 2-36 v Middx (Lord's) 2019 (RLC). T20 HS 40. T20 BB – .

SALTER, Andrew Graham (Milford Haven SFC; Cardiff Met U), b Haverfordwest 1 Jun 1993. 5'9''. RHB, OB. Squad No 21. Cardiff MCCU 2012-14. Glamorgan debut 2013. Wales MC 2010-11. HS 88 v Glos (Cardiff) 2017. BB 4-80 v Warwks (Birmingham) 2018. LO HS 51 v Pakistan A (Newport) 2016. LO BB 2-41 v Notts (Nottingham) 2012 (CB40) and 2-41 v Notts (Lord's) 2013 (Y40). T20 HS 39*. T20 BB 4-12.

SELMAN, Nicholas James (Matthew Flinders Anglican C, Buderim), b Brisbane, Australia 18 Oct 1995. 6'4''. RHB, RM. Squad No 9. Debut (Glamorgan) 2016. Kent 2nd XI debut 2014. Gloucestershire 2nd XI 2015. HS 150 v Glos (Newport) 2019. BB 1-22 v Northants (Cardiff) 2019. LO HS 92 v Kent (Canterbury) 2018 (RLC). T20 HS 66.

SISODIYA, Prem (Clifton C; Cardiff Met U), b Cardiff 21 Sep 1998. RHB, SLA. Squad No 32. Debut (Glamorgan) 2018. Cardiff MCCU 2019. Wales MC 2017. HS 38 and CC BB 3-54 v Derbys (Swansea) 2018. BB 4-79 CfU v Somerset (Taunton) 2019. T20 BB 1-45.

NQSMITH, Ruaidhri Alexander James (Llandaff Cathedral S; Shrewsbury S; Bristol U), b Glasgow, Scotland 5 Aug 1994. 6'1''. RHB, RM. Squad No 20. Debut (Glamorgan) 2013. Scotland 2017. **LOI** (Scot): 2 (2016); HS 10 and BB 1-34 v Afg (Edinburgh) 2016. **IT20** (Scot): 2 (2018-19); HS 9* v Netherlands (Al Amerat) 2018-19; BB – . HS 57* v Glos (Bristol) 2014. BB 5-87 v Durham (Cardiff) 2018. LO HS 14 v Hants (Swansea) 2018 (RLC). LO BB 4-7 v Oman (Al Amerat) 2018-19. T20 HS 22*. T20 BB 4-6.

TAYLOR, Callum Zinzan (The Southport S), b Newport, Monmouths 19 Jun 1998. RHB, OB. Squad No 42. Glamorgan 2nd XI debut 2017. Wales MC 2017. Awaiting f-c debut. T20 HS 16*. T20 BB – .

NQvan der GUGTEN, Timm, b Hornsby, Sydney, Australia 25 Feb 1991. 6'1½''. RHB, RFM. Squad No 64. New South Wales 2011-12. Netherlands 2012 to date. Glamorgan debut 2016; cap 2018. Big Bash: HH 2014-15. **LOI** (Neth): 4 (2011-12 to 2013); HS 2 (twice); BB 5-24 v Canada (King City, NW) 2013. **IT20** (Neth): 39 (2011-12 to 2019-20); HS 40* v PNG (Dubai, ICCA) 2019-20; BB 3-9 v Singapore (Dubai, ICCA) 2019-20. HS 60* v Glos (Cardiff) 2018. 50 wkts (1): 56 (2016). BB 7-42 v Kent (Cardiff) 2018. LO HS 36 Neth v Nepal (Amstelveen) 2016; LO BB 5-24 (*see LOI*). T20 HS 40*. T20 BB 5-21.

WAGG, Graham Grant (Ashlawn S, Rugby), b Rugby, Warwks 28 Apr 1983. 6'0". RHB, LM. Squad No 8. Warwickshire 2002-04. Derbyshire 2006-10; cap 2007. Glamorgan debut 2011; cap 2013; testimonial 2019. F-c Tour (Eng A): 1 2003-04. HS 200 v Surrey (Guildford) 2015. 50 wkts (2); most – 59 (2008). BB 6-29 v Surrey (Oval) 2014. LO HS 68 v Hants (Southampton) 2019 (RLC). LO BB 4-35 De v Durham (Derby) 2008 (FPT). T20 HS 62. T20 BB 5-14 v Worcs (Worcester) 2013 – Gm record.

WALKER, Roman Isaac (Ysgol Bryn Alyn), b Wrexham 6 Aug 2000. RHB, RFM. Squad No 37. Glamorgan 2nd XI debut 2016. Wales MC 2018. Awaiting f-c debut. LO HS 7* v Sussex (Hove) 2019 (RLC). T20 HS 1. T20 BB 3-39.

RELEASED/RETIRED

(Having made a County 1st XI appearance in 2019)

NQ**BRATHWAITE, Kraigg** Clairmonte (Combermere S), b Belfield, St Michael, Barbados 1 Dec 1992. RHB, OB. Barbados 2008-09 to date. Yorkshire 2017. Nottinghamshire 2018; cap 2018. Glamorgan 2019. **Tests** (WI): 59 (2011 to 2019-20); HS 212 v B (Kingstown) 2014; BB 6-29 v SL (Colombo, PSS) 2015-16. **LOI** (WI): 10 (2016-17); HS 78 v Z (Bulawayo) 2016-17; BB 1-56 v SL (Bulawayo) 2016-17. F-c Tours (WI): E 2010 (WI A), 2017; A 2015-16; SA 2014-15; NZ 2013-14, 2017-18; I 2011-12, 2013-14 (WI A), 2018-19, 2019-20 (v Afg); SL 2014-15 (WI A), 2015-16; Z 2017-18; B 2011-12, 2018-19; UAE (v P) 2016-17. HS 212 (see Tests). CC HS 103* v Leics (Cardiff) 2019. BB 6-29 (see Tests). LO HS 108 Bar v ICC Americas (Lucas Street) 2016-17. LO BB 2-54 WI A v Sri Lanka A (Dambulla) 2014-15.

NQ**FAKHAR ZAMAN**, b Mardan, NWFP, Pakistan 10 Apr 1990. LHB, SLA. Karachi Blues 2012-13 to 2013-14. Habib Bank 2014-15 to 2017-18. Khyber Pakhtunkhwa 2019-20. Glamorgan 2019 (T20 only). **Tests** (P): 3 (2018-19); HS 94 v A (Abu Dhabi) 2018-19. **LOI** (P): 46 (2017 to 2019-20); HS 210* v Z (Bulawayo) 2018 – P record; BB 1-19 v NZ (Wellington) 2017-18. **IT20** (P): 34 (2016-17 to 2019-20); HS 91 v A (Harare) 2018; BB – . F-c Tours (P): E 2016 (PA); SA 2018-19; Z 2016-17; UAE (v A) 2018-19. HS 205 HB v Fed Admin Tribal Areas (Sialkot) 2015-16. BB 2-2 KP v Baluchistan (Karachi) 2019-20. LO HS 210* (see LOI). LO BB 5-27 PA v EL (Dubai) 2015-16. T20 HS 100*. T20 BB 1-3.

LAWLOR, Jeremy Lloyd (Monmouth S; Cardiff Met U), b Cardiff 4 Nov 1995. Son of P.J.Lawlor (Glamorgan 1981). 6'0". RHB, RM. Cardiff MCCU 2015-17. Glamorgan 2015-19. Wales MC 2013. HS 81 CfU v Hants (Southampton) 2016. Gm HS 25 v Derbys (Derby) 2019. BB 3-59 v Sussex (Hove) 2018. LO HS 48 v Sussex (Hove) 2019 (RLC). T20 HS 43.

NQ**MARSH, Shaun** Edward, b Narrogin, WA, Australia 9 Jul 1983. Son of G.R.Marsh (WA and Australia 1977-78 to 1993-94) and elder brother of M.R.Marsh (see MIDDLESEX). 6'0". LHB, SLA. Western Australia 2000-01 to date. Yorkshire 2017. Glamorgan 2018-19. IPL: KXIP 2007-08 to 2017. Big Bash: PS 2011-12 to 2018-19. MR 2019-20. **Tests** (A): 38 (2011 to 2018-19); HS 182 v WI (Hobart) 2015-16. **LOI** (A): 73 (2008 to 2019); HS 151 v Scotland (Edinburgh) 2013. **IT20** (A): 15 (2008 to 2015-16); HS 47* v SL (Melbourne) 2012-13. F-c Tours (A): E 2015; SA 2011-12, 2013 (Aus A), 2013-14, 2017-18; I 2016-17; SL 2011, 2016; UAE 2018-19 (v P). HS 214 WA v Vic (Perth) 2019-20. CC HS 125* Y v Surrey (Oval) 2017. Gm HS 111 v Glos (Bristol) 2018. BB 2-20 WA v NSW (Sydney) 2003-04. LO HS 186 WA v Cricket Australia (Sydney) 2015-16. LO BB 1-14 WA v Vic (Perth) 2002-03. T20 HS 115. T20 BB – .

J.R.Murphy and K.B.Szymanski left the staff without making a County 1st XI appearance in 2019.

GLAMORGAN 2019

RESULTS SUMMARY

	Place	Won	Lost	Drew	Tied	NR
Specsavers County Champ (2nd Division)	4th	4	3	7		
All First-Class Matches		4	3	7		
Royal London One-Day Cup (South Group)	6th	3	4			1
Vitality Blast (South Group)	9th	1	8		1	4

SPECSAVERS COUNTY CHAMPIONSHIP AVERAGES

BATTING AND FIELDING

Cap		M	I	NO	HS	Runs	Avge	100	50	Ct/St
2019	M.Labuschagne	10	18	1	182	1114	65.52	5	5	12
	K.C.Brathwaite	3	4	1	103*	166	55.33	1	–	2
2016	C.B.Cooke	7	10	2	96	368	46.00	–	2	18/2
	T.van der Gugten	8	10	7	30*	135	45.00	–	–	2
	W.T.Root	14	22	1	229	768	36.57	2	1	4
	T.N.Cullen	9	12	3	63	319	35.44	–	4	29
	N.J.Selman	14	24	2	150	752	34.18	1	6	10
	K.S.Carlson	3	4	–	111	130	32.50	1	–	2
2013	G.G.Wagg	10	16	3	100	418	32.15	1	1	2
	C.R.Hemphrey	10	18	1	75	546	32.11	–	5	7
	S.R.Patel	4	6	–	66	187	31.16	–	2	1
2019	D.L.Lloyd	14	23	1	97	668	30.36	–	4	16
2013	M.G.Hogan	11	12	6	54	166	27.66	–	1	3
	L.J.Carey	9	12	3	62*	230	25.55	–	2	–
	D.A.Douthwaite	7	12	–	63	298	24.83	–	1	1
	J.L.Lawlor	2	4	–	25	74	18.50	–	–	3
	A.O.Morgan	4	6	1	43	82	16.40	–	–	1
2019	M.de Lange	8	10	1	45*	127	14.11	–	–	2
	R.A.J.Smith	3	5	–	18	35	7.00	–	–	–

Also batted: K.A.Bull (1 match) 2, 5 (1 ct); S.E.Marsh (1) 8, 9 (1 ct); A.G.Salter (2) 0, 26, 21.

BOWLING

	O	M	R	W	Avge	Best	5wI	10wM
M.G.Hogan	349	85	974	46	21.17	5-62	1	–
S.R.Patel	122.1	40	292	12	24.33	4-58	–	–
D.A.Douthwaite	132.1	10	612	17	36.00	4-48	–	–
M.de Lange	244.4	33	950	26	36.53	4-64	–	–
M.Labuschagne	192.2	16	724	19	38.10	3-52	–	–
L.J.Carey	242.3	50	766	19	40.31	4-54	–	–
D.L.Lloyd	128.1	22	437	10	43.70	2-35	–	–
G.G.Wagg	236	35	789	17	46.41	3-59	–	–
T.van der Gugten	198	26	705	15	47.00	3-44	–	–

Also bowled:

	O	M	R	W	Avge	Best
R.A.J.Smith	67	11	224	7	32.00	3-43

K.A.Bull 36-6-100-2; K.S.Carlson 15-2-52-0; C.R.Hemphrey 43-4-163-2; J.L.Lawlor 6-1-15-0; A.O.Morgan 31-2-108-0; W.T.Root 19-4-69-2; A.G.Salter 45-12-103-4 N.J.Selman 3.3-0-22-1.

Glamorgan played no first-class fixtures outside the County Championship in 2019. The First-Class Averages (pp 226–241) give the records of Glamorgan players in all first-class county matches, with the exception of K.S.Carlson, D.A.Douthwaite, M.Labuschagne and S.R.Patel, whose first-class figures for Glamorgan are as above.

GLAMORGAN RECORDS

FIRST-CLASS CRICKET

Highest Total	For 718-3d		v	Sussex	Colwyn Bay	2000
	V 750		by	Northants	Cardiff	2019
Lowest Total	For 22		v	Lancashire	Liverpool	1924
	V 33		by	Leics	Ebbw Vale	1965
Highest Innings	For 309*	S.P.James	v	Sussex	Colwyn Bay	2000
	V 322*	M.B.Loye	for	Northants	Northampton	1998

Highest Partnership for each Wicket

1st	374	M.T.G.Elliott/S.P.James	v	Sussex	Colwyn Bay	2000
2nd	291	N.J.Selman/M.Labuschagne	v	Sussex	Hove	2019
3rd	313	D.E.Davies/W.E.Jones	v	Essex	Brentwood	1948
4th	425*	A.Dale/I.V.A.Richards	v	Middlesex	Cardiff	1993
5th	264	M.Robinson/S.W.Montgomery	v	Hampshire	Bournemouth	1949
6th	240	J.Allenby/M.A.Wallace	v	Surrey	The Oval	2009
7th	211	P.A.Cottey/O.D.Gibson	v	Leics	Swansea	1996
8th	202	D.Davies/J.J.Hills	v	Sussex	Eastbourne	1928
9th	203*	J.J.Hills/J.C.Clay	v	Worcs	Swansea	1929
10th	143	T.Davies/S.A.B.Daniels	v	Glos	Swansea	1982

Best Bowling	For 10- 51	J.Mercer	v	Worcs	Worcester	1936
(Innings)	V 10- 18	G.Geary	for	Leics	Pontypridd	1929
Best Bowling	For 17-212	J.C.Clay	v	Worcs	Swansea	1937
(Match)	V 16- 96	G.Geary	for	Leics	Pontypridd	1929

Most Runs – Season	2276	H.Morris	(av 55.51)		1990
Most Runs – Career	34056	A.Jones	(av 33.03)		1957-83
Most 100s – Season	10	H.Morris			1990
Most 100s – Career	54	M.P.Maynard			1985-2005
Most Wkts – Season	176	J.C.Clay	(av 17.34)		1937
Most Wkts – Career	2174	D.J.Shepherd	(av 20.95)		1950-72
Most Career W-K Dismissals	933	E.W.Jones	(840 ct; 93 st)		1961-83
Most Career Catches in the Field	656	P.M.Walker			1956-72

LIMITED-OVERS CRICKET

Highest Total	50ov	429	v	Surrey	The Oval	2002
	40ov	328-4	v	Lancashire	Colwyn Bay	2011
	T20	240-3	v	Surrey	The Oval	2015
Lowest Total	50ov	68	v	Lancashire	Manchester	1973
	40ov	42	v	Derbyshire	Swansea	1979
	T20	44	v	Surrey	The Oval	2019
Highest Innings	50ov	169*	J.A.Rudolph	v	Sussex	Hove	2014
	40ov	155*	J.H.Kallis	v	Surrey	Pontypridd	1999
	T20	116*	I.J.Thomas	v	Somerset	Taunton	2004
Best Bowling	50ov	6-20	S.D.Thomas	v	Comb Univs	Cardiff	1995
	40ov	7-16	S.D.Thomas	v	Surrey	Swansea	1998
	T20	5-14	G.G.Wagg	v	Worcs	Worcester	2013

GLOUCESTERSHIRE

Formation of Present Club: 1871
Inaugural First-Class Match: 1870
Colours: Blue, Gold, Brown, Silver, Green and Red
Badge: Coat of Arms of the City and County of Bristol
County Champions (since 1890): (0); best – 2nd 1930, 1931, 1947, 1959, 1969, 1986
Gillette/NatWest/C&G Trophy Winners: (5) 1973, 1999, 2000, 2003, 2004
Benson and Hedges Cup Winners: (3) 1977, 1999, 2000
Pro 40/National League (Div 1) Winners: (1) 2000
Royal London One-Day Cup Winners: (1) 2015
Twenty20 Cup Winners: (0); best – Finalist 2007

Chief Executive: Will Brown, Bristol County Ground, Nevil Road, Bristol BS7 9EJ • Tel: 0117 910 8000 • Email: info@gloscricket.co.uk • Web: www.gloscricket.co.uk • Twitter: @Gloscricket (62,732 followers)

Head Coach: Richard Dawson. **Asst Head Coach**: Ian Harvey. **Captain**: C.D.J.Dent. **Vice-Captain**: J.M.R.Taylor. **Overseas Players**: C.A.Pujara and Qais Ahmad. **2020 Testimonial**: None. **Head Groundsman**: Sean Williams. **Scorer**: Adrian Bull. ‡ New registration. NQ Not qualified for England.

Gloucestershire revised their capping policy in 2004 and now award players with their County Caps when they make their first-class debut.

BRACEY, James Robert (Filton CS), b Bristol 3 May 1997. Younger brother of S.N.Bracey (Cardiff MCCU 2014-15). 6'1". LHB, WK, occ RM. Squad No 25. Debut (Gloucestershire) 2016; cap 2016. Loughborough MCCU 2017-18. Gloucestershire 2nd XI debut 2015. F-c Tour (EL): A 2019-20. HS 156 v Glamorgan (Cardiff) 2017. BB – . LO HS 113* and LO BB 1-23 v Essex (Chelmsford) 2019 (RLC). T20 HS 64.

CHARLESWORTH, Ben Geoffrey (St Edward's S), b Oxford 19 Nov 2000. Son of G.M.Charlesworth (Griqualand W and Cambridge U 1989-90 to 1993). 6'2½". LHB, RM/OB. Squad No 64. Debut (Gloucestershire) 2018; cap 2018. Gloucestershire 2nd XI debut 2016. Oxfordshire 2016. England U19 2018 to 2018-19. HS 77* and BB 3-25 v Middx (Bristol) 2018. HS 77* v Northants (Bristol) 2019. LO HS 14 v Australia A (Bristol) 2019.

COCKBAIN, Ian Andrew (Maghull HS), b Bootle, Liverpool 17 Feb 1987. Son of I.Cockbain (Lancs and Minor Cos 1979-94). 6'0". RHB, RM. Squad No 28. Debut (Gloucestershire) 2011; cap 2011; testimonial 2019. MCC YC 2008-10. HS 151* v Surrey (Bristol) 2014. BB 1-23 v Durham MCCU (Bristol) 2016. LO HS 108* v Middx (Lord's) 2017 (RLC). T20 HS 123.

DENT, Christopher David James (Backwell CS; Alton C), b Bristol 20 Jan 1991. 5'9". LHB, WK, occ SLA. Squad No 15. Debut (Gloucestershire) 2010; cap 2010; captain 2018 to date. 1000 runs (4); most – 1336 (2016). HS 268 v Glamorgan (Bristol) 2015. BB 2-21 v Sussex (Hove) 2016. LO HS 151* v Glamorgan (Cardiff) 2013 (Y40). LO BB 4-43 v Leics (Bristol) 2012 (CB40). T20 HS 63*. T20 BB 1-4.

DRISSELL, George Samuel (Bedminster Down SS; Filton C), b Bristol 20 Jan 1999. 6'1½". RHB, OB. Squad No 20. Debut (Gloucestershire) 2017; cap 2017. Gloucestershire 2nd XI debut 2016. HS 19 v Warwks (Birmingham) 2018. BB 4-83 v Glamorgan (Newport) 2019. LO HS 0 and LO BB – v Middx (Bristol) 2018 (RLC).

GOODMAN, Dominic Charles (Dr Challoner's GS), b Ashford, Kent 23 Oct 2000. RHB, RM. Gloucestershire 2nd XI debut 2019. Awaiting 1st XI debut.

HAMMOND, Miles Arthur Halhead (St Edward's S, Oxford), b Cheltenham 11 Jan 1996. 5'11". LHB, OB. Squad No 88. Debut (Gloucestershire) 2013; cap 2013. England U19 2012-13. Gloucestershire 2nd XI debut 2010, aged 14y 120d. F-c Tour (MCC): Nepal 2019-20. HS 123* v Middx (Bristol) 2018. BB 1-29 MCC v Nepal (Kirtipur) 2019-20. Gs BB 1-96 v Glamorgan (Bristol) 2013. LO HS 95 v Sussex (Eastbourne) 2019 (RLC). LO BB 2-18 v Northants (Northampton) 2015 (RLC). T20 HS 63. T20 BB – .

HANKINS, George Thomas (Millfield S), b Bath, Somerset 4 Jan 1997. Elder brother of H.J.Hankins (*see below*). 6'1½". RHB, OB. Squad No 21. Debut (Gloucestershire) 2016; cap 2016. Gloucestershire 2nd XI debut 2014. England U19 2016. HS 116 v Northants (Northampton) 2016. BB – . LO HS 92 v Kent (Beckenham) 2018 (RLC). T20 HS 14.

HANKINS, Harry John (Beechen Cliff S), b Bath, Somerset 24 Apr 1999. Younger brother of G.T.Hankins (*see above*). 6'2". RHB, RMF. Debut (Gloucestershire) 2019; cap 2019. Gloucestershire 2nd XI debut 2018. HS 9 v Derbys (Bristol) 2019 – only 1st XI appearance.

HIGGINS, Ryan Francis (Bradfield C), b Harare, Zimbabwe 6 Jan 1995. 5'10". RHB, RM. Squad No 29. Middlesex 2017. Gloucestershire debut/cap 2018. HS 199 v Leics (Leicester) 2019. 50 wkts (1): 50 (2019). BB 5-21 v Sussex (Hove) 2018. LO HS 81* v Surrey (Oval) 2018 (RLC). LO BB 4-50 ECB XI v India A (Leeds) 2018. T20 HS 77*. T20 BB 5-13.

HOWELL, Benny Alexander Cameron (The Oratory S), b Bordeaux, France 5 Oct 1988. Son of J.B.Howell (Warwickshire 2nd XI 1978). 5'11". RHB, RM. Squad No 13. Hampshire 2011. Middlesex 2011. Gloucestershire debut/cap 2012. Berkshire 2007. HS 163 v Glamorgan (Cardiff) 2017. BB 5-57 v Leics (Leicester) 2013. LO HS 122 v Surrey (Croydon) 2011 (CB40). LO BB 3-37 v Yorks (Leeds) 2015 (RLC). T20 HS 57. T20 BB 5-18 v Glamorgan (Cheltenham) 2019 – Gs record.

PAYNE, David Alan (Lytchett Minster S), b Poole, Dorset, 15 Feb 1991. 6'2". RHB, LMF. Squad No 14. Debut (Gloucestershire) 2011; cap 2011. Dorset 2009. HS 67* v Glamorgan (Cardiff) 2016. BB 6-26 v Leics (Bristol) 2011. LO HS 36* v Glamorgan (Bristol) 2019 (RLC). LO BB 7-29 v Essex (Chelmsford) 2010 (CB40), inc 4 wkts in 4 balls and 6 wkts in 9 balls – Gs record. T20 HS 10. T20 BB 5-24.

PRICE, Oliver James (Magdalen Coll S), b Oxford 12 Jun 2001. Younger brother of T.J.Price (*see below*). RHB, OB. Gloucestershire 2nd XI debut 2018. Oxfordshire 2018-19. Awaiting 1st XI debut.

PRICE, Thomas James (Magdalen Coll S), b Oxford 2 Jan 2000. Elder brother of O.J.Price (*see above*). 6'1". RHB, RM. Gloucestershire 2nd XI debut 2015. Oxfordshire 2018-19. Awaiting f-c debut. LO HS 0. LO BB – . Only 1st XI appearance.

‡NOPUJARA, Cheteshwar Arvindbhai, b Rajkot, India 25 Jan 1988. 5'11". RHB, LB. Son of A.S.Pujara (Saurashtra 1976-77 to 1979-80), nephew of B.S.Pujara (Saurashtra 1983-84 to 1996-97). Saurashtra 2005-06 to date. Derbyshire 2014. Yorkshire 2015-18. Nottinghamshire 2017; cap 2017. IPL: KKR 2009-10. RCB 2011-13. KXIP 2014. **Tests** (I): 77 (2010-11 to 2019-20); 1000 runs (1): 1140 (2017); HS 206* v E (Ahmedabad) 2012-13. **LOI** (I): 5 (2013 to 2014); HS 27 v B (Dhaka) 2014. F-c Tours (I): E 2010 (I A), 2014, 2018; A 2006 (I A), 2014-15, 2018-19; SA 2010-11, 2013 (I A), 2013-14, 2017-18; WI 2012 (I A), 2016, 2019; NZ 2013-14, 2019-20; SL 2015, 2017; Z/Ken 2007-08 (I A). 1000 runs (0+3); most – 2064 (2016-17). HS 352 Saur v Karnataka (Rajkot) 2012-13. CC HS 133* Y v Hants (Leeds) 2015. BB 2-4 Saur v Rajasthan (Jaipur) 2007-08. LO HS 158* Ind B v India A (Rajkot) 2012-13. T20 HS 100*.

‡NOQAIS AHMAD Kamawal, b Nangarhar, Afghanistan 15 Aug 2000. RHB, LB. Squad No 32. Speen Ghar Region 2017-18 to 2018-19. Big Bash: HH 2018-19 to date. **Tests** (Afg): 1 (2019); HS 14 and BB 1-22 v B (Chittagong) 2019. HS 46* Afg A v Bangladesh A (Khulna) 2019. BB 7-41 SGR v Band-e-Amir (Ghazi Amanullah Khan) 2019. LO HS 66 Afg Emerging Players v Oman (Colombo, CCC) 2018-19. LO BB 3-53 SGR v Kabul Region (Kabul) 2018. T20 HS 33. T20 BB 5-18.

RODERICK, Gareth Hugh (Maritzburg C), b Durban, South Africa 29 Aug 1991. 6'0". RHB, WK. Squad No 27. UK passport, qualifying for England in October 2018. KZN 2010-11 to 2011-12. Gloucestershire debut/cap 2013; captain 2016-17. HS 171 v Leics (Bristol) 2014. LO HS 104 v Leics (Leicester) 2015 (RLC). T20 HS 32.

‡SCOTT, George Frederick Buchan (Beechwood Park S; St Albans S; Leeds U), b Hemel Hempstead, Herts 6 Nov 1995. Younger brother of J.E.B.Scott (Hertfordshire 2013-18); elder brother of C.F.B.Scott (Durham MCCU 2019) and P.E.B.Scott (Hertfordshire 2014-17). 6'2". RHB, RM. Squad No 17. Leeds/Bradford MCCU 2015-16. Middlesex 2018-19. Hertfordshire 2011-14. HS 55 M v Leics (Lord's) 2019. BB 2-49 M v Derbys (Derby) 2019. LO HS 63 M v Essex (Chelmsford) 2019 (RLC). LO BB 1-65 M v Lancs (Lord's) 2019 (RLC). T20 HS 38*. T20 BB 1-14.

SHAW, Joshua (Crofton HS, Wakefield; Skills Exchange C), b Wakefield, Yorks 3 Jan 1996. Son of C.Shaw (Yorkshire 1984-88). 6'1". RHB, RMF. Squad No 5. Debut (Gloucestershire) 2016 (on loan). Yorkshire 2016-19. England U19 2012-13 to 2014. HS 42 Y v Somerset (Leeds) 2018. Gs HS 38* v Worcs (Worcester) 2019. BB 5-79 v Sussex (Bristol) 2016. LO BB – . T20 HS 1. T20 BB 1-42.

SMITH, Thomas Michael John (Seaford Head Community C; Sussex Downs C), b Eastbourne, Sussex 29 Aug 1987. 5'9". RHB, SLA. Squad No 6. Sussex 2007-09. Surrey 2009 (l-o only). Middlesex 2010-13. Gloucestershire debut/cap 2013. HS 84 v Leics (Cheltenham) 2019. BB 4-35 v Kent (Canterbury) 2014. LO HS 65 Sy v Leics (Leicester) 2009 (P40). LO BB 4-26 v Sussex (Cheltenham) 2016 (RLC). T20 HS 36*. T20 BB 5-24.

TAYLOR, Jack Martin Robert (Chipping Norton S), b Banbury, Oxfordshire 12 Nov 1991. Elder brother of M.D.Taylor (see below). 5'11". RHB, OB. Squad No 10. Debut (Gloucestershire) 2010; cap 2010. Oxfordshire 2009-11. HS 156 v Northants (Cheltenham) 2015. BB 4-16 v Glamorgan (Bristol) 2016. LO HS 75 v Glamorgan (Bristol) 2019 (RLC). LO BB 4-38 v Hants (Bristol) 2014 (RLC). T20 HS 80. T20 BB 4-16.

‡NQTAYLOR, Jerome Everton, b St Elizabeth, Jamaica 22 Jun 1984. 5'11". RHB, RF. Jamaica 2002-03 to 2018-19. Leicestershire 2007. Sussex 2017 (l-o only). Somerset 2018-19 (T20 only). IPL: PW 2011. Big Bash: HH 2018-19. Joins Gloucestershire as a Kolpak signing. **Tests** (WI): 46 (2003 to 2015-16); HS 106 v NZ (Dunedin) 2008-09; BB 6-47 v A (Kingston) 2015. **LOI** (WI): 90 (2003 to 2017); HS 43* v SA (Durban) 2007-08; BB 5-48 v Z (Bulawayo) 2007-08. **IT20** (WI): 30 (2005-06 to 2017-18); HS 21 v P (Dubai, DSC) 2016-17; BB 3-6 v SA (Port Elizabeth) 2007-08. F-c Tours (WI): E 2007, 2009; A 2009-10, 2015-16; SA 2007-08, 2014-15; NZ 2005-06, 2008-09; P 2006-07; SL 2015-16; Z 2003-04. HS 106 (*see Tests*). CC HS 40 Le v Derbys (Leicester) 2007. BB 8-59 Jamaica v T&T (Port of Spain) 2002-03. CC BB 6-35 Le v Middx (Southgate) 2007. LO HS 43* (*see LOI*). LO BB 5-40 Jamaica v Guyana (Bridgetown) 2016-17. T20 HS 21. T20 BB 5-10.

TAYLOR, Matthew David (Chipping Norton S), b Banbury, Oxfordshire 8 Jul 1994. Younger brother of J.M.R.Taylor (*see above*). 6'0". RHB, LMF. Squad No 36. Debut (Gloucestershire) 2013; cap 2013. Oxfordshire 2011-12. HS 48 v Glamorgan (Bristol) 2018. BB 5-15 v Cardiff MCCU (Bristol) 2018. CC BB 5-57 v Lancs (Cheltenham) 2019. LO HS 16 v Kent (Canterbury) 2016 (RLC). LO BB 3-39 v Sussex (Eastbourne) 2019 (RLC). T20 HS 9*. T20 BB 3-16.

van BUUREN, Graeme Lourens, b Pretoria, South Africa 22 Aug 1990. 5'6". RHB, SLA. Squad No 12. Northerns 2009-10 to 2015-16. Titans 2012-13 to 2014-15. Gloucestershire debut/cap 2016. Qualified for England in May 2019. HS 235 Northerns v EP (Centurion) 2014-15. Gs HS 172* v Worcs (Worcester) 2016. BB 4-12 Northerns v SW Districts (Oudtshoorn) 2012-13. Gs BB 4-18 v Durham MCCU (Bristol) 2017. CC BB 3-15 v Glamorgan (Bristol) 2016. LO HS 119* Northerns v EP (Pt Elizabeth, Grey HS) 2013-14. LO BB 5-35 Northerns v SW Districts (Pretoria) 2011-12. T20 HS 64. T20 BB 5-8.

NQWHITTINGHAM, Stuart Gordon (Christ's Hospital, Horsham; Loughborough U), b Derby 10 Feb 1994. 6'0". RHB, RFM. Squad No 19. Loughborough MCCU 2015. Sussex 2016-18. MCC Universities 2013. Joined Gloucestershire in 2019 – no 1st XI appearances. LOI (Scot): 5 (2017-18 to 2019-20); HS 3* and BB 3-58 v Ire (Dubai, ICCA) 2017-18. IT20 (Scot): 5 (2018); HS – ; BB 2-33 v Ire (Deventer) 2018. HS 22 Sx v Notts (Hove) 2017. BB 5-70 Scot v Ire (Dubai, DSC) 2017-18. CC BB 5-80 Sx v Derbys (Hove) 2017. LO HS 3* (*see LOI*). LO BB 3-35 Scot v Nepal (Bulawayo) 2017-18. T20 HS – . T20 BB 2-33.

RELEASED/RETIRED

(Having made a County 1st XI appearance in 2019)

ALLISON, B.M.J. – *see ESSEX*.

NQGABRIEL, Shannon Terry, b Trinidad 28 Apr 1988. RHB, RFM. Trinidad & Tobago 2009-10 to 2018-19. Worcestershire 2015. Gloucestershire 2019; cap 2019. **Tests** (WI): 45 (2012 to 2019); HS 20* v E (St George's) 2015; BB 8-62 v SL (Gros Islet) 2018. **LOI** (WI): 25 (2016 to 2019); HS 12* v NZ (Christchurch) 2017-18; BB 3-17 v SA (Bridgetown) 2016. **IT20** (WI): 2 (2012-13 to 2013); HS – ; BB 3-44 v P (Kingstown) 2013. F-c Tours (WI): E 2012, 2017; A 2015-16; SA 2014-15; NZ 2013-14, 2017-18; I 2013-14, 2018-19; SL 2014-15 (WI A), 2015-16; Z 2017-18; B 2018-19; UAE (v P) 2016-17. HS 20* (*see Tests*). Gs HS 2* and Gs BB 2-20 v Worcs (Worcester) 2019. BB 8-62 (*see Tests*). CC BB 5-31 Wo v Middx (Worcester) 2015. LO HS 12* (*see LOI*). LO BB 5-33 T&T v Windward Is (Coolidge) 2016-17. T20 HS 2*. T20 BB 3-19.

NQKLINGER, Michael (Scopus Memorial C, Kew), b Kew, Melbourne, Australia 4 Jul 1980. 5'10½". RHB. Victoria 1999-00 to 2007-08. S Australia 2008-09 to 2013-14. Worcestershire 2012; cap 2012. Gloucestershire 2013-16; cap 2013; captain 2013-15; T20 captain 2016-19. W Australia 2014-15 to 2016-17. Big Bash: AS 2011-12 to 2013-14. PS 2014-15 to 2018-19. **IT20** (A): 3 (2016-17); HS 62 v SL (Adelaide) 2016-17. 1000 runs (1+2); most – 1203 (2008-09). HS 255 SA v WA (Adelaide) 2008-09. Gs HS 163 v Hants (Bristol) 2013. LO HS 166* v Hants (Bristol) 2016 (RLC). T20 HS 126* v Essex (Bristol) 2015 – Gs record.

LIDDLE, Christopher John (Nunthorpe CS; Teesside Tertiary C), b Middlesbrough, Yorks 1 Feb 1984. 6'5". RHB, LFM. Leicestershire 2005-06. Sussex 2007-15. Gloucestershire 2017-18; cap 2017. HS 53 Sx v Worcs (Hove) 2007. Gs HS 21 v Durham (Bristol) 2017. BB 3-42 Le v Somerset (Leicester) 2006. Gs BB 2-23 v Cardiff MCCU (Bristol) 2018. LO HS 26 v Hants (Southampton) 2019 (RLC). LO BB 5-18 Sx v Netherlands (Amstelveen) 2011 (CB40). T20 HS 16. T20 BB 5-17.

NQSAYERS, Chadd James (b Henley Beach, S Australia 31 Aug 1987. Son of D.K.Sayers (S Australia 1981-82). 5'11". RHB, RM. S Australia 2010-11 to date. Gloucestershire 2019; cap 2019. **Tests** (A): 1 (2017-18); HS 0; BB 2-78 v A (Johannesburg) 2017-18. F-c Tours (Aus A): E 2013; SA 2013, 2017-18 (A). HS 58* SA v WA (Adelaide) 2019-20. Gs HS 33* v Leics (Cheltenham) 2019. 50 wkts (0+1): 62 (2016-17). BB 8-64 (13-131 match) SA v NSW (Adelaide) 2019-20. Gs BB 3-60 v Middx (Northwood) 2019. LO HS 14 SA v NSW (Brisbane, AB) 2014-15. LO BB 2-41 SA v Tas (Sydney, BO) 2013-14.

NQTYE, Andrew James (Padbury Senior HS, WA), b Perth, Australia 12 Dec 1986. 6'4". RHB, RMF. W Australia 2014-15 to date. Gloucestershire 2016-19 (T20 only). IPL: GL 2017. KXIP 2018-19. Big Bash: ST 2013-14. PS 2014-15 to 2018-19. **LOI** (A): 7 (2017-18 to 2018); HS 19 v E (Oval) 2018; BB 5-46 v E (Perth) 2017-18. **IT20** (A): 26 (2015-16 to 2018-19); HS 20 v E (Birmingham) 2018; BB 4-23 v NZ (Sydney) 2017-18. HS 10 WA v Tas (Hobart) 2014-15. BB 3-47 WA v Q (Brisbane) 2014-15. LO HS 28* WA v NSW (Sydney) 2013-14. LO BB 6-46 WA v Q (Sydney, HO) 2018-19. T20 HS 42. T20 BB 5-17.

WILLOWS, Gregory Peter (Millfield S), b Dorchester, Dorset 15 Feb 1999. Son of A. Willows (Sussex 1980-83). RHB, RM. Gloucestershire 2nd XI debut 2018. Awaiting f-c debut. LO HS 10 v Australia A (Bristol) 2019 – only 1st XI appearance.

NQWORRALL, Daniel James (Kardina International C; U of Melbourne), b Melbourne, Australia 10 Jul 1991. RHB, RFM. S Australia 2012-13 to date. Gloucestershire 2018; cap 2018. Big Bash: MS 2013-14 to date. **LOI** (A): 3 (2016-17); HS 6* v SA (Centurion) 2016-17; BB 1-43 v SA (Benoni) 2016-17. HS 50 v Glamorgan (Bristol) 2018. BB 7-64 (10-148 match) SA v WA (Adelaide) 2018-19. Gs BB 4-45 v Sussex (Hove) 2018. LO HS 16 SA v Tas (N Sydney) 2017-18. LO BB 5-62 SA v Vic (Hobart) 2017-18. T20 HS 16. T20 BB 4-23.

W.A.Tavaré left the staff without making a County 1st XI appearance in 2019.

GLOUCESTERSHIRE 2019

RESULTS SUMMARY

	Place	Won	Lost	Drew	Tied	NR
Specsavers County Champ (2nd Division)	3rd	5	3	6		
All First-Class Matches		5	3	6		
Royal London One-Day Cup (South Group)	4th	5	3			
Vitality Blast (South Group)	QF	7	4		1	3

SPECSAVERS COUNTY CHAMPIONSHIP AVERAGES
BATTING AND FIELDING

Cap†		M	I	NO	HS	Runs	Avge	100	50	Ct/St
2018	R.F.Higgins	14	21	5	199	958	59.87	4	3	4
2010	C.D.J.Dent	14	24	1	176	1087	47.26	4	4	8
2016	G.L.van Buuren	10	13	3	93	363	36.30	–	2	4
2016	J.R.Bracey	13	22	2	152	677	33.85	2	2	23
2013	T.M.J.Smith	5	8	–	84	261	32.62	–	2	3
2013	G.H.Roderick	14	24	3	158	654	31.14	1	2	41/1
2012	B.A.C.Howell	10	15	–	76	369	24.60	–	2	12
2018	B.G.Charlesworth	5	7	1	77*	145	24.16	–	1	3
2013	M.D.Taylor	9	10	7	28*	67	22.33	–	–	–
2010	J.M.R.Taylor	9	13	–	99	279	21.46	–	1	3
2013	M.A.H.Hammond	14	23	1	82	418	19.00	–	2	14
2011	D.A.Payne	12	15	4	43	205	18.63	–	–	4
2019	C.J.Sayers	4	4	1	33*	55	18.33	–	–	–
2016	J.Shaw	9	12	2	38*	107	10.70	–	–	3
2016	G.T.Hankins	4	6	–	14	23	3.83	–	–	–

Also batted: B.M.J.Allison (1 match – cap 2019) 0; E.R.Bamber (2 – cap 2019) 15, 3, 12*; G.S.Drissell (1 – cap 2017) 1; S.T.Gabriel (3 – cap 2019) 1, 2, 2*; H.J.Hankins (1 – cap 2019) 9.

BOWLING

	O	M	R	W	Avge	Best	5wI	10wM
R.F.Higgins	453.4	110	1182	50	23.64	5-54	2	–
J.Shaw	225.2	43	737	30	24.56	4-33	–	–
D.A.Payne	403.5	94	1113	43	25.88	4-40	–	–
M.D.Taylor	245	43	760	29	26.20	5-57	1	–
C.J.Sayers	149.4	39	400	11	36.36	3-60	–	–

Also bowled:

E.R.Bamber	85.3	15	206	8	25.75	3-53		
B.A.C.Howell	97.2	23	262	7	37.42	2-19		

B.M.J.Allison 41-9-139-4; J.R.Bracey 10-0-35-0; B.G.Charlesworth 18-1-84-3; C.D.J.Dent 2.2-0-18-1; G.S.Drissell 41.1-5-174-4; S.T.Gabriel 32.5-0-180-2; M.A.H.Hammond 33-0-121-0; H.J.Hankins 23-4-101-0; T.M.J.Smith 76-14-217-4; J.M.R.Taylor 9-0-51-0; G.L.van Buuren 119-16-343-3.

Gloucestershire played no first-class fixtures outside the County Championship in 2019. The First-Class Averages (pp 226–241) give the records of Gloucestershire players in all first-class county matches, with the exception of E.R.Bamber; J.R.Bracey and J.Shaw, whose first-class figures for Gloucestershire are as above.

† Gloucestershire revised their capping policy in 2004 and now award players with their County Caps when they make their first-class debut.

GLOUCESTERSHIRE RECORDS

FIRST-CLASS CRICKET

Highest Total	For	695-9d		v	Middlesex	Gloucester	2004
	V	774-7d		by	Australians	Bristol	1948
Lowest Total	For	17		v	Australians	Cheltenham	1896
	V	12		by	Northants	Gloucester	1907
Highest Innings	For	341	C.M.Spearman	v	Middlesex	Gloucester	2004
	V	319	C.J.L.Rogers	for	Northants	Northampton	2006

Highest Partnership for each Wicket

1st	395	D.M.Young/R.B.Nicholls	v	Oxford U	Oxford	1962
2nd	256	C.T.M.Pugh/T.W.Graveney	v	Derbyshire	Chesterfield	1960
3rd	392	G.H.Roderick/A.P.R.Gidman	v	Leics	Bristol	2014
4th	321	W.R.Hammond/W.L.Neale	v	Leics	Gloucester	1937
5th	261	W.G.Grace/W.O.Moberley	v	Yorkshire	Cheltenham	1876
6th	320	G.L.Jessop/J.H.Board	v	Sussex	Hove	1903
7th	248	W.G.Grace/E.L.Thomas	v	Sussex	Hove	1896
8th	239	W.R.Hammond/A.E.Wilson	v	Lancashire	Bristol	1938
9th	193	W.G.Grace/S.A.P.Kitcat	v	Sussex	Bristol	1896
10th	137	C.N.Miles/L.C.Norwell	v	Worcs	Cheltenham	2014

Best Bowling	For	10-40	E.G.Dennett	v	Essex	Bristol	1906
(Innings)	V	10-66	A.A.Mailey	for	Australians	Cheltenham	1921
		10-66	K.Smales	for	Notts	Stroud	1956
Best Bowling	For	17-56	C.W.L.Parker	v	Essex	Gloucester	1925
(Match)	V	15-87	A.J.Conway	for	Worcs	Moreton-in-M	1914

Most Runs – Season	2860	W.R.Hammond	(av 69.75)	1933
Most Runs – Career	33664	W.R.Hammond	(av 57.05)	1920-51
Most 100s – Season	13	W.R.Hammond		1938
Most 100s – Career	113	W.R.Hammond		1920-51
Most Wkts – Season	222	T.W.J.Goddard	(av 16.80)	1937
	222	T.W.J.Goddard	(av 16.37)	1947
Most Wkts – Career	3170	C.W.L.Parker	(av 19.43)	1903-35
Most Career W-K Dismissals	1054	R.C.Russell	(950 ct; 104 st)	1981-2004
Most Career Catches in the Field	719	C.A.Milton		1948-74

LIMITED-OVERS CRICKET

Highest Total	50ov	401-7		v	Bucks	Wing	2003
	40ov	344-6		v	Northants	Cheltenham	2001
	T20	254-3		v	Middlesex	Uxbridge	2011
Lowest Total	50ov	82		v	Notts	Bristol	1987
	40ov	49		v	Middlesex	Bristol	1978
	T20	68		v	Hampshire	Bristol	2010
Highest Innings	50ov	177	A.J.Wright	v	Scotland	Bristol	1997
	40ov	153	C.M.Spearman	v	Warwicks	Gloucester	2003
	T20	126*	M.Klinger	v	Essex	Bristol	2015
Best Bowling	50ov	6-13	M.J.Proctor	v	Hampshire	Southampton[1]	1977
	40ov	7-29	D.A.Payne	v	Essex	Chelmsford	2010
	T20	5-18	B.A.C.Howell	v	Glamorgan	Cheltenham	2019

HAMPSHIRE

Formation of Present Club: 12 August 1863
Inaugural First-Class Match: 1864
Colours: Blue, Gold and White
Badge: Tudor Rose and Crown
County Champions: (2) 1961, 1973
NatWest/C&G/FP Trophy Winners: (3) 1991, 2005, 2009
Benson and Hedges Cup Winners: (2) 1988, 1992
Sunday League Winners: (3) 1975, 1978, 1986
Clydesdale Bank Winners: (1) 2012
Royal London One-Day Cup: (1) 2018
Twenty20 Cup Winners: (2) 2010, 2012

HAMPSHIRE
CRICKET

CEO: David Mann, The Ageas Bowl, Botley Road, West End, Southampton SO30 3XH •
Tel: 023 8047 2002 • Email: enquiries@ageasbowl.com • Web: www.ageasbowl.com •
Twitter: @hantscricket (81,933 followers)

Cricket Operations Manager: Tim Tremlett. **Director of Cricket**: Giles White. **1st XI Manager**: Adrian Birrell. **Assistant Coaches**: Alfonso Thomas and Jimmy Adams. **Captain**: J.M.Vince. **Overseas Players**: N.M.Lyon, Shaheen Shah Afridi (T20 only) and J.W.Wells (T20 only). **2020 Testimonial**: None. **Head Groundsman**: Simon Lee. **Scorer**: Kevin Baker. ‡ New registration. NQ Not qualified for England.

NQABBOTT, Kyle John (Kearnsey C, KZN), b Empangeni, South Africa 18 Jun 1987. 6'3½". RHB, RFM. Squad No 11. KwaZulu-Natal 2008-09 to 2009-10. Dolphins 2008-09 to 2014-15. Hampshire debut 2014; cap 2017 (Kolpak signing). Worcestershire 2016. IPL: KXIP 2016. **Tests** (SA): 11 (2012-13 to 2016-17); HS 17 v A (Adelaide) 2016-17; BB 7-29 v P (Centurion) 2012-13. **LOI** (SA): 28 (2012-13 to 2016-17); HS 23 v Z (Bulawayo) 2014; BB 4-21 v I (Canberra) 2014-15. **IT20** (SA): 21 (2012-13 to 2015-16); HS 9* v NZ (Centurion) 2015; BB 3-20 v B (Dhaka) 2015. F-c Tours (SA): A 2016-17; I 2015-16. HS 97* v Lancs (Manchester) 2017. 50 wkts (3+1): 72 (2019). BB 9-40 (17-86 match) v Somerset (Southampton) 2019 – 4th best match figures in CC history. Hat-trick v Worcs (Worcester) 2018. LO HS 56 v Surrey (Oval) 2017 (RLC). LO BB 4-21 (*see LOI*). T20 HS 30. T20 BB 5-14.

ALSOP, Thomas Philip (Lavington S), b High Wycombe, Bucks 26 Nov 1995. Younger brother of O.J.Alsop (Wiltshire 2010-12). 5'11". LHB, WK, occ SLA. Squad No 9. Debut (Hampshire) 2014. MCC 2017. Hampshire 2nd XI debut 2013. England U19 2014 to 2015. F-c Tours (EL): SL 2016-17. UAE 2016-17 (v Afg). HS 150 v Warwks (Birmingham) 2019. BB 2-59 v Yorks (Leeds) 2016. LO HS 130* v Glamorgan (Southampton) 2019 (RLC). T20 HS 85.

BARKER, Keith Hubert Douglas (Moorhead HS; Fulwood C, Preston), b Manchester 21 Oct 1986. Son of K.H.Barker (British Guiana 1960-61 to 1963-64). Played football for Blackburn Rovers and Rochdale. 6'3". LHB, LMF. Squad No 10. Warwickshire 2009-18; cap 2013. Hampshire debut 2019. HS 125 Wa v Surrey (Guildford) 2013. H HS 64 v Yorks (Southampton) 2019. 50 wkts (3); most – 62 (2016). BB 6-40 Wa v Somerset (Taunton) 2012. H BB 5-48 v Kent (Canterbury) 2019. LO HS 56 Wa v Scotland (Birmingham) 2011 (CB40). LO BB 4-33 Wa v Scotland (Birmingham) 2010 (CB40). T20 HS 46. T20 BB 4-19.

CAME, Harry Robert Charles (Bradfield C), b Basingstoke 27 Aug 1998. Son of P.R.C.Came (Hampshire 2nd XI 1986-87); grandson of K.C.Came (Free Foresters 1957); great-grandson of R.W.V.Robins (Middlesex, Cambridge U & England 1925-58). 5'9". RHB, OB. Squad No 4. Debut (Hampshire) 2019. Hampshire 2nd XI debut 2017. Kent 2nd XI 2017-18. HS 23* v Surrey (Oval) 2019 – only 1st XI appearance.

CRANE, Mason Sydney (Lancing C), b Shoreham-by-Sea, Sussex 18 Feb 1997. 5'7". RHB, LB. Squad No 32. Debut (Hampshire) 2015. NSW 2016-17. MCC 2017. Hampshire 2nd XI debut 2013. **Test**: 1 (2017-18); HS 4 and BB 1-193 v A (Sydney) 2017-18 **IT20**: 2 (2017); HS – ; BB 1-39 v SA (Cardiff) 2017. F-c Tours: A 2017-18; WI 2017-18 (EL). HS 29 v Somerset (Taunton) 2017. BB 5-35 v Warwks (Southampton) 2015. LO HS 28* v Somerset (Lord's) 2019 (RLC). LO BB 4-30 v Middx (Southampton) 2015 (RLC). T20 HS 5*. T20 BB 3-15.

CURRIE, Scott William (St Edward's RC & C of E S), b Poole, Dorset 2 May 2001. Younger brother of B.J.Currie (Dorset 2016 to date). 6'5". RHB, RMF. Hampshire 2nd XI debut 2018. Dorset 2017-19. Awaiting 1st XI debut.

DALE, Ajeet Singh (Wellington C), b Slough, Berks 3 Jul 2000. 6'1". RHB, RFM. Hampshire 2nd XI debut 2018. Awaiting 1st XI debut.

DAWSON, Liam Andrew (John Bentley S, Calne), b Swindon, Wilts 1 Mar 1990. 5'8". RHB, SLA. Squad No 8. Debut (Hampshire) 2007; cap 2013. Mountaineers 2011-12. Essex 2015 (on loan). Wiltshire 2006-07. **Tests**: 3 (2016-17 to 2017); HS 66* v I (Chennai) 2016-17; BB 2-34 v SA (Lord's) 2017. **LOI**: 3 (2016 to 2018-19); HS 10 and BB 2-70 v P (Cardiff) 2016. **IT20**: 6 (2016 to 2017-18); HS 10 v NZ (Hamilton) 2017-18; BB 3-27 v SL (Southampton) 2016. F-c Tour: I 2016-17. HS 169 v Somerset (Southampton) 2011. BB 7-51 Mountaineers v ME (Mutare) 2011-12 (also scored 110* in same match). H BB 5-29 v Leics (Southampton) 2012. LO HS 113* SJD v Kalabagan (Savar) 2014-15. LO BB 6-47 v Sussex (Southampton) 2015 (RLC). T20 HS 82. T20 BB 5-17.

DONALD, Aneurin Henry Thomas (Pontarddulais CS), b Swansea, Glamorgan 20 Dec 1996. 6'2". RHB, OB. Squad No 12. Glamorgan 2014-18. Hampshire debut 2019. MC 2012. 1000 runs (1): 1088 (2016). HS 234 Gm v Derbys (Colwyn Bay) 2016, in 123 balls, equalling world record for fastest 200, inc 15 sixes, going from 0-127* between lunch and tea, and 127-234 after tea. H HS 173 v Warwks (Southampton) 2019, sharing H record 5th wkt partnership of 262 with I.G.Holland. LO HS 57 v Somerset (Taunton) 2019 (RLC). T20 HS 76.

[NQ]**EDWARDS, Fidel** Henderson (St James's SS), b Gays, St Peter, Barbados 6 Feb 1982. 5'11". RHB, RFM. Squad No 20. Half-brother of P.T.Collins (Barbados, Surrey, Middlesex & West Indies 1996-97 to 2011-12). Barbados 2001-02 to 2013-14. Hampshire debut 2015 (Kolpak signing); cap 2018. MCC 2018. IPL: DC 2009 to 2009-10. Big Bash: ST 2011-12. Warwickshire 2019 (T20 only). **Tests** (WI): 55 (2003 to 2012-13); HS 30 v I (Roseau) 2011; BB 7-87 v NZ (Napier) 2008-09. **LOI** (WI): 50 (2003-04 to 2009); HS 13 v NZ (Wellington) 2008-09; BB 6-22 v Z (Harare) 2003-04 – on debut. **IT20** (WI): 20 (2007-08 to 2012-13); HS 7* v E (Oval) 2011; BB 3-23 v A (Bridgetown) 2011-12. F-c Tours (WI): E 2004, 2007, 2009, 2012; A 2005-06; SA 2003-04, 2007-08; NZ 2005-06, 2008-09; I 2011-12, 2013-14 (WI A); P 2006-07; Z 2003-04; B 2011-12, 2012-13. HS 40 Bar v Jamaica (Bridgetown) 2007-08. H HS 20 v Surrey (Southampton) 2017. 50 wkts (2); most – 54 (2018). BB 7-87 (see Tests). H BB 6-50 v Notts (Southampton) 2018. LO HS 21* Bar v Jamaica (Providence) 2007-08. LO BB 6-22 (see LOI). T20 HS 11*. T20 BB 5-22.

FULLER, James Kerr (Otago U, NZ), b Cape Town, South Africa 24 Jan 1990. UK passport. 6'3". RHB, RFM. Squad No 26. Otago 2009-10 to 2012-13. Gloucestershire 2011-15; cap 2011. Middlesex 2016-18. Hampshire debut 2019. HS 93 M v Somerset (Taunton) 2016. H HS 54* and H BB 3-51 v Yorks (Leeds) 2019. BB 6-24 (10-79 match) Otago v Wellington (Dunedin) 2012-13. CC BB 6-47 Gs v Surrey (Oval) 2014. Hat-trick Gs v Worcs (Cheltenham) 2013. LO HS 55* v Somerset (Lord's) 2019 (RLC). LO BB 6-35 M v Netherlands (Amstelveen) 2012 (CB40). T20 HS 46*. T20 BB 6-28 M v Hants (Southampton) 2018 – M record.

HOLLAND, Ian Gabriel (Ringwood Secondary C, Melbourne), b Stevens Point, Wisconsin, USA 3 Oct 1990. 6'0". RHB, RMF. Squad No 22. England qualified at the start of the 2020 season. Victoria 2015-16. Hampshire debut 2017. **LOI** (USA): 8 (2019-20); HS 75 v Nepal (Kirtipur) 2019-20; BB 3-11 v UAE (Dubai, ICCA) 2019-20. HS 143 v Warwks (Southampton) 2019, sharing H record 5th wkt partnership of 262 with A.H.T.Donald. BB 4-16 v Somerset (Southampton) 2017. LO HS 75 (*see LOI*). LO BB 3-11 (*see LOI*). T20 HS 11*. T20 BB 1-33.

‡ᴺQ**LYON, Nathan** Michael, b Young, NSW, Australia 20 Nov 1987. 5'9". RHB, OB. Squad No 67. S Australia 2010-11 to 2012-13. New South Wales 2013-14 to date. Big Bash: AS 2011-12 to 2012-13. SS 2013-14 to date. Worcestershire 2017. **Tests** (A): 96 (2011 to 2019-20); HS 47 v SA (Cape Town) 2017-18; 50 wkts (1): 63 (2017); BB 8-50 v I (Bangalore) 2016-17. **LOI** (A): 29 (2011-12 to 2019); HS 30 v SA (Providence) 2016; BB 4-44 v Z (Harare) 2014. **IT20** (A): 2 (2015-16 to 2018-19); HS 4* and BB 1-33 v P (Dubai, DSC) 2018-19. F-c Tours (A): E 2012 (Aus A), 2013, 2015, 2019; SA 2011-12, 2013-14, 2017-18; WI 2011-12, 2015; NZ 2015-16; I 2012-13, 2016-17; SL 2011, 2016; B 2017; UAE (v P) 2014-15, 2018-19. HS 75 NSW v Vic (Alice Springs) 2015-16. CC HS 6* Wo v Glamorgan (Worcester) 2017. BB 8-50 (*see Tests*). CC BB Wo 3-94 v Northants (Northampton) 2017. LO HS 37* SA v WA (Adelaide) 2011-12. LO BB 4-10 NSW v Q (Sydney) 2016-17. T20 HS 11. T20 BB 5-23.

McMANUS, Lewis David (Clayesmore S, Bournemouth), b Poole, Dorset 9 Oct 1994. 5'10". RHB, WK. Squad No 18. Debut (Hampshire) 2015. Dorset 2011-13. HS 132* v Surrey (Southampton) 2016. LO HS 47 v Barbados (Bridgetown) 2017-18. T20 HS 59.

‡ᴺQ**MUNSEY, Henry George** (Loretto S), b Oxford 22 Feb 1993. LHB, RMF. Northamptonshire 2015. Scotland 2017 to 2017-18. Leicestershire 2019 (l-o only). **LOI** (Scot): 25 (2016-17 to 2019-20); HS 61 v SL (Edinburgh) 2019. **IT20** (Scot): 38 (2015 to 2019-20); HS 127* v Neth (Dublin) 2019. HS 100* Scot v Namibia (Alloway) 2017. LO HS 96 Scot v Oman (Al Amerat) 2018-19. T20 HS 127*.

NORTHEAST, Sam Alexander (Harrow S), b Ashford, Kent 16 Oct 1989. 5'11". RHB, LB. Squad No 17. Kent 2007-17; cap 2012; captain 2016-17. Hampshire debut 2018; cap 2019. MCC 2013, 2018. 1000 runs (4); most – 1402 (2016). HS 191 K v Derbys (Canterbury) 2016. H HS 169 v Essex (Southampton) 2019. BB 1-60 K v Glos (Cheltenham) 2013. LO HS 132 K v Somerset (Taunton) 2014 (RLC). T20 HS 114.

ORGAN, Felix Spencer (Canford S), b Sydney, Australia 2 Jun 1999. 5'9". RHB, OB. Squad No 3. Debut (Hampshire) 2017. Hampshire 2nd XI debut 2015. HS 100 v Kent (Southampton) 2019. BB 5-25 v Surrey (Southampton) 2019. LO HS 0. LO BB 1-6 v CC&C (Lucas Street) 2017-18.

ᴺQ**ROSSOUW, Rilee** Roscoe, b Bloemfontein, South Africa, 9 Oct 1989. 6'1". LHB, OB. Squad No 30. Free State 2007-08 to 2012-13. Eagles 2008-09 to 2009-10. Knights 2010-11 to 2016-17. Hampshire debut 2017 (Kolpak signing). IPL: RCB 2014-15. **LOI** (SA): 36 (2014 to 2016-17); HS 132 v WI (Centurion) 2014-15; BB 1-17 v Z (Harare) 2014. **IT20** (SA): 15 (2014-15 to 2015-16); HS 78 v A (Adelaide) 2014-15. F-c Tours (SA A): A 2014; SL 2010; B 2010. 1000 runs (0+1): 1261 (2009-10). HS 319 Eagles v Titans (Centurion) 2009-10, sharing in 3rd highest 2nd wkt partnership in all f-c cricket of 480 with D.Elgar. H HS 120* v Lancs (Manchester) 2018. BB 1-1 Knights v Cobras (Cape Town) 2013-14. LO HS 156 v Somerset (Taunton) 2017 (RLC). LO BB 1-17 (*see LOI*). T20 HS 100*. T20 BB 1-3.

SCRIVEN, Thomas Antony Rhys (Magdalen Coll S), b Oxford 18 Nov 1998. 6'0½". RHB, RMF. Awaiting f-c debut. Hampshire 2nd XI debut 2016. T20 BB – . No 1st XI appearances in 2019.

‡**NQSHAHEEN** Shah **AFRIDI**, b Khyber Agency, Pakistan 6 Apr 2000. 6'4½". LHB, LFM. Khan Research Laboratories 2017-18. Northern Areas 2019-20. Joins Hampshire for T20 only in 2020. **Tests** (P): 8 (2018-19 to 2019-20); HS 14 v SA (Cape Town) 2018-19; BB 5-77 v SL (Karachi) 2019-20. **LOI** (P): 19 (2018-19 to 2019); HS 19* v E (Leeds) 2019; BB 6-35 v S (Lord's) 2019. **IT20** (P): 12 (2017-18 to 2019-20); HS 0*; BB 3-20 v NZ (Dubai, DSC) 2018-19. F-c Tours (P): A 2019-20; SA 2018-19. HS 25 P v Australia A (Perth, OS) 2019-20. BB 8-39 KRL v Rawalpindi (Rawalpindi) 2017-18 – on f-c debut, aged 17y 174d. LO HS 19* (*see LOI*). LO BB 6-35 (*see LOI*). T20 HS 4. T20 BB 5-4.

SOAMES, Oliver Courtenay (Cheltenham C; Loughborough U), b Kingston upon Thames, Surrey, 27 Oct 1995. 5'8". RHB, RM/OB. Squad No 27. Loughborough MCCU 2018. Hampshire debut 2018. Hampshire 2nd XI debut 2017. HS 62 v Warwks (Birmingham) 2019.

STEVENSON, Ryan Anthony (King Edward VI Community C), b Torquay, Devon 2 Apr 1992. 6'2". RHB, RMF. Squad No 47. Debut (Hampshire) 2015. Devon 2015. HS 51 v Surrey (Oval) 2019. BB 1-15 v Notts (Nottingham) 2015. LO HS 0. LO BB 1-28 v Essex (Southampton) 2016 (RLC). T20 HS 4*. T20 BB 2-28.

TAYLOR, Bradley Jacob (Eggar's S, Alton), b Winchester 14 Mar 1997. 5'11". RHB, OB. Squad No 93. Debut (Hampshire) 2013. Hampshire 2nd XI debut 2013. England U19 2014 to 2014-15. HS 36 v Cardiff MCCU (Southampton) 2016. CC HS 20 and BB 4-64 v Lancs (Southport) 2013. LO HS 69 v CC&C (Bridgetown) 2017-18. LO BB 4-26 v CC&C (Lucas Street) 2017-18. T20 HS 9*. T20 BB 2-20.

VINCE, James Michael (Warminster S), b Cuckfield, Sussex 14 Mar 1991. 6'2". RHB, RM. Squad No 14. Debut (Hampshire) 2009; cap 2013; captain 2016 to date. Wiltshire 2007-08. Big Bash: ST 2016-17 to 2017-18. SS 2018-19 to date. **Tests**: 13 (2016 to 2017-18); HS 83 v A (Brisbane) 2017-18; BB – . **LOI**: 13 (2015 to 2019); HS 51 v SL (Cardiff) 2016. **IT20**: 12 (2015-16 to 2019-20); HS 59 v NZ (Christchurch) 2019-20. F-c Tours: A 2017-18; SA 2014-15 (EL); NZ 2017-18; SL 2013-14 (EL). 1000 runs (2); most - 1525 (2014). HS 240 v Essex (Southampton) 2014. BB 5-41 v Loughborough MCCU (Southampton) 2013. CC BB 2-2 v Lancs (Southport) 2013. LO HS 190 v Glos (Southampton) 2019 (RLC) – H record. LO BB 1-18 EL v Australia A (Sydney) 2012-13. T20 HS 107*. T20 BB 1-5.

WEATHERLEY, Joe James (King Edward VI S, Southampton), b Winchester 19 Jan 1997. 6'1". RHB, OB. Squad No 5. Debut (Hampshire) 2016. Kent 2017 (on loan). Hampshire 2nd XI debut 2014. England U19 2014-15. HS 126* v Lancs (Manchester) 2018. BB 1-2 v Notts (Southampton) 2018. LO HS 105* v Kent (Southampton) 2018 (RLC). LO BB 4-25 v T&T (Cave Hill) 2017-18. T20 HS 43. T20 BB – .

‡**NQWELLS, Jon**athan Wayne, b Hobart, Australia 13 Aug 1988. RHB, RM. Tasmania 2008-09 to 2014-15. W Australia 2015-16 to 2018-19. Big Bash: HH 2011-12 to 2016-17. AS 2017-18 to date. HS 120 WA v Tas (Perth) 2016-17. BB 1-28 Tas v Vic (Hobart) 2009-10. LO HS 121* Tas v Q (Hobart) 2011-12. LO BB 1-6 Tas v NSW (Sydney, BO) 2014-15. T20 HS 72.

NQWHEAL, Bradley Thomas James (Clifton C), b Durban, South Africa 28 Aug 1996. 5'9". RHB, RMF. Squad No 58. Debut (Hampshire) 2015. **LOI** (Scot): 13 (2015-16 to 2019); HS 14 v Ire (Harare) 2017-18; BB 3-34 v WI (Harare) 2017-18. **IT20** (Scot): 5 (2015-16 to 2016-17); HS 2* and BB 3-20 v Hong Kong (Mong Kok) 2015-16. HS 25* v Somerset (Taunton) 2018. BB 6-51 v Notts (Nottingham) 2016. LO HS 18* v CC&C (Bridgetown) 2017-18. LO BB 4-38 v Kent (Southampton) 2016 (RLC). T20 HS 16. T20 BB 3-20.

WOOD, Christopher Philip (Alton C), b Basingstoke 27 June 1990. 6'2''. RHB, LM. Squad No 25. Debut (Hampshire) 2010; cap 2018. HS 105* v Leics (Leicester) 2012. BB 5-39 v Kent (Canterbury) 2014. LO HS 41 v Essex (Southampton) 2013 (Y40). LO BB 5-22 v Glamorgan (Cardiff) 2012 (CB40). T20 HS 27. T20 BB 5-32.

RELEASED/RETIRED

(Having made a County 1st XI appearance in 2019)

BERG, G.K. – *see NORTHAMPTONSHIRE.*

NO**MARKRAM, Aiden** Kyle, b Pretoria, South Africa 4 Oct 1994. RHB, OB. Northerns 2014-15 to 2016-17. Titans 2016-17 to date. Durham 2018. Hampshire 2019. **Tests** (SA): 20 (2017-18 to 2019-20); HS 152 v A (Johannesburg) 2017-18; BB – . **LOI** (SA): 26 (2017-18 to 2019); HS 67* v SL (Cape Town) 2018-19; BB 2-18 v B (East London) 2017-18. **IT20** (SA): 2 (2018-19); HS 15 v SL (Johannesburg) 2018-19. F-c Tours (SA): E 2017 (SAA); I 2019-20; SL 2018. 1000 runs (0+1): 1439 (2017-18). HS 182 Northerns v WP (Cape Town) 2015-16. CC HS 94 and BB 1-1 Du v Leics (Chester-le-St) 2018. H HS 63 v Essex (Southampton) 2019. LO HS 183 Titans v Lions (Johannesburg) 2016-17. LO BB 4-45 SAA v EL (Northampton) 2017. T20 HS 82. T20 BB 3-21.

NO**MORRIS, Chris**topher Henry, b Pretoria, South Africa 20 Apr 1987. Son of W.F.Morris (N Transvaal 1979-80 to 1991-92). RHB, RFM. North West 2009-10 to 2011-12. Lions 2011-12 to 2014-15. Titans 2015-16 to date. Surrey 2016 (T20 only). Hampshire 2019 (T20 only). IPL: CSK 2013. RR 2015. DD 2016-18. DCa 2019. Big Bash: ST 2019-20. **Tests** (SA): 4 (2015-16 to 2017); HS 69 v E (Cape Town) 2015-16 – on debut; BB 3-38 v E (Nottingham) 2017. **LOI** (SA): 42 (2013 to 2019); HS 62 v E (Johannesburg) 2015-16; BB 4-31 v SL (Centurion) 2016-17. **IT20** (SA): 23 (2012-13 to 2018-19); HS 55* v P (Centurion) 2018-19; BB 4-27 v Afg (Mumbai) 2015-16. F-c Tour (SA): E 2017. HS 154 NW v Easterns (Potchefstroom) 2010-11. BB 8-44 (12-101 match) Lions v Dolphins (Johannesburg) 2012-13. LO HS 90* NW v SW Districts (Potchefstroom) 2010-11. LO BB 4-23 Titans v Cobras (Centurion) 2018-19. T20 HS 82*. T20 BB 4-9.

NO**RAHANE, Ajinkya** Madhukar, b Ashwi Khurd, India 6 Jun 1988. RHB, RM. Mumbai 2007-08 to date. Hampshire 2019. IPL: MI 2007-08 to 2009. RR 2011 to date. RPS 2016-17. **Tests** (I): 65 (2012-13 to 2019-20); HS 188 v NZ (Indore) 2016-17. **LOI** (I): 90 (2011 to 2017-18); HS 111 v SL (Cuttack) 2014-15. **IT20** (I): 20 (2011 to 2016); HS 61 v E (Manchester) 2011. F-c Tours (I): E 2010 (IA), 2014, 2018; A 2014-15, 2018-19; SA 2013 (IA), 2013-14, 2017-18; WI 2012 (IA), 2016, 2019; NZ 2013-14, 2018-19 (IA), 2019-20; SL 2015, 2017; B 2015. 1000 runs (0+3): most – 1390 (2008-09). HS 265* Mumbai v Hyderabad (Hyderabad) 2009-10. H HS 119 v Notts (Newport, IoW) 2019. BB – . LO HS 187 Mumbai v Maharashtra (Pune) 2007-08. LO BB 2-36 Mumbai v Tamil Nadu (Agartala) 2008-09. T20 HS 105*. T20 BB 1-5.

NO**SHAMSI, Tabraiz**, b Johannesburg, South Africa 18 Feb 1990. RHB, SLC. Gauteng 2009-10. Lions 2009-10. Dolphins 2010-11 to 2013-14. KwaZulu-Natal 2010-11. KZN Inland 2011-12 to 2013-14. Easterns 2014-15 to 2015-16. Titans 2015-16 to date. Warriors 2017-18. Northamptonshire 2017 (T20 only). Hampshire 2019 (T20 only). IPL: RCB 2016. **Tests** (SA): 2 (2016-17 to 2018); HS 18* v A (Adelaide) 2016-17; BB 3-91 v SL (Galle) 2018. **LOI** (SA): 22 (2016 to 2019-20); HS 0*; BB 4-33 v SL (Dambulla) 2018. **IT20** (SA): 22 (2017 to 2019-20); HS 2* (twice); BB 2-16 v SL (Centurion) 2018-19. F-c Tours (SA): A 2016-17; SL 2018. HS 30* KZN Inland v Easterns (Benoni) 2012-13. 50 wkts (0+2); most – 57 (2015-16). BB 8-85 (13-120 match) KZN Inland v KZN (Chatsworth) 2014-15. LO HS 15* Titans v Dolphins (Pietermaritzburg) 2017-18. LO BB 5-40 Titans v Lions (Benoni) 2017-18. T20 HS 15*. T20 BB 4-10.

HAMPSHIRE 2019

RESULTS SUMMARY

	Place	Won	Lost	Drew	Tied	NR
Specsavers County Champ (1st Division)	3rd	5	3	6		
All First-Class Matches		5	3	7		
Royal London One-Day Cup (South Group)	Finalists 8	2				
Vitality Blast (South Group)	7th	5	6		1	2

SPECSAVERS COUNTY CHAMPIONSHIP AVERAGES
BATTING AND FIELDING

Cap		M	I	NO	HS	Runs	Avge	100	50	Ct/St
2019	S.A.Northeast	13	22	3	169	969	51.00	3	5	5
2013	L.A.Dawson	8	12	1	103	561	51.00	1	5	6
2013	J.M.Vince	6	10	1	142	365	40.55	1	1	3
	A.H.T.Donald	9	15	1	173	554	39.57	1	2	4
	R.R.Rossouw	10	17	1	92	595	37.18	–	5	2
	J.K.Fuller	4	5	1	54*	138	34.50	–	1	1
	I.G.Holland	9	16	1	143	478	31.86	1	3	5
	L.D.McManus	7	10	1	61	267	29.66	–	1	20/1
	J.J.Weatherley	8	13	2	66	322	29.27	–	2	8
	F.S.Organ	6	11	–	100	300	27.27	1	2	4
	T.P.Alsop	10	16	3	150	347	26.69	1	1	11
	K.H.D.Barker	13	18	4	64	357	25.50	–	1	2
	A.M.Rahane	7	13	–	119	307	23.61	1	1	6
2017	K.J.Abbott	13	16	2	72	207	14.78	–	1	1
	O.C.Soames	5	9	–	62	124	13.77	–	1	2
2016	G.K.Berg	5	8	–	33	79	9.87	–	–	1
	M.S.Crane	6	8	1	20	65	9.28	–	–	
2018	F.H.Edwards	14	17	9	8*	32	4.00	–	–	3

Also batted: H.R.C.Came (1 match) 23*; A.K.Markram (2) 63, 45, 7; R.A.Stevenson (1) 51 (1 ct).

BOWLING

	O	M	R	W	Avge	Best	5wI	10wM
K.J.Abbott	362.5	78	1117	71	15.73	9- 40	6	1
F.H.Edwards	353.1	55	1240	48	25.83	5- 49	4	–
K.H.D.Barker	348	70	984	37	26.59	5- 48	1	–
L.A.Dawson	210.1	39	538	10	53.80	3-184	–	–
Also bowled:								
F.S.Organ	45.5	9	125	8	15.62	5- 25	1	–
J.K.Fuller	80.4	15	302	9	33.55	3- 51	–	–
G.K.Berg	116	24	361	9	40.11	2- 41	–	–
I.G.Holland	146.1	33	378	5	75.60	1- 14	–	–
M.S.Crane	106.5	9	539	5	107.80	3-122	–	–

T.P.Alsop 1-0-3-0; R.A.Stevenson 25-1-87-1; J.M.Vince 6-0-17-0; J.J.Weatherley 16-0-67-1.

The First-Class Averages (pp 226–241) give the records of Hampshire players in all first-class county matches (Hampshire's other opponents being Oxford MCCU), with the exception of:
G.K.Berg 6-10-1-33-94-10.44-0-0-1ct. 127-32-365-11-33.18-2/4-0-0.
S.A.Northeast 14-23-3-169-1087-54.35-4-5-5ct. Did not bowl.

HAMPSHIRE RECORDS

FIRST-CLASS CRICKET

Highest Total	For 714-5d		v	Notts	Southampton[2]	2005
	V 742		by	Surrey	The Oval	1909
Lowest Total	For 15		v	Warwicks	Birmingham	1922
	V 23		by	Yorkshire	Middlesbrough	1965
Highest Innings	For 316	R.H.Moore	v	Warwicks	Bournemouth	1937
	V 303*	G.A.Hick	for	Worcs	Southampton[1]	1997

Highest Partnership for each Wicket

1st	347	V.P.Terry/C.L.Smith	v	Warwicks	Birmingham	1987
2nd	373	J.H.K.Adams/M.A.Carberry	v	Somerset	Taunton	2011
3rd	523	M.A.Carberry/N.D.McKenzie	v	Yorkshire	Southampton[2]	2011
4th	367	J.H.K.Adams/S.M.Ervine	v	Warwicks	Southampton[2]	2017
5th	262	I.G.Holland/A.H.T.Donald	v	Warwicks	Southampton[2]	2019
6th	411	R.M.Poore/E.G.Wynyard	v	Somerset	Taunton	1899
7th	325	G.Brown/C.H.Abercrombie	v	Essex	Leyton	1913
8th	257	N.Pothas/A.J.Bichel	v	Glos	Cheltenham	2005
9th	230	D.A.Livingstone/A.T.Castell	v	Surrey	Southampton[1]	1962
10th	192	H.A.W.Bowell/W.H.Livsey	v	Worcs	Bournemouth	1921

Best Bowling	For 9- 25	R.M.H.Cottam	v	Lancashire	Manchester	1965
(Innings)	V 10- 46	W.Hickton	for	Lancashire	Manchester	1870
Best Bowling	For 17- 86	K.J.Abbott	v	Somerset	Southampton[2]	2019
(Match)	V 17-103	W.Mycroft	for	Derbyshire	Southampton	1876

Most Runs – Season	2854	C.P.Mead	(av 79.27)	1928
Most Runs – Career	48892	C.P.Mead	(av 48.84)	1905-36
Most 100s – Season	12	C.P.Mead		1928
Most 100s – Career	138	C.P.Mead		1905-36
Most Wkts – Season	190	A.S.Kennedy	(av 15.61)	1922
Most Wkts – Career	2669	D.Shackleton	(av 18.23)	1948-69
Most Career W-K Dismissals	700	R.J.Parks	(630 ct; 70 st)	1980-92
Most Career Catches in the Field	629	C.P.Mead		1905-36

LIMITED-OVERS CRICKET

Highest Total	50ov	371-4		v	Glamorgan	Southampton[1]	1975
	40ov	353-8		v	Middlesex	Lord's	2005
	T20	249-8		v	Derbyshire	Derby	2017
Lowest Total	50ov	50		v	Yorkshire	Leeds	1991
	40ov	43		v	Essex	Basingstoke	1972
	T20	85		v	Sussex	Southampton[2]	2008
Highest Innings	50ov	190	J.M.Vince	v	Glos	Southampton[2]	2019
	40ov	172	C.G.Greenidge	v	Surrey	Southampton[1]	1987
	T20	124*	M.J.Lumb	v	Essex	Southampton[2]	2009
Best Bowling	50ov	7-30	P.J.Sainsbury	v	Norfolk	Southampton[1]	1965
	40ov	6-20	T.E.Jesty	v	Glamorgan	Cardiff	1975
	T20	5-14	A.D.Mascarenhas	v	Sussex	Hove	2004

[1] County Ground (Northlands Road) [2] Ageas Bowl

118

KENT

Formation of Present Club: 1 March 1859
Substantial Reorganisation: 6 December 1870
Inaugural First-Class Match: 1864
Colours: Maroon and White
Badge: White Horse on a Red Ground
County Champions: (6) 1906, 1909, 1910, 1913, 1970, 1978
Joint Champions: (1) 1977
Gillette Cup Winners: (2) 1967, 1974
Benson and Hedges Cup Winners: (3) 1973, 1976, 1978
Pro 40/National League (Div 1) Winners: (1) 2001
Sunday League Winners: (4) 1972, 1973, 1976, 1995
Twenty20 Cup Winners: (1) 2007

Cricket Chief Executive: Simon Storey, The Spitfire Ground, Old Dover Road, Canterbury, CT1 3NZ • Tel: 01227 456886 • Email: feedback.kent@ecb.co.uk • Web: www.kentcricket.co.uk • Twitter: @kentcricket (85,353 followers)

Director of Cricket: Paul Downton. **Head Coach**: Matt Walker. **Batting Coach**: Michael Yardy. **Bowling Coach**: Simon Cook. **Captain**: S.W.Billings. **Vice-Captain**: J.L.Denly. **Overseas Players**: M.J.Henry and Mohammad Nabi (T20 only). **2020 Testimonial**: None. **Head Groundsman**: Adrian Llong. **Scorer**: Lorne Hart. **Blast Team Name**: Kent Spitfires. ‡ New registration. ^NQ Not qualified for England.

BELL-DRUMMOND, Daniel James (Millfield S), b Lewisham, London 4 Aug 1993. 5'10". RHB, RMF. Squad No 23. Debut (Kent) 2011; cap 2015. MCC 2014, 2018. 1000 runs (1): 1058 (2014). HS 206* v Loughborough MCCU (Canterbury) 2016. CC HS 166 v Warwks (Canterbury) 2019. BB 2-6 v Loughborough MCCU (Canterbury) 2019. CC HS 2-7 v Yorks (Leeds) 2019. LO HS 171* EL v Sri Lanka A (Canterbury) 2016. LO BB 2-22 v Surrey (Oval) 2019 ((RLC). T20 HS 112*. T20 BB 2-19.

BILLINGS, Samuel William (Haileybury S; Loughborough U), b Pembury 15 Jun 1991. 5'11". RHB, WK. Squad No 7. Loughborough MCCU 2011, scoring 131 v Northants (Loughborough) on f-c debut. Kent debut 2011; cap 2015; captain 2018 to date. MCC 2015. IPL: DD 2016-17. CSK 2018-19. Big Bash: SS 2016-17 to 2017-18. LOI: 15 (2015 to 2018); HS 62 v B (Chittagong) 2016-17. IT20: 26 (2015 to 2019-20); HS 87 v WI (Basseterre) 2018-19 – world record IT20 score by a No 6 batsman. F-c Tours (EL): I 2018-19; UAE 2018-19 (v P). HS 171 v Glos (Bristol) 2016. LO HS 175 EL v Pakistan A (Canterbury) 2016. T20 HS 95*.

BLAKE, Alexander James (Hayes SS; Leeds Met U), b Farnborough 25 Jan 1989. 6'1". LHB, RMF. Squad No 10. Debut (Kent) 2008; cap 2017. Leeds/Bradford UCCE 2009-11 (not f-c). HS 105* v Yorks (Leeds) 2010. BB 2-9 v Pakistanis (Canterbury) 2010. CC BB 1-60 v Hants (Southampton) 2010. LO HS 116 v Somerset (Taunton) 2017 (RLC). LO BB 2-13 v Yorks (Leeds) 2011 (CB40). T20 HS 71*.

COX, Jordan Matthew (Felsted S), b Margate 21 Oct 2000. 5'8". RHB, WK. Squad No 22. Debut (Kent) 2019. Kent 2nd XI debut 2017. England U19 2018-19. HS 27 v Hants (Southampton) 2019. LO HS 21 v Pakistanis (Beckenham) 2019. T20 HS 23*.

CRAWLEY, Zak (Tonbridge S), b Bromley 3 Feb 1998. 6'6". RHB, RM. Squad No 16. Debut (Kent) 2017; cap 2019. **Tests**: 4 (2019-20); HS 66 v SA (Johannesburg) 2019-20. F-c Tours: SA 2019-20; NZ 2019-20; SL 2019-20. HS 168 v Glamorgan (Canterbury) 2018. LO HS 120 v Middx (Canterbury) 2019 (RL). T20 HS 89.

DENLY, Joseph Liam (Chaucer TC), b Canterbury 16 Mar 1986. 6'0". RHB, LB. Squad No 6. Kent debut 2004; cap 2008; testimonial 2019. Middlesex 2012-14; cap 2012. MCC 2013. PCA 2018. **ECB L-O Central Contract 2019-20. Tests:** 14 (2018-19 to 2019-20); HS 94 v A (Oval) 2019; BB 2-42 v SA (Cape Town) 2019-20. **LOI:** 16 (2009 to 2019-20); HS 87 v SA (Cape Town) 2019-20; BB 1-24 v Ire (Dublin) 2019. **IT20:** 12 (2009 to 2019-20); HS 30 v WI (Gros Islet) 2018-19; BB 4-19 v SL (Colombo, RPS) 2018-19. F-c Tours: SA 2019-20; WI 2018-19; NZ 2008-09 (Eng A), 2019-20; I 2007-08 (Eng A); SL 2019-20. 1000 runs (4); most – 1266 (2017). HS 227 v Worcs (Worcester) 2017. BB 4-36 v Derbys (Derby) 2018. LO HS 150* v Glamorgan (Canterbury) 2018 (RLC) – K record. LO BB 4-35 v Jamaica (North Sound) 2017-18. T20 HS 127 v Essex (Chelmsford) 2017 – K record. T20 BB 4-19.

DICKSON, Sean Robert, b Johannesburg, South Africa 2 Sep 1991. 5'10". RHB, RM. Squad No 58. Northerns 2013-14 to 2014-15. Kent debut 2015. UK passport holder; England qualified. HS 318 v Northants (Beckenham) 2017, 2nd highest score in K history, sharing K record 2nd wkt partnership of 382 with J.L.Denly. BB 1-15 Northerns v GW (Centurion) 2014-15. K BB - . LO HS 99 v Middx (Lord's) 2016 (RLC). T20 HS 53. T20 BB 1-9.

‡**GROENEWALD, Tim**othy Duncan (Maritzburg C; South Africa U), b Pietermaritzburg, South Africa 10 Jan 1984. 6'0". RHB, RFM. Squad No 36. Debut Cambridge UCCE 2006. Warwickshire 2006-08. Derbyshire 2009-14; cap 2011. Somerset 2014-19; cap 2016. HS 78 Wa v Bangladesh A (Birmingham) 2008. CC HS 76 Wa v Durham (Chester-le-St) 2006. BB 6-50 De v Surrey (Croydon) 2009. Hat-trick De v Essex (Chelmsford) 2014. LO HS 57 Sm v Warwks (Birmingham) 2014 (RLC). LO BB 4-22 De v Worcs (Worcester) 2011 (CB40). T20 HS 41. T20 BB 4-21.

HAGGETT, Calum John (Millfield S), b Taunton, Somerset 30 Oct 1990. 6'3". LHB, RMF. Squad No 25. Debut (Kent) 2013. No 1st XI appearances in 2019. HS 80 v Surrey (Oval) 2015. BB 4-15 v Derbys (Derby) 2016. LO HS 45 v Leeward Is (Coolidge) 2016-17. LO BB 4-59 v Windward Is (Coolidge) 2016-17. T20 HS 20. T20 BB 2-12.

‡**HAMIDULLAH QADRI** (Derby Moor S; Chellaston Ac), b Kandahar, Afghanistan 5 Dec 2000. 5'9". RHB, OB. Squad No 75. Derbyshire 2017-19, taking 5-60 v Glamorgan (Cardiff), the youngest to take 5 wkts on CC debut, and the first born this century to play f-c cricket in England. England U19 2018-19. HS 17* De v Lancs (Manchester) 2019. BB 5-60 (*see above*). LO HS 4 De v Notts (Nottingham) 2018 (RLC). LO BB 1-31 De v Northants (Northampton) 2018 (RLC). T20 BB – .

ᴺᴼ**HENRY, Matt**hew James (St Bede's S), b Christchurch, New Zealand 14 Dec 1991. RHB, RFM. Squad No 24. Canterbury 2010-11 to date. Worcestershire 2016. Kent debut 2018; cap 2018. Derbyshire 2017 (T20 only). IPL: KXIP 2017. **Tests** (NZ): 12 (2015 to 2019-20); HS 66 v A (Christchurch) 2015-16; BB 4-93 v E (Lord's) 2015 and 4-93 v SA (Hamilton) 2016-17. **LOI** (NZ): 52 (2013-14 to 2019); HS 48* v P (Wellington) 2015-16; BB 5-30 v P (Abu Dhabi) 2014-15. **IT20** (NZ): 6 (2014-15 to 2016-17); HS 10 v P (Auckland) 2015-16; BB 3-44 v SL (Mt Maunganui) 2015-16. F-c Tours (NZ): E 2014 (NZA), 2015; A 2015-16, 2019-20; I 2016-17, 2017-18 (NZA); SL 2013-14 (NZA). HS 81 v Derbys (Derby) 2018. 50 wkts (1): 75 (2018). BB 7-42 (11-114 match) v Northants (Canterbury) 2018. LO HS 48* (*see LOI*). LO BB 6-45 Canterbury v Auckland (Auckland) 2012-13. T20 HS 42. T20 BB 4-43.

[NQ]**KLAASSEN, Fred**erick Jack (Sacred Heart C, Auckland, NZ), b Haywards Heath, Sussex 13 Nov 1992. 6'4". RHB, LMF. Squad No 18. Debut (Kent) 2019. **LOI** (Neth): 4 (2018 to 2019); HS 13 v Nepal (Amstelveen) 2018; BB 3-30 v Nepal (Amstelveen) 2018 – separate matches. **IT20** (Neth): 21 (2018 to 2019-20); HS 13 v Z (Rotterdam) 2019; BB 3-31 v Ire (Al Amerat) 2018-19. HS 14* v Loughborough MCCU (Canterbury) 2019. CC HS 13 and BB 1-44 v Yorks (Canterbury) 2019. LO HS 13 (*see LOI*). LO BB 3-30 (*see LOI*). T20 HS 13. T20 BB 3-31.

[NQ]**KUHN, Heino** Gunther, b Piet Relief, Mpumalanga, South Africa 1 Apr 1984. 5'10". RHB, WK. Squad No 4. Northerns 2004-05 to 2015-16. Titans 2005-06 to date. Kent debut 2018 (Kolpak signing); cap 2018. **Tests** (SA): 4 (2017); HS 34 v E (Nottingham) 2017. **IT20** (SA): 7 (2009-10 to 2016-17); HS 29 v SL (Johannesburg) 2016-17. F-c Tours (SAA): E 2017 (SA); A 2014; SL 2010; Z 2016; B 2010; Ire 2012. 1000 runs (0+1): 1159 (2015-16). HS 244* Titans v Lions (Benoni) 2014-15. Scored 200* SAA v Hants (Southampton) 2017 on UK debut. K HS 96* v Leics (Leicester) 2018. LO HS 141* SAA v Bangladesh A (Benoni) 2011. T20 HS 83*.

‡**LEANING, Jack** Andrew (Archbishop Holgate's S, York; York C), b Bristol, Glos 18 Oct 1993. 5'10". RHB, RMF. Squad No 34. Yorkshire 2013-19; cap 2016. YC 2015. HS 123 Y v Somerset (Taunton) 2014. BB 2-20 Y v Hants (Southampton) 2019. LO HS 131* Y v Leics (Leicester) 2016 (RLC). LO BB 5-22 Y v Unicorns (Leeds) 2013 (Y40). T20 HS 64. T20 BB 1-15.

MILNES, Matthew Edward (West Bridgford CS; Durham U), b Nottingham 29 Jul 1994. 6'1". RHB, RMF. Squad No 8. Durham MCCU 2014. Nottinghamshire 2018. Kent 2019. MCC Univs 2015. HS 43 Nt v Yorks (Nottingham) 2018. K HS 31 v Essex (Canterbury) 2019. 50 wkts (1): 58 (2019). BB 5-68 v Notts (Tunbridge W) 2019. LO HS 26 and LO BB 5-79 v Hants (Canterbury) 2019 (RLC). T20 BB – .

[NQ]**MOHAMMAD NABI** Eisakhil, b Peshawar, Pakistan 7 Mar 1985. 6'3". RHB, OB. Squad No 77. MCC 2007-11. Pakistan Customs 2007-08 to 2009-10. Leicestershire 2018 (T20 only). Kent debut 2019 (T20 only). IPL: SH 2017-18. Big Bash: MR 2017-18 to date. **Tests** (Afg): 3 (2018 to 2019); HS 24 v I (Bengalaru) 2018; BB 3-36 v Ire (Dehradun) 2018-19. **LOI** (Afg): 124 (2009 to 2019-20); HS 116 v Z (Bulawayo) 2015-16; BB 4-30 v Ire (Greater Noida) 2016-17 and 4-30 v SL (Cardiff) 2019. **IT20** (Afg): 78 (2009-10 to 2019-20); HS 89 v Ire (Greater Noida) 2016-17; BB 4-10 v Ire (Dubai, DSC) 2016-17. HS 117 Afg v UAE (Sharjah) 2011-12. BB 6-33 Afg v Namibia (Windhoek) 2013. LO HS 146 MSC v PDSC (Bogra) 2013-14. LO BB 5-12 Afg v Namibia (Windhoek) 2013. T20 HS 89. T20 BB 4-10.

O'RIORDAN, Marcus Kevin (Tonbridge S), b Pembury 25 Jan 1998. 5'10". RHB, OB. Squad No 55. Debut (Kent) 2019. Kent 2nd XI debut 2014. HS 12 v Notts (Nottingham) 2019. BB – . T20 BB – .

PODMORE, Harry William (Twyford HS), b Hammersmith, London 23 Jul 1994. 6'3". RHB, RMF. Squad No 1. Glamorgan 2016-17 (on loan). Middlesex 2016 to 2016-17. Derbyshire 2017 (on loan). Kent debut 2018; cap 2019. HS 66* De v Sussex (Hove) 2017. K HS 54* v Essex (Canterbury) 2019. 50 wkts (1): 54 (2019). BB 6-36 v Middx (Canterbury) 2018. LO HS 40 v Hants (Canterbury) 2019 (RLC). LO BB 4-57 v Notts (Nottingham) 2018 (RLC). T20 HS 9. T20 BB 3-13.

QAYYUM, Imran (Villiers HS, Southall; Greenford SFC; City U), b Ealing, Middx 23 May 1993. 6'0". RHB, SLA. Squad No 11. Debut (Kent) 2016. HS 39 v Leics (Canterbury) 2017. BB 3-158 v Northants (Northampton) 2016. LO HS 26* v Pakistanis (Beckenham) 2019. LO BB 4-33 v USA (North Sound) 2017-18. T20 HS 21*. T20 BB 5-21.

ROBINSON, Oliver Graham (Hurtsmere S, Greenwich), b Sidcup 1 Dec 1998. 5'8". RHB, WK, occ RM. Squad No 21. Debut (Kent) 2018. Kent 2nd XI debut 2015. England U19 2017 to 2018. HS 143 v Warwks (Birmingham) 2019. LO HS 49 v Pakistanis (Beckenham) 2019. T20 HS 53.

ROUSE, Adam Paul (Perrins Community Sports C; Peter Symonds C, Winchester), b Harare, Zimbabwe 30 Jun 1992. 5'10". RHB, WK. Squad No 12. Hampshire 2013. Gloucestershire 2014; cap 2014. Kent debut 2016. Surrey 2018 (on loan). Sussex 2019 (on loan). HS 95* v Derbys (Canterbury) 2017. LO HS 75* v Jamaica (North Sound) 2017-18. T20 HS 35*.

STEVENS, Darren Ian (Hinckley C), b Leicester 30 Apr 1976. 5'11". RHB, RM. Squad No 3. Leicestershire 1997-2004; cap 2002. Kent debut/cap 2005; benefit 2016. MCC 2002. F-c Tour (ECB Acad): SL 2002-03. 1000 runs (3); most – 1304 (2013). HS 237 v Yorks (Leeds) 2019, sharing K record 6th wkt partnership of 346 with S.W.Billings. 50 wkts (4); most – 63 (2017). BB 8-75 v Leics (Canterbury) 2017. HS 147 v Glamorgan (Swansea) 2017 (RLC). LO BB 6-25 v Surrey (Beckenham) 2018 (RLC). T20 HS 90. T20 BB 4-14.

NQ**STEWART, Grant** (All Saints C, Maitland; U of Newcastle), b Kalgoorlie, W Australia 19 Feb 1994. 6'2". RHB, RMF. Squad No 9. UK qualified due to Italian mother. Debut (Kent) 2017. HS 103 and BB 6-22 v Middx (Canterbury) 2018. LO HS 44 v USA (North Sound) 2017-18. LO BB 3-17 v Guyana (Coolidge) 2017-18. T20 HS 5*. T20 BB 2-23.

THOMAS, Ivan Alfred Astley (John Roan S, Blackheath; Leeds U), b Greenwich, London 25 Sep 1991. 6'4". RHB, RMF. Squad No 5. Leeds/Bradford MCCU 2012-14. Kent debut 2012. Missed entire 2019 season due to injury. HS 13 v Australians (Canterbury) 2015. CC HS 7* v Glos (Bristol) 2015. BB 5-91 v Leics (Leicester) 2018. LO HS 6 v Guyana (North Sound) 2017-18. LO BB 4-30 v Jamaica (North Sound) 2017-18. T20 HS 3*. T20 BB 2-42.

RELEASED/RETIRED

(Having made a County 1st XI appearance in 2019)

CLAYDON, M.E. – see SUSSEX.

NQ**Du PLESSIS**, Francois ('**Faf**') (Affies BS, Pretoria), b Pretoria, South Africa 13 Jul 1984. 6'0". RHB, LB. Northerns 2003-04 to 2005-06. Titans 2005-06 to date. Lancashire 2008-09. Kent 2019. IPL: CSK 2012-19. RPS 2016-17. Big Bash: MR 2012-13. **Tests** (SA): 65 (2012-13 to 2019-20, 36 as captain); HS 137 v NZ (Port Elizabeth) 2012-13; BB – . **LOI** (SA): 143 (2010-11 to 2019, 39 as captain); HS 185 v SL (Cape Town) 2016-17; BB 1-8 v E (Nottingham) 2012. **IT20** (SA): 47 (2012 to 2019-20, 40 as captain); HS 119 v WI (Johannesburg) 2014-15. F-c Tours (SA)(C=Captain): E 2017C; A 2012-13, 2016-17C; NZ 2016-17C; I 2015-16, 2019-20C; SL 2014, 2018C; B 2015; Z 2014; UAE (v P) 2013-14. HS 176 Titans v Lions (Centurion) 2008-09. CC HS 86* La v Hants (Southampton) 2009. K HS 36 v Yorks (Leeds) 2019. BB 4-39 Northerns v FS (Pretoria) 2004-05. CC BB 3-61 La v Yorks (Manchester) 2008. LO HS 185 (see LOI). LO BB 4-47 Northerns v Easterns (Pretoria) 2005-06. T20 HS 119. T20 BB 5-19.

NQ**MILNE, Adam** Fraser, b Palmerston North, New Zealand 13 Apr 1992. RHB, RF. Central Districts 2009-10 to 2018-19. Kent 2017; cap 2019. IPL: RCB 2016-17. **LOI** (NZ): 40 (2012-13 to 2017-18); HS 36 v A (Wellington) 2015-16; BB 3-49 v P (Auckland) 2015-16. **IT20** (NZ): 21 (2010-11 to 2018-19); HS 10* v SA (Centurion) 2015; BB 4-37 v P (Auckland) 2015-16. F-c Tour (NZ A): SL 2013-14. HS 97 and BB 5-47 CD v Otago (Napier) 2012-13. K HS 51 v Notts (Nottingham) 2017. K BB 4-68 v Durham (Chester-le-St) 2017. LO HS 45 NZA v Sri Lanka A (Lincoln) 2015-16. LO BB 5-61 NZA v Sri Lanka A (Pallekele) 2013-14. T20 HS 18*. T20 BB 5-11 v Somerset (Taunton) 2017 – K record.

NOMULDER, Peter Wiaan Adriaan, b Johannesburg, South Africa 19 Feb 1998. RHB, RM. Lions 2016-17 to date. Gauteng 2017-18 to 2018-19. Kent 2019. **Tests** (SA): 1 (2018-19); HS 9 and BB 1-6 v SL (Port Elizabeth) 2018-19. **LOI** (SA): 10 (2017-18 to 2018-19); HS 19* v SL (Dambulla) 2018; BB 2-59 v SL (Colombo, RPS) 2018. F-c Tour (SA A): E 2017. HS 146 Lions v Knights (Bloemfontein) 2018-19. K HS 68* and K BB 4-118 v Surrey (Beckenham) 2019. BB 7-25 Lions v Dolphins (Potchefstroom) 2016-17. LO HS 66 SA A v India A (Pretoria) 2017. LO BB 3-32 Lions v Knights (Potchefstroom) 2017-18. T20 HS 63. T20 BB 2-13.

NORENSHAW, Matthew Thomas, b Middlesbrough, Yorks 28 Mar 1996. 6'0". LHB, OB. Queensland 2014-15 to date. Somerset 2018. Kent 2019. Big Bash: BH 2017-18 to date. **Tests** (A): 11 (2016-17 to 2017-18); HS 184 v P (Sydney) 2016-17; BB – . F-c Tours (A): SA 2017-18; I 2016-17, 2018-19 (Aus A); P 2018-19 (v P). HS 184 (see Tests). CC HS 112 Sm v Yorks (Taunton) 2018. K HS 48* v Warwks (Birmingham) 2019. BB 1-12 Q v Vic (Melbourne) 2017-18. LO HS 109 v Sussex (Beckenham) 2019 (RLC). LO BB 2-17 v Surrey (Oval) 2019 (RLC). T20 HS 90*. T20 BB 1-2.

RILEY, Adam Edward Nicholas (Beths GS, Bexley; Loughborough U), b Sidcup 23 Mar 1992. 6'2". RHB, OB. Kent 2011-19. Loughborough MCCU 2012-14. MCC 2015. F-c Tour (EL): SA 2014-15. HS 34 v Derbys (Canterbury) 2015. 50 wkts (1): 57 (2014). BB 7-150 v Hants (Southampton) 2013. LO HS 21* v Leeward Is (Coolidge) 2016-17. LO BB 4-40 v Leeward Is (Coolidge) 2017-18. T20 HS 5*. T20 BB 4-22.

NOVILJOEN, GC ('Hardus') b Witbank, South Africa 6 Mar 1989. 6'5". RHB, RF. Easterns 2008-09 to 2011-12. Titans 2009-10 to date. Lions 2012-13 to 2017-18. Kent 2016 (T20 only in 2019). Derbyshire 2017-18. IPL: KXIP 2019. **Tests** (SA): 1 (2015-16); HS 20* and BB 1-79 v E (Johannesburg) 2015-16. F-c Tours (SA A): A 2014, 2016; I 2015; Z 2016. HS 132 Titans v Cobras (Cape Town) 2019-20. CC HS 63 v Northants (Beckenham) 2016. 50 wkts (0+1): 68 (2010-11). BB 8-90 (15-170 match – best match figs for De since 1952) v Sussex (Hove) 2017. LO HS 54* Easterns v Boland (Paarl) 2011-12. LO BB 6-19 Lions v Titans (Centurion) 2012-13. T20 HS 41*. T20 BB 5-16.

RELEASED/RETIRED (continued from p 96)

(Having made a County 1st XI appearance in 2019)

BOPARA, R.S. – see SUSSEX.

COLES, Matthew Thomas (Maplesden Noakes S; Mid-Kent C), b Maidstone, Kent 26 May 1990. 6'3". LHB, RFM. Kent 2009-17; cap 2012. Hampshire 2013-14. Essex 2018-19. Northamptonshire 2019. HS 103* K v Yorks (Leeds) 2012. Ex HS 15* v Cambridge MCCU (Cambridge) 2019. 50 wkts (2); most – 67 (2015). BB 6-51 K v Northants (Northampton) 2012. Ex BB 5-123 v Surrey (Oval) 2018. LO HS 100 K v Surrey (Oval) 2015 (RLC). LO BB 6-32 K v Yorks (Leeds) 2012 (CB40). T20 HS 54. T20 BB 4-27.

NOMOHAMMAD AMIR, b Gujar Khan, Punjab, Pakistan 13 Apr 1992. LHB, LF. Federal Areas 2008-09. National Bank 2008-09 to 2009-10. SSGC 2015-16 to 2017-18. Essex 2017-19. **Tests** (P): 36 (2009 to 2018-19); HS 48 v A (Brisbane) 2016-17; BB 6-44 v WI (Kingston) 2017. **LOI** (P): 61 (2009 to 2019-20); HS 73* v NZ (Abu Dhabi) 2009-10; BB 5-30 v A (Taunton) 2019. **IT20** (P): 48 (2009 to 2019-20); HS 21* v A (Birmingham) 2010; BB 4-13 v SL (Lahore) 2017-18. F-c Tours (P): E 2010, 2016, 2018; A 2009-10, 2016-17; SA 2018-19; WI 2017; NZ 2009-10, 2016-17; WI 2017; SL 2009; Ire 2018. HS 66 SSGC v Lahore Blues (Lahore) 2015-16. Ex HS 28 v Kent (Canterbury) 2019. 50 wkts (0+1): 56 (2008-09). BB 7-61 (10-97 match) NBP v Lahore Shalimar (Lahore) 2008-09. Ex BB 5-18 (10-72 match) v Yorks (Scarborough) 2017. LO HS 73* (see LOI). LO BB 5-30 (see LOI). T20 HS 21*. T20 BB 6-17.

KENT 2019

RESULTS SUMMARY

	Place	Won	Lost	Drew	NR
Specsavers County Champ (1st Division)	4th	5	5	4	
All First-Class Matches		5	5	5	
Royal London One-Day Cup (South Group)	7th	2	5		1
Vitality Blast (South Group)	5th	6	6		2

SPECSAVERS COUNTY CHAMPIONSHIP AVERAGES

BATTING AND FIELDING

Cap		M	I	NO	HS	Runs	Avge	100	50	Ct/St
2015	S.W.Billings	4	7	1	138	366	61.00	3	–	1
2008	J.L.Denly	6	11	2	167*	504	56.00	2	1	1
2015	D.J.Bell-Drummond	14	26	–	166	892	35.68	1	5	4
2019	Z.Crawley	13	24	–	111	820	34.16	2	5	16
	O.G.Robinson	14	25	2	143	765	33.26	2	3	54
2005	D.I.Stevens	12	19	1	237	597	33.16	1	2	2
	P.W.A.Mulder	3	6	2	68*	114	28.50	–	1	–
	S.R.Dickson	11	21	–	161	557	26.52	2	1	13
2018	H.G.Kuhn	14	24	–	95	605	25.20	–	5	11
	M.T.Renshaw	3	6	1	48*	118	23.60	–	–	3
	G.Stewart	5	7	2	59	113	22.60	–	1	–
	J.M.Cox	3	4	–	27	71	17.75	–	–	1
2019	H.W.Podmore	14	21	6	54*	265	17.66	–	1	4
	O.P.Rayner	8	10	1	40*	152	16.88	–	–	5
2016	M.E.Claydon	6	7	4	13*	50	16.66	–	–	–
	A.J.Blake	5	9	–	34	136	15.11	–	–	2
	M.E.Milnes	14	19	6	31	174	13.38	–	–	5

Also batted: F.du Plessis (1 match) 0, 36 (3 ct); I.Qayyum (1) 14*, 1*; F.J.Klaassen (1) 10, 13 (1 ct); M.K.O'Riordan (1) 12, 9; A.E.N.Riley (2) 3*, 0*, 7 (4 ct).

BOWLING

	O	M	R	W	Avge	Best	5wI	10wM
D.I.Stevens	403	126	914	52	17.57	5- 20	5	1
M.E.Claydon	130.2	20	466	19	24.52	5- 46	1	–
M.E.Milnes	386.4	68	1383	55	25.14	5- 68	2	–
H.W.Podmore	473.3	105	1380	52	26.53	5- 41	2	–
O.P.Rayner	166.3	76	292	10	29.20	2- 7	–	–
P.W.A.Mulder	91.5	22	307	10	30.70	4-118	–	–
G.Stewart	135.3	16	514	15	34.26	3- 37	–	–

Also bowled:

	O	M	R	W	Avge	Best	5wI	10wM
D.J.Bell-Drummond	60.2	11	163	6	27.16	2- 7	–	–

A.J.Blake 1-0-9-0; Z.Crawley 11-2-33-0; J.L.Denly 72-20-184-4; S.R.Dickson 4-0-9-0; I.Qayyum 8-0-43-0; F.J.Klaassen 29-0-132-2; M.K.O'Riordan 7-0-33-0; M.T.Renshaw 16-2-53-0; A.E.N.Riley 56-10-182-2.

The First-Class Averages (pp 226–241) give the records of Kent players in all first-class county matches (Kent's other opponents being Loughborough MCCU), with the exception of J.L.Denly and O.P.Rayner, whose first-class figures for Kent are as above, and:
Z.Crawley 14-26-0-111-916-35.23-2-6-17ct. 11-2-33-0.

KENT RECORDS

FIRST-CLASS CRICKET

Highest Total	For	803-4d		v	Essex	Brentwood	1934
	V	676		by	Australians	Canterbury	1921
Lowest Total	For	18		v	Sussex	Gravesend	1867
	V	16		by	Warwicks	Tonbridge	1913
Highest Innings	For	332	W.H.Ashdown	v	Essex	Brentwood	1934
	V	344	W.G.Grace	for	MCC	Canterbury	1876

Highest Partnership for each Wicket

1st	300	N.R.Taylor/M.R.Benson	v	Derbyshire	Canterbury	1991
2nd	382	S.R.Dickson/J.L.Denly	v	Northants	Beckenham	2017
3rd	323	R.W.T.Key/M.van Jaarsveld	v	Surrey	Tunbridge Wells	2005
4th	368	P.A.de Silva/G.R.Cowdrey	v	Derbyshire	Maidstone	1995
5th	277	F.E.Woolley/L.E.G.Ames	v	N Zealanders	Canterbury	1931
6th	346	S.W.Billings/D.I.Stephens	v	Yorkshire	Leeds	2019
7th	248	A.P.Day/E.Humphreys	v	Somerset	Taunton	1908
8th	222	S.A.Northeast/J.C.Tredwell	v	Essex	Chelmsford	2016
9th	171	M.A.Ealham/P.A.Strang	v	Notts	Nottingham	1997
10th	235	F.E.Woolley/A.Fielder	v	Worcs	Stourbridge	1909

Best Bowling	For	10- 30	C.Blythe	v	Northants	Northampton	1907
(Innings)	V	10- 48	C.H.G.Bland	for	Sussex	Tonbridge	1899
Best Bowling	For	17- 48	C.Blythe	v	Northants	Northampton	1907
(Match)	V	17-106	T.W.J.Goddard	for	Glos	Bristol	1939

Most Runs – Season	2894	F.E.Woolley	(av 59.06)		1928
Most Runs – Career	47868	F.E.Woolley	(av 41.77)		1906-38
Most 100s – Season	10	F.E.Woolley		1928, 1934
Most 100s – Career	122	F.E.Woolley			1906-38
Most Wkts – Season	262	A.P.Freeman	(av 14.74)		1933
Most Wkts – Career	3340	A.P.Freeman	(av 17.64)		1914-36
Most Career W-K Dismissals	1253	F.H.Huish	(901 ct; 352 st)	1895-1914
Most Career Catches in the Field	773	F.E.Woolley			1906-38

LIMITED-OVERS CRICKET

Highest Total	50ov	384-6		v	Berkshire	Finchampstead	1994
		384-8		v	Surrey	Beckenham	2018
	40ov	337-7		v	Sussex	Canterbury	2013
	T20	231-7		v	Surrey	The Oval	2015
		231-5		v	Somerset	Canterbury	2018
Lowest Total	50ov	60		v	Somerset	Taunton	1979
	40ov	83		v	Middlesex	Lord's	1984
	T20	72		v	Hampshire	Southampton[2]	2011
Highest Innings	50ov	150*	J.L.Denly	v	Glamorgan	Canterbury	2018
	40ov	146	A.Symonds	v	Lancashire	Tunbridge Wells	2004
	T20	127	J.L.Denly	v	Essex	Chelmsford	2017
Best Bowling	50ov	8-31	D.L.Underwood	v	Scotland	Edinburgh	1987
	40ov	6- 9	R.A.Woolmer	v	Derbyshire	Chesterfield	1979
	T20	5-11	A.F.Milne	v	Somerset	Taunton	2017

LANCASHIRE

Formation of Present Club: 12 January 1864
Inaugural First-Class Match: 1865
Colours: Red, Green and Blue
Badge: Red Rose
County Champions (since 1890): (8) 1897, 1904, 1926, 1927, 1928, 1930, 1934, 2011
Joint Champions: (1) 1950
Gillette/NatWest Trophy Winners: (7) 1970, 1971, 1972, 1975, 1990, 1996, 1998
Benson and Hedges Cup Winners: (4) 1984, 1990, 1995, 1996
Pro 40/National League (Div 1) Winners: (1) 1999.
Sunday League Winners: (4) 1969, 1970, 1989, 1998
Twenty20 Cup Winners: (1) 2015

Chief Executive: Daniel Gidney, Emirates Old Trafford, Talbot Road, Manchester M16 0PX • Tel: 0161 282 4000 • Email: enquiries@lancashirecricket.co.uk • Web: www.lancashirecricket.co.uk • Twitter: @lancscricket (112,545 followers)

Director of Cricket: Paul Allott. **Head Coach**: Glen Chapple. **Assistant Coach/Development Director**: Mark Chilton. **Captain**: D.J.Vilas. **Overseas Players**: J.P.Faulkner (T20 only), G.J.Maxwell and B.J.Watling. **2020 Testimonial**: S.D.Parry. **Head Groundsman**: Matthew Merchant. **Scorer**: Chris Rimmer. **Blast Team Name**: Lancashire Lightning. ‡ New registration. ^NQ^ Not qualified for England.

ANDERSON, James Michael (St Theodore RC HS and SFC, Burnley), b Burnley 30 Jul 1982. 6'2". LHB, RFM. Squad No 9. Debut (Lancashire) 2002; cap 2003; benefit 2012. Auckland 2007-08. YC 2003. *Wisden* 2008. OBE 2015. **ECB Test Central Contract 2019-20. Tests**: 151 (2003 to 2019-20); HS 81 v I (Nottingham) 2014, sharing a world Test record 10th wkt partnership of 198 with J.E.Root; 50 wkts (3); most – 57 (2010); BB 7-42 v WI (Lord's) 2017. **LOI**: 194 (2002-03 to 2014-15); HS 28 v NZ (Southampton) 2013; BB 5-23 v SA (Port Elizabeth) 2009-10. Hat-trick v P (Oval) 2003 – 1st for E in 373 LOI. **IT20**: 19 (2006-07 to 2009-10); HS 1* v A (Sydney) 2006-07; BB 3-23 v Netherlands (Lord's) 2009. F-c Tours: A 2006-07, 2010-11, 2013-14, 2017-18; SA 2004-05, 2009-10, 2015-16, 2019-20; WI 2003-04, 2005-06 (Eng A) (*part*), 2008-09, 2014-15, 2018-19; NZ 2007-08, 2012-13, 2017-18; I 2005-06 (*part*), 2008-09, 2012-13, 2016-17; SL 2003-04, 2007-08, 2011-12, 2018-19; UAE 2011-12 (v P), 2015-16 (v P). HS 81 (*see Tests*). La HS 42 v Surrey (Manchester) 2015. 50 wkts (4); most – 60 (2005, 2017). BB 7-42 (*see Tests*). La BB 7-77 v Essex (Chelmsford) 2015. Hat-trick v Essex (Manchester) 2003. LO HS 28 (*see LOI*). LO BB 5-23 (*see LOI*). T20 HS 16. T20 BB 3-23.

BAILEY, Thomas Ernest (Our Lady's Catholic HS, Preston), b Preston 21 Apr 1991. 6'4". RHB, RMF. Squad No 8. Debut (Lancashire) 2012; cap 2018. F-c Tour (EL): I 2018-19. HS 68 v Northants (Manchester) 2019. 50 wkts (1): 65 (2018). BB 5-12 v Leics (Leicester) 2015. LO HS 33 v Yorks (Manchester) 2018 (RLC). LO BB 3-31 v Middx (Blackpool) 2015 (RLC). T20 HS 10. T20 BB 2-24.

BALDERSON, George Philip (Cheadle Hulme HS), b Manchester 11 Oct 2000. 5'11". LHB, RM. Lancashire 2nd XI debut 2018. England U19 2018-19. Awaiting 1st XI debut.

BOHANNON, Joshua James (Harper Green HS), b Bolton 9 Apr 1997. 5'8". RHB, RM. Squad No 20. Debut (Lancashire) 2018. Lancashire 2nd XI debut 2014. HS 174 v Derbys (Manchester) 2019. BB 3-46 v Hants (Southampton) 2018. LO HS 55* v Yorks (Leeds) 2019 (RLC). LO BB 1-33 v Notts (Nottingham) 2019. T20 HS 23.

BUTTLER, Joseph Charles (King's C, Taunton), b Taunton, Somerset 8 Sep 1990. 6'0". RHB, WK. Squad No 6. Somerset 2009-13; cap 2013. Lancashire debut 2014; cap 2018. IPL: MI 2016-17. RR 2018-19. Big Bash: MR 2013-14. ST 2017-18 to 2018-19. *Wisden* 2018. MBE 2020. **ECB Test & L-O Central Contract 2019-20. Tests:** 41 (2014 to 2019-20); HS 106 v I (Nottingham) 2018. **LOI:** 142 (2011-12 to 2019); HS 150 v WI (St George's) 2018-19. **IT20:** 69 (2011 to 2019-20); HS 73* v SL (Southampton) 2016. F-c Tours: SA 2019-20; WI 2015, 2018-19; NZ 2019-20; I 2016-17; SL 2018-19, 2019-20; UAE 2015-16 (v P). HS 144 Sm v Hants (Southampton) 2010. La HS 100* v Durham (Chester-le-St) 2014. BB – . LO HS 150 (*see LOI*). T20 HS 95*.

CROFT, Steven John (Highfield HS, Blackpool; Myerscough C), b Blackpool 11 Oct 1984. 5'10". RHB, OB. Squad No 15. Debut (Lancashire) 2005; cap 2010; captain 2017; testimonial 2018. Auckland 2008-09. HS 156 v Northants (Manchester) 2014. BB 6-41 v Worcs (Manchester) 2012. LO HS 127 v Warwks (Birmingham) 2017 (RLC). LO BB 4-24 v Scotland (Manchester) 2008 (FPT). T20 HS 94*. T20 BB 3-6.

DAVIES, Alexander Luke (Queen Elizabeth GS, Blackburn), b Darwen 23 Aug 1994. 5'7". RHB, WK. Squad No 17. Debut (Lancashire) 2012; cap 2017. F-c Tour (EL): WI 2017-18. 1000 runs (1): 1046 (2017). HS 147 v Northants (Northampton) 2019. LO HS 147 v Durham (Manchester) 2018 (RLC). T20 HS 94*.

^{NQ}**FAULKNER, James** Peter, b Launceston, Tasmania, Australia 29 Apr 1990. Son of P.I.Faulkner (Tasmania 1982-83 to 1989-90). 6'1". RHB, LMF. Squad No 44. Tasmania 2008-09 to date. Lancashire debut 2015; cap 2019. IPL: PW 2012. KXIP 2012. RR 2013-15. GL 2016-17 Big Bash: MS 2011-12 to 2017-18. HH 2018-19 to date. **Tests:** 1 (2013); HS 23 and BB 4-51 (Oval) 2013. **LOI** (A): 69 (2012-13 to 2017-18); HS 116 v I (Bangalore) 2013-14; BB 4-32 v P (Brisbane) 2014-15. **IT20** (A): 24 (2011-12 to 2016-17); HS 41* v SA (Adelaide) 2014-15; BB 5-27 v P (Mohali) 2015-16. F-c Tour (A): E 2013. HS 121 v Surrey (Oval) 2015. BB 5-5 Tas v SA (Hobart) 2010-11. La BB 5-39 v Essex (Manchester) 2015. LO HS 116 (*see LOI*). LO BB 4-20 Tas v Vic (Melbourne) 2010-11. T20 HS 73. T20 BB 5-16.

GLEESON, Richard James (Baines HS), b Blackpool, Lancs 2 Dec 1987. 6'3". RHB, RFM. Squad No 11. Northamptonshire 2015-18. Lancashire debut 2018. MCC 2018. Cumberland 2010-15. F-c Tour (EL): WI 2017-18. HS 31 Nh v Glos (Bristol) 2016. La HS 11 v Leics (Liverpool) 2019. BB 6-43 v Leics (Leicester) 2019. Hat-trick MCC v Essex (Bridgetown) 2017-18. LO HS 13 EL v West Indies A (Coolidge) 2017-18. LO BB 5-47 Nh v Worcs (Worcester) 2016 (RLC). T20 HS 7*. T20 BB 3-12.

GUEST, Brooke David (Kent Street Senior HS, Perth, WA; Murdoch U, Perth), b Whitworth Park, Manchester 14 May 1997. 5'11". RHB, WK. Squad No 29. Debut (Lancashire) 2018. Lancashire 2nd XI debut 2016. HS 17 v Middx (Lord's) 2019. LO HS 36 v Worcs (Manchester) 2019 (RLC).

HARTLEY, Tom William (Merchant Taylors S), b Ormskirk 3 May 1999. LHB, SLA. Squad No 2. Lancashire 2nd XI debut 2018. Awaiting 1st XI debut.

HURT, Liam Jack (Balshaw's CE HS, Leyland), b Preston 15 Mar 1994. 6'4". RHB, RMF. Squad No 22. Debut (Lancashire) 2019. Leicestershire 2015 (l-o only). HS 38 v Leics (Leicester) 2019. BB – . LO HS 15* v Yorks (Leeds) 2019 (RLC). LO BB 2-24 v Leics (Manchester) 2019 (RLC).

JENNINGS, Keaton Kent (King Edward VII S, Johannesburg), b Johannesburg, South Africa 19 Jun 1992. Son of R.V.Jennings (Transvaal 1973-74 to 1992-93), brother of D.Jennings (Gauteng and Easterns 1999 to 2003-04), nephew of K.E.Jennings (Northern Transvaal 1981-82 to 1982-83). 6'4". LHB, RM. Squad No 1. Gauteng 2011-12. Durham 2012-17; captain 2017 (l-o only). Lancashire debut/cap 2018. **Tests:** 17 (2016-17 to 2018-19); HS 146* v SL (Galle) 2018; scored 112 v I (Mumbai) on debut; BB – . F-c Tours (C=Captain): A 2019-20 (EL)C; WI 2017-18 (EL)C, 2018-19; I 2016/17; SL 2016-17 (EL), 2018-19. 1000 runs (1): 1602 (2016), inc seven hundreds (Du record). HS 221* Du v Yorks (Chester-le-St) 2016. La HS 177 v Worcs (Worcester) 2018. BB 3-37 Du v Sussex (Chester-le-St) 2017. La BB 1-8 v Durham (Sedbergh) 2018. LO HS 139 Du v Warwks (Birmingham) 2017 (RLC). LO BB 2-19 v Worcs (Worcester) 2018 (RLC). T20 HS 88. T20 BB 4-37.

JONES, Robert Peter (Bridgewater HS), b Warrington, Cheshire 3 Nov 1995. 5'10". RHB, LB. Squad No 12. Debut (Lancashire) 2016. Lancashire 2nd XI debut 2013. Cheshire 2014. England U19 2014. HS 122 v Middx (Lord's) 2019. BB 1-18 v Worcs (Worcester) 2018. LO HS 65 v Yorks (Leeds) 2019 (RLC). LO BB 1-3 v Leics (Manchester) 2019 (RLC). T20 HS – .

LAMB, Daniel John (St Michael's HS, Chorley; Cardinal Newman C, Preston), b Preston 7 Sep 1995. 6'0". RHB, RM. Squad No 26. Debut (Lancashire) 2018. Lancashire 2nd XI debut 2013. HS 49 and BB 4-70 v Glamorgan (Colwyn B) 2019. LO HS 4* and LO BB 2-51 v Durham (Chester-le-St) 2017 (RLC). T20 HS 24. T20 BB 3-30.

LAVELLE, George Isaac Davies (Merchant Taylors S), b Ormskirk 24 Mar 2000. 5'8". LHB. WK. Lancashire 2nd XI debut 2017. England U19 2018. Awaiting 1st XI debut.

LESTER, Toby James (Rossall S; Loughborough U), b Blackpool 5 Apr 1993. 6'4". LHB, LMF. Squad No 5. Loughborough MCCU 2012-14. Lancashire debut 2015. Warwickshire 2019 (on loan). MCC Univs 2012-14. HS 8 (twice) v Worcs (Southport) 2018. BB 4-41 Wa v Surrey (Oval) 2019. La BB 3-50 v Essex (Manchester) 2015. T20 HS 7*. T20 BB 4-25.

LIVINGSTONE, Liam Stephen (Chetwynde S, Barrow-in-Furness), b Barrow-in-Furness, Cumberland 4 Aug 1993. 6'1". RHB, LB. Squad No 7. Debut (Lancashire) 2016; cap 2017; captain 2018. IPL: RR 2019. Big Bash: PS 2019-20. **IT20:** 2 (2017); HS 16 v SA (Taunton) 2017. F-c Tours (EL): WI 2017-18; SL 2016-17. HS 224 v Warwks (Manchester) 2017. BB 6-52 v Surrey (Manchester) 2017. LO HS 129 EL v South Africa A (Northampton) 2017. LO BB 3-51 v Yorks (Manchester) 2016 (RLC). T20 HS 100. T20 BB 4-17.

MAHMOOD, Saqib (Matthew Moss HS, Rochdale), b Birmingham, Warwks 25 Feb 1997. 6'3". RHB, RFM. Squad No 25. Debut (Lancashire) 2016. England U19 2014. **LOI:** 1 (2019-20); HS – ; BB 1-17 v SA (Johannesburg) 2019-20. **IT20:** 3 (2019-20); HS 4 v NZ (Wellington) 2019-20; BB 1-20 v NZ (Auckland) 2019-20. F-c Tour (EL): WI 2017-18. HS 34 v Middx (Manchester) 2019. BB 4-48 v Glos (Cheltenham) 2019. LO HS 45 v Warwks (Birmingham) 2019 (RLC). LO BB 6-37 v Northants (Manchester) 2019 (RLC). T20 HS 4. T20 BB 4-14.

^{NQ}**MAXWELL, Glenn** James, b Kew, Melbourne, Australia 14 Oct 1988. 5'9". RHB, OB. Squad No 32. Victoria 2010-11 to date. Hampshire 2014. Yorkshire 2015. Lancashire debut 2019. IPL: DD 2012-18. MI 2013. KXIP 2014-17. Big Bash: MR 2011-12. MS 2012-13 to date. **Tests** (A): 7 (2012-13 to 2017); HS 104 v I (Ranchi) 2016-17; BB 4-127 v I (Hyderabad) 2012-13. **LOI** (A): 110 (2012 to 2019); HS 102 v SL (Sydney) 2014-15; BB 4-46 v E (Perth) 2014-15. **IT20** (A): 61 (2012 to 2019-20); HS 145* v SL (Pallekele) 2016; BB 3-10 v E (Hobart) 2017-18. F-c Tours (A): I 2012-13, 2016-17; SA/Z 2013 (Aus A); B 2017; UAE 2014-15 (v P). HS 278 Vic v NSW (Sydney, NO) 2017-18. CC HS 140 Y v Durham (Scarborough) 2015. La HS 59 v Sussex (Manchester) 2019. BB 5-40 v Middx (Lord's) 2019. LO HS 146 H v Lancs (Manchester) 2014 (RLC). LO BB 4-46 (*see LOI*). T20 HS 145*. T20 BB 3-10.

MORLEY, Jack Peter (Siddal Moor Sports C), b Rochdale 25 Jun 1991. LHB, SLA. Lancashire 2nd XI debut 2018. England U19 2018-19. Awaiting 1st XI debut.

ONIONS, Graham (St Thomas More RC S, Blaydon), b Gateshead, Tyne & Wear 9 Sep 1982. 6'1". RHB, RFM. Squad No 99. Durham 2004-17; benefit 2015. Dolphins 2013-14. Lancashire debut/cap 2018. MCC 2007-08, 2015-16. *Wisden* 2009. **Tests**: 9 (2009 to 2012); HS 17* v A (Lord's) 2009; BB 5-38 v WI (Lord's) 2009 – on debut. **LOI**: 4 (2009 to 2009-10); HS 1 v A (Centurion) 2009-10; BB 2-58 v SL (Johannesburg) 2009-10. F-c Tours: SA 2009-10; NZ 2012-13; I 2007-08 (EL), 2012-13; SL 2013-14; B 2006-07 (Eng A); UAE 2011-12 (*part*). HS 65 Du v Notts (Chester-le-St) 2016. La HS 41 v Essex (Manchester) 2018. 50 wkts (8); most – 73 (2013). BB 9-67 Du v Notts (Nottingham) 2012. La BB 6-55 v Notts (Nottingham) 2018. LO HS 30* v Worcs (Worcester) 2018 (RLC). LO BB 4-45 Du v Lancs (Chester-le-St) 2013 (Y40). T20 HS 31. T20 BB 3-15.

PARKINSON, Matthew William (Bolton S), b Bolton 24 Oct 1996. Twin brother of C.F.Parkinson (*see LEICESTERSHIRE*). 6'0". RHB, LB. Squad No 28. Debut (Lancashire) 2016; cap 2019. Lancashire 2nd XI debut 2013. Staffordshire 2014. England U19 2016. **LOI**: 2 (2019-20); HS – ; BB – . **IT20**: 2 (2019-20); HS – ; BB 4-47 v NZ (Napier) 2019-20. F-c Tour: SL 2019-20. HS 22 E v SLPB (Colombo, PSS) 2019-20. La HS 14 v Middx (Manchester) 2019. BB 6-23 (10-165 match) v Sussex (Manchester) 2019. LO HS 15* EL v West Indies A (Coolidge) 2017-18. LO BB 5-51 v Worcs (Manchester) 201 (RLC). T20 HS 7*. T20 BB 4-23.

PARRY, Stephen David (Audenshaw HS), b Manchester 12 Jan 1986. 6'0". RHB, SLA. Squad No 4. Debut (Lancashire) 2007, taking 5-23 v Durham (v Durham) cap 2015; testimonial 2020. MCC 2019. Cumberland 2005-06. Big Bash: BH 2014-15. **LOI**: 2 (2013-14); HS – ; BB 3-32 v WI (North Sound) 2013-14. **IT20**: 5 (2013-14 to 2015-16); HS 1 v Netherlands (Chittagong) 2013-14; BB 2-33 v P (Dubai, DSC) 2015-16. HS 44 v Somerset (Manchester) 2017. BB 5-23 (*see above*). CC BB 5-45 v Middx (Southport) 2017. LO HS 31 v Essex (Chelmsford) 2009 (FPT). LO BB 5-17 v Surrey (Manchester) 2013 (Y40). T20 HS 15*. T20 BB 5-13 v Worcs (Manchester) 2016 – La record.

^{NQ}**VILAS, Dane** James, b Johannesburg, South Africa 10 Jun 1985. 6'2". RHB, WK. Squad No 33. Gauteng 2006-07 to 2009-10. Lions 2008-09 to 2009-10. W Province 2010-11. Cape Cobras 2011-12 to 2016-17. Lancashire debut 2017 (Kolpak signing); cap 2018; captain 2019 to date. Dolphins 2017-18 to 2018-19. **Tests** (SA): 6 (2015 to 2015-16); HS 26 v E (Johannesburg) 2015-16. **IT20** (SA): 1 (2011-12); HS – . F-c Tours (SA): A 2016 (SA A), I 2015 (SA A), 2015-16; Z 2016 (SA A), B 2015. 1000 runs (1): 1036 (2019). HS 266 v Glamorgan (Colwyn B) 2019. LO HS 166 v Notts (Nottingham) 2019 (RLC). T20 HS 75*.

‡^{NQ}**WATLING**, Bradley-John ('**BJ**'), b Durban, S Africa 9 Jul 1985. RHB, WK. N Districts 2004-05 to date. Durham 2019. **Tests** (NZ): 70 (2009-10 to 2019-20); HS 205 v E (Mt Maunganui) 2019-20. **LOI** (NZ): 28 (2010 to 2018-19); HS 96* v SL (Pallekele) 2012-13. **IT20** (NZ): 5 (2009-10 to 2014); HS 22 v P (Dubai) 2009-10. F-c Tours (NZ): E 2013, 2014 (NZA), 2015; A 2015-16, 2019-20; SA 2012-13, 2016; WI 2012, 2014; I 2008-09 (NZA), 2010-11, 2016-17; SL 2019; Z 2011-12, 2016; B 2013-14; UAE (v P) 2014-15, 2018-19. HS 205 (see Tests). CC HS 104* Du v Glamorgan (Chester-le-St) 2019. LO HS 145* ND v Auckland (Auckland, CN) 2009-10. T20 HS 75.

‡**WOOD, Luke** (Portland CS, Worksop), b Sheffield, Yorks 2 Aug 1995. 5'9". LHB, LFM. Squad No 14. Nottinghamshire 2014-19. Worcestershire 2018 (on loan). Northamptonshire 2019 (on loan). England U19 2014. HS 100 Nt v Sussex (Nottingham) 2015. BB 5-40 Nt v Cambridge MCCU (Cambridge) 2016. CC BB 5-67 Nt v Yorks (Scarborough) 2019. LO HS 52 Nt v Leics (Leicester) 2016 (RLC). LO BB 2-36 Nt v Worcs (Worcester) 2019 (RLC). T20 HS 11. T20 BB 3-16.

RELEASED/RETIRED

(Having made a County 1st XI appearance in 2019)

^{NQ}**BURNS, Joseph** Antony, b Herston, Brisbane, Australia 6 Sep 1989. RHB, RM. Queensland 2010-11 to date. Leicestershire 2013. Middlesex 2015. Lancashire 2019. Glamorgan 2018 (T20 only). Big Bash: BH 2012-13 to date. **Tests** (A): 21 (2014-15 to 2019-20); HS 180 v SL (Canberra) 2018-19. **LOI** (A): 6 (2015); HS 69 v Ire (Belfast) 2015. F-c Tours (A): E 2012 (Aus A), 2019 (Aus A); SA 2017-18; NZ 2015-16; I 2015 (Aus A); SL 2016. HS 202* Q v SA (Cairns) 2017-18. CC HS 87 M v Worcs (Uxbridge) 2015. La HS 10 v Northants (Manchester) 2019. BB 1-0 Q v Tas (Brisbane) 2016-17. LO HS 154 Aus A v India A (Chennai) 2015. LO BB 1-20 Q v WA (Sydney, HO) 2018-19. T20 HS 81*. T20 BB 1-8.

HAMEED, H. – see NOTTINGHAMSHIRE.

^{NQ}**LEHMANN, Jake** Scott (Charles Campbell SS), b Melbourne, Australia 8 Jul 1992. Son of D.S.Lehmann (S Australia, Victoria, Yorkshire and Australia 1987-88 to 2007-08), nephew of C.White (Yorkshire, Victoria and England 1990-2007). LHB, SLA. S Australia 2014-15 to date. Yorkshire 2016. Lancashire 2019. Big Bash: AS 2015-16 to 2018-19. HS 205 SA v Tas (Hobart) 2015-16. CC HS 116 Y v Somerset (Leeds) 2016. La HS 22 v Leics (Liverpool) 2019. BB 2-17 SA v NSW (Sydney) 2018-19. LO HS 87 SA v NSW (Perth) 2018-19. T20 HS 46. T20 BB 1-5.

LANCASHIRE 2019

RESULTS SUMMARY

	Place	Won	Lost	Drew	NR
Specsavers County Champ (2nd Division)	1st	8		6	
All First-Class Matches		8		6	
Royal London One-Day Cup (North Group)	SF	6	4		
Vitality Blast (North Group)	QF	8	3		4

SPECSAVERS COUNTY CHAMPIONSHIP AVERAGES
BATTING AND FIELDING

Cap		M	I	NO	HS	Runs	Avge	100	50	Ct/St
2018	D.J.Vilas	14	17	4	266	1036	79.69	2	7	47/1
	J.J.Bohannon	11	12	3	174	472	52.44	1	2	4
2010	S.J.Croft	11	12	2	78	472	47.20	–	4	4
2017	L.S.Livingstone	11	14	1	114	599	46.07	1	5	7
	R.P.Jones	14	19	2	122	624	36.70	1	4	11
2017	A.L.Davies	10	14	1	147	468	36.00	1	2	–
2018	K.K.Jennings	14	21	2	97	588	30.94	–	6	17
2016	H.Hameed	10	15	3	117	341	28.41	1	1	5
2018	T.E.Bailey	9	10	–	68	207	20.70	–	2	5
	G.J.Maxwell	4	5	–	59	96	19.20	–	1	3
	S.Mahmood	9	10	2	34	136	17.00	–	–	–
	J.S.Lehmann	3	4	–	22	35	8.75	–	–	–
	R.J.Gleeson	9	8	4	11	34	8.50	–	–	2
2018	G.Onions	10	10	1	18	34	8.50	–	–	2
2003	J.M.Anderson	6	6	2	18	65	7.22	–	–	1
2019	M.W.Parkinson	4	4	–	14	19	4.75	–	–	3

Also batted (1 match each): J.A.Burns 10; B.D.Guest 17, 11 (5 ct); L.J.Hurt 38; D.J.Lamb 49; S.D.Parry 0.

BOWLING

	O	M	R	W	Avge	Best	5wI	10wM
J.M.Anderson	159.4	61	281	30	9.36	5-18	2	–
M.W.Parkinson	143.5	33	381	20	19.05	6-23	1	1
G.Onions	306.1	66	881	45	19.57	5-38	3	–
R.J.Gleeson	273.1	61	948	47	20.17	6-43	5	1
G.J.Maxwell	109.5	27	287	14	20.50	5-40	1	–
T.E.Bailey	289.2	81	777	37	21.00	5-41	3	–
L.S.Livingstone	135.1	42	249	10	24.90	2-17	–	–
S.Mahmood	196.3	31	660	21	31.42	4-48	–	–
Also bowled:								
D.J.Lamb	26	5	89	6	14.83	4-70	–	–
S.D.Parry	55	5	156	5	31.20	3-59	–	–
J.J.Bohannon	109.4	20	365	5	73.00	1-31	–	–

S.J.Croft 26-6-60-1; A.L.Davies 1-0-6-0; L.J.Hurt 25-6-66-0; K.K.Jennings 26-3-68-1; R.P.Jones 5-1-15-0.

Lancashire played no first-class fixtures outside the County Championship in 2019. The First-Class Averages (pp 226–241) give the records of their players in all first-class county matches, with the exception of J.M.Anderson and J.A.Burns, whose first-class figures for Lancashire are as above.

LANCASHIRE RECORDS

FIRST-CLASS CRICKET

Highest Total	For	863		v	Surrey	The Oval	1990
	V	707-9d		by	Surrey	The Oval	1990
Lowest Total	For	25		v	Derbyshire	Manchester	1871
	V	20		by	Essex	Chelmsford	2013
Highest Innings	For	424	A.C.MacLaren	v	Somerset	Taunton	1895
	V	315*	T.W.Hayward	for	Surrey	The Oval	1898

Highest Partnership for each Wicket

1st	368	A.C.MacLaren/R.H.Spooner	v	Glos	Liverpool	1903
2nd	371	F.B.Watson/G.E.Tyldesley	v	Surrey	Manchester	1928
3rd	501	A.N.Petersen/A.G.Prince	v	Glamorgan	Colwyn Bay	2015
4th	358	S.P.Titchard/G.D.Lloyd	v	Essex	Chelmsford	1996
5th	360	S.G.Law/C.L.Hooper	v	Warwicks	Birmingham	2003
6th	278	J.Iddon/H.R.W.Butterworth	v	Sussex	Manchester	1932
7th	248	G.D.Lloyd/I.D.Austin	v	Yorkshire	Leeds	1997
8th	158	J.Lyon/R.M.Ratcliffe	v	Warwicks	Manchester	1979
9th	142	L.O.S.Poidevin/A.Kermode	v	Sussex	Eastbourne	1907
10th	173	J.Briggs/R.Pilling	v	Surrey	Liverpool	1885

Best Bowling	For	10-46	W.Hickton	v	Hampshire	Manchester	1870
(Innings)	V	10-40	G.O.B.Allen	for	Middlesex	Lord's	1929
Best Bowling	For	17-91	H.Dean	v	Yorkshire	Liverpool	1913
(Match)	V	16-65	G.Giffen	for	Australians	Manchester	1886

Most Runs – Season	2633	J.T.Tyldesley	(av 56.02)	1901
Most Runs – Career	34222	G.E.Tyldesley	(av 45.20)	1909-36
Most 100s – Season	11	C.Hallows		1928
Most 100s – Career	90	G.E.Tyldesley		1909-36
Most Wkts – Season	198	E.A.McDonald	(av 18.55)	1925
Most Wkts – Career	1816	J.B.Statham	(av 15.12)	1950-68
Most Career W-K Dismissals	925	G.Duckworth	(635 ct; 290 st)	1923-38
Most Career Catches in the Field	556	K.J.Grieves		1949-64

LIMITED-OVERS CRICKET

Highest Total	50ov	406-9		v	Notts	Nottingham	2019
	40ov	324-4		v	Worcs	Worcester	2012
	T20	231-4		v	Yorkshire	Manchester	2015
Lowest Total	50ov	59		v	Worcs	Worcester	1963
	40ov	68		v	Yorkshire	Leeds	2000
		68		v	Surrey	The Oval	2002
	T20	91		v	Derbyshire	Manchester	2003
Highest Innings	50ov	166	D.J.Vilas	v	Notts	Nottingham	2019
	40ov	143	A.Flintoff	v	Essex	Chelmsford	1999
	T20	103*	A.N.Petersen	v	Leics	Leicester	2016
Best Bowling	50ov	6-10	C.E.H.Croft	v	Scotland	Manchester	1982
	40ov	6-25	G.Chapple	v	Yorkshire	Leeds	1998
	T20	5-13	S.D.Parry	v	Worcs	Manchester	2016

LEICESTERSHIRE

Formation of Present Club: 25 March 1879
Inaugural First-Class Match: 1894
Colours: Dark Green and Scarlet
Badge: Gold Running Fox on Green Ground
County Champions: (3) 1975, 1996, 1998
Benson and Hedges Cup Winners: (3) 1972, 1975, 1985
Sunday League Champions: (2) 1974, 1977
Twenty20 Cup Winners: (3) 2004, 2006, 2011

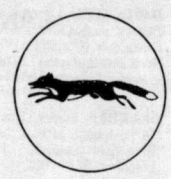

Chief Executive: tba, Fischer County Ground, Grace Road, Leicester LE2 8EB • Tel: 0116 283 2128 • Email: enquiries@leicestershireccc.co.uk • Web: www.leicestershireccc.co.uk • Twitter: @leicsccc (59,995 followers)

Head Coach: Paul Nixon. **Assistant Coach**: Tom Smith. **Captains**: P.J.Horton (f-c and l-o) and C.N.Ackermann (T20). **Overseas Players**: C.N.Ackermann and J.N.Malan. **2020 Testimonial**: None. **Head Groundsman**: Andy Ward. **Scorer**: Paul Rogers. **Blast Team Name**: Leicestershire Foxes. ‡ New registration. NQ Not qualified for England.

NQACKERMANN, Colin Niel (Grey HS, Port Elizabeth; U of SA), b George, South Africa 4 Apr 1991. RHB, OB. Squad No 48. Eastern Province 2010-11 to 2015-16. Warriors 2013-14 to 2018-19. Leicestershire debut 2017; cap 2019; captain 2020 (T20 only). **IT20** (Neth): 11 (2019-20); HS 43* and BB 1-6 v Bermuda (Dubai, DSC) 2019-20. 1000 runs (0+1): 1200 (2013-14). HS 196* v Middx (Leicester) 2018. BB 5-69 v Sussex (Hove) 2019. LO HS 152* v Worcs (Leicester) 2019 (RLC). LO BB 4-48 Warriors v Dolphins (Durban) 2017-18. T20 HS 79*. T20 BB 7-18 v Warwks (Leicester) 2019 – world record T20 figures.

AZAD, Mohammad Hasan (Fernwood S, Nottingham; Bilborough SFC; Loughborough U), b Quetta, Pakistan 7 Jan 1994. Son of Imran Azad (Public Works 1986-87). LHB, OB. Squad No 42. Loughborough MCCU 2015-16. Leicestershire debut 2019, scoring 139 v Loughborough MCCU (Leicester), sharing then Le record 2nd wkt partnership of 309 with A.Javid. 1000 runs (1): 1189 (2019). HS 139 (see above). CC HS 137 v Glos (Leicester) 2019, sharing Le record 2nd wkt partnership of 320 with N.J.Dexter.

BOWLEY, Nathan John (Woodvale S, Loughborough; Loughborough C), b Nottingham 3 Aug 2001. LHB, OB. Leicestershire 2nd XI debut 2018. Awaiting 1st XI debut.

BUTCHART, Donald Norton (Oakham S), b Harare, Zimbabwe 18 Dec 1998. Son of I.P.Butchart (Zimbabwe & Mashonaland 1980-81 to 1994-95). RHB, RM. Awaiting f-c debut. Leicestershire 2nd XI debut 2017. LO HS 12 v India A (Leicester) 2018. No 1st XI appearances in 2019.

NQCOSGROVE, Mark James, b Elizabeth, Adelaide, S Australia 14 Jun 1984. 5'9". LHB, RM. Squad No 55. S Australia 2002-03 to 2015-16. Glamorgan 2006-10; cap 2006. Tasmania 2010-11 to 2013-14. Leicestershire debut/cap 2015; captain 2015-17. **LOI** (A): 3 (2005-06 to 2006-07); HS 74 v B (Fatullah) 2005-06 – on debut; BB 1-1 v WI (Kuala Lumpur) 2006-07. 1000 runs (4): most – 1279 (2016). HS 233 Gm v Derbys (Derby) 2006. Le HS 188 v Derbys (Derby) 2017. BB 3-3 SA v Tas (Adelaide) 2006-07. CC BB Gm 3-30 v Derbys (Derby) 2009. Le BB 2-14 v Worcs (Worcester) 2016. LO HS 121 SA v WA (Perth) 2005-06. LO BB 2-21 SA v Q (Brisbane) 2005-06. T20 HS 89. T20 BB 2-11.

DAVIS, William Samuel (Stafford GS), b 6 Mar 1996. 6'1". RHB, RFM. Squad No 44. Derbyshire 2015-18. Leicestershire debut 2019. Derbyshire 2nd XI debut 2013. HS 39* v Glamorgan (Cardiff) 2019. BB 7-146 De v Glamorgan (Colwyn Bay) 2016. Le BB 4-73 v Northants (Leicester) 2019. LO HS 15* v Durham (Chester-le-St) 2019 (RLC). LO BB 1-60 v Worcs (Leicester) 2019 (RLC). T20 HS 2. T20 BB 3-24.

DEARDEN, Harry Edward (Tottington HS), b Bury, Lancs 7 May 1997. LHB, OB. Squad No 5. Debut (Leicestershire) 2016. Lancashire 2nd XI 2014-15. Cheshire 2016. HS 87 v Glamorgan (Leicester) 2017. BB 1-0 v Kent (Leicester) 2017. LO HS 91 v Worcs (Leicester) 2019 (RLC). T20 HS 61.

EVANS, Huw Alexander (Bedford Modern S; Leeds Beckett U), b Bedford 9 Aug 2000. LHB, RFM. Loughborough MCCU 2019. Leicestershire debut 2019. Leicestershire 2nd XI debut 2018. Bedfordshire 2017. HS 7* and BB 3-49 LU v Kent (Canterbury) 2019. Le HS 5* and Le BB 1-14 v Northants (Leicester) 2019 – only 1st XI appearance.

EVANS, Samuel Thomas (Lancaster S, Leicester; Wyggeston & QE I C; Leicester U), b Leicester 20 Dec 1997. RHB, OB. Squad No 21. Loughborough MCCU 2017-18. Leicestershire debut 2017. Leicestershire 2nd XI debut 2015. HS 114 LU v Northants (Northampton) 2017. Le HS 29 v Northants (Leicester) 2017 and 29 v Derbys (Derby) 2018. LO HS 20 v India A (Leicester) 2018.

GRIFFITHS, Gavin Timothy (St Mary's C, Crosby), b Ormskirk, Lancs 19 Nov 1993. 6'2". RHB, RMF. Debut (Leicestershire) 2017. Lancashire 2014-15 (l-o only). Hampshire 2016 (T20 only). HS 40 v Middx (Leicester) 2018. BB 6-49 (10-83 match) v Durham (Chester-le-St) 2018. LO HS 15* v Notts (Leicester) 2018 (RLC). LO BB 4-30 v Northants (Northampton) 2018 (RLC). T20 HS 11. T20 BB 3-14.

HILL, Lewis John (Hastings HS, Hinckley; John Cleveland C), b Leicester 5 Oct 1990. 5'7½". RHB, WK, occ RM. Squad No 23. Debut (Leicestershire) 2015. Unicorns 2012-13. HS 126 v Surrey (Oval) 2015. LO HS 118 v Worcs (Leicester) 2019 (RLC). T20 HS 58.

HORTON, Paul James (St Margaret's HS, Liverpool), b Sydney, Australia 20 Sep 1982. 5'10". RHB, RM. Squad No 2. UK resident since 1997. Lancashire 2003-15; cap 2007. Matabeleland Tuskers 2010-11 to 2011-12. Leicestershire debut 2016; captain 2018 (*part*) to date. 1000 runs (3); most – 1116 (2007). HS 209 MT v SR (Masvingo) 2010-11. CC HS 173 La v Somerset (Taunton) 2009. Le HS 117* v Worcs (Worcester) 2016. BB 2-6 v Sussex (Leicester) 2016. LO HS 111* La v Derbys (Manchester) 2009 (FPT). LO BB 1-7 v Lancs (Leicester) 2016 (RLC). T20 HS 71*.

ᴺᴼKLEIN, Dieter (Hoerskool, Lichtenburg), b Lichtenburg, South Africa 31 Oct 1988. 5'10". RHB, LMF. Squad No 77. North West 2007-08 to 2015-16. Lions 2012-13 to 2013-14. Leicestershire debut 2016. **IT20** (Ger): 2 (2019-20); HS 31* and BB 1-12 v Spain (Almeria) 2019-20. HS 94 v Glamorgan (Cardiff) 2018. BB 8-72 NW v Northerns (Potchefstroom) 2014-15. Le BB 6-80 v Northants (Northampton) 2017. LO HS 46 v Durham (Chester-le-St) 2019 (RLC). LO BB 5-35 NW v Northerns (Pretoria) 2012-13. T20 HS 31*. T20 BB 3-27.

LILLEY, Arron Mark (Mossley Hollins HS; Ashton SFC), b Tameside, Lancs 1 Apr 1991. 6'1". RHB, OB. Squad No 19. Lancashire 2013-18. Leicestershire debut 2019. HS 63 and BB 5-23 La v Derbys (Southport) 2015. Le BB 2-22 v Loughborough MCCU (Leicester) 2019. LO HS 25 v Yorks (Leeds) 2019 (RLC). LO BB 4-30 La v Derbys (Manchester) 2013 (Y40). T20 HS 66. T20 BB 3-31.

‡**NQ****MALAN**, Johannes Nieuwoudt ('**Janneman**') (Waterkloof HS), b Nelspruit, South Africa 18 Apr 1996. Younger brother of P.J.Malan (Northerns, Titans, W Province, Cape Cobras and South Africa 2006-07 to date) and A.J.Malan (Northerns, North West, W Province 2010-11 to date). RHB, LB. Squad No 18. North West 2015-16 to 2017-18. Cape Cobras 2018-19 to date. **LOI** (SA): 3 (2019-20); HS 129* v A (Bloemfontein) 2019-20. **IT20** (SA): 2 (2018-19); HS 33 v P (Johannesburg) 2018-19. 1000 runs (0+1): 1046 (2017-18). HS 208* NW v WP (Potchefstroom) 2017-18. LO HS 170* NW v KZN (Potchefstroom) 2016-17. T20 HS 128*.

MIKE, Benjamin Wentworth Munro (Loughborough GS), b Nottingham 24 Aug 1998. Son of G.W.Mike (Nottinghamshire 1989-96). RHB, RM. Squad No 8. Debut (Leicestershire) 2018. Warwickshire 2019 (on loan). Leicestershire 2nd XI debut 2017. HS 72 Wa v Hants (Southampton) 2019. Le HS 39 v Warwks (Leicester) 2018. BB 5-37 (9-94 match) v Sussex (Hove) 2018 – on debut. LO HS 41 and LO BB 1-47 v Northants (Leicester) 2019 (RLC). T20 HS 37. T20 BB 3-38.

PARKINSON, Callum Francis (Bolton S), b Bolton, Lancs 24 Oct 1996. Twin brother of M.W.Parkinson (*see LANCASHIRE*). RHB, SLA. Squad No 10. Derbyshire 2016. Leicestershire debut 2015-16. HS 75 v Kent (Canterbury) 2017. BB 8-148 (10-185 match) v Worcs (Worcester) 2017. LO HS 52* v Notts (Leicester) 2018 (RLC). LO BB 1-34 v Derbys (Derby) 2018 (RLC). T20 HS 27*. T20 BB 4-20.

RHODES, George Harry (Chase HS & SFC, Malvern), b Birmingham 26 Oct 1993. Son of S.J.Rhodes (Yorkshire, Worcestershire & England 1981-2004) and grandson of W.E.Rhodes (Nottinghamshire 1961-64). 6'0". RHB, OB. Worcestershire 2016-19. Leicestershire debut 2019. HS 61* v Northants (Leicester) 2019. BB 2-83 Wo v Kent (Canterbury) 2016. Le BB – . LO HS 106 v Yorks (Worcester) 2019 (RLC). LO BB 2-34 v Yorks (Leeds) 2016 (RLC). T20 HS 17*. T20 BB 4-13.

SWINDELLS, Harry John (Brockington C; Lutterworth C), b Leicester 21 Feb 1999. 5'7". RHB, WK. Squad No 28. Debut (Leicestershire) 2019. Leicestershire 2nd XI debut 2015. England U19 2017. HS 37 v Lancs (Liverpool) 2019. LO HS 28 v India A (Leicester) 2018. T20 HS 63.

TAYLOR, Thomas Alex Ian (Trentham HS, Stoke-on-Trent), b Stoke-on-Trent, Staffs 21 Dec 1994. Elder brother of J.P.A.Taylor (*see SURREY*). 6'2". RHB, RMF. Squad No 16. Derbyshire 2014-17. Leicestershire debut 2018. HS 80 De v Kent (Derby) 2016. Le HS 57 v Worcs (Leicester) 2019. BB 6-47 (10-122 match) v Sussex (Hove) 2014. LO HS 98* v Warwks (Leicester) 2019 (RLC). LO BB 3-48 De v Worcs (Worcester) 2014 (RLC).

WRIGHT, Christopher Julian Clement (Eggars S, Alton; Anglia Ruskin U), b Chipping Norton, Oxon 14 Jul 1985. 6'3". RHB, RFM. Squad No 31. Cambridge UCCE 2004-05. Middlesex 2004-07. Tamil Union 2005-06. Essex 2008-11. Warwickshire 2011-18; cap 2013. Leicestershire debut 2019. F-c Tour (MCC): Nepal 2019-20. HS 77 Ex v Cambridge MCCU (Cambridge) 2011. CC HS 72 Wa v Derbys (Birmingham) 2018. Le HS 60 v Glamorgan (Cardiff) 2019. 50 wkts (2); most – 67 (2012). BB 6-22 Ex v Leics (Leicester) 2008. Le BB 5-30 v Durham (Leicester) 2019. LO HS 42 Ex v Glos (Cheltenham) 2011 (CB40). LO BB 4-20 Ex v Unicorns (Chelmsford) 2011 (CB40). T20 HS 6*. T20 BB 4-24.

RELEASED/RETIRED

(Having made a County 1st XI appearance in 2019)

ALI, Aadil Masud (Lancaster S, Leicester; Q Elizabeth C), b Leicester 29 Dec 1994. 5'11". RHB, OB. Leicestershire 2015-17. HS 80 v Glos (Leicester) 2015. BB 1-10 v Worcs (Worcester) 2017. LO HS 88 v Worcs (Leicester) 2017 (RLC). LO BB 1-31 v Notts (Mkt Warsop) 2017 (RLC). T20 HS 35*. T20 BB 2-22.

RELEASED/RETIRED continued on p 142

LEICESTERSHIRE 2019

RESULTS SUMMARY

	Place	Won	Lost	Drew	NR
Specsavers County Champ (2nd Division)	10th	1	6	7	
All First-Class Matches		2	6	7	
Royal London One-Day Cup (North Group)	9th	2	6		
Vitality Blast (North Group)	9th	4	7		3

SPECSAVERS COUNTY CHAMPIONSHIP AVERAGES

BATTING AND FIELDING

Cap		M	I	NO	HS	Runs	Avge	100	50	Ct/St
	M.H.Azad	14	26	4	137	1189	54.04	3	8	7
2019	C.N.Ackermann	14	25	6	70*	675	35.52	–	7	19
2015	M.J.Cosgrove	13	23	3	107*	697	34.85	1	6	2
	G.H.Rhodes	3	6	2	61*	128	32.00	–	1	1
	N.J.Dexter	8	12	–	180	359	29.91	1	1	1
	P.J.Horton	14	26	1	100*	744	29.76	1	3	11
	T.A.I.Taylor	3	4	–	57	115	28.75	–	1	1
	C.F.Parkinson	4	7	–	37	158	22.57	–	–	
	D.Klein	6	6	–	87	122	20.33	–	1	
	H.E.Dearden	13	19	–	61	375	19.73	–	1	6
	L.J.Hill	7	11	1	67	196	19.60	–	1	23/1
	H.J.Swindells	7	10	–	37	168	16.80	–	–	12/1
	C.J.C.Wright	14	21	3	60	295	16.38	–	1	3
	W.S.Davis	10	17	8	39*	142	15.77	–	–	1
	A.Javid	4	8	–	69	113	14.12	–	1	–
	B.W.M.Mike	5	8	1	16	73	10.42	–	–	
	G.T.Griffiths	4	7	–	22	41	5.85	–	1	
2018	Mohammad Abbas	9	11	3	11	22	2.75	–	–	4

Also batted: (1 match each): H.A.Evans 0, 5*; S.T.Evans 1.

BOWLING

	O	M	R	W	Avge	Best	5wI	10wM
T.A.I.Taylor	98	16	344	14	24.57	6- 47	1	1
Mohammad Abbas	281.5	81	747	29	25.75	4- 72	–	–
D.Klein	112	15	467	16	29.18	4-113	–	–
C.J.C.Wright	424.2	78	1455	47	30.95	5- 30	2	–
W.S.Davis	264.5	59	871	23	37.86	4- 73	–	–
B.W.M.Mike	104.3	14	486	11	44.18	3- 41	–	–
C.N.Ackermann	180	22	703	12	58.58	5- 69	1	–
Also bowled:								
G.T.Griffiths	110.3	19	380	9	42.22	3- 71	–	–
C.F.Parkinson	64.4	9	237	5	47.40	2- 0	–	–

M.J.Cosgrove 17.1-5-36-0; H.E.Dearden 2-0-13-0; N.J.Dexter 120.3-25-426-3; H.A.Evans 21-3-79-4; A.Javid 3-0-8-0; G.H.Rhodes 4.4-0-23-0.

The First-Class Averages (pp 226–241) give the records of Leicestershire players in all first-class county matches (Leicestershire's other opponents being Loughborough MCCU), with the exception of H.A.Evans, B.W.M.Mike and G.H.Rhodes, whose first-class figures for Leicestershire are as above, and:
M.H.Azad 15-27-4-139-1328-57.73-4-8-8ct. Did not bowl.

LEICESTERSHIRE RECORDS

FIRST-CLASS CRICKET

Highest Total	For 701-4d		v	Worcs	Worcester	1906
	V 761-6d		by	Essex	Chelmsford	1990
Lowest Total	For 25		v	Kent	Leicester	1912
	V 24		by	Glamorgan	Leicester	1971
	24		by	Oxford U	Oxford	1985
Highest Innings	For 309*	H.D.Ackerman	v	Glamorgan	Cardiff	2006
	V 355*	K.P.Pietersen	for	Surrey	The Oval	2015

Highest Partnership for each Wicket

1st	390	B.Dudleston/J.F.Steele	v	Derbyshire	Leicester	1979
2nd	320	M.H.Azad/N.J.Dexter	v	Glos	Leicester	2019
3rd	436*	D.L.Maddy/B.J.Hodge	v	L'boro UCCE	Leicester	2003
4th	360*	J.W.A.Taylor/A.B.McDonald	v	Middlesex	Leicester	2010
5th	330	J.W.A.Taylor/S.J.Thakor	v	L'boro MCCU	Leicester	2011
6th	284	P.V.Simmons/P.A.Nixon	v	Durham	Chester-le-St[2]	1996
7th	219*	J.D.R.Benson/P.Whitticase	v	Hampshire	Bournemouth	1991
8th	195	J.W.A.Taylor/J.K.H.Naik	v	Derbyshire	Leicester	2009
9th	160	R.T.Crawford/ W.W.Odell	v	Worcs	Leicester	1902
10th	228	R.Illingworth/K.Higgs	v	Northants	Leicester	1977

Best Bowling	For	10- 18	G.Geary	v	Glamorgan	Pontypridd	1929
(Innings)	V	10- 32	H.Pickett	for	Essex	Leyton	1895
Best Bowling	For	16- 96	G.Geary	v	Glamorgan	Pontypridd	1929
(Match)	V	16-102	C.Blythe	for	Kent	Leicester	1909

Most Runs – Season	2446	L.G.Berry	(av 52.04)		1937
Most Runs – Career	30143	L.G.Berry	(av 30.32)		1924-51
Most 100s – Season	7	L.G.Berry			1937
	7	W.Watson			1959
	7	B.F.Davison			1982
Most 100s – Career	45	L.G.Berry			1924-51
Most Wkts – Season	170	J.E.Walsh	(av 18.96)		1948
Most Wkts – Career	2131	W.E.Astill	(av 23.18)		1906-39
Most Career W-K Dismissals	905	R.W.Tolchard	(794 ct; 111 st)		1965-83
Most Career Catches in the Field	426	M.R.Hallam			1950-70

LIMITED-OVERS CRICKET

Highest Total	50ov	406-5		v	Berkshire	Leicester	1996
	40ov	344-4		v	Durham	Chester-le-St[2]	1996
	T20	229-5		v	Warwicks	Birmingham	2018
Lowest Total	50ov	56		v	Northants	Leicester	1964
		56		v	Minor Cos	Wellington	1982
	40ov	36		v	Sussex	Leicester	1973
	T20	90		v	Notts	Nottingham	2014
Highest Innings	50ov	201	V.J.Wells	v	Berkshire	Leicester	1996
	40ov	154*	B.J.Hodge	v	Sussex	Horsham	2004
	T20	113	B.A.Raine	v	Warwicks	Birmingham	2018
Best Bowling	50ov	6-16	C.M.Willoughby	v	Somerset	Leicester	2005
	40ov	6-17	K.Higgs	v	Glamorgan	Leicester	1973
	T20	7-18	C.N.Ackermann	v	Warwicks	Leicester	2019

MIDDLESEX

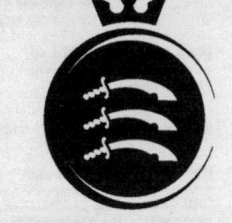

Formation of Present Club: 2 February 1864
Inaugural First-Class Match: 1864
Colours: Blue
Badge: Three Seaxes
County Champions (since 1890): (11) 1903, 1920, 1921, 1947, 1976, 1980, 1982, 1985, 1990, 1993, 2016
Joint Champions: (2) 1949, 1977
Gillette/NatWest Trophy Winners: (4) 1977, 1980, 1984, 1988
Benson and Hedges Cup Winners: (2) 1983, 1986
Sunday League Winners: (1) 1992
Twenty20 Cup Winners: (1) 2008

Chief Executive: Richard Goatley, Lord's Cricket Ground, London NW8 8QN • Tel: 020 7289 1300 • Email: enquiries@middlesexccc.com • Web: www.middlesexccc.com • Twitter: @Middlesex_CCC (80,299 followers)

Managing Director of Cricket: Angus Fraser MBE. **Head Coach**: Stuart Law. **Assistant Coaches**: Nic Pothas and Alan Coleman. **T20 Bowling Coach**: Dimitri Mascarenhas. **Captains**: P.S.P.Handscomb (f-c and l-o) and E.J.G.Morgan (T20). **Overseas Players**: P.S.P.Handscomb, M.R.Marsh (T20 only) and Mujeeb Zadran (T20 only). **2020 Testimonial**: E.J.G.Morgan. **Head Groundsman**: Karl McDermott. **Scorer**: Don Shelley. ‡ New registration. ᴺᵠ Not qualified for England.

ANDERSSON, Martin Kristoffer (Reading Blue Coat S), b Reading, Berks 6 Sep 1996. 6'1". RHB, RM. Squad No 24. Debut (Leeds/Bradford MCCU) 2017. Derbyshire 2018 (on loan). Middlesex debut 2018. Middlesex 2nd XI debut 2013. Berkshire 2015-16. HS 83 v Lancs (Manchester) 2019. BB 4-25 De v Glamorgan (Derby) 2018. M BB 2-15 v Durham (Chester-le-St) 2018. T20 HS 1. T20 BB – .

BAMBER, Ethan Read (Mill Hill S), b Westminster 17 Dec 1998. 5'11". RHB, RMF. Squad No 54. Debut (Middlesex) 2018. Gloucestershire 2019 (on loan). Middlesex 2nd XI debut 2015. Berkshire 2017. HS 27* v Glos (Bristol) 2018. BB 5-93 v Derbys (Lord's) 2019. T20 HS 0*. T20 BB 1-38.

CRACKNELL, Joseph Benjamin (London Oratory S), b Enfield 16 Mar 2000. 5'9". RHB, WK. Squad No 48. Middlesex 2nd XI debut 2017. Berkshire 2018. Awaiting 1st XI debut.

CULLEN, Blake Carlton (Hampton S), b Hounslow 19 Feb 2002. 6'1". RHB, RMF. Squad No 19. Middlesex 2nd XI debut 2017, aged 15y 142d. Awaiting Middlesex 1st XI debut.

ᴺᵠ**CUMMINS, Miguel** Lamar, b St Michael, Barbados 5 Sep 1990. 6'2". LHB, RF. Squad No 41. Barbados 2011-12 to date. Worcestershire 2016. Middlesex debut 2019. **Tests** (WI): 14 (2016 to 2019); HS 24* v I (Kingston) 2016; BB 6-48 v I (Gros Islet) 2016. **LOI** (WI): 11 (2013-14 to 2017); HS 5 v Afg (Gros Islet) 2017; BB 3-82 v E (Bristol) 2017. F-c Tours (WI): E 2017; NZ 2017-18; I 2013-14 (WIA); SL 2014-15 (WIA); UAE (v P) 2016-17. HS 29* Barbados v Leeward Is (Basseterre) 2015-16. CC HS 25 and CC BB 7-84 (12-166 match) Wo v Sussex (Hove) 2016. M HS 22* v Durham (Lord's) 2019. BB 7-45 Barbados v T&T (Port of Spain) 2012-13. M BB 4-77 v Lancs (Manchester) 2019. LO HS 20 Barbados v CC&C (Cave Hill) 2018-19. LO BB 4-27 Barbados v Windward Is (Bridgetown) 2017-18. T20 HS 10. T20 BB 3-19.

DAVIES, Jack Leo Benjamin (Wellington C), b Reading, Berks 30 Mar 2000. Son of A.G.Davies (Cambridge U 1982-89). 5'10". LHB, WK. Squad No 23. Middlesex 2nd XI debut 2017. Berkshire 2017-19. England U19 2018. Awaiting 1st XI debut.

ESKINAZI, Stephen Sean (Christ Church GS, Claremont; U of WA), b Johannesburg, South Africa 28 Mar 1994. 6'2". RHB, WK. Squad No 28. Debut (Middlesex) 2015; cap 2018. UK passport. HS 179 v Warwks (Birmingham) 2017. LO HS 107* v Glos (Lord's) 2019 (RLC). T20 HS 57*.

FINN, Steven Thomas (Parmiter's S, Garston), b Watford, Herts 4 Apr 1989. 6'7½". RHB, RFM. Squad No 9. Debut (Middlesex) 2005; cap 2009. Otago 2011-12. YC 2010. **Tests**: 36 (2009-10 to 2016-17); HS 56 v NZ (Dunedin) 2012-13; BB 6-79 v A (Birmingham) 2015. **LOI**: 69 (2010-11 to 2017); HS 35 v A (Brisbane) 2010-11; BB 5-33 v I (Brisbane) 2014-15. **IT20**: 21 (2011 to 2015); HS 8* v I (Colombo, RPS) 2012-13; BB 3-16 v NZ (Pallekele) 2012-13. F-c Tours: A 2010-11, 2013-14; SA 2015-16; NZ 2012-13; I 2012-13; SL 2011-12; B 2009-10, 2016-17; UAE 2011-12 v P. HS 56 (*see Tests*) and 56 v Sussex (Hove) 2019. 50 wkts (2); most – 64 (2010). BB 9-37 (14-106 match) v Worcs (Worcester) 2010. LO HS 42* v Glamorgan (Cardiff) 2014 (RLC). LO BB (*see LOI*) and 5-33 v Derbys (Lord's) 2011 (CB40). T20 HS 8*. T20 BB 5-16.

GUBBINS, Nicholas Richard Trail (Radley C; Leeds U), b Richmond, Surrey 31 Dec 1993. 6'0½". LHB, LB. Squad No 18. Leeds/Bradford MCCU 2013-15. Middlesex debut 2014; cap 2016. F-c Tours (EL): WI 2017-18; SL 2016-17; UAE 2016-17 (v Afg), 2018-19 (v PA). 1000 runs (1): 1409 (2016). HS 201* v Lancs (Lord's) 2016. BB – . LO HS 141 v Sussex (Hove) 2015 (RLC). T20 HS 75.

‡NOHANDSCOMB, Peter Stephen Patrick (Mt Waverley SC; Deakin U, Melbourne), b Melbourne, Australia 26 Apr 1991. RHB, WK. Squad No 29. British passport (English parents). Victoria 2011-12 to date. Gloucestershire 2015; cap 2015. Yorkshire 2017. Durham 2019. Joins Middlesex in 2020 as f-c and 50-over captain. IPL: RPS 2016. Big Bash: MS 2012-13 to date. **Tests** (A): 16 (2016-17 to 2018-19); HS 110 v P (Sydney) 2016-17. **LOI** (A): 22 (2016-17 to 2019); HS 117 v I (Mohali) 2018-19. **IT20** (A): 2 (2018-19); HS 208 v I (Bengaluru) 2018-19. F-c Tours (A): SA 2017-18; I 2015 (Aus A), 2016-17, 2018-19; B 2017. HS 215 Vic v NSW (Sydney) 2016-17. CC HS 101* Y v Lancs (Manchester) 2017. LO HS 140 Y v Derbys (Leeds) 2017 (RLC). T20 HS 103*.

HARRIS, James Alexander Russell (Pontardulais CS; Gorseinon C), b Morriston, Swansea, Glamorgan 16 May 1990. 6'0". RHB, RMF. Squad No 5. Glamorgan 2007-14, making debut aged 16y 351d – youngest Gm player to take an f-c wicket; cap 2010. Middlesex debut 2013; cap 2015. Kent 2017 (on loan). MCC 2016. Wales MC 2005-08. F-c Tours (EL): WI 2010-11; SL 2013-14. HS 87* Gm v Notts (Swansea) 2007. M HS 80 v Sussex (Lord's) 2019. 50 wkts (3); most – 73 (2015). BB 9-34 (13-103 match) v Durham (Lord's) 2015 – record innings and match analysis v Durham. Took 12-118 in match for Gm v Glos (Bristol) 2007 – youngest (17y 3d) to take 10 wickets in any CC match. LO HS 117 v Lancs (Lord's) 2019 (RLC). LO BB 4-38 v Glamorgan (Lord's) 2015 (RLC). T20 HS 18. T20 BB 4-23.

HELM, Thomas George (Misbourne S, Gt Missenden), b Stoke Mandeville Hospital, Bucks 7 May 1994. 6'4". RHB, RMF. Squad No 7. Debut (Middlesex) 2013; cap 2019. Glamorgan 2014 (on loan). Buckinghamshire 2011. F-c Tour (EL): SL 2016-17. HS 52 v Derbys (Derby) 2018. BB 5-36 v Worcs (Worcester) 2019. LO HS 30 v Surrey (Lord's) 2018 (RLC). LO BB 5-33 EL v Sri Lanka A (Colombo, CCC) 2016-17. T20 HS 28*. T20 BB 5-11.

HOLDEN, Max David Edward (Sawston Village C; Hills Road SFC, Cambridge), b Cambridge 18 Dec 1997. 5'11". LHB, OB. Squad No 4. Middlesex 2nd XI debut 2013. Northamptonshire 2017 (on loan). Middlesex debut 2017. England U19 2014-15 to 2016-17. F-c Tour (EL): I 2018-19. HS 153 and BB 2-59 Nh v Kent (Beckenham) 2017. M HS 119* v Derbys (Lord's) 2018. M BB 1-15 v Leics (Leicester) 2018. LO HS 166 v Kent (Canterbury) 2019 (RLC) – M record. LO BB 1-29 v Australians (Lord's) 2018. T20 HS 84. T20 BB – .

HOLLMAN, Luke Barnaby Kurt (Acland Burghley S), b Islington 16 Sep 2000. 6'2". LHB, LB. Squad No 56. Middlesex 2nd XI debut 2017. Berkshire 2019. England U19 2018 to 2018-19. Awaiting 1st XI debut.

LACE, Thomas Cresswell (Millfield S), b Hammersmith, Middx 27 May 1998. 5'8". RHB, WK. Squad No 27. Derbyshire 2018-19 (on loan). Middlesex debut 2019. Middlesex 2nd XI debut 2015. HS 143 De v Glamorgan (Swansea) 2019. M HS 51 v Leics (Lord's) 2019. LO HS 48 De v Durham (Chester-le-St) 2019 (RLC).

LINCOLN, Daniel John (Edgbarrow S, Crowthorne), b Frimley, Surrey 26 May 1995. 6'1". RHB, RM. Squad No 43. Awaiting f-c debut. Middlesex 2nd XI debut 2018. Berkshire 2012-19. Played as a goalkeeper for Reading and Arsenal junior sides, and as 12th man for England in 2019 Ashes. T20 HS 30.

‡**NQMARSH, Mitchell** Ross, b Attadale, Perth, W Australia 20 Oct 1991. Son of G.R.Marsh (W Australia and Australia 1977-78 to 1993-94) and younger brother of S,E.Marsh (*see GLAMORGAN*). 6'3". RHB, RMF. Squad No 8. W Australia 2009-10 to date. IPL: DC 2009-10. PW 2011-13. RPS 2016. Big Bash: PS 2011-12 to date. **Tests** (A): 32 (2014-15 to 2019); HS 181 v E (Perth) 2017-18; BB 5-46 v E (Oval) 2019. **LOI** (A): 57 (2011-12 to 2019-20); HS 102* v I (Sydney) 2015-16; BB 5-33 v E (Melbourne) 2014-15. **IT20** (A): 14 (2011-12 to 2019-20); HS 36 v SA (Johannesburg) 2011-12; BB 2-6 v P (Dubai, DSC) 2018-19. F-c Tours (A): E 2015, 2019; SA 2013 (Aus A), 2017-18; WI 2015; NZ 2015-16; I 2016-17, 2018-19; SL 2016; Z 2011 (Aus A); UAE 2014-15, 2018-19 (v P). HS 211 Aus A v India A (Brisbane, AB) 2014. BB 6-84 WA v Q (Perth) 2011-12. LO HS 124 WA v S Aus (Sydney, DO) 2017-18. LO BB 5-33 (*see LOI*). T20 HS 93*. T20 BB 4-6.

MORGAN, Eoin Joseph Gerard (Catholic University S), b Dublin, Ireland 10 Sep 1986. 6'0". LHB, RM. Squad No 16. UK passport. Ireland 2004 to 2007-08. Middlesex debut 2006; cap 2008; l-o captain 2014-15; T20 captain 2020. IPL: RCB 2009-10. KKR 2011-13. SH 2015-16. KXIP 2017. Big Bash: ST 2013-14 to 2016-17. *Wisden* 2010. CBE 2020. **ECB L-O Central Contract 2019-20. Tests**: 16 (2010 to 2011-12); HS 130 v P (Nottingham) 2010. **LOI** (E/Ire): 236 (23 for Ire 2006 to 2008-09; 213 for E 2009 to 2019-20, 114 as captain); HS 148 v Afg (Manchester) 2019, inc world record 17 sixes. **IT20**: 89 (2009 to 2019-20, 46 as captain); HS 91 v NZ (Napier) 2019-20. F-c Tours (Ire): A 2010-11 (E); NZ 2008-09 (Eng A); Namibia 2005-06; UAE 2006-07, 2007-08, 2011-12 (v P). 1000 runs (1): 1085 (2008). HS 209* Ire v UAE (Abu Dhabi) 2006-07. M HS 191 v Notts (Nottingham) 2014. BB 2-24 v Notts (Lord's) 2007. LO HS 161 v Kent (Canterbury) 2009 (FPT). LO BB – . T20 HS 91.

NQMUJEEB ZADRAN (also known as Mujeeb Ur Rahman), b Khost, Afghanistan 28 Mar 2001. 5'11". RHB, OB. Squad No 88. Hampshire 2018 (T20 only). Middlesex debut 2019 (T20 only). IPL: KXIP 2018-19. Big Bash: BH 2018-19 to date. **Tests** (Afg): 1 (2018); HS 15 and BB 1-75 v I (Bengalaru) 2018. **LOI** (Afg): 40 (2017-18 to 2019-20); HS 15 v Z (Sharjah) 2017-18; BB 5-50 v Z (Sharjah) 2017-18 – separate matches. **IT20** (Afg): 19 (2017-18 to 2019-20); HS 8* v WI (Lucknow) 2019-20; BB 4-15 v B (Dhaka) 2019-20. F-c Tour (Afg): I 2018. HS 15 (*see Tests*). LO HS 15 (*see LOI*). LO BB 5-50 (*see LOI*). T20 HS 27. T20 BB 4-12.

NQMURTAGH, Timothy James (John Fisher S; St Mary's C), b Lambeth, London 2 Aug 1981. Elder brother of C.P.Murtagh (Loughborough UCCE and Surrey 2005-09), nephew of A.J.Murtagh (Hampshire and EP 1973-77). 6'0". LHB, RMF. Squad No 34. British U 2000-03. Surrey 2001-06. Middlesex debut 2007; cap 2008; benefit 2015. Ireland 2012-13 to date. MCC 2010. **Tests** (Ire): 3 (2018 to 2019); HS 54* v Afg (Dehradun) 2018-19; BB 5-13 v E (Lord's) 2019. **LOI** (Ire): 50 (2012 to 2019); HS 23* v Scotland (Belfast) 2013; BB 5-21 v Z (Belfast) 2019. **IT20** (Ire): 14 (2012 to 2015-16); HS 12* v UAE (Abu Dhabi) 2015-16; BB 3-23 v PNG (Townsville) 2015-16. HS 74* Sy v Middx (Oval) 2004 and 74* Sy v Warwks (Croydon) 2005. M HS 55 v Leics (Leicester) 2011, sharing M record 9th wkt partnership of 172 with G.K.Berg. 50 wkts (8); most – 85 (2011). BB 7-82 v Derbys (Derby) 2009. LO HS 35* v Surrey (Lord's) 2008 (FPT). LO BB 5-21 (*see LOI*). T20 HS 40*. T20 BB 6-24 Sy v Middx (Lord's) 2005 – Sy record.

ROBSON, Sam David (Marcellin C, Randwick), b Paddington, Sydney, Australia 1 Jul 1989. Elder brother of A.J.Robson (see *DURHAM*). 6'0". RHB, LB. Squad No 12. Qualified for England in April 2013. Debut (Middlesex) 2009; cap 2013. **Tests**: 7 (2014); HS 127 v SL (Leeds) 2014. F-c Tours (EL): SA 2014-15; SL 2013-14. 1000 runs (2); most – 1180 (2013). HS 231* v Warwks (Lord's) 2013. BB 2-4 v Lancs (Lord's) 2019. LO HS 106 v Somerset (Radlett) 2019 (RLC). LO BB 1-27 v Glamorgan (Lord's) 2019 (RLC). T20 HS 28*. T20 BB 3-31.

ROLAND-JONES, Tobias Skelton ('Toby') (Hampton S; Leeds U), b Ashford 29 Jan 1988. 6'4". RHB, RFM. Squad No 21. Debut (Middlesex) 2010; cap 2012. MCC 2011. *Wisden* 2016. Leeds/Bradford UCCE 2009 (not f-c). **Tests**: 4 (2017); HS 25 and BB 5-57 v SA (Oval) 2017. **LOI**: 1 (2017); HS 37* and BB 1-34 v SA (Lord's) 2017. F-c Tours (EL): WI 2017-18; SL 2016-17; UAE 2016-17 (v Afg). HS 103* v Yorks (Lord's) 2015. 50 wkts (2); most – 64 (2012). BB 7-52 (10-79 match) v Glos (Northwood) 2019. Hat-tricks (2): v Derbys (Lord's) 2013, and v Yorks (Lord's) 2016 – at end of match to secure the Championship. LO HS 65 v Glos (Lord's) 2017 (RLC). LO BB 4-10 v Hants (Southampton) 2017 (RLC). T20 HS 40. T20 BB 5-21.

SIMPSON, John Andrew (St Gabriel's RC HS), b Bury, Lancs 13 Jul 1988. 5'10". LHB, WK. Squad No 20. Debut (Middlesex) 2009; cap 2011. MCC 2018. Cumberland 2007. HS 167* v Lancs (Manchester) 2019. LO HS 82* v Sussex (Lord's) 2017 (RLC). T20 HS 84*.

SOWTER, Nathan Adam (Hill Sport HS, NSW), b Penrith, NSW, Australia 12 Oct 1992. 5'10". RHB, LB. Squad No 72. Debut (Middlesex) 2017. HS 57* v Glamorgan (Cardiff) 2019. BB 3-42 v Lancs (Manchester) 2017. LO HS 31 v Surrey (Oval) 2019 (RLC). LO BB 6-62 v Essex (Chelmsford) 2019 (RLC). T20 HS 13*. T20 BB 4-23.

WALALLAWITA, Thilan Nipuna (Oaklands S), b Colombo, Sri Lanka 23 Jun 1998. 5'9". LHB, SLA. Squad No 32. Moved to UK in 2004. Middlesex 2nd XI debut 2015. Awaiting 1st XI debut.

WHITE, Robert George (Harrow S; Loughborough U), b Ealing 15 Sep 1995. 5'9". RHB, WK, occ RM. Squad No 14. Loughborough MCCU 2015-17. Middlesex debut 2018. Essex 2019 (on loan). Middlesex 2nd XI debut 2013. HS 69 LU v Northants (Northampton) 2017. CC HS 39 Ex v Surrey (Oval) 2019. M HS 35 v Northants (Northampton) 2018. LO HS 21* Ex v Sussex (Chelmsford) 2019 (RLC). T20 HS 11*.

RELEASED/RETIRED

(Having made a County 1st XI appearance in 2019)

BARBER, T.E. – see *NOTTINGHAMSHIRE*.

[NQ]**De VILLIERS, Abraham** Benjamin ('AB'), b Pretoria, South Africa 17 Feb 1984. RHB, RM, WK. Northerns 2003-04. Titans 2004-05 to 2017-18. Middlesex 2019 (T20 only). IPL: DD 2007-08 to 2009-10. RCB 2011-19. Big Bash: BH 2019-20. **Tests** (SA): 114 (2004-05 to 2017-18, 3 as captain); 1000 runs (2); most – 1061 (2008); HS 278* v P (Abu Dhabi) 2010-11; BB 2-49 v WI (St John's) 2015. **LOI** (SA): 223 (+ 5 for Africa; 2004-05 to 2017-18, 103 as captain); 1000 runs (3); most – 1209 (2007); HS 176 v B (Paarl) 2017-18; BB 2-15 v UAE (Wellington) 2014-15. **IT20** (SA): 78 (2005-06 to 2017-18, 18 as captain); HS 79* v Scotland (Oval) 2009. F-c Tours (SA): E 2008, 2012; A 2005-06, 2008-09, 2012-13; WI 2005, 2010; NZ 2011-12; I 2008, 2009-10, 2015-16; P 2007-08; SL 2006, 2014; Z 2014; B 2007-08; UAE 2010-11 (v P), 2013-14 (v P). 1000 runs (0+1): 1122 (2004-05). HS 278* (see *Tests*). BB 2-49 (see *Tests*). LO HS 176 (see *LOI*). LO BB 2-15 (see *LOI*). T20 HS 133*.

MALAN, D.J. – see *YORKSHIRE*.

NQMOHAMMAD HAFEEZ, b Sargodha, Pakistan 17 Oct 1980. RHB, OB. Sargodha 1998-99 to 2002-03. SNGPL 2001-02 to 2018-19. Faisalabad 2003-05 to 2005-06. Middlesex 2019 (T20 only). IPL: 2007-08. Big Bash: MS 2013-14. **Tests** (P): 55 (2003 to 2018-19); HS 224 v K (Khulna) 2015; BB 4-16 v SA (Johannesburg) 2012-13. **LOI** (P): 218 (2002-03 to 2019); HS 140* v SL (Sharjah) 2013-14; BB 4-41 v SL (Dambulla) 2015. **IT20** (P): 91 (2006 to 2019-20); HS 86 v SA (Centurion) 2012-13; BB 4-10 v Z (Harare) 2011. F-c Tours (P): E 2006, 2016; A 2006 (PA), 2009 (PA); SA 2006-07, 2012-13; WI 2011; NZ 2010-11; I 2008-09; SL 2012, 2015; Z 2011, 2013; B 2011-12, 2014-15. 1000 runs: 0+1 (2009-10). HS 224 (*see* Tests). BB 8-57 (10-87 match) Faisalabad v Quetta (Faisalabad) 2004-05. LO HS 140* (*see LOI*). LO BB 4-23 SNGPL v PIA (Karachi) 2001-02. T20 HS 102*. T20 BB 4-10.

RAYNER, Oliver Philip (St Bede's S, Upper Dicker), b Fallingbostel, W Germany, 1 Nov 1985. 6'5". RHB, OB. Sussex 2006-11, scoring 101 v Sri Lankans (Hove) – first hundred on debut for Sussex since 1920. Middlesex 2011-19; cap 2015. Hampshire 2018 (on loan). Kent 2019 (on loan). MCC 2014. F-c Tours (EL): SL 2013-14, 2016-17; UAE 2016-17 (v Afg). HS 143* v Notts (Nottingham) 2012. 50 wkts (1): 51 (2016). BB 8-46 (15-118 match) v Surrey (Oval) 2013. LO HS 61 Sx v Lancs (Hove) 2006 (P40). LO BB 4-35 v Notts (Lord's) 2015 (RLC). T20 HS 41*. T20 BB 5-18.

SCOTT, G.F.B. – *see GLOUCESTERSHIRE.*

STIRLING, P.R. – *see NORTHAMPTONSHIRE.*

NQTAYLOR, Luteru **Ross** Poutoa Lote (Palmerston North BHS; Wairarapa C), b Lower Hutt, Wellington, New Zealand 8 Mar 1984. 6'0". RHB, OB. Central Districts 2002-03 to date. Sussex 2016. Nottinghamshire 2018; cap 2018. Middlesex 2019 (l-o only). IPL: RCB 2007-08 to 2009-10. RR 2011. DD 2012-14. PW 2013. **Tests** (NZ): 101 (2007-08 to 2019-20, 14 as captain); HS 290 v A (Perth) 2015-16; BB 2-4 v I (Ahmedabad) 2010-11. **LOI** (NZ): 232 (2005-06 to 2019-20, 20 as captain); 1000 runs (1): 1046 (2015); HS 181* v E (Dunedin) 2017-18; BB – . **IT20** (NZ): 100 (2006-07 to 2018-19, 13 as captain); HS 63 v WI (Auckland) 2008-09. F-c Tours (NZ) (C=Captain): E 2008, 2013, 2015; A 2008-09, 2011-12C, 2015-16, 2019-20; SA 2004 (NZ A), 2007-08, 2016; WI 2012C; I 2010-11, 2012C, 2014, 2016-17; SL 2009, 2012-13C, 2019; Z 2011-12C, 2016; B 2008-09, 2013-14; UAE 2014-15 (v P), 2018-19 (v P). HS 290 (*see* Tests). CC HS 146 Nt v Essex (Chelmsford) 2018. BB 2-4 (*see* Tests). LO HS 181* (*see LOI*). LO BB 1-13 CD v Canterbury (Christchurch) 2005-06. T20 HS 111*. T20 BB 3-28.

RELEASED/RETIRED (continued from p 135)

DEXTER, Neil John (Northwood HS, Durban; Varsity C; U of South Africa), b Johannesburg, South Africa 21 Aug 1984. 6'0". RHB, RMF. Kent 2005-08. Essex 2008. Middlesex 2009-15; cap 2010; captain 2010 (*part*) to 2013. Qualified for England in 2010. HS 180 v Glos (Leicester) 2019, sharing Le record 2nd wkt partnership of 320 with M.H.Azad. BB 6-63 M v Lancs (Lord's) 2014. Le BB 5-52 v Sussex (Leicester) 2016. LO HS 135* K v Glamorgan (Cardiff) 2006 (CGT). LO BB 4-22 v Lancs (Leicester) 2016 (RLC). T20 HS 73. T20 BB 4-21.

JAVID, Ateeq (Aston Manor S), b Birmingham 15 Oct 1991. 5'8". RHB, OB. Squad No 99. Warwickshire 2009-17. Leicestershire 2018-19. HS 142 v Loughborough MCCU (Leicester) 2019. Le HS 133 Wa v Somerset (Birmingham) 2013. BB 1-1 Wa v Lancs (Manchester) 2014. Le BB 1-30 v Sussex (Leicester) 2018. LO HS 43 Wa v Kent (Canterbury) 2013 (Y40). LO BB 4-42 Wa v Yorks (Leeds) 2016 (RLC). T20 HS 51*. T20 BB 4-17.

MOHAMMAD ABBAS – *see NOTTINGHAMSHIRE.*

MUNSEY, H.G. – *see HAMPSHIRE.*

MIDDLESEX 2019

RESULTS SUMMARY

	Place	Won	Lost	Drew	NR
Specsavers County Champ (2nd Division)	8th	3	5	6	
All First-Class Matches		3	5	7	
Royal London One-Day Cup (South Group)	QF	6	3		
Vitality Blast (South Group)	QF	7	7		1

SPECSAVERS COUNTY CHAMPIONSHIP AVERAGES

BATTING AND FIELDING

Cap		M	I	NO	HS	Runs	Avge	100	50	Ct/St
2016	P.R.Stirling	3	4	1	138	150	50.00	1	–	2
2010	D.J.Malan	13	22	1	199	1005	47.85	4	2	17
2011	J.A.Simpson	14	22	3	167*	773	40.68	2	4	35
2013	S.D.Robson	14	24	1	140*	858	37.30	2	4	9
2015	J.A.R.Harris	9	16	3	80	435	33.46	–	3	2
2009	S.T.Finn	7	9	3	56	155	25.83	–	1	2
2019	T.G.Helm	7	9	1	46	187	23.37	–	–	1
2012	T.S.Roland-Jones	11	17	3	54	327	23.35	–	2	3
2008	E.J.G.Morgan	2	4	1	36*	69	23.00	–	–	1
2016	N.R.T.Gubbins	14	24	–	91	530	22.08	–	3	3
	G.F.B.Scott	7	11	1	55	204	20.40	–	1	3
2018	S.S.Eskinazi	12	21	–	75	403	19.19	–	1	12
	N.A.Sowter	7	11	1	57*	184	18.40	–	2	4
	M.D.E.Holden	9	16	–	54	218	13.62	–	1	1
2008	T.J.Murtagh	11	15	4	33	149	13.54	–	–	2
2015	O.P.Rayner	2	4	1	28*	29	9.66	–	–	2
	M.L.Cummins	3	5	1	22*	34	8.50	–	–	3
	R.G.White	2	4	–	10	22	5.50	–	–	
	E.R.Bamber	5	8	2	8	30	5.00	–	–	1

Also batted: M.K.Andersson (2 matches) 4, 83, 8; T.C.Lace (1) 51, 4.

BOWLING

	O	M	R	W	Avge	Best	5wI	10wM
T.J.Murtagh	295.3	93	757	43	17.60	6-51	4	–
T.G.Helm	208	39	600	24	25.00	5-36	2	–
T.S.Roland-Jones	302.5	60	963	33	29.18	7-52	3	1
S.T.Finn	149.5	25	548	17	32.23	5-75	1	–
E.R.Bamber	125	31	381	11	34.63	5-93	1	–
J.A.R.Harris	247	41	876	22	39.81	4-98	–	–
N.A.Sowter	180.4	23	650	14	46.42	3-42	–	–

Also bowled:

M.L.Cummins	81	19	266	8	33.25	4-77	–	–
O.P.Rayner	72	16	183	5	36.60	4-58	–	–

S.S.Eskinazi 2-0-4-0; M.D.E.Holden 14-1-66-0; D.J.Malan 42-3-134-4; E.J.G.Morgan 3-1-4-0; S.D.Robson 9.5-0-44-2; G.F.B.Scott 39-6-123-3; J.A.Simpson 1-0-2-0; P.R.Stirling 8-0-29-2.

The First-Class Averages (pp 226–241) give the records of Middlesex players in all first-class county matches (Middlesex's other opponents being Oxford MCCU), with the exception of E.R.Bamber, T.C.Lace, O.P.Rayner, P.R.Stirling and R.G.White, whose first-class figures for Middlesex are as above, and:
T.J.Murtagh 12-15-4-33-149-13.54-0-0-2ct. 321.3-108-792-49-16.16-6/51-4-0.

MIDDLESEX RECORDS

FIRST-CLASS CRICKET

Highest Total	For 642-3d		v	Hampshire	Southampton[1]	1923
	V 850-7d		by	Somerset	Taunton	2007
Lowest Total	For 20		v	MCC	Lord's	1864
	V 31		by	Glos	Bristol	1924
Highest Innings	For 331*	J.D.B.Robertson	v	Worcs	Worcester	1949
	V 341	C.M.Spearman	for	Glos	Gloucester	2004

Highest Partnership for each Wicket

1st	372	M.W.Gatting/J.L.Langer	v	Essex	Southgate	1998
2nd	380	F.A.Tarrant/J.W.Hearne	v	Lancashire	Lord's	1914
3rd	424*	W.J.Edrich/D.C.S.Compton	v	Somerset	Lord's	1948
4th	325	J.W.Hearne/E.H.Hendren	v	Hampshire	Lord's	1919
5th	338	R.S.Lucas/T.C.O'Brien	v	Sussex	Hove	1895
6th	270	J.D.Carr/P.N.Weekes	v	Glos	Lord's	1994
7th	271*	E.H.Hendren/F.T.Mann	v	Notts	Nottingham	1925
8th	182*	M.H.C.Doll/H.R.Murrell	v	Notts	Lord's	1913
9th	172	G.K.Berg/T.J.Murtagh	v	Leics	Leicester	2011
10th	230	R.W.Nicholls/W.Roche	v	Kent	Lord's	1899

Best Bowling (Innings)	For 10- 40	G.O.B.Allen	v	Lancashire	Lord's	1929
	V 9- 38	R.C.R.Glasgow†	for	Somerset	Lord's	1924
Best Bowling (Match)	For 16-114	G.Burton	v	Yorkshire	Sheffield	1888
	16-114	J.T.Hearne	v	Lancashire	Manchester	1898
	V 16-100	J.E.B.B.P.Q.C.Dwyer	for	Sussex	Hove	1906

Most Runs – Season	2669	E.H.Hendren	(av 83.41)	1923
Most Runs – Career	40302	E.H.Hendren	(av 48.81)	1907-37
Most 100s – Season	13	D.C.S.Compton		1947
Most 100s – Career	119	E.H.Hendren		1907-37
Most Wkts – Season	158	F.J.Titmus	(av 14.63)	1955
Most Wkts – Career	2361	F.J.Titmus	(av 21.27)	1949-82
Most Career W-K Dismissals	1223	J.T.Murray	(1024 ct; 199 st)	1952-75
Most Career Catches in the Field	561	E.H.Hendren		1907-37

LIMITED-OVERS CRICKET

Highest Total	50ov	380-5		v	Kent	Canterbury	2019
	40ov	350-6		v	Lancashire	Lord's	2012
	T20	227-4		v	Somerset	Taunton	2019
Lowest Total	50ov	41		v	Essex	Westcliff	1972
	40ov	23		v	Yorkshire	Leeds	1974
	T20	92		v	Surrey	Lords	2013
Highest Innings	50ov	166	M.D.E.Holden	v	Kent	Canterbury	2019
	40ov	147*	M.R.Ramprakash	v	Worcs	Lord's	1990
	T20	129	D.T.Christian	v	Kent	Canterbury	2014
Best Bowling	50ov	7-12	W.W.Daniel	v	Minor Cos E	Ipswich	1978
	40ov	6- 6	R.W.Hooker	v	Surrey	Lord's	1969
	T20	6-28	J.K.Fuller	v	Hampshire	Southampton[2]	2018

† R.C.Robertson-Glasgow

NORTHAMPTONSHIRE

Formation of Present Club: 31 July 1878
Inaugural First-Class Match: 1905
Colours: Maroon
Badge: Tudor Rose
County Champions: (0); best – 2nd 1912, 1957, 1965, 1976
Gillette/NatWest/C&G/FP Trophy Winners: (2) 1976, 1992
Benson and Hedges Cup Winners: (1) 1980
Twenty20 Cup Winners: (2) 2013, 2016

est. 1878
NORTHAMPTONSHIRE
COUNTY CRICKET CLUB

Chief Executive: Ray Payne, County Ground, Abington Avenue, Northampton, NN1 4PR • Tel: 01604 514455 • Email: reception@nccc.co.uk • Web: www.northantscricket.com • Twitter: @NorthantsCCC (60,595 followers)

Head Coach: David Ripley. **Assistant Coach/Batting Lead**: John Sadler. **Bowling Lead**: Chris Liddle. **Captains**: A.M.Rossington (f-c) and J.J.Cobb (l-o and T20). **Overseas Players**: Faheem Ashraf, K.A.Pollard and P.R.Stirling (both T20 only). **2020 Testimonial**: A.G.Wakely. **Head Groundsman**: Craig Harvey. **Scorer**: Tony Kingston. **Blast Team Name**: Northamptonshire Steelbacks. ‡ New registration. NQ Not qualified for England.

BERG, Gareth Kyle (South African College S), b Cape Town, South Africa 18 Jan 1981. 6'0". RHB, RMF. Squad No 13. England qualified through residency. Middlesex 2008-14; cap 2010. Hampshire 2015-19; cap 2016. Northamptonshire debut 2019. Italy 2011-12 to date (l-o and T20 only). HS 130* M v Leics (Leicester) 2011, sharing M record 9th wkt partnership of 172 with T.J.Murtagh. Nh HS 5 v Leics (Leicester) 2019 BB 6-56 H v Yorks (Southampton) 2016. LO HS 75 M v Glamorgan (Lord's) 2013 (Y40). LO BB 5-26 H v Lancs (Southampton) 2019 (RLC). T20 HS 90. T20 BB 4-20.

BUCK, Nathan Liam (Newbridge HS; Ashby S), b Leicester 26 Apr 1991. 6'2" RHB, RMF. Squad No 11. Leicestershire 2009-14; cap 2011. Lancashire 2015-16. Northamptonshire debut 2017. F-c Tour (EL): WI 2010-11. HS 53 v Glamorgan (Cardiff) 2019. BB 6-34 v Durham (Chester-le-St) 2017. LO HS 21 Le v Glamorgan (Leicester) 2009 (P40). LO BB 4-39 EL v Sri Lanka A (Dambulla) 2011-12. T20 HS 11*. T20 BB 4-26.

COBB, Joshua James (Oakham S), b Leicester 17 Aug 1990. Son of R.A.Cobb (Leics and N Transvaal 1980-89). 5'11½". RHB, OB. Squad No 4. Leicestershire 2007-14; l-o captain 2014. Northamptonshire debut 2015; cap 2018; captain 2020 (l-o and T20 only). HS 148* Le v Middx (Lord's) 2008. Nh HS 139 v Durham MCCU (Northampton) 2019. BB 2-11 Le v Glos (Leicester) 2008. Nh BB 2-44 v Loughborough MCCU (Northampton) 2017. LO HS 146* v Pakistanis (Northampton) 2019. LO BB 3-34 Le v Glos (Leicester) 2013 (Y40). T20 HS 103. T20 BB 4-22.

CURRAN, Benjamin Jack (Wellington C), b Northampton 7 Jun 1996. Son of K.M.Curran (Glos, Natal, Northants, Boland and Zimbabwe 1980-81 to 1999); grandson of K.P.Curran (Rhodesia 1947-48 to 1954-55); younger brother of T.K.Curran (see SURREY) and elder brother of S.M.Curran (see SURREY). LHB, OB. Squad No 57. Debut (Northamptonshire) 2018. Nottinghamshire 2nd XI 2016. Surrey 2nd XI 2016. Warwickshire 2nd XI 2017. Leicestershire 2nd XI 2017. HS 83* v Sussex (Northampton) 2018. LO HS 69 v Leics (Leicester) 2019 (RLC). T20 HS 29.

NQFAHEEM ASHRAF, b Punjab, Pakistan 16 Jan 1994. LHB, RFM. Squad No 41. Faisalabad 2013-14. Faisalabad Wolves 2014-15. National Bank 2015-16. Habib Bank 2016-17 to 2018-19. Central Punjab 2019-20. Northamptonshire debut 2019 (T20 only). **Tests** (P): 4 (2018 to 2018-19); HS 83 v Ire (Dublin) 2018 – on debut; BB 3-42 v SA (Johannesburg) 2018-19. **LOI** (P): 23 (2017 to 2019); HS 28 v A (Sharjah) 2018-19; BB 5-22 v Z (Bulawayo) 2018. **IT20** (P): 27 (2017 to 2019-20); HS 21 v A (Harare) 2018; BB 3-5 v Scot (Edinburgh) 2018. HS 116 Faisalabad v Multan (Faisalabad) 2013-14 – on debut. BB 6-65 HB v KRL (Karachi) 2016-17. LO HS 71 Faisalabad W v Hyderabad Hawks (Lahore) 2014-15. LO BB 5-22 (*see LOI*). T20 HS 54*. T20 BB 6-19.

GAY, Emilio Nico (Bedford S), b Bedford May 2000. LHB, RM. Squad No 19. Debut (Northamptonshire) 2019 – did not bat or bowl. Northamptonshire 2nd XI debut 2018.

‡NQGLOVER, Brandon Dale (St Stithians C), b Johannesburg, South Africa 3 Apr 1997. RHB, RFM. Squad No 20. Boland 2016-17 to 2018-19. **LOI** (Neth): 1 (2019); HS – ; BB 1-37 v Z (Deventer) 2019. **IT20** (Neth): 19 (2019 to 2019-20); HS – ; BB 4-12 v UAE (Dubai, DSC) 2019-20. HS 12* Boland v Gauteng (Paarl) 2018-19. BB 4-83 Boland v FS (Bloemfontein) 2017-18. LO HS 27 Boland v Easterns (Benoni) 2017-18. LO BB 2-60 Boland v Namibia (Paarl) 2016-17. T20 HS 1*. T20 BB 4-12.

HUTTON, Brett Alan (Worksop C), b Doncaster, Yorks 6 Feb 1993. 6'2". RHB, RM. Squad No 16. Nottinghamshire 2011-17. Northamptonshire debut 2018. HS 74 Nt v Durham (Nottingham) 2016. Nh HS 34* v Durham (Chester-le-St) 2019. BB 8-57 v Glos (Northampton) 2018. LO HS 34* v Leics (Northampton) 2018 (RLC). LO BB 3-72 Nt v Kent (Nottingham) 2015 (RLC). T20 HS 18*. T20 BB 2-28.

KEOGH, Robert Ian (Queensbury S; Dunstable C), b Luton, Beds 21 Oct 1991. 5'11". RHB, OB. Squad No 21. Debut (Northamptonshire) 2012; cap 2019. Bedfordshire 2009-10. HS 221 v Hants (Southampton) 2013. BB 9-52 (13-125 match) v Glamorgan (Northampton) 2016. LO HS 134 v Durham (Northampton) 2016 (RLC). LO BB 2-26 v Yorks (Leeds) 2018 (RLC). T20 HS 59*. T20 BB 3-30.

NQLEVI, Richard Ernst, b Johannesburg, South Africa 14 Jan 1988. 5'11". RHB, RM. Squad No 88. W Province 2006-07 to 2016-17. Cape Cobras 2008-09 to 2015-16. Northamptonshire debut 2014 (Kolpak signing); cap 2017. IPL: MI 2012. **IT20** (SA): 13 (2011-12 to 2012-13); HS 117* v NZ (Hamilton) 2011-12. HS 168 v Essex (Northampton) 2015. LO HS 166 Cobras v Titans (Paarl) 2012-13. T20 HS 117*.

NQMUZARABANI, Blessing (Churchill S), b Harare, Zimbabwe 2 Oct 1996. Younger brother of T.Muzarabani (Centrals, MWR, SR, ME, HME 2006-07 to 2017-18). 6'6". RHB, RMF. Squad No 40. Rising Stars 2017-18. Northamptonshire debut 2019 (Kolpak deal). Eagles 2019-20. **Tests** (Z): 1 (2017-18); HS 10 and BB – v SA (Port Elizabeth) 2017-18. **LOI** (Z): 18 (2017-18 to 2018); HS 7 v Scot (Bulawayo) 2017-18; BB 4-47 v Afg (Bulawayo) 2018. **IT20** (Z): 6 (2017-18 to 2018); HS 1* v A (Harare) 2018; BB 3-21 v A (Harare) 2018 – separate matches. HS 23 RS v Midlands Rhinos (Kwekwe) 2017-18. Nh HS 1* v Glamorgan (Cardiff) 2019. BB 5-32 RS v BMT (Kwekwe) 2017-18. Nh BB 2-29 v Durham MCCU (Northampton) 2019. CC BB 2-47 v Worcs (Northampton) 2019. LO HS 18 v Derbys (Derby) 2019 (RLC). LO BB 4-47 (*see LOI*). T20 HS 9. T20 BB 3-21.

NEWTON, Robert Irving (Framlingham C), b Taunton, Somerset 18 Jan 1990. 5'8". RHB, OB. Squad No 10. Debut (Northamptonshire) 2010; cap 2017. 1000 runs (1): 1060 (2017). HS 202* v Leics (Northampton) 2016. BB 1-82 v Derbys (Derby) 2017. LO HS 107 v Worcs (Northampton) 2017 (RLC). T20 HS 38.

‡**NQPOLLARD, Kieron** Adrian, b Tacarigua, Trinidad 12 May 1987. RHB, RMF. Trinidad & Tobago 2006-07 to 2014-15, scoring 126 (inc 7 sixes) v Barbados on debut. Somerset 2010-11 (T20 only). IPL: 2009-10 to date. Big Bash: AS 2012-13 to 2016-17. MR 2017-18. **LOI** (WI): 113 (2006-07 to 2019-20); HS 119 v I (Chennai) 2011-12; BB 3-27 v SA (Roseau) 2010. **IT20** (WI): 73 (2008 to 2019-20); HS 68 v I (Mumbai) 2019-20; BB 4-25 v Ire (Basseterre) 2019-20. HS 174 T&T v Barbados (Pointe-a-Pierre) 2008-09. BB 2-29 T&T v Windward Is (Couva) 2014-15. LO HS 119 (*see LOI*). LO BB 4-32 T&T v Jamaica (Kingston) 2006-07. T20 HS 104. T20 BB 4-15.

PROCTER, Luke Anthony (Counthill S, Oldham), b Oldham, Lancs 24 June 1988. 5'11". LHB, RM. Squad No 2. Lancashire 2010-17. Northamptonshire debut 2017. Cumberland 2007. HS 137 v Hants (Manchester) 2016. Nh HS 94 v Leics (Leicester) 2017. BB 7-71 La v Surrey (Liverpool) 2012. Nh BB 5-33 v Durham (Chester-le-St) 2017. LO HS 97 v West Indies A (Manchester) 2010. LO BB 3-29 v Unicorns (Colwyn Bay) 2010 (CB40). T20 HS 25*. T20 BB 3-22.

ROSSINGTON, Adam Matthew (Mill Hill S), b Edgware, Middx 5 May 1993. 5'11". RHB, WK, occ RM. Squad No 7. Middlesex 2010-14. Northamptonshire debut 2014; cap 2019; captain 2020. HS 138* v Sussex (Arundel) 2016. Won 2013 Walter Lawrence Trophy with 55-ball century v Cambridge MCCU (Cambridge). LO HS 97 v Notts (Nottingham) 2016 (RLC). T20 HS 85.

SANDERSON, Ben William (Ecclesfield CS; Sheffield C), b Sheffield, Yorks 3 Jan 1989. 6'0". RHB, RMF. Squad No 26. Yorkshire 2008-10. Northamptonshire debut 2015; cap 2018. Shropshire 2013-15. HS 42 v Kent (Canterbury) 2015. 50 wkts (3); most – 61 (2019). BB 8-73 v Glos (Northampton) 2016. LO HS 31 v Derbys (Derby) 2019 (RLC). LO BB 3-36 v Durham (Chester-le-St) 2017 (RLC). T20 HS 12*. T20 BB 4-21.

SOLE, Thomas Barclay (Merchiston Castle S; Cardiff Met U), b Edinburgh, Scotland 12 Jun 1996. Younger brother of C.B.Sole (Scotland 2016 to 2017-18); son of D.M.B.Sole (Scotland Grand Slam-winning rugby union captain); nephew of C.R.Trembath (Gloucestershire 1982-84). RHB, OB. Squad No 90. Northamptonshire 2nd XI debut 2015. Awaiting f-c debut. **LOI** (Scot): 10 (2017-18 to 2019); HS 20 v Ire (Dubai, ICCA) 2017-18; BB 4-15 v Hong Kong (Bulawayo) 2017-18. **IT20** (Scot): 9 (2019 to 2019-20); HS 33* v Kenya (Dubai, ICCA) 2019-20; BB 2-15 v Neth (Dublin) 2019. LO HS 54 v S Africans (Northampton) 2017. LO BB 4-15 (*see LOI*). T20 HS 41*. T20 BB 2-15.

‡**NQSTIRLING, Paul** Robert (Belfast HS), b Belfast, N Ireland 3 Sep 1990. Father Brian Stirling was an international rugby referee. 5'10". RHB, OB. Squad No 39. Ireland 2007-08 to date. Middlesex 2013-19; cap 2016. **Tests** (Ire): 3 (2018 to 2019); HS 36 v E (Lord's) 2019; BB – . **LOI** (Ire): 117 (2008 to 2019-20); HS 177 v Canada (Toronto) 2010 – Ire record; BB 6-55 v Afg (Greater Noida) 2016-17 – Ire record. **IT20** (Ire): 78 (2009 to 2019-20); HS 95 v WI (St George's) 2019-20; BB 3-21 v B (Belfast) 2012. F-c Tours (Ire): WI 2009-10; Kenya 2011-12; Z 2015-16; UAE 2013-14. HS 146 Ire v UAE (Dublin) 2015. CC HS 138 and BB 2-21 M v Glamorgan (Radlett) 2019. LO HS 177 (*see LOI*). LO BB 6-55 (*see LOI*). T20 HS 109. T20 BB 4-10.

THURSTON, Charles Oliver (Bedford S; Loughborough U), b Cambridge 17 Aug 1996. RHB, RM. Squad No 96. Loughborough MCCU 2016-18. Northamptonshire debut 2018. Bedfordshire 2014-17. Middlesex 2nd XI 2013-14. Northamptonshire 2nd XI debut 2015. HS 126 LU v Northants (Northampton) 2017. Nh HS 29 v Sussex (Northampton) 2018. BB – . LO HS 53 v Yorks (Leeds) 2018 (RLC). T20 HS 41.

NQVASCONCELOS, Ricardo Surrador (St Stithians), b Johannesburg, South Africa 27 Oct 1997. LHB, WK. Squad No 27. Boland 2016-17 to 2017-18. Northamptonshire debut 2018. South Africa U19 2016. Portuguese passport. HS 184 v Glamorgan (Cardiff) 2019. LO HS 112 v Yorks (Northampton) 2019. T20 HS 45*.

WAKELY, Alexander George (Bedford S), b Hammersmith, London 3 Nov 1988. 6'2''. RHB, RM. Squad No 8. Debut (Northamptonshire) 2007; cap 2012; captain 2015-19; testimonial 2020. Bedfordshire 2004-05. HS 123 v Leics (Northampton) 2015. BB 2-62 v Somerset (Taunton) 2007. LO HS 109* v Lancs (Liverpool) 2017 (RLC). LO BB 2-14 v Lancs (Northampton) 2007 (P40). T20 HS 64. T20 BB – .

WHITE, Curtley-Jack (Ullswater Comm C; Queen Elizabeth GS, Penrith), b Kendal, Cumberland 19 Feb 1992. LHB, RFM. Northamptonshire 2nd XI debut 2018. Cumberland 2013. Cheshire 2016-17. Awaiting 1st XI debut.

WHITE, Graeme Geoffrey (Stowe S), b Milton Keynes, Bucks 18 Apr 1987. 5'11''. RHB, SLA. Squad No 87. Debut (Northamptonshire) 2006. Nottinghamshire 2010-13. HS 65 v Glamorgan (Colwyn Bay) 2007. BB 6-44 v Glamorgan (Northampton) 2016. LO HS 41* v Yorks (Leeds) 2018 (RLC). LO BB 6-37 v Lancs (Northampton) 2016 (RLC). T20 HS 34. T20 BB 5-22 Nt v Lancs (Nottingham) 2013 – Nt record.

ZAIB, Saif Ali (RGS High Wycombe), b High Wycombe, Bucks 22 May 1998. LHB, SLA. Squad No 18. Debut (Northamptonshire) 2015. Northamptonshire 2nd XI debut 2013, aged 15y 90d. HS 65* v Glamorgan (Swansea) 2016. BB 6-115 v Loughborough MCCU (Northampton) 2017 CC BB 5-148 v Leics (Northampton) 2016. LO HS 17 and LO BB 2-22 v South Africans (Northampton) 2017. T20 HS 6. T20 BB – .

RELEASED/RETIRED

(Having made a County 1st XI appearance in 2019, even if not formally contracted. Some may return in 2020.)

AZHARULLAH, Mohammad, b Burewala, Punjab, Pakistan 25 Dec 1983. 5'7''. RHB, RFM. Multan 2004-05 to 2006-07. WAPDA 2004-05 to 2012-13. Quetta 2005-06. Baluchistan 2007-08 to 2008-09. Northamptonshire 2013-17; cap 2015. Pakistan Television 2018-19. UK qualified through residency and British wife. HS 58* v Kent (Canterbury) 2015. BB 7-74 Quetta v Lahore Ravi (Quetta) 2005-06. Nh BB 7-76 (10-158 match) v Sussex (Northampton) 2014. LO HS 9 (twice). LO BB 5-38 v Hants (Southampton) 2014 (RLC). T20 HS 6*. T20 BB 4-14.

NQBAVUMA, Temba, b Cape Town, South Africa 17 May 1990. Cousin of P.V.Mntungwa (Boland 2017-18). RHB, RM. Gauteng 2008-09 to 2013-14. Lions 2010-11 to date. Cape Cobras 2017-18. Northamptonshire 2019. **Tests** (SA): 40 (2014-15 to 2019-20); HS 102* v E (Cape Town) 2015-16; BB 1-29 v A (Perth) 2016-17. **LOI** (SA): 6 (2016-17 to 2019-20); HS 113 v Ire (Benoni) 2016-17. **IT20** (SA): 5 (2019 to 2019-20); HS 49 v E (Centurion) 2019-20. F-c Tours (SA): E 2017; A 2014 (SAA), 2016 (SAA), 2016-17; NZ 2016-17; I 2015 (SAA), 2019-20; SL 2018; B 2015; Ire 2012 (SAA). HS 180 Lions v Dolphins (Pietermaritzburg) 2019-20. Nh HS 134 v Derbys (Chesterfield) 2019. BB 2-34 Gauteng v NW (Potchefstroom) 2010-11. Nh BB – . LO HS 117* Lions v Titans (Potchefstroom) 2018-19. LO BB – . T20 HS 104.

^{NQ}**BRACEWELL, Douglas** Andrew John, b Tauranga, New Zealand 28 Sep 1990. Son of B.P.Bracewell (Central Districts, Otago, Northern Districts & NZ 1977-78 to 1989-90); nephew of J.G.Bracewell (Otago, Auckland & NZ 1978-79 to 1989-90), D.W.Bracewell (Canterbury and Central Districts 1974-75 to 1979-80) and M.A.Bracewell (Otago 1977-78); cousin of M.G.Bracewell (Otago and Wellington 2010-11 to date). RHB, RM. Central Districts 2008-09 to date. Northamptonshire 2018-19. IPL: DD 2012. **Tests** (NZ): 27 (2011-12 to 2016); HS 47 v SL (Dunedin) 2015-16; BB 6-40 v A (Hobart) 2011-12. **LOI** (NZ): 19 (2011-12 to 2018-19); HS 57 v I (Mt Maunganui) 2018-19; BB 4-55 v WI (Whangarei) 2017-18. **IT20** (NZ): 18 (2011-12 to 2018-19); HS 44 v SL (Auckland) 2018-19; BB 3-25 v Z (Harare) 2011-12. F-c Tours (NZ): E 2013, 2015; A 2011-12, 2015-16; SA 2012-13, 2016; WI 2012; I 2012, 2013-14 (NZA); SL 2012-13, 2013-14 (NZA); Z 2011-12; B 2013-14. HS 105 CD v Otago (Queenstown) 2014-15. Nh HS 81 and Nh BB 4-71 v Warwks (Birmingham) 2018. BB 7-35 CD v Canterbury (Rangiora) 2012-13. LO HS 80 CD v ND (Whangarei) 2015-16. LO BB 4-43 CD v Canterbury (Rangiora) 2010-11. T20 HS 44. T20 BB 3-21.

^{NQ}**HOLDER, Jason** Omar, b St George, Barbados 5 Nov 1991. RHB, RMF. Barbados 2008-09 to date. CC&C 2011-12. Northamptonshire 2019. IPL: CSK 2013. SH 2014. KKR 2016. **Tests** (WI): 40 (2014 to 2019-20, 32 as captain); HS 202* v E (Bridgetown) 2018-19; BB 6-59 v B (Kingston) 2018. **LOI** (WI): 115 (2012-13 to 2019-20, 86 as captain); HS 99* v PNG (Harare) 2017-18; BB 5-27 v I (North Sound) 2017. **IT20** (WI): 17 (2013-14 to 2019-20, 3 as captain); HS 26* v P (Port of Spain) 2016-17; BB 2-23 v Afg (Lucknow) 2019-20. F-c Tours (WI)(C=Captain): E 2017C; A 2015-16C; SA 2014-15; NZ 2017-18C; I 2018-19C 2019-20 (v Afg)C; SL 2015-16C; Z 2017-18C; UAE (v P) 2016-17C. HS 202* (*see Tests*). Nh HS 40 and Nh BB 2-62 v Middx (Northampton) 2019. BB 6-59 (*see Tests*). LO HS 99* (*see LOI*). LO BB 5-27 (*see LOI*). T20 HS 54. T20 BB 4-27.

^{NQ}**PRETORIUS, Dwaine**, b Randfontein, South Africa 29 Mar 1989. RHB, RMF. North West 2010-11 to 2013-14. Lions 2014-15 to date. Northamptonshire 2019. **Tests** (SA): 3 (2019-20); HS 37 v E (Johannesburg) 2019-20; BB 2-26 v E (Cape Town) 2019-20. **LOI** (SA): 22 (2016-17 to 2019); HS 50 v NZ (Christchurch) 2016-17; BB 3-5 v NZ (Wellington) 2016-17. **IT20** (SA): 11 (2017 to 2019-20); HS 77* and BB 1-12 v SL (Johannesburg) 2018-19. F-c Tours (SAA): I 2018; Z 2016. HS 177 NW v SW Districts (Potchefstroom) 2012-13. Nh HS 111 and Nh BB 1-21 v Worcs (Northampton) 2019 – on UK debut. BB 6-38 (10-75 match) Lions v Dolphins (Johannesburg) 2018-19. LO HS 115 Lions v Knights (Kimberley) 2014-15. LO BB 4-35 Lions v Knights (Bloemfontein) 2014-15. T20 HS 77*. T20 BB 4-22.

B.D.Cotton left the staff without making a County 1st XI appearance in 2019.

NORTHAMPTONSHIRE 2019

RESULTS SUMMARY

	Place	Won	Lost	Drew	NR
Specsavers County Champ (2nd Division)	2nd	5	2	7	
All First-Class Matches		5	2	8	
Royal London One-Day Cup (North Group)	8th	2	6		
Vitality Blast (North Group)	7th	4	6		4

SPECSAVERS COUNTY CHAMPIONSHIP AVERAGES

BATTING AND FIELDING

Cap		M	I	NO	HS	Runs	Avge	100	50	Ct/St
	R.S.Vasconcelos	10	18	2	184	750	46.87	2	3	16
2019	A.M.Rossington	13	19	2	82	787	46.29	–	8	32/2
	T.Bavuma	8	15	–	134	566	37.73	2	1	7
2012	A.G.Wakely	12	16	1	102	548	36.53	1	2	12
	L.A.Procter	14	21	7	86*	510	36.42	–	2	4
2019	R.I.Keogh	14	22	–	150	744	33.81	2	2	4
	S.A.Zaib	3	5	–	54	163	32.60	–	1	–
	N.L.Buck	10	13	4	53	287	31.88	–	3	2
2018	J.J.Cobb	6	10	–	68	314	31.40	–	3	2
2017	R.E.Levi	4	6	1	60	144	28.80	–	1	2
	B.J.Curran	7	11	1	52	273	27.30	–	1	3
	M.T.Coles	4	5	1	41*	98	24.50	–	–	3
2017	R.I.Newton	10	19	2	105	396	23.29	1	1	3
	L.Wood	4	6	1	66	116	23.20	–	1	3
	B.A.Hutton	10	15	4	34*	203	18.45	–	–	9
2018	B.W.Sanderson	14	17	5	28	162	14.72	–	–	–

Also played: G.K.Berg (3 matches) 5, 3, 1; D.A.J.Bracewell (3) 38, 1, 15; E.N.Gay (1) did
not bat (1 ct); J.O.Holder (2) 40, 3 (4 ct); B.Muzarabani (2) 1*, 1 (1 ct); J.Overton (2) 6, 0,
19 (2 ct); D.Pretorius (1) 111.

BOWLING

	O	M	R	W	Avge	Best	5wI	10wM
B.W.Sanderson	448.2	118	1179	60	19.65	6-37	3	1
B.A.Hutton	263.3	72	700	35	20.00	6-57	2	–
N.L.Buck	207.1	38	814	22	37.00	5-54	1	–
L.A.Procter	204.1	43	697	17	41.00	4-26	–	–
R.I.Keogh	225.2	37	804	13	61.84	3-43	–	–
Also bowled:								
G.K.Berg	59.3	18	153	8	19.12	2-17	–	–
M.T.Coles	69	13	268	9	29.77	3-51	–	–
L.Wood	110	18	332	9	36.88	5-72	1	–
J.Overton	55.2	3	223	6	37.16	3-79	–	–

T.Bavuma 1-0-2-0; D.A.J.Bracewell 54-7-212-4; J.J.Cobb 27-4-91-1; J.O.Holder
52-6-199-4; B.Muzarabani 31-2-160-4; D.Pretorius 20-6-54-2; A.M.Rossington 5-0-20-0;
R.S.Vasconcelos 1.3-0-9-0; S.A.Zaib 4-0-16-0.

The First-Class Averages (pp 226–241) give the records of Northamptonshire players in all
first-class county matches (Northamptonshire's other opponents being Durham MCCU),
with the exception of G.K.Berg, M.T.Coles, J.Overton and L.Wood, whose first-class figures
for Northamptonshire are as above.

NORTHAMPTONSHIRE RECORDS

FIRST-CLASS CRICKET

Highest Total	For 781-7d			v Notts	Northampton	1995
	V 701-7d			by Kent	Beckenham	2017
Lowest Total	For 12			v Glos	Gloucester	1907
	V 33			by Lancashire	Northampton	1977
Highest Innings	For 331*	M.E.K.Hussey		v Somerset	Taunton	2003
	V 333	K.S.Duleepsinhji	for	Sussex	Hove	1930

Highest Partnership for each Wicket

1st	375	R.A.White/M.J.Powell	v	Glos	Northampton	2002
2nd	344	G.Cook/R.J.Boyd-Moss	v	Lancashire	Northampton	1986
3rd	393	A.Fordham/A.J.Lamb	v	Yorkshire	Leeds	1990
4th	370	R.T.Virgin/P.Willey	v	Somerset	Northampton	1976
5th	401	M.B.Loye/D.Ripley	v	Glamorgan	Northampton	1998
6th	376	R.Subba Row/A.Lightfoot	v	Surrey	The Oval	1958
7th	293	D.J.G.Sales/D.Ripley	v	Essex	Northampton	1999
8th	179	A.J.Hall/J.D.Middlebrook	v	Surrey	The Oval	2011
9th	156	R.Subba Row/S.Starkie	v	Lancashire	Northampton	1955
10th	148	B.W.Bellamy/J.V.Murdin	v	Glamorgan	Northampton	1925

Best Bowling	For 10-127	V.W.C.Jupp		v Kent	Tunbridge W	1932
(Innings)	V 10- 30	C.Blythe	for	Kent	Northampton	1907
Best Bowling	For 15- 31	G.E.Tribe		v Yorkshire	Northampton	1958
(Match)	V 17- 48	C.Blythe	for	Kent	Northampton	1907

Most Runs – Season	2198	D.Brookes	(av 51.11)		1952
Most Runs – Career	28980	D.Brookes	(av 36.13)		1934-59
Most 100s – Season	8	R.A.Haywood			1921
Most 100s – Career	67	D.Brookes			1934-59
Most Wkts – Season	175	G.E.Tribe	(av 18.70)		1955
Most Wkts – Career	1102	E.W.Clark	(av 21.26)		1922-47
Most Career W-K Dismissals	810	K.V.Andrew	(653 ct; 157 st)		1953-66
Most Career Catches in the Field	469	D.S.Steele			1963-84

LIMITED-OVERS CRICKET

Highest Total	50ov	425		v Notts	Nottingham	2016
	40ov	324-6		v Warwicks	Birmingham	2013
	T20	231-5		v Warwicks	Birmingham	2018
Lowest Total	50ov	62		v Leics	Leicester	1974
	40ov	41		v Middlesex	Northampton	1972
	T20	47		v Durham	Chester-le-St[2]	2011
Highest Innings	50ov	161	D.J.G.Sales	v Yorkshire	Northampton	2006
	40ov	172*	W.Larkins	v Warwicks	Luton	1983
	T20	111*	L.Klusener	v Worcs	Kidderminster	2007
Best Bowling	50ov	7-10	C.Pietersen	v Denmark	Brondby	2005
	40ov	7-39	A.Hodgson	v Somerset	Northampton	1976
	T20	6-21	A.J.Hall	v Worcs	Northampton	2008

151

NOTTINGHAMSHIRE

Formation of Present Club: March/April 1841
Substantial Reorganisation: 11 December 1866
Inaugural First-Class Match: 1864
Colours: Green and Gold
County Champions (since 1890): (6) 1907, 1929, 1981, 1987, 2005, 2010
NatWest Trophy Winners: (1) 1987
Benson and Hedges Cup Winners: (1) 1989
Sunday League Winners: (1) 1991
Yorkshire Bank 40 Winners: (1) 2013
Royal London Cup Winners: (1) 2017
Twenty20 Cup Winners: (1) 2017

Chief Executive: Lisa Pursehouse, Trent Bridge, West Bridgford, Nottingham NG2 6AG • Tel: 0115 982 3000 • Email: questions@nottsccc.co.uk • Web: www.trentbridge.co.uk • Twitter: @TrentBridge (86,929 followers)

Director of Cricket: Mick Newell. **Head Coach**: Peter Moores. **Assistant Head Coach**: Paul Franks. **Bowling Coach**: Andy Pick. **Captains**: S.J.Mullaney (f-c & l-o) and D.T.Christian (T20). **Overseas Players**: D.T.Christian (T20 only) and Mohammad Abbas. **2020 Testimonial**: None. **Head Groundsman**: Steve Birks. **Scorer**: Roger Marshall and Anne Cusworth. **Blast Team Name**: Notts Outlaws. ‡ New registration. NQ Not qualified for England.

BALL, Jacob Timothy ('**Jake**') (Meden CS), b Mansfield 14 Mar 1991. Nephew of B.N.French (Notts and England 1976-95). 6'0". RHB, RFM. Squad No 28. Debut (Nottinghamshire) 2011; cap 2016. MCC 2016. **Tests**: 4 (2016 to 2017-18); HS 31 and BB 1-47 v I (Mumbai) 2016-17. **LOI**: 18 (2016-17 to 2018); HS 28 v B (Dhaka) 2016-17; BB 5-51 v B (Dhaka) 2016-17 – different games. **IT20**: 2 (2018); HS – ; BB 1-39 v I (Bristol) 2018. F-c Tours: A 2017-18; I 2016-17. HS 49* v Warwks (Nottingham) 2015. 50 wkts (1): 54 (2016). BB 6-49 v Sussex (Nottingham) 2015. Hat-trick v Middx (Nottingham) 2016. LO HS 28 (*see LOI*). BB 5-51 (*see LOI*). T20 HS 8*. T20 BB 3-27.

‡BARBER, Thomas Edward (Bournemouth GS), b Poole, Dorset 31 May 1994. 6'3". RHB, LFM. Squad No 18. Middlesex 2018. Hampshire 2014 (l-o only). Dorset 2016. HS 3 and BB – M v Sussex (Hove) 2018. LO HS 1 South v North (Cave Hill) 2017-18. LO BB 3-62 M v Australians (Lord's) 2018. T20 HS 2. T20 BB 4-28.

BLATHERWICK, Jack Morgan (Holgate Ac, Hucknall; Central C, Nottingham), b Nottingham 4 June 1998. RHB, RMF. Squad No 47. Debut (Nottinghamshire) 2019. Nottinghamshire 2nd XI Champions 2016. England U19 2017. HS 4* v Warwks (Nottingham) 2019. BB 1-82 v Surrey (Oval) 2019. LO HS 3* v Warwks (Nottingham) 2018 (RLC). LO BB 1-55 Nh v Australia A (Northampton) 2019.

BROAD, Stuart Christopher John (Oakham S), b Nottingham 24 Jun 1986. Squad No 8. Son of B.C.Broad (Glos, Notts, OFS and England 1979-94). 6'6". LHB, RFM. Debut (Leicestershire) 2005; cap 2007. Nottinghamshire debut/cap 2008; testimonial 2019. MCC 2019. Big Bash: HH 2016-17. YC 2006. *Wisden* 2009. **ECB Test Central Contract 2019-20. Tests**: 138 (2007-08 to 2019-20); HS 169 v P (Lord's) 2010, sharing in record Test and UK f-c 8th wkt partnership of 332 with I.J.L.Trott; 50 wkts (2); most – 62 (2013); BB 8-15 v A (Nottingham) 2015. Hat-tricks (2): v I (Nottingham) 2011, and v SL (Leeds) 2014. **LOI**: 121 (2006 to 2015-16, 3 as captain); HS 45* v I (Manchester) 2007; BB 5-23 v SA (Nottingham) 2008. **IT20**: 56 (2006 to 2013-14, 27 as captain); HS 18* v SA (Chester-le-St) 2012 and 18* v A (Melbourne) 2013-14; BB 4-24 v NZ (Auckland) 2012-13. F-c Tours: A 2010-11, 2013-14, 2017-18; SA 2009-10, 2015-16, 2019-20; WI 2005-06 (Eng A), 2008-09, 2014-15, 2018-19; NZ 2007-08, 2012-13, 2017-18, 2019-20; I 2008-09, 2012-13, 2016-17; SL 2007-08, 2011-12, 2018-19; B 2006-07 (Eng A), 2009-10, 2016-17; UAE 2011-12 (v P), 2015-16 (v P). HS 169 (*see Tests*). CC HS 91* Le v Derbys (Leicester) 2007. Nt HS 60 v Worcs (Nottingham) 2009. BB 8-15 (*see Tests*). CC BB 8-52 (11-131 match) Nt v Warwks (Birmingham) 2010. LO HS 45* (*see LOI*). LO BB 5-23 (*see LOI*). T20 HS 18*. T20 BB 4-24.

BUDINGER, Solomon George (Southport S), b Colchester, Essex 21 Aug 1999. LHB, OB, occ WK. Squad No 1. Sussex 2nd XI 2016-17. Nottinghamshire 2nd XI debut 2018. Awaiting 1st XI debut.

CARTER, Matthew (Branston S), b Lincoln 26 May 1996. Younger brother of A.Carter (*see WORCESTERSHIRE*). RHB, OB. Squad No 20. Debut (Nottinghamshire) 2015, taking 7-56 v Somerset (Taunton) – the best debut figures for Nt since 1914. Nottinghamshire 2nd XI debut 2013. Lincolnshire 2013-17. HS 33 v Sussex (Hove) 2018. BB 7-56 (10-195 match) (*see above*). LO HS 21* v Warwks (Birmingham) 2019 (RLC). LO BB 4-40 v Warwks (Nottingham) 2018 (RLC). T20 HS 16*. T20 BB 3-14.

CHAPPELL, Zachariah John ('Zak') (Stamford S), b Grantham, Lincs 21 Aug 1996. 6'4". RHB, RFM. Squad No 32. Leicestershire 2015-18. Nottinghamshire debut 2019. HS 96 Le v Derbys (Derby) 2015. Nt HS 29 v Warwks (Nottingham) 2019. BB 6-44 Le v Northants (Northampton) 2018. BB – . LO HS 59* Le v Durham (Gosforth) 2017 (RLC). LO BB 3-45 Le v Durham (Leicester) 2018 (RLC). T20 HS 16. T20 BB 3-23.

NQCHRISTIAN, Daniel Trevor, b Camperdown, NSW, Australia 4 May 1983. RHB, RFM. Squad No 54. S Australia 2007-08 to 2012-13. Hampshire 2010. Gloucestershire 2013; cap 2013. Victoria 2013-14 to 2017-18. Nottinghamshire debut 2016, having joined in 2015 for l-o and T20 only; cap 2015; captain 2016 to date (T20 only). IPL: DC 2011-12. RCB 2013. RPS 2017. DD 2018. Big Bash: BH 2011-12 to 2014-15. HH 2015-16 to 2017-18. MR 2018-19 to date. **LOI** (A): 19 (2011-12 to 2013-14); HS 39 v I (Adelaide) 2011-12; BB 5-31 v SL (Melbourne) 2011-12. **IT20** (A): 16 (2009-10 to 2017-18); HS 9 v I (Ranchi) 2017-18; BB 3-27 v WI (Gros Islet) 2011-12. HS 131* SA v NSW (Adelaide) 2011-12. CC HS 36 and CC BB 2-115 H v Somerset (Taunton) 2010. Nt HS 31 v Hants (Southampton) 2016. BB 5-24 SA v WA (Perth) (2009-10). Nt BB 1-22 v Warwks (Birmingham) 2016. LO HS 117 Vic v NSW (Sydney) 2013-14. LO BB 6-48 SA v Vic (Geelong) 2010-11. T20 HS 129 M v Kent (Canterbury) 2014 – M record. T20 BB 5-14.

CLARKE, Joe Michael (Llanfyllin HS), b Shrewsbury, Shrops 26 May 1996. 5'11". RHB, WK. Squad No 33. Worcestershire 2015-18. Nottinghamshire debut 2019. MCC 2017. Shropshire 2012-13. England U19 2014. F-c Tours (EL): WI 2017-18; UAE 2016-17 (v Afg). 1000 runs (1): 1325 (2016). HS 194 Wo v Derbys (Worcester) 2016. Nt HS 125 (and 112) v Warwks (Nottingham) 2019. BB – . LO HS 139 v Lancs (Nottingham) 2019 (RLC). T20 HS 124*.

COMPTON, Benjamin Garnet (Clifton C, Durban), b Durban, S Africa 29 Mar 1994. Son of P.M.D.Compton (Natal 1979-80); grandson of D.S.C.Compton (Middlesex and England 1936-58); cousin of N.R.D.Compton (Middlesex, Somerset, ME, Worcs and England 2004-17). LHB, OB. Squad No 7. Debut (Nottinghamshire) 2019. HS 16* v Surrey (Oval) 2019.

DUCKETT, Ben Matthew (Stowe S), b Farnborough, Kent 17 Oct 1994. 5'7". LHB, WK, occ OB. Squad No 17. Northamptonshire 2013-18; cap 2016. Nottinghamshire debut 2018. MCC 2017. Big Bash: HH 2018-19. PCA 2016. YC 2016. *Wisden* 2016. **Tests**: 4 (2016-17); HS 56 v B (Dhaka) 2016-17. **LOI**: 3 (2016-17); HS 63 v B (Chittagong) 2016-17. **IT20**: 1 (2019); HS 9 v P (Cardiff) 2019. F-c Tours: I 2016-17; B 2016-17. 1000 runs (2); most – 1338 (2016). HS 282* Nh v Sussex (Northampton) 2016. Nt HS 216 v Cambridge MCCU (Cambridge) 2019. BB 1-21 Nh v Kent (Beckenham) 2017. LO HS 220* EL v Sri Lanka A (Canterbury) 2016. T20 HS 96.

EVISON, Joseph David Michael (Stamford S), b Peterborough, Cambs 14 Nov 2001. Son of G.M.Evison (Lincolnshire 1993-97); younger brother of S.H.G.Evison (Lincolnshire 2017-18). RHB, RM. Squad No 90. Debut (Nottinghamshire) 2019. Nottinghamshire 2nd XI debut 2017. HS 45 v Warwks (Nottingham) 2019 – only 1st XI appearance.

FLETCHER, Luke Jack (Henry Mellish S, Nottingham), b Nottingham 18 Sep 1988. 6'6". RHB, RMF. Squad No 19. Debut (Nottinghamshire) 2008; cap 2014. Surrey 2015 (on loan). Derbyshire 2016 (on loan). HS 92 v Hants (Southampton) 2009 and 92 v Durham (Chester-le-St) 2017. BB 5-27 v Worcs (Worcester) 2018. LO HS 53* v Kent (Nottingham) 2018 (RLC). LO BB 5-56 v Derbys (Derby) 2019 (RLC). T20 HS 27. T20 BB 4-30.

GURNEY, Harry Frederick (Garendon HS; Loughborough GS; Leeds U), b Nottingham 25 Oct 1986. 6'2". RHB, LFM. Squad No 11. Leicestershire 2007-11. Nottinghamshire debut 2012; cap 2014. MCC 2014. Bradford/Leeds UCCE 2006-07 (not f-c). IPL: KKR 2019. Big Bash: MR 2018-19 to date. **LOI**: 10 (2014 to 2014-15); HS 6* v SL (Colombo, RPS) 2014-15; BB 4-55 v SL (Lord's) 2014. **IT20**: 2 (2014); BB 2-26 v SL (Oval) 2014. HS 42* v Sussex (Hove) 2017. BB 6-25 v Lancs (Manchester) 2018. Hat-trick v Sussex (Hove) 2013. LO HS 13* v Durham (Chester-le-St) 2012 (CB40). LO BB 5-24 Le v Hants (Leicester) 2010 (CB40). T20 HS 6. T20 BB 5-30.

HALES, Alexander Daniel (Chesham HS), b Hillingdon, Middx 3 Jan 1989. 6'5". RHB, OB, occ WK. Squad No 10. Debut (Nottinghamshire) 2008; cap 2011. Agreed white-ball-only contract in 2018. Worcestershire 2014 (1 game, on loan). Buckinghamshire 2006-07. IPL: SH 2018. Big Bash: MR 2012-13. AS 2013-14. HH 2014-15. ST 2019-20. **Tests**: 11 (2015-16 to 2016); HS 94 v SL (Lord's) 2016; BB – . **LOI**: 70 (2014 to 2018-19); HS 171 v P (Nottingham) 2016. **IT20**: 60 (2011 to 2018-19); HS 116* v SL (Chittagong) 2013-14 – E record. 1000 runs (3); most – 1127 (2011). HS 236 v Yorks (Nottingham) 2015. BB 2-63 v Yorks (Nottingham) 2009. LO HS 187* v Surrey (Lord's) 2017 (RLC) – Nt record. T20 HS 116*.

‡**HAMEED, Haseeb** (Bolton S), b Bolton, Lancs 17 Jan 1997. 6'2". RHB, LB. Squad No 99. Lancashire 2015-19; cap 2016. Lancashire 2nd XI debut 2013. England U19 2014-15 to 2015. **Tests**: 3 (2016-17); HS 82 v I (Rajkot) 2016-17 – on debut. F-c Tours: WI 2017-18 (EL); I 2016-17; SL 2016-17 (EL). 1000 runs (1): 1198 (2016). HS 122 La v Notts (Nottingham) 2016. BB – . LO HS 88 La v Leics (Manchester) 2017 (RLC).

JAMES, Lyndon Wallace (Oakham S), b Worksop 27 Dec 1998. RHB, RMF. Squad No 45. Debut (Nottinghamshire) 2018. Nottinghamshire 2nd XI debut 2017. HS 13 and BB 3-54 v Essex (Nottingham) 2018. LO HS 0.

‡**NQMOHAMMAD ABBAS**, b Sialkot, Pakistan 10 Mar 1990. RHB, RMF. Squad No 27. Sialkot 2008-09 to 2012-13. KRL 2015-16 to 2016-17. SNGPL 2017-18 to 2018-19. Leicestershire 2018-19; cap 2018. Southern Punjab 2019-20. **Tests** (P): 18 (2017 to 2019-20); HS 29 v A (Adelaide) 2019-20; BB 5-33 v A (Abu Dhabi) 2018-19. **LOI** (P): 3 (2018-19); HS – ; BB 1-44 v A (Sharjah) 2018-19. F-c Tours (P): E 2018; A 2019-20; SA 2018-19; WI 2017; Ire 2018. HS 40 and BB 8-46 (14-93 match) KRL v Karachi Whites (Karachi) 2016-17. CC HS 32* Le v Sussex (Hove) 2018. 50 wkts (1+2); most – 71 (2016-17). CC BB 6-48 Le v Kent (Leicester) 2018. LO HS 15* KRL v HB (Karachi) 2016-17. LO BB 4-31 KRL v SNGPL (Karachi) 2016-17. T20 HS 15*. T20 BB 3-22.

MOORES, Thomas James (Loughborough GS), b Brighton, Sussex 4 Sep 1996. Son of P.Moores (Worcestershire, Sussex & OFS 1983-98); nephew of S.Moores (Cheshire 1995). LHB, WK. Squad No 23. Lancashire 2016 (on loan). Nottinghamshire debut 2016. Nottinghamshire 2nd XI debut 2014. HS 103 v Somerset (Taunton) 2018. LO HS 76 v Leics (Leicester) 2018. T20 HS 80*.

MULLANEY, Steven John (St Mary's RC S, Astley), b Warrington, Cheshire 19 Nov 1986. 5'9". RHB, RM. Squad No 5. Lancashire 2006-08. Nottinghamshire debut 2010, scoring 100* v Hants (Southampton); cap 2013; captain 2018 to date. F-c Tour (EL): I 2018-19. 1000 runs (1): 1148 (2016). HS 179 v Warwks (Nottingham) 2019. BB 5-32 v Glos (Nottingham) 2017. LO HS 124 v Durham (Chester-le-St) 2018 (RLC). LO BB 4-29 v Kent (Nottingham) 2013 (Y40). T20 HS 55. T20 BB 4-19.

NASH, Christopher David (Collyer's SFC; Loughborough U), b Cuckfield, Sussex 19 May 1983. 5'11". RHB, OB. Squad No 3. Sussex 2002-17; cap 2008; testimonial 2017. Nottinghamshire debut 2018. Loughborough UCCE 2003-04. British U 2004. 1000 runs (4); most – 1321 (2009). HS 184 Sx v Leics (Leicester) 2010. Nt HS 139 and Nt BB 2-4 v Worcs (Nottingham) 2018. BB 4-12 Sx v Glamorgan (Cardiff) 2010. LO HS 124* Sx v Kent (Canterbury) 2011 (CB40). LO BB 4-40 Sx v Yorks (Hove) 2009 (FPT). T20 HS 112*. T20 BB 4-7.

PATEL, Samit Rohit (Worksop C), b Leicester 30 Nov 1984. Elder brother of A.Patel (Derbyshire and Notts 2007-11). 5'8". RHB, SLA. Squad No 21. Debut (Nottinghamshire) 2002; cap 2008; testimonial 2017. Glamorgan 2019 (on loan). MCC 2014, 2016. PCA 2017. **Tests**: 6 (2011-12 to 2015-16); HS 42 v P (Sharjah) 2015-16; BB 2-27 v SL (Galle) 2011-12. **LOI**: 36 (2008 to 2012-13); HS 70* v I (Mohali) 2011-12; BB 5-41 v SA (Oval) 2008. **IT20**: 18 (2011 to 2012-13); HS 67 v SL (Pallekele) 2012-13; BB 2-6 v Afg (Colombo, RPS) 2012-13. F-c Tours: NZ 2008-09 (Eng A); I 2012-13; SL 2011-12; UAE 2015-16 (v P). 1000 runs (2); most – 1125 (2014). HS 257* v Glos (Bristol) 2017. BB 7-68 (11-111 match) v Hants (Southampton) 2011. LO HS 136* v Northants (Northampton) 2019 (RLC). LO BB 6-13 v Ireland (Dublin) 2009 (FPT). T20 HS 90*. T20 BB 4-5.

PATTERSON-WHITE, Liam Anthony (Worksop C), b Sunderland, Co Durham 8 Nov 1998. LHB, SLA. Squad No 22. Debut (Nottinghamshire) 2019. Nottinghamshire 2nd XI debut 2016. England U19 2016-17. HS 58* v Yorks (Scarborough) 2019. BB 5-73 v Somerset (Taunton) 2019 – on debut.

SLATER, Benjamin Thomas (Netherthorpe S; Leeds Met U), b Chesterfield, Derbys 26 Aug 1991. 5'10". LHB, OB. Squad No 26. Debut (Leeds/Bradford MCCU) 2012. Southern Rocks 2012-13. Derbyshire 2013-18. Nottinghamshire debut 2018. HS 130 v Cambridge MCCU (Cambridge) 2019. CC HS 119 (and 104) De v Leics (Derby) 2014. BB – . LO HS 148* De v Northants (Northampton) 2016 (RLC). T20 HS 57.

‡**TREGO, Peter** David (Wyvern CS, W-s-M), b Weston-super-Mare, Somerset 12 Jun 1981. 6'0". RHB, RMF. Squad No 77. Somerset 2000-18; cap 2007; benefit 2015. Kent 2003. Middlesex 2005. C Districts 2013-14. MCC 2013, 2019. Herefordshire 2005. 1000 runs (1): 1070 (2016). HS 154* Sm v Lancs (Manchester) 2016, sharing Sm record 8th wkt partnership of 236 with R.C.Davies. 50 wkts (1): 50 (2012). BB 7-84 (11-153 match) Sm v Yorks (Leeds) 2014. LO HS 147 Sm v Glamorgan (Taunton) 2010 (CB40). LO BB 5-40 EL v West Indies A (Worcester) 2010. T20 HS 94*. T20 BB 4-27.

RELEASED/RETIRED

(Having made a County 1st XI appearance in 2019)

ASHWIN, R. – *see YORKSHIRE*.

COUGHLIN, P. – *see DURHAM*.

NQ**IMAD WASIM**, b Swansea, Glamorgan 18 Dec 1988. LHB, SLA. Islamabad 2006-07 to 2017-18. Federal Areas 2008-09 to 2011-12. Islamabad Leopards 2014-15. Northern Areas 2019-20. Nottinghamshire 2019 (T20 only). **LOI** (P): 53 (2015 to 2019-20, 2 as captain); HS 63* v E (Lord's) 2016; BB 5-14 v Ire (Dublin) 2016. **IT20** (P): 43 (2015 to 2019-20); HS 47 v SL (Lahore) 2019-20; BB 5-14 v WI (Dubai, DSC) 2016-17. F-c Tour (PA): SL 2015. HS 207 Leopards v Multan Tigers (Multan) 2014-15. BB 8-81 (12-104 match) Islamabad v Multan (Karachi) 2013-14. LO HS 117* P v Kent (Beckenham) 2019. LO BB 5-14 (*see LOI*). T20 HS 64. T20 BB 5-14.

LIBBY, J.D. – *see WORCESTERSHIRE*.

NQ**PATTINSON, James** Lee, b Melbourne, Australia 3 May 1990. Younger brother of D.J.Pattinson (Victoria, Nottinghamshire and England 2006-07 to 2011-12). LHB, RFM. Victoria 2008-09 to date. Nottinghamshire 2017-19; cap 2017. Big Bash: MR 2013-14 to 2016-17. BH 2018-19 to date. **Tests** (A): 21 (2011-12 to 2019-20); HS 47* v E (Birmingham) 2019; BB 5-27 v NZ (Brisbane) 2011-12 and 5-27 v WI (Hobart) 2015-16. **LOI** (A): 15 (2011 to 2015); HS 13 v E (Manchester) 2012; BB 4-51 v SL (Melbourne) 2011-12. **IT20** (A): 4 (2011-12); HS 5* and BB 2-17 v SA (Johannesburg) 2011-12. F-c Tours (A): E 2013, 2019; SA 2013-14; WI 2011-12; NZ 2015-16; I 2012-13. HS 89* v Leics (Leicester) 2017. BB 6-32 Vic v Q (Brisbane) 2012-13. Nt BB 6-73 v Kent (Tunbridge W) 2019. LO HS 44 Vic v Q (Sydney) 2015-16. LO BB 6-48 Vic v NSW (Sydney) 2009-10. T20 HS 27*. T20 BB 5-33.

WOOD, L. – *see LANCASHIRE*.

M.H.A.Footitt left the staff without making a County 1st XI appearance in 2019.

NOTTINGHAMSHIRE 2019

RESULTS SUMMARY

		Place	Won	Lost	Drew	NR
Specsavers County Champ (1st Division)		8th		10	4	
All First-Class Matches				10	5	
Royal London One-Day Cup (North Group)	SF	6	2			1
Vitality Blast (North Group)		SF	7	5		4

SPECSAVERS COUNTY CHAMPIONSHIP AVERAGES
BATTING AND FIELDING

Cap		M	I	NO	HS	Runs	Avge	100	50	Ct/St
2019	R.Ashwin	5	10	1	66*	339	37.66	–	2	2
	J.M.Clarke	12	21	1	125	621	31.05	3	1	6
	C.D.Nash	12	22	1	85	641	30.52	–	6	4
2013	S.J.Mullaney	13	24	–	194	694	28.91	2	2	13
	B.M.Duckett	13	23	–	140	630	27.39	1	2	7
	P.Coughlin	5	7	–	49	167	23.85	–	–	7
	B.T.Slater	13	24	1	76	471	20.47	–	1	6
	J.D.Libby	5	10	–	77	189	18.90	–	1	3
2017	J.L.Pattinson	3	5	2	22	55	18.33	–	–	–
2008	S.R.Patel	9	16	1	52	258	17.20	–	1	2
	L.A.Patterson-White	5	8	2	58*	91	15.16	–	1	3
	T.J.Moores	13	23	–	48	323	14.04	–	–	29/1
2016	J.T.Ball	10	16	11	15*	67	13.40	–	–	3
2008	S.C.J.Broad	7	13	4	30	109	12.11	–	–	3
	Z.J.Chappell	3	6	1	29	59	11.80	–	–	1
	L.Wood	5	9	1	52	87	10.87	–	–	–
2014	L.J.Fletcher	12	22	1	25*	209	9.95	–	–	2
	M.Carter	5	7	–	23	51	7.28	–	–	5

Also batted: J.M.Blatherwick (2 matches) 4*, 2*; B.G.Compton (2) 14, 13, 16* (1 ct); J.D.M.Evison (1) 45, 12 (1 ct).

BOWLING

	O	M	R	W	Avge	Best	5wI	10wM
L.A.Patterson-White	134.5	17	420	20	21.00	5-73	1	–
R.Ashwin	297.4	73	836	34	24.58	6-69	4	1
L.J.Fletcher	326.4	89	926	35	26.45	5-50	2	–
S.C.J.Broad	195.4	44	509	17	29.94	5-73	1	–
L.Wood	93	12	349	11	31.72	5-67	1	–
S.J.Mullaney	166	32	536	13	41.23	4-48	–	–
P.Coughlin	135.4	19	530	11	48.18	3-37	–	–
J.T.Ball	246.5	42	878	15	58.53	2-57	–	–

Also bowled:

J.L.Pattinson	74	12	235	8	29.37	6-73	–	–
S.R.Patel	117.5	18	391	7	55.85	3-31	–	–
M.Carter	137.4	14	529	6	88.16	3-68	–	–

J.M.Blatherwick 34.4-3-192-2; Z.J.Chappell 40.4-3-178-0; B.M.Duckett 4-0-16-0; J.D.M.Evison 9-0-33-0; J.D.Libby 4-0-32-0.

The First-Class Averages (pp 226–241) give the records of Nottinghamshire players in all first-class county matches (Nottinghamshire's other opponents being Cambridge MCCU), with the exception of S.C.J.Broad and J.L.Pattinson, whose first-class figures for Nottinghamshire are as above, and:
S.R.Patel 10-18-2-52-319-19.93-0-1-3ct. 128.5-22-414-10-41.40-3/21-0-0.
L.Wood 6-10-2-52-106-13.25-0-1-0ct. 106.1-18-380-14-27.14-5/67-1-0.

NOTTINGHAMSHIRE RECORDS

FIRST-CLASS CRICKET

Highest Total	For 791		v	Essex	Chelmsford	2007
	V 781-7d		by	Northants	Northampton	1995
Lowest Total	For 13		v	Yorkshire	Nottingham	1901
	V 16		by	Derbyshire	Nottingham	1879
	16		by	Surrey	The Oval	1880
Highest Innings	For 312*	W.W.Keeton	v	Middlesex	The Oval	1939
	V 345	C.G.Macartney	for	Australians	Nottingham	1921

Highest Partnership for each Wicket

1st	406*	D.J.Bicknell/G.E.Welton	v	Warwicks	Birmingham	2000
2nd	398	A.Shrewsbury/W.Gunn	v	Sussex	Nottingham	1890
3rd	367	W.Gunn/J.R.Gunn	v	Leics	Nottingham	1903
4th	361	A.O.Jones/J.R.Gunn	v	Essex	Leyton	1905
5th	359	D.J.Hussey/C.M.W.Read	v	Essex	Nottingham	2007
6th	372*	K.P.Pietersen/J.E.Morris	v	Derbyshire	Derby	2001
7th	301	C.C.Lewis/B.N.French	v	Durham	Chester-le-St[2]	1993
8th	220	G.F.H.Heane/R.Winrow	v	Somerset	Nottingham	1935
9th	170	J.C.Adams/K.P.Evans	v	Somerset	Taunton	1994
10th	152	E.B.Alletson/W.Riley	v	Sussex	Hove	1911
	152	U.Afzaal/A.J.Harris	v	Worcs	Nottingham	2000

Best Bowling	For 10-66	K.Smales	v	Glos	Stroud	1956
(Innings)	V 10-10	H.Verity	for	Yorkshire	Leeds	1932
Best Bowling	For 17-89	F.C.L.Matthews	v	Northants	Nottingham	1923
(Match)	V 17-89	W.G.Grace	for	Glos	Cheltenham	1877

Most Runs – Season	2620	W.W.Whysall	(av 53.46)	1929
Most Runs – Career	31592	G.Gunn	(av 35.69)	1902-32
Most 100s – Season	9	W.W.Whysall		1928
	9	M.J.Harris		1971
	9	B.C.Broad		1990
Most 100s – Career	65	J.Hardstaff jr		1930-55
Most Wkts – Season	181	B.Dooland	(av 14.96)	1954
Most Wkts – Career	1653	T.G.Wass	(av 20.34)	1896-1920
Most Career W-K Dismissals	983	C.M.W.Read	(939 ct; 44 st)	1998-2017
Most Career Catches in the Field	466	A.O.Jones		1892-1914

LIMITED-OVERS CRICKET

Highest Total	50ov	445-8	v	Northants	Nottingham	2016
	40ov	296-7	v	Somerset	Taunton	2002
	T20	227-3	v	Derbyshire	Nottingham	2017
Lowest Total	50ov	74	v	Leics	Leicester	1987
	40ov	57	v	Glos	Nottingham	2009
	T20	91	v	Lancashire	Manchester	2006
Highest Innings	50ov	187*	A.D.Hales	v	Surrey	Lord's	2017
	40ov	150*	A.D.Hales	v	Worcs	Nottingham	2009
	T20	113*	D.T.Christian	v	Northants	Northampton	2018
Best Bowling	50ov	6-10	K.P.Evans	v	Northumb	Jesmond	1994
	40ov	6-12	R.J.Hadlee	v	Lancashire	Nottingham	1980
	T20	5-22	G.G.White	v	Lancashire	Nottingham	2013

SOMERSET

Formation of Present Club: 18 August 1875
Inaugural First-Class Match: 1882
Colours: Black, White and Maroon
Badge: Somerset Dragon
County Champions: (0); best – 2nd (Div 1) 2001, 2010, 2012, 2016, 2018, 2019
Gillette/NatWest/C&G Trophy Winners: (3) 1979, 1983, 2001
Benson and Hedges Cup Winners: (2) 1981, 1982
Sunday League Winners: (1) 1979
Royal London One-Day Cup Winners: (1) 2019
Twenty20 Cup Winners: (1) 2005

Chief Executive: Gordon Hollins, Cooper Associates County Ground, Taunton TA1 1JT • Tel: 01823 425301 • Email: enquiries@somersetcountycc.co.uk • Web: www.somersetcountycc.co.uk • Twitter: @SomersetCCC (131,447 followers)

Director of Cricket: Andy Hurry. **Head Coach**: Jason Kerr. **Assistant Coaches**: Greg Kennis and Marcus Trescothick. **Captains**: T.B.Abell (f-c and l-o) and L.Gregory (T20). **Overseas Players**: C.J.Anderson (T20 only), Babar Azam and M.S.Wade. **2020 Testimonial**: None. **Groundsman**: Simon Lee. **Scorer**: Polly Rhodes. ‡ New registration. [NQ] Not qualified for England.

ABELL, Thomas Benjamin (Taunton S; Exeter U), b Taunton 5 Mar 1994. 5'10". RHB, RM. Squad No 28. Debut (Somerset) 2014; captain 2017 to date; cap 2018. MCC 2019. F-c Tour (EL): A 2019-20. HS 135 v Lancs (Manchester) 2016. BB 4-39 v Warwks (Birmingham) 2019. Hat-trick v Notts (Nottingham) 2018. LO HS 106 v Sussex (Taunton) 2016 (RLC). LO BB 2-19 v Hants (Lord's) 2019 (RLC). T20 HS 101*. T"0 BB 1-11.

ALDRIDGE, Kasey Luke (Millfield S), b Bristol 24 Dec 2000. RHB, RMF. Squad No 5. Somerset 2nd XI debut 2019. Devon 2019. England U19 2018-19. Awaiting 1st XI debut.

[NQ]**ANDERSON, Corey** James (b Christchurch, New Zealand 13 Dec 1990. LHB, LMF. Squad No 78. Canterbury 2006-07 to 2009-10. Northern Districts 2011-12 to 2017-18. Somerset debut 2017 (T20 only). IPL: MI 2014-15. DD 2017. RCB 2018. **Tests** (NZ): 13 (2013-14 to 2015-16); HS 116 v B (Dhaka) 2013-14; BB 3-47 v WI (Hamilton) 2013-14. **LOI** (NZ): 49 (2013 to 2017); HS 131* v WI (Queenstown) 2013-14; BB 5-63 v I (Auckland) 2013-14. **IT20** (NZ): 31 (2012-13 to 2018-19); HS 94* v B (Mt Maunganui) 2014-15; BB 2-17 v P (Wellington) 2015-16. F-c Tours (NZ): E 2015; I 2013-14 (NZA); SL 2013-14 (NZA); B 2013-14; UAE 2014-15 (v P). HS 167 ND v Otago (Hamilton) 2012-13. BB 5-22 ND v Canterbury (Hamilton) 2009-10. LO HS 131* (see LOI). LO BB 5-26 ND v Canterbury (Hamilton) 2009-10. T20 HS 95*. T20 BB 2-17.

[NQ]**BABAR AZAM**, Mohammad, b Lahore, Pakistan 15 Oct 1994. RHB, OB. Squad No 56. ZT Bank 2010-11 to 2013-14. Islamabad 2012-13. State Bank of Pak 2014-15. SSGC 2015-16 to 2017-18. Somerset debut 2019. Central Punjab 2019-20. **Tests** (P): 26 (2015-16 to 2019-20); HS 143 v B (Rawalpindi) 2019-20. **LOI** (P): 74 (2015 to 2019); HS 125* v WI (Providence) 2017. **IT20** (P): 38 (2016 to 2019-20); HS 97* v WI (Karachi) 2017-18. F-c Tours (P): E 2016 (P A), 2018; A 2016-17, 2019-20; SA 2018-19; WI 2016-17; NZ 2016-17; Ire 2018. HS 266 State Bank v HB (Faisalabad) 2014-15. Sm HS 40 Warwks (Birmingham) 2019. BB 1-13 ZT v UB (Islamabad) 2012-13. LO HS 142* State Bank v Karachi Dolphins (Karachi) 2014-15. LO BB 2-20 P A v Glamorgan (Newport) 2016. T20 HS 102*. T20 BB 2-20.

BANTON, Thomas (Bromsgrove S), b Chiltern, Bucks 11 Nov 1998. Son of C.Banton (Nottinghamshire 1995). 6'2". RHB, WK. Squad No 18. Debut (Somerset) 2018. Warwickshire 2nd XI 2015. Somerset 2nd XI debut 2016. England U19 2018. **LOI**: 3 (2019-20); HS 32 v SA (Johannesburg) 2019-20. **IT20**: 3 (2019-20); HS 31 v NZ (Napier) 2019-20. HS 79 v Hants (Taunton) 2019. LO HS 112 v Worcs (Worcester) 2019 (RLC). T20 HS 100.

BARTLETT, George Anthony (Millfield S), b Frimley, Surrey 14 Mar 1998. 6'0". RHB, OB. Squad No 14. Debut (Somerset) 2017. Somerset 2nd XI debut 2015. England U19 2016 to 2017. HS 137 v Surrey (Guildford) 2019. BB – . LO HS 57* v Surrey (Taunton) 2019 (RLC).

BESS, Dominic Mark (Blundell's S), b Exeter, Devon 22 Jul 1997. Cousin of Z.G.G.Bess (Devon 2015 to date), J.J.Bess (Devon 2007-18) and L.F.O.Bess (Devon 2017 to date). RHB, OB. Squad No 22. Debut (Somerset) 2016. Yorkshire 2019 (on loan). MCC 2018, 2019. Somerset 2nd XI debut 2013. Devon 2015-16. **Tests**: 4 (2018 to 2019-20); HS 57 v P (Lord's) 2018; BB 5-51 v SA (Port Elizabeth) 2019-20. F-c Tours: A 2019-20 (EL); SA 2019-20; WI 2017-18 (EL); I 2018-19 (EL); SL 2019-20. HS 107 MCC v Essex (Bridgetown) 2018. Sm HS 92 v Hants (Taunton) 2018. BB 7-117 (10-162 match) v Hants (Taunton) 2017. LO HS 24* South v North (Cave Hill) 2017-18. LO BB 3-35 EL v Pakistan A (Abu Dhabi) 2018-19. T20 HS 5*. T20 BB 2-30.

BROOKS, Jack Alexander (Wheatley Park S), b Oxford 4 Jun 1984. 6'2". RHB, RFM. Squad No 70. Northamptonshire 2009-12; cap 2012. Yorkshire 2013-18; cap 2013. Somerset debut 2019. Oxfordshire 2004-09. F-c Tour (EL): SA 2014-15. HS 109* Y v Lancs (Manchester) 2017. Sm HS 35* v Kent (Taunton) 2019. 50 wkts (4); most – 71 (2014). BB 6-65 Y v Middx (Lord's) 2016. Sm BB 5-33 v Surrey (Guildford) 2019. LO HS 10 Nh v Middx (Uxbridge) 2009 (P40). LO BB 3-30 Y v Hants (Southampton) 2014 (RLC). T20 HS 33*. T20 BB 5-21.

BYROM, Edward James (St John's C, Harare), b Harare, Zimbabwe 17 Jun 1997. 5'11". LHB, OB. Squad No 97. Irish passport. Debut (Somerset) 2017. Rising Stars 2017-18. Somerset 2nd XI debut 2015. HS 152 RS v MT (Kwekwe) 2017-18. Sm HS 115* v Cardiff MCCU (Taunton) 2019. CC HS 56 v Middx (Taunton) 2017. BB – . T20 HS 54*.

[NQ]DAVEY, Joshua Henry (Culford S), b Aberdeen, Scotland 3 Aug 1990. 5'11". RHB, RMF. Squad No 38. Middlesex 2010-12. Scotland 2011-12 to 2016. Somerset debut 2015. Suffolk 2014. **LOI** (Scot): 31 (2010 to 2019-20); HS 64 v Afg (Sharjah) 2012-13; BB 6-28 v Afg (Abu Dhabi) 2014-15 – Scot record. **IT20** (Scot): 21 (2012 to 2019-20); HS 24 v Z (Nagpur) 2015-16; BB 4-34 v Netherlands (Abu Dhabi) 2016-17. HS 72 M v Oxford MCCU (Oxford) 2010 – on debut. CC HS 61 M v Glos (Bristol) 2010. Sm HS 47 v Middx (Lord's) 2017. Sm BB 5-21 v Yorks (Taunton) 2019. LO HS 91 Scot v Warwks (Birmingham) 2011 (CB40). LO BB 6-28 (*see LOI*). T20 HS 24. T20 BB 4-34.

DAVIES, Steven Michael (King Charles I S, Kidderminster), b Bromsgrove, Worcs 17 Jun 1986. 5'10". LHB, WK. Squad No 11. Worcestershire 2005-09. Surrey 2010-16; cap 2011. Somerset debut/cap 2017. MCC 2006-07, 2011. **LOI**: 8 (2009-10 to 2010-11); HS 87 v P (Chester-le-St) 2010. **IT20**: 5 (2008-09 to 2010-11); HS 33* v P (Cardiff) 2010. F-c Tours: A 2010-11; B 2006-07 (Eng A); UAE 2011-12 (v P). 1000 runs (6); most – 1147 (2016). HS 200* Sy v Glamorgan (Cardiff) 2015. Sm HS 142 v Surrey (Taunton) 2017. LO HS 127* Sy v Hants (Oval) 2013 (Y40). T20 HS 99*.

GILCHRIST, Nathan Nicholas (St Stithian's C; King's C, Taunton), b Harare, Zimbabwe 11 Jun 2000. RHB, RFM. Squad No 21. Somerset 2nd XI debut 2016. Awaiting 1st XI debut.

GOLDSWORTHY, Lewis Peter (Cambourne Science & Int Ac), b Cornwall 8 Jan 2001. RHB, SLA. Squad No 44. Somerset 2nd XI debut 2017. Cornwall 2017-19. England U19 2018-19. Awaiting 1st XI debut.

GREEN, Benjamin George Frederick (Exeter S), b Exeter, Devon 28 Sep 1997. 6'2". RHB, RFM. Squad No 54. Debut (Somerset) 2018. Somerset 2nd XI debut 2014. Devon 2014-18. England U19 2014-15 to 2017. No 1st XI appearances in 2019. HS 26 and BB 1-8 v Hants (Southampton) 2018. LO HS 26* v Kent (Canterbury) 2018 (RLC). LO BB 1-52 v Hants (Southampton) 2018 (RLC). T20 HS 12*.

GREGORY, Lewis (Hele's S, Plympton), b Plymouth, Devon 24 May 1992. 6'0". RHB, RMF. Squad No 24. Debut (Somerset) 2011; cap 2015; T20 captain 2018 to date. MCC 2017. Devon 2008. **IT20:** 5 (2019-20); HS 15 and BB 1-10 v NZ (Wellington) 2019-20. HS 137 v Middx (Lord's) 2017. 50 wkts (1): 59 (2019). BB 6-32 (11-53 match) v Kent (Canterbury) 2019. LO HS 105* v Durham (Taunton) 2014 (RLC). LO BB 4-23 v Essex (Chelmsford) 2016 (RLC). T20 HS 76*. T20 BB 4-15.

HILDRETH, James Charles (Millfield S), b Milton Keynes, Bucks 9 Sep 1984. 5'10", RHB, RMF. Squad No 25. Debut (Somerset) 2003; cap 2007; testimonial 2017. MCC 2015. F-c Tour (EL): WI 2010-11. 1000 runs (7); most – 1620 (2015). HS 303* v Warwks (Taunton) 2009. BB 2-39 v Hants (Taunton) 2004. LO HS 159 v Glamorgan (Taunton) 2018 (RLC). LO BB 2-26 v Worcs (Worcester) 2008 (FPT). T20 HS 107*. T20 BB 3-24.

LAMMONBY, Thomas Alexander (Exeter S), b Exeter, Devon 2 Jun 2000. LHB, LM. Squad No 15. Somerset 2nd XI debut 2015. Devon 2016-18. England U19 2018-19. Awaiting f-c debut. T20 HS 31. T20 BB 2-32.

LEACH, Matthew Jack (Bishop Fox's Community S, Taunton; Richard Huish C; UWIC), b Taunton 22 Jun 1991. 6'0". LHB, SLA. Squad No 17. Cardiff MCCU 2012. Somerset debut 2012; cap 2017. MCC 2017. Dorset 2011. **ECB Incremental Contract 2019-20. Tests:** 10 (2017-18 to 2019-20); HS 92 v Ire (Lord's) 2019; BB 5-83 v SL (Pallekele) 2018-19. F-c Tours: WI 2017-18 (EL); NZ 2017-18, 2019-20; SL 2016-17 (EL), 2018-19, 2019-20; UAE 2016-17 (v Afg)(EL). HS 92 (*see Tests*). Sm HS 66 v Lancs (Manchester) 2018. 50 wkts (2); most – 68 (2016). BB 8-85 (10-112 match) v Essex (Taunton) 2018. LO HS 18 v Surrey (Oval) 2014 (RLC). LO BB 3-7 EL v UAE (Dubai, DSC) 2016-17.

OVERTON, Craig (West Buckland S), b Barnstaple, Devon 10 Apr 1994. Twin brother of Jamie Overton (*see below*). 6'5". RHB, RMF. Squad No 12. Debut (Somerset) 2012; cap 2016. MCC 2017. Devon 2010-11. **Tests:** 4 (2017-18 to 2019); HS 41* and BB 3-105 v A (Adelaide) 2017-18. F-c Tours: A 2017-18, 2019-20 (EL); NZ 2017-18. HS 138 v Hants (Taunton) 2016. BB 6-24 v Cardiff MCCU (Taunton) 2019. CC BB 6-74 v Warwks (Birmingham) 2015. LO HS 66* and LO BB 5-18 v Kent (Taunton) 2019 (RLC). T20 HS 35*. T20 BB 3-17.

OVERTON, Jamie (West Buckland S), b Barnstaple, Devon 10 Apr 1994. Twin brother of Craig Overton (*see above*). 6'5". RHB, RFM. Squad No 8. Debut (Somerset) 2012; cap 2019. Northamptonshire 2019 (on loan). Devon 2011. F-c Tour (EL): UAE 2018-19 (v PA). HS 56 v Warwks (Birmingham) 2014. BB 6-95 v Middx (Taunton) 2013. Hat-trick v Notts (Nottingham) 2018. LO HS 40* v Glos (Taunton) 2016 (RLC). LO BB 4-42 v Durham (Chester-le-St) 2012 (CB40). T20 HS 31. T20 BB 5-47.

NQPHILANDER, Vernon Darryl, b Bellville, Cape Province, South Africa 24 Jun 1985. RHB, RMF. Squad No 1. Western Province 2003-04 to 2015-16. WP Boland 2004-05. Cape Cobras 2005-06 to 2018-19. Middlesex 2008. Somerset debut 2012; rejoins on a Kolpak deal. Kent 2013. Nottinghamshire 2015; cap 2015. Sussex 2017. Devon 2004. **Tests** (SA): 64 (2011-12 to 2019-20); HS 74 v P (Centurion) 2012-13; BB 6-21 v A (Johannesburg) 2017-18. **LOI** (SA): 30 (2007 to 2015); HS 30* v NZ (Potchefstroom) 2015; BB 4-12 v Ireland (Belfast) 2007 – on debut. **IT20** (SA): 7 (2007-08); HS 6 v E (Cape Town) 2007-08; BB 2-23 v B (Cape Town) 2007-08. F-c Tours (SA): E 2012, 2017; A 2012-13, 2016-17; NZ 2011-12, 2016-17; I 2015-16, 2019-20; SL 2010 (SA A), 2014, 2018; Z 2014, 2016; B 2010 (SA A), 2015; UAE (v P) 2013-14. HS 168 WP v GW (Kimberley) 2004-05. CC HS 73* Sx v Kent (Tunbridge Wells) 2017 and 73* Sx v Leics (Leicester) 2017. Sm HS 38 v Warwks (Birmingham) 2012. 50 wkts (0+2); most – 59 (2009-10). BB 7-61 Cobras v Knights (Cape Town) 2011-12. CC BB 5-43 v Middx (Taunton) 2012. LO HS 79* SA A v Bangladesh A (East London) 2010-11. LO BB 4-12 (*see LOI*). T20 HS 56*. T20 BB 5-17.

SALE, Oliver Richard Trethowan (Sherborne S), b Newcastle-under-Lyme, Staffs 30 Sep 1995. 6'1". RHB, RFM. Squad No 82. Somerset 2nd XI debut 2014. Awaiting f-c debut. T20 HS 1. T20 BB – .

NQVAN DER MERWE, Roelof Erasmus (Pretoria HS), b Johannesburg, South Africa 31 Dec 1984. RHB, SLA. Squad No 52. Northerns 2006-07 to 2013-14. Titans 2007-08 to 2014-15. Netherlands 2015 to 2017-18. Somerset debut 2016; cap 2018. IPL: RCB 2009 to 2009-10. DD 2011-13. Big Bash: BH 2011-12. **LOI** (SA/Neth): 15 (13 for SA 2008-09 to 2010; 2 for Neth 2019); HS 57 v Z (Deventer) 2019; BB 3-27 v Z (Centurion) 2009-10. **IT20** (SA/Neth): 43 (13 for SA 2008-09 to 2010; 30 for Neth 2015 to 2019-20); HS 75* v Z (Rotterdam) 2019; BB 4-35 v Z (Rotterdam) 2019 – separate games. HS 205* Titans v Warriors (Benoni) 2014-15. Sm HS 102* v Hants (Taunton) 2016. BB 4-22 v Middx (Taunton) 2016. LO HS 165* v Surrey (Taunton) 2017 (RLC). LO BB 5-26 Titans v Knights (Centurion) 2012-13. T20 HS 89*. T20 BB 5-32.

‡NQWADE, Matthew Scott, b Lauderdale, Australia 26 Dec 1987. 5'7". LHB, RM, WK. Squad No 13. Victoria 2007-08 to 2016-17. Tasmania 2017-18 to date. Warwickshire 2016 (T20 only). IPL: DD 2011. Big Bash: MS 2011-12 to 2013-14. MR 2014-15 to 2015-16. HH 2017-18 to date. **Tests** (A): 32 (2012 to 2019-20); HS 117 v E (Oval) 2019. **LOI** (A): 94 (2011-12 to 2017-18); HS 100* v P (Brisbane) 2016-17. **IT20** (A): 29 (2011-12 to 2019-20); HS 72 v I (Sydney) 2011-12. F-c Tours: E 2013, 2019; WI 2012; I 2012-13, 2015 (Aus A), 2016-17; B 2017. 1000 runs (0+1): 1021 (2018-19). HS 152 Vic v Q (Brisbane) 2014-15. BB 3-13 Tas v Q (Brisbane) 2017-18. LO HS 155 Aus A v Derbys (Derby) 2019. T20 HS 130*.

WALLER, Maximilian Thomas Charles (Millfield S; Bournemouth U), b Salisbury, Wiltshire 3 March 1988. 6'0". RHB, LB. Squad No 10. Debut (Somerset) 2009. Dorset 2007-08. HS 28 v Hants (Southampton) 2009. BB 3-33 v Cardiff MCCU (Taunton Vale) 2012. CC BB 2-27 v Sussex (Hove) 2009. LO HS 25* v Glamorgan (Taunton) 2013 (Y40). LO BB 3-37 v Glos (Bristol) 2017 (RLC). T20 HS 17. T20 BB 4-16.

YOUNG, Samuel Jack (Millfield S), b Plymouth, Devon 30 Jul 2000. RHB, OB. Squad No 77. Somerset 2nd XI debut 2018. Awaiting 1st team debut.

RELEASED/RETIRED

(Having made a County 1st XI appearance in 2019)

^{NQ}**AZHAR ALI**, b Lahore, Pakistan 19 Feb 1985. RHB, LB. Lahore Blues 2001-02. KRL 2002-03 to 2011-12. Lahore 2003-04. SNGPL 2012-13 to 2018-19. Somerset 2018-19; cap 2019. Central Punjab 2019-20. **Tests** (P): 78 (2010 to 2019-20, 6 as captain); 1000 runs (1): 1198 (2016); HS 302* v WI (Dubai, DSC) 2016-17; BB 2-35 v SL (Pallekele) 2015. **LOI** (P): 53 (2011 to 2017-18, 31 as captain); HS 102 v Z (Lahore) 2015; BB 2-26 v E (Dubai, DSC) 2015-16. F-c Tours (P)(C=Captain): E 2010, 2016, 2018; A 2009 (PA), 2016-17, 2019-20C; SA 2012-13, 2018-19; WI 2011, 2016-17; NZ 2010-11, 2016-17; SL 2009 (PA), 2012, 2014, 2015; Z 2011, 2013; B 2011-12, 2014-15; Ire 2018. HS 302* (*see* **Tests**). Sm HS 125 v Worcs (Worcester) 2018 – on debut. BB 4-34 KRL v Peshawar (Peshawar) 2002-03. Sm BB 1-5 v Essex (Taunton) 2018. LO HS 132* SNGPL v Lahore Blues (Islamabad) 2015-16. LO BB 5-23 Lahore Whites v Peshawar (Karachi) 2001 – on debut. T20 HS 72. T20 BB 3-10.

GROENEWALD, T.D. – *see KENT.*

TAYLOR, J.E. – *see GLOUCESTERSHIRE.*

TREGO, P.D. – *see NOTTINGHAMSHIRE.*

TRESCOTHICK, Marcus Edward (Sir Bernard Lovell S), b Keynsham 25 Dec 1975. 6'2". LHB, RM, occ WK. Somerset 1993-2019; cap 1999; joint captain 2002; benefit 2008; captain 2010-15; testimonial 2018. PCA 2000, 2009, 2011. *Wisden* 2004. MBE 2005. **Tests**: 76 (2000 to 2006, 2 as captain); HS 219 v SA (Oval) 2003; BB 1-34 v P (Karachi) 2000-01. **LOI**: 123 (2000 to 2006, 10 as captain); HS 137 v P (Lord's) 2001; BB 2-7 v Z (Manchester) 2000. **IT20**: 3 (2005 to 2006); HS 72 v SL (Southampton) 2006. F-c Tours: A 2002-03; SA 2004-05; WI 2003-04; NZ 1999-00 (Eng A), 2001-02; I 2001-02, 2005-06 (*part*); P 2000-01, 2005-06; SL 2000-01, 2003-04; B 1999-00 (Eng A), 2003-04. 1000 runs (8); most – 1817 (2009). HS 284 v Northants (Northampton) 2007. BB 4-36 (inc hat-trick) v Young A (Taunton) 1995. CC BB 4-82 v Yorks (Leeds) 1998. Hat-trick 1995 (*see above*). LO HS 184 v Glos (Taunton) 2008 (P40) – Sm 1-o record. LO BB 4-50 v Northants (Northampton) 2000 (NL). T20 HS 108*.

^{NQ}**VIJAY, Murali**, b Madras, India 1 Apr 1984. RHB, OB. Tamil Nadu 2006-07 to date. Central Districts 2008-09. Essex 2018. Somerset 2019. IPL: CSK 2009-19. DD 2014. KXIP 2015-16. **Tests** (I): 61 (2008-09 to 2018-19); HS 167 v A (Hyderabad) 2012-13; BB 1-12 v E (Lord's) 2014. **LOI** (I): 17 (2009-10 to 2015); HS 72 v Z (Harare) 2013; BB 1-19 v Z (Harare) 2015 – different matches. **IT20** (I): 9 (2010 to 2015); HS 48 v Afg (Gros Islet) 2010. F-c Tours (I): E 2014, 2018; A 2011-12, 2014-15, 2018-19; SA 2010-11, 2013 (IA), 2013-14, 2017-18; WI 2011, 2016; NZ 2008-09 (IA), 2013-14; SL 2010, 2015; B 2009-10, 2015. 1000 runs (0+1): 1024 (2012-13). HS 266 Rest of India v Rajasthan (Bangalore) 2012-13. CC HS 100 Ex v Notts (Nottingham) 2018 – on debut. Sm HS 29 v Hants (Southampton) 2019. BB 3-46 India Green v India Red (Lucknow) 2017. LO HS 155 India B v India A (Rajkot) 2012-13. LO BB 3-13 TN v Karnataka (Visakhapatnam) 2008-09. T20 HS 127. T20 BB – .

T.D.Rouse and P.A.van Meekeren left the staff without making a County 1st XI appearance in 2019.

SOMERSET 2019

RESULTS SUMMARY

	Place	Won	Lost	Drew	NR
Specsavers County Champ (1st Division)	2nd	9	3	2	
All First-Class Matches		10	3	2	
Royal London One-Day Cup (South Group) **Winners**	8	3			
Vitality Blast (South Group)	6th	6	7		1

SPECSAVERS COUNTY CHAMPIONSHIP AVERAGES
BATTING AND FIELDING

Cap		M	I	NO	HS	Runs	Avge	100	50	Ct/St
2018	T.B.Abell	14	25	1	101	756	31.50	1	5	13
	G.A.Bartlett	14	24	1	137	718	31.21	2	3	1
	T.Banton	10	18	–	79	533	29.61	–	5	6
2015	L.Gregory	11	18	2	129*	465	29.06	1	1	10
2017	S.M.Davies	14	24	1	109	642	27.91	1	3	47/3
2018	R.E.van der Merwe	4	6	1	60	132	26.40	–	1	7
2019	Azhar Ali	9	16	2	79	344	24.57	–	3	3
	D.M.Bess	7	13	3	52*	233	23.30	–	2	3
2007	J.C.Hildreth	14	24	–	105	553	23.04	1	3	17
2019	J.Overton	8	14	2	52*	252	21.00	–	1	16
2016	C.Overton	10	15	1	40	230	16.42	–	–	12
	J.H.Davey	5	9	1	36	92	11.50	–	–	1
	J.A.Brooks	8	12	6	35*	68	11.33	–	–	2
1999	M.E.Trescothick	5	8	–	23	86	10.75	–	–	9
2016	T.D.Groenewald	7	13	3	17	100	10.00	–	–	3
	M.Vijay	3	5	–	29	42	8.40	–	–	5
2017	M.J.Leach	9	13	4	11*	53	5.88	–	–	7

Also batted: (1 match each): Babar Azam 0, 40; E.J.Byrom 6, 14 (2 ct).

BOWLING

	O	M	R	W	Avge	Best	5wI	10wM
L.Gregory	284.1	81	804	51	15.76	6-32	4	1
M.J.Leach	250.3	71	596	34	17.52	6-36	2	–
J.H.Davey	107.5	29	301	17	17.70	5-21	1	–
R.E.van der Merwe	66.5	21	177	10	17.70	4-41	–	–
J.Overton	156.5	29	521	28	18.60	5-70	1	–
C.Overton	282.3	64	810	37	21.89	5-31	2	–
D.M.Bess	174.3	44	447	19	23.52	5-59	1	–
T.B.Abell	103.2	30	313	13	24.07	4-39	–	–
T.D.Groenewald	163.3	32	472	18	26.22	5-51	1	–
J.A.Brooks	214.1	51	728	25	29.12	5-33	1	–

Also bowled:
Azhar Ali 2-2-0-0.

The First-Class Averages (pp 226–241) give the records of Somerset players in all first-class county matches (Somerset's other opponents being Cardiff MCCU), with the exceptions of D.M.Bess and J.Overton, whose first-class figures for Somerset are as above, and:
L.Gregory 12-19-2-129*-491-28.88-1-1-11ct. 297.1-86-832-55-15.12/6/32-4-1.
M.J.Leach 10-14-4-11*-56-5.60-0-0-9ct. 258.3-72-608-34-17.88-6/36-2-0.
C.Overton 11-16-1-58-288-19.20-0-1-12ct. 297.5-66-849-45-18.86-6/24-3-0.

SOMERSET RECORDS
FIRST-CLASS CRICKET

Highest Total	For 850-7d		v	Middlesex	Taunton	2007
	V 811		by	Surrey	The Oval	1899
Lowest Total	For 25		v	Glos	Bristol	1947
	V 22		by	Glos	Bristol	1920
Highest Innings	For 342	J.L.Langer	v	Surrey	Guildford	2006
	V 424	A.C.MacLaren	for	Lancashire	Taunton	1895

Highest Partnership for each Wicket

1st	346	L.C.H.Palairet/ H.T.Hewett	v	Yorkshire	Taunton	1892
2nd	450	N.R.D.Compton/J.C.Hildreth	v	Cardiff MCCU	Taunton Vale	2012
3rd	319	P.M.Roebuck/M.D.Crowe	v	Leics	Taunton	1984
4th	310	P.W.Denning/I.T.Botham	v	Glos	Taunton	1980
5th	320	J.D.Francis/I.D.Blackwell	v	Durham UCCE	Taunton	2005
6th	265	W.E.Alley/K.E.Palmer	v	Northants	Northampton	1961
7th	279	R.J.Harden/G.D.Rose	v	Sussex	Taunton	1997
8th	236	P.D.Trego/R.C.Davies	v	Lancashire	Manchester	2016
9th	183	C.H.M.Greetham/H.W.Stephenson	v	Leics	Weston-s-Mare	1963
	183	C.J.Tavaré/N.A.Mallender	v	Sussex	Hove	1990
10th	163	I.D.Blackwell/N.A.M.McLean	v	Derbyshire	Taunton	2003

Best Bowling	For 10-49	E.J.Tyler	v	Surrey	Taunton	1895
(Innings)	V 10-35	A.Drake	for	Yorkshire	Weston-s-Mare	1914
Best Bowling	For 16-83	J.C.White	v	Worcs	Bath	1919
(Match)	V 17-86	K.J.Abbott	for	Hampshire	Southampton[2]	2019

Most Runs – Season	2761	W.E.Alley	(av 58.74)	1961
Most Runs – Career	21142	H.Gimblett	(av 36.96)	1935-54
Most 100s – Season	11	S.J.Cook		1991
Most 100s – Career	52	M.E.Trescothick		1993-2018
Most Wkts – Season	169	A.W.Wellard	(av 19.24)	1938
Most Wkts – Career	2165	J.C.White	(av 18.03)	1909-37
Most Career W-K Dismissals	1007	H.W.Stephenson	(698 ct; 309 st)	1948-64
Most Career Catches in the Field	443	M.E.Trescothick		1993-2019

LIMITED-OVERS CRICKET

Highest Total	50ov	413-4		v	Devon	Torquay	1990
	40ov	377-9		v	Sussex	Hove	2003
	T20	250-3		v	Glos	Taunton	2006
Lowest Total	50ov	58		v	Middlesex	Southgate	2000
	40ov	58		v	Essex	Chelmsford	1977
	T20	82		v	Kent	Taunton	2010
Highest Innings	50ov	177	S.J.Cook	v	Sussex	Hove	1990
	40ov	184	M.E.Trescothick	v	Glos	Taunton	2008
	T20	151*	C.H.Gayle	v	Kent	Taunton	2015
Best Bowling	50ov	8-66	S.R.G.Francis	v	Derbyshire	Derby	2004
	40ov	6-16	Abdur Rehman	v	Notts	Taunton	2012
	T20	6- 5	A.V.Suppiah	v	Glamorgan	Cardiff	2011

SURREY

Formation of Present Club: 22 August 1845
Inaugural First-Class Match: 1864
Colours: Chocolate
Badge: Prince of Wales' Feathers
County Champions (since 1890): (19) 1890, 1891, 1892, 1894, 1895, 1899, 1914, 1952, 1953, 1954, 1955, 1956, 1957, 1958, 1971, 1999, 2000, 2002, 2018
Joint Champions: (1) 1950
NatWest Trophy Winners: (1) 1982
Benson and Hedges Cup Winners: (3) 1974, 1997, 2001
Pro 40/National League (Div 1) Winners: (1) 2003
Sunday League Winners: (1) 1996
Clydesdale Bank 40 Winners: (1) 2011
Twenty20 Cup Winners: (1) 2003

Chief Executive: Richard Gould, The Kia Oval, London, SE11 5SS • Tel: 0203 946 0100 • Email: enquiries@surreycricket.com • Web: www.kiaoval.com • Twitter: @surreycricket (95,042 followers)

Director of Cricket: Alec Stewart. **Head Coach**: Michael Di Venuto. **Assistant Coaches**: Richard Johnson and Vikram Solanki. **Captains**: R.J.Burns (f-c and l-o) and J.W.Dernbach (T20). **Overseas Players**: M.G.Neser, Shadab Khan and D.J.M.Short (both T20 only). **2020 Testimonial**: None. **Head Groundsman**: Lee Fortiss. **Scorer**: Philip Makepeace. ‡ New registration. ^{NQ} Not qualified for England.

^{NQ}**AMLA, Hashim** Mahomed, b Durban, South Africa 31 Mar 1983. Younger brother of A.M.Amla (Natal B, KZN, Dolphins 1997-98 to 2012-13). 6'0". RHB, RM/OB. Squad No 1. KZN 1999-00 to 2003-04. Dolphins 2004-05 to 2011-12. Essex 2009. Nottinghamshire 2010; cap 2010. Surrey debut 2013; returns in 2020 on Kolpak deal. Derbyshire 2015. Cape Cobras 2015-16 to 2018-19. Hampshire 2018. IPL: KXIP 2016-17. *Wisden* 2012. **Tests** (SA): 124 (2004-05 to 2018-19, 14 as captain); 1000 runs (3); most – 1249 (2010); HS 311* v E (Oval) 2012; BB – . **LOI** (SA): 181 (2007-08 to 2019, 9 as captain); 1000 runs (2); most – 1062 (2015); HS 159 v Ire (Canberra) 2014-15. **IT20** (SA): 44 (2008-09 to 2018, 2 as captain); HS 97* v A (Cape Town) 2015-16. F-c Tours (SA) (C=Captain): E 2008, 2012, 2017; A 2008-09, 2012-13, 2016-17; WI 2010; NZ 2011-12, 2016-17; I 2004-05, 2007-08 (SA A), 2007-08, 2009-10, 2015-16C; P 2007-08; SL 2005-06 (SA A), 2006, 2014C, 2018; Z 2004 (SA A), 2007 (SA A), 2014C; B 2007-08, 2015C; UAE 2010-11, 2013-14 (v P). 1000 runs (0+2); most – 1126 (2005-06). HS 311* (*see Tests*). CC HS 181 Ex v Glamorgan (Chelmsford) 2009 – on debut. Sy HS 151 v Yorks (Oval) 2013. BB 1-10 SA A v India A (Kimberley) 2001-02. LO HS 159 (*see LOI*). T20 HS 104*.

ATKINSON, Angus ('Gus') Alexander Patrick (Bradfield C), b Chelsea, Middx 19 Jan 1998. 6'2". RHB, RM. Squad No 37. Surrey 2nd XI debut 2016. Awaiting 1st XI debut.

BATTY, Gareth Jon (Bingley GS), b Bradford, Yorks 13 Oct 1977. Younger brother of J.D.Batty (Yorkshire and Somerset 1989-96). 5'11". RHB, OB. Squad No 13. Yorkshire 1997. Surrey debut 1999; cap 2011; captain 2015-17; testimonial 2017. Worcestershire 2002-09. MCC 2012. **Tests**: 9 (2003-04 to 2016-17); HS 38 v SL (Kandy) 2003-04; BB 3-55 v SL (Galle) 2003-04. Took wicket with his third ball in Test cricket. **LOI**: 10 (2002-03 to 2008-09); HS 17 v WI (Bridgetown) 2008-09; BB 2-40 v WI (Gros Islet) 2003-04. **IT20**: 1 (2008-09); HS 4 v WI (Port of Spain) 2008-09. F-c Tours: WI 2003-04, 2005-06; NZ 2003-04 (Eng A); I 2016-17; SL 2002-03 (ECB Acad), 2003-04; B 2003-04, 2016-17. HS 133 Wo v Surrey (Oval) 2004. Sy HS 110* v Hants (Southampton) 2016, sharing Sy record 8th wkt partnership of 222* with B.T.Foakes. 50 wkts (2); most – 60 (2003). BB 8-64 (10-111 match) v Warwks (Birmingham) 2019. Hat-tricks (2): v Derbys (Oval) 2015 and v Warwks (Birmingham) 2019. LO HS 83* v Yorks (Oval) 2001 (NL). LO BB 5-35 Wo v Hants (Southampton) 2009 (FPT). T20 HS 87. T20 BB 4-13.

BORTHWICK, Scott George (Farringdon Community Sports C, Sunderland), b Sunderland, Co Durham 19 Apr 1990. 5'9''. LHB, LBG. Squad No 6. Durham 2009-16. Wellington 2015-16 to 2016-17. Surrey debut 2017; cap 2018. **Tests**: 1 (2013-14); HS 4 and BB 3-33 v A (Sydney) 2013-14. **LOI**: 2 (2011 to 2011-12); HS 15 v Ire (Dublin) 2011; BB – . **IT20**: 1 (2011); HS 14 and BB 1-15 v WI (Oval) 2011. F-c Tours: A 2013-14; SL 2013-14 (EL). 1000 runs (5); most – 1390 (2015). HS 216 Du v Middx (Chester-le-St) 2014, sharing Du record 2nd wkt partnership of 274 with M.D.Stoneman. Sy HS 175* and Sy BB 2-35 v West Indies A (Oval) 2018. BB 6-70 Du v Surrey (Oval) 2013. LO HS 87 and LO BB 5-38 Du v Leics (Leicester) 2015 (RLC). T20 HS 62. T20 BB 4-18.

BURNS, Rory Joseph (City of London Freemen's S), b Epsom 26 Aug 1990. 5'10''. LHB, WK, occ RM. Squad No 17. Debut (Surrey) 2011; cap 2014; captain 2018 to date. MCC 2016. MCC Univs 2010. *Wisden* 2018. **ECB Test Central Contract 2019-20. Tests**: 15 (2018-19 to 2019-20); HS 133 v A (Birmingham) 2019. 1000 runs (6); most – 1402 (2018). HS 219* v Hants (Oval) 2017. BB 1-18 v Middx (Lord's) 2013. LO HS 95 v Glos (Bristol) 2015 (RLC). T20 HS 50.

CLARK, Jordan (Sedbergh S), b Whitehaven, Cumbria 14 Oct 1990. Elder brother of G.Clark (*see DURHAM*). 6'4''. RHB, RMF, occ WK. Squad No 8. Lancashire 2015-18. Surrey debut 2019. Big Bash: HH 2018-19. HS 140 La v Surrey (Oval) 2017. Sy HS 54 v Notts (Nottingham) 2019. BB 5-58 La v Yorks (Manchester) 2018. Sy BB 5-77 v Yorks (Scarborough) 2019. Hat-trick La v Yorks (Manchester) 2018, dismissing J.E.Root, K.S.Williamson and J.M.Bairstow. LO HS 79* and LO BB 4-34 La v Worcs (Manchester) 2017 (RLC). T20 HS 60. T20 BB 4-22.

CLARKE, Rikki (Broadwater SS; Godalming C), b Orsett, Essex 29 Sep 1981. 6'4''. RHB, RMF. Squad No 81. Debut (Surrey) 2002, scoring 107* v Cambridge U (Cambridge); cap 2005. Derbyshire cap/captain 2008. Warwickshire 2008-17; cap 2011. MCC 2006, 2016. YC 2002. **Tests**: 2 (2003-04); HS 55 and BB 2-7 v B (Chittagong) 2003-04. **LOI**: 20 (2003 to 2006); HS 39 v P (Lord's) 2006; BB 2-28 v B (Dhaka) 2003-04. F-c Tours: WI 2003-04, 2005-06; SL 2002-03 (ECB Acad), 2004-05; B 2003-04. 1000 runs (1): 1027 (2006). HS 214 v Somerset (Guildford) 2006. BB 7-55 v Somerset (Oval) 2017. Took seven catches in an innings Wa v Lancs (Liverpool) 2011 to equal world record. LO HS 98* v Derbys (Derby) 2002 (NL). LO BB 5-26 Wa v Worcs (Birmingham) 2016 (RLC). T20 HS 79*. T20 BB 4-16

CURRAN, Samuel Matthew (Wellington C), b Northampton 3 Jun 1998. Son of K.M.Curran (Glos, Natal, Northants, Boland and Zimbabwe 1980-81 to 1999), grandson of K.P.Curran (Rhodesia 1947-48 to 1954-55), younger brother of T.K.Curran (*see below*) and B.J.Curran (*see NORTHAMPTONSHIRE*). 5'9''. LHB, LMF. Squad No 58. Debut (Surrey) 2015, taking 5-101 v Kent (Oval); cap 2018. Surrey 2nd XI debut 2013. YC 2018. *Wisden* 2018. **ECB Test Central Contract 2019-20. Tests**: 17 (2018 to 2019-20); HS 78 v I (Southampton) 2018; BB 4-58 v SA (Centurion) 2019-20. **LOI**: 4 (2018 to 2019-20); HS 15 and BB 2-44 v A (Manchester) 2018. **IT20**: 5 (2019-20); HS 24 v NZ (Auckland) 2019-20; BB 2-22 v NZ (Wellington) 2019-20. F-c Tours: SA 2019-20; WI 2018-19; NZ 2019-20; SL 2016-17 (EL), 2018-19, 2019-20; UAE 2016-17 (v Afg)(EL). HS 96 v Lancs (Oval) 2016. BB 7-58 v Durham (Chester-le-St) 2016. LO HS 57 v Glos (Oval) 2016 (RLC). LO BB 4-32 v Northants (Oval) 2015 (RLC). T20 HS 55*. T20 BB 4-11.

CURRAN, Thomas Kevin (Hilton C, Durban), b Cape Town, South Africa 12 Mar 1995. Son of K.M.Curran (Glos, Natal, Northants, Boland and Zimbabwe 1980-81 to 1999), grandson of K.P.Curran (Rhodesia 1947-48 to 1954-55), elder brother of S.M.Curran (*see above*) and B.J.Curran (*see NORTHAMPTONSHIRE*). 6'0". RHB, RFM. Squad No 59. Debut (Surrey) 2014; cap 2016. IPL: KKR 2018. Big Bash: SS 2018-19 to date. **ECB Incremental Contract 2019-20. Tests**: 2 (2017-18); HS 39 v A (Sydney) 2017-18; BB 1-65 v A (Melbourne) 2017-18. **LOI**: 20 (2017 to 2019-20); HS 47* v Ire (Dublin) 2019; BB 5-35 v A (Perth) 2017-18. **IT20**: 18 (2017 to 2019-20); HS 14* v NZ (Nelson) 2019-20; BB 4-36 v WI (Gros Islet) 2018-19. F-c Tours: A 2017-18; SL 2016-17 (EL); UAE 2016-17 (v Afg)(EL). HS 60 v Leics (Leicester) 2015. 50 wkts (1): 76 (2015). BB 7-20 v Glos (Oval) 2015. LO HS 47* (*see LOI*). LO BB 5-16 EL v UAE (Dubai, DSC) 2016-17. T20 HS 62. T20 BB 4-22.

DERNBACH, Jade Winston (St John the Baptist S, Woking), b Johannesburg, South Africa 3 Mar 1986. 6'1½". RHB, RFM. Squad No 16. Italian passport. UK resident since 1998. Debut (Surrey) 2003; cap 2011; captain 2018 to date (T20 only); testimonial 2019. Big Bash: MS 2011-12. **LOI**: 24 (2011 to 2013); HS 5 v SL (Leeds) 2011; BB 4-45 v P (Dubai) 2011-12. **IT20**: 34 (2011 to 2013-14); HS 12 v I (Colombo, RPS) 2012-13; BB 4-22 v I (Manchester) 2011. F-c Tour (EL): WI 2010-11. HS 56* v Northants (Northampton) 2010. 50 wkts (1): 51 (2010). BB 6-47 v Leics (Leicester) 2009. LO HS 31 v Somerset (Taunton) 2010 (CB40). LO BB 6-35 v Glos (Lord's) 2015 (RLC). T20 HS 24*. T20 BB 4-22.

DUNN, Matthew Peter (Bearwood C, Wokingham), b Egham 5 May 1992. 6'1". LHB, RFM. Squad No 4. Debut (Surrey) 2010. MCC 2015. HS 31* v Kent (Guildford) 2014. BB 5-43 v Somerset (Guildford) 2019. LO HS – . LO BB 2-32 Eng Dev XI v Sri Lanka A (Manchester) 2011. T20 HS 2. BB 3-8.

FOAKES, Benjamin Thomas (Tendring TC), b Colchester, Essex 15 Feb 1993. 6'1". RHB, WK. Squad No 7. Essex 2011-14. Surrey debut 2015; cap 2016. MCC 2016. **Tests**: 5 (2018-19); HS 107 v SL (Galle) 2018-19 – on debut. F-c Tours: WI 2017-18 (EL), 2018-19; SL 2013-14 (EL), 2016-17 (EL), 2018-19; UAE 2016-17 (v Afg)(EL). HS 141* v Hants (Southampton) 2016, sharing Sy record 8th wkt partnership of 222* with G.J.Batty. LO HS 92 v Somerset (Taunton) 2016 (RLC). T20 HS 75*.

JACKS, William George (St George's C, Weybridge), b Chertsey 21 Nov 1998. 6'1". RHB, RM. Squad No 9. Debut (Surrey) 2018. Surrey 2nd XI debut 2016. England U19 2016-17 to 2017. F-c Tour (EL): I 2018-19. HS 120 v Kent (Beckenham) 2019. BB – . LO HS 121 v Glos (Oval) 2018 (RLC). LO BB 2-32 v Middx (Oval) 2019 (RLC). T20 HS 63. T20 BB – .

‡**KIMBER, Nicholas** John Henry (William Farr C of E S), b Lincoln 16 Jan 2001. Younger brother of L.P.J.Kimber (Loughborough MCCU 2019) and J.F.Kimber (Lincolnshire 2016-18). 5'11". RHB, RMF. Squad No 12. Nottinghamshire 2nd XI 2019. Awaiting 1st XI debut.

McKERR, Conor (St John's C, Johannesburg), b Johannesburg, South Africa 19 Jan 1998. 6'6". RHB, RFM. Squad No 83. UK passport, qualified for England in March 2020. Derbyshire 2017 (on loan), taking wkt of J.D.Libby with 4th ball in f-c cricket. Surrey debut 2017. Surrey 2nd XI debut 2016. HS 29 v Yorks (Oval) 2018. BB 5-54 (10-141 match) De v Northants (Northampton) 2017. Sy BB 4-26 v Notts (Oval) 2018. LO HS 26* v Glamorgan (Cardiff) 2019 (RLC). LO BB 3-56 v Somerset (Taunton) 2019 (RLC).

MORIARTY, Daniel Thornhill (Rondesbosch Boys' HS), b Reigate 2 Dec 1999. 6'0". LHB, SLA. Squad No 21. Surrey 2nd XI debut 2019. Essex 2nd XI 2019. MCC YC 2019. South Africa U19 2016. Awaiting 1st XI debut.

NQMORKEL, Morne (Hoerskool, Vereeniging), b Vereeniging, South Africa 6 Oct 1984. Younger brother of J.A.Morkel (Easterns, Titans, Durham and South Africa 1999-00 to 2015-16). 6'4". LHB, RF. Squad No 65. Easterns 2003-04 to 2017-18. Titans 2004-05 to 2017-18. Yorkshire 2008 (1 match). Surrey debut/cap 2018 (Kolpak signing). Kent 2007 (T20 only). IPL: RR 2009 to 2009-10. DD 2011-13. KKR 2014-16. Big Bash: PS 2019-20. **Tests** (SA): 86 (2006-07 to 2017-18); HS 40 v A (Sydney) 2008-09 and 40 v NZ (Wellington) 2016-17; BB 6-23 v NZ (Wellington) 2011-12. **LOI** (SA): 114 (+ 3 Africa XI 2007) (2007 to 2017-18); HS 32* v WI (Bridgetown) 2016; BB 5-21 v A (Perth) 2014-15. **IT20** (SA): 41 (+ 3 World XI 2017) (2007 to 2017); HS 8* v P (Johannesburg) 2013-14; BB 4-17 v NZ (Durban) 2007. F-c Tours: SA 2008-09, 2012-13; WI 2010; NZ 2011-12, 2016-17; I 2007-08, 2009-10, 2015-16; SL 2014; Z 2014; B 2007-08, 2015; UAE (v P) 2010-11, 2013-14. HS 82* (and 1-56 match) Titans v Warriors (E London) 2006-07. Sy HS 29 v Yorks (Scarborough) 2018 and 29 v Lancs (Oval) 2018. 50 wkts (1): 63 (2018). BB 6-23 (see Tests). Sy BB 6-57 v Lancs (Oval) 2018. LO HS 35 Easterns v Northerns (Pretoria) 2005-06. LO BB 5-21 (see LOI). T20 HS 23*. T20 BB 4-17.

‡NQNESER, Michael Gertges, b Pretoria, South Africa 29 Mar 1990. 6'0". RHB, RMF. Squad No 18. Queensland 2010-11 to date. IPL: KXIP 2013. Big Bash: BH 2011-12. AS 2012-13 to date. **LOI** (A): 2 (2018); HS 6 and BB 2-46 v E (Oval) 2018. F-c Tours (Aus A): E 2019; I 2018-19; UAE (v P) 2018-19. HS 77 Q v WA (Perth) 2012-13. BB 6-57 Q v Tas (Hobart) 2017-18. LO HS 122 Q v WA (Sydney, DO) 2017-18. LO BB 4-41 Q v SA (Perth) 2016-17. T20 HS 44. T20 BB 3-24.

PATEL, Ryan Samir (Whitgift S), b Sutton 26 Oct 1997. 5'10". LHB, RMF. Squad No 26. Debut (Surrey) 2017. Surrey 2nd XI debut 2016. England U19 2017. HS 100* v Essex (Oval) 2019. BB 6-5 v Somerset (Guildford) 2018. LO HS 41* v Surrey (Taunton) 2019 (RLC). LO BB 2-65 v Hants (Oval) 2019 (RLC). T20 HS 5*. T20 BB – .

PLUNKETT, Liam Edward (Nunthorpe SS; Teesside Tertiary C), b Middlesbrough, Yorks 6 Apr 1985. 6'3". RHB, RF. Squad No 28. Durham 2003-12. Dolphins 2007-08. Yorkshire 2013-17; cap 2013. Surrey debut 2019. MCC 2017. IPL: DD 2018. Big Bash: MS 2019-20. **Tests**: 13 (2005-06 to 2014); HS 55* v I (Lord's) 2014; BB 5-64 v SL (Leeds) 2014. **LOI**: 89 (2005-06 to 2019); HS 56 v P (Lahore) 2005-06; BB 5-52 v WI (Bristol) 2017. **IT20**: 22 (2006 to 2018-19); HS 18 v WI (Chester-le-St) 2017; BB 3-21 v P (Dubai, DSC) 2015-16. F-c Tours (EL): SA 2014-15; WI 2010-11; NZ 2008-09; I 2005-06 (E), 2007-08 (P); P 2005-06 (E); SL 2013-14. HS 126 Y v Hants (Leeds) 2016. Sy HS 2 v Essex (Chelmsford) 2019. 50 wkts (3); most – 60 (2009). BB 6-33 Y v Leeds/Bradford MCCU (Leeds) 2013 on Y debut. CC BB 6-63 (11-119 match) Du v Worcs (Chester-le-St) 2009. Sy BB 1-85 v Essex (Oval) 2019. LO HS 72 Du v Somerset (Chester-le-St) 2008 (P40). LO BB 5-52 (see LOI). T20 HS 41. T20 BB 5-31.

POPE, Oliver John Douglas (Cranleigh S), b Chelsea, Middx 2 Jan 1998. 5'9". RHB, WK. Squad No 32. Debut (Surrey) 2017; cap 2018. Surrey 2nd XI debut 2015. England U19 2016 to 2016-17. **Tests**: 7 (2018 to 2019-20); HS 135* v SA (Port Elizabeth) 2019-20. F-c Tours: SA 2019-20; NZ 2019-20; I 2018-19 (EL); SL 2019-20. 1000 runs (1): 1098 (2018). HS 251 v MCC (Dubai, ICCA) 2018-19. CC HS 221* v Hants (Oval) 2019. LO HS 93* EL v Pakistan A (Abu Dhabi) 2018-19. T20 HS 48.

REIFER, Nico (Queen's C, Bridgetown; Whitgift S), b Bridgetown, Barbados 11 Nov 2000. 5'11". RHB, RM. Squad No 27. Surrey 2nd XI debut 2018. Awaiting 1st XI debut.

ROY, Jason Jonathan (Whitgift S), b Durban, South Africa 21 Jul 1990. 6'0". RHB, RM. Squad No 20. Debut (Surrey) 2010; cap 2014. IPL: GL 2017. DD 2018. Big Bash: ST 2014-15. SS 2016-17 to 2017-18. **ECB L-O Central Contract 2019-20. Tests**: 5 (2019); HS 72 v Ire (Lord's) 2019. **LOI**: 87 (2015 to 2019-20); HS 180 v A (Melbourne) 2017-18 – E record. **IT20**: 35 (2014 to 2019-20); HS 78 v NZ (Delhi) 2015-16. 1000 runs (1): 1078 (2014). HS 143 v Lancs (Oval) 2015. BB 3-9 v Glos (Bristol) 2014. LO HS 180 (see LOI). LO BB – . T20 HS 122*. T20 BB 1-23.

‡**NOSHADAB KHAN**, b Mianwali, Punjab, Pakistan 4 Oct 1998. 5'10". RHB, LBG. Rawalpindi 2016-17. SNGPL 2017-18. Big Bash: BH 2017-18. **Tests** (P): 5 (2017 to 2018-19); HS 56 v E (Leeds) 2018; BB 3-31 v Ire (Dublin) 2018. **LOI** (P): 43 (2017 to 2019-20); HS 54 v NZ (Wellington) 2017-18; BB 4-28 v Z (Bulawayo) 2018. **IT20** (P): 40 (2016-17 to 2019-20); HS 29 v A (Harare) 2018; BB 4-14 v WI (Port of Spain) 2016-17. F-c Tours (P): E 2016 (PA), 2018; SA 2018-19; WI 2017; Z 2016-17 (PA); Ire 2018. HS 132 PA v Zimbabwe A (Bulawayo) 2016-17. BB 6-77 (10-157 match) P v Northants (Northampton) 2018. LO HS 56 Rawalpindi v FATA (Islamabad) 2016-17. LO BB 4-28 (*see LOI*). T20 HS 77. T20 BB 4-14.

‡**NOSHORT, D'Arcy** John Matthew, b Katherine, N Territory, Australia 9 Aug 1990. 5'11". LHB, SLC. W Australia 2016-17 to date. Durham 2019 (T20 only). IPL: RR 2018. Big Bash: HH 2016-17 to date. **LOI** (A): 8 (2018 to 2019-20); HS 69 v SA (Bloemfontein) 2019-20; BB – . **IT20** (A): 20 (2017-18 to 2018-19); HS 76 v NZ (Auckland) 2017-18 and 76 v P (Harare) 2018; BB 1-13 v P (Abu Dhabi) 2018-19. HS 66 WA v SA (Adelaide, GS) 2017-18. BB 3-78 WA v Vic (Melbourne) 2017-18. LO HS 257 (inc world record 23 sixes) WA v Q (Sydney, HO) 2018-19 – 3rd highest l-o score on record. LO BB 3-53 WA v Vic (Perth) 2017-18. T20 HS 122*. T20 BB 5-21.

SMITH, Jamie Luke (Whitgift S), b Epsom 12 Jul 2000. 5'10". RHB, WK. Squad No 11. Debut (Surrey) 2018-19, scoring 127 v MCC (Dubai, ICCA). Surrey 2nd XI debut. England U19 2018-19. HS 127 (*see above*). CC HS 57 v Notts (Nottingham) 2019. LO HS 40 v Somerset (Taunton) 2019 (RLC). T20 HS 7*.

STONEMAN, Mark Daniel (Whickham CS), b Newcastle upon Tyne, Northumb 26 Jun 1987. 5'10". LHB, OB. Squad No 23. Durham 2007-16; captain (l-o only) 2015-16. Surrey debut 2017; cap 2018. **Tests**: 11 (2017 to 2018); HS 60 v NZ (Christchurch) 2017-18. F-c Tour: A 2017-18; NZ 2017-18. 1000 runs (5); most – 1481 (2017). HS 197 v Essex (Guildford) 2017. BB – . LO HS 144* v Notts (Lord's) 2017 (RLC). LO BB 1-8 Du v Derbys (Derby) 2016 (RLC). T20 HS 89*.

‡**TAYLOR, James** Philip Arthur (Trentham HS), b Stoke-on-Trent, Staffs 19 Jan 2001. Younger brother of T.A.I.Taylor (*see LEICESTERSHIRE*). 6'3". RHB, RM. Squad No 25. Derbyshire 2017-19. Derbyshire 2nd XI debut 2016. HS 11* and BB 3-26 De v Leeds/Brad MCCU (Derby) 2019. LO HS 6* and LO BB 2-66 De v Australia A (Derby) 2019.

‡**TOPLEY, Reece** James William (Royal Hospital S, Ipswich), b Ipswich, Suffolk 21 February 1994. Son of T.D.Topley (Surrey, Essex, GW 1985-94) and nephew of P.A.Topley (Kent 1972-75). 6'7". RHB, LMF. Squad No 24. Essex 2011-15; cap 2013. Hampshire 2016-17. Sussex 2019. **LOI**: 10 (2015 to 2015-16); HS 6 v A (Manchester) 2015; BB 4-50 v SA (Port Elizabeth) 2015-16. **IT20**: 6 (2015 to 2015-16); HS 1* v SA (Johannesburg) 2015-16; BB 3-24 v P (Dubai, DSC) 2015-16. F-c Tour (EL): SL 2013-14. HS 16 H v Yorks (Southampton) 2017. BB 6-29 (11-85 match) Ex v Worcs (Chelmsford) 2013. LO HS 19 Ex v Somerset (Taunton) 2011 (CB40). LO BB 4-16 EL v West Indies A (Northampton) 2018. T20 HS 5*. T20 BB 4-26.

VIRDI, Guramar Singh ('**Amar**') (Guru Nanak Sikh Ac, Hayes), b Chiswick, Middx 19 Jul 1998. 5'10". RHB, OB. Squad No 19. Debut (Surrey) 2017. Surrey 2nd XI debut 2016. England U19 2016 to 2017. HS 21* v Somerset (Taunton) 2018. BB 8-61 (14-139 match) v Notts (Nottingham) 2019.

(Having made a County 1st XI appearance in 2019)

NQ**ELGAR, Dean**, b Welkom, OFS, South Africa 11 Jun 1987. 5'8". LHB, SLA. Free State 2005-06 to 2010-11. Eagles 2006-07 to 2009-10. Knights 2010-11 to 2013-14. Somerset 2013-17; cap 2017. Titans 2014-15 to date. **Tests** (SA): 63 (2012-13 to 2019-20); 1000 runs (1): 1128 (2017); HS 199 v B (Potchefstroom) 2017-18; BB 4-22 v I (Mohali) 2015-16. **LOI** (SA): 8 (2012 to 2019-19); HS 42 v E (Oval) 2012; BB 1-11 v E (Southampton) 2012. F-c Tours (SA): E 2017; A 2012-13, 2016 (SA A), 2016-17; NZ 2016-17; I 2015-16, 2019-20; SL 2010 (SA A), 2014, 2018; Z 2014; B 2010 (SA A), 2015; UAE (v P) 2013-14; Ire 2012 (SA A). 1000 runs (0+2); most – 1193 (2009-10). HS 268 SA A v Australia A (Pretoria) 2013. CC HS 158 Sm v Middx (Lord's) 2017. Sy HS 110 v Somerset (Taunton) 2018. CC BB 1-4 Sm v Essex (Taunton) 2017. Sy BB 1-17 v Kent (Beckenham) 2019. LO HS 137 Titans v Lions (Potchefstroom) 2018-19. LO BB 4-37 Titans v Dolphins (Durban) 2018-19. T20 HS 88*. T20 BB 4-23.

NQ**FINCH, Aaron** James, b Colac, Victoria, Australia 17 Nov 1986. 5'9". RHB, SLA. Victoria 2007-08 to date. Yorkshire 2014-15. Surrey 2016-19; cap 2018. IPL: RR: 2009-10. DD 2011-12. PW 2013. SH 2014. MI 2015. GL 2016-17. KXIP 2018. Big Bash: MR 2011-12 to date. **Tests** (A): 5 (2018-19); HS 62 v P (Dubai, DSC) 2018-19; BB – . **LOI** (A): 126 (2012-13 to 2019-20); HS 153* v P (Sharjah) 2018-19; BB 1-2 v I (Pune) 2013-14. **IT20** (A): 61 (2010-11 to 2019-20); HS 172 v Z (Harare) 2018 – world record IT20 score. F-c Tours (Aus A): SA/Z 2013; Z 2011; UAE 2018-19 (v P)(A). HS 288* Cricket A v New Zealanders (Sydney) 2015-16. CC HS 110 Y v Warwks (Birmingham) 2014 and 110 v Warwks (Guildford) 2016. BB 1-0 Vic v WA (Perth) 2013-14. CC BB 1-20 Y v Sussex (Arundel) 2014. LO HS 188* Vic v Q (Melbourne) 2019-20. LO BB 2-44 Aus A v EL (Hobart) 2012-13. T20 HS 172. T20 BB 1-9.

NQ**IMRAN TAHIR,** Mohammad (Government Pakistan Angels HS and MAO College, Lahore), b Lahore, Pakistan 4 Jun 1979. 5'11". RHB, LB. Lahore City 1996-97 to 1997-98. WAPDA 1998-99. REDCO 1999-00. Lahore Whites 2000-01. SNGPL 2001-02 to 2003-04. Sialkot 2002-03. Middlesex 2003. Lahore Blues 2004-05. PIA 2004-05 to 2006-07. Lahore Ravi 2005-06. Yorkshire (1 match) 2007. Titans 2007-08 to 2009-10. Hampshire 2008-09; cap 2009. Easterns 2008-09 to 2009-10. Warwickshire 2010; cap 2010. Dolphins 2010-11 to 2016-17. Lions 2012-13 to 2013-14. Nottinghamshire 2015-16; cap 2015. Derbyshire 2017. Durham 2018 (T20 only). Surrey 2019 (T20 only). IPL: DD 2014-16. RPS 2017. CSK 2018-19. Staffordshire 2004-05. Qualified for SA on 1 Apr 2009. **Tests** (SA): 20 (2011-12 to 2015-16); HS 29* v SL (Centurion) 2011-12; BB 5-32 v P (Dubai) 2013-14. **LOI** (SA): 107 (2010-11 to 2019); HS 29 v WI (Bridgetown) 2016; LO BB 7-45 v WI (Basseterre) 2016. **IT20** (SA): 38 (2013 to 2018-19); HS 9* v Netherlands (Chittagong) 2013-14; BB 5-23 v Z (East London) 2018-19. F-c Tours (SA): E 2012; A 2012-13; NZ 2011-12; I 2015-16; SL 2004-05 (Pak A), 2014; UAE 2013-14 (v P). HS 77* H v Somerset (Southampton) 2009. 50 wkts (2+2); most – 74 (2004-05). BB 8-42 (12-133 match) Dolphins v Knights (Kimberley) 2015-16. UK BB 7-66 (12-189 match) H v Lancs (Manchester) 2008. LO HS 41* Staffs v Lancs (Stone) 2004 (CGT). LO BB 7-45 (see LOI). T20 HS 23. T20 BB 5-23.

MEAKER, S.C. – see *SUSSEX*.

VAN DEN BERGH, Frederick Oliver Edward (Whitgift S, Croydon; Hatfield C, Durham U), b Farnborough, Kent 14 Jun 1992. 6'0". RHB, SLA. Surrey 2011-19. Durham MCCU 2013-14. HS 34 and BB 4-84 DU v Notts (Nottingham) 2013. Sy HS 16* v Leeds/Bradford MCCU (Oval) 2012. CC HS 16 v Essex (Oval) 2019. Sy BB 3-79 v Cambridge MCCU (Cambridge) 2011. CC BB 3-84 v Yorks (Oval) 2017. LO HS 29* v Sussex (Oval) 2014 (RLC). LO BB – . T20 HS 19*. T20 BB – .

A.Harinath left the staff without making a County 1st XI appearance in 2019.

SURREY 2019

RESULTS SUMMARY

		Place	Won	Lost	Tied	Drew	NR
Specsavers County Champ (1st Division)		6th	2	6		6	
All First-Class Matches			2	6		6	
Royal London One-Day Cup (South Group)	9th		1	7			
Vitality Blast (South Group)		8th	5	7	1		1

SPECSAVERS COUNTY CHAMPIONSHIP AVERAGES

BATTING AND FIELDING

Cap		M	I	NO	HS	Runs	Avge	100	50	Ct/St
2018	O.J.D.Pope	5	8	1	221*	561	80.14	2	2	4
2014	R.J.Burns	8	16	–	107	603	37.68	1	2	8
2005	R.Clarke	14	25	–	88	662	33.10	–	3	18
2018	S.G.Borthwick	13	23	–	137	705	30.65	2	2	16
2018	M.D.Stoneman	13	23	–	100	685	29.78	1	4	5
2018	S.M.Curran	5	9	–	80	265	29.44	–	2	–
	D.Elgar	10	19	–	103	555	29.21	1	5	6
	G.S.Virdi	5	6	5	14*	28	28.00	–	–	–
	W.G.Jacks	10	16	–	120	427	26.68	1	3	13
2016	B.T.Foakes	13	23	1	69	575	26.13	–	5	39/6
	J.L.Smith	8	14	1	57	338	26.00	–	2	4/1
	J.Clark	9	15	4	54	268	24.36	–	1	1
	R.S.Patel	8	14	1	100*	292	22.46	1	1	3
2011	G.J.Batty	8	15	4	29	123	11.18	–	–	2
	C.McKerr	4	5	1	17*	35	8.75	–	–	1
2018	M.Morkel	14	22	3	27	131	6.89	–	–	3
	M.P.Dunn	3	5	3	2*	3	1.50	–	–	–

Also batted: T.K.Curran (1 match – cap 2016) 8, 22*; A.J.Finch (1 cap 2018) 90 (1 ct);
L.E.Plunkett (3) 0, 0, 2; F.O.E.van den Bergh (1) 16.

BOWLING

	O	M	R	W	Avge	Best	5wI	10wM
G.S.Virdi	140	34	452	23	19.65	8-61	2	1
M.P.Dunn	90.2	18	277	13	21.30	5-43	1	–
R.Clarke	332	73	1031	43	23.97	7-74	2	–
G.J.Batty	234.3	43	678	26	26.07	8-64	1	1
S.M.Curran	156.5	28	510	19	26.84	3-50	–	–
M.Morkel	413	94	1297	44	29.47	4-43	–	–
J.Clark	151.4	17	636	21	30.28	5-77	1	–

Also bowled:
C.McKerr | 89 | 11 | 366 | 7 | 52.28 | 3-94 | – | –

S.G.Borthwick 22-1-113-0; R.J.Burns 1-1-0-0; T.K.Curran 28-6-118-3; D.Elgar
15.4-2-57-2; W.G.Jacks 1-1-0-0; R.S.Patel 56.3-6-213-4; L.E.Plunkett 33-5-160-1;
M.D.Stoneman 2-0-15-0; F.O.E.van den Bergh 21.4-1-88-1.

Surrey played no first-class fixtures outside the County Championship in 2019. The
First-Class Averages (pp 226–241) give the records of Surrey players in all first-class county
matches, with the exception of R.J.Burns, S.M.Curran and B.T.Foakes, whose first-class
figures for Surrey are as above.

SURREY RECORDS

FIRST-CLASS CRICKET

Highest Total	For	811		v	Somerset	The Oval	1899
	V	863		by	Lancashire	The Oval	1990
Lowest Total	For	14		v	Essex	Chelmsford	1983
	V	16		by	MCC	Lord's	1872
Highest Innings	For	357*	R.Abel	v	Somerset	The Oval	1899
	V	366	N.H.Fairbrother	for	Lancashire	The Oval	1990

Highest Partnership for each Wicket

1st	428	J.B.Hobbs/A.Sandham	v	Oxford U	The Oval	1926
2nd	371	J.B.Hobbs/E.G.Hayes	v	Hampshire	The Oval	1909
3rd	413	D.J.Bicknell/D.M.Ward	v	Kent	Canterbury	1990
4th	448	R.Abel/T.W.Hayward	v	Yorkshire	The Oval	1899
5th	318	M.R.Ramprakash/Azhar Mahmood	v	Middlesex	The Oval	2005
6th	298	A.Sandham/H.S.Harrison	v	Sussex	The Oval	1913
7th	262	C.J.Richards/K.T.Medlycott	v	Kent	The Oval	1987
8th	222*	B.T.Foakes/G.J.Batty	v	Hampshire	Southampton[2]	2016
9th	168	E.R.T.Holmes/E.W.J.Brooks	v	Hampshire	The Oval	1936
10th	173	A.Ducat/A.Sandham	v	Essex	Leyton	1921

Best Bowling	For	10-43	T.Rushby	v	Somerset	Taunton	1921
(Innings)	V	10-28	W.P.Howell	for	Australians	The Oval	1899
Best Bowling	For	16-83	G.A.R.Lock	v	Kent	Blackheath	1956
(Match)	V	15-57	W.P.Howell	for	Australians	The Oval	1899

Most Runs – Season	3246	T.W.Hayward	(av 72.13)	1906
Most Runs – Career	43554	J.B.Hobbs	(av 49.72)	1905-34
Most 100s – Season	13	T.W.Hayward		1906
	13	J.B.Hobbs		1925
Most 100s – Career	144	J.B.Hobbs		1905-34
Most Wkts – Season	252	T.Richardson	(av 13.94)	1895
Most Wkts – Career	1775	T.Richardson	(av 17.87)	1892-1904
Most Career W-K Dismissals	1221	H.Strudwick	(1035 ct; 186 st)	1902-27
Most Career Catches in the Field	605	M.J.Stewart		1954-72

LIMITED-OVERS CRICKET

Highest Total	50ov	496-4		v	Glos	The Oval	2007
	40ov	386-3		v	Glamorgan	The Oval	2010
	T20	250-6		v	Kent	Canterbury	2018
Lowest Total	50ov	74		v	Kent	The Oval	1967
	40ov	64		v	Worcs	Worcester	1978
	T20	88		v	Kent	The Oval	2012
Highest Innings	50ov	268	A.D.Brown	v	Glamorgan	The Oval	2002
	40ov	203	A.D.Brown	v	Hampshire	Guildford	1997
	T20	131*	A.J.Finch	v	Sussex	Hove	2018
Best Bowling	50ov	7-33	R.D.Jackman	v	Yorkshire	Harrogate	1970
	40ov	7-30	M.P.Bicknell	v	Glamorgan	The Oval	1999
	T20	6-24	T.J.Murtagh	v	Middlesex	Lord's	2005

173

SUSSEX

Formation of Present Club: 1 March 1839
Substantial Reorganisation: August 1857
Inaugural First-Class Match: 1864
Colours: Dark Blue, Light Blue and Gold
Badge: County Arms of Six Martlets
County Champions: (3) 2003, 2006, 2007
Gillette/NatWest/C&G Trophy Winners: (5) 1963, 1964, 1978, 1986, 2006
Pro 40/National League (Div 1) Winners: (2) 2008, 2009
Sunday League Winners: (1) 1982
Twenty20 Cup Winners: (1) 2009

Chief Executive: Rob Andrew, The 1st Central County Ground, Eaton Road, Hove BN3 3AN • Tel: 0844 264 0202 • Email: info@sussexcricket.co.uk • Web: www.sussexcricket.co.uk • Twitter: @SussexCCC (93,969 followers)

Director of Cricket: Keith Greenfield. **Head Coach**: Jason Gillespie. **Lead Batting Coach**: Jason Swift. **Lead Bowling Coach**: James Kirtley. **Lead Spin Coach**: Ian Salisbury. **Captains**: B.C.Brown (f-c and l-o) and L.J.Wright (T20). **Overseas Players**: T.M.Head and Rashid Khan. **2020 Testimonial**: None. **Head Groundsman**: Ben Gibson. **Scorer**: Graham Irwin. **Vitality Blast Name**: Sussex Sharks. ‡ New registration. NQ Not qualified for England.

ARCHER, Jofra Chioke (Christchurch Foundation), b Bridgetown, Barbados 1 Apr 1995. 6'3". RHB, RF. Squad No 22. Debut (Sussex) 2016; cap 2017. IPL: RR 2018. Big Bash: HH 2017-18 to date. Qualified for England at the start of the 2019 season. **ECB Test & L-O Central Contract 2019-20**. Tests: 7 (2019 to 2019-20); HS 30 v NZ (Mt Maunganui) 2019-20; BB 6-45 v A (Leeds) 2019. LOI: 14 (2019); HS 7* and BB 3-27 v SA (Oval) 2019. IT20: 1 (2019); HS – ; BB 2-29 v P (Cardiff) 2019. F-c Tours: SA 2019-20; NZ 2019-20. HS 81* v Northants (Northampton) 2017. 50 wkts (1): 61 (2017). BB 7-67 v Kent (Hove) 2017. LO HS 45 v Essex (Chelmsford) 2017 (RLC). LO BB 5-42 v Somerset (Taunton) 2016 (RLC). T20 HS 36. T20 BB 4-18.

BEER, William Andrew Thomas (Reigate GS; Collyer's C, Horsham), b Crawley 8 Oct 1988. 5'10". RHB, LB. Squad No 18. Debut (Sussex) 2008. HS 97 v Glos (Arundel) 2019. BB 6-29 (11-91 match) v South Africa A (Arundel) 2017. CC BB 3-31 v Worcs (Worcester) 2010. LO HS 75 v Essex (Chelmsford) 2019 (RLC). LO BB 3-27 v Warwks (Hove) 2012 (CB40). T20 HS 37. T20 BB 3-14.

‡BOPARA, Ravinder Singh (Brampton Manor S; Barking Abbey Sports C), b Newham, London 4 May 1985. 5'8". RHB, RM. Squad No 23. Essex 2002-19; cap 2005; benefit 2015; captain (l-o only) 2016. Auckland 2009-10. Dolphins 2010-11. MCC 2006, 2008. IPL: KXIP 2009 to 2009-10. SH 2015. Big Bash: SS 2013-14. YC 2008. Tests: 13 (2007-08 to 2012); HS 143 v WI (Lord's) 2009; BB 1-39 v SL (Galle) 2007-08. LOI: 120 (2006-07 to 2014-15); HS 101* v Ire (Dublin) 2013; BB 4-38 v B (Birmingham) 2010. IT20: 38 (2008 to 2014); HS 65* v A (Hobart) 2013-14; BB 4-10 v WI (Oval) 2011. F-c Tours: WI 2008-09, 2010-11 (EL); SL 2007-08, 2011-12. 1000 runs (1): 1256 (2008). HS 229 Ex v Northants (Chelmsford) 2007. BB 5-49 Ex v Derbys (Chelmsford) 2016. LO HS 201* Ex v Leics (Leicester) 2008 (FPT) – Ex record. LO BB 5-63 Dolphins v Warriors (Pietermaritzburg) 2010-11. T20 HS 105*. T20 BB 6-16.

BRIGGS, Danny Richard (Isle of Wight C), b Newport, IoW, 30 Apr 1991. 6'2". RHB, SLA. Squad No 21. Hampshire 2009-15; cap 2012. Sussex debut 2016. **LOI**: 1 (2011-12); BB 2-39 v P (Dubai) 2011-12. **IT20**: 7 (2012 to 2013-14); HS 0*; BB 2-25 v A (Chester-le-St) 2013. F-c Tours (EL): WI 2010-11; I 2018-19. HS 120* v South Africa A (Arundel) 2017. CC HS 54 H v Glos (Bristol) 2013. BB 6-45 EL v Windward Is (Roseau) 2010-11. CC BB 6-65 H v Notts (Southampton) 2011. Sx BB 5-93 v Glos (Bristol) 2016. LO HS 37* v Essex (Chelmsford) 2019 (RLC). LO BB 4-32 H v Glamorgan (Cardiff) 2012 (CB40). T20 HS 13. T20 BB 5-19.

BROWN, Ben Christopher (Ardingly C), b Crawley 23 Nov 1988. 5'8". RHB, WK. Squad No 26. Debut (Sussex) 2007; cap 2014; captain 2017 to date. 1000 runs (2); most – 1031 (2015, 2018). HS 163 v Durham (Hove) 2014. BB 1-48 v Essex (Colchester) 2016. LO HS 73* v Kent (Hove) 2018 (RLC). T20 HS 68.

CLARK, Thomas Geoffrey Reeves (Ardingly C), b Haywards Heath 2 July 2001. 6'2". LHB, RM. Squad No 27. Debut (Sussex) 2019. Sussex 2nd XI debut 2017. HS 13 v Worcs (Hove) 2019 – only 1st XI appearance.

‡**CLAYDON, Mitchell** Eric (Westfield Sports HS, Sydney), b Fairfield, NSW, Australia 25 Nov 1982. 6'4". LHB, RMF. Squad No 4. Yorkshire 2005-06. Durham 2007-13. Canterbury 2010-11. Kent 2013-19; cap 2016. HS 77 K v Leics (Leicester) 2014. 50 wkts (2); most – 59 (2014). BB 6-104 Du v Somerset (Taunton) 2011. LO HS 19 Du v Glos (Bristol) 2009 (FPT) and 19 K v Middx (Canterbury) 2017 (RLC). LO BB 5-31 K v Guyana (North Sound) 2017-18. T20 HS 19. T20 BB 5-26.

EVANS, Laurie John (Whitgift S; The John Fisher S; St Mary's C, Durham U), b Lambeth, London 12 Oct 1987. 6'0". RHB, RM. Squad No 32. Durham UCCE 2007. MCC 2007. Surrey 2009-10. Warwickshire 2010-16. Northamptonshire 2016 (on loan). Sussex debut 2017. HS 213* and BB 1-29 Wa v Sussex (Birmingham) 2015, sharing Wa 6th wkt record partnership of 327 with T.R.Ambrose. Sx HS 113 v Worcs (Kidderminster) 2010. LO HS 134* v Kent (Canterbury) 2017 (RLC). LO BB 1-29 v Middx (Lord's) 2019 (RLC). T20 HS 104*. T20 BB 1-5.

FINCH, Harry Zachariah (St Richard's Catholic C, Bexhill; Eastbourne C), b Hastings 10 Feb 1995. 5'8". RHB, RM. Squad No 6. Debut (Sussex) 2013. HS 135* and BB 1-9 v Leeds/Bradford MCCU (Hove) 2016. CC HS 103 v Middx (Hove) 2018. CC BB 1-30 v Northants (Arundel) 2016. LO HS 108 v Hants (Hove) 2018 (RLC). LO BB – . T20 HS 35*.

GARTON, George Henry Simmons (Hurstpierpoint C), b Brighton 15 Apr 1997. 5'10½". LHB, LF. Squad No 15. Debut (Sussex) 2016. Sussex 2nd XI debut 2014. HS 59* v Worcs (Hove) 2019. BB 3-20 v Durham (Chester-le-St) 2017. LO HS 38 v Essex (Chelmsford) 2019 (RLC). LO BB 4-43 EL v Sri Lanka A (Canterbury) 2016. T20 HS 2*. T20 BB 4-16.

HAINES, Thomas Jacob (Tanbridge House S, Horsham; Hurstpierpoint C), b Crawley 28 Oct 1998. 5'10". LHB, RM. Squad No 20. Debut (Sussex) 2016. Sussex 2nd XI debut 2014. HS 124 v Durham (Arundel) 2018. BB 1-9 v Durham (Chester-le-St) 2019.

‡[NQ]**HEAD, Travis** Michael, b Adelaide, Australia 29 Dec 1993. 5'9". LHB, OB. Squad No 62. S Australia 2011-12 to date. Yorkshire 2016. Worcestershire 2018. IPL: RCB 2016-17. Big Bash: AS 2012-13 to date. **Tests** (A): 17 (2018-19 to 2019-20); HS 161 v SL (Canberra) 2018-19; BB – . **LOI** (A): 42 (2016 to 2018-19); HS 128 v P (Adelaide) 2016-17; BB 2-22 v SL (Pallekele) 2016-17. **IT20** (A): 16 (2015-16 to 2018); HS 48* v I (Guwahati) 2017-18; BB 1-16 v SL (Adelaide) 2016-17. F-c Tours (A): E 2019; I 2015 (Aus A), 2018-19 (Aus A); UAE 2018-19 (v P). HS 192 SA v Tas (Adelaide) 2015-16. CC HS 62 Wo v Essex (Worcester) 2018. BB 3-42 SA v NSW (Adelaide) 2015-16. LO HS 202 SA v WA (Sydney) 2015-16. LO BB 2-9 SA v NSW (Brisbane) 2014-15. T20 HS 101*. T20 BB 3-16.

HOOPER, Elliot Owen (Bede's, Upper Dicker; Loughborough U), b Eastbourne 22 Mar 1996. LHB, SLA. Debut (Sussex) 2019. Sussex 2nd XI debut 2013. HS 20 and BB 1-65 v Middx (Hove) 2019 – only 1st XI appearance.

JORDAN, Christopher James (Comber Mere S, Barbados; Dulwich C), b Christ Church, Barbados 4 Oct 1988. 6'0''. RHB, RFM. Squad No 8. Surrey 2007-12. Barbados 2011-12 to 2012-13. Sussex debut 2013; cap 2014. IPL: RCB 2016. SH 2017-18. Big Bash: AS 2016-17. ST 2018-19. PS 2019-20. **Tests**: 8 (2014 to 2014-15); HS 35 v SL (Lord's) 2014; BB 4-18 v I (Oval) 2014. **LOI**: 34 (2013 to 2019-20); HS 38* v SL (Oval) 2014; BB 5-29 v SL (Manchester) 2014. **IT20**: 46 (2013-14 to 2019-20); HS 36 v NZ (Wellington) 2019-20; BB 4-6 v WI (Basseterre) 2018-19 – E record. F-c Tour: WI 2014-15. HS 166 v Northants (Northampton) 2019. 50 wkts (1): 61 (2013). BB 7-43 Barbados v CC&C (Bridgetown) 2012-13. Sx BB 6-48 v Yorks (Leeds) 2013. LO HS 55 v Surrey (Guildford) 2016 (RLC). LO BB 5-28 v Middx (Hove) 2016 (RLC). T20 HS 45*. T20 BB 4-6.

‡MEAKER, Stuart Christopher (Cranleigh S), b Johannesburg, South Africa 21 Jan 1989. Moved to UK in 2001. 6'1''. RHB, RFM. Squad No 12. Surrey 2008-18; cap 2012. Auckland 2017-18. **LOI**: 2 (2011-12); HS 1 and BB 1-45 v I (Mumbai) 2011-12. **IT20**: 2 (2012-13); BB 1-28 v I (Pune) 2013-14. F-c Tour: I 2012-13. HS 94 Sy v Bangladeshis (Oval) 2010. CC HS 72 Sy v Essex (Colchester) 2009. 50 wkts (1): 51 (2012). BB 8-52 (11-167 match) Sy v Somerset (Oval) 2012. LO HS 50 v Glamorgan (Cardiff) 2019 (RLC). LO BB 4-37 Sy v Kent (Oval) 2017 (RLC). T20 HS 17. T20 BB 4-30.

MILLS, Tymal Solomon (Mildenhall TC), b Dewsbury, Yorks 12 Aug 1992. 6'1''. RHB, LF. Squad No 7. Essex 2011-14. Sussex debut 2016; has played T20 only since start of 2016. IPL: RCB 2017. Big Bash: BH 2016-17. HH 2017-18. **IT20**: 4 (+1 ICC World XI 2018) (2016 to 2016-17); HS 0; BB 1-27 v I (Kanpur) 2016-17. F-c Tour: SL 2013-14. HS 31* EL v Sri Lanka A (Colombo, RPS) 2013-14. CC HS 30 Ex v Kent (Canterbury) 2014. Sx HS 8 v Worcs (Hove) 2015. BB 4-25 Ex v Glamorgan (Cardiff) 2012. Sx BB 2-28 v Hants (Southampton) 2015. LO HS 3* v Notts (Hove) 2015 (RLC). LO BB 3-23 Ex v Durham (Chelmsford) 2013 (Y40). T20 HS 8*. T20 BB 4-22.

NORASHID KHAN Arman, b Nangarhar, Afghanistan 20 Sep 1998. RHB, LBG. Squad No 1. Afghanistan 2016-17 to date. Sussex debut 2018 (T20 only). IPL: SH 2017 to date. Big Bash: AS 2017-18 to date. **Tests** (Afg): 4 (2018 to 2019-20); HS 51 and BB 6-49 (11-104 match) v B (Chittagong) 2019. **LOI** (Afg): 71 (2015-16 to 2019-20); HS 60* v Ire (Belfast) 2016; BB 7-18 v WI (Gros Islet) 2017 – 4th best analysis in all LOI. **IT20** (Afg): 48 (2015-16 to 2019-20); HS 33 v WI (Basseterre) 2017; BB 5-3 v Ire (Greater Noida) 2016-17. HS 52 and BB 8-74 (12-122 match) Afg v EL (Abu Dhabi) 2017-18. LO HS 60* (*see LOI*). LO BB 7-18 (*see LOI*). T20 HS 56*. T20 BB 5-3.

RAWLINS, Delray Millard Wendell (Bede's S, Upper Dicker), b Bermuda 14 Sep 1997. 6'1''. LHB, SLA. Squad No 9. Debut (Sussex) 2017. MCC 2018. Bermuda (l-o and T20) 2019 to date. Sussex 2nd XI debut 2015. Oxfordshire 2017. England U19 2016-17. **IT20** (Ber): 11 (2019 to 2019-20); HS 63 v USA (Hamilton) 2019; BB 2-22 v USA (Hamilton) 2019 – separate matches. HS 100 v Lancs (Manchester) 2019. BB 3-19 v Durham (Hove) 2019. LO HS 53 South v North (Bridgetown) 2017-18 and 53 Bermuda v Uganda (Al Amerat) 2019-20. LO BB 1-27 Bermuda v Italy (Al Amerat) 2019-20. T20 HS 69. T20 BB 2-19.

ROBINSON, Oliver Edward (King's S, Canterbury), b Margate, Kent 1 Dec 1993. 6'1''. RHB, RMF/OB. Squad No 25. Debut (Sussex) 2015; cap 2019. F-c Tour (EL): A 2019-20. HS 110 v Durham (Chester-le-St) 2015, on debut, sharing Sx record 10th wkt partnership of 164 with M.E.Hobden. 50 wkts (2); most – 81 (2018). BB 8-34 (14-135 match) v Middx (Hove) 2019. LO HS 30 v Kent (Canterbury) 2015 (RLC). LO BB 3-31 v Kent (Hove) 2018 (RLC). T20 HS 18*. T20 BB 4-15.

SALT, Philip Dean (Reed's S, Cobham), b Bodelwyddan, Denbighs 28 Aug 1996. 5'10''. RHB, OB. Squad No 28. Debut (Sussex) 2013. Sussex 2nd XI debut 2014. Big Bash: AS 2019-20. HS 148 v Derbys (Hove) 2018. BB 1-32 v Warwks (Hove) 2018. LO HS 137* v Kent (Beckenham) 2019 (RLC). T20 HS 78*.

SHEFFIELD, William Arthur (Aldridge Ac, Saltdean), b Haywards Heath 26 Aug 2000. 6'4''. LHB, LMF. Sussex 2nd XI debut 2018. Awaiting 1st XI debut.

THOMASON, Aaron Dean (Barr Beacon S, Walsall), b Birmingham 26 Jun 1997. 5'10". RHB, RMF. Squad No 24. Debut (Sussex) 2019. Warwickshire (l-o and T20 only) 2014-19. Warwickshire 2nd XI debut 2014. England U19 2015. HS 90 v Worcs (Kidderminster) 2019 – on debut. BB 2-107 v Australia A (Arundel) 2019. CC BB 1-33 v Northants (Hove) 2019. LO HS 28 Wa v Durham (Birmingham) 2017 (RLC). LO BB 4-45 v Notts (Nottingham) 2018 (RLC). T20 HS 42. T20 BB 3-33.

^{NQ}**VAN ZYL, Stiaan**, b Cape Town, South Africa 19 Sep 1987. 5'11½". LHB, RM. Squad No 74. Boland 2006-07 to 2010-11. Cape Cobras 2007-08 to 2017-18. W Province 2014-15 to 2016-17. Sussex debut 2017 (Kolpak signing); cap 2019. **Tests** (SA): 12 (2014-15 to 2016); HS 101* v WI (Centurion) 2014-15 – on debut; BB 3-20 v E (Durban) 2015-16. F-c Tours (SA): A 2016 (SA A), I 2015 (SA A), 2015-16; SL 2010 (SA A); B 2010 (SA A), 2015; Ire 2012 (SA A). 1000 runs (1): 1023 (2017). HS 228 Cobras v Lions (Paarl) 2017-18. Sx 173 v Middx (Lord's) 2019. BB 5-32 Boland v Northerns (Paarl) 2010-11. Sx BB 3-16 v Glos (Hove) 2018. LO HS 114* Cobras v Eagles (Kimberley) 2009-10. LO BB 4-24 Boland v Gauteng (Stellenbosch) 2010-11. T20 HS 86*. T20 BB 2-14.

WELLS, Luke William Peter (St Bede's, Upper Dicker), b Eastbourne 29 Dec 1990. Son of A.P.Wells (Border, Kent, Sussex and England 1981-2000); elder brother of D.A.C.Wells (Oxford MCCU 2017); nephew of C.M.Wells (Border, Derbyshire, Sussex and WP 1979-96). 6'4". LHB, LB. Squad No 31. Debut (Sussex) 2010; cap 2016. Colombo CC 2011-12. 1000 runs (2); most – 1292 (2017). HS 258 v Durham (Hove) 2017. BB 5-63 v Glamorgan (Hove) 2019. LO HS 62 v Kent (Hove) 2018 (RLC). BB 3-19 v Netherlands (Amstelveen) 2011 (CB40). T20 HS 11.

^{NQ}**WIESE, David** (Witbank HS), b Roodepoort, South Africa 18 May 1985. 6'3". RHB, RMF. Squad No 96. Easterns 2005-06 to 2011-12. Titans 2009-10 to 2016-17. Sussex debut/cap 2016 (Kolpak signing). IPL: RCB 2015-16. **LOI** (SA): 6 (2015 to 2015-16); HS 41* and BB 3-50 v E (Cape Town) 2015-16. **IT20** (SA): 20 (2013 to 2015-16); HS 28 v WI (Nagpur) 2015-16; BB 5-23 v WI (Durban) 2015-16. F-c Tour (SA A): A 2014. HS 208 Easterns v GW (Benoni) 2008-09. Sx HS 139 v Cardiff MCCU (Hove) 2019. CC HS 106 v Warwks (Birmingham) 2018. BB 6-58 Titans v Knights (Centurion) 2014-15. Sx BB 5-26 v Middx (Lord's) 2019. LO HS 171 v Hants (Southampton) 2019 (RLC) – Sx record. LO BB 5-25 Easterns v Boland (Benoni) 2010-11. T20 HS 71*. T20 BB 5-19.

WRIGHT, Luke James (Belvoir HS; Ratcliffe C; Loughborough U), b Grantham, Lincs 7 Mar 1985. Younger brother of A.S.Wright (Leicestershire 2001-02). 5'11". RHB, RMF. Squad No 10. Leicestershire 2003 (one f-c match). Sussex debut 2004; cap 2007; T20 captain & benefit 2015; captain 2017; captain 2020 (T20 only). IPL: PW 2012-13. Big Bash: MS 2011-12 to 2017-18. **LOI**: 50 (2007 to 2013-14); HS 52 v NZ (Birmingham) 2008; BB 2-34 v NZ (Bristol) 2008 and 2-34 v A (Southampton) 2010. **IT20**: 51 (2007-08 to 2013-14); HS 99* v Afg (Colombo, RPS) 2012-13; BB 2-24 v NZ (Hamilton) 2012-13. F-c Tour (EL): NZ 2008-09. 1000 runs (1): 1220 (2015). HS 226* v Worcs (Worcester) 2015, sharing Sx record 6th wkt partnership of 335 with B.C.Brown. BB 5-65 v Derbys (Derby) 2010. LO HS 166 vMiddx (Lord's) 2019 (RLC). LO BB 4-12 v Middx (Hove) 2004 (NL). T20 HS 153* v Essex (Chelmsford) 2014 – Sx record. T20 BB 3-17.

RELEASED/RETIRED

(Having made a County 1st XI appearance in 2019)

^{NQ}**BEHRENDORFF, Jason** Paul (Alfred Deakin HS; Canberra C), b Camden, NSW, Australia 20 Apr 1990. RHB, LFM. W Australia 2011-12 to 2017-18. Sussex 2019 (T20 only). IPL: MI 2019. Big Bash: PS 2012-13 to 2018-19. **LOI** (A): 11 (2018-19 to 2019); HS 11* v SA (Manchester) 2019; BB 5-44 v E (Lord's) 2019. **IT20** (A): 7 (2017-18 to 2018-19); HS – ; BB 4-21 v I (Guwahati) 2017-18. HS 39* WA v Q (Perth) 2017-18. BB 9-37 (14-89 match) WA v Vic (Perth) 2016-17. LO HS 24* WA v Q (Sydney, BO) 2013-14. LO BB 5-27 WA v NSW (Sydney) 2014-15. T20 HS 26. T20 BB 4-21.

RELEASED/RETIRED continued on p 190

SUSSEX 2019

RESULTS SUMMARY

	Place	Won	Lost	Drew	NR
Specsavers County Champ (2nd Division)	6th	4	5		5
All First-Class Matches		4	6		6
Royal London One-Day Cup (South Group)	5th	4	4		
Vitality Blast (South Group)	QF	8	4	1	2

SPECSAVERS COUNTY CHAMPIONSHIP AVERAGES
BATTING AND FIELDING

Cap		M	I	NO	HS	Runs	Avge	100	50	Ct/St
	G.H.S.Garton	3	4	2	59*	112	56.00	–	2	2
2019	S.van Zyl	12	20	3	173	820	48.23	2	4	4
2014	B.C.Brown	14	22	3	156	812	42.73	3	3	52/1
	D.M.W.Rawlins	6	10	1	100	328	36.44	1	2	5
	P.D.Salt	10	19	1	122	603	33.50	2	3	13
	W.A.T.Beer	10	15	2	97	377	29.00	–	3	1
2014	C.J.Jordan	11	16	1	166	429	28.60	1	1	17
	D.R.Briggs	4	5	2	24	80	26.66	–	–	2
2016	D.Wiese	14	20	–	77	527	26.35	–	5	1
	L.J.Evans	7	11	–	113	264	24.00	1	1	6
2016	L.W.P.Wells	14	25	3	98*	527	23.95	–	2	5
2019	O.E.Robinson	11	16	4	59	255	21.25	–	1	3
	A.D.Thomason	3	6	–	90	113	18.83	–	1	1
	V.Chopra	2	4	–	32	74	18.50	–	–	2
	T.J.Haines	6	11	–	39	159	14.45	–	–	2
	H.Z.Finch	8	14	1	48	161	12.38	–	–	12
	A.Sakande	5	7	3	15	38	9.50	–	–	2
	Mir Hamza	6	7	2	8	14	2.80	–	–	2

Also played: M.G.K.Burgess (1 match) 9; A.T.Carey (1) 56, 69* (1 ct); T.G.R.Clark (1) 13; E.O.Hooper (1) 20; R.J.W.Topley (2) 1*, 5; J.D.Warner (2) 1*, 13*.

BOWLING

	O	M	R	W	Avge	Best	5wI	10wM
O.E.Robinson	380.3	83	1036	63	16.44	8-34	6	3
Mir Hamza	195	48	577	21	27.47	4-51	–	–
D.M.W.Rawlins	89	10	330	10	33.00	3-19	–	–
D.Wiese	339.3	68	1048	30	34.93	5-26	2	–
C.J.Jordan	297	58	919	26	35.34	4-58	–	–
L.W.P.Wells	148.4	21	497	11	45.18	5-63	1	–

Also bowled:

	O	M	R	W	Avge	Best	5wI	10wM
R.J.W.Topley	22.3	4	81	6	13.50	4-58	–	–
T.J.Haines	70	17	198	5	39.60	1- 9	–	–
A.Sakande	111.3	11	458	9	50.88	3-74	–	–
W.A.T.Beer	150.1	24	474	8	59.25	2-76	–	–

D.R.Briggs 83.3-11-255-4; B.C.Brown 2-0-15-0; L.J.Evans 1-0-11-0; H.Z.Finch 2-0-9-0; G.H.S.Garton 30.5-2-107-4; E.O.Hooper 20.5-5-65-1; A.D.Thomason 52-2-239-2; J.D.Warner 30.2-4-141-4.

The First-Class Averages (pp 226–241) give the records of Sussex players in all first-class county matches (Sussex's other opponents being Cardiff MCCU and Australia A), with the exception of A.T.Carey, whose first-class figures for Sussex are as above, and:
M.G.K.Burgess 2-2-0-95-104-52.00-0-1-1ct. Did not bowl.
V.Chopra 3-6-0-32-121-20.16-0-0-3ct. Did not bowl.
O.E.Robinson 12-17-4-59-260-20.00-0-1-3ct. 392.3-86-1072-63-17.01-8/34-6-3.

178

SUSSEX RECORDS

FIRST-CLASS CRICKET

Highest Total	For 742-5d			v	Somerset	Taunton	2009
	V 726			by	Notts	Nottingham	1895
Lowest Total	For 19			v	Surrey	Godalming	1830
	19			v	Notts	Hove	1873
	V 18			by	Kent	Gravesend	1867
Highest Innings	For 344*	M.W.Goodwin		v	Somerset	Taunton	2009
	V 322	E.Paynter		for	Lancashire	Hove	1937

Highest Partnership for each Wicket

1st	490	E.H.Bowley/J.G.Langridge	v	Middlesex	Hove	1933
2nd	385	E.H.Bowley/M.W.Tate	v	Northants	Hove	1921
3rd	385*	M.H.Yardy/M.W.Goodwin	v	Warwicks	Hove	2006
4th	363	M.W.Goodwin/C.D.Hopkinson	v	Somerset	Taunton	2009
5th	297	J.H.Parks/H.W.Parks	v	Hampshire	Portsmouth	1937
6th	335	L.J.Wright/B.C.Brown	v	Durham	Hove	2014
7th	344	K.S.Ranjitsinhji/W.Newham	v	Essex	Leyton	1902
8th	291	R.S.C.Martin-Jenkins/M.J.G.Davis	v	Somerset	Taunton	2002
9th	178	H.W.Parks/A.F.Wensley	v	Derbyshire	Horsham	1930
10th	164	O.E.Robinson/M.E.Hobden	v	Durham	Chester-le-St[2]	2015

Best Bowling	For 10- 48	C.H.G.Bland	v	Kent	Tonbridge	1899
(Innings)	V 9- 11	A.P.Freeman	for	Kent	Hove	1922
Best Bowling	For 17-106	G.R.Cox	v	Warwicks	Horsham	1926
(Match)	V 17- 67	A.P.Freeman	for	Kent	Hove	1922

Most Runs – Season	2850	J.G.Langridge	(av 64.77)		1949
Most Runs – Career	34150	J.G.Langridge	(av 37.69)		1928-55
Most 100s – Season	12	J.G.Langridge			1949
Most 100s – Career	76	J.G.Langridge			1928-55
Most Wkts – Season	198	M.W.Tate	(av 13.47)		1925
Most Wkts – Career	2211	M.W.Tate	(av 17.41)		1912-37
Most Career W-K Dismissals	1176	H.R.Butt	(911 ct; 265 st)		1890-1912
Most Career Catches in the Field	779	J.G.Langridge			1928-55

LIMITED-OVERS CRICKET

Highest Total	50ov	384-9		v	Ireland	Belfast	1996
	40ov	399-4		v	Worcs	Horsham	2011
	T20	242-5		v	Glos	Bristol	2016
Lowest Total	50ov	49		v	Derbyshire	Chesterfield	1969
	40ov	59		v	Glamorgan	Hove	1996
	T20	67		v	Hampshire	Hove	2004
Highest Innings	50ov	171	D.Wiese	v	Hampshire	Southampton[2]	2019
	40ov	163	C.J.Adams	v	Middlesex	Arundel	1999
	T20	153*	L.J.Wright	v	Essex	Chelmsford	2014
Best Bowling	50ov	6- 9	A.I.C.Dodemaide	v	Ireland	Downpatrick	1990
	40ov	7-41	A.N.Jones	v	Notts	Nottingham	1986
	T20	5-11	Mushtaq Ahmed	v	Essex	Hove	2005

WARWICKSHIRE

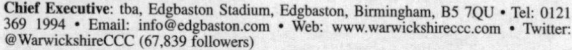

Formation of Present Club: 8 April 1882
Substantial Reorganisation: 19 January 1884
Inaugural First-Class Match: 1894
Colours: Dark Blue, Gold and Silver
Badge: Bear and Ragged Staff
County Champions: (7) 1911, 1951, 1972, 1994, 1995, 2004, 2012
Gillette/NatWest Trophy Winners: (5) 1966, 1968, 1989, 1993, 1995
Benson and Hedges Cup Winners: (2) 1994, 2002
Sunday League Winners: (3) 1980, 1994, 1997
Clydesdale Bank 40 Winners: (1) 2010
Royal London Cup Winners: (1) 2015
Twenty20 Cup Winners: (1) 2014

Chief Executive: tba, Edgbaston Stadium, Edgbaston, Birmingham, B5 7QU • Tel: 0121 369 1994 • Email: info@edgbaston.com • Web: www.warwickshireccc.com • Twitter: @WarwickshireCCC (67,839 followers)

Sport Director: Paul Farbrace. **1st Team Coach**: Jim Troughton. **Batting Coach**: Tony Frost. **Bowling Coach**: Graeme Welch. **Captains**: W.H.M.Rhodes (f-c and l-o) and C.J.Green (T20). **Vice-Captain**: D.P.Sibley. **Overseas Players**: C.J.Green and J.S.Patel. **2020 Testimonial**: None. **Head Groundsman**: Gary Barwell. **Scorer**: Mel Smith. **T20 Blast Name**: Birmingham Bears. ‡ New registration. ^{NQ} Not qualified for England.

AMBROSE, Timothy Raymond (Merewether HS, NSW; TAFE C), b Newcastle, NSW, Australia 1 Dec 1982. ECB qualified – British/EU passport. 5'7". RHB, WK. Squad No 11. Sussex 2001-05; cap 2003. Warwickshire debut 2006; cap 2007; benefit 2016. **Tests**: 11 (2007-08 to 2008-09); HS 102 v NZ (Wellington) 2007-08. **LOI**: 5 (2008); HS 6 v NZ (Oval) 2008. **IT20**: 1 (2008); HS – . F-c Tours: WI 2008-09; NZ 2007-08. HS 251* v Worcs (Worcester) 2007. LO HS 135 v Durham (Birmingham) 2007 (FPT). T20 HS 77.

BANKS, Liam (Newcastle-under-Lyme S & SFC), b Newcastle-under-Lyme, Staffs 3 Jun 1999. 5'10". RHB, OB. Squad No 8. Debut (Warwickshire) 2017. Warwickshire 2nd XI debut 2015. England U19 2017 to 2018. HS 50 v Essex (Chelmsford) 2019. BB – . LO HS 61 v Lancs (Birmingham) 2019 (RLC). T20 HS 24*.

BELL, Ian Ronald (Princethorpe C), b Walsgrave-on-Sowe 11 Apr 1982. 5'9". RHB, RM. Squad No 4. Debut (Warwickshire) 1999; cap 2001; benefit 2011; captain 2016-17. MCC 2004, 2016. YC 2004. MBE 2005. *Wisden* 2007. Missed entire 2019 season due to knee injury. **Tests**: 118 (2004 to 2015-16); 1000 runs (1): 1005 (2013); HS 235 v I (Oval) 2011; BB 1-33 v P (Faisalabad) 2005-06. **LOI**: 161 (2004-05 to 2014-15); 1000 runs (1): 1080 (2007); HS 141 v A (Hobart) 2014-15; BB 3-9 v Z (Bulawayo) 2004-05 – taking a wicket with his third ball in LOI. **IT20**: 8 (2006 to 2014); HS 60* v NZ (Manchester) 2008. F-c Tours: A 2006-07, 2010-11, 2013-14; SA 2009-10; WI 2000-01 (Eng A), 2008-09, 2014-15; NZ 2007-08, 2012-13; I 2005-06, 2008-09, 2012-13; P 2005-06; SL 2002-03 (ECB Acad), 2004-05, 2007-08, 2011-12; B 2009-10; UAE 2011-12 (v P), 2015-16 (v P). 1000 runs (5); most – 1714 (2004). HS 262* v Sussex (Horsham) 2004. BB 4-4 v Middx (Lord's) 2004. LO HS 158 EL v India A (Worcester) 2010. LO BB 5-41 v Essex (Chelmsford) 2003 (NL). T20 HS 131. T20 BB 1-12.

BROOKES, Ethan Alexander (Solihull S & SFC), b Solihull 23 May 2001. Younger brother of H.J.H.Brookes (*see below*). RHB, RMF. Squad No 77. Debut (Warwickshire) 2019. Warwickshire 2nd XI debut 2018. Staffordshire 2019. HS 0 and BB – v Essex (Birmingham) 2019.

BROOKES, Henry James Hamilton (Tudor Grange Acad, Solihull), b Solihull 21 Aug 1999. Elder brother of E.A.Brookes (*see above*). 6'3". RHB, RMF. Squad No 10. Debut (Warwickshire) 2017. Warwickshire 2nd XI debut 2016. England U19 2016-17 to 2017. HS 840 v Kent (Birmingham) 2019. BB 4-54 v Northants (Birmingham) 2018. LO HS 12* v Derbys (Derby) 2019 (RLC). LO BB 3-50 v Yorks (Birmingham) 2019 (RLC). T20 HS 9. T20 BB 3-26.

BURGESS, Michael Gregory Kerran (Cranleigh S; Loughborough U), b Epsom, Surrey 8 Jul 1994. RHB, RM, occ WK. Squad No 5. Loughborough MCCU 2014-15. Leicestershire 2016. Sussex 2017-19. Warwickshire debut 2019. HS 146 Sx v Notts (Hove) 2017. Wa HS 64 v Essex (Chelmsford) 2019. LO HS 58 Sx v Glamorgan (Cardiff) 2018 (RLC). T20 HS 56.

FURRER, George William (Barker C; U of New South Wales) b London 10 Oct 1998. RHB, LFM. Warwickshire 2nd XI debut 2019. Awaiting 1st XI debut.

GARRETT, George Anthony (Shrewsbury S), Harpenden, Herts 4 Mar 2000. RHB, RM. Squad No 44. Debut (Warwickshire) 2019. Warwickshire 2nd XI debut 2019. HS 24 v Essex (Birmingham) 2019. BB 2-53 v Notts (Nottingham) 2019. T20 BB 1-19.

‡^{NQ}**GREEN, Chris**topher James (Knox GS, Wahroonga), b Durban, South Africa 1 Oct 1993. RHB, OB. Awaiting f-c debut. New South Wales (l-o only) 2014-15 to 2018-19. Warwickshire debut 2019 (T20 only); captain 2020 (T20 only). Big Bash: ST 2014-15 to date. LO HS 24 NSW v Tas (Sydney, NS) 2018-19. LO BB 5-53 NSW v Q (Sydney, DO) 2018-19. T20 HS 49. T20 BB 4-14.

HAIN, Samuel Robert (Southport S, Gold Coast), b Hong Kong 16 July 1995. 5'10". RHB, OB. Squad No 16. Debut (Warwickshire) 2014; cap 2018. MCC 2018. Warwickshire 2nd XI debut 2011. UK passport (British parents). HS 208 v Northants (Birmingham) 2014. LO HS 145* EL v West Indies A (Derby) 2018. T20 HS 95.

HANNON-DALBY, Oliver James (Brooksbank S, Leeds Met U) b Halifax, Yorkshire 20 Jun 1989. 6'7". LHB, RMF. Squad No 20. Yorkshire 2008-12. Warwickshire debut 2013; cap 2019. F-c Tour (MCC): Nepal 2019-20. HS 40 v Somerset (Taunton) 2014. BB 5-11 MCC v Nepal (Kirtipur) 2019-20. Wa BB 5-18 v Somerset (Taunton) 2019. LO HS 21* Y v Warwks (Scarborough) 2012 (CB40). LO BB 5-27 v Glamorgan (Birmingham) 2015 (RLC). T20 HS 14*. T20 BB 4-20.

HOSE, Adam John (Carisbrooke S), b Newport, IoW 25 Oct 1992. 6'2". RHB, RMF. Squad No 21. Somerset 2016-17. Warwickshire debut 2018. HS 111 v Notts (Birmingham) 2019. LO HS 101* Sm v Glos (Bristol) 2017 (RLC). T20 HS 76.

LAMB, Matthew James (North Bromsgrove HS; Bromsgrove S), b Wolverhampton, Staffs 19 July 1996. 6'1". RHB, RM. Squad No 7. Debut (Warwickshire) 2016. Warwickshire 2nd XI debut 2015. HS 173 and BB 1-15 v Essex (Birmingham) 2019. LO HS 47 v West Indies A (Birmingham) 2018. LO BB – . T20 HS 35.

MILES, Craig Neil (Bradon Forest S, Swindon; Filton C, Bristol), b Swindon, Wilts 20 July 1994. Brother of A.J.Miles (Cardiff MCCU 2012). 6'4". RHB, RMF. Squad No 18. Gloucestershire 2011-18; cap 2011. Warwickshire debut 2019. HS 62* Gs v Worcs (Cheltenham) 2014. Wa HS 27 v Yorks (York) 2019. 50 wkts (3); most – 58 (2018). BB 6-63 Gs v Northants (Northampton) 2015. Wa BB 5-91 v Surrey (Oval) 2019. Hat-trick Gs v Essex (Cheltenham) 2016. LO HS 31 v Leics (Leicester) 2019 (RLC). LO BB 4-29 Gs v Yorks (Scarborough) 2015 (RLC). T20 HS 8. T20 BB 3-25.

MOUSLEY, Daniel Richard (Bablake S, Coventry), b Birmingham 8 Jul 2001. LHB, OB. Squad No 80. Debut (Warwickshire) 2019. Staffordshire 2019. England U19 2018-19. HS 3 v Essex (Chelmsford) 2019.

NORWELL, Liam Connor (Redruth SS), b Bournemouth, Dorset 27 Dec 1991. 6'3". RHB, RMF. Squad No 24. Gloucestershire 2011-18, taking 6-46 v Derbys (Bristol) on debut; cap 2011. Warwickshire debut 2019. HS 102 Gs v Derbys (Bristol) 2016. Wa HS 64 v Surrey (Birmingham) 2019. 50 wkts (2); most – 68 (2015). BB 8-43 (10-95 match) Gs v Leics (Leicester) 2017. Wa BB 7-41 v Somerset (Taunton) 2019. LO HS 16 Gs v Somerset (Bristol) 2017 (RLC). LO BB 6-52 Gs v Leics (Leicester) 2012 (CB40). T20 HS 2*. T20 BB 3-27.

NQPATEL, Jeetan Shashi, b Wellington, New Zealand 7 May 1980. 5'10". RHB, OB. Squad No 5. Wellington 1999-00 to date. Warwickshire debut 2009; cap 2012; captain 2018-19. *Wisden* 2014. **Tests** (NZ): 24 (2006-07 to 2016-17); HS 47 v I (Kolkata) 2016-17; BB 5-110 v WI (Napier) 2008-09. **LOI** (NZ): 43 (2005 to 2017); HS 34 v SL (Kingston) 2006-07; BB 3-11 v SA (Mumbai, BS) 2006-07. **IT20** (NZ): 11 (2005-06 to 2008-09); HS 5 v E (Auckland) 2012-13; BB 3-20 v SA (Johannesburg) 2005-06. F-c Tours (NZ): E 2008; SA 2005-06, 2012-13; I 2010-11, 2012, 2016-17; SL 2009, 2012-13; Z 2010-11, 2011-12; B 2008-09. HS 120 v Yorks (Birmingham) 2009. 50 wkts (7); most – 69 (2016). BB 8-36 (12-89 match) v Surrey (Birmingham) 2019. LO HS 50 v Kent (Birmingham) 2013 (Y40). LO BB 5-43 v Somerset (Birmingham) 2016 (RLC). T20 HS 34*. T20 BB 4-11.

POLLOCK, Edward John (RGS Worcester; Shrewsbury S; Collingwood C, Durham U), b High Wycombe, Bucks 10 Jul 1995. Son of A.J.Pollock (Cambridge U 1982-84); younger brother of A.W.Pollock (Cambridge MCCU & U 2013-15). 5'10". LHB, OB. Squad No 28. Durham MCCU 2015-17. Awaiting Warwickshire f-c debut. Durham 2nd XI 2015. Warwickshire 2nd XI debut 2015. Herefordshire 2014-16. HS 52 DU v Glos (Bristol) 2017. LO HS 57 v Leics (Leicester) 2019 (RLC). T20 HS. 77.

RHODES, William Michael Henry (Cottingham HS, Cottingham SFC, Hull), b Nottingham 2 Mar 1995. 6'2". LHB, RMF. Squad No 35. Yorkshire 2014-15 to 2016. Essex 2016 (on loan). Warwickshire debut 2018; captain 2020. MCC 2019. England U19 2014. F-c Tour (MCC): Nepal 2019-20. HS 137 v Glos (Birmingham) 2018. BB 5-17 v Essex (Chelmsford) 2019. LO HS 69 v Worcs (Birmingham) 2018 (RLC) and 69 v West Indies A (Birmingham) 2018. LO BB 2-22 Y v Essex (Chelmsford) 2015 (RLC). T20 HS 45. T20 BB 3-27.

SIBLEY, Dominic Peter (Whitgift S, Croydon), b Epsom, Surrey 5 Sep 1995. 6'2". RHB, OB. Squad No 45. Surrey 2013-17. Warwickshire debut 2017; cap 2019. MCC 2019. England U19 2012-13 to 2014. **Tests**: 6 (2019-20); HS 133* v SA (Cape Town) 2019-20. F-c Tours: SA 2019-20; NZ 2019-20; SL 2019-20. 1000 runs (1): 1428 (2019). HS 244 v Kent (Canterbury) 2019. BB 2-103 Sy v Hants (Southampton) 2016. Wa BB – . LO HS 115 v West Indies A (Birmingham) 2018. LO BB 1-20 Sy v Essex (Chelmsford) 2016 (RLC). T20 HS 74*. T20 BB 2-33.

SIDEBOTTOM, Ryan Nathan, b Shepparton, Victoria, Australia 14 Aug 1989. UK passport. 6'0". RHB, RMF. Squad No 22. Victoria 2012-13. Warwickshire debut 2017. HS 27* v Kent (Birmingham) 2019. BB 6-35 (10-96 match) v Northants (Northampton) 2018.

STONE, Oliver Peter (Thorpe St Andrew HS), b Norwich, Norfolk 9 Oct 1993. 6'1". RHB, RF. Squad No 6. Northamptonshire 2012-16. Warwickshire debut 2017. Norfolk 2011. **Tests**: 1 (2019); HS 19 and BB 3-29 v Ire (Lord's) 2019. **LOI**: 4 (2018-19); HS 9* and BB 1-23 v SL (Dambulla) 2018-19. HS 60 Nh v Kent (Northampton) 2016. Wa HS 42* v Glamorgan (Colwyn Bay) 2018. BB 8-80 v Sussex (Birmingham) 2018. LO HS 24* Nh v Derbys (Derby) 2015 (RLC). LO BB 4-71 v Worcs (Birmingham) 2018 (RLC). T20 HS 8*. T20 BB 3-22.

THOMSON, Alexander Thomas (Kings S, Macclesfield; Denstone C; Cardiff Met U), b Macclesfield, Cheshire 30 Oct 1993. 6'2". RHB, OB. Squad No 29. Cardiff MCCU 2014-16. Warwickshire debut 2017. Staffordshire 2013-16. F-c Tour (MCC): Nepal 2019-20. HS 26 v Hants (Birmingham) 2017. BB 6-138 CfU v Hants (Southampton) 2016. Wa BB 1-21 v Yorks (Birmingham) 2019. LO HS 68* v Derbys (Derby) 2019 (RLC). LO BB 3-27 v Lancs (Birmingham) 2019 (RLC). T20 HS 14. T20 BB 4-35.

WOAKES, Christopher Roger (Barr Beacon Language S, Walsall), b Birmingham 2 March 1989. 6'2". RHB, RFM. Squad No 19. Debut (Warwickshire) 2006; cap 2009. Wellington 2012-13. MCC 2009. IPL: KKR 2017. RCB 2018. Big Bash: ST 2013-14. Herefordshire 2006-07. *Wisden* 2016. **ECB Test & LO Central Contract 2019-20. Tests**: 33 (2013 to 2019-20); HS 137* v I (Lord's) 2018; BB 6-17 v Ire (Lord's) 2017. **LOI**: 101 (2010-11 to 2019-20); HS 95* v SL (Nottingham) 2016; BB 6-45 v A (Brisbane) 2010-11. **IT20**: 8 (2010-11 to 2015-16); HS 37 v P (Sharjah) 2015-16; BB 2-40 v P (Dubai, DSC) 2015-16. F-c Tours: A 2017-18; SA 2015-16, 2019-20; WI 2010-11 (EL); NZ 2017-18, 2019-20; I 2016-17; SL 2013-14 (EL), 2019-20; B 2016-17; UAE 2015-16 (v P). HS 152* v Derbys (Derby) 2013. 50 wkts (3); most – 59 (2016). BB 9-36 v Durham (Birmingham) 2016. LO HS 95* (*see LOI*). LO BB 6-45 (*see LOI*). T20 HS 57*. T20 BB 4-21.

YATES, Robert Michael (Warwick S), b Solihull 19 Sep 1999. 6'0". LHB, OB. Squad No 17. Debut (Warwickshire) 2019. Warwickshire 2nd XI debut 2017. Staffordshire 2018. HS 141 v Somerset (Birmingham) 2019. LO HS 66 v Leics (Leicester) 2019.

RELEASED/RETIRED

(Having made a County 1st XI appearance in 2019)

NQAGAR, Ashton Charles (De La Salle C), b Melbourne, Australia 14 Oct 1993. Elder brother of W.A.Agar (S Australia, Victoria (l-o only) and AS 2016-17 to date). LHB, SLA. W Australia 2012-13 to date. Middlesex 2018 (T20 only). Warwickshire 2019 (T20 only). Big Bash: PS 2013-14 to date. **Tests** (A): 4 (2013 to 2017); HS 98 v E (Nottingham) 2013 – on debut, a record score for a No 11, sharing a then world record 10th wkt partnership of 163 with P.J.Hughes; BB 3-46 v B (Dhaka) 2017. **LOI** (A): 13 (2015 to 2019); HS 46 v E (Cardiff) 2018; BB 2-48 v E (Chester-le-St) 2018. **IT20** (A): 24 (2015-16 to 2019-20); HS 29 v E (Birmingham) 2018; BB 5-24 v SA (Johannesburg) 2019-20. F-c Tours: A (A): E 2013; I 2012-13, 2015 (Aus A); B 2017; Ire/Scot 2013 (Aus A). HS 106 WA v Tas (Perth) 2015-16. BB 6-110 (10-141 match) WA v NSW (Sydney) 2016-17. LO HS 64 WA v Tas (Sydney, NS) 2014-15. LO BB 5-39 Aus A v India A (Chennai) 2015. T20 HS 68. T20 BB 5-24.

MELLOR, Alexander James (Westwood C, Leek; Staffordshire U), b Stoke-on-Trent, Staffs 22 Jul 1991. 5'10". LHB, WK. Derbyshire 2016. Warwickshire 2016-17. Staffordshire 2014-15. HS 59 v Oxford MCCU (Oxford) 2017. CC HS 44 De v Essex (Derby) 2016. LO HS 58 v Derbys (Derby) 2018 (RLC). T20 HS 18*.

MILNES, Thomas Patrick (Heart of England S, Coventry), b Stourbridge, Worcs 6 Oct 1992. 5'11". RHB, RMF. Warwickshire 2011-19. Derbyshire 2015-17. HS 56 De v Glos (Derby) 2016. Wa HS 52* and BB 7-39 v Oxford MCCU (Oxford) 2013. CC BB 6-93 De v Essex (Derby) 2016. LO HS 16 v Worcs (Birmingham) 2013 (Y40). LO BB 2-73 v Northants (Birmingham) 2013 (Y40). T20 HS 0. T20 BB – .

PANAYI, George David (Shrewsbury S), b Enfield, Middx 23 Sep 1997. 6'3". RHB, RFM. Warwickshire 2017. Warwickshire 2nd XI debut 2015. England U19 2017. HS 16 and BB 3-41 v Lancs (Birmingham) 2017. LO HS 26 v Derbys (Derby) 2019 (RLC). LO BB 2-44 v Warwks (Birmingham) 2019 (RLC).

THOMASON, A.D. – *see SUSSEX.*

WAINMAN, James Charles (Leeds GS), b Harrogate 25 Jan 1993. 6'4". RHB, LMF. Warwickshire 2019. HS – and BB 3-112 v Kent (Canterbury) 2019. LO HS 33 and LO BB 3-51 v Sri Lanka A (Leeds) 2014. T20 HS 12*. T20 BB 1-27.

WARWICKSHIRE 2019

RESULTS SUMMARY

	Place	Won	Lost	Tied	Drew	NR
Specsavers County Champ (1st Division)	7th	3	6		5	
All First-Class Matches		3	6		5	
Royal London One-Day Cup (North Group)	7th	2	5	1		
Vitality Blast (North Group)	8th	4	7	1		2

SPECSAVERS COUNTY CHAMPIONSHIP AVERAGES

BATTING AND FIELDING

Cap		M	I	NO	HS	Runs	Avge	100	50	Ct/St
2019	D.P.Sibley	13	21	2	244	1324	69.68	5	5	5
2018	S.R.Hain	12	19	3	129*	822	51.37	2	3	16
	M.G.K.Burgess	5	7	1	64	248	41.33	–	3	4
	W.M.H.Rhodes	14	23	–	109	770	33.47	1	5	13
	R.M.Yates	12	19	–	141	570	30.00	1	2	10
	L.C.Norwell	4	6	2	64	120	30.00	–	1	1
	M.J.Lamb	5	8	1	173	208	29.71	1	–	1
2012	J.S.Patel	14	22	4	70*	365	20.27	–	2	8
2007	T.R.Ambrose	12	20	–	107	399	19.95	1	–	39/3
	H.J.H.Brookes	11	17	2	84	285	19.00	–	1	4
	A.J.Hose	11	20	–	111	340	17.00	1	–	3
	L.Banks	8	13	–	50	220	16.92	–	1	14
	G.A.Garrett	3	4	2	24	32	16.00	–	–	1
	C.N.Miles	5	8	1	27	77	11.00	–	–	2
2019	O.J.Hannon-Dalby	12	15	5	17*	102	10.20	–	–	2
	O.P.Stone	2	4	–	21	22	5.50	–	–	–

Also played: E.A.Brookes (1 match) 0; T.J.Lester (2) 0*, 0* (1 ct); B.W.M.Mike (2) 45*, 7, 72; T.P.Milnes (1) 12, 1; D.R.Mousley 3, 0; R.N.Sidebottom (1) 27*, 4*; A.T.Thomson (2) 9, 18; J.C.Wainman did not bat.

BOWLING

	O	M	R	W	Avge	Best	5wI	10wM
O.J.Hannon-Dalby	399	108	1129	44	25.65	5- 18	2	–
L.C.Norwell	110.5	30	360	14	25.71	7- 41	1	–
J.S.Patel	635.1	182	1712	64	26.75	8- 36	4	2
W.M.H.Rhodes	149.1	37	425	15	28.33	5- 17	1	–
C.N.Miles	118.4	14	542	17	31.88	5- 91	1	–
H.J.H.Brookes	315.3	52	1350	32	42.18	3-100	–	–
Also bowled:								
G.A.Garrett	84.5	19	302	8	37.75	2- 53	–	–
O.P.Stone	66.3	10	270	7	38.57	5- 93	1	–
T.J.Lester	55	11	233	5	46.60	4- 41	–	–

L.Banks 3-0-9-0; E.A.Brookes 12-2-41-0; M.J.Lamb 34.2-3-166-3; B.W.M.Mike 36-1-163-1; T.P.Milnes 13-2-50-0; R.N.Sidebottom 34-6-119-2; A.T.Thomson 10-0-54-1; J.C.Wainman 23-4-112-3.

Warwickshire played no first-class fixtures outside the County Championship in 2019. The First-Class Averages (pp 226–241) give the records of Warwickshire players in all first-class county matches, with the exception of M.G.K.Burgess, S.R.Hain, B.W.M.Mike, D.P.Sibley and O.P.Stone, whose first-class figures for Warwickshire are as above.

WARWICKSHIRE RECORDS

FIRST-CLASS CRICKET

Highest Total	For 810-4d		v	Durham	Birmingham	1994
	V 887		by	Yorkshire	Birmingham	1896
Lowest Total	For 16		v	Kent	Tonbridge	1913
	V 15		by	Hampshire	Birmingham	1922
Highest Innings	For 501*	B.C.Lara	v	Durham	Birmingham	1994
	V 322	I.V.A.Richards	for	Somerset	Taunton	1985

Highest Partnership for each Wicket

1st	377*	N.F.Horner/K.Ibadulla	v	Surrey	The Oval	1960
2nd	465*	J.A.Jameson/R.B.Kanhai	v	Glos	Birmingham	1974
3rd	327	S.P.Kinneir/W.G.Quaife	v	Lancashire	Birmingham	1901
4th	470	A.I.Kallicharran/G.W.Humpage	v	Lancashire	Southport	1982
5th	335	J.O.Troughton/T.R.Ambrose	v	Hampshire	Birmingham	2009
6th	327	L.J.Evans/T.R.Ambrose	v	Sussex	Birmingham	2015
7th	289*	I.R.Bell/T.Frost	v	Sussex	Horsham	2004
8th	228	A.J.W.Croom/R.E.S.Wyatt	v	Worcs	Dudley	1925
9th	233	I.J.L.Trott/J.S.Patel	v	Yorkshire	Birmingham	2009
10th	214	N.V.Knight/A.Richardson	v	Hampshire	Birmingham	2002

Best Bowling	For 10-41	J.D.Bannister	v	Comb Servs	Birmingham	1959
(Innings)	V 10-36	H.Verity	for	Yorkshire	Leeds	1931
Best Bowling	For 15-76	S.Hargreave	v	Surrey	The Oval	1903
(Match)	V 17-92	A.P.Freeman	for	Kent	Folkestone	1932

Most Runs – Season	2417	M.J.K.Smith	(av 60.42)	1959
Most Runs – Career	35146	D.L.Amiss	(av 41.64)	1960-87
Most 100s – Season	9	A.I.Kallicharran		1984
	9	B.C.Lara		1994
Most 100s – Career	78	D.L.Amiss		1960-87
Most Wkts – Season	180	W.E.Hollies	(av 15.13)	1946
Most Wkts – Career	2201	W.E.Hollies	(av 20.45)	1932-57
Most Career W-K Dismissals	800	E.J.Smith	(662 ct; 138 st)	1904-30
Most Career Catches in the Field	422	M.J.K.Smith		1956-75

LIMITED-OVERS CRICKET

Highest Total	**50ov**	392-5		v	Oxfordshire	Birmingham	1984
	40ov	321-7		v	Leics	Birmingham	2010
	T20	242-2		v	Derbyshire	Birmingham	2015
Lowest Total	**50ov**	94		v	Glos	Bristol	2000
	40ov	59		v	Yorkshire	Leeds	2001
	T20	73		v	Somerset	Taunton	2013
Highest Innings	**50ov**	206	A.I.Kallicharran	v	Oxfordshire	Birmingham	1984
	40ov	137	I.R.Bell	v	Yorkshire	Birmingham	2005
	T20	158*	B.B.McCullum	v	Derbyshire	Birmingham	2015
Best Bowling	**50ov**	7-32	R.G.D.Willis	v	Yorkshire	Birmingham	1981
	40ov	6-15	A.A.Donald	v	Yorkshire	Birmingham	1995
	T20	5-19	N.M.Carter	v	Worcs	Birmingham	2005

WORCESTERSHIRE

Formation of Present Club: 11 March 1865
Inaugural First-Class Match: 1899
Colours: Dark Green and Black
Badge: Shield Argent a Fess between three Pears Sable
County Championships: (5) 1964, 1965, 1974, 1988, 1989
NatWest Trophy Winners: (1) 1994
Benson and Hedges Cup Winners: (1) 1991
Pro 40/National League (Div 1) Winners: (1) 2007
Sunday League Winners: (3) 1971, 1987, 1988
Twenty20 Cup Winners: (1) 2018

Chief Executive: tba, County Ground, Blackfinch New Road, Worcester, WR2 4QQ • Tel: 01905 748474 Email: info@wccc.co.uk • Web: www.wccc.co.uk • Twitter: @WorcsCCC (76,426 followers)

Head of Player and Coaches Development: Kevin Sharp. **First Team Coach**: Alex Gidman. **Head Bowling Coach**: Alan Richardson. **Captains**: J.Leach (f-c and l-o) and M.M.Ali (T20). **Overseas Players**: H.D.Rutherford and A.J.Turner (T20 only). **2020 Testimonial**: none. **Head Groundsman**: Tim Packwood. **Scorer**: Sue Drinkwater (home) and Philip Mellish (away). **Vitality Blast Name**: Worcestershire Rapids. ‡ New registration. NQ Not qualified for England.

Worcestershire revised their capping policy in 2002 and now award players with their County Colours when they make their Championship debut.

ALI, Moeen Munir (Moseley S), b Birmingham, Warwks 18 Jun 1987. Brother of A.K.Ali (Worcs, Glos and Leics 2000-12), cousin of Kabir Ali (Worcs, Rajasthan, Hants and Lancs 1999-2014). 6'0". LHB, OB. Squad No 8. Warwickshire 2005-06. Worcestershire debut 2007. Moors SC 2011-12. MT 2012-13. MCC 2012. IPL: RCB 2018-19. PCA 2013. *Wisden* 2014. **ECB L-O Central Contract 2019-20. Tests**: 60 (2014 to 2019); 1000 runs (1): 1078 (2016); HS 155* v SL (Chester-le-St) 2016; BB 6-53 v SA (Lord's) 2017. Hat-trick v SA (Oval) 2017. **LOI**: 102 (2013-14 to 2019-20); HS 128 v Scotland (Christchurch) 2014-15; BB 4-46 v A (Manchester) 2018. **IT20**: 28 (2013-14 to 2019-20); HS 72* v A (Cardiff) 2015; BB 2-21 v I (Kanpur) 2016-17. F-c Tours: A 2017-18; SA 2015-16; WI 2014-15, 2018-19; NZ 2017-18; I 2016-17; SL 2013-14 (EL), 2018-19; B 2016-17; UAE 2015-16 (v P). 1000 runs (2); most – 1420 (2013). HS 250 v Glamorgan (Worcester) 2013. BB 6-29 (12-96 match) v Lancs (Manchester) 2012. LO HS 158 v Sussex (Horsham) 2011 (CB40); BB 4-46 v A (Manchester) 2018. LO HS 158 v Sussex (Horsham) 2011 (CB40); BB 4-33 v Notts (Nottingham) 2018 (RLC). T20 HS 121*. T20 BB 5-34.

BARNARD, Edward George (Shrewsbury S), b Shrewsbury, Shrops 20 Nov 1995. Younger brother of M.R.Barnard (Oxford MCCU 2010). 6'1". RHB, RMF. Squad No 30. Debut (Worcestershire) 2015. Shropshire 2012. England U19 2012-13 to 2014. HS 75 v Durham (Worcester) 2017. BB 6-37 (11-89 match) v Somerset (Taunton) 2018. LO HS 61 v Leics (Leicester) 2019 (RLC). LO BB 3-26 v Yorks (Worcester) 2019 (RLC). T20 HS 42*. T20 BB 3-29.

BROWN, Patrick Rhys (Bourne GS, Lincs), b Peterborough, Cambs 23 Aug 1998. 6'2". RHB, RMF. Squad No 36. Debut (Worcestershire) 2017. Worcestershire 2nd XI debut 2016. Lincolnshire 2016. **IT20**: 4 (2019-20); HS 4* v NZ (Wellington) 2019-20; BB 1-29 v NZ (Napier) 2019-20. HS 5* v Sussex (Worcester) 2017. BB 2-15 v Leics (Worcester) 2017. LO HS 3 v Somerset (Worcester) 2019 (RLC). LO BB 3-53 v Kent (Worcester) 2018 (RLC). T20 HS 4*. T20 BB 4-21.

COX, Oliver Ben (Bromsgrove S), b Wordsley, Stourbridge 2 Feb 1992. 5'10". RHB, WK. Squad No 10. Debut (Worcestershire) 2009. MCC 2017, 2019. HS 124 v Glos (Cheltenham) 2017. LO HS 122* v Kent (Worcester) 2018 (RLC). T20 HS 59*.

DELL, Joshua Jamie (Cheltenham C), b Tenbury Wells 26 Sep 1997. 6'3". RHB, RMF. Squad No 52. Debut (Worcestershire) 2019. Worcestershire 2nd XI debut 2015. England U19 2016. HS 61 v Durham (Worcester) 2019. LO HS 46 v West Indies A (Worcester) 2018.

D'OLIVEIRA, Brett Louis (Worcester SFC), b Worcester 28 Feb 1992. Son of D.B.D'Oliveira (Worcs 1982-95), grandson of B.L.D'Oliveira (Worcs, EP and England 1964-80). 5'9". RHB, LB. Squad No 15. Debut (Worcestershire) 2012. MCC 2018. HS 202* v Glamorgan (Cardiff) 2016. BB 7-92 v Glamorgan (Cardiff) 2019. LO HS 79 North v South (Bridgetown) 2017-18. LO BB 3-35 v Warwks (Worcester) 2013 (Y40). T20 HS 64. T20 BB 4-26.

FELL, Thomas Charles (Oakham S; Oxford Brookes U), b Hillingdon, Middx 17 Oct 1993. 6'1". RHB, WK, occ OB. Squad No 29. Oxford MCCU 2013. Worcestershire debut 2013. 1000 runs (1): 1127 (2015). HS 171 v Middx (Worcester) 2015. LO HS 116* v Lancs (Worcester) 2016 (RLC). T20 HS 28.

FINCH, Adam William (Kingswinford S; Oldswinford Hospital SFC), b Wordsley, Stourbridge 28 May 2000. 6'4". RHB, RMF. England U19 2018 to 2018-19. Debut (Worcestershire) 2019. Worcestershire 2nd XI debut 2017. HS 18* v Australians (Worcester) 2019. CC HS 17 and BB 2-23 v Glos (Worcester) 2019.

HAYNES, Jack Alexander (Malvern C), b Worcester 30 Jan 2001. Son of G.R.Haynes (Worcestershire 1991-99); younger brother of J.L.Haynes (Worcestershire 2nd XI 2015-16). 6'1". RHB, OB. Squad No 17. Debut (Worcestershire) 2019. Worcestershire 2nd XI debut 2016. England U19 2018. HS 31 v Glamorgan (Worcester) 2019. LO HS 33 v West Indies A (Worcester) 2018.

LEACH, Joseph (Shrewsbury S; Leeds U), b Stafford 30 Oct 1990. Elder brother of S.G.Leach (Oxford MCCU 2014-16). 6'1". RHB, RMF. Squad No 23. Leeds/Bradford MCCU 2012. Worcestershire debut 2012; captain 2017 to date. Staffordshire 2008-09. HS 114 v Glos (Cheltenham) 2013. 50 wkts (2): 69 (2017). BB 6-73 v Warwks (Birmingham) 2015. LO HS 63 v Yorks (Leeds) 2016 (RLC). LO BB 4-30 v Northants (Worcester) 2015 (RLC). T20 HS 24. T20 BB 5-33.

‡**LIBBY, Jacob** ('Jake') Daniel (Plymouth C; UWIC), b Plymouth, Devon 3 Jan 1993. 5'9". RHB, OB. Squad No 2. Cardiff MCCU 2014. Nottinghamshire 2014-19, scoring 108 v Sussex (Nottingham) on debut. Northamptonshire 2016 (on loan). Cornwall 2011-14. HS 144 Nt v Durham (Chester-le-St) 2016. BB 1-13 Nh v Leics (Leicester) 2014. LO HS 66 Nt v Leics (Nottingham) 2019 (RLC). T20 HS 58. T20 BB 1-11.

MILTON, Alexander Geoffrey (Malvern C; Cardiff U), b Redhill, Surrey 19 May 1996. 5'7". RHB, LB, occ WK. Squad No 12. Cardiff MCCU 2016-18. Worcestershire debut 2018. Worcestershire 2nd XI debut 2015. Glamorgan 2nd XI 2015. Herefordshire 2016. HS 104* v Somerset (Worcester) 2018 – on county f-c debut, sharing Wo record 10th wkt partnership of 136 with S.J.Magoffin. LO HS 0.

MITCHELL, Daryl Keith Henry (Prince Henry's HS; University C, Worcester), b Badsey, near Evesham 25 Nov 1983. 5'10". RHB, RM. Squad No 27. Debut (Worcestershire) 2005; captain 2011-16; benefit 2016. Mountaineers 2011-12. MCC 2015. 1000 runs (5); most – 1334 (2014). HS 298 v Somerset (Taunton) 2009. BB 4-49 v Yorks (Leeds) 2009. LO HS 107 v Sussex (Hove) 2013 (Y40). LO BB 4-19 v Northants (Milton Keynes) 2014 (RLC). T20 HS 68*. T20 BB 5-28.

MORRIS, Charles Andrew John (King's C, Taunton; Oxford Brookes U), b Hereford 6 Jul 1992. 6'0". RHB, RMF. Squad No 31. Oxford MCCU 2012-14. Worcestershire debut 2013. MCC Univs 2012. Devon 2011-12. HS 53* v Australians (Worcester) 2019. CC HS 29* v Glos (Worcester) 2019. 50 wkts (2); most – 56 (2014). BB 7-45 v Leics (Leicester) 2019. LO HS 16* v Northants (Milton Keynes) 2014 (RLC). LO BB 4-33 v Durham (Gosforth) 2018 (RLC). T20 HS 3. T20 BB 2-30.

NQ**PARNELL, Wayne** Dillon (Grey HS), b Port Elizabeth, South Africa 30 Jul 1989. 6'1". LHB, LFM. Squad No 7. E Province 2006-07 to 2010-11. Warriors 2008-09 to 2014-15. Kent 2009-17. Sussex 2011. Cape Cobras 2015-16 to 2016-17. Worcestershire debut 2018 (Kolpak signing). Glamorgan 2015 (T20 only). IPL: PW 2011-13. DD 2014. **Tests** (SA): 6 (2009-10 to 2017-18); HS 23 and BB 4-51 v SL (Johannesburg) 2016-17. **LOI** (SA): 65 (2008-09 to 2017); HS 56 v P (Sharjah) 2013-14; BB 5-48 v E (Cape Town) 2009-10. **IT20** (SA): 40 (2008-09 to 2017); HS 29* v A (Johannesburg) 2011-12; BB 4-13 v WI (Oval) 2009. F-c Tours (SA A): A 2016; I 2009-10 (SA), 2015; Ire 2012. HS 111* Cobras v Warriors (Paarl) 2015-16. CC HS 90 K v Glamorgan (Canterbury) 2009. Wo HS 63 and CC BB 5-47 v Lancs (Manchester) 2019. BB 7-51 Cobras v Dolphins (Cape Town) 2015-16. LO HS 129 Warriors v Lions (Potchefstroom) 2013-14. LO BB 6-51 Warriors v Knights (Kimberley) 2013-14. T20 HS 99. T20 BB 4-13.

PENNINGTON, Dillon Young (Wrekin C), b Shrewsbury, Shrops 26 Feb 1999. 6'2". RHB, RMF. Squad No 22. Debut (Worcestershire) 2018. Worcestershire 2nd XI debut 2017. Shropshire 2017. HS 37 v Somerset (Worcester) 2018. BB 4-53 v Yorks (Scarborough) 2018. LO HS 4* and LO BB 5-67 v West Indies A (Worcester) 2018. T20 HS 6*. T20 BB 4-9.

NQ**RUTHERFORD, Hamish** Duncan, b Dunedin, New Zealand 27 Apr 1989. Son of K.R.Rutherford (Gauteng, Otago, Transvaal & New Zealand 1982-83 to 1999-00). Nephew of I.A.Rutherford (C Districts, Otago & Worcestershire 1974-75 to 1983-84). 5'10". LHB, SLA. Squad No 72. Otago 2008-09 to date. Essex 2013. Derbyshire 2015-16. Worcestershire debut 2019. **Tests** (NZ): 16 (2012-13 to 2014-15); HS 171 v E (Dunedin) 2012-13 – on debut. **LOI** (NZ): 4 (2012-13 to 2013-14); HS 11 v E (Napier) 2012-13. **IT20** (NZ): 7 (2012-13 to 2013-14); HS 62 v E (Oval) 2013. F-c Tours (NZ): E 2013, 2014 (NZ A); WI 2014; B 2013-14. 1000 runs (0+1): 1077 (2012-13). HS 239 Otago v Wellington (Dunedin) 2011-12. CC HS 123 v Leics (Leicester) 2019 – on Wo debut. BB –. LO HS 155 Otago v CD (Dunedin) 2019-20. LO BB 1-4 Otago v Wellington (Dunedin) 2017-18. T20 HS 106.

SCRIMSHAW, George Louis Sheridan (John Taylor HS, Burton), b Burton-on-Trent, Staffs 10 Feb 1998. 6'6". RHB, RMF. Squad No 9. Worcestershire 2nd XI debut 2016. Awaiting f-c debut. Missed entire 2018 and 2019 seasons through injury. T20 HS 1*. T20 BB 1-20.

TONGUE, Joshua Charles (King's S, Worcester; Worcester SFC), b Redditch 15 Nov 1997. 6'5". RHB, RM. Squad No 24. Debut (Worcestershire) 2016. Worcestershire 2nd XI debut 2015. HS 41 and BB 6-97 v Glamorgan (Worcester) 2017. LO HS 34 v Warwks (Worcester) 2019 (RLC). LO BB 2-35 v Lancs (Manchester) 2019 (RLC). T20 HS 2*. T20 BB 2-32.

‡**NQTURNER, Ashton** James, b Perth, Australia 25 Jan 1993. 6'3". RHB, OB. Squad No 70. W Australia 2013-14 to date. IPL: RR 2019. Big Bash: PS 2013-14 to date. Joins Worcestershire in 2020 (T20 only). **LOI** (A): 6 (2018-19 to 2019-20); HS 84* v I (Mohali) 2018-19. **IT20** (A): 11 (2016-17 to 2019-20); HS 22* v SL (Melbourne) 2019-20; BB 2-12 v SL (Melbourne) 2016-17. HS 110 WA v Tas (Perth) 2016-17. BB 6-111 WA v NSW (Perth) 2016-17. LO HS 84* (*see LOI*). LO BB 2-26 WA v NSW (Sydney, NS) 2016-17. T20 HS 73. T20 BB 2-3.

TWOHIG, Benjamin Jake (Malvern C), b Dewsbury, Yorks 13 Apr 1998. 5'9". RHB, SLA. Squad No 42. Debut (Worcestershire) 2018. Worcestershire 2nd XI debut 2014. Missed entire 2019 season with anterior cruciate ligament injury. HS 35 v Notts (Nottingham) 2018. BB 2-47 v Yorks (Worcester) 2018. LO HS 1 and LO BB – v West Indies A (Worcester) 2018.

WESSELS, Mattheus Hendrik ('**Riki**') (Woodridge C, Pt Elizabeth; Northampton U), b Marogudoore, Queensland, Australia 12 Nov 1985. Left Australia when 2 months old. Qualified for England after gaining a UK passport in July 2016. Son of K.C.Wessels (OFS, Sussex, WP, NT, Q, EP, GW, Australia and South Africa 1973-74 to 1999-00). 5'11". RHB, WK. Squad No 99. MCC 2004. Northamptonshire 2005-09. Nondescripts 2007-08. MWR 2009-10 to 2011-12. Nottinghamshire 2011-18; cap 2014. Worcestershire debut 2019. Big Bash: SS 2014-15. 1000 runs (2); most – 1213 (2014). HS 202* Nt v Sussex (Nottingham) 2017. Wo HS 118 v Durham (Worcester) 2019. BB 1-10 MWR v MT (Bulawayo) 2009-10. LO HS 146 Nt v Northants (Nottingham) 2016 (RLC). LO BB 1-0 MWR v MT (Bulawayo) 2009-10. T20 HS 110.

WESTBURY, Oliver ('**Olly**') Edward (Ellowes Hall Sports C, Dudley; Shrewsbury S), b Dudley, Warwicks 2 Jul 1997. 5'10". RHB, OB. Squad No 19. Debut (Worcestershire) 2018. Worcestershire 2nd XI debut 2015. England U19 2016. No 1st XI appearances in 2019. HS 22 v Essex (Chelmsford) 2018. BB – . LO HS 8 v West Indies A (Worcester) 2018. T20 HS 24.

WHITELEY, Ross Andrew (Repton S), b Sheffield, Yorks 13 Sep 1988. 6'2". LHB, LM. Squad No 44. Derbyshire 2008-13. Worcestershire debut 2013. HS 130* De v Kent (Derby) 2011. Wo HS 101 v Yorks (Scarborough) 2015. BB 2-6 De v Hants (Derby) 2012. Wo BB 2-35 v Middx (Worcester) 2019. LO HS 131 v Leics (Leicester) 2019 (RLC). LO BB 1-11 v Lancs (Manchester) 2019 (RLC). T20 HS 91*. T20 BB 1-10.

RELEASED/RETIRED

(Having made a County 1st XI appearance in 2019)

NQFERGUSON, Callum James, b North Adelaide, Australia 21 Nov 1984. RHB, RM. S Australia 2004-05 to date. Worcestershire 2019. IPL: PW 2011-12. Big Bash: AS 2011-12 to 2013-14. MR 2014-15 to 2016-17. ST 2017-18 to date. **Tests** (A): 1 (2016-17); HS 3 v SA (Hobart) 2016-17. **LOI** (A): 30 (2008-09 to 2010-11); HS 71* v E (Oval) 2009. **IT20** (A): 3 (2008-09 to 2009); HS 8 (twice). F-c Tours (Aus A): I 2015; Z 2011. HS 213 SA v Tas (Hobart) 2015-16. Wo HS 127 v Derbys (Kidderminster) 2019. BB 2-32 SA v Tas (Hobart) 2013-14. HS 192 v Leics (Worcester) 2018 (RLC) – Wo record on county debut. LO BB 1-8 SA v Vic (Sydney, BO) 2015-16. T20 HS 113*.

^{NQ}**GUPTILL, Martin** James (Avondale C), b Auckland, New Zealand 30 Sep 1986. 6'3". RHB, OB. Auckland 2005-06 to date. Derbyshire 2011-15; cap 2012. Worcestershire 2018. Lancashire 2016 (l-o and T20 only). IPL: MI 2016. KXIP 2017. SH 2019. Big Bash: ST 2012-13. **Tests** (NZ): 47 (2008-09 to 2016-17); HS 189 v B (Hamilton) 2009-10; BB 3-11 v Z (Bulawayo) 2016. **LOI** (NZ): 183 (2008-09 to 2019-20); 1000 runs (1): 1489 (2015); HS 237* v WI (Wellington) 2014-15, 2nd highest score in all LOI; BB 2-6 v I (Delhi) 2016-17. **IT20** (NZ): 88 (2008-09 to 2019-20); HS 105 v A (Auckland) 2017-18; BB – . F-c Tours (NZ): E 2013, 2015; A 2011-12, 2015-16; SA 2012-13, 2016; WI 2012; I 2008-09 (NZ A), 2010-11, 2012, 2016-17; SL 2009, 2012-13; Z 2010-11 (NZ A), 2011-12, 2016. HS 227 De v Glos (Bristol) 2015. Wo HS 111 v Lancs (Worcester) 2018. BB 3-11 (*see Tests*). Wo BB 1-12 v Notts (Nottingham) 2018. LO HS 237* (*see LOI*). LO BB 2-6 (*see LOI*). T20 HS 120*. T20 BB – .

RHODES, G.H. – *see LEICESTERSHIRE.*

MIDDLESEX RELEASED/RETIRED (continued from p 177)

BURGESS, M.G.K. – *see WARWICKSHIRE.*

^{NQ}**CAREY, Alex** Tyson, b Loxton, S Australia 27 Aug 1991. LHB, WK, occ RMF. S Australia 2012-13 to date. Sussex 2019. Big Bash: AS 2016-17 to date. **LOI** (A): 36 (2017-18 to 2019-20); HS 85 v SA (Manchester) 2019. **IT20** (A): 28 (2017-18 to 2019-20); HS 37* v P (Harare) 2018. F-c Tours (A): E 2019; I 2018-19 (Aus A). HS 143 SA v WA (Perth) 2019-20. Sx HS 69* v Middx (Hove) 2019. LO HS 92 SA v Vic (Hobart) 2017-18. T20 HS 100.

KAPIL, Aneesh (Denstone C), b Wolverhampton 3 Aug 1993. 5'10". RHB, RFM. Worcestershire 2011-13. Surrey 2014-15. Sussex 2019. HS 104* Sy v New Zealand A (Oval) 2014. CC HS 54 Wo v Sussex (Horsham) 2011. Sx HS 33* v Australia A (Arundel) 2019. BB 3-17 Wo v Notts (Worcester) 2012. LO HS 59 Sy v Somerset (Oval) 2014 (RLC). LO BB 1-18 Wo v Netherlands (Worcester) 2011 (CB40). T20 HS 13. T20 BB 3-9.

^{NQ}**MIR HAMZA**, b Karachi, Pakistan 10 Sep 1992. LHB, LMF. Karachi Whites 2012-13 to 2013-14. Karachi Dolphins 2014-15. United Bank 2015-16 to 2017-18. National Bank 2018-19. Sussex 2019. Sindh 2019-20. **Tests** (P): 1 (2018-19); HS 4* and BB 1-40 v A (Abu Dhabi) 2018-19. HS 25 NBP v Peshawar (Faisalabad) 2018-19. Sx HS 8 v Durham (Chester-le-St) 2019. BB 7-59 UB v SSGC (Sialkot) 2016-17. Sx BB 4-51 v Northants (Northampton) 2019. LO HS 49 KD v Rawalpindi Rams (Karachi) 2014-15. LO BB 4-27 KD v Hyderabad Hawks (Karachi) 2013-14. T20 HS 5. T20 BB 4-28.

SAKANDE, Abidine (Ardingly C; St John's C, Oxford), b Chester 22 Sep 1994. 6'1". RHB, RFM. Oxford U 2014-15. Oxford MCCU 2015-16. Sussex 2016-19. HS 33 OU v Cambridge U (Cambridge) 2015. Sx HS 17 and BB 5-43 v South Africa A (Arundel) 2017. CC HS 15 v Lancs (Manchester) 2019. CC BB 3-44 v Northants (Northampton) 2018. LO HS 7* v South Africans (Hove) 2017. LO BB 2-53 v Somerset (Taunton) 2018 (RLC).

TOPLEY, R.J.W. – *see SURREY.*

WORCESTERSHIRE 2019

RESULTS SUMMARY

	Place	Won	Lost	Drew	NR
Specsavers County Champ (2nd Division)	9th	3	7	4	
All First-Class Matches		3	7	5	
Royal London One-Day Cup (North Group)	QF	6	3		
Vitality Blast (North Group)	Finalists 8	6			3

SPECSAVERS COUNTY CHAMPIONSHIP AVERAGES
BATTING AND FIELDING

Cap†		M	I	NO	HS	Runs	Avge	100	50	Ct/St
2019	H.D.Rutherford	4	5	–	123	220	44.00	1	1	3
2012	B.L.D'Oliveira	7	9	1	103	298	37.25	1	1	3
2007	M.M.Ali	2	4	–	42	126	31.50	–	–	2
2019	C.J.Ferguson	9	17	1	127	503	31.43	1	3	8
2019	M.H.Wessels	14	23	2	118	593	28.23	1	3	21
2009	O.B.Cox	14	22	2	100*	531	26.55	–	3	38/1
2012	J.Leach	12	20	4	54*	420	26.25	–	2	1
2013	R.A.Whiteley	10	16	1	88	391	26.06	–	3	4
2018	W.D.Parnell	7	8	–	63	205	25.62	–	1	2
2005	D.K.H.Mitchell	14	24	2	139	559	25.40	2	2	18
2015	E.G.Barnard	14	21	2	56	429	22.57	–	2	11
2013	T.C.Fell	5	7	–	40	136	19.42	–	–	4
2019	J.A.Haynes	4	6	–	31	95	15.83	–	–	1
2019	J.J.Dell	6	11	–	61	158	14.36	–	1	5
2014	C.A.J.Morris	11	15	8	29*	96	13.71	–	–	–
2017	J.C.Tongue	4	5	1	20*	51	12.75	–	–	–
2016	G.H.Rhodes	3	6	–	28	59	9.83	–	–	–
2019	A.W.Finch	7	9	4	17	43	8.60	–	–	–
2018	D.Y.Pennington	4	8	–	18	44	5.50	–	–	–
2018	A.G.Milton	3	6	–	12	17	2.83	–	–	4

BOWLING

	O	M	R	W	Avge	Best	5wI	10wM
J.C.Tongue	113.3	23	322	17	18.94	5- 37	1	–
C.A.J.Morris	293	67	945	44	21.47	7- 45	3	–
E.G.Barnard	371	100	993	44	22.56	6- 42	1	–
W.D.Parnell	157.4	42	507	22	23.04	5- 47	1	–
J.Leach	384.4	83	1081	41	26.36	6- 79	1	–
B.L.D'Oliveira	170.4	22	556	14	39.71	7- 92	1	–
A.W.Finch	152.2	26	583	11	53.00	2- 23	–	–
Also bowled:								
M.M.Ali	55.3	10	210	7	30.00	3-126	–	–
D.Y.Pennington	115	29	301	8	37.62	2- 92	–	–
R.A.Whiteley	79.4	5	303	8	37.87	2- 35	–	–

D.K.H.Mitchell 34-7-79-1; G.H.Rhodes 22.2-2-90-0.

The First-Class Averages (pp 226–241) give the records of Worcestershire players in all first-class county matches (Worcestershire's other opponents being the Australians), with the exception of M.M.Ali, whose first-class figures for Worcestershire are as above, and: G.H.Rhodes 4-7-0-28-70-10.00-0-0-Oct. 37.2-2-143-0.

† Worcestershire revised their capping policy in 2002 and now award players with their County Colours when they make their Championship debut.

WORCESTERSHIRE RECORDS

FIRST-CLASS CRICKET

Highest Total	For 701-6d		v	Surrey	Worcester	2007
	V 701-4d		by	Leics	Worcester	1906
Lowest Total	For 24		v	Yorkshire	Huddersfield	1903
	V 30		by	Hampshire	Worcester	1903
Highest Innings	For 405*	G.A.Hick	v	Somerset	Taunton	1988
	V 331*	J.D.B.Robertson	for	Middlesex	Worcester	1949

Highest Partnership for each Wicket

1st	309	H.K.Foster/F.L.Bowley	v	Derbyshire	Derby	1901
2nd	316	S.C.Moore/V.S.Solanki	v	Glos	Cheltenham	2008
3rd	438*	G.A.Hick/T.M.Moody	v	Hampshire	Southampton[1]	1997
4th	330	B.F.Smith/G.A.Hick	v	Somerset	Taunton	2006
5th	393	E.G.Arnold/W.B.Burns	v	Warwicks	Birmingham	1909
6th	265	G.A.Hick/S.J.Rhodes	v	Somerset	Taunton	1988
7th	256	D.A.Leatherdale/S.J.Rhodes	v	Notts	Nottingham	2002
8th	184	S.J.Rhodes/S.R.Lampitt	v	Derbyshire	Kidderminster	1991
9th	181	J.A.Cuffe/R.D.Burrows	v	Glos	Worcester	1907
10th	136	A.G.Milton/S.J.Magoffin	v	Somerset	Worcester	2018

Best Bowling (Innings)	For 9- 23	C.F.Root	v	Lancashire	Worcester	1931
	V 10- 51	J.Mercer	for	Glamorgan	Worcester	1936
Best Bowling (Match)	For 15- 87	A.J.Conway	v	Glos	Moreton-in-M	1914
	V 17-212	J.C.Clay	for	Glamorgan	Swansea	1937

Most Runs – Season	2654	H.H.I.H.Gibbons	(av 52.03)	1934
Most Runs – Career	34490	D.Kenyon	(av 34.18)	1946-67
Most 100s – Season	10	G.M.Turner		1970
	10	G.A.Hick		1988
Most 100s – Career	106	G.A.Hick		1984-2008
Most Wkts – Season	207	C.F.Root	(av 17.52)	1925
Most Wkts – Career	2143	R.T.D.Perks	(av 23.73)	1930-55
Most Career W-K Dismissals	1095	S.J.Rhodes	(991 ct; 104 st)	1985-2004
Most Career Catches in the Field	528	G.A.Hick		1984-2008

LIMITED-OVERS CRICKET

Highest Total	50ov	404-3		v	Devon	Worcester	1987
	40ov	376-6		v	Surrey	The Oval	2010
	T20	227-6		v	Northants	Kidderminster	2007
Lowest Total	50ov	58		v	Ireland	Worcester	2009
	40ov	86		v	Yorkshire	Leeds	1969
	T20	53		v	Lancashire	Manchester	2016
Highest Innings	50ov	192	C.J.Ferguson	v	Leics	Worcester	2018
	40ov	160	T.M.Moody	v	Kent	Worcester	1991
	T20	127	T.Kohler-Cadmore	v	Durham	Worcester	2004
Best Bowling	50ov	7-19	N.V.Radford	v	Beds	Bedford	1991
	40ov	6-16	Shoaib Akhtar	v	Glos	Worcester	2005
	T20	5-24	A.Hepburn	v	Notts	Worcester	2017

YORKSHIRE

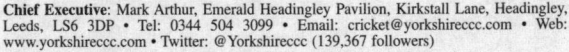

Formation of Present Club: 8 January 1863
Substantial Reorganisation: 10 December 1891
Inaugural First-Class Match: 1864
Colours: Dark Blue, Light Blue and Gold
Badge: White Rose
County Championships (since 1890): (32) 1893, 1896, 1898, 1900, 1901, 1902, 1905, 1908, 1912, 1919, 1922, 1923, 1924, 1925, 1931, 1932, 1933, 1935, 1937, 1938, 1939, 1946, 1959, 1960, 1962, 1963, 1966, 1967, 1968, 2001, 2014, 2015
Joint Champions: (1) 1949
Gillette/C&G Trophy Winners: (3) 1965, 1969, 2002
Benson and Hedges Cup Winners: (1) 1987
Sunday League Winners: (1) 1983
Twenty20 Cup Winners: (0); best – Finalist 2012

Chief Executive: Mark Arthur, Emerald Headingley Pavilion, Kirkstall Lane, Headingley, Leeds, LS6 3DP • Tel: 0344 504 3099 • Email: cricket@yorkshireccc.com • Web: www.yorkshireccc.com • Twitter: @Yorkshireccc (139,367 followers)

Director of Cricket: Martyn Moxon. **1st XI Coach**: Andrew Gale. **Batting Coach**: Paul Grayson. **Bowling Coach**: Richard Pyrah. **Captains**: S.A.Patterson (f-c and l-o) and D.J.Willey (T20). **Overseas Players**: R.Ashwin, K.A.Maharaj and N.Pooran (T20 only). **2020 Testimonial**: A.Lyth. **Head Groundsman**: Andy Fogarty. **Scorer**: John Potter. **Vitality Blast Name**: Yorkshire Vikings. ‡ New registration. ^{NQ} Not qualified for England.

‡^{NQ}ASHWIN, Ravichandran, b Madras, India 17 Sep 1986. 6'2". RHB, OB. Squad No 99. Tamil Nadu 2006-07 to date. Worcestershire 2017. Nottinghamshire 2019; cap 2019. IPL: CSK 2009-15. RPS 2016. KXIP 2018-19. **Tests** (I): 71 (2011-12 to 2019-20); HS 124 v WI (Kolkata) 2013-14; 50 wkts (3); most 72 (2016); BB 7-59 (13-140 match) v NZ (Indore) 2016-17. **LOI** (I): 111 (2010 to 2017); HS 65 v NZ (Auckland) 2013-14; BB 4-25 v UAE (Perth) 2014-15. **IT20** (I): 46 (2010 to 2017); HS 31* v SL (Pune) 2015-16; BB 4-8 v SL (Visakhapatnam) 2015-16. F-c Tours (I): E 2014, 2018; A 2011-12, 2014-15, 2018-19; SA 2013-14, 2017-18; WI 2016; NZ 2019-20; SL 2007-08 (TN), 2015, 2017; B 2015. HS 124 (*see Tests*). CC HS 82 Wo v Durham (Worcester) 2017. 50 wkts (0+1): 82 (2016-17). BB 7-59 (*see Tests*). CC BB 6-69 (12-144 match) Nt v Surrey (Nottingham) 2019. LO HS 79 South Zone v Central Zone (Vadodara) 2009-10. LO BB 4-25 (*see LOI*). T20 HS 46. T20 BB 4-8.

BAIRSTOW, Jonathan Marc (St Peter's S, York; Leeds Met U), b Bradford 26 Sep 1989. Son of D.L.Bairstow (Yorkshire, GW and England 1970-90); brother of A.D.Bairstow (Derbyshire 1995). 6'0". RHB, WK, occ RM. Squad No 21. Debut (Yorkshire) 2009; cap 2011. Inaugural winner of Young Wisden Schools Cricketer of the Year 2008. YC 2011. **ECB Test & L-O Central Contract 2019-20. Tests**: 70 (2012 to 2019-20); 1000 runs (1): 1470 (2016); HS 167* v SL (Lord's) 2016. Took a world record 70 dismissals in 2016, as well as scoring a record number of runs in a calendar year for a keeper. **LOI**: 77 (2011 to 2019-20); 1000 runs (1): 1025 (2018); HS 141* v WI (Southampton) 2018. **IT20**: 37 (2011 to 2019-20); HS 68 v WI (Gros Islet) 2018-19. F-c Tours: A 2013-14, 2017-18; SA 2014-15 (EL), 2015-16, 2019-20; WI 2010-11 (EL), 2018-19; NZ 2017-18; I 2012-13, 2016-17; SL 2013-14 (EL), 2018-19; B 2016-17; UAE 2015-16 (v P). 1000 runs (3); most – 1286 (2016). HS 246 v Hants (Leeds) 2016. LO HS 174 v Durham (Leeds) 2017 (RLC). T20 HS 114.

BALLANCE, Gary Simon (Peterhouse S, Marondera, Zimbabwe; Harrow S; Leeds Met U), b Harare, Zimbabwe 22 Nov 1989. Nephew of G.S.Ballance (Rhodesia B 1978-79) and D.L.Houghton (Rhodesia/Zimbabwe 1978-79 to 1997-98). 6'0''. LHB, LB. Squad No 19. Debut (Yorkshire) 2008; cap 2012; captain 2017 to 2018 (part). MWR 2010-11 to 2011-12. *Wisden* 2014. **Tests**: 23 (2013-14 to 2017); HS 156 v I (Southampton) 2014; BB – . **LOI**: 16 (2013 to 2014-15); HS 79 v A (Melbourne) 2013-14. F-c Tours: A 2013-14; WI 2014-15; B 2016-17. 1000 runs (4+1); most – 1363 (2013). HS 210 MWR v SR (Masvingo) 2011-12. Y HS 203* v Hants (Southampton) 2017. BB – . LO HS 156 v Leics (Leeds) 2019 (RLC). T20 HS 79.

BARNES, Edward (King James S, Knaresborough), b York 26 Nov 1997. 6'0''. RHB, RFM. Squad No 62. Yorkshire 2nd XI debut 2016. England U19 2016. Awaiting 1st XI debut.

BIRKHEAD, Benjamin David (Huddersfield New C), b Halifax 28 Oct 1998. 5'9½''. RHB, WK. Squad No 30. Yorkshire 2nd XI debut 2016. Awaiting f-c debut. LO HS – .

BRESNAN, Timothy Thomas (Castleford HS and TC; Pontefract New C), b Pontefract 28 Feb 1985. 6'0''. RHB, RFM. Squad No 16. Debut (Yorkshire) 2003; cap 2006; benefit 2014. MCC 2006, 2009. Big Bash: HH 2014-15. PS 2016-17 to 2017-18. *Wisden* 2011. **Tests**: 23 (2009 to 2013-14); HS 91 v B (Dhaka) 2009-10; BB 5-48 v I (Nottingham) 2011. **LOI**: 85 (2006 to 2015); HS 80 v SA (Centurion) 2009-10; BB 5-48 v I (Bangalore) 2010-11. **IT20**: 34 (2006 to 2013-14); HS 47* v WI (Bridgetown) 2013-14; BB 3-10 v P (Cardiff) 2010. F-c Tours: A 2010-11, 2013-14; I 2012-13; SL 2011-12; B 2006-07 (Eng A), 2009-10. HS 169* v Durham (Chester-le-St) 2015, sharing Y record 7th wkt partnership of 366* with J.M.Bairstow. BB 5-28 v Hants (Leeds) 2018. LO HS 95* v Notts (Scarborough) 2016 (RLC). BB 5-48 (see *LOI*). T20 HS 51. T20 BB 6-19 v Lancs (Leeds) 2017 – Y record.

BROOK, Harry Cherrington (Sedbergh S), b Keighley 22 Feb 1999. 5'11''. RHB, RM. Squad No 88. Debut (Yorkshire) 2016. Yorkshire 2nd XI debut 2015. England U19 2016-17 to 2017. HS 124 v Essex (Chelmsford) 2018. BB 1-54 v Somerset (Scarborough) 2017. LO HS 103 v Leics (Leeds) 2019 (RLC). T20 HS 44.

COAD, Benjamin Oliver (Thirsk S & SFC), b Harrogate 10 Jan 1994. 6'2''. RHB, RM. Squad No 10. Debut (Yorkshire) 2016; cap 2018. HS 48 v Surrey (Scarborough) 2019. 50 wkts (1): 53 (2017). BB 6-25 v Lancs (Leeds) 2017. LO HS 9 v Hants (Southampton) 2018 (RLC). LO BB 4-63 v Derbys (Leeds) 2017 (RLC). T20 HS 2*. T20 BB 2-24.

FISHER, Matthew David (Easingwold SS), b York 9 Nov 1997. 6'1''. RHB, RFM. Squad No 7. Debut (Yorkshire) 2015. MCC 2018. Yorkshire 2nd XI debut 2013, aged 15y 201d. England U19 2014. HS 47* v Kent (Leeds) 2019. BB 5-54 v Warwks (Leeds) 2017. LO HS 36* v Worcs (Worcester) 2017 (RLC). LO BB 3-32 v Leics (Leeds) 2015 (RLC). T20 HS 17*. T20 BB 5-22.

FRAINE, William Alan Richard (Silcoates S; Bromsgrove SFC; Durham U), b Huddersfield, Yorks 13 Jun 1996. 6'2''. RHB, RM. Squad No 31. Durham MCCU 2017-18. Nottinghamshire 2018. Yorkshire debut 2019. Worcestershire 2nd XI 2015-16. Nottinghamshire 2nd XI 2017-18. Herefordshire 2016. HS 106 v Surrey (Scarborough) 2019. LO HS 13 Nt v Lancs (Manchester) 2018 (RLC). T20 HS 16.

KOHLER-CADMORE, Tom (Malvern C), b Chatham, Kent 19 Aug 1994. 6'2''. RHB, OB. Squad No 32. Worcestershire debut 2014-15. Yorkshire debut 2017; cap 2019. 1000 runs (1): 1004 (2019). HS 176 v Leeds/Brad MCCU (Leeds) 2016. CC HS 169 Wo v Glos (Worcester) 2016. LO HS 164 v Durham (Chester-le-St) 2018 (RLC). T20 HS 127 Wo v Durham (Worcester) 2016 – Wo record, winning Walter Lawrence Trophy for fastest 100 (43 balls).

LOGAN, James Edwin Graham (Normanton Freestone HS; Pontefract New C), b Wakefield 12 Oct 1997. 6'1". LHB, SLA. Squad No 11. Debut (Yorkshire) 2018. Yorkshire 2nd XI debut 2014. HS 20* and BB 4-22 v Warwks (York) 2019.

LOTEN, Thomas William (Pocklington S), b York 8 Jan 1999. 6'5". RHB, RMF. Squad No 40. Debut (Yorkshire) 2019. Yorkshire 2nd XI debut 2018. HS 58 v Warwks (Birmingham) 2019. LO HS – .

LYTH, Adam (Caedmon S, Whitby; Whitby Community C), b Whitby 25 Sep 1987. 5'8". LHB, RM. Squad No 9. Debut (Yorkshire) 2007; cap 2010; testimonial 2020. MCC 2017. PCA 2014. *Wisden* 2014. **Tests**: 7 (2015); HS 107 v NZ (Leeds) 2015. F-c Tours (EL): SA 2014-15; WI 2010-11. 1000 runs (3); most – 1619 (2014). HS 251 v Lancs (Manchester) 2014, sharing in Y record 6th wicket partnership of 296 with A.U.Rashid. BB 2-9 v Middx (Scarborough) 2016. LO HS 144 v Lancs (Manchester) 2018 (RLC). LO BB 2-27 v Derbys (Leeds) 2019 (RLC). T20 HS 161 v Northants (Leeds) 2017 – Y & UK record; 5th highest score in all T20 cricket. T20 BB 5-31.

NQMAHARAJ, Keshav Athmanand, b Durban, South Africa 7 Feb 1990. 5'10". RHB, SLA. Squad No 27. KwaZulu-Natal 2006-07 to 2014-15. Dolphins 2009-10 to date. Lancashire 2018. Yorkshire debut 2019. **Tests** (SA): 30 (2016-17 to 2019-20); HS 72 v I (Pune) 2019-20; BB 9-129 (match 12-283) v SL (Colombo, SSC) 2018 – 2nd best innings analysis for SA. **LOI** (SA): 7 (2017 to 2019-20); HS 17 v SL (Pallekele) 2018; BB 3-25 v E (Lord's) 2017. F-c Tours (SA): E 2017; A 2016-17; NZ 2016-17; I 2015 (SAA), 2019-20; SL 2018; Z 2016 (SA A). HS 114* KZN v Northerns (Pretoria) 2012-13. CC HS 85 v Essex (Chelmsford) 2019. BB 9-129 (*see Tests*). CC BB 7-37 (11-102 match) La v Somerset (Taunton) 2018. Y BB 7-52 (10-127 match) v Somerset (Leeds) 2019. LO HS 50* Dolphins v Cobras (Cape Town) 2019-20. LO BB 5-34 KZN v Border (Durban) 2014-15. T20 HS 45*. T20 BB 3-7.

‡MALAN, Dawid Johannes (Paarl HS), b Roehampton, Surrey 3 Sep 1987. Son of D.J.Malan (WP B and Transvaal B 1978-79 to 1981-82), elder brother of C.C.Malan (Loughborough MCCU 2009-10). 6'0". LHB, LB. Squad No 29. Boland 2005-06. Middlesex 2008-19, scoring 132* v Northants (Uxbridge) on debut; cap 2010; T20 captain 2016-19; captain 2018-19. MCC 2010-11, 2013. **Tests**: 15 (2017 to 2018); HS 140* v A (Perth) 2017-18; BB – . **LOI**: 1 (2019); HS 24 v Ire (Dublin) 2019. **IT20**: 10 (2017 to 2019-20); HS 103* v NZ (Napier) 2019-20; BB 1-27 v NZ (Hamilton) 2017-18. F-c Tours: A 2017-18; NZ 2017-18. 1000 runs (3); most – 1137 runs (2014). HS 199 M v Derbys (Derby) 2019. BB 5-61 M v Lancs (Liverpool) 2012. LO HS 185* EL v Sri Lanka A (Northampton) 2016. LO BB 4-25 PDSC v Partex (Savar) 2014-15. T20 HS 117. T20 BB 2-10.

NQOLIVIER, Duanne, b Groblersdal, South Africa 9 May 1992. 6'4". RHB, RFM. Squad No 74. Free State 2010-11 to 2017-18. Knights 2013-14 to 2018-19. Derbyshire 2018. Yorkshire debut 2019 (Kolpak deal). **Tests** (SA): 10 (2016-17 to 2018-19); HS 10* v P (Cape Town) 2018-19; BB 6-37 (11-96 match) v P (Centurion) 2018-19. **LOI** (SA): 2 (2018-19); HS – ; BB 2-73 v P (Port Elizabeth) 2018-19. F-c Tours (SA): E 2017; A 2016 (SAA); I 2018 (SAA); Z 2016 (SAA). HS 72 FS v Namibia (Bloemfontein) 2014-15. CC HS 40* De v Warwks (Birmingham) 2018. Y HS 24 v Kent (Leeds) 2019. 50 wkts (0+3); most – 64 (2016-17). BB 6-37 (*see Tests*). CC BB 5-20 (10-125 match) De v Durham (Chester-le-St) 2018. Y BB 5-96 v Notts (Nottingham) 2019. LO HS 25* and LO BB 4-34 Knights v Lions (Kimberley) 2017-18. T20 HS 15*. T20 BB 4-28.

PATTERSON, Steven Andrew (Malet Lambert CS; St Mary's SFC, Hull; Leeds U), b Beverley 3 Oct 1983. 6'4". RHB, RMF. Squad No 17. Debut (Yorkshire) 2005; cap 2012; testimonial 2017; captain 2018 (*part*) to date. Bradford/Leeds UCCE 2003 (not f-c). HS 63* v Warwks (Birmingham) 2016. 50 wkts (2). most – 53 (2012). BB 6-40 v Essex (Chelmsford) 2018. LO HS 25* v Worcs (Leeds) 2006 (P40). LO BB 6-32 v Derbys (Leeds) 2010. T20 HS 3*. T20 BB 4-30.

[NQ]**PILLANS, Mathew** William (Pretoria BHS; U of Pretoria), b Durban, South Africa 4 Jul 1991. Qualifies for England in 2023, ancestral visa. 6'6". RHB, RF. Squad No 13. Northerns 2012-13. KwaZulu-Natal Inland 2013-14 to 2015-16. Dolphins 2013-14 to 2015-16. Surrey 2016-18. Leicestershire 2017 (on loan). Yorkshire debut 2018. HS 56 Le v Northants (Northampton) 2017. Y HS 8 v Notts (Nottingham) 2018. BB 6-67 (10-129 match) Dolphins v Knights (Durban) 2014-15. CC BB 3-63 Le v Sussex (Arundel) 2017. Y BB 2-34 v Leeds/Brad MCCU (Leeds) 2019. LO HS 31 v Worcs (Worcester) 2019 (RLC). LO BB 5-29 v Leics (Leeds) 2019 (RLC). T20 HS 34*. T20 BB 3-15.

[NQ]**POORAN, Nicolas**, b Trinidad 2 Oct 1995. LHB, WK. Squad No 39. Trinidad & Tobago 2014-15. Yorkshire debut 2019 (T20 only). IPL: KXIP 2019. **LOI** (WI): 25 (2018-19 to 2019-20); HS 118 v SL (Chester-le-St) 2019. **IT20** (WI): 21 (2016 to 2019-20); HS 58 v E (Gros Islet) 2018-19. HS 55 T&T v Jamaica (Port of Spain) 2014-15. LO HS 118 (*see LOI*). T20 HS 81.

POYSDEN, Joshua Edward (Cardinal Newman S, Hove; Anglia RU), b Shoreham-by-Sea, Sussex 8 Aug 1991. 5'9". LHB, LB. Squad No 14. Cambridge MCCU 2011-13. Warwickshire 2015-18. Yorkshire debut 2018. Unicorns (l-o) 2013. HS 47 CU v Surrey (Cambridge) 2011. CC HS 20* v Lancs (Manchester) 2018. BB 5-29 Wa v Glamorgan (Birmingham) 2018. Y BB 3-128 v Worcs (Scarborough) 2018. LO HS 10* Unicorns v Glos (Wormsley) 2013 (Y40). LO BB 3-33 Unicorns v Middx (Lord's) 2013 (Y40). T20 BB 9*. T20 BB 4-51.

RASHID, Adil Usman (Belle Vue S, Bradford), b Bradford 17 Feb 1988. 5'8". RHB, LBG. Squad No 3. Debut (Yorkshire) 2006; cap 2008; testimonial 2018. Signed white ball only contract for 2020. MCC 2007-09. Big Bash: AS 2015-16. YC 2007. Match double (114, 48, 8-157 and 2-45) for England U19 v India U19 (Taunton) 2006. **ECB L-O Central Contract 2019-20**. **Tests**: 19 (2015-16 to 2018-19), taking 5-64 v P (Abu Dhabi) on debut; HS 61 v P (Dubai, DSC) 2015-16; BB 5-49 v SL (Colombo, SSC) 2018-19. **LOI**: 100 (2009 to 2019-20); HS 69 v NZ (Birmingham) 2015; BB 5-27 v Ire (Bristol) 2017. **IT20**: 43 (2009 to 2019-20); HS 9* v SA (Nottingham) 2009; BB 3-11 v SL (Colombo, RPS) 2018-19. F-c Tours: WI 2010-11 (EL), 2018-19; I 2007-08 (EL), 2016-17; SL 2018-19; B 2006-07 (Eng A), 2016-17; UAE 2015-16 (v P). HS 180 v Somerset (Leeds) 2013. 50 wkts (2); most – 65 (2008). BB 7-107 v Hants (Southampton) 2008. LO HS 71 v Glos (Leeds) 2014 (RLC). LO BB 5-27 (*see LOI*). T20 HS 36*. T20 BB 4-19.

REVIS, Matthew Liam (Ilkley GS), b Steeton 15 Nov 2001. 6'4½". RHB, RM. Debut (Yorkshire) 2019. Yorkshire 2nd XI debut 2019. HS 9 v Kent (Leeds) 2019 – only 1st XI appearance.

ROOT, Joseph Edward (King Ecgbert S, Sheffield; Worksop C), b Sheffield 30 Dec 1990. Elder brother of W.T.Root (*see GLAMORGAN*). 6'0". RHB, OB. Squad No 66. Debut (Yorkshire) 2010; cap 2012. YC 2012. **ECB Test & L-O Central Contract 2019-20. Tests**: 92 (2012-13 to 2019-20, 39 as captain); 1000 runs (2); most – 1477 (2016); HS 254 v P (Manchester) 2016; BB 4-87 v SA (Port Elizabeth) 2019-20. **LOI**: 146 (2012-13 to 2019-20); HS 133* v B (Oval) 2017; BB 3-52 v Ire (Lord's) 2017. **IT20**: 32 (2012-13 to 2019); HS 90* v A (Southampton) 2013; BB 2-9 v WI (Kolkata) 2015-16. F-c Tours(C=Captain): A 2013-14, 2017-18C; SA 2015-16, 2019-20C; WI 2014-15, 2018-19C; NZ 2012-13, 2017-18C, 2019-20C; I 2012-13, 2016-17; SL 2018-19C, 2019-20C; B 2016-17; UAE 2015-16 (v P). 1000 runs (3); most – 1228 (2013). HS 254 (*see Tests*). CC HS 236 v Derbys (Leeds) 2013. BB 4-5 v Lancs (Manchester) 2018. LO HS 133* (*see LOI*). LO BB 3-52 (*see LOI*). T20 HS 92*. T20 BB 2-9.

SHUTT, Jack William (Kirk Balk S; Thomas Rotherham C), b Barnsley 24 Jun 1997. 6'0". RHB, OB. Squad No 24. Yorkshire 2nd XI debut 2016. Awaiting f-c debut. T20 HS 0*. T20 BB 5-11.

TATTERSALL, Jonathan Andrew (King James S, Knaresborough), b Harrogate 15 Dec 1994. 5'8". RHB, LB. Squad No 12. Debut (Yorkshire) 2018. HS 135* v Leeds/Brad MCCU (Leeds) 2019. HS 92 v Notts (Scarborough) 2019. LO HS 89 v Hants (Southampton) 2018 (RLC). T20 HS 53*.

THOMPSON, Jordan Aaron (Benton Park S), b Leeds 9 Oct 1996. 5'11". LHB, RM. Squad No 44. Debut (Yorkshire) 2019. Yorkshire 2nd XI debut 2014. HS 34 v Surrey (Guildford) 2019. BB 2-28 Warwks (York) 2019. LO BB – . T20 HS 50. T20 BB 3-23.

WAITE, Matthew James (Brigshaw HS), b Leeds 24 Dec 1995. 6'0". RHB, RFM. Squad No 6. Debut (Yorkshire) 2017. Yorkshire 2nd XI debut 2014. HS 42 and CC BB 3-91 v Notts (Nottingham) 2018. HS 5-16 v Leeds/Brad MCCU (Leeds) 2019. LO HS 71 v Warwks (Birmingham) 2017 (RLC). LO BB 4-65 v Worcs (Worcester) 2017 (RLC). T20 HS 19*. T20 BB 1-6.

WARNER, Jared David (Kettleborough Park HS; Silcoates SFC), b Wakefield 14 Nov 1996. 6'1". RHB, RFM. Squad No 45. Debut (Sussex) 2019 (on loan). Yorkshire 2nd XI debut 2015. England U19 2014-15 to 2015. HS 13* Sx v Middx (Hove) 2019. BB 3-35 v Glamorgan (Hove) 2019. LO BB – .

WILLEY, David Jonathan (Northampton S), b Northampton 28 Feb 1990. Son of P.Willey (Northants, Leics and England 1966-91). 6'1". LHB, LMF. Squad No 15. Northamptonshire 2009-15; cap 2013. Yorkshire debut/cap 2016; captain 2020 (T20 only). Bedfordshire 2008. IPL: CSK 2018. Big Bash: PS 2015-16 to 2018-19. **LOI**: 46 (2015 to 2019); HS 50 v I (Lord's) 2018; BB 4-34 v SL (Cardiff) 2016. **IT20**: 28 (2015 to 2019); HS 29* v I (Manchester) 2018; BB 4-7 v WI (Basseterre) 2018-19. HS 104* Nh v Glos (Northampton) 2015. Y HS 46 v Warwks (York) 2019. BB 5-29 (10-75 match) Nh v Glos (Northampton) 2011. Y BB 3-55 v Surrey (Leeds) 2016. LO HS 167 Nh v Warwks (Birmingham) 2013 (Y40). LO BB 5-62 EL v New Zealand A (Bristol) 2014. T20 HS 118. T20 BB 4-7.

RELEASED/RETIRED

(Having made a County 1st XI appearance in 2019)

LEANING, J.A. – see KENT.

[NQ]**PATEL, Ajaz** Yunus, b Bombay, India 21 Oct 1988. LHB, SLA. Central Districts 2012-13 to date. Yorkshire 2019. **Tests** (NZ): 8 (2018-19 to 2019-20); HS 14 v SL (Galle) 2019; BB 5-59 v P (Abu Dhabi) 2018-19 – on debut. **IT20** (NZ): 2 (2018-19); HS – ; BB 1-27 v P (Abu Dhabi) 2018-19. F-c Tours (NZ): SL 2019; UAE (v P) 2018-19. HS 45 CD v Otago (Dunedin) 2016-17. Y HS 20 and Y BB 1-112 v Kent (Leeds) 2019. BB 6-48 CD v ND (Mt Maunganui) 2017-18. LO HS 31* CD v Otago (Palmerston North) 2016-17. LO BB 3-43 CD v ND (New Plymouth) 2016-17. T20 HS 12*. T20 BB 3-20.

SHAW, J. – see GLOUCESTERSHIRE.

K.Carver left the staff without making a County 1st XI appearance in 2019.

YORKSHIRE 2019

RESULTS SUMMARY

		Place	Won	Lost	Tied	Drew	NR
Specsavers County Champ (1st Division)		5th	5	4		5	
All First-Class Matches			6	4		5	
Royal London One-Day Cup (North Group)	6th		2	3	2		1
Vitality Blast (North Group)		5th	4	5	1		4

SPECSAVERS COUNTY CHAMPIONSHIP AVERAGES

BATTING AND FIELDING

Cap		M	I	NO	HS	Runs	Avge	100	50	Ct/St
2012	G.S.Ballance	14	23	2	159	975	46.42	5	3	4
2019	T.Kohler-Cadmore	14	22	1	165*	828	39.42	2	3	30
	D.M.Bess	4	5	1	91*	156	39.00	–	1	1
2010	A.Lyth	14	25	2	95	804	34.95	–	7	26
	M.D.Fisher	4	5	1	47*	115	28.75	–	–	1
2016	D.J.Willey	5	7	1	46	171	28.50	–	–	3
	W.A.R.Fraine	8	15	1	106	393	28.07	1	–	8
2016	J.A.Leaning	8	12	1	77*	295	26.81	–	3	3
	K.A.Maharaj	5	9	–	85	239	26.55	–	2	1
	J.A.Tattersall	14	21	1	92	523	26.15	–	3	32/3
	H.C.Brook	10	16	–	101	353	22.06	1	–	7
	D.Olivier	13	17	11	24	130	21.66	–	–	3
2006	T.T.Bresnan	4	8	–	58	143	17.87	–	1	1
2018	B.O.Coad	11	14	2	48	196	16.33	–	–	–
2012	S.A.Patterson	14	20	2	60	271	15.05	–	1	6

Also batted: J.E.G.Logan (1 match) 20*, 7; T.W.Loten (1) 58; A.Y.Patel (2) 20, 0*; M.L.Revis (1) 9, 0 (1 ct); J.E.Root (2 – cap 2012) 73, 130*, 94 (2 ct); J.Shaw (1) 6; J.A.Thompson (2) 34, 0, 2; M.J.Waite (2) 22, 5* (1 ct).

BOWLING

	O	M	R	W	Avge	Best	5wI	10wM
K.A.Maharaj	266	76	719	38	18.92	7-52	4	2
B.O.Coad	340	82	955	37	25.81	6-52	1	–
M.D.Fisher	82	16	288	11	26.18	3-59	–	–
D.J.Willey	88.2	21	316	11	28.72	3-71	–	–
S.A.Patterson	396.4	111	1050	36	29.16	5-81	1	–
D.Olivier	365.5	66	1390	43	32.32	5-96	2	–
Also bowled:								
J.A.Thompson	40	10	105	5	21.00	2-28	–	–
D.M.Bess	97	24	234	7	33.42	3-45	–	–
M.J.Waite	59	5	235	6	39.16	2-38	–	–
T.T.Bresnan	82	17	262	6	43.66	2-47	–	–

J.A.Leaning 30-8-96-3; J.E.G.Logan 21-6-41-4; A.Lyth 25-3-79-1; A.Y.Patel 35-0-231-2; J.E.Root 43-2-158-0; J.Shaw 8-3-24-0.

The First-Class Averages (pp 226–241) give the records of Yorkshire players in all first-class county matches (Yorkshire's other opponents being Leeds/Bradford MCCU), with the exception of D.M.Bess, J.E.Root and J.Shaw, whose first-class figures for Yorkshire are as above.

YORKSHIRE RECORDS

FIRST-CLASS CRICKET

Highest Total	For	887		v	Warwicks	Birmingham	1896
	V	681-7d		by	Leics	Bradford	1996
Lowest Total	For	23		v	Hampshire	Middlesbrough	1965
	V	13		by	Notts	Nottingham	1901
Highest Innings	For	341	G.H.Hirst	v	Leics	Leicester	1905
	V	318*	W.G.Grace	for	Glos	Cheltenham	1876

Highest Partnership for each Wicket

1st	555	P.Holmes/H.Sutcliffe	v	Essex	Leyton	1932
2nd	346	W.Barber/M.Leyland	v	Middlesex	Sheffield	1932
3rd	346	J.J.Sayers/A.McGrath	v	Warwicks	Birmingham	2009
4th	372	J.E.Root/J.M.Bairstow	v	Surrey	Leeds	2016
5th	340	E.Wainwright/G.H.Hirst	v	Surrey	The Oval	1899
6th	296	A.Lyth/A.U.Rashid	v	Lancashire	Manchester	2014
7th	366*	J.M.Bairstow/T.T.Bresnan	v	Durham	Chester-le-St[2]	2015
8th	292	R.Peel/Lord Hawke	v	Warwicks	Birmingham	1896
9th	246	T.T.Bresnan/J.N.Gillespie	v	Surrey	The Oval	2007
10th	149	G.Boycott/G.B.Stevenson	v	Warwicks	Birmingham	1982

Best Bowling	For	10-10	H.Verity	v	Notts	Leeds	1932
(Innings)	V	10-37	C.V.Grimmett	for	Australians	Sheffield	1930
Best Bowling	For	17-91	H.Verity	v	Essex	Leyton	1933
(Match)	V	17-91	H.Dean	for	Lancashire	Liverpool	1913

Most Runs – Season	2883	H.Sutcliffe	(av 80.08)	1932
Most Runs – Career	38558	H.Sutcliffe	(av 50.20)	1919-45
Most 100s – Season	12	H.Sutcliffe		1932
Most 100s – Career	112	H.Sutcliffe		1919-45
Most Wkts – Season	240	W.Rhodes	(av 12.72)	1900
Most Wkts – Career	3597	W.Rhodes	(av 16.02)	1898-1930
Most Career W-K Dismissals	1186	D.Hunter	(863 ct; 323 st)	1888-1909
Most Career Catches in the Field	665	J.Tunnicliffe		1891-1907

LIMITED-OVERS CRICKET

Highest Total	50ov	411-6		v	Devon	Exmouth	2004
	40ov	352-6		v	Notts	Scarborough	2001
	T20	260-4		v	Northants	Leeds	2017
Lowest Total	50ov	76		v	Surrey	Harrogate	1970
	40ov	54		v	Essex	Leeds	1985
	T20	90-9		v	Durham	Chester-le-St[2]	2009
Highest Innings	50ov	175	T.M.Head	v	Leics	Leicester	2016
	40ov	191	D.S.Lehmann	v	Notts	Scarborough	2001
	T20	161	A.Lyth	v	Northants	Leeds	2017
Best Bowling	50ov	7-27	D.Gough	v	Ireland	Leeds	1997
	40ov	7-15	R.A.Hutton	v	Worcs	Leeds	1969
	T20	6-19	T.T.Bresnan	v	Lancashire	Leeds	2017

FIRST-CLASS UMPIRES 2020

† New appointment. See page 79 for key to abbreviations.

BAILEY, Robert John (Biddulph HS), b Biddulph, Staffs 28 Oct 1963. 6'3". RHB, OB. Northamptonshire 1982-99; cap 1985; benefit 1993; captain 1996-97. Derbyshire 2000-01; cap 2000. Staffordshire 1980. YC 1984. **Tests**: 4 (1988 to 1989-90); HS 43 v WI (Oval) 1988. **LOI**: 4 (1984-85 to 1989-90); HS 43* v SL (Oval) 1988. F-c Tours: SA 1991-92 (Nh); WI 1989-90; Z 1994-95 (Nh). 1000 runs (13); most – 1987 (1990). HS 224* Nh v Glamorgan (Swansea) 1986. BB 5-54 Nh v Notts (Northampton) 1993. F-c career: 374 matches; 21844 runs @ 40.52, 47 hundreds; 121 wickets @ 42.51; 272 ct. Appointed 2006. Umpired 23 LOI (2011 to 2019). **ICC International Panel 2011-19.**

BAINTON, Neil Laurence, b Romford, Essex 2 October 1970. No f-c appearances. Appointed 2006.

BALDWIN, Paul Kerr, b Epsom, Surrey 18 Jul 1973. No f-c appearances. Umpired 18 LOI (2006 to 2009). Reserve List 2010-14. Appointed 2015.

BLACKWELL, Ian David (Brookfield Community S), b Chesterfield, Derbys 10 Jun 1978. 6'2". LHB, SLA. Derbyshire 1997-99. Somerset 2000-08; cap 2001; captain 2006 (*part*). Durham 2009-12. Warwickshire 2012 (on loan). MCC 2012. **Tests**: 1 (2005-06); HS 4 and BB-v I (Nagpur) 2005-06. **LOI**: 34 (2002-03 to 2005-06); HS 82 v I (Colombo) 2002-03; BB 3-26 v A (Adelaide) 2002-03. F-c Tour: I 2005-06. 1000 runs (3); most – 1256 (2005). HS 247* Sm v Derbys (Taunton) 2003 – off 156 balls and including 204 off 98 balls in reduced post-lunch session. BB 7-52 Du v Australia A (Chester-le-St) 2012. CC BB 7-85 Du v Lancs (Manchester) 2009. F-c career: 210 matches; 11595 runs @ 39.57, 27 hundreds; 398 wickets @ 35.91; 66 ct. Reserve List 2015-17. Appointed 2018.

BURNS, Michael (Walney CS), b Barrow-in-Furness, Lancs 6 Feb 1969. 6'0". RHB, RM, WK. Warwickshire 1992-96. Somerset 1997-2005; cap 1999; captain 2003-04. 1000 runs (2); most – 1133 (2003). HS 221 Sm v Yorks (Bath) 2001. BB 6-54 Sm v Leics (Taunton) 2001. F-c career: 154 matches; 7648 runs @ 32.68, 8 hundreds; 68 wickets @ 42.42; 142 ct, 7 st. Appointed 2016. **ICC International Panel 2020.**

COOK, Nicholas Grant Billson (Lutterworth GS), b Leicester 17 Jun 1956. 6'0". RHB, SLA. Leicestershire 1978-85; cap 1982. Northamptonshire 1986-94; cap 1987; benefit 1995. **Tests**: 15 (1983 to 1989); HS 31 v A (Oval) 1989; BB 6-65 (11-83 match) v P (Karachi) 1983-84. **LOI**: 3 (1983-84 to 1989-90); HS – ; BB 2-18 v P (Peshawar) 1987-88. F-c Tours: NZ 1979-80 (DHR), 1983-84; P 1983-84, 1987-88; SL 1985-86 (Eng B); Z 1980-81 (Le), 1984-85 (EC). HS 75 Le v Somerset (Taunton) 1984. 50 wkts (8); most – 90 (1982). BB 7-34 (10-97 match) Nh v Essex (Chelmsford) 1992. F-c career: 356 matches; 3137 runs @ 11.66; 879 wickets @ 29.01; 197 ct. Appointed 2009.

DEBENHAM, Benjamin John, b Chelmsford, Essex 11 Oct 1967. LHB. No f-c appearances. Reserve List 2012-17. Appointed 2018.

EVANS, Jeffrey Howard, b Llanelli, Carms 7 Aug 1954. No f-c appearances. Appointed 2001. Umpired in Indian Cricket League 2007-08.

GOUGH, Michael Andrew (English Martyrs RCS; Hartlepool SFC), b Hartlepool, Co Durham 18 Dec 1979. Son of M.P.Gough (Durham 1974-77). 6'5". RHB, OB. Durham 1998-2003. F-c Tours (Eng A): NZ 1999-00; B 1999-00. HS 123 Du v CU (Cambridge) 1998. CC HS 103 Du v Essex (Colchester) 2002. BB 5-56 Du v Middx (Chester-le-St) 2001. F-c career: 67 matches; 2952 runs @ 25.44, 2 hundreds; 30 wickets @ 45.00; 57 ct. Reserve List 2006-08. Appointed 2009. Umpired 14 Tests (2016 to 2019-20) and 62 LOI (2013 to 2019-20). **ICC Elite Panel 2020.**

GOULD, Ian James (Westgate SS, Slough), b Taplow, Bucks 19 Aug 1957. 5'8". LHB, WK. Middlesex 1975 to 1980-81, 1996; cap 1977. Auckland 1979-80. Sussex 1981-90; cap 1981; captain 1987; benefit 1990. MCC YC. **LOI:** 18 (1982-83 to 1983); HS 42 v A (Sydney) 1982-83. F-c Tours: A 1982-83; P 1980-81 (Int); Z 1980-81 (M). HS 128 M v Worcs (Worcester) 1978. BB 3-10 Sx v Surrey (Oval) 1989. Middlesex coach 1991-2000. Reappeared in one match (v OU) 1996. F-c career: 298 matches; 8756 runs @ 26.05, 4 hundreds; 7 wickets @ 52.14; 603 dismissals (536 ct, 67 st). Appointed 2002. Umpired 74 Tests (2008-09 to 2018-19) and 140 LOI (2006 to 2019). **ICC Elite Panel 2009-19.**

HARTLEY, Peter John (Greenhead GS; Bradford C), b Keighley, Yorks 18 Apr 1960. 6'0". RHB, RMF. Warwickshire 1982. Yorkshire 1985-97; cap 1987; benefit 1996. Hampshire 1998-2000; cap 1998. F-c Tours (Y): SA 1991-92; WI 1986-87; Z 1995-96. HS 127* Y v Lancs (Manchester) 1988. 50 wkts (7); most – 81 (1995). BB 9-41 (inc hat-trick, 4 wkts in 5 balls and 5 in 9; 11-68 match) Y v Derbys (Chesterfield) 1995. Hat-trick 1995. F-c career: 232 matches; 4321 runs @ 19.91, 2 hundreds; 683 wickets @ 30.21; 68 ct. Appointed 2003. Umpired 6 LOI (2007 to 2009). **ICC International Panel 2006-09.**

ILLINGWORTH, Richard Keith (Salts GS), b Bradford, Yorks 23 Aug 1963. 5'11". RHB, SLA. Worcestershire 1982-2000; cap 1986; benefit 1997. Natal 1988-89. Derbyshire 2001. Wiltshire 2005. **Tests:** 9 (1991 to 1995-96); HS 28 v SA (Pt Elizabeth) 1995-96; BB 4-96 v WI (Nottingham) 1995. Took wicket of P.V.Simmons with his first ball in Tests – v WI (Nottingham) 1991. **LOI:** 25 (1991 to 1995-96); HS 14 v P (Melbourne) 1991-92; BB 3-33 v Z (Albury) 1991-92. F-c Tours: SA 1995-96; NZ 1991-92; P 1990-91 (Eng A); SL 1990-91 (Eng A); Z 1989-90 (Eng A), 1990-91 (Wo), 1993-94 (Wo), 1996-97 (Wo). HS 120* Wo v Warwks (Worcester) 1987 – as night-watchman. Scored 106 for England A v Z (Harare) 1989-90 – also as night-watchman. 50 wkts (5); most – 75 (1990). BB 7-50 Wo v OU (Oxford) 1985. F-c career: 376 matches; 7027 runs @ 22.45, 4 hundreds; 831 wickets @ 31.54; 161 ct. Appointed 2006. Umpired 47 Tests (2012-13 to 2019-20) and 68 LOI (2010 to 2019-20). **ICC Elite Panel 2013 to date.**

KETTLEBOROUGH, Richard Allan (Worksop C), b Sheffield, Yorks 15 Mar 1973. 6'0". LHB, RM. Yorkshire 1994-97. Middlesex 1998-99. F-c Tour (Y): Z 1995-96. HS 108 Y v Essex (Leeds) 1996. BB 2-26 Y v Notts (Scarborough) 1996. F-c career: 33 matches; 1258 runs @ 25.16, 1 hundred; 3 wickets @ 81.00; 20 ct. Appointed 2006. Umpired 64 Tests (2010-11 to 2019-20) and 89 LOI (2009 to 2019-20). **ICC Elite Panel 2011 to date.**

LLONG, Nigel James (Ashford North S), b Ashford, Kent 11 Feb 1969. 6'0". LHB, OB. Kent 1990-98; cap 1993. F-c Tour (K): Z 1992-93. HS 130 K v Hants (Canterbury) 1996. BB 5-21 K v Middx (Canterbury) 1996. F-c career: 68 matches; 3024 runs @ 31.17, 6 hundreds; 35 wickets @ 35.97; 59 ct. Appointed 2002. Umpired 62 Tests (2007-08 to 2019-20) and 130 LOI (2006 to 2019-20). **ICC Elite Panel 2012 to date.**

LLOYD, Graham David (Hollins County HS), b Accrington, Lancs 1 Jul 1969. Son of D.Lloyd (Lancs and England 1965-83). 5'9". RHB, RM. Lancashire 1988-2002; cap 1992; benefit 2001. **LOI:** 6 (1996 to 1998-99); HS 22 v A (Oval) 1997. F-c Tours: A 1992-93 (Eng A); WI 1995-96 (La). 1000 runs (5); most – 1389 (1992). HS 241 La v Essex (Chelmsford) 1996. BB 1-4. F-c career: 203 matches; 11279 runs @ 38.23, 24 hundreds; 2 wickets @ 220.00; 140 ct. Reserve List 2009-13. Appointed 2014.

LLOYDS, Jeremy William (Blundell's S), b Penang, Malaya 17 Nov 1954. 6'0". LHB, OB. Somerset 1979-84; cap 1982. Gloucestershire 1985-91; cap 1985. OFS 1983-84 to 1987-88. F-c Tour (Gl): SL 1986-87. 1000 runs (3); most – 1295 (1986). HS 132* Sm v Northants (Northampton) 1982. BB 7-88 Sm v Essex (Chelmsford) 1982. F-c career: 267 matches; 10679 runs @ 31.04, 10 hundreds; 333 wickets @ 38.86; 229 ct. Appointed 1998. Umpired 5 Tests (2003-04 to 2004-05) and 18 LOI (2000 to 2005-06). **ICC International Panel 2003-06.**

MALLENDER, Neil Alan (Beverley GS), b Kirk Sandall, Yorks 13 Aug 1961. 6'0". RHB, RFM. Northamptonshire 1980-86 and 1995-96; cap 1984. Somerset 1987-94; cap 1987; benefit 1994. Otago 1983-84 to 1992-93; captain 1990-91 to 1992-93. **Tests:** 2 (1992); HS 4 v P (Oval) 1992; BB 5-50 v P (Leeds) 1992 – on debut. F-c Tour (Nh): Z 1994-95. HS 100* Otago v CD (Palmerston N) 1991-92. UK HS 87* Sm v Sussex (Hove) 1990. 50 wkts (6); most – 56 (1983). BB 7-27 Otago v Auckland (Auckland) 1984-85. UK BB 7-41 Nh v Derbys (Northampton) 1982. F-c career: 345 matches; 4709 runs @ 17.18, 1 hundred; 937 wickets @ 26.31; 111 ct. Appointed 1999. Umpired 3 Tests (2003-04) and 22 LOI (2001 to 2003-04), including 2002-03 World Cup. **ICC Elite Panel 2004.**

MILLNS, David James (Garibaldi CS; N Notts C; Nottingham Trent U), b Clipstone, Notts 27 Feb 1965. 6'3". LHB, RF. Nottinghamshire 1988-89, 2000-01; cap 2000. Leicestershire 1990-99; cap 1991; benefit 1999. Tasmania 1994-95. Boland 1996-97. F-c Tours: A 1992-93 (Eng A); SA 1996-97 (Le). HS 121 Le v Northants (Northampton) 1997. 50 wkts (4); most – 76 (1994). BB 9-37 (12-91 match) Le v Derbys (Derby) 1991. F-c career: 171 matches; 3082 runs @ 22.01, 3 hundreds; 553 wickets @ 27.35; 76 ct. Reserve List 2007-08. Appointed 2009. **ICC International Panel 2020.**

O'SHAUGHNESSY, Steven Joseph (Harper Green SS, Franworth), b Bury, Lancs 9 Sep 1961. 5'10½". RHB, RM. Lancashire 1980-87; cap 1985. Worcestershire 1988-89. Scored 100 in 35 min to equal world record for La v Leics (Manchester) 1983. 1000 runs (1): 1167 (1984). HS 159* La v Somerset (Bath) 1984. BB 4-66 La v Notts (Nottingham) 1982. F-c career: 112 matches; 3720 runs @ 24.31, 5 hundreds; 114 wickets @ 36.03; 57 ct. Reserve List 2009-10. Appointed 2011.

POLLARD, Paul Raymond (Gedling CS), b Carlton, Nottingham 24 Sep 1968. 5'11". LHB, RM. Nottinghamshire 1987-98; cap 1992. Worcestershire 1999-2001. F-c Tour (Nt): SA 1996-97. 1000 runs (3); most – 1463 (1993). HS 180 Nt v Derbys (Nottingham) 1993. BB 2-79 Nt v Glos (Bristol) 1993. F-c career: 192 matches; 9685 runs @ 31.44, 15 hundreds; 4 wkts @ 68.00; 158 ct. Reserve List 2012-17. Appointed 2018.

ROBINSON, Robert Timothy (Dunstable GS; High Pavement SFC; Sheffield U), b Sutton in Ashfield, Notts 21 Nov 1958. 6'0". RHB, RM. Nottinghamshire 1978-99; cap 1983; captain 1988-95; benefit 1992. *Wisden* 1985. **Tests:** 29 (1984-85 to 1989); HS 175 v A (Leeds) 1985. **LOI:** 26 (1984-85 to 1988); HS 83 v P (Sharjah) 1986-87. F-c Tours: A 1987-88; SA 1989-90 (Eng XI), 1996-97 (Nt); NZ 1987-88; WI 1985-86; I/SL 1984-85; P 1987-88. 1000 runs (14) inc 2000 (1): 2032 (1984). HS 220* Nt v Yorks (Nottingham) 1990. BB 1-22. F-c career: 425 matches; 27571 runs @ 42.15, 63 hundreds; 4 wickets @ 72.25; 257 ct. Appointed 2007. Umpired 16 LOI (2013 to 2019). **ICC International Panel 2012-19.**

SAGGERS, Martin John (Springwood HS, King's Lynn; Huddersfield U), b King's Lynn, Norfolk 23 May 1972. 6'2". RHB, RMF. Durham 1996-98. Kent 1999-2009; cap 2001; benefit 2009. MCC 2004. Essex 2007 (on loan). Norfolk 1995-96. **Tests**: 3 (2003-04 to 2004); HS 1 and BB 2-29 v B (Chittagong) 2003-04 – on debut. F-c Tour: B 2003-04. HS 64 K v Worcs (Canterbury) 2004. 50 wkts (4); most – 83 (2002). BB 7-79 K v Durham (Chester-le-St) 2000. F-c career: 119 matches; 1165 runs @ 11.20; 415 wickets @ 25.33; 27 ct. Reserve List 2010-11. Appointed 2012. **ICC International Panel 2020.**

TAYLOR, Billy Victor (Bitterne Park S, Southampton), b Southampton 11 Jan 1977. Younger brother of J.L.Taylor (Wiltshire 1998-2002). 6'3". LHB, RMF. Wiltshire 1996-98. Hampshire 2004-09; cap 2006; testimonial 2010. Wiltshire 1996-98. HS 40 v Essex (Southampton) 2004. BB 6-32 v Middlesex (Southampton) 2006 (inc hat-trick). F-c career: 54 matches; 431 runs @10.26; 136 wickets @ 33.34; 6 ct. Reserve List 2011-16. Appointed 2017.

WARREN, Russell John (Kingsthorpe Upper S), b Northampton 10 Sep 1971. 6'1''. RHB, OB, WK. Northamptonshire 1992-2002; cap 1995. Nottinghamshire 2003-06; cap 2004. 1000 runs (1): 1030 (2001). HS 201* Nh v Glamorgan (Northampton) 2001. F-c career: 146 matches; 7776 runs @ 36.67, 15 hundreds; 128 ct, 5 st. Reserve List: 2015-17. Appointed 2018.

WHARF, Alexander George (Buttershaw Upper S; Thomas Danby C), b Bradford, Yorks 4 Jun 1975. 6'5''. RHB, RMF. Yorkshire 1994-97. Nottinghamshire 1998-99. Glamorgan 2000-08, scoring 100* v OU (Oxford) on debut; cap 2000; benefit 2009. **LOI**: 13 (2004 to 2004-05); HS 9 v India (Lord's) 2004; BB 4-24 v Z (Harare) 2004-05. F-c Tour (Eng A): WI 2005-06. HS 128* Gm v Glos (Bristol) 2007. 50 wkts (1): 52 (2003). BB 6-59 Gm v Glos (Bristol) 2005. F-c career: 121 matches; 3570 runs @ 23.03, 6 hundreds; 293 wickets @ 37.34; 63 ct. Reserve List 2011-13. Appointed 2014. Umpired 3 LOI (2018 to 2019). **ICC International Panel 2018 to date.**

RESERVE FIRST-CLASS LIST: Hassan M.S.Adnan, Tom Lungley, James D.Middlebrook, Mark Newell, Neil J.Pratt, Ian N.Ramage, Christopher M.Watts, Robert A.White.

Test Match and LOI statistics to 11 March 2020.

TOURING TEAMS REGISTER 2019

Some players appeared for both Australia and Australia A during the summer.

AUSTRALIA

Full Names	Birthdate	Birthplace	Team	Type	F-C Debut
BANCROFT, Cameron Timothy	19.11.92	Perth	W Australia	RHB/RM	2013-14
CAREY, Alex Tyson	27.08.91	Loxton	S Australia	LHB/WK	2012-13
CUMMINS, Patrick James	08.05.93	Sydney	NSW	RHB/RF	2010-11
HARRIS, Marcus Sinclair	21.07.92	Perth	Victoria	LHB/OB	2010-11
HAZLEWOOD, Josh Reginald	08.01.91	Tamworth	NSW	LHB/RFM	2008-09
HEAD, Travis Michael	29.12.93	Adelaide	S Australia	RHB/OB	2011-12
KHAWAJA, Usman Tariq	18.12.86	Islamabad, Pak	Queensland	LHB/RM	2007-08
LABUSCHAGNE, Marnus	22.06.94	Klerksdorp, SA	Queensland	RHB/LB	2014-15
LYON, Nathan Michael	20.11.87	Young	NSW	RHB/OB	2010-11
MARSH, Mitchell Ross	20.10.91	Perth	W Australia	RHB/RMF	2009-10
NESER, Michael Gertges	29.03.90	Pretoria SA	Queensland	RHB/RM	2010-11
PAINE, Timothy David	08.12.84	Hobart	Tasmania	RHB/WK	2005-06
PATTINSON, James Lee	03.05.90	Melbourne	Victoria	LHB/RFM	2008-09
SIDDLE, Peter Matthew	25.11.84	Traralgon	Victoria	RHB/RFM	2005-06
SMITH, Steven Peter Devereux	02.06.89	Sydney	NSW	RHB/LB	2007-08
STARC, Mitchell Aaron	30.01.90	Sydney	NSW	LHB/LF	2008-09
WADE, Matthew Scott	26.12.87	Lauderdale	Tasmania	LHB/WK	2007-08
WARNER, David Andrew	27.10.86	Paddington	NSW	LHB/LB	2008-09

AUSTRALIA A

Full Names	Birthdate	Birthplace	Team	Type	F-C Debut
BIRD, Jackson Munro	11.12.86	Sydney	Tasmania	RHB/RFM	2011-12
BURNS, Joseph Anthony	06.09.89	Brisbane	Queensland	RHB/RM	2010-11
HOLLAND, Jonathan Mark	29.05.87	Sandringham	Victoria	RHB/SLA	2008-09
PATTERSON, Kurtis Robert	05.05.93	Hurstville	NSW	LHB/OB	2011-12
PUCOVSKI, William Jan	02.02.98	Malvern	Victoria	RHB/OB	2016-17
TREMAIN, Christopher Peter	10.08.91	Dubbo, NSW	Victoria	RHB/RMF	2011-12

For the Ireland register, go to page 322 for further details.

THE 2019 FIRST-CLASS SEASON
STATISTICAL HIGHLIGHTS

FIRST TO INDIVIDUAL TARGETS

1000 RUNS	M.Labuschagne	Glamorgan	2 July
2000 RUNS	–	Most – 1530 M.Labuschagne (Australia, Glamorgan)	
50 WICKETS	S.R.Harmer	Essex	3 July
100 WICKETS	–	Most – 86 S.R.Harmer (Essex)	

TEAM HIGHLIGHTS († *Team record*)
HIGHEST INNINGS TOTALS

750	Northamptonshire v Glamorgan	Cardiff
598-5d	Derbyshire v Glamorgan	Swansea
585-7d	Kent v Warwickshire	Canterbury
579-7d	Surrey v Hampshire	The Oval

HIGHEST FOURTH INNINGS TOTAL

362-9	England (set 359) v Australia (*3rd Test*)	Leeds

LOWEST INNINGS TOTALS

38†	Ireland v England	Lord's
40	Kent v Essex	Canterbury
46	Cardiff MCCU v Somerset	Taunton
59	Kent v Somerset	Canterbury
67	England v Australia (*3rd Test*)	Leeds
75	Middlesex v Sussex	Hove
84	Derbyshire v Lancashire	Derby
85	England v Ireland	Lord's
88	Hampshire v Essex	Chelmsford
94	Leeds/Bradford MCCU v Derbyshire	Derby
97	Nottinghamshire v Warwickshire	Birmingham
98	Worcestershire v Lancashire	Worcester

HIGHEST MATCH AGGREGATES

1517-32	Nottinghamshire (498 & 260) v Warwicks (488 & 271-2)	Nottingham
1417-30	Sussex (422 & 339-4d) v Northants (368 & 288-6)	Northampton

BATSMEN'S MATCH (Qualification: 1200 runs, average 60 per wicket)

(73.15) 1390-19	Glamorgan (570-8d & 70-1) v Northamptonshire (750)	Cardiff
(63.45) 1269-20	Leicestershire (487 & 211-0d) v Gloucestershire (571)	Leicester

LARGE MARGINS OF VICTORY

568 runs†	Somerset (387-4d & 345-9d) beat Cardiff MCCU (118 & 46)	Taunton
UK record winning margin by runs.		
433 runs	Kent (482-8d & 337-7d) beat Yorkshire (269 & 117)	Leeds
393 runs	Northamptonshire (273 & 331) beat Sussex (106 & 105)	Hove
336 runs	Derbys (398-5d & 232-5d) beat Leeds/Brad MCCU (200 & 94)	Derby
314 runs	Hampshire (354 & 302-5d) beat Warwicks (233 & 109)	Birmingham
313 runs	Somerset (408 & 358-8d) beat Hampshire (349 & 104)	Taunton
Inns & 220 runs	Leics (524-5d) beat Loughboro MCCU (153 & 151)	Leicester

NARROW MARGINS OF VICTORY

13 runs	Gloucestershire (354 & 184) beat Worcs (293 & 232)	Cheltenham
1 wkt	England (67 & 362-9) beat Australia (179 & 246)	Leeds

MOST EXTRAS IN AN INNINGS

	B	LB	W	NB			
61	18	25	2	16	Northamptonshire (750) v Glamorgan	Cardiff
60	7	7	–	46	Sussex (370) v Gloucestershire	Bristol

Under ECB regulations, Test matches excluded, two penalty extras were scored for each no-ball.

SIX FIFTIES IN AN INNINGS

Northamptonshire (750) v Glamorgan   Cardiff

BATTING HIGHLIGHTS
DOUBLE HUNDREDS

B.M.Duckett	216	Nottinghamshire v Cambridge MCCU	Cambridge
B.A.Godleman	227	Derbyshire v Glamorgan	Swansea
W.L.Madsen	204*	Derbyshire v Gloucestershire	Bristol
O.J.D.Pope	221*	Surrey v Hampshire	The Oval
W.T.Root	229	Glamorgan v Northamptonshire	Northampton
D.P.Sibley (2)	244	Warwickshire v Kent	Canterbury
	215*	Warwickshire v Nottinghamshire	Nottingham
S.P.D.Smith	211	Australia v England (*4th Test*)	Manchester
D.I.Stevens	237	Kent v Yorkshire	Leeds
D.J.Vilas	266	Lancashire v Glamorgan	Colwyn Bay

HUNDREDS IN THREE CONSECUTIVE INNINGS

S.W.Billings		100	Kent v Nottinghamshire	Nottingham
	138	122*	Kent v Yorkshire	Leeds

DOUBLE HUNDRED AND A HUNDRED IN A MATCH

D.P.Sibley	215*	109	Warwickshire v Nottinghamshire	Nottingham

HUNDRED IN EACH INNINGS OF A MATCH

M.H.Azad	137	100*	Leicestershire v Gloucestershire	Leicester
S.W.Billings	138	122*	Kent v Yorkshire	Leeds
J.M.Clarke	125	112	Nottinghamshire v Warwickshire	Nottingham
S.R.Hain	129*	104	Warwickshire v Hampshire	Southampton
M.Labuschagne	106	100	Glamorgan v Worcestershire	Cardiff
S.P.D.Smith	144	142	Australia v England (*1st Test*)	Birmingham

FASTEST HUNDRED AGAINST GENUINE BOWLING

D.Wiese	(139) 80 balls Sussex v Cardiff MCCU	Hove

SCORING HUNDRED BEFORE LUNCH

B.M.Duckett (0-148*) Nottinghamshire v Cambridge MCCU   Cambridge

200 RUNS IN A DAY

B.M.Duckett (0-216)	Nottinghamshire v Cambridge MCCU	Cambridge
W.T.Root (0-229)	Glamorgan v Northamptonshire	Northampton
D.I.Stevens (0-237)	Kent v Yorkshire	Leeds
D.J.Vilas (0-266)	Lancashire v Glamorgan	Colwyn Bay

150 RUNS OR MORE FROM BOUNDARIES IN AN INNINGS

Runs 6s 4s

Runs	6s	4s			
176	6	35	D.J.Vilas	Lancashire v Glamorgan	Colwyn Bay
166	9	28	D.I.Stevens	Kent v Yorkshire	Leeds
160	4	34	B.M.Duckett	Nottinghamshire v Cambridge MCCU	Cambridge

HUNDRED ON FIRST-CLASS DEBUT

G.T.Hargrave	146	Oxford University v Cambridge U	Cambridge

HUNDRED ON FIRST-CLASS DEBUT IN BRITAIN

M.S.Harris	109	Australia A v Sussex	Arundel
D.Pretorius	111	Northamptonshire v Worcestershire	Northampton

CARRYING BAT THROUGH COMPLETED INNINGS

A.Z.Lees	107*	Durham (242) v Derbyshire	Chester-le-Street
S.D.Robson	140*	Middlesex (342) v Glamorgan	Cardiff
N.J.Selman	75*	Glamorgan (186) v Sussex	Hove
D.P.Sibley (2)	109*	Warwickshire (233) v Hampshire	Birmingham
	215*	Warwickshire (488) v Nottinghamshire	Nottingham

60% OF A COMPLETE INNINGS TOTAL

62.83%	J.M.Vince	Hampshire (142/226) v Somerset	Southampton

LONG INNINGS (Qualification 600 mins and/or 400 balls)

Mins Balls

Mins	Balls			
640	491	D.P.Sibley (244)	Warwickshire v Kent	Canterbury
531	420	D.P.Sibley (215*)	Warwickshire v Notts	Nottingham

NOTABLE PARTNERSHIPS

Qualifications: 1st-4th wkts: 250 runs; 5th-6th: 225; 7th: 200; 8th: 175; 9th: 150; 10th: 100. († Team record)

First Wicket

325	B.T.Slater/B.M.Duckett	Notts v Cambridge MCCU	Cambridge
303	R.S.Vasconcelos/R.I.Newton	Northamptonshire v Glamorgan	Cardiff
274	L.M.Reece/B.A.Godleman	Derbyshire v Sussex	Derby

Second Wicket

320†	M.H.Azad/N.J.Dexter	Leicestershire v Glos	Leicester
309	A.Javid/Hasan Azad	Leics v Loughboro MCCU	Leicester
291†	N.J.Selman/M.Labuschagne	Glamorgan v Sussex	Hove

Third Wicket

291	B.A.Godleman/T.C.Lace	Derbyshire v Glamorgan	Swansea
257	A.M.Rahane/S.A.Northeast	Hampshire v Nottinghamshire	Newport, IoW
253*	G.S.Ballance/J.E.Root	Yorkshire v Nottinghamshire	Nottingham

Fourth Wicket

278*	W.L.Madsen/A.L.Hughes	Derbyshire v Gloucestershire	Bristol

Fifth Wicket

262†	I.G.Holland/A.H.T.Donald	Hampshire v Warwickshire	Southampton

Sixth Wicket

346†	S.W.Billings/D.I.Stevens	Kent v Yorkshire	Leeds
318	C.D.J.Dent/R.F.Higgins	Gloucestershire v Leics	Leicester
282†	C.T.Bancroft/E.J.H.Eckersley	Durham v Sussex	Hove

Seventh Wicket

309	B.C.Brown/C.J.Jordan	Sussex v Northamptonshire	Northampton
224	D.J.Malan/J.A.Simpson	Middlesex v Derbyshire	Derby
220	M.G.K.Burgess/D.Wiese	Sussex v Cardiff MCCU	Hove

Ninth Wicket

167	G.G.Wagg/L.J.Carey	Glamorgan v Derbyshire	Swansea

BOWLING HIGHLIGHTS

EIGHT OR MORE WICKETS IN AN INNINGS

K.J.Abbott (2)	9-40	Hampshire v Somerset (*1st inns*)	Southampton
	8-46	Hampshire v Somerset (*2nd inns*)	Southampton
G.J.Batty	8-64	Surrey v Warwickshire	Birmingham
S.R.Harmer	8-98	Essex v Kent	Chelmsford
J.S.Patel	8-36	Warwickshire v Surrey	Birmingham
O.E.Robinson	8-34	Sussex v Middlesex	Hove
G.S.Virdi	8-61	Surrey v Nottinghamshire	Nottingham

TEN OR MORE WICKETS IN A MATCH

K.J.Abbott	17- 86	Hampshire v Somerset	Southampton

The 4th best analysis in County Championship history

R.Ashwin	12-144	Nottinghamshire v Surrey	Nottingham
T.E.Bailey	10-119	Lancashire v Middlesex	Manchester
G.J.Batty	10-111	Surrey v Warwickshire	Birmingham
S.J.Cook	12- 65	Essex v Kent	Canterbury
R.J.Gleeson	10-113	Lancashire v Northamptonshire	Manchester
L.Gregory	11- 53	Somerset v Kent	Canterbury
S.R.Harmer (2)	11-170	Essex v Kent	Chelmsford
	12- 61	Essex v Hampshire	Chelmsford
K.A.Maharaj (2)	10-127	Yorkshire v Somerset	Leeds
	10-176	Yorkshire v Somerset	Taunton
M.W.Parkinson	10-165	Lancashire v Sussex	Manchester
J.S.Patel (2)	12- 89	Warwickshire v Surrey	Birmingham
	10- 88	Warwickshire v Nottinghamshire	Birmingham
O.E.Robinson (3)	10-148	Sussex v Middlesex	Lord's
	10-132	Sussex v Northamptonshire	Hove
	14-135	Sussex v Middlesex	Hove
T.S.Roland-Jones	10- 79	Middlesex v Gloucestershire	Northwood
C.Rushworth	10- 67	Durham v Worcestershire	Chester-le-Street
B.W.Sanderson	10- 55	Northamptonshire v Sussex	Hove
D.I.Stevens	10- 92	Kent v Nottinghamshire	Nottingham
T.A.I.Taylor	10-122	Leicestershire v Sussex	Hove
G.S.Virdi	14-139	Surrey v Nottinghamshire	Nottingham

FIVE WICKETS IN AN INNINGS ON FIRST-CLASS DEBUT

L.A.Patterson-White	5-73	Nottinghamshire v Somerset	Taunton

HAT-TRICK

G.J.Batty		Surrey v Warwickshire	Birmingham

BOWLING UNCHANGED THROUGHOUT A COMPLETED INNINGS

C.Overton (8-0-24-6)/J.H.Davey (8-0-21-4)	Somerset v Cardiff MCCU	Taunton
S.C.J.Broad (8-3-19-4)/C.R.Woakes 7.4-2-17-6)	England v Ireland	Lord's

MOST RUNS CONCEDED IN AN INNINGS

| L.A.Dawson | 60-4-184-3 | Hampshire v Yorkshire | | Southampton |

60 OVERS BOWLED IN AN INNINGS

| R.Ashwin | 60-17-162-3 | Nottinghamshire v Essex | Nottingham |
| L.A.Dawson | 60-4-184-3 | Hampshire v Yorkshire | Southampton |

WICKET-KEEPING HIGHLIGHTS

SIX WICKET-KEEPING DISMISSALS IN AN INNINGS

| S.W.Poynter | 6ct | Durham v Durham MCCU | Chester-le-Street |
| O.G.Robinson | 6ct | Kent v Surrey | The Oval |

NINE OR MORE WICKET-KEEPING DISMISSALS IN A MATCH

| S.W.Poynter | 9ct | Durham v Durham MCCU | Chester-le-Street |

FIELDING HIGHLIGHTS

FOUR OR MORE CATCHES IN THE FIELD IN AN INNINGS

T.Kohler-Cadmore	6ct	Yorkshire v Kent	Canterbury
R.J.Burns	4ct	Surrey v Warwickshire	Birmingham
R.Clarke	4ct	Surrey v Hampshire	Southampton
T.Kohler-Cadmore	4ct	Yorkshire v Hampshire	Southampton
D.L.Lloyd	4ct	Glamorgan v Leicestershire	Cardiff
J.Overton	4ct	Somerset v Yorkshire	Leeds
S.P.D.Smith	4ct	Australia v England (*5th Test*)	The Oval
D.A.Warner	4ct	Australia v England (*3rd Test*)	Leeds

SIX OR MORE CATCHES IN THE FIELD IN A MATCH

T.Kohler-Cadmore	7ct	Yorkshire v Hampshire	Southampton
T.Kohler-Cadmore	6ct	Yorkshire v Kent	Canterbury
S.P.D.Smith	6ct	Australia v England (*5th Test*)	The Oval
D.A.Warner	6ct	Australia v England (*3rd Test*)	Leeds

ALL-ROUND HIGHLIGHTS

HUNDRED AND FIVE WICKETS IN AN INNINGS

B.L.D'Oliveira	103	7-92	Worcestershire v Glamorgan	Cardiff
R.F.Higgins	101	5-54	Gloucestershire v Derbyshire	Derby
L.M.Reece	184	5-63	Derbyshire v Sussex	Derby
D.I.Stevens	237	5-20	Kent v Yorkshire	Leeds

SPECSAVERS COUNTY CHAMPIONSHIP 2019
FINAL TABLES

DIVISION 1

		P	W	L	T	D	Bat	Bowl	Points	Points
							Bonus	Points	Deduct	Total
1	ESSEX (3)	14	9	1	–	4	26	38	–	228
2	Somerset (2)	14	9	3	–	2	25	38	1	217
3	Hampshire (5)	14	5	3	–	6	31	36	1	176
4	Kent (-)	14	5	5	–	4	36	36	–	172
5	Yorkshire (4)	14	5	4	–	5	24	36	–	165
6	Surrey (1)	14	2	6	–	6	33	38	–	133
7	Warwickshire (-)	14	3	6	–	5	26	32	–	131
8	Nottinghamshire (6)	14	–	10	–	4	16	32	1	67

DIVISION 2

		P	W	L	T	D	Bat	Bowl	Points	Points
							Bonus	Points	Deduct	Total
1	Lancashire (-)	14	8	–	–	6	34	41	–	233
2	Northamptonshire (9)	14	5	2	–	7	35	38	–	188
3	Gloucestershire (5)	14	5	3	–	6	36	36	–	182
4	Glamorgan (10)	14	4	3	–	7	35	34	1	167
5	Durham (8)	14	5	5	–	4	21	36	–	157
6	Sussex (4)	14	4	5	–	5	32	35	–	156
7	Derbyshire (7)	14	4	6	–	4	23	38	–	145
8	Middlesex (4)	14	3	5	–	6	24	33	2	133
9	Worcestershire (-)	14	3	7	–	4	20	37	–	125
10	Leicestershire (6)	14	1	6	–	7	24	32	–	107

2018 positions in brackets.
Glamorgan, Hampshire and Nottinghamshire deducted 1 point each for slow over rate.
Middlesex deducted 2 points for slow over rates.

SCORING OF CHAMPIONSHIP POINTS 2019

(a) For a win, 16 points, plus any points scored in the first innings.

(b) In a tie, each side to score eight points, plus any points scored in the first innings.

(c) In a drawn match, each side to score five points, plus any points scored in the first innings (see also paragraph (e) below).

(d) If the scores are equal in a drawn match, the side batting in the fourth innings to score eight points plus any points scored in the first innings, and the opposing side to score three points plus any points scored in the first innings.

(e) First Innings Points (awarded only for performances **in the first 110 overs** of each first innings and retained whatever the result of the match).

    (i) A maximum of five batting points to be available as under:
200 to 249 runs – 1 point; 250 to 299 runs – 2 points; 300 to 349 runs – 3 points; 350 to 399 runs – 4 points; 400 runs or over – 5 points.

    (ii) A maximum of three bowling points to be available as under:
3 to 5 wickets taken – 1 point; 6 to 8 wickets taken – 2 points; 9 to 10 wickets taken – 3 points.

(f) If a match is abandoned without a ball being bowled, each side to score five points.

(g) The side which has the highest aggregate of points gained at the end of the season shall be the Champion County of their respective Division. Should any sides in the Championship table be equal on points, the following tie-breakers will be applied in the order stated: most wins, fewest losses, team achieving most points in contests between teams level on points, most wickets taken, most runs scored. At the end of the season, the top three teams from the Second Division will be promoted and the bottom team from the First Division will be relegated.

COUNTY CHAMPIONS

The English County Championship was not officially constituted until December 1889. Prior to that date there was no generally accepted method of awarding the title; although the 'least matches lost' method existed, it was not consistently applied. Rules governing playing qualifications were agreed in 1873 and the first unofficial points system 15 years later.

Research has produced a list of champions dating back to 1826, but at least seven different versions exist for the period from 1864 to 1889 (see *The Wisden Book of Cricket Records*). Only from 1890 can any authorised list of county champions commence.

That first official Championship was contested between eight counties: Gloucestershire, Kent, Lancashire, Middlesex, Nottinghamshire, Surrey, Sussex and Yorkshire. The remaining counties were admitted in the following seasons: 1891 – Somerset, 1895 – Derbyshire, Essex, Hampshire, Leicestershire and Warwickshire, 1899 – Worcestershire, 1905 – Northamptonshire, 1921 – Glamorgan, and 1992 – Durham.

The Championship pennant was introduced by the 1951 champions, Warwickshire, and the Lord's Taverners' Trophy was first presented in 1973. The first sponsors, Schweppes (1977-83), were succeeded by Britannic Assurance (1984-98), PPP Healthcare (1999-2000), CricInfo (2001), Frizzell (2002-05), Liverpool Victoria (2006-15) and Specsavers (from 2016). Based on their previous season's positions, the 18 counties were separated into two divisions in 2000. From 2000 to 2005 the bottom three Division 1 teams were relegated and the top three Division 2 sides promoted. This was reduced to two teams from the end of the 2006 season.

1890	Surrey	1935	Yorkshire	1979	Essex
1891	Surrey	1936	Derbyshire	1980	Middlesex
1892	Surrey	1937	Yorkshire	1981	Nottinghamshire
1893	Yorkshire	1938	Yorkshire	1982	Middlesex
1894	Surrey	1939	Yorkshire	1983	Essex
1895	Surrey	1946	Yorkshire	1984	Essex
1896	Yorkshire	1947	Middlesex	1985	Middlesex
1897	Lancashire	1948	Glamorgan	1986	Essex
1898	Yorkshire	1949	{ Middlesex	1987	Nottinghamshire
1899	Surrey		Yorkshire	1988	Worcestershire
1900	Yorkshire	1950	{ Lancashire	1989	Worcestershire
1901	Yorkshire		Surrey	1990	Middlesex
1902	Yorkshire	1951	Warwickshire	1991	Essex
1903	Middlesex	1952	Surrey	1992	Essex
1904	Lancashire	1953	Surrey	1993	Middlesex
1905	Yorkshire	1954	Surrey	1994	Warwickshire
1906	Kent	1955	Surrey	1995	Warwickshire
1907	Nottinghamshire	1956	Surrey	1996	Leicestershire
1908	Yorkshire	1957	Surrey	1997	Glamorgan
1909	Kent	1958	Surrey	1998	Leicestershire
1910	Kent	1959	Yorkshire	1999	Surrey
1911	Warwickshire	1960	Yorkshire	2000	Surrey
1912	Yorkshire	1961	Hampshire	2001	Yorkshire
1913	Kent	1962	Yorkshire	2002	Surrey
1914	Surrey	1963	Yorkshire	2003	Sussex
1919	Yorkshire	1964	Worcestershire	2004	Warwickshire
1920	Middlesex	1965	Worcestershire	2005	Nottinghamshire
1921	Middlesex	1966	Yorkshire	2006	Sussex
1922	Yorkshire	1967	Yorkshire	2007	Sussex
1923	Yorkshire	1968	Yorkshire	2008	Durham
1924	Yorkshire	1969	Glamorgan	2009	Durham
1925	Yorkshire	1970	Kent	2010	Nottinghamshire
1926	Lancashire	1971	Surrey	2011	Lancashire
1927	Lancashire	1972	Warwickshire	2012	Warwickshire
1928	Lancashire	1973	Hampshire	2013	Durham
1929	Nottinghamshire	1974	Worcestershire	2014	Yorkshire
1930	Lancashire	1975	Leicestershire	2015	Yorkshire
1931	Yorkshire	1976	Middlesex	2016	Middlesex
1932	Yorkshire	1977	{ Kent	2017	Essex
1933	Yorkshire		Middlesex	2018	Surrey
1934	Lancashire	1978	Kent	2019	Essex

COUNTY CHAMPIONSHIP RESULTS 2019

DIVISION 1

	ESSEX	HANTS	KENT	NOTTS	SOM'T	SURREY	WARWKS	YORKS
ESSEX		C'ford	C'ford	C'ford	C'ford	C'ford	C'ford	C'ford
		E I/8	E 113	E 8w	E 151	E I/40	E 187	E 8w
HANTS	So'ton		So'ton	Newport	So'ton	So'ton	So'ton	So'ton
	H I/87		Drawn	H 244	H 136	H 272	Drawn	Y I/44
KENT	Cant	Cant		Tun W	Cant	Beck	Cant	Cant
	E 3w	Drawn		K 285	Sm 10w	Drawn	Drawn	Y 172
NOTTS	N'ham	Mansf'd	N'ham		N'ham	N'ham	N'ham	N'ham
	E I/123		K 227		Sm I/14	Sy 167	Wa 8w	Drawn
SOM'T	Taunton	Taunton	Taunton	Taunton		Taunton	Taunton	Taunton
	Drawn	Sm 313	Sm 74	Sm 132		Drawn	Sm 49	Sm 298
SURREY	Oval	Oval	Oval	Oval	G'ford		Oval	G'ford
	Drawn	Drawn	K 5w	Drawn	Sm 102		Sy 74	Drawn
WARWKS	Birm	Birm	Birm	Birm	Birm	Birm		Birm
	Drawn	H 314	K 8w	Drawn	Sm 5w	Wa 130		Drawn
YORKS	Leeds	Leeds	Leeds	Scar	Leeds	Scar	York	
	Drawn	Drawn	K 433	Y 143	Y I/73	Y 123	Wa 3w	

DIVISION 2

	DERBYS	DURHAM	GLAM	GLOS	LANCS	LEICS	MIDDX	N'HANTS	SUSSEX	WORCS
DERBYS		Derby	Derby	Derby	Derby		Derby	C'field	Derby	
		De 125	Gm 2w	Gs 8w	La 10w		Drawn	Nh 72	De 181	
DURHAM	C-le-St		C-le-St	C-le-St			C-le-St		C-le-St	C-le-St
	Du 29		Drawn	Gs 6w			Drawn		Sx 6w	Du 109
GLAM	Swan			Newport	Col B	Cardiff	Cardiff	Cardiff		Cardiff
	Drawn			Drawn	La I/50	Gm 291	M 256			Drawn
GLOS	Bristol		Bristol			Chelt	Chelt	Bristol	Bristol	Chelt
	Drawn		Gm 4w			Drawn	Gs 6w	Drawn	Sx 8w	Gs 13
LANCS	Man	Sedbergh				L'pool	Man	Man	Man	Man
	La I/45	Drawn				Drawn	La 104	La 10w	La I/51	La 6w
LEICS	Leics	Leics		Leics	Leics		Leics	Leics	Leics	Leics
	De 65	Du 119					Drawn	Nh 7w		Wo I/18
MIDDX	Lord's	Lord's	Radlett	N'wood	Lord's	Lord's			Lord's	
	Drawn	Du 44	Drawn	M 78	La 7w	Drawn			Sx I/50	
N'HANTS		No'ton	No'ton		No'ton	No'ton	No'ton		No'ton	No'ton
		Nh 169	Gm I/143		Drawn	Drawn	Drawn		Drawn	Nh 10w
SUSSEX		Hove	Hove	Arundel		Hove	Hove	Hove		Hove
		Du 196	Drawn	Drawn		Le 7w	Sx 7w	Nh 393		Drawn
WORCS	Kidder	Worcs	Worcs	Worcs	Worcs		Worcs		Kidder	
	De 82	Wo 5w	Wo 155	Gs 6w	Drawn		M 127		Drawn	

COUNTY CHAMPIONSHIP FIXTURES 2020

DIVISION 1

	ESSEX	GLOS	HANTS	KENT	LANCS	N'HANTS	SOM'T	SURREY	WARWKS	YORKS
ESSEX		C'ford	C'ford	C'ford	C'ford	C'ford	C'ford			C'ford
GLOS			Chelt		Bristol	Bristol	Bristol	Bristol	Bristol	Chelt
HANTS		So'ton		So'ton	So'ton	So'ton	So'ton		So'ton	So'ton
KENT	Cant	Cant	Cant		Cant	Cant	Cant	Beck		
LANCS	Man	Man		Man			Man	Man	Man	Man
N'HANTS	No'ton	No'ton		No'ton	No'ton			No'ton	No'ton	No'ton
SOM'T	Taunton	Taunton	Taunton			Taunton		Taunton	Taunton	Taunton
SURREY	Oval		Oval	Oval		G'ford	Oval		Oval	Oval
WARWKS	Birm		Birm	Birm	Birm	Birm	Birm	Birm		
YORKS	Leeds	Leeds	Leeds	Leeds	Scar			Leeds	Scar	

DIVISION 2

	DERBYS	DURHAM	GLAM	LEICS	MIDDX	NOTTS	SUSSEX	WORCS
DERBYS		Derby	Derby	Derby	Derby	Derby	Derby	C'field
DURHAM	C-le-St		C-le-St	C-le-St	C-le-St	C-le-St	C-le-St	C-le-St
GLAM	Cardiff	Swan		Cardiff	Cardiff	Col B	Cardiff	Cardiff
LEICS	Leics	Leics	Leics		Leics	Leics	Leics	Leics
MIDDX	Lord's	Lord's	N'wood	Lord's		Lord's	Lord's	Lord's
NOTTS	N'ham	N'ham	N'ham	N'ham	N'ham		N'ham	N'ham
SUSSEX	Arundel	Hove	Hove	Hove	Hove	Hove		Hove
WORCS	Worcs	Worcs	Worcs	Worcs	Worcs	Worcs	Worcs	

ROYAL LONDON ONE-DAY CUP 2019

This latest format of limited-overs competition was launched in 2014, and is now the only List-A tournament played in the UK. The top team from each group went through to the semi-finals, with a home draw; the second team from each group (drawn at home) played off against the third team from the other division to qualify for the semi-finals. The winner is decided in the final at Lord's.

NORTH GROUP	P	W	L	T	NR	Pts	Net RR
1 Nottinghamshire (2)	8	6	1	–	1	13	+0.61
2 Worcestershire (1)	8	6	2	–	–	12	+1.08
3 Lancashire (6)	8	5	3	–	–	10	+0.34
4 Durham (9)	8	4	2	–	2	10	+0.47
5 Derbyshire (5)	8	3	4	1	–	7	–0.07
6 Yorkshire (3)	8	2	3	2	1	7	–0.09
7 Warwickshire (4)	8	2	5	1	–	5	–0.91
8 Northamptonshire (7)	8	2	6	–	–	4	+0.06
9 Leicestershire (8)	8	2	6	–	–	4	–1.31

SOUTH GROUP	P	W	L	T	NR	Pts	Net RR
1 Hampshire (1)	8	7	1	–	–	14	+1.02
2 Middlesex (6)	8	6	2	–	–	12	+0.13
3 Somerset (4)	8	5	3	–	–	10	+0.50
4 Gloucestershire (7)	8	5	3	–	–	10	+0.27
5 Sussex (8)	8	4	4	–	–	8	+0.01
6 Glamorgan (9)	8	3	4	–	1	7	–0.29
7 Kent (3)	8	2	5	–	1	5	–0.96
8 Essex (2)	8	2	6	–	–	4	+0.32
9 Surrey (5)	8	1	7	–	–	2	–1.00

Win = 2 points. Tie (T)/No Result (NR) = 1 point. 2018 positions in brackets.

Positions of counties finishing equal on points are decided by most wins or, if equal, the team that achieved the most points in the matches played between them; if still equal, the team with the higher net run rate (ie deducting from the average runs per over scored by that team in matches where a result was achieved, the average runs per over scored against that team). In the event the teams still cannot be separated, the winner will be decided by drawing lots.

Statistical Highlights in 2019

Highest total	433-7		Nottinghamshire v Leics	Nottingham
Biggest victory (runs)	264		Somerset (358-9) beat Kent (94)	Taunton
Most runs	521 (ave 74.42)	B.A.Godleman (Derbyshire)		
Highest innings	190	J.M.Vince	Hampshire v Glos	Southampton
Most sixes (inns)	11	M.H.Wessels	Worcestershire v Derbys	Derby
Highest partnership	234	C.B.Cooke/W.T.Root	Glamorgan v Glos	Bristol
Most wickets	28 (ave 18.50)	S.Mahmood (Lancashire)		
Best bowling	6-37	S.Mahmood	Lancashire v Northants	Manchester
Most economical	10-3-14-5	S.Mahmood	Lancashire v Leics	Manchester
Most expensive	10-0-93-0	C.J.Liddle	Gloucestershire v Kent	Bristol
	9-0-93-1	D.Klein	Leicestershire v Notts	Nottingham
Most w/k dismissals	19	T.P.Alsop (Hampshire)		
Most w/k dismissals (inns)	5	R.G.White	Essex v Glamorgan	Cardiff
	5	R.G.White	Essex v Middlesex	Chelmsford
Most catches	12	R.E.van der Merwe (Somerset)		
Most catches (inns)	4	J.A.Porter	Essex v Hampshire	Chelmsford

2019 ROYAL LONDON ONE-DAY CUP FINAL
HAMPSHIRE v SOMERSET

At Lord's, London, on 25 May.
Result: **SOMERSET** won by six wickets.
Toss: Hampshire. Award: J.Overton.

HAMPSHIRE

		Runs	Balls	4/6	Fall
† T.P.Alsop	c Hildreth b Davey	16	27	2	2- 31
A.H.T.Donald	c van der Merwe b Davey	11	11	2	1- 16
J.J.Weatherley	b Gregory	12	25	–	3- 50
* S.A.Northeast	b Abell	56	89	4	6-164
R.R.Rossouw	b J.Overton	28	17	6	4- 96
G.K.Berg	c Bartlett b J.Overton	27	42	2	5-145
J.K.Fuller	not out	55	48	4/2	
C.P.Wood	c Bartlett b J.Overton	0	2	–	7-165
K.J.Abbott	b Abell	2	10	–	8-180
M.S.Crane	not out	28	29	3	
F.H.Edwards					
Extras	(LB 3, W 6)	9			
Total	(8 wkts; 50 overs)	**244**			

SOMERSET

		Runs	Balls	4/6	Fall
† T.Banton	c Alsop b Edwards	69	67	9/1	1-112
Azhar Ali	c Rossouw b Edwards	45	53	6	2-121
P.D.Trego	c Wood b Fuller	29	40	1	3-170
J.C.Hildreth	not out	69	68	3	
* T.B.Abell	c Donald b Edwards	14	11	3	4-203
G.A.Bartlett	not out	14	22	1	
L.Gregory					
R.E.van der Merwe					
C.Overton					
J.Overton					
J.H.Davey					
Extras	(LB 4, W 1)	5			
Total	(4 wkts; 43.3 overs)	**245**			

SOMERSET

	O	M	R	W	HAMPSHIRE	O	M	R	W
C.Overton	10	0	52	0	Edwards	9.3	0	69	3
Davey	8	0	28	2	Abbott	9	0	43	0
Gregory	8	0	42	1	Wood	6	1	28	0
J.Overton	10	1	48	3	Berg	4	0	13	0
Van der Merwe	9	0	52	0	Crane	10	0	62	0
Abell	5	0	19	2	Fuller	5	0	26	1

Umpires: R.J.Bailey and M.J.Saggers

SEMI-FINALS

At Rose Bowl, Southampton, on 12 May. Toss: Lancashire. **HAMPSHIRE** won by four wickets. Lancashire 241 (47.4; K.K.Jennings 63, J.S.Lehmann 62, G.K.Berg 5-26). Hampshire 245-6 (49; R.R.Rossouw 85, J.M.Vince 79, S.Mahmood 3-46). Award: G.K.Berg.
At Trent Bridge, Nottingham, on 12 May. Toss: Nottinghamshire. **SOMERSET** won by 115 runs. Somerset 337 (50; P.D.Trego 73, Azhar Ali 72, T.Banton 59, J.T.Ball 4-62). Nottinghamshire 222 (38.2; B.T.Slater 58, A.D.Hales 54, R.E.van der Merwe 3-29).

PRINCIPAL LIST A RECORDS 1963-2019

These records cover all the major limited-overs tournaments played by the counties since the inauguration of the Gillette Cup in 1963.

Highest Totals		496-4	Surrey v Glos	The Oval	2007
		445-8	Notts v Northants	Nottingham	2016
Highest Total Batting Second		429	Glamorgan v Surrey	The Oval	2002
Lowest Totals		23	Middlesex v Yorks	Leeds	1974
		36	Leics v Sussex	Leicester	1973
Largest Victory (Runs)		346	Somerset beat Devon	Torquay	1990
		304	Sussex beat Ireland	Belfast	1996
Highest Scores	268	A.D.Brown	Surrey v Glamorgan	The Oval	2002
	206	A.I.Kallicharran	Warwicks v Oxfords	Birmingham	1984
	203	A.D.Brown	Surrey v Hampshire	Guildford	1997
	201*	R.S.Bopara	Essex v Leics	Leicester	2008
	201	V.J.Wells	Leics v Berkshire	Leicester	1996
Fastest Hundred	36 balls	G.D.Rose	Somerset v Devon	Torquay	1990
	43 balls	R.R.Watson	Scotland v Somerset	Edinburgh	2003
	44 balls	M.A.Ealham	Kent v Derbyshire	Maidstone	1995
	44 balls	T.C.Smith	Lancashire v Worcs	Worcester	2012
	44 balls	D.I.Stevens	Kent v Sussex	Canterbury	2013
Most Sixes (Inns)	15	R.N.ten Doeschate	Essex v Scotland	Chelmsford	2013
Highest Partnership for each Wicket					
1st	342	M.J.Lumb/M.H.Wessels	Notts v Northants	Nottingham	2016
2nd	302	M.E.Trescothick/C.Kieswetter	Somerset v Glos	Taunton	2008
3rd	309*	T.S.Curtis/T.M.Moody	Worcs v Surrey	The Oval	1994
4th	234*	D.I.Lloyd/C.H.Lloyd	Lancashire v Glos	Manchester	1978
5th	221*	R.R.Sarwan/M.A.Hardinges	Glos v Lancashire	Manchester	2005
6th	232	D.Wiese/B.C.Brown	Sussex v Hampshire	Southampton	2019
7th	170	D.R.Brown/A.F.Giles	Warwicks v Essex	Birmingham	2003
8th	174	R.W.T.Key/J.C.Tredwell	Kent v Surrey	The Oval	2007
9th	155	C.M.W.Read/A.J.Harris	Notts v Durham	Nottingham	1984
10th	82	G.Chapple/P.J.Martin	Lancashire v Worcs	Manchester	1996
Best Bowling	8-21	M.A.Holding	Derbyshire v Sussex	Hove	1988
	8-26	K.D.Boyce	Essex v Lancashire	Manchester	1971
	8-31	D.L.Underwood	Kent v Scotland	Edinburgh	1987
	8-66	S.R.G.Francis	Somerset v Derbys	Derby	2004
Four Wkts in Four Balls		A.Ward	Derbyshire v Sussex	Derby	1970
		S.M.Pollock	Warwickshire v Leics	Birmingham	1996
		V.C.Drakes	Notts v Derbyshire	Nottingham	1999
		D.A.Payne	Gloucestershire v Essex	Chelmsford	2010
		G.R.Napier	Essex v Surrey	Chelmsford	2013
Most Economical Analyses					
	8-8-0-0	B.A.Langford	Somerset v Essex	Yeovil	1969
	8-7-1-1	D.R.Doshi	Notts v Northants	Northampton	1977
	12-9-3-1	J.Simmons	Lancashire v Suffolk	Bury St Eds	1985
	8-6-2-3	F.J.Titmus	Middlesex v Northants	Northampton	1972
Most Expensive Analyses					
	9-0-108-3	S.D.Thomas	Glamorgan v Surrey	The Oval	2002
	10-0-107-0	J.W.Dernbach	Surrey v Essex	The Oval	2008
	11-0-103-0	G.Welch	Warwicks v Lancs	Birmingham	1995
	10-0-101-1	M.J.J.Critchley	Derbyshire v Worcs	Worcester	2016
Century and Five Wickets in an Innings					
	154*, 5-26	M.J.Procter	Glos v Somerset	Taunton	1972
	206, 6-32	A.I.Kallicharran	Warwicks v Oxfords	Birmingham	1984
	103, 5-41	C.L.Hooper	Kent v Essex	Maidstone	1993
	125, 5-41	I.R.Bell	Warwicks v Essex	Chelmsford	2003
Most Wicket-Keeping Dismissals in an Innings					
	8 (8 ct)	D.J.S.Taylor	Somerset v British Us	Taunton	1982
	8 (8 ct)	D.J.Pipe	Worcs v Herts	Hertford	2001
Most Catches in an Innings by a Fielder					
	5	J.M.Rice	Hampshire v Warwicks	Southampton	1978
	5	D.J.G.Sales	Northants v Essex	Northampton	2007

VITALITY BLAST 2019

In 2019, the Twenty20 competition was sponsored by Vitality. Between 2003 and 2009, three regional leagues competed to qualify for the knockout stages, but this was reduced to two leagues in 2010, before returning to the three-division format in 2012. In 2014, the competition reverted to two regional leagues. (2018's positions in brackets.)

NORTH GROUP

	P	W	L	T	NR	Pts	Net RR
Lancashire (3)	14	8	3	–	4	20	+0.75
Nottinghamshire (4)	14	6	4	–	4	16	+0.33
Derbyshire (7)	14	7	5	–	2	16	+0.22
Worcestershire (1)	14	6	5	–	3	15	+0.20
Yorkshire (5)	14	4	5	1	4	13	+0.33
Durham (2)	14	5	7	–	2	12	–0.04
Northamptonshire (9)	14	4	6	–	4	12	–0.54
Warwickshire (6)	14	4	7	1	2	11	–0.46
Leicestershire (8)	14	4	7	–	3	11	–0.47

SOUTH GROUP

	P	W	L	T	NR	Pts	Net RR
Sussex (3)	14	8	3	1	2	19	+0.80
Gloucestershire (4)	14	7	3	1	3	18	+0.24
Middlesex (9)	14	7	6	–	1	15	+0.21
Essex (7)	14	5	4	1	4	15	–0.46
Kent (2)	14	6	6	–	2	14	0.00
Somerset (1)	14	6	7	–	1	13	+0.44
Hampshire (8)	14	5	6	1	2	13	+0.02
Surrey (5)	14	5	7	1	1	12	–0.24
Glamorgan (6)	14	3	9	–	2	7	–1.38

QUARTER-FINALS: ESSEX beat Lancashire by six wickets at Chester-le-Street.
NOTTINGHAMSHIRE beat Middlesex by ten wickets at Nottingham.
WORCESTERSHIRE beat Sussex by eight wickets at Hove.
DERBYSHIRE beat Gloucestershire by seven wickets at Bristol.

SEMI-FINALS: WORCESTERSHIRE beat Nottinghamshire by 1 run at Birmingham.
ESSEX beat Derbyshire by 34 runs at Birmingham.

LEADING AGGREGATES AND RECORDS 2019

BATTING (500 runs)

	M	I	NO	HS	Runs	Avge	100	50	R/100b	Sixes
Babar Azam (Somerset)	13	13	2	102*	578	52.54	1	4	149.3	14
T.Banton (Somerset)	13	13	–	100	549	42.23	1	1	161.4	23

BOWLING (20 wkts)

	O	M	R	W	Avge	BB	4w	R/Over
R.Rampaul (Derbys)	54.0	1	362	23	15.73	3-17	–	6.70
H.F.Gurney (Notts)	44.0	–	396	22	18.00	5-30	1	9.00
M.W.Parkinson (Lancs)	41.0	–	307	21	14.61	4-30	1	7.48
K.J.Abbott (Hants)	43.3	–	356	20	17.80	3-15	–	8.18

Highest total	255-2		Yorkshire v Leicestershire	Leicester
Highest innings	129	C.S.Delport	Essex v Surrey	Chelmsford
Most sixes	30	M.M.Ali (Worcestershire)		
Highest partnership	177	M.H.Wessels/M.M.Ali	Worcestershire v Sussex	Hove
Best bowling	7-18	C.N.Ackermann	Leicestershire v Warwicks	Leicester
Most economical	4-0-9-3	C.N.Ackermann	Leicestershire v Derbyshire	Derby
Most expensive	4-0-67-2	C.P.Wood	Hampshire v Glamorgan	Cardiff
Most w/k dismissals	11	O.B.Cox (Worcestershire)		
Most catches	13	P.D.Salt (Sussex)		
Most catches (inns)	4	G.J.Maxwell	Lancashire v Nottinghamshire	Manchester
	4	H.C.Brook	Yorkshire v Northants	Leeds

2019 VITALITY BLAST FINAL
ESSEX v WORCESTERSHIRE

At Edgbaston, Birmingham, on 21 September (floodlit).
Result: **ESSEX** won by four wickets.
Toss: Essex. Award: S.R.Harmer.

WORCESTERSHIRE		**Runs**	**Balls**	**4/6**	**Fall**
H.D.Rutherford	b Lawrence	4	3	1	1- 5
M.H.Wessels	run out	31	34	2/1	5-112
* M.M.Ali	c and b Harmer	32	26	3/2	2- 61
† O.B.Cox	lbw b Harmer	0	1	–	3- 61
W.D.Parnell	b Harmer	19	19	1/1	4- 90
D.K.H.Mitchell	c Delport b Lawrence	19	15	3	6-119
R.A.Whiteley	c Harmer b Delport	7	6	–/1	7-127
B.L.D'Oliveira	c Lawrence b Bopara	10	9	1	9-145
E.G.Barnard	c Westley b Bopara	5	5	–	8-136
P.R.Brown	not out	1	2	–	
C.A.J.Morris					
Extras	(B 4, LB 2, W 11)	17			
Total	(9 wkts; 20 overs)	**145**			

ESSEX		**Runs**	**Balls**	**4/6**	**Fall**
T.Westley	c Brown b Parnell	36	31	4	3- 65
C.S.Delport	c Wessels b Parnell	1	7	–	1- 9
† A.J.A.Wheater	b Mitchell	15	15	1	2- 47
D.W.Lawrence	c Wessels b Ali	23	18	1/1	5- 82
R.N.ten Doeschate	c Mitchell b Ali	1	4	–	4- 75
R.S.Bopara	not out	36	22	2/2	
P.I.Walter	b Brown	14	16	1	6-129
* S.R.Harmer	not out	18	7	3	
A.S.S.Nijjar					
A.P.Beard					
S.J.Cook					
Extras	(LB 3, W 1)	4			
Total	(6 wkts; 20 overs)	**148**			

ESSEX	O	M	R	W	**WORCESTERSHIRE**	O	M	R	W
Lawrence	4	0	26	2	Ali	4	0	22	2
Cook	2	0	19	0	Morris	2	0	17	0
Beard	1	0	7	0	Parnell	4	0	34	2
Bopara	4	0	30	2	Brown	4	0	28	1
Harmer	4	0	16	3	Barnard	2	0	17	0
Nijjar	4	0	31	0	D'Oliveira	2	0	15	0
Delport	1	0	10	1	Mitchell	2	0	12	1

Umpires: D.J.Millns and A.G.Wharf

TWENTY20 CUP WINNERS

2003	Surrey	2009	Sussex	2015	Lancashire
2004	Leicestershire	2010	Hampshire	2016	Northamptonshire
2005	Somerset	2011	Leicestershire	2017	Nottinghamshire
2006	Leicestershire	2012	Hampshire	2018	Worcestershire
2007	Kent	2013	Northamptonshire	2019	Essex
2008	Middlesex	2014	Warwickshire		

PRINCIPAL TWENTY20 CUP RECORDS 2003-19

Highest Total	260-4		Yorkshire v Northants	Leeds	2017
Highest Total Batting 2nd	231-5		Warwickshire v Northants	Birmingham	2018
Lowest Total	44		Glamorgan v Surrey	The Oval	2019
Largest Victory (Runs)	143		Somerset v Essex	Chelmsford	2011
Largest Victory (Balls)	75		Hampshire v Glos	Bristol	2010
Highest Scores	161	A.Lyth	Yorkshire v Northants	Leeds	2017
	158*	B.B.McCullum	Warwickshire v Derbys	Birmingham	2015
	153*	L.J.Wright	Sussex v Essex	Chelmsford	2014
	152*	G.R.Napier	Essex v Sussex	Chelmsford	2008
	151*	C.H.Gayle	Somerset v Kent	Taunton	2015
Fastest Hundred	34 balls	A.Symonds	Kent v Middlesex	Maidstone	2004
Most Sixes (Innings)	16	G.R.Napier	Essex v Sussex	Chelmsford	2008
Most Runs in Career	4087	L.J.Wright	Sussex		2004-19

Highest Partnership for each Wicket

1st	207	J.L.Denly/D.J.Bell-Drummond	Kent v Essex	Chelmsford	2017
2nd	186	J.L.Langer/C.L.White	Somerset v Glos	Taunton	2006
3rd	171	I.R.Bell/A.J.Hose	Warwickshire v Northants	Birmingham	2018
4th	159*	L.J.Wright/M.W.Machan	Sussex v Essex	Chelmsford	2014
5th	117*	M.N.W.Spriegel/G.C.Wilson	Surrey v Middlesex	Lord's	2012
	117*	R.N.ten Doeschate/R.S.Bopara	Essex v Surrey	The Oval	2019
6th	126*	C.S.MacLeod/J.W.Hastings	Durham v Northants	Chester-le-St	2014
7th	80	D.T.Christian/T.S.Roland-Jones	Middlesex v Kent	Canterbury	2014
8th	86*	J.A.Simpson/T.G.Southee	Middlesex v Hampshire	Southampton	2017
9th	69	C.J.Anderson/J.H.Davey	Somerset v Surrey	The Oval	2017
10th	59	H.H.Streak/J.E.Anyon	Warwickshire v Worcs	Birmingham	2005
Best Bowling	7-18	C.N.Ackermann	Leics v Warwicks	Leicester	2019
	6- 5	A.V.Suppiah	Somerset v Glamorgan	Cardiff	2011
	6-16	T.G.Southee	Essex v Glamorgan	Chelmsford	2011
	6-19	T.T.Bresnan	Yorkshire v Lancashire	Leeds	2017
	6-21	A.J.Hall	Northants v Worcs	Northampton	2008
	6-24	T.J.Murtagh	Surrey v Middlesex	Lord's	2005
	6-28	J.K.Fuller	Middlesex v Hampshire	Southampton	2018
Most Wkts in Career	160	D.R.Briggs	Hampshire, Sussex		2010-19

Most Economical Innings Analyses (Qualification: 4 overs)

4-2-5-2	A.C.Thomas	Somerset v Hampshire	Southampton	2010
4-0-5-3	D.R.Briggs	Hampshire v Kent	Canterbury	2010

Most Maiden Overs in an Innings

4-2-9-1	M.Morkel	Kent v Surrey	Beckenham	2007
4-2-5-2	A.C.Thomas	Somerset v Hampshire	Southampton	2010
4-2-14-1	S.M.Curran	Surrey v Sussex	Hove	2018

Most Expensive Innings Analyses

4-0-77-0	B.W.Sanderson	Northants v Yorkshire	Leeds	2017
4-0-67-1	R.J.Kirtley	Sussex v Essex	Chelmsford	2008
4-0-67-2	C.P.Wood	Hampshire v Glamorgan	Cardiff	2019

Most Wicket-Keeping Dismissals in Career

114	J.S.Foster	Essex		2003-17

Most Wicket-Keeping Dismissals in an Innings

5 (5 ct)	M.J.Prior	Sussex v Middlesex	Richmond	2006
5 (4 ct, 1 st)	G.L.Brophy	Yorkshire v Durham	Chester-le-St	2008
5 (3 ct, 2 st)	B.J.M.Scott	Worcs v Yorkshire	Worcester	2011
5 (4 ct, 1 st)	G.C.Wilson	Surrey v Hampshire	The Oval	2014
5 (5 ct)	N.J.O'Brien	Leics v Northants	Leicester	2014
5 (3 ct, 2 st)	J.A.Simpson	Middlesex v Surrey	Lord's	2014
5 (4 ct, 1 st)	C.B.Cooke	Glamorgan v Surrey	Cardiff	2016

Most Catches in Career

102	S.J.Croft	Lancashire	2006-19

Most Catches in an Innings by a Fielder

5	M.W.Machan	Sussex v Glamorgan	Hove	2016

THE HUNDRED REGISTER

BIRMINGHAM PHOENIX

Venues: Edgbaston, Birmingham (men); New Road, Worcester (women). **Men's Head Coach**: Andrew McDonald. **Women's Head Coach**: Ben Sawyer. **Men's Captain**: Moeen Ali. **Women's Captain**: Sophie Devine.

ALI, Moeen Munir – *see WORCESTERSHIRE*. £125,000. Local icon.

BOPARA, Ravinder Singh – *see SUSSEX*. £100,000.

BROOKES, Henry James Hamilton – *see WARWICKSHIRE*. £40,000.

BROWN, Patrick Rhys – *see WORCESTERSHIRE*. £60,000. Local icon.

COOKE, Christopher Barry – *see GLAMORGAN*. £30,000.

DELPORT, Cameron Scott – *see ESSEX*. £50,000.

HELM, Thomas George – *see MIDDLESEX*. £75,000.

HOSE, Adam John – *see WARWICKSHIRE*. £50,000.

HOWELL, Benny Alexander Cameron – *see GLOUCESTERSHIRE*. £75,000.

LIVINGSTONE, Liam Stephen – *see LANCASHIRE*. £125,000.

NQSHAHEEN SHAH AFRIDI – *see HAMPSHIRE*. £60,000.

WESSELS, Mattheus Hendrik ('**Riki**') – *see WORCESTERSHIRE*. £30,000.

NQWILLIAMSON, Kane Stuart (Tauranga Boys' C), b Tauranga, New Zealand 8 Aug 1990. Cousin of D.Cleaver (C Districts 2010-11 to date). 5'8". RHB, OB. N Districts 2007-08 to date. Gloucestershire 2011-12; cap 2011. Yorkshire 2013-18. IPL: SH 2015-19. **Tests** (NZ): 80 (2010-11 to 2019-20, 32 as captain); 1000 runs (1): 1172 (2015); HS 242* v SL (Wellington) 2014-15; scored 131 v I (Ahmedabad) 2010-11 on debut; BB 4-44 v E (Auckland) 2012-13. **LOI** (NZ): 151 (2010 to 2019-20, 77 as captain); 1000 runs (1): 1376 (2015); HS 148 v WI (Manchester) 2019; BB 4-22 v SA (Paarl) 2012-13. **IT20** (NZ): 57 (2011-12 to 2018-19, 39 as captain); HS 73* v B (Napier) 2016-17; BB 2-16 v B (Mt Maunganui) 2016-17. F-c Tours (NZ)(C=Captain): E 2013, 2015; A 2011-12, 2015-16, 2019-20C; SA 2012-13, 2016C; WI 2012, 2014; I 2010-11, 2012, 2016-17C; SL 2012-13, 2019C; Z 2011-12, 2016C; B 2013-14; UAE 2014-15 (v P), 2018-19C (v P). HS 284* ND v Wellington (Lincoln) 2011-12. CC HS 189 Y v Sussex (Scarborough) 2014. BB 5-75 ND v Canterbury (Christchurch) 2008-09. CC BB 3-58 Gs v Northants (Northampton) 2012. LO HS 148 (*see LOI*). LO BB 5-51 ND v Auckland (Auckland) 2009-10. T20 HS 101*. T20 BB 3-33. £100,000.

WOAKES, Christopher Roger – *see WARWICKSHIRE*. Central.

NQZAMPA, Adam – *see ESSEX*. £40,000.

LONDON SPIRIT

Venues: Lord's Cricket Ground, London (men); Cloud FM County Ground, Chelmsford (women); County Ground, Northampton (women). **Men's Head Coach**: Shane Warne. **Women's Head Coach**: Trevor Griffin. **Men's Captain**: Eoin Morgan. **Women's Captain**: Heather Knight.

ABBOTT, Kyle John – *see HAMPSHIRE*. £50,000. Kolpak.

BURNS, Rory Joseph – *see SURREY*. Central.

CRANE, Mason Sydney – *see HAMPSHIRE*. £50,000.

CRAWLEY, Zak – *see KENT*. £40,000.

DENLY, Joseph Liam – *see KENT.* £60,000.

DERNBACH, Jade Winston – *see SURREY.* £30,000.

LAWRENCE, Daniel William – *see ESSEX.* £60,000. Local icon.

^{NQ}**MAXWELL, Glenn** James – *see LANCASHIRE.* £125,000.

^{NQ}**MOHAMMAD AMIR** – *see ESSEX.* £100,000.

^{NQ}**MOHAMMAD NABI** – *see KENT.* £100,000.

MORGAN, Eoin Joseph Gerard – *see MIDDLESEX.* £125,000. Local icon.

REECE, Luis Michael – *see DERBYSHIRE.* £30,000.

ROSSINGTON, Adam Matthew – *see NORTHAMPTONSHIRE.* £40,000.

VAN DER MERWE, Roelof Erasmus – *see SOMERSET.* £75,000.

WOOD, Mark Andrew – *see DURHAM.* £75,000.

MANCHESTER ORIGINALS

Venues: Old Trafford, Manchester (both); Sedbergh School (women). **Men's Head Coach**: Simon Katich. **Women's Head Coach**: tba. **Men's Captain**: Jos Buttler. **Women's Captain**: Kathryn Cross.

ABELL, Thomas Benjamin – *see SOMERSET.* £100,000.

BUTTLER, Joseph Charles – *see LANCASHIRE.* Central.

BYROM, Edward James – *see SOMERSET.* £30,000.

^{NQ}**CHRISTIAN, Dan**iel Trevor – *see NOTTINGHAMSHIRE.* £60,000.

CLARKE, Joe Michael – *see NOTTINGHAMSHIRE.* £40,000.

De LANGE, Marchant – *see GLAMORGAN.* £40,000.

^{NQ}**IMRAN TAHIR** – *see SURREY.* £125,000.

MADSEN, Wayne Lee – *see DERBYSHIRE.* £60,000.

MAHMOOD, Saqib – *see LANCASHIRE.* £75,000. Local icon.

PARKINSON, Matthew William – *see LANCASHIRE.* Local icon.

PARNELL, Wayne Dillon – *see WORCESTERSHIRE.* £50,000. Kolpak.

POLLOCK, Edward John – *see WARWICKSHIRE.* £30,000.

SALT, Philip Dean – *see SUSSEX.* £100,000.

^{NQ}**SANTNER, Mitchell** Josef, b Hamilton, New Zealand 5 Feb 1992. LHB, SLA. N Districts 2011-12 to date. Worcestershire 2016; 2017 (T20 only). IPL: CSK 2019. **Tests** (NZ): 22 (2015-16 to 2019-20); HS 126 and BB 3-53 v E (Mt Maunganui) 2019-20. **LOI** (NZ): 72 (2015 to 2019-20); HS 67 v E (Christchurch) 2017-18; BB 5-50 v Ire (Dublin) 2017. **IT20** (NZ): 44 (2015 to 2019-20); HS 37 v P (Auckland) 2017-18; BB 4-11 v I (Nagpur) 2015-16. F-c Tours (NZ): E 2015; A 2015-16, 2019-20; SA 2016; I 2016-17; SL 2019; Z 2016. HS 126 (*see Tests*). CC HS 23* Wo v Glamorgan (Cardiff) 2016. BB 3-27 ND v CD (Napier) 2018-19. LO HS 86 ND v CD (New Plymouth) 2014-15. LO BB 5-50 (*see LOI*). T20 HS 45*. T20 BB 4-11. £50,000.

VILAS, Dane James – *see LANCASHIRE.* £125,000. Kolpak.

NORTHERN SUPERCHARGERS

Venues: Emerald Headingley, Leeds (both); South Northumberland CC, Gosforth (women); York CC (women). **Men's Head Coach:** Darren Lehmann. **Women's Head Coach:** Danielle Hazell. **Men's Captain:** Aaron Finch. **Women's Captain:** Lauren Winfield.

BARNARD, Edward George – *see WORCESTERSHIRE*. £30,000.

CARSE, Brydon Alexander – *see DURHAM*. £40,000.

^{NQ}**FINCH, Aaron** James – *see SURREY*. £125,000.

FOAKES, Benjamin Thomas – *see SURREY*. £60,000.

GLEESON, Richard James – *see LANCASHIRE*. £60,000.

KOHLER-CADMORE, Tom – *see YORKSHIRE*. £50,000.

^{NQ}**LYNN, Chris**topher Austin, b Herston, Brisbane, Australia 10 Apr 1990. RHB, SLA. Queensland 2009-10 to 2016-17. IPL: DC 2012. KKR 2014 to date. Big Bash: BH 2011-12 to date. **LOI** (A): 4 (2016-17 to 2018-19); HS 44 v SA (Adelaide) 2018-19. **IT20** (A): 18 (2013-14 to 2018-19); HS 44 v NZ (Sydney) 2017-18. HS 250 Q v Vic (Brisbane) 2014-15. BB – . LO HS 135 Q v NSW (Sydney, DO) 2018-19. LO BB 1-3 Q v WA (Sydney, BO) 2013-14. T20 HS 101. T20 BB 2-15. £100,000.

LYTH, Adam – *see YORKSHIRE*. £75,000.

^{NQ}**MUJEEB ZADRAN** – *see MIDDLESEX*. £125,000.

RASHID, Adil Usman – *see YORKSHIRE*. £100,000. Local icon.

RIMMINGTON, Nathan John – *see DURHAM*. £40,000.

SIMPSON, John Andrew – *see MIDDLESEX*. £30,000.

STOKES, Benjamin Andrew – *see DURHAM*. Central.

WIESE, David – *see SUSSEX*. £50,000. Kolpak.

WILLEY, David Jonathan – *see YORKSHIRE*. £75,000. Local icon.

OVAL INVINCIBLES

Venues: The Kia Oval, London (both); County Ground, Beckenham (women). **Men's Head Coach:** Tom Moody. **Women's Head Coach:** Lydia Greenway. **Men's Captain:** tba. **Women's Captain:** tba.

^{NQ}**ALLEN, Fabian** Anthony, b Kingston, Jamaica 7 May 1995. RHB, SLA. Jamaica 2016-17 to date. **LOI** (WI): 14 (2018-19 to 2019-20); HS 51 v SL (Chester-le-Street) 2019; BB 2-40 v I (Port of Spain) 2019. **IT20** (WI): 13 (2018-19 to 2019-20); HS 27 v I (Kolkata) 2018-19; BB 2-19 v B (Dhaka) 2018-19. HS 169* Jam v T&T (Tarouba) 2017-18. BB 4-47 Jam v Barbados (Bridgetown) 2016-17. LO HS 62* Jam v USA (North Sound) 2017-18. LO BB 2-18 Jam v USA (Bridgetown) 2018-19. T20 HS 64*. T20 BB 2-19. £50,000.

BILLINGS, Samuel William – *see KENT*. £100,000.

BLAKE, Alexander James – *see KENT*. £50,000.

CURRAN, Samuel Matthew – *see SURREY*. Central.

CURRAN, Thomas Kevin – *see SURREY*. £75,000. Local icon.

EVANS, Laurie John – *see SUSSEX*. £30,000.

JACKS, William George – *see SURREY*. £40,000.

NQLAMICHHANE, Sandeep, b Syangja, Nepal 2 Aug 2000. RHB, LBG. Nepal 2019-20. IPL: DD 2018. DC 2019. Big Bash: MS 2018-19 to date. **LOI** (Nepal): 10 (2018 to 2019-20); HS 28 v Oman (Kirtipur) 2019-20; BB 6-16 v USA (Kirtipur) 2019-20. **IT20** (Nepal): 20 (+ 1 ICC World XI 2018) (2018 to 2019-20); HS 9 v Qatar (Singapore) 2019; BB 4-20 v Neth (Al Amerat) 2019-20. HS 39* and BB 3-84 Nepal v MCC (Kirtipur) 2019-20. LO HS 28 (see *LOI*). LO BB 6-16 (see *LOI*). T20 HS 10*. T20 BB 4-10. £100,000.

NQNARINE, Sunil Philip, b Arima, Trinidad 26 May 1988. LHB, OB. Trinidad & Tobago 2008-09 to 2012-13. IPL: KKR 2012 to date. Big Bash: SS 2012-13. MR 2016-17. **Tests** (WI): 6 (2012 to 2013-14); HS 22* v B (Dhaka) 2012-13; BB 6-91 v NZ (Hamilton) 2013-14. **LOI** (WI): 65 (2011-12 to 2016-17); HS 36 v B (Khulna) 2012-13; BB 6-27 v SA (Providence) 2016. **IT20** (WI): 51 (2011-12 to 2019); HS 30 v P (Dubai, DSC) 2016-17; BB 4-12 v NZ (Lauderhill) 2012. F-c Tours (WI): E 2012; NZ 2013-14; B 2012-13. HS 40* WI A v Bangladesh A (Gros Islet) 2011-12. BB 8-17 (13-39 match) T&T v CC&C (Cave Hill) 2011-12. LO HS 51 T&T v Barbados (Bridgetown) 2017-18. LO BB 6-9 T&T v Guyana (Port of Spain) 2014-15. T20 HS 79. T20 BB 5-19. £125,000.

ROSSOUW, Rilee Roscoe – *see HAMPSHIRE*. £75,000.

ROY, Jason Jonathan – *see SURREY*. £125,000. Local icon.

SOWTER, Nathan Adam – *see MIDDLESEX*. £30,000.

TOPLEY, Reece James William – *see SURREY*. £60,000.

VILJOEN, GC 'Hardus' – *see KENT*. £60,000. Kolpak.

WOOD, Christopher Philip – *see HAMPSHIRE*. £40,000.

SOUTHERN BRAVE

Venues: Ageas Bowl, Southampton (both); 1st Central County Ground, Hove (women).
Men's Head Coach: Mahela Jayawardena. **Women's Head Coach**: Charlotte Edwards.
Men's Captain: tba. **Women's Captain**: tba.

ARCHER, Jofra Chioke – *see SUSSEX*. Central.

DAVIES, Alexander Luke – *see LANCASHIRE*. £40,000.

DAWSON, Liam Andrew – *see HAMPSHIRE*. £100,000.

GARTON, George Henry Simmons – *see SUSSEX*. £40,000.

JORDAN, Christopher James – *see SUSSEX*. £75,000. Local icon.

MILLS, Tymal Solomon – *see SUSSEX*. £60,000.

OVERTON, Craig – *see SOMERSET*. £30,000.

POPE, Oliver John Douglas – *see SURREY*. £50,000.

RAWLINS, Delray Millard Wendell – *see SUSSEX*. £50,000.

NQRUSSELL, Andre Dwayne, b Jamaica 29 Apr 1988. RHB, RF. Jamaica 2006-07 to 2013-14. IPL: DD 2012-13. KKR 2014 to date. Big Bash: MR 2014-15. ST 2015-16 to 2016-17. Worcestershire 2013 (T20 only). Nottinghamshire 2016 (T20 only). **Tests** (WI): 1 (2010-11); HS 2 and BB 1-73 v SL (Galle). **LOI** (WI): 56 (2010-11 to 2019); HS 92* v I (North Sound) 2011; BB 4-35 v I (Kingston) 2011. **IT20** (WI): 49 (2011 to 2019-20); HS 47 v B (Lauderhill) 2018; BB 2-10 v B (Dhaka) 2013-14. F-c Tours (WI): E 2010 (WI A); SL 2010-11. HS 128 WI A v Bangladesh A (North Sound) 2011-12. BB 5-36 WI A v Bangladesh A (Gros Islet) 2011-12. LO HS 132* (in 56 balls, inc 13 sixes) Sagicor HPC v Bangladesh A (Bridgetown) 2014. LO BB 6-28 Sagicor HPC v Bangladesh A (Lucas Street) 2014. T20 HS 121*. T20 BB 4-11. £125,000.

NQSHADAB KHAN – see SURREY. £75,000.

VINCE, James Michael – *see HAMPSHIRE*. £100,000. Local icon.

WALLER, Maximilian Thomas Charles – *see SOMERSET*. £30,000.

NQ**WARNER, David** Andrew, b Paddington, Sydney, NSW, Australia 27 Oct 1986. 5'7". LHB, LBG. NSW 2008-09 to date. IPL: DD 2009-13. SH 2014 to date. Big Bash: ST 2011-12 to 2013-14. SS 2012-13. Durham 2009 (T20 only). Middlesex 2010 (T20 and one l-o match). **Tests** (A): 84 (2011-12 to 2019-20); HS 335* v P (Adelaide) 2019-20; BB 2-45 v WI (Bridgetown) 2012. **LOI** (A): 123 (2008-09 to 2019-20); HS 179 v P (Adelaide) 2016-17. **IT20** (A): 79 (2008-09 to 2019-20); HS 100* v SL (Adelaide) 2019-20. In 2008-09, he became the first man to play for Australia before making f-c debut since 1877. HS 335* (*see Tests*). BB 2-45 (*see Tests*). LO HS 197 NSW v Vic (Sydney, NS) 2013-14. LO BB 1-11 NSW v Q (Brisbane) 2009-10. T20 HS 135*. £125,000.

WHITELEY, Ross Andrew – *see WORCESTERSHIRE*. £60,000.

TRENT ROCKETS

Venues: Trent Bridge, Nottingham (both); Fischer County Ground, Leicester (women); Pattonair County Ground, Derby (women). **Men's Head Coach**: Stephen Fleming. **Women's Head Coach**: Salliann Briggs. **Men's Captain**: Lewis Gregory. **Women's Captain**: Nat Sciver.

CARTER, Matthew – *see NOTTINGHAMSHIRE*. £60,000.

NQ**COULTER-NILE, Nathan** Mitchell, b Perth, Australia 11 Oct 1987. 6'3". RHB, RF. W Australia 2009-10 to 2017-18. IPL: MI 2013. DD 2014-16. KKR 2017. Big Bash: PS 2011-12 to 2018-19. MS 2019-20. **LOI** (A): 32 (2013 to 2019); HS 92 v WI (Nottingham) 2019; BB 4-48 v SA (Perth) 2014-15. **IT20** (A): 28 (2012-13 to 2018-19); HS 34 v P (Abu Dhabi) 2018-19; BB 4-31 v E (Hobart) 2013-14. F-c Tours (Aus A): E 2012; SA 2013. HS 64 WA v Tas (Perth) 2014-15. BB 6-84 WA v Q (Brisbane) 2012-13. LO HS 92 (*see LOI*). LO BB 5-26 WA v Vic (Sydney, BOP) 2014-15. T20 HS 42*. T20 BB 4-20. £75,000.

COX, Oliver **Ben** – *see WORCESTERSHIRE*. £40,000.

FLETCHER, Luke Jack – *see NOTTINGHAMSHIRE*. £30,000.

GREGORY, Lewis – *see SOMERSET*. £100,000.

GURNEY, Harry Frederick – *see NOTTINGHAMSHIRE*. Local icon.

HALES, Alexander Daniel – *see NOTTINGHAMSHIRE*. £100,000. Local icon.

MALAN, Dawid Johannes – *see YORKSHIRE*. £40,000.

MOORES, Thomas James – *see NOTTINGHAMSHIRE*. £50,000.

MULLANEY, Steven John – *see NOTTINGHAMSHIRE*. £60,000.

NQ**RASHID KHAN** – *see SUSSEX*. £125,000.

ROOT, Joseph Edward – *see YORKSHIRE*. Central.

NQ**SHORT, D'Arcy** John Matthew – *see SURREY*. £125,000.

WOOD, Luke – *see LANCASHIRE*. £50,000.

WRIGHT, Luke James – *see SUSSEX*. £30,000.

WELSH FIRE

Venues: Sophia Gardens, Cardiff (both); Bristol County Ground; Cooper Associates County Ground, Taunton (women). **Men's Head Coach**: Gary Kirsten. **Women's Head Coach**: Matthew Mott. **Men's Captain**: S.P.D.Smith. **Women's Captain**: tba.

BAIRSTOW, Jonathan Marc – *see YORKSHIRE*. Central.

BANTON, Thomas – *see SOMERSET*. £100,000. Local icon.

BRIGGS, Danny Richard – *see SUSSEX*. £30,000.

DUCKETT, Ben Matthew – *see NOTTINGHAMSHIRE*. £75,000.

Du PLOOY, Jacobus Leus – *see DERBYSHIRE*. £30,000. Kolpak.

HARMER, Simon Ross – *see ESSEX*. £60,000. Kolpak.

HIGGINS, Ryan Francis – *see GLOUCESTERSHIRE*. £40,000.

INGRAM, Colin Alexander – *see GLAMORGAN*. £100,000. Local icon. Kolpak.

PAYNE, David Alan – *see GLOUCESTERSHIRE*. £40,000.

PLUNKETT, Liam Edward – *see SURREY*. £50,000.

ᴺᵒQAIS AHMAD Kamawal – *see GLOUCESTERSHIRE*. £60,000.

RAMPAUL, Ravi – *see DERBYSHIRE*. £75,000. Kolpak.

ᴺᵒSMITH, Steven Peter Devereux, b Kogarah, Sydney, NSW, Australia 2 Jun 1989. RHB, LBG. NSW 2007-08 to date. IPL: PW 2012-13. RR 2014-19. RPS 2016-17. Big Bash: SS 2011-12 to date. Worcestershire 2010 (T20 only). **Tests** (A): 73 (2010 to 2019-20, 34 as captain); 1000 runs (4); most – 1474 (2015); HS 239 v E (Perth) 2017-18; BB 3-18 v E (Lord's) 2013. **LOI** (A): 125 (2009-10 to 2019-20, 51 as captain); 1000 runs (1): 1154 (2016); HS 164 v NZ (Sydney) 2016-17; BB 3-16 v Z (Harare) 2014. **IT20** (A): 39 (2009-10 to 2019-20, 8 as captain); HS 90 v E (Cardiff) 2015; BB 3-20 v WI (Gros Islet) 2010. F-c Tours (A)(C=Captain): E 2010 (v P), 2013, 2015, 2019; SA 2013-14; 2017-18C; WI 2015; NZ 2015-16C; I 2010-11, 2012-13, 2016-17C; SL 2016C; B 2017C; UAE (v P) 2014-15. HS 239 (*see Tests*). BB 7-64 NSW v SA (Sydney) 2009-10. LO HS 164 (*see LOI*). LO BB 3-16 (*see LOI*). T20 HS 101. T20 BB 4-13. £125,000.

ᴺᵒSTARC, Mitchell Aaron, b Baulkham Hills, Sydney, Australia 13 Jan 1990. 6'5". LHB, LF. New South Wales 2008-09 to date. Yorkshire 2012. IPL: RCB 2014-15. Big Bash: SS 2011-12 to 2014-15. **Tests** (A): 57 (2011-12 to 2019-20); 50 wkts (1): 50 (2016); HS 99 v I (Mohali) 2012-13; BB 6-50 v SL (Galle) 2016. **LOI** (A): 91 (2010-11 to 2019-20); HS 52* v SL (Sydney) 2012-13; BB 6-28 v NZ (Auckland) 2014-15. **IT20** (A): 31 (2012 to 2019-20); HS 7* v SA (Johannesburg) 2019-20; BB 3-11 v P (Dubai, DSC) 2012. F-c Tours (A): E 2012 (Aus A), 2013, 2015, 2019; SA 2017-18; WI 2011-12, 2015; I 2012-13, 2016-17; SL 2016; Z 2011 (Aus A); UAE (v P) 2014-15, 2018-19. HS 99 (*see Tests*). BB 8-73 (10-119 match) NSW v SA (Adelaide) 2017-18. LO HS 52* (*see LOI*). LO BB 6-25 NSW v Cricket Australia (Sydney, BO) 2015-16. T20 HS 29. T20 BB 4-15. £125,000.

Ten DOESCHATE, Ryan Neil – *see ESSEX*. £50,000.

YOUNG CRICKETER OF THE YEAR

This annual award, made by The Cricket Writers' Club, is currently restricted to players qualified for England, Andrew Symonds meeting that requirement at the time of his award, and under the age of 23 on 1st May. In 1986 their ballot resulted in a dead heat. Up to 18 March 2020 their selections have gained a tally of 2,787 international Test match caps (shown in brackets).

1950	R.Tattersall (16)	1974	P.H.Edmonds (51)	1997	B.C.Hollioake (2)
1951	P.B.H.May (66)	1975	A.Kennedy	1998	A.Flintoff (79)
1952	F.S.Trueman (67)	1976	G.Miller (34)	1999	A.J.Tudor (10)
1953	M.C.Cowdrey (114)	1977	I.T.Botham (102)	2000	P.J.Franks
1954	P.J.Loader (13)	1978	D.I.Gower (117)	2001	O.A.Shah (6)
1955	K.F.Barrington (82)	1979	P.W.G.Parker (1)	2002	R.Clarke (2)
1956	B.Taylor	1980	G.R.Dilley (41)	2003	J.M.Anderson (151)
1957	M.J.Stewart (8)	1981	M.W.Gatting (79)	2004	I.R.Bell (118)
1958	A.C.D.Ingleby-Mackenzie	1982	N.G.Cowans (19)	2005	A.N.Cook (161)
1959	G.Pullar (28)	1983	N.A.Foster (29)	2006	S.C.J.Broad (138)
1960	D.A.Allen (39)	1984	R.J.Bailey (4)	2007	A.U.Rashid (19)
1961	P.H.Parfitt (37)	1985	D.V.Lawrence (5)	2008	R.S.Bopara (13)
1962	P.J.Sharpe (12)	1986 {	A.A.Metcalfe	2009	J.W.A.Taylor (7)
1963	G.Boycott (108)		J.J.Whitaker (1)	2010	S.T.Finn (36)
1964	J.M.Brearley (39)	1987	R.J.Blakey (2)	2011	J.M.Bairstow (70)
1965	A.P.E.Knott (95)	1988	M.P.Maynard (4)	2012	J.E.Root (92)
1966	D.L.Underwood (86)	1989	N.Hussain (96)	2013	B.A.Stokes (63)
1967	A.W.Greig (58)	1990	M.A.Atherton (115)	2014	A.Z.Lees
1968	R.M.H.Cottam (4)	1991	M.R.Ramprakash (52)	2015	J.A.Leaning
1969	A.Ward (5)	1992	I.D.K.Salisbury (15)	2016	B.M.Duckett (4)
1970	C.M.Old (46)	1993	M.N.Lathwell (1)	2017	D.W.Lawrence
1971	J.Whitehouse	1994	J.P.Crawley (37)	2018	S.M.Curran (17)
1972	D.R.Owen-Thomas	1995	A.Symonds (26 - Australia)	2019	T.Banton
1973	M.Hendrick (30)	1996	C.E.W.Silverwood (6)		

THE PROFESSIONAL CRICKETERS' ASSOCIATION

PLAYER OF THE YEAR

Founded in 1967, the Professional Cricketers' Association introduced this award, decided by their membership, in 1970. The award, now known as the Reg Hayter Cup, is presented at the PCA's Annual Awards Dinner in London.

1970 {	M.J.Procter	1986	C.A.Walsh	2003	Mushtaq Ahmed
	J.D.Bond	1987	R.J.Hadlee	2004	A.Flintoff
1971	L.R.Gibbs	1988	G.A.Hick	2005	A.Flintoff
1972	A.M.E.Roberts	1989	S.J.Cook	2006	M.R.Ramprakash
1973	P.G.Lee	1990	G.A.Gooch	2007	O.D.Gibson
1974	B.Stead	1991	Waqar Younis	2008	M.van Jaarsveld
1975	Zaheer Abbas	1992	C.A.Walsh	2009	M.E.Trescothick
1976	P.G.Lee	1993	S.L.Watkin	2010	N.M.Carter
1977	M.J.Procter	1994	B.C.Lara	2011	M.E.Trescothick
1978	J.K.Lever	1995	D.G.Cork	2012	N.R.D.Compton
1979	J.K.Lever	1996	P.V.Simmons	2013	M.M.Ali
1980	R.D.Jackman	1997	S.P.James	2014	A.Lyth
1981	R.J.Hadlee	1998	M.B.Loye	2015	C.Rushworth
1982	M.D.Marshall	1999	S.G.Law	2016	B.M.Duckett
1983	K.S.McEwan	2000	M.E.Trescothick	2017	S.R.Patel
1984	R.J.Hadlee	2001	D.P.Fulton	2018	J.L.Denly
1985	N.V.Radford	2002	M.P.Vaughan	2019	B.A.Stokes

2019 FIRST-CLASS AVERAGES

These averages involve the 501 players who appeared in the 149 first-class matches played by 29 teams in England and Wales during the 2019 season.

'Cap' denotes the season in which the player was awarded a 1st XI cap by the county he represented in 2019. If he played for more than one county in 2019, the county(ies) who awarded him his cap is (are) underlined. Durham abolished both their capping and 'awards' system after the 2005 season. Glamorgan's capping system is based on a player's number of appearances. Gloucestershire now cap players on first-class debut. Worcestershire now award county colours when players make their Championship debut.

Team abbreviations: A – Australia(ns); AA – Australia A; CU – Cambridge University/ Cambridge MCCU; CfU – Cardiff MCCU; De – Derbyshire; Du – Durham; DU – Durham MCCU; E – England; EL – England Lions; Ex – Essex; Gm – Glamorgan; Gs – Gloucestershire; H – Hampshire; Ire – Ireland; K – Kent; La – Lancashire; LBU – Leeds/Bradford MCCU; Le – Leicestershire; LU – Loughborough MCCU; M – Middlesex; Nh – Northamptonshire; Nt – Nottinghamshire; OU – Oxford University/Oxford MCCU; Sm – Somerset; Sy – Surrey; Sx – Sussex; Wa – Warwickshire; Wo – Worcestershire; Y – Yorkshire.

† Left-handed batsman. Cap: a dash (–) denotes a non-county player. A blank denotes uncapped by his current county.

BATTING AND FIELDING

	Cap	M	I	NO	HS	Runs	Avge	100	50	Ct/St
K.J.Abbott (H)	2017	14	18	4	72	229	16.35	–	1	1
T.B.Abell (Sm)	2018	14	25	1	101	756	31.50	1	5	13
C.N.Ackermann (Le)	2019	14	25	6	70*	675	35.52	–	7	19
H.R.D.Adair (OU)	–	1	2	–	6	6	3.00	–	–	1
M.R.Adair (Ire)	–	1	2	–	8	11	5.50	–	–	1
Z.Akhter (OU)	–	1	1	1	11*	11	–	–	–	–
† M.M.Ali (E/Wo)	2007	4	8	–	42	139	17.37	–	–	2
B.M.J.Allison (Gs)	2019	1	1	–	0	0	0.00	–	–	–
† T.P.Alsop (H)		11	18	3	150	353	23.53	1	1	14
T.R.Ambrose (Wa)	2007	12	20	–	107	399	19.95	1	–	39/3
A.R.Amin (CU)	–	1	2	–	24	24	12.00	–	–	3
† J.M.Anderson (E/La)	2003	7	8	3	9*	32	6.40	–	–	4
M.K.Andersson (M)		2	3	–	83	95	31.66	–	1	–
W.F.Angus (DU)	–	1	1	–	0	0	0.00	–	–	–
J.C.Archer (E)		4	7	–	15	48	6.85	–	–	–
S.T.Ashraf (LBU)	–	2	4	–	62	109	27.25	–	1	1
R.Ashwin (Nt)	2019	5	10	1	66*	339	37.66	–	2	2
† M.H.Azad (Le/LU)		16	28	4	139	1353	56.37	4	8	9
Azhar Ali (Sm)	2019	10	18	2	79	339	24.93	–	3	3
Babar Azam (Sm)		1	2	–	40	40	20.00	–	–	–
T.E.Bailey (La)	2018	9	10	–	68	207	20.70	–	2	5
J.M.Bairstow (E)	–	6	12	1	52	214	19.45	–	1	21/2
V.Bajaj (CU)	–	2	3	–	20	39	13.00	–	–	1
A.Balbirnie (Ire)	–	1	2	–	55	60	30.00	–	1	1
T.W.Balderson (CU)	–	1	2	–	17	17	8.50	–	–	–
J.T.Ball (Nt)	2016	11	17	11	15*	67	11.16	–	–	3
† G.S.Ballance (Y)	2012	15	24	2	159	1014	46.09	5	3	4
E.R.Bamber (Gs/M)	2019	7	11	3	15	60	7.50	–	–	–
C.T.Bancroft (A/Du)		13	24	2	158	846	38.45	2	3	22
L.Banks (Wa)		8	13	–	50	220	16.92	–	1	14
T.Banton (Sm)		10	18	–	79	533	29.61	–	5	6
† K.H.D.Barker (H)		14	19	4	64	401	26.73	–	1	2
E.G.Barnard (Wo)	2015	14	21	2	56	429	22.57	–	2	11
G.A.Bartlett (Sm)		15	26	1	137	772	30.88	2	3	1

	Cap	M	I	NO	HS	Runs	Avge	100	50	Ct/St
O.R.Batchelor (LBU)	–	2	4	–	21	23	5.75	–	–	–
G.J.Batty (Sy)	2011	8	15	4	29	123	11.18	–	–	2
T.Bavuma (Nh)		8	15	–	134	566	37.73	2	1	7
† A.P.Beard (Ex)		8	9	4	41	112	22.40	–	–	3
L.Bedford (DU)	–	2	3	–	2	2	0.66	–	–	–
W.A.T.Beer (Sx)		11	17	3	97	417	29.78	–	3	1
S.J.D.Bell (Du)		1	1	–	1	1	1.00	–	–	–
D.J.Bell-Drummond (K)	2015	15	28	2	166	987	37.96	1	6	4
C.G.Benjamin (DU)	–	2	3	–	33	46	15.33	–	–	2
G.K.Berg (H/Nh)	2016	9	13	1	33	103	8.58	–	–	1
D.M.Bess (Sm/Y)		11	18	4	91*	389	27.78	–	3	4
J.M.M.Bevin (OU)	–	1	2	1	29	47	47.00	–	–	1
B.J.Bhabra (LU)		2	3	–	10	14	4.66	–	–	–
S.W.Billings (K)	2015	4	7	1	138	366	61.00	3	–	1
J.M.Bird (AA)	–	2	3	–	17	32	10.66	–	–	1
† A.J.Blake (K)		6	10	–	34	137	13.70	–	–	2
J.M.Blatherwick (Nt)		2	2	2	4*	6	–	–	–	–
J.J.Bohannon (La)		11	12	3	174	472	52.44	1	2	4
R.S.Bopara (Ex)	2005	11	16	1	135	570	38.00	2	3	10
S.G.Borthwick (Sy)	2018	13	23	–	137	705	30.65	2	2	16
D.A.J.Bracewell (Nh)		3	3	–	38	54	18.00	–	–	–
† J.R.Bracey (EL/Gs)	2016	14	24	2	152	745	33.86	2	2	23
K.C.Brathwaite (Gm)		3	4	1	103*	166	55.33	1	–	2
T.T.Bresnan (Y)	2006	4	8	–	58	143	17.87	–	1	1
D.R.Briggs (Sx)		4	5	2	24	80	26.66	–	–	2
† S.C.J.Broad (E/Nt)	2008	13	24	9	30	194	12.93	–	–	4
H.C.Brook (Y)		11	17	–	101	370	21.76	1	–	7
E.A.Brookes (Wa)		1	1	–	0	0	0.00	–	–	–
H.J.H.Brookes (Wa)		11	17	2	84	285	19.00	–	1	4
J.A.Brooks (Sm)		9	13	7	35*	79	13.16	–	–	2
B.C.Brown (Sx)	2014	15	24	4	156	908	45.40	3	4	54/1
† N.L.J.Browne (Ex)	2015	15	25	1	163	710	29.58	1	3	13
N.L.Buck (Nh)		11	14	5	53	287	31.88	–	3	2
K.A.Bull (Gm)		1	2	–	5	7	3.50	–	–	1
M.G.K.Burgess (Sx/Wa)		7	9	1	95	352	44.00	–	4	5
J.T.A.Burnham (Du)		13	23	1	86	598	27.18	–	4	4
J.A.Burns (AA/La)		3	5	1	133	171	42.75	1	–	1
† R.J.Burns (E/Sy)	2014	14	28	–	133	1005	35.89	2	4	15
J.C.Buttler (E)		5	10	–	70	247	24.70	–	1	5
† E.J.Byrom (Sm)		2	4	2	115*	193	96.50	1	1	5
H.R.C.Came (H)		1	1	1	23*	23	–	–	–	–
J.O.I.Campbell (Du/DU)		3	4	2	2	2	1.00	–	–	–
J.J.Cantrell (CU)	–	2	3	–	19	46	15.33	–	–	1
S.Cantwell (LBU)	–	2	4	3	43	73	73.00	–	1	2
† A.T.Carey (A/Sx)		2	2	1	69*	125	125.00	–	2	5
L.J.Carey (Gm)		9	12	3	62*	230	25.55	–	2	–
K.S.Carlson (CfU/Gm)		4	5	–	111	130	26.00	1	–	4
B.A.Carse (Du)		10	15	3	77*	246	20.50	–	1	1
M.Carter (Nt)		5	7	–	23	51	7.28	–	–	5
L.J.Chapman (CU)	–	2	3	–	5	9	3.00	–	–	1
Z.J.Chappell (Nt)		3	6	1	29	59	11.80	–	–	1
† B.G.Charlesworth (Gs)	2018	5	7	1	77*	145	24.16	–	1	3
V.Chopra (Ex/Sx)	2018	4	8	–	32	177	22.12	–	–	4
G.Clark (Du)		4	8	1	26	79	11.28	–	–	4
J.Clark (Sy)		9	15	4	54	268	24.36	–	1	1
† T.G.R.Clark (Sx)		1	1	–	13	13	13.00	–	–	–

227

Name	Cap	M	I	NO	HS	Runs	Avge	100	50	Ct/St
J.M.Clarke (Nt)		13	23	1	125	643	29.22	3	1	6
R.Clarke (Sy)	2005	14	25	5	88	662	33.10	–	3	18
T.H.Claughton (OU)	–	1	1	–	8	8	8.00	–	–	6/1
† M.E.Claydon (K)	2016	6	7	4	13*	50	16.66	–	–	–
B.O.Coad (Y)	2018	12	15	3	48	206	17.16	–	–	–
J.J.Cobb (Nh)	2018	7	11	–	139	453	41.18	1	3	3
M.T.Coles (Ex/Nh)		5	7	3	41*	116	29.00	–	–	4
† B.G.Compton (Nt)		2	3	1	16*	43	21.50	–	–	1
S.Conners (Sm)		3	2	1	14	20	20.00	–	–	1
A.N.Cook (Ex)	2005	15	25	5	150*	1063	53.15	2	7	17
S.J.Cook (Ex)		9	10	2	37*	54	6.75	–	–	2
C.B.Cooke (Gm)	2016	7	10	2	96	368	46.00	–	2	18/2
† T.R.Cornall (LBU)		2	4	–	19	43	10.75	–	–	2
† M.J.Cosgrove (Le)	2015	13	23	3	107*	697	34.85	1	6	2
J.Coughlin (Du)		1	1	–	24	24	24.00	–	–	–
P.Coughlin (Nt)		6	9	1	49	200	25.00	–	–	7
J.M.Cox (K)		3	4	–	27	71	17.75	–	–	1
O.B.Cox (Wo)	2009	14	22	2	100*	531	26.55	1	3	38/1
M.S.Crane (H)		6	8	1	20	65	9.28	–	–	–
Z.Crawley (EL/K)	2019	15	28	–	111	974	34.78	2	6	17
M.J.J.Critchley (De)	2019	16	27	4	79*	540	23.47	–	3	14
S.J.Croft (La)	2010	11	12	2	78	472	47.20	–	4	4
J.O.Cross-Zamirski (CU)	–	1	2	1	6*	6	6.00	–	–	–
T.N.Cullen (Gm)		9	12	3	63	319	35.44	–	4	29
† M.L.Cummins (M)		3	5	1	22*	34	8.50	–	–	3
P.J.Cummins (A)		5	9	2	26*	71	10.14	–	–	2
† B.J.Curran (Nh)		8	13	2	64	368	33.45	–	2	3
† S.M.Curran (E/EL/Sy)	2018	8	15	1	80	458	32.71	–	4	1
T.K.Curran (Sy)	2016	1	2	1	22*	30	30.00	–	–	1
† A.E.C.Dahl (LBU)		2	4	–	46	106	26.50	–	–	–
A.K.Dal (De)		11	19	4	92	295	19.66	–	2	7
J.H.Davey (Sm)		6	10	1	36	99	11.00	–	–	1
A.L.Davies (La)	2017	10	14	1	147	468	36.00	1	2	4
† S.M.Davies (Sm)	2017	15	26	1	109	688	27.52	1	3	48/3
W.S.Davis (Le)		11	17	8	39*	142	15.77	–	–	1
L.A.Dawson (H)	2013	9	13	1	103	643	53.58	1	6	6
M.de Lange (Gm)	2019	8	10	1	45*	127	14.11	–	–	2
† H.E.Dearden (Le)		14	20	–	61	431	21.55	–	2	7
J.J.Dell (Wo)	2019	7	12	–	61	158	13.16	–	1	5
J.L.Denly (E/K)	2008	12	23	2	167*	849	40.42	2	4	5
† C.D.J.Dent (Gs)	2010	14	24	1	176	1087	47.26	4	4	8
A.H.J.Dewes (DU)	–	2	3	–	6	11	3.66	–	–	–
A.C.H.Dewhurst (CU)	–	1	2	–	28	44	22.00	–	–	1
N.J.Dexter (Le)		9	13	–	180	441	33.92	1	2	5
S.R.Dickson (K)		12	23	2	161	668	31.80	3	1	13
J.Diwakar (OU)	–	1	2	–	24	45	22.50	–	–	–
B.L.D'Oliveira (Wo)	2012	7	9	1	103	298	37.25	1	1	3
A.H.T.Donald (Gm)		9	15	1	173	554	39.57	1	2	4
D.A.Douthwaite (CfU/Gm)		9	15	1	100*	443	31.64	1	1	1
G.S.Drissell (Gs)	2017	1	1	–	1	1	1.00	–	–	–
F.du Plessis (K)		1	2	–	36	36	18.00	–	–	–
† J.L.du Plooy (De)		11	19	3	118	677	42.31	2	3	9
† B.M.Duckett (Nt)		14	25	–	216	928	37.12	2	3	8
† M.P.Dunn (Sy)		3	5	3	2*	3	1.50	–	–	–
E.J.H.Eckersley (Du)		13	22	4	118	720	40.00	1	4	42
F.H.Edwards (H)	2018	15	17	9	8*	32	4.00	–	–	3

	Cap	M	I	NO	HS	Runs	Avge	100	50	Ct/St
† D.Elgar (Sy)		10	19	–	103	555	29.21	1	5	6
J.F.Emanuel (DU)	–	1	1	–	20	20	20.00	–	–	–
S.S.Eskinazi (M)	2018	13	22	–	125	528	24.00	1	1	13
B.N.Evans (CfU)	–	2	3	1	3*	3	1.50	–	–	–
† H.A.Evans (Le/LU)		3	5	3	7*	16	8.00	–	–	1
L.J.Evans (Sx)		8	13	–	113	282	21.69	1	1	6
S.T.Evans (Le)		1	1	–	1	1	1.00	–	–	–
J.D.M.Evison (Nt)		1	2	–	45	57	28.50	–	–	1
J.B.Fallows (LBU)	–	2	3	1	19	32	16.00	–	–	1
M.J.Fanning (OU)	–	1	1	–	1	1	1.00	–	–	–
T.C.Fell (Wo)	2013	6	8	–	40	136	17.00	–	–	5
C.J.Ferguson (Wo)	2019	10	18	1	127	509	29.94	1	3	8
A.J.Finch (Sy)	2018	1	1	–	90	90	90.00	–	1	1
A.W.Finch (Wo)	2019	8	10	5	18*	61	12.20	–	–	–
H.Z.Finch (Sx)		9	16	1	48	179	11.93	–	–	12
S.T.Finn (M)	2009	8	9	3	56	155	25.83	–	1	2
M.D.Fisher (Y)		4	5	1	47*	155	28.75	–	–	1
L.J.Fletcher (Nt)	2014	13	22	1	25*	209	9.95	–	–	2
B.T.Foakes (EL/Sy)	2016	14	25	1	69	590	24.58	–	5	41/6
† F.J.H.Foster (OU)	–	1	1	–	1	1	1.00	–	–	1
M.T.Foster (CfU)	–	1	1	–	6	6	6.00	–	–	–
W.A.R.Fraine (Y)		8	15	1	106	393	28.07	1	–	–
J.K.Fuller (H)		4	5	1	54*	138	34.50	–	1	1
S.T.Gabriel (Gs)	2019	3	3	1	2*	5	2.50	–	–	–
G.A.Garrett (Wa)		3	4	2	24	32	16.00	–	–	1
† G.H.S.Garton (Sx)		3	4	2	59*	112	56.00	–	2	2
† E.N.Gay (Nh)		1	–	–	–	–	–	–	–	–
J.H.Gibbs (CfU)	–	1	1	–	0	0	0.00	–	–	–
A.F.Gleadall (De)		1	2	–	0	0	0.00	–	–	–
R.J.Gleeson (La)		9	8	4	11	34	8.50	–	–	2
† B.A.Godleman (De)	2015	16	30	–	227	1087	36.23	4	2	2
† B.W.M.Graves (DU)	–	2	3	–	66	106	35.33	–	1	1
A.D.Greenidge (CU)	–	2	3	–	24	49	16.33	–	–	2
R.L.Greenwell (Du)		1	2	–	31	35	17.50	–	–	–
L.Gregory (EL/Sm)	2015	13	20	2	129*	491	27.27	1	1	11
G.T.Griffiths (Le)		5	7	–	22	41	5.85	–	–	1
T.D.Groenewald (Sm)	2016	7	13	3	17	100	10.00	–	–	3
† N.R.T.Gubbins (M)	2016	15	26	–	105	668	25.69	1	3	4
B.D.Guest (La)		1	2	–	17	28	14.00	–	–	5
C.J.Guest (CU)	–	2	3	–	34	47	15.66	–	–	2
S.R.Hain (EL/Wa)	2018	13	21	4	129*	914	53.76	2	4	17
† T.J.Haines (Sx)		7	12	–	93	252	21.00	–	1	5
H.Hameed (La)	2016	10	15	3	117	341	28.41	1	1	7
Hamidullah Qadri (De)		3	6	2	17*	28	7.00	–	–	2
M.A.H.Hammond (Gs)	2013	14	23	1	82	418	19.00	–	2	14
N.A.Hammond (LU)	–	2	2	–	9	10	5.00	–	–	4
† P.S.P.Handscomb (Du)		2	3	–	54	86	28.66	–	1	4
G.T.Hankins (Gs)	2016	4	6	–	14	23	3.83	–	–	–
H.J.Hankins (Gs)	2019	1	1	–	9	9	9.00	–	–	–
† O.J.Hannon-Dalby (Wa)	2019	12	15	5	17*	102	10.20	–	–	2
G.H.I.Harding (Du)		1	1	–	36	36	36.00	–	–	–
G.T.Hargrave (OU)	–	1	2	–	146	151	75.50	1	–	–
S.R.Harmer (Ex)	2018	15	21	3	62	382	21.22	–	2	16
J.A.R.Harris (M)	2015	10	17	4	80	469	36.07	–	3	2
† M.S.Harris (A/AA)	–	7	13	1	109	408	34.00	1	3	2
C.G.Harrison (OU)	–	2	3	1	37*	65	32.50	–	–	1

	Cap	M	I	NO	HS	Runs	Avge	100	50	Ct/St
G.J.Harte (Du)		12	23	2	108*	569	27.09	1	3	2
J.A.Haynes (Wo)	2019	5	7	–	31	119	17.00	–	–	1
† J.L.Haynes (LBU)	–	2	4	–	20	38	9.50	–	–	1
T.S.Haynes (LU)	–	1	2	–	13	19	9.50	–	–	–
† J.R.Hazlewood (A/AA)	–	6	6	4	5	14	7.00	–	–	3
† T.M.Head (A/AA)	–	7	12	3	139*	485	53.88	2	1	2
T.D.Heathfield (OU)	–	2	3	–	47	76	25.33	–	–	–
T.G.Helm (M)	2019	7	9	1	46	187	23.37	–	–	1
C.R.Hemphrey (Gm)		10	18	1	75	546	32.11	–	5	7
R.F.Higgins (Gs)	2018	14	21	5	199	958	59.87	4	3	4
J.C.Hildreth (Sm)	2007	15	26	1	158*	731	29.24	2	3	17
L.J.Hill (Le)		8	12	2	67	232	23.20	–	1	28/1
M.G.Hogan (Gm)	2013	11	12	6	54	166	27.66	–	1	3
† M.D.E.Holden (M)		10	18	–	54	227	12.61	–	1	1
J.O.Holder (Nh)		2	2	–	40	43	21.50	–	–	4
I.G.Holland (H)		9	16	1	143	478	31.86	1	3	5
J.M.Holland (AA)	–	2	3	2	2*	2	2.00	–	–	–
† J.B.R.Holling (LBU)	–	2	4	–	13	16	4.00	–	–	–
† E.O.Hooper (Sx)		1	1	–	20	20	20.00	–	–	–
P.J.Horton (Le)		15	27	1	100*	751	28.88	1	3	13
A.J.Hose (Wa)		11	20	–	111	340	17.00	1	–	3
H.R.Hosein (De)		16	28	4	138*	783	32.62	1	5	33/2
B.A.C.Howell (Gs)	2012	10	15	–	76	369	24.60	–	2	12
F.J.Hudson-Prentice (De)		7	12	2	99	342	34.20	–	2	1
A.L.Hughes (De)	2017	13	24	1	109*	578	25.13	1	1	12
L.J.Hurt (La)		1	1	–	38	38	38.00	–	–	–
B.A.Hutton (Nh)		10	15	4	34*	203	18.45	–	–	9
E.R.B.Hyde (CU)	–	3	5	1	19	48	12.00	–	–	7
D.A.Ironside (LBU)	–	2	4	–	24	52	13.00	–	–	–
W.G.Jacks (Sy)		10	16	–	120	427	26.68	1	3	13
A.Javid (Le)		5	9	–	143	256	28.44	1	1	–
† K.K.Jennings (La)	2018	14	21	2	97	588	30.94	1	6	17
N.R.Johns (CU)	–	1	2	–	14	24	12.00	–	–	–
M.A.Jones (Du)		2	3	–	9	9	3.00	–	–	–
R.P.Jones (La)		14	19	2	122	624	36.70	1	4	11
C.J.Jordan (Sx)	2014	12	17	2	166	444	29.60	1	1	18
A.Kapil (Sx)		1	2	1	33*	33	33.00	–	–	–
J.B.R.Keeping (CU)	–	1	1	–	10	10	10.00	–	–	–
J.S.Kendall (LU)	–	2	3	1	37*	95	47.50	–	–	–
R.I.Keogh (Nh)	2019	15	23	–	150	811	35.26	2	3	4
† U.T.Khawaja (A)	–	5	8	–	72	251	31.37	–	2	3
L.P.J.Kimber (LU)	–	2	3	–	62	99	33.00	–	1	1
† A.E.King (LU)	–	2	3	–	33	53	17.66	–	–	2
F.J.Klaassen (K)		2	3	1	14*	37	18.50	–	–	2
D.Klein (Le)		6	6	–	87	122	20.33	–	1	–
T.Kohler-Cadmore (Y)	2019	15	23	1	176	1004	45.63	3	3	33
O.M.D.Kolk (CfU)	–	2	3	–	33	42	14.00	–	–	2
H.G.Kuhn (K)	2018	14	24	–	95	605	25.20	–	5	11
M.Labuschagne (A/Gm)	2019	16	28	3	182	1530	61.20	5	9	18
T.C.Lace (De/M)		12	23	1	143	865	39.31	3	4	11
D.J.Lamb (La)		1	1	–	49	49	49.00	–	–	–
M.J.Lamb (Wa)		5	8	1	173	208	29.71	1	–	1
J.L.Lawlor (Gm)		2	4	–	25	74	18.50	–	–	3
D.W.Lawrence (Ex)	2017	14	22	3	147	725	38.15	1	5	9
J.Leach (Wo)	2012	13	21	4	54*	420	24.70	–	2	1
† M.J.Leach (E/EL/Sm)	2017	16	24	8	92	203	12.68	–	1	12

	Cap	M	I	NO	HS	Runs	Avge	100	50	Ct/St
J.A.Leaning (Y)	2016	9	13	1	77*	315	26.25	–	3	4
† A.Z.Lees (Du)		15	27	1	181	973	37.42	3	4	11
† J.S.Lehmann (La)		3	4	–	22	35	8.75	–	–	–
† T.J.Lester (Wa)		2	2	2	0*	0	–	–	–	1
R.E.Levi (Nh)	2017	5	8	1	60	159	26.50	–	1	3
J.D.Libby (Nt)		5	10	–	77	189	18.90	–	1	3
A.M.Lilley (Le)		1	–	–	–	–	–	–	–	–
L.S.Livingstone (La)	2017	11	14	1	114	599	46.07	1	5	7
D.L.Lloyd (Gm)	2019	14	23	1	97	668	30.36	–	4	16
† J.E.G.Logan (Y)		1	2	1	20*	27	27.00	–	–	1
T.W.Loten (Y)		1	1	–	58	58	58.00	–	1	–
J.H.Ludlow (CfU)	–	2	3	–	4	9	3.00	–	–	4
N.M.Lyon (A)	–	5	7	2	26*	80	16.00	–	–	2
† A.Lyth (Y)	2010	15	26	2	95	816	34.00	–	7	27
C.J.McBride (OU)	–	2	3	–	28	35	11.66	–	–	–
† A.R.McBrine (Ire)	–	1	2	–	11	11	5.50	–	–	–
J.A.McCollum (Ire)	–	1	2	–	19	30	15.00	–	–	2
N.C.MacDonagh (DU)	–	1	1	–	17	17	17.00	–	–	1/1
C.McKerr (Sy)		4	5	1	17*	35	8.75	–	–	1
M.H.McKiernan (De)		1	2	–	7	7	3.50	–	–	3
L.D.McManus (H)		7	10	1	61	267	29.66	–	1	20/1
L.Machado (CfU)	–	2	3	–	19	25	8.33	–	–	1/1
W.L.Madsen (De)	2011	14	25	1	204*	917	38.20	2	3	26
K.A.Maharaj (Y)		5	9	–	85	239	26.55	–	2	1
S.Mahmood (La)		9	10	2	34	136	17.00	–	–	–
† D.J.Malan (M)	2010	14	23	–	199	1059	48.13	4	3	17
A.K.Markram (H)	–	2	3	–	63	115	38.33	–	1	–
M.R.Marsh (A)	–	4	7	1	74	231	38.50	–	1	2
† S.E.Marsh (Gm)		1	2	–	9	17	8.50	–	–	1
G.J.Maxwell (A)		4	5	–	59	96	19.20	–	1	3
D.R.Melton (De)		3	4	2	1*	1	0.50	–	–	1
B.W.M.Mike (Le/Wa)		7	11	2	72	197	21.88	–	1	4
C.N.Miles (Wa)		5	8	1	27	77	11.00	–	–	2
M.E.Milnes (K)		15	20	6	31	183	13.07	–	–	6
T.P.Milnes (Wa)		1	2	–	12	13	6.50	–	–	–
A.G.Milton (Wo)	2018	4	7	–	74	91	13.00	–	1	6
† Mir Hamza (Sx)		7	9	2	10	24	3.42	–	–	2
D.K.H.Mitchell (Wo)	2005	14	24	4	139	559	25.40	2	2	18
Mohammad Abbas (Le)	2018	9	11	3	11	22	2.75	–	–	4
† Mohammad Amir (Ex)		1	1	–	28	32	32.00	–	–	–
† Mohammad Rizvi (OU)	–	1	1	–	2	2	2.00	–	–	1
T.J.Moores (Nt)		14	25	–	48	347	13.88	–	–	31/1
A.O.Morgan (Gm)		4	6	1	43	82	16.40	–	–	1
† E.J.G.Morgan (M)	2008	3	5	2	61*	130	43.33	–	1	3
† M.Morkel (Sy)	2018	14	22	3	27	131	6.89	–	–	3
C.A.J.Morris (Wo)	2014	12	16	9	53*	149	21.28	–	1	–
† D.R.Mousley (Wa)		1	2	–	3	3	1.50	–	–	–
P.W.A.Mulder (K)		3	6	2	68*	114	28.50	–	1	1
S.J.Mullaney (Nt)	2013	14	26	–	179	824	31.69	2	4	14
† T.J.Murtagh (Ire/M)	2008	13	17	4	33	167	12.84	–	–	2
B.Muzarabani (Nh)		3	2	1	1*	2	2.00	–	–	1
C.D.Nash (Nt)		13	24	1	95	667	29.00	–	6	4
A.J.Neal (LBU)	–	2	4	–	15	28	7.00	–	–	–
M.G.Neser (A/AA)	–	4	3	–	32	33	11.00	–	–	–
R.I.Newton (Nh)	2017	11	20	2	118	514	28.55	2	1	1
† A.S.S.Nijjar (Ex)		2	1	–	2	2	2.00	–	–	2

231

	Cap	M	I	NO	HS	Runs	Avge	100	50	Ct/St
S.A.Northeast (EL/H)	2019	15	25	3	169	1123	51.04	4	5	6
L.C.Norwell (Wa)		4	6	2	64	120	30.00	–	1	1
K.J.O'Brien (Ire)		1	2	1	28*	32	32.00	–	–	–
Y.J.Odedra (CfU)		1	2	–	4	4	2.00	–	–	–
D.Olivier (Y)		14	17	11	24	130	21.66	–	–	3
G.Onions (La)	2018	10	10	1	18	65	7.22	–	–	1
F.S.Organ (H)		6	11	–	100	300	27.27	1	2	4
M.K.O'Riordan (K)		1	2	–	12	21	10.50	–	–	–
C.Overton (E/Sm)	2016	12	18	1	58	314	18.47	–	1	12
J.Overton (Nh/Sm)	2019	10	17	2	52*	277	18.46	–	1	18
X.G.Owen (DU)		1	2	1	24	31	31.00	–	–	–
T.D.Paine (A/AA)		8	13	1	58	238	19.83	–	1	29/1
A.P.Palladino (De)	2012	11	16	3	58	238	18.30	–	1	–
C.F.Parkinson (Le)		4	7	–	37	158	22.57	–	–	–
M.W.Parkinson (La)	2019	4	4	–	14	19	4.75	–	–	3
J.C.H.Park-Johnson (CU)		2	3	–	12	28	9.33	–	–	1
† W.D.Parnell (Wo)	2018	7	8	–	63	205	25.62	–	1	2
S.D.Parry (La)	2015	1	1	–	0	0	0.00	–	–	–
† A.Y.Patel (Y)		2	2	1	20	20	20.00	–	–	–
J.S.Patel (Wa)	2012	14	22	4	70*	365	20.27	–	2	8
R.K.Patel (CU/Ex)		6	8	–	35	146	18.25	–	–	6
† R.S.Patel (Sy)		8	14	1	100*	292	22.46	1	1	3
S.R.Patel (Gm/Nt)	2008	14	24	2	66	506	23.00	–	3	4
K.R.Patterson (AA)		2	3	–	38	74	24.66	–	–	3
S.A.Patterson (Y)	2012	15	21	2	60	310	16.31	–	1	6
† L.A.Patterson-White (Nt)		5	8	2	58*	91	15.16	–	1	3
† J.L.Pattinson (A/AA/Nt)	2017	6	10	3	47*	137	19.57	–	–	1
D.A.Payne (Gs)	2011	12	15	4	43	205	18.63	–	–	4
S.J.Pearce (CfU)		2	3	–	11	20	6.66	–	–	–
D.Y.Pennington (Wo)	2018	4	8	–	18	44	5.50	–	–	–
M.S.Pepper (Ex)		1	2	–	7	8	4.00	–	–	6
W.J.N.Pereira (LU)		2	3	–	4	4	1.33	–	–	–
T.H.S.Pettman (OU)		3	3	–	13	16	5.33	–	–	3
M.W.Pillans (Y)		1	1	–	3	3	3.00	–	–	–
L.E.Plunkett (Sy)		3	3	–	2	2	0.66	–	–	–
H.W.Podmore (K)	2019	15	22	6	54*	279	17.43	–	1	4
O.J.D.Pope (Sy)	2018	5	8	1	221*	561	80.14	2	2	4
J.A.Porter (EL/Ex)	2015	15	16	5	17	32	2.90	–	–	3
† W.T.S.Porterfield (Ire)		1	2	–	14	16	8.00	–	–	–
M.J.Potts (Du)		3	5	1	20	46	11.50	–	–	1
T.B.Powe (DU)		2	3	–	33	74	24.66	–	–	–
S.W.Poynter (Du)		2	4	–	80	97	24.25	–	1	12
D.Pretorius (Nh)		1	1	–	111	111	111.00	1	–	4
R.D.Pringle (Du)		3	5	–	30	44	8.80	–	–	1
† L.A.Procter (Nh)		15	23	8	86*	559	37.26	–	2	4
W.J.Pucovski (AA)		1	1	–	13	13	13.00	–	–	–
Y.Punja (CfU)		1	2	–	9	9	4.50	–	–	–
I.Qayyum (K)		1	2	2	14*	15	–	–	–	–
M.R.Quinn (Ex)		4	5	2	10	23	7.66	–	–	2
A.J.W.Rackow (OU)		1	2	1	52	84	84.00	–	1	1
A.M.Rahane (H)		7	13	–	119	307	23.61	1	1	6
† B.A.Raine (Du)		15	24	2	82	486	22.09	–	2	1
† R.Rampaul (De)	2019	13	19	5	30	186	13.28	–	–	2
† W.B.Rankin (Ire)		1	2	1	7	7	7.00	–	–	–
† D.M.W.Rawlins (Sx)		7	12	1	100	397	36.09	1	3	5
O.P.Rayner (K/M)	2015	10	14	2	40*	181	15.08	–	–	7

232

	Cap	M	I	NO	HS	Runs	Avge	100	50	Ct/St
J.Read (LBU)	–	2	4	–	15	34	8.50	–	–	5
† L.M.Reece (De)	2019	16	30	–	184	944	31.46	2	2	6
† S.J.Reingold (CfU)	–	2	3	–	22	29	9.66	–	–	–
† M.T.Renshaw (K)		3	6	1	48*	118	23.60	–	–	3
M.L.Revis (Y)		1	2	–	9	9	4.50	–	–	1
G.H.Rhodes (Le/Wo)	2016	7	13	2	61*	198	18.00	–	1	1
† W.M.H.Rhodes (Wa)		14	23	–	109	790	33.47	1	5	13
M.J.Richardson (Du)		1	2	–	7	12	6.00	–	–	5
A.E.N.Riley (K)		3	3	2	7	10	10.00	–	–	4
N.J.Rimmington (Du)		7	10	2	92	232	29.00	–	2	3
† S.E.Rippington (CU)	–	2	3	1	8*	11	5.50	–	–	–
† W.J.R.Robertson (OU)	–	2	2	1	8*	8	8.00	–	–	–
O.E.Robinson (Sx)	2019	13	18	5	59	275	21.15	–	1	5
O.G.Robinson (K)		15	26	2	143	786	32.75	2	3	54
A.J.Robson (Du)		4	6	–	64	97	16.16	–	1	6
S.D.Robson (M)	2013	15	25	1	140*	900	37.50	2	4	10
G.H.Roderick (Gs)	2013	14	24	3	158	654	31.14	1	2	41/1
O.J.W.Rogers (OU)	–	1	1	–	0	0	0.00	–	–	2
T.S.Roland-Jones (M)	2012	12	18	4	54	336	24.00	–	2	3
J.E.Root (E/Y)	2012	8	15	1	130*	655	46.78	1	6	14
† W.T.Root (Gm)		14	22	1	229	768	36.57	2	1	4
A.M.Rossington (Nh)	2019	14	21	2	82	803	42.26	–	8	34/2
† R.R.Rossouw (H)		11	19	1	92	620	34.44	–	5	2
A.P.Rouse (K/Sx)		2	3	–	20	33	11.00	–	–	6
J.J.Roy (E)	–	5	10	–	72	187	18.70	–	1	1
C.Rushworth (Du)		15	20	9	12*	66	6.00	–	–	4
† H.D.Rutherford (Wo)	2019	4	5	–	123	220	44.00	1	1	3
A.Sakande (Sx)		7	10	4	15	47	7.83	–	–	2
M.E.T.Salisbury (Du)		5	10	1	23	76	8.44	–	–	–
P.D.Salt (Sx)		12	23	1	122	727	33.04	2	4	13
A.G.Salter (Gm)	–	2	3	–	26	47	15.66	–	–	–
C.W.G.Sanders (LU)	–	2	3	–	18	18	6.00	–	–	–
B.W.Sanderson (Nh)		15	17	6	28	162	14.72	–	–	4
C.J.Sayers (Gs)	2019	4	4	1	33*	55	18.33	–	–	–
C.F.B.Scott (DU)	–	2	3	–	32	40	13.33	–	–	–
D.N.C.Scott (OU)	–	1	1	–	0	0	0.00	–	–	–
G.F.B.Scott (M)		7	11	1	55	204	20.40	–	1	3
B.M.A.Seabrook (CU)	–	2	3	1	44*	94	47.00	–	–	1
C.J.Searle (OU)	–	3	3	1	8	14	7.00	–	–	–
N.J.Selman (Gm)		14	24	2	150	752	34.18	1	6	10
J.C.Seward (OU)	–	2	3	–	28	50	16.66	–	–	1
J.Shaw (Gs/Y)	2016	10	13	2	38*	113	10.27	–	–	3
L.J.P.Shaw (OU)	–	2	2	–	11	11	5.50	–	–	1
D.P.Sibley (EL/Wa)	2019	14	23	2	244	1428	68.00	5	6	6
P.M.Siddle (A/Ex)		12	15	5	60	311	31.10	–	1	5
R.N.Sidebottom (Wa)		1	2	2	27*	31	–	–	–	–
B.D.Sidwell (DU)	–	1	2	1	42*	45	45.00	–	–	–
J.A.Simpson (M)	2011	15	24	4	167*	853	42.65	2	5	37
† A.R.Singh (DU)	–	1	2	–	31	33	16.50	–	–	2
P.Sisodiya (CfU)	–	2	3	–	33	42	14.00	–	–	1
B.T.Slater (Nt)		14	25	1	130	601	25.04	1	1	6
J.L.Smith (Sy)		8	14	1	57	338	26.00	–	2	4/1
M.J.E.Smith (CU)	–	1	2	–	17	17	8.50	–	–	–
R.A.J.Smith (Gm)		3	5	–	18	35	7.00	–	–	–
S.P.D.Smith (A)	–	5	8	–	211	797	99.62	3	3	12
T.M.J.Smith (Gs)	2013	5	8	–	84	261	32.62	–	2	3

	Cap	M	I	NO	HS	Runs	Avge	100	50	Ct/St
W.R.Smith (Du)		2	4	1	179	198	66.00	1	–	1
O.C.Soames (H)		6	11	–	62	148	13.45	–	1	2
J.H.Sookias (DU)		1	2	–	1	1	0.50	–	–	3
N.A.Sowter (M)		7	11	1	57*	184	18.40	–	2	4
† M.A.Starc (A)	–	3	2	2	54*	57	–	–	1	1
C.T.Steel (Du)		6	10	–	39	133	13.30	–	–	2
S.Steel (Du)		2	4	–	39	48	12.00	–	–	1
D.I.Stevens (K)	2005	13	20	1	237	597	31.42	1	2	3
R.A.Stevenson (H)		1	1	–	51	51	51.00	–	1	1
G.Stewart (K)		5	7	2	59	113	22.60	–	1	–
P.R.Stirling (Ire/M)	2016	4	6	1	138	186	37.20	1	–	3
† B.A.Stokes (E)		5	10	2	135*	441	55.12	2	2	4
O.P.Stone (E/Wa)		3	6	–	21	41	6.83	–	–	1
† M.D.Stoneman (Sy)	2018	13	23	–	100	685	29.78	1	4	5
J.Subramanyan (DU)		1	1	–	11	11	11.00	–	–	–
K.Suresh (CU)		1	2	–	54	54	27.00	–	1	–
† B.Swanson (OU)		1	1	–	3	3	3.00	–	–	2
H.J.Swindells (Le)		7	10	–	37	168	16.80	–	–	12/1
J.A.Tattersall (Y)		15	22	2	135*	658	32.90	1	3	36/4
J.M.R.Taylor (Gs)	2010	9	13	–	99	279	21.46	–	1	3
J.P.A.Taylor (De)		1	1	1	11*	11	–	–	–	–
M.D.Taylor (Gs)	2013	9	10	7	28*	67	22.33	–	–	–
M.J.Taylor (OU)	–	2	3	1	61*	101	50.50	–	1	1
N.P.Taylor (CU)	–	1	2	–	59	59	29.50	–	1	1
T.A.I.Taylor (Le)		4	5	1	57	125	31.25	–	1	2
R.N.ten Doeschate (Ex)	2006	14	19	1	130	483	26.83	2	1	8
A.D.Thomason (Sx)		4	8	–	90	129	16.12	–	1	1
† J.A.Thompson (Y)		2	3	–	34	36	12.00	–	–	–
† S.R.Thompson (Ire)	–	1	2	–	4	4	2.00	–	–	–
A.T.Thomson (Wa)		2	2	–	18	27	13.50	–	–	–
A.D.Tillcock (LU)	–	2	3	–	60	80	26.66	–	1	–
J.C.Tongue (Wo)	2017	5	6	1	20*	53	10.60	–	–	4
R.J.W.Topley (Sx)		2	2	1	5	6	6.00	–	–	–
C.P.Tremain (AA)	–	1	2	1	18*	18	18.00	–	–	–
† M.E.Trescothick (Sm)	1999	6	10	–	37	145	14.50	–	–	10
† L.Trevaskis (Du)		10	17	1	64	392	24.50	–	2	2
S.A.Turner (CU)	–	1	2	–	38	43	21.50	–	–	–
L.V.van Beek (De)		9	12	3	34*	127	14.11	–	–	5
G.L.van Buuren (Gs)	2016	10	13	3	93	363	36.30	–	2	4
F.O.E.van den Bergh (Sy)		1	1	–	16	16	16.00	–	–	–
T.van der Gugten (Gm)	2018	8	10	7	30*	135	45.00	–	–	2
R.E.van der Merwe (Sm)		4	6	1	60	132	26.40	–	1	7
† S.van Zyl (Sx)	2019	13	22	3	173	931	49.00	3	4	4
† R.S.Vasconcelos (Nh)		11	20	2	184	805	44.72	2	3	16
M.Vijay (Sm)		3	5	–	29	42	8.40	–	–	5
D.J.Vilas (La)	2018	14	17	4	266	1036	79.69	2	7	47/1
J.M.Vince (H)	2013	7	11	1	142	504	50.40	2	1	4
G.S.Virdi (Sy)		5	6	5	14*	28	28.00	–	–	–
J.C.Vitali (CU)	–	1	2	1	46*	61	61.00	–	–	–
M.S.Wade (A)	–	8	14	2	117	485	40.41	3	–	7
G.G.Wagg (Gm)	2013	10	16	3	100	418	32.15	1	1	2
J.C.Wainman (Wa)		1	–	–	–	–	–	–	–	–
M.J.Waite (Y)		3	3	1	22	42	21.00	–	–	1
A.G.Wakely (Nh)	2012	12	16	1	102	548	36.53	1	2	12
† D.A.Warner (A)	–	5	10	–	61	95	9.50	–	1	8
J.D.Warner (Sx)		2	2	2	13*	14	–	–	–	–

	Cap	M	I	NO	HS	Runs	Avge	100	50	Ct/St
B.J.Watling (Du)		2	3	1	104*	139	69.50	1	–	1
J.J.Weatherley (H)		9	15	2	66	341	26.23	–	2	8
† W.J.Weighell (Du)		3	5	–	24	37	7.40	–	–	1
N.R.Welch (LU)		2	3	–	44	67	22.33	–	–	–
† L.W.P.Wells (Sx)	2016	16	29	4	98*	620	24.80	–	3	6
M.H.Wessels (Wo)	2019	15	24	2	118	602	27.36	1	3	21
T.Westley (Ex)	2013	14	23	1	141	794	36.09	1	3	11
A.J.A.Wheater (Ex)		11	13	1	130	307	25.58	1	–	29/3
R.G.White (Ex/M)		4	6	–	39	63	10.50	–	–	4/2
R.A.Whiteley (Wo)	2013	10	16	1	88	391	26.06	–	3	4
D.Wiese (Sx)	2016	15	21	–	139	666	31.71	1	5	1
D.J.Willey (Y)	2016	5	7	1	46	171	28.50	–	–	3
G.C.Wilson (Ire)	–	1	2	–	0	0	0.00	–	–	6
C.R.Woakes (E)	–	5	9	1	37*	133	16.62	–	–	–
† L.Wood (Nh/Nt)		10	16	3	66	222	17.07	–	2	3
† A.J.Woodland (CfU)	–	1	2	–	11	11	5.50	–	–	–
C.J.C.Wright (Le)		15	21	3	60	295	16.38	–	1	3
† R.M.Yates (Wa)		12	19	–	141	570	30.00	1	2	10
† S.A.Zaib (Nh)		3	5	–	54	163	32.60	–	1	–

BOWLING

See BATTING AND FIELDING section for details of matches and caps

	Cat	O	M	R	W	Avge	Best	5wI	10wM
K.J.Abbott (H)	RFM	376.5	79	1163	72	16.15	9- 40	6	1
T.B.Abell (Sm)	RM	103.2	30	313	13	24.07	4- 39	–	–
C.N.Ackermann (Le)	OB	180	22	703	12	58.58	5- 69	1	–
M.R.Adair (Ire)	RFM	27.4	8	98	6	16.33	3- 32	–	–
Z.Akhter (OU)	RM	26	1	112	0				
M.M.Ali (E/Wo)	OB	101.5	15	396	11	36.00	3-126	–	–
B.M.J.Allison (Gs)	RFM	41	9	139	4	34.75	3-109	–	–
T.P.Alsop (H)	SLA	1	0	3	0				
A.R.Amin (CU)		27.1	7	82	6	13.66	4- 56	–	–
J.M.Anderson (E/La)	RFM	163.4	64	282	30	9.40	5- 18	2	–
W.F.Angus (DU)	RMF	24	0	102	2	51.00	2- 71	–	–
J.C.Archer (E)	RF	156	34	446	22	20.27	6- 45	2	–
R.Ashwin (Nt)	OB	297.4	73	836	34	24.58	6- 69	4	1
Azhar Ali (Sm)	LB	2	2	0	0				
T.E.Bailey (La)	RMF	289.2	81	777	37	21.00	5- 41	3	1
T.W.Balderson (CU)	SLA	28.4	9	65	1	65.00	1- 55	–	–
J.T.Ball (Nt)	RFM	259.5	46	904	18	50.22	3- 26	–	–
E.R.Bamber (Gs/M)	RMF	210.3	46	587	19	30.89	5- 93	1	–
L.Banks (Wa)	OB	3	0	9	0				
K.H.D.Barker (H)	LMF	362	85	1001	38	26.34	5- 48	1	–
E.G.Barnard (Wo)	RMF	371	100	993	44	22.56	6- 42	1	–
G.J.Batty (Sy)	OB	234.3	43	678	26	26.07	8- 64	1	1
T.Bavuma (Nh)	RM	1	0	2	0				
A.P.Beard (Ex)	RFM	129	22	450	21	21.42	4- 23	–	–
W.A.T.Beer (Sx)	LB	151.1	22	478	8	59.75	2- 76	–	–
D.J.Bell-Drummond (K)	RMF	67.2	13	169	8	21.12	2- 6	–	–
G.K.Berg (H/Nh)	RMF	186.3	50	518	19	27.26	2- 4	–	–
D.M.Bess (Sm/Y)	OB	271.3	68	681	26	26.19	5- 59	1	–
B.J.Bhabra (LU)	RMF	37.4	5	149	1	149.00	1-101	–	–
J.M.Bird (AA)	RFM	58	13	178	8	22.25	3- 18	–	–
A.J.Blake (K)	RMF	1	0	9	0				
J.M.Blatherwick (Nh)	RFM	34.4	3	192	2	96.00	1- 82	–	–

	Cat	O	M	R	W	Avge	Best	5wI	10wM
J.J.Bohannon (La)	RM	109.4	20	365	5	73.00	1- 31	–	–
R.S.Bopara (Ex)	RM	84	13	274	9	30.44	2- 35	–	–
S.G.Borthwick (Sy)	LBG	22	1	113	0				
D.A.J.Bracewell (Nh)	RM	54	7	212	4	53.00	2- 44	–	–
J.R.Bracey (Gs/EL)	RM	10	0	35	0				
T.T.Bresnan (Y)	RFM	82	17	262	6	43.66	2- 47	–	–
D.R.Briggs (Sx)	SLA	83.3	11	255	4	63.75	2- 40	–	–
S.C.J.Broad (E/Nt)	RFM	397.5	81	1201	47	25.55	5- 73	2	–
E.A.Brookes (Wa)	RMF	12	2	41	0				
H.J.H.Brookes (Wa)	RMF	315.3	52	1350	32	42.18	3-100	–	–
J.A.Brooks (Sm)	RFM	228.1	53	762	28	27.21	5- 33	1	–
B.C.Brown (Sx)	(WK)	2	0	15	0				
P.R.Brown (Wo)	RMF	20	3	67	1	67.00	1- 53	–	–
N.L.J.Browne (Ex)	LB	1	0	4	0				
N.L.Buck (Nh)	RMF	219.1	41	842	25	33.68	5- 54	1	–
K.A.Bull (Gm)	OB	36	6	100	2	50.00	2- 42	–	–
J.T.A.Burnham (Du)	RM	10.1	2	17	0				
R.J.Burns (E/Sy)	RM	1	1	0	0				
J.O.I.Campbell (Du/DU)	LMF	78	14	261	1	261.00	1- 43	–	–
J.J.Cantrell (CU)	LB	40	3	177	2	88.50	1- 40	–	–
S.Cantwell (LBU)	RFM	55	10	185	2	92.50	1- 67	–	–
L.J.Carey (Gm)	RFM	242.3	50	766	19	40.31	4- 54	–	–
K.S.Carlson (CfU/Gm)	OB	27	3	110	0				
B.A.Carse (Du)	RF	250.4	42	940	35	26.85	6- 26	3	–
M.Carter (Nt)	OB	137.4	14	529	6	88.16	3- 68	–	–
L.J.Chapman (CU)	OB	57	6	263	4	65.75	2-133	–	–
Z.J.Chappell (Nt)	RFM	40.4	3	178	0				
B.G.Charlesworth (Gs)	RM/OB	18	1	84	3	28.00	2- 27	–	–
G.Clark (Du)	LB	2	0	7	0				
J.Clark (Sy)	RMF	151.4	17	636	21	30.28	5- 77	1	–
R.Clarke (Sy)	RMF	332	73	1031	43	23.97	7- 74	2	–
M.E.Claydon (K)	RMF	130.2	20	466	19	24.52	5- 46	1	–
B.O.Coad (Y)	RMF	366.5	91	1013	42	24.11	6- 52	1	–
J.J.Cobb (Nh)	OB	27	4	91	1	91.00	1- 21	–	–
M.T.Coles (Ex/Nh)	RMF	82	16	298	10	29.80	3- 51	–	–
S.Conners (De)	RM	37	6	113	5	22.60	2- 13	–	–
S.J.Cook (Ex)	RFM	235.5	61	673	32	21.03	7- 23	3	1
M.J.Cosgrove (Le)	RM	17.1	5	36	0				
J.Coughlin (Du)	RM	21	5	67	2	33.50	1- 28	–	–
P.Coughlin (Nt)	RM	144.4	19	582	11	52.90	3- 37	–	–
M.S.Crane (H)	LB	106.5	8	539	5	107.80	3-122	–	–
Z.Crawley (EL/K)	RM	11	2	33	0				
M.J.J.Critchley (De)	LB	256.5	29	935	23	40.65	4-107	–	–
S.J.Croft (La)	RMF	26	6	60	1	60.00	1- 17	–	–
J.O.Cross-Zamirski (CU)	RMF	17	0	67	0				
M.L.Cummins (M)	RF	81	19	266	8	33.25	4- 77	–	–
P.J.Cummins (A)	RF	211	61	569	29	19.62	4- 32	–	–
S.M.Curran (E/EL/Sy)	LMF	225.5	45	727	31	23.45	6- 95	1	–
T.K.Curran (Sy)	RFM	28	6	118	3	39.33	3-118	–	–
A.E.C.Dahl (LBU)	SLA	32	4	128	2	64.00	2- 41	–	–
A.K.Dal (De)	RM	62.4	11	180	9	20.00	3- 11	–	–
J.H.Davey (Sm)	RMF	123.5	30	341	22	15.50	5- 21	1	–
A.L.Davies (La)	(WK)	1	0	6	0				
W.S.Davis (Le)	RFM	288.5	63	954	29	32.89	4- 73	–	–
L.A.Dawson (H)	SLA	224.1	48	549	14	39.21	4- 11	–	–
M.de Lange (Gm)	RF	244.4	33	950	26	36.53	4- 64	–	–

	Cat	O	M	R	W	Avge	Best	5wI	10wM
H.E.Dearden (Le)	OB	2	0	13	0			–	–
J.L.Denly (E/K)	LB	93	25	271	4	67.75	3- 48	–	–
C.D.J.Dent (Gs)	SLA	2.2	0	18	1	18.00	1- 1	–	–
A.J.H.Dewes (DU)		22	5	75	3	25.00	1- 1	–	–
N.J.Dexter (Le)	RMF	124.3	27	428	3	142.66	1- 15	–	–
S.R.Dickson (K)	RM	4	0	9	0			–	–
B.L.D'Oliveira (Wo)	LB	170.4	22	556	14	39.71	7- 92	1	–
D.A.Douthwaite (CfU/Gm)	RMF	190.1	16	902	21	42.95	4- 48	–	–
G.S.Drissell (Gs)	OB	41.1	5	174	4	43.50	4- 83	–	–
B.M.Duckett (Nt)	OB	4	0	16	0			–	–
M.P.Dunn (Sy)	RFM	90.2	18	277	13	21.30	5- 43	1	–
J.L.du Plooy (De)	SLA	49.3	2	190	5	38.00	2- 24	–	–
F.H.Edwards (H)	RFM	366.1	57	1266	50	25.32	5- 49	4	–
D.Elgar (Sy)	SLA	15.4	2	57	2	28.50	1- 17	–	–
J.F.Emanuel (DU)		23	1	89	2	44.50	2- 81	–	–
S.S.Eskinazi (M)	(WK)	2	0	4	0				
B.N.Evans (CfU)	RMF	52	8	208	3	69.33	2- 76	–	–
H.A.Evans (Le/LU)	RFM	42	16	229	7	32.71	3- 49	–	–
L.J.Evans (Sx)	RM	2	0	11	0				
J.D.M.Evison (Nt)	RM	9	0	33	0				
J.B.Fallows (LBU)	RMF	44	8	155	0				
M.J.Fanning (OU)	RFM	33.5	9	82	3	27.33	3- 47	–	–
A.W.Finch (Wo)	RM	177.2	31	682	12	56.83	2- 23	–	–
H.Z.Finch (Sx)	RM	2	0	9	0				
S.T.Finn (M)	RFM	171.4	29	600	20	30.00	5- 75	1	–
M.D.Fisher (Y)	RMF	82	16	288	11	26.18	3- 59	–	–
L.J.Fletcher (Nt)	RMF	326.4	68	926	35	26.45	5- 50	2	–
F.J.H.Foster (OU)		38	17	80	3	26.66	2- 36	–	–
M.T.Foster (CfU)	RFM	10	1	59	1	59.00	1- 59	–	–
J.K.Fuller (H)	RMF	80.4	15	302	9	33.55	3- 51	–	–
S.T.Gabriel (Gs)	RF	32.5	0	180	2	90.00	2- 20	–	–
G.A.Garrett (Wa)	RM	84.5	19	302	8	37.75	2- 53	–	–
G.H.S.Garton (Sx)	LF	30.5	2	107	4	26.75	2- 29	–	–
J.H.Gibbs (CfU)	RMF	24.3	1	116	2	58.00	2- 54	–	–
A.F.Gleadall (M)	RMF	12	0	60	0				
R.J.Gleeson (La)	RFM	273.1	61	948	47	20.17	6- 43	5	1
B.W.M.Graves (DU)	SLA	57.2	10	219	3	73.00	2- 56	–	–
L.Gregory (EL/Sm)	RMF	332	97	927	59	15.71	6- 32	4	1
G.T.Griffiths (Le)	RMF	128.2	24	439	11	39.90	3- 71	–	–
T.D.Groenewald (Sm)	RFM	163.3	32	472	18	26.22	5- 51	1	–
C.J.Guest (CU)	OB	70.3	18	217	7	31.00	3-100	–	–
T.J.Haines (Sx)	RM	76	19	212	6	35.33	1- 9	–	–
Hamidullah Qadri (De)	OB	53.3	7	219	5	43.80	2- 24	–	–
M.A.H.Hammond (Gs)	OB	22	0	121	0				
H.J.Hankins (Gs)	RMF	33	4	101	0				
O.J.Hannon-Dalby (Wa)	RMF	399	108	1129	44	25.65	5- 18	2	–
G.H.I.Harding (Du)	SLA	11	4	29	2	14.50	2- 9	–	–
S.R.Harmer (Ex)	OB	617.5	181	1561	86	18.15	8- 98	10	2
J.A.R.Harris (M)	RMF	273	45	932	23	40.52	4- 98	–	–
C.G.Harrison (OU)	LBG	27	5	113	3	37.66	1- 30	–	–
G.J.Harte (Du)	RM	94	23	281	10	28.10	4- 15	–	–
J.L.Haynes (LBU)	SLA	53	4	193	4	48.25	3- 37	–	–
J.L.Hazlewood (A/AA)	RFM	201.2	56	524	23	22.78	5- 30	1	–
T.M.Head (A/AA)	OB	14	3	65	0				
T.D.Heathfield (OU)	RMF	39	0	189	2	94.50	2- 57	–	–
T.G.Helm (M)	RMF	208	39	600	24	25.00	5- 36	2	–

	Cat	O	M	R	W	Avge	Best	5wI	10wM
C.R.Hemphrey (Gm)	OB	43	4	163	2	81.50	1- 17	–	–
R.F.Higgins (Gs)	RM	453.4	110	1182	50	23.64	5- 54	2	–
M.G.Hogan (Gm)	RFM	349	85	974	46	21.17	5- 62	1	–
M.D.E.Holden (M)	OB	23	1	104	0				
J.O.Holder (Nh)	RMF	52	6	199	4	49.75	2- 62	–	–
I.G.Holland (H)	RMF	146.1	33	378	5	75.60	1- 14	–	–
J.M.Holland (AA)	SLA	73.5	15	216	8	27.00	3- 30	–	–
J.B.R.Holling (LBU)	LM	39	4	192	4	48.00	3- 56	–	–
E.O.Hooper (Sx)	SLA	20.5	5	65	1	65.00	1- 65	–	–
B.A.C.Howell (Gs)	RMF	97.2	23	262	7	37.42	2- 19	–	–
F.J.Hudson-Prentice (De)	RMF	148	38	465	20	23.25	3- 27	–	–
A.L.Hughes (De)	RM	92	17	239	3	79.66	1- 11	–	–
L.J.Hurt (La)	RMF	25	6	66	0				
B.A.Hutton (Nh)	RM	263.3	72	700	35	20.00	6- 57	2	–
D.A.Ironside (LBU)	OB	6	0	40	2	20.00	2- 20	–	–
W.G.Jacks (Sy)	RM	1	1	0	0				
A.Javid (Le)	OB	3	0	8	0				
K.K.Jennings (La)	RM	26	3	68	1	68.00	1- 8	–	–
R.P.Jones (La)	LB	5	1	18	0				
C.J.Jordan (Sx)	RFM	311	61	972	31	31.35	5- 53	1	–
J.B.R.Keeping (CU)		6	0	23	1	23.00	1- 23	–	–
R.I.Keogh (Nh)	OB	234.4	39	819	17	48.17	4- 15	–	–
L.P.J.Kimber (LU)	OB	23.3	1	86	2	43.00	1- 34	–	–
F.J.Klaassen (K)	LMF	45	2	170	2	85.00	1- 44	–	–
D.Klein (Le)	LMF	112	15	467	16	29.18	4-113	–	–
M.Labuschagne (A/Gm)	LB	235.4	23	876	24	36.50	3- 52	–	–
D.J.Lamb (La)	RM	26	5	89	6	14.83	4- 70	–	–
M.J.Lamb (Wa)	RM	34.2	3	166	3	55.33	1- 15	–	–
J.L.Lawlor (Gm)	OB	6	1	15	0				
D.W.Lawrence (Ex)	LB	23	4	52	0				
J.Leach (Wo)	RMF	410.4	89	1145	42	27.26	6- 79	1	–
M.J.Leach (E/EL/Sm)	SLA	409	97	1128	51	22.11	6- 36	3	–
J.A.Leaning (Y)	RMF	41	8	128	4	32.00	2- 20	–	–
A.Z.Lees (Du)	LB	0.1	0	0	0				
T.J.Lester (Wa)	LFM	55	11	233	5	46.60	4- 41	–	–
J.D.Libby (Nt)	OB	4	0	32	0				
A.M.Lilley (Le)	OB	10	1	22	2	11.00	2- 22	–	–
L.S.Livingstone (La)	LB	135.1	42	249	10	24.90	2- 17	–	–
D.L.Lloyd (Gm)	OB	128.1	22	437	10	43.70	2- 35	–	–
J.E.G.Logan (Y)	SLA	28.2	6	41	4	10.25	4- 22	–	–
N.M.Lyon (A)	OB	242.3	44	668	20	33.40	6- 49	1	–
A.Lyth (Y)	RM	28.2	4	88	1	88.00	1- 25	–	–
C.J.McBride (OU)	RM/LB	5	0	15	1	15.00	1- 15	–	–
A.R.McBrine (Ire)	OB	10	1	47	0				
C.McKerr (Sy)	RFM	89	11	366	7	52.28	3- 94	–	–
W.L.Madsen (De)	OB	59	12	188	4	47.00	1- 12	–	–
K.A.Maharaj (SLA)	SLA	266	76	719	38	18.92	7- 52	4	2
S.Mahmood (La)	RFM	196.3	31	660	21	31.42	4- 48	–	–
D.J.Malan (M)	LB	47	5	139	4	34.75	3- 60	–	–
M.R.Marsh (A)	RMF	71.2	16	201	12	16.75	5- 46	1	–
G.J.Maxwell (La)	OB	109.5	27	287	14	20.50	5- 40	1	–
D.R.Melton (De)	RFM	31.5	5	149	2	74.50	1- 24	–	–
B.W.M.Mike (Le/Wa)	RM	140.3	15	649	12	54.08	3- 41	–	–
C.N.Miles (Wa)	RMF	118.4	14	542	17	31.88	5- 91	1	–
M.E.Milnes (K)	RMF	408.2	70	1478	58	25.48	5- 68	2	–
T.P.Milnes (Wa)	RFM	13	2	50	0				

	Cat	O	M	R	W	Avge	Best	5wI	10wM
Mir Hamza (Sx)	LMF	212	51	633	24	26.37	4- 51	–	–
D.K.H.Mitchell (Wo)	RM	34	7	79	1	79.00	1- 20	–	–
A.J.Moen (CU)	RM	3	0	16	0				
Mohammad Abbas (Le)	RMF	281.5	81	747	29	25.75	4- 72	–	–
Mohammad Amir (Ex)	LF	30	8	64	6	10.66	4- 48	–	–
Mohammed Rizvi (OU)	LB	9	1	46	0				
A.O.Morgan (Gm)	SLA	31	2	108	0				
E.J.G.Morgan (M)	RM	3	1	4	0				
M.Morkel (Sy)	RF	413	94	1297	44	29.47	4- 43	–	–
C.A.J.Morris (Wo)	RMF	317	72	1035	47	22.02	7- 45	3	–
P.W.A.Mulder (K)	RFM	91.5	22	307	10	30.70	4-118	–	–
S.J.Mullaney (Nt)	RM	173	36	545	14	38.92	4- 48	–	–
T.J.Murtagh (Ire/M)	RMF	348.3	113	857	55	15.58	6- 51	5	–
B.Muzurabani (Nh)	RFM	41	3	189	6	31.50	2- 29	–	–
A.J.Neal (LBU)	LM	51	8	199	4	49.75	3- 77	–	–
M.G.Neser (A/AA)	RM	76	18	218	12	18.16	3- 31	–	–
A.S.S.Nijjar (Ex)	SLA	10.2	0	46	3	15.33	2- 28	–	–
L.C.Norwell (Wa)	RMF	110.5	30	360	14	25.71	7- 41	1	–
Y.J.Odedra (CfU)		21	0	95	2	47.50	1- 41	–	–
D.Olivier (Y)	RF	390.3	75	1458	47	31.02	5- 96	2	–
G.Onions (La)	RFM	306.1	66	881	45	19.57	5- 38	3	–
F.S.Organ (H)	OB	45.5	9	125	8	15.62	5- 25	1	–
M.K.O'Riordan (K)	OB	7	0	33	0				
C.Overton (E/Sm)	RMF	331.4	70	956	47	20.34	6- 24	3	–
J.Overton (Nh/Sm)	RFM	212.1	32	744	34	21.88	5- 70	1	–
X.G.Owen (DU)	RM	27.4	8	80	4	20.00	3- 60	–	–
A.P.Palladino (De)	RMF	295.5	102	686	27	25.40	5- 29	1	–
C.F.Parkinson (Le)	SLA	64.4	9	237	5	47.40	2- 0	–	–
M.W.Parkinson (La)	LB	143.5	33	381	20	19.05	6- 23	1	1
J.C.H.Park-Johnson (CU)	RM	43	4	236	1	236.00	1- 69	–	–
W.D.Parnell (Wo)	LFM	157.4	42	507	22	23.04	5- 47	1	–
S.D.Parry (La)	SLA	550	5	156	5	31.20	3- 59	–	–
A.Y.Patel (Y)	SLA	35	0	231	2	115.50	1-112	–	–
J.S.Patel (Wa)	OB	635.1	182	1712	64	26.75	8- 36	4	2
R.S.Patel (Sy)	RMF	56.3	6	213	4	53.25	2- 35	–	–
S.R.Patel (Gm/Nt)	SLA	251	62	704	22	32.00	4- 58	–	–
S.A.Patterson (Y)	RMF	415.4	118	1095	37	29.59	5- 81	1	–
L.A.Patterson-White (Nt)	SLA	134.5	17	420	20	21.00	5- 73	1	–
J.L.Pattinson (A/AA/Nt)	RMF	165.4	33	479	20	23.95	6- 73	1	–
D.A.Payne (Gs)	LMF	403.5	94	1113	43	25.88	4- 40	–	–
S.J.Pearce (CfU)	LB	14	0	58	0				
D.Y.Pennington (Wo)	RMF	115	29	301	8	37.62	2- 92	–	–
W.J.N.Pereira (LU)	LFM	48	11	140	3	46.66	3- 61	–	–
T.H.S.Pettman (OU)	RFM	97	29	264	14	18.85	5- 19	1	–
M.W.Pillans (Y)	RF	14	2	59	2	29.50	2- 34	–	–
L.E.Plunkett (Sy)	RF	33	5	160	1	160.00	1- 85	–	–
H.W.Podmore (K)	RMF	499.3	114	1444	54	26.74	5- 41	2	–
J.A.Porter (EL/Ex)	RFM	443.1	97	1376	53	25.96	5- 51	2	–
M.J.Potts (Du)	RM	68	13	213	2	106.50	1- 97	–	–
T.B.Powe (DU)	OB	1	0	3	0				
D.Pretorius (Nh)	RMF	20	6	54	2	27.00	1- 21	–	–
R.D.Pringle (Du)	OB	19.4	6	41	2	20.50	2- 16	–	–
L.A.Procter (Nh)	RM	217.1	49	722	17	42.47	4- 26	–	–
Y.Punja (CfU)	RM	7.3	2	26	0				
I.Qayyum (K)	SLA	8	0	43	0				
M.R.Quinn (Ex)	RMF	109	17	384	7	54.85	3-104	–	–

	Cat	O	M	R	W	Avge	Best	5wI	10wM
B.A.Raine (Du)	RMF	486.5	130	1230	60	20.50	6- 27	3	–
R.Rampaul (De)	RFM	393	87	1180	49	24.08	5- 77	–	–
W.B.Rankin (Ire)	RFM	20	1	91	4	22.75	2- 5	–	–
D.M.W.Rawlins (Sx)	SLA	109	12	396	10	39.60	3- 19	–	–
O.P.Rayner (K/M)	OB	238.3	92	475	15	31.66	4- 58	–	–
L.M.Reece (De)	LM	386	109	1071	55	19.47	6- 58	3	–
S.J.Reingold (CfU)	OB	55	4	256	3	85.33	2- 64	–	–
M.T.Renshaw (K)	OB	16	2	53	0			–	–
G.H.Rhodes (Le/Wo)	OB	42	2	166	0			–	–
W.M.H.Rhodes (Wa)	RMF	149.1	37	425	15	28.33	5- 17	1	–
A.E.N.Riley (K)	OB	60	11	190	2	95.00	1- 45	–	–
N.J.Rimmington (Du)	RFM	158.2	31	446	18	24.77	4- 42	–	–
S.E.Rippington (CU)	LM	68	5	336	6	56.00	3-120	–	–
W.J.R.Robertson (OU)	RM	55.2	7	212	5	42.40	3- 32	–	–
O.E.Robinson (EL/Sx)	RMF	427.3	92	1211	64	18.92	8- 34	6	3
S.D.Robson (M)	LB	14.5	0	62	2	31.00	2- 4	–	–
O.J.W.Rogers (OU)	LB	1	0	9	0				
T.S.Roland-Jones (M)	RFM	328.5	64	1044	37	28.21	7- 52	3	1
J.E.Root (E/Y)	OB	71	4	280	3	93.33	2- 26	–	–
W.T.Root (Gm)	OB	19	4	69	2	34.50	2- 63	–	–
A.M.Rossington (Nh)	RM	5	0	20	0				
C.Rushworth (Du)	RMF	505.4	134	1317	75	17.56	6- 39	4	1
A.Sakande (Sx)	RFM	146.2	21	568	13	43.69	3- 74	–	–
M.E.T.Salisbury (Du)	RMF	137.1	27	448	19	23.57	4- 67	–	–
A.G.Salter (Gm)	OB	45	12	103	4	25.75	3- 6	–	–
C.W.G.Sanders (LU)	RFM	52	8	200	2	100.00	1- 72	–	–
B.W.Sanderson (Nh)	RMF	460.2	122	1197	61	19.62	6- 37	1	–
C.J.Sayers (Gs)	RM	149.4	39	400	11	36.36	3- 60	–	–
D.N.C.Scott (OU)	RM	1	0	8	0				
G.F.B.Scott (M)	RM	39	6	123	3	41.00	2- 49		
B.M.A.Seabrook (CU)	RM	10	0	53	0				
C.J.Searle (OU)	RMF	78.2	16	302	6	50.33	2- 31	–	–
N.J.Selman (Gm)	RM	3.3	0	22	1	22.00	1- 22	–	–
J.Shaw (Gs/Y)	RMF	233.2	46	761	30	25.36	4- 33	–	–
P.M.Siddle (A/Ex)	RFM	376.4	98	1010	44	22.95	6-104	2	–
R.N.Sidebottom (Wa)	RMF	34	6	119	2	59.50	2- 90	–	–
B.D.Sidwell (M)	RM	39.2	11	84	1	84.00	1- 58	–	–
J.A.Simpson (M)	(WK)	1	0	2	0				
A.R.Singh (DU)	SLA	41	2	186	3	62.00	3-117	–	–
P.Sisodiya (CfU)	SLA	58.3	6	218	8	27.25	4- 79	–	–
M.J.E.Smith (CU)		15.3	3	54	1	54.00	1- 34	–	–
R.A.J.Smith (Gm)	RM	67	11	224	7	32.00	3- 43	–	–
S.P.D.Smith (A)	LBG	6	1	20	0				
T.M.J.Smith (Gs)	SLA	76	14	217	4	54.25	2- 73	–	–
W.R.Smith (Du)	OB	7	2	31	0				
N.A.Sowter (M)	LB	180.4	23	650	14	46.42	3- 42	–	–
M.A.Starc (A)	LF	80.3	19	267	13	20.53	4- 39	–	–
C.T.Steel (Du)	LB	10	1	35	2	17.50	2- 35	–	–
S.Steel (Du)	OB	7	3	16	0				
D.I.Stevens (K)	RM	422	134	937	54	17.35	5- 20	5	1
R.A.Stevenson (H)	RMF	25	1	87	1	87.00	1- 87	–	–
G.Stewart (K)	RMF	135.3	16	514	15	34.26	3- 37	–	–
P.R.Stirling (Ire/M)	OB	8	0	29	2	14.50	2- 21	–	–
B.A.Stokes (E)	RFM	95.1	15	362	8	45.25	3- 56	–	–
O.P.Stone (E/Wa)	RF	78.3	13	299	10	29.90	5- 93	1	–
M.D.Stoneman (Sy)	OB	2	0	15	0				

	Cat	O	M	R	W	Avge	Best	5wI	10wM
J.Subramanyan (DU)	LB	49	5	182	3	60.66	2- 42	–	–
K.Suresh (CU)	RFM	20	5	76	2	38.00	2- 59	–	–
B.Swanson (OU)	SLA	24	12	42	1	42.00	1- 26	–	–
J.M.R.Taylor (Gs)	OB	9	0	51	0				
J.P.A.Taylor (De)	RM	23	6	74	6	12.33	3- 26	–	–
M.D.Taylor (Gs)	LMF	245	43	760	29	26.20	5- 57	1	–
T.A.I.Taylor (Le)	RMF	127.2	26	410	20	20.50	6- 47	1	1
R.N.ten Doeschate (Ex)	RMF	7	0	21	0				
A.D.Thomason (Sx)	RMF	75.1	2	358	4	89.50	2-107	–	–
J.A.Thompson (Y)	RM	40	10	105	5	21.00	2- 28	–	–
S.R.Thompson (Ire)	RM	16.5	1	74	3	24.66	3- 44	–	–
A.T.Thomson (Wa)	OB	10	0	54	1	54.00	1- 21	–	–
A.D.Tillcock (LU)	SLA	46.2	5	157	0				
J.C.Tongue (Wo)	RM	137.3	30	402	19	21.15	5- 37	1	–
R.J.W.Topley (Sx)	LMF	22.3	4	81	6	13.50	4- 58	–	–
C.P.Tremain (AA)	RMF	30.1	6	101	4	25.25	4- 70	–	–
L.Trevaskis (Du)	RMF	149.3	36	410	6	68.33	2- 96	–	–
L.V.van Beek (De)	RMF	219.2	34	726	19	38.21	3- 20	–	–
G.L.van Buuren (Gs)	SLA	119	16	343	3	114.33	3- 46	–	–
F.O.E.van den Bergh (Sy)	SLA	21.4	1	88	1	88.00	1- 88	–	–
T.van der Gugten (Gm)	RFM	198	26	705	15	47.00	3- 44	–	–
R.E.van der Merwe (Sm)	SLA	68.5	21	177	10	17.70	4- 41	–	–
R.S.Vasconcelos (Nh)	(WK)	1.3	0	9	0				
J.M.Vince (H)	RM	6	0	17	0				
G.S.Virdi (Sy)	OB	140	34	452	23	19.65	8- 61	2	1
J.C.Vitali (CU)	RM	20	4	58	2	29.00	2- 50	–	–
M.S.Wade (A)	RM	1	0	7	0				
G.G.Wagg (Gm)	LM	236	35	789	17	46.41	3- 59	–	–
J.C.Wainman (Wa)	LM	23	4	112	3	37.33	3-112	–	–
M.J.Waite (Y)	RFM	84	15	292	12	24.33	5- 16	1	–
J.D.Warner (Sx)	RFM	30.2	4	141	4	35.25	3- 35	–	–
J.J.Weatherley (H)	OB	17	1	67	1	67.00	1- 12	–	–
W.J.Weighell (Du)	RMF	75.1	17	222	9	24.66	3- 41	–	–
L.W.P.Wells (Sx)	LB	167.4	25	571	15	38.06	5- 63	1	–
T.Westley (Ex)	OB	15	2	58	0				
R.A.Whiteley (Wo)	LM	79.4	5	303	8	37.87	2- 35	–	–
D.Wiese (Sx)	RMF	346.1	69	1082	31	34.90	5- 26	2	–
D.J.Willey (Y)	LMF	88.2	21	316	11	28.72	3- 71	–	–
C.R.Woakes (E)	RFM	112.4	21	382	16	23.87	6- 17	1	–
L.Wood (Nh/Nt)	LFM	216.1	36	712	23	30.95	5- 67	2	–
A.J.Woodland (CfU)	RM	9	1	53	0				
C.J.C.Wright (Le)	RFM	450.2	90	1501	51	29.43	5- 30	2	–
S.A.Zaib (Nh)	SLA	4	0	16	0				

FIRST-CLASS CAREER RECORDS

Compiled by Philip Bailey

The following career records are for all players who appeared in first-class and county cricket during the 2019 season, and are complete to the end of that season. Some players who did not appear in 2019 but may do so in 2020 are included.

BATTING AND FIELDING

'1000' denotes instances of scoring 1000 runs in a season. Where these have been achieved outside the British Isles they are shown after a plus sign.

	M	I	NO	HS	Runs	Avge	100	50	1000	Ct/St
Abbott, K.J.	114	157	30	97*	2427	19.11	–	9	–	18
Abbott, S.A.	48	70	6	79	1050	16.40	–	3	–	25
Abell, T.B.	74	134	13	135	3852	31.83	5	23	–	48
Ackermann, C.N.	125	219	25	196*	7864	40.53	17	48	0+1	112
Adair, H.R.D.	2	2	–	6	6	3.00	–	–	–	1
Adair, M.R.	11	15	2	91	331	25.46	–	1	–	10
Agar, A.C.	52	77	9	106	1742	25.61	2	9	–	19
Akhter, Z.	1	1	1	11*	11	–	–	–	–	0
Ali, A.M.	15	25	1	80	639	26.62	–	3	–	6
Ali, M.M.	194	332	27	250	11202	36.72	20	69	2	111
Allen, F.A.	13	23	2	169*	696	33.14	2	4	–	9
Allison, B.M.J.	1	1	–	0	0	0.00	–	–	–	0
Alsop, T.P.	44	74	4	150	1835	26.21	2	13	–	60
Ambrose, T.R.	251	383	34	251*	11349	32.51	18	65	–	678/43
Amin, A.R.	1	2	–	24	24	12.00	–	–	–	3
Amla, H.M.	237	396	31	311*	17765	48.67	52	88	0+2	185
Anderson, C.J.	53	89	10	167	2862	36.22	4	13	–	39
Anderson, J.M.	246	316	127	81	1822	9.64	–	1	–	144
Andersson, M.K.	8	15	2	83	194	14.92	–	1	–	6
Angus, W.F.	1	1	–	0	0	0.00	–	–	–	0
Archer, J.C.	32	48	9	81*	1051	26.94	–	6	–	19
Ashraf, S.T.	2	4	–	62	109	27.25	–	1	–	1
Ashwin, R.	114	159	27	124	4130	31.28	6	21	–	45
Azad, M.H.	24	38	5	139	1659	50.27	4	10	1	11
Azhar Ali	187	328	28	302*	11581	38.60	35	51	–	140
Azharullah	115	156	78	58*	1000	12.82	–	1	–	25
Babar Azam	53	89	9	266	2960	37.00	3	22	–	33
Bailey, T.E.	56	76	12	68	1128	17.62	–	5	–	14
Bairstow, J.M.	180	297	33	246	11566	43.81	24	62	3	468/24
Bajaj, V.	2	3	–	20	39	13.00	–	–	–	1
Balbirnie, A.	30	42	3	205*	1296	33.23	2	8	–	28
Balderson, T.W.	2	4	1	10	20	6.66	–	–	–	0
Ball, J.T.	63	96	23	49*	964	13.20	–	–	–	10
Ballance, G.S.	160	262	24	210	11282	47.40	40	51	4+1	119
Bamber, E.R.	13	21	6	27*	136	9.06	–	–	–	2
Bancroft, C.T.	93	171	14	228*	6148	39.15	14	26	–	129/1
Banks, L.	10	17	–	50	277	16.29	–	1	–	15
Banton, T.	12	21	–	79	570	27.14	–	5	–	7
Barber, T.E.	2	3	1	3	3	1.50	–	–	–	0
Barker, K.H.D.	127	169	29	125	3955	28.25	6	17	–	35
Barnard, E.G.	60	90	14	75	2028	26.68	–	12	–	35
Bartlett, G.A.	25	45	2	137	1178	27.39	3	3	–	6
Batchelor, O.R.	2	4	–	21	23	5.75	–	–	–	0

242

	M	I	NO	HS	Runs	Avge	100	50	1000	Ct/St
Batty, G.J.	261	389	68	133	7399	23.04	3	30	–	163
Bavuma, T.	140	234	29	162	7580	36.97	14	40	–	77
Beard, A.P.	17	18	9	58*	191	21.22	–	1	–	4
Bedford, L.	2	3	–	2	0.66		–	–	–	1
Bedingham, D.G.	26	45	4	147	1823	44.46	6	5	–	27
Beer, W.A.T.	27	34	7	97	755	27.96	–	4	–	6
Behardien, F.	107	170	16	150*	6203	40.27	9	42	–	70
Behrendorff, J.P.	31	45	13	39*	389	12.15	–	–	–	11
Bell, S.J.D.	1	1	–	1	1	1.00	–	–	–	0
Bell-Drummond, D.J.	112	192	16	206*	5812	33.02	10	30	1	44
Benjamin, C.G.	2	3	–	33	46	15.33	–	–	–	2
Berg, G.K.	131	197	23	130*	4948	28.43	2	27	–	66
Bess, D.M.	38	60	9	107	1238	24.27	1	6	–	20
Bevin, J.M.M.	1	2	1	29	47	47.00	–	–	–	0
Bhabra, B.J.	2	3	–	10	14	4.66	–	–	–	0
Billings, S.W.	68	102	11	171	3158	34.70	6	14	–	165/11
Bird, J.M.	83	113	34	50	966	12.22	–	1	–	39
Blake, A.J.	46	72	6	105*	1511	22.89	1	6	–	25
Blatherwick, J.M.	2	2	2	4*	6	–	–	–	–	0
Bohannon, J.J.	16	21	4	174	727	42.76	1	4	–	6
Bopara, R.S.	221	357	40	229	12821	40.44	31	55	1	118
Borthwick, S.G.	164	275	25	216	9096	36.38	19	48	4	216
Bracewell, D.A.J.	101	151	21	105	3436	26.43	2	18	–	46
Bracey, J.R.	37	64	6	156	2027	34.94	5	7	–	45
Brathwaite, K.C.	147	262	20	212	9358	38.66	22	48	–	89
Bresnan, T.T.	198	272	41	169*	6599	28.56	6	34	–	102
Briggs, D.R.	108	138	37	120*	1769	17.51	1	1	–	38
Broad, S.C.J.	216	305	49	169	5119	19.99	1	24	–	78
Brook, H.C.	28	47	–	124	1027	21.85	2	3	–	15
Brookes, E.A.	1	1	–	0	0	0.00	–	–	–	0
Brookes, H.J.H.	17	25	3	84	465	21.13	–	3	–	7
Brooks, J.A.	128	158	56	109*	1688	16.54	1	4	–	31
Brown, B.C.	140	219	34	163	7403	40.01	18	40	2	397/17
Brown, P.R.	5	6	4	5*	14	7.00	–	–	–	2
Browne, N.L.J.	91	149	10	255	5531	39.79	15	23	3	69
Buck, N.L.	94	131	36	53	1345	14.15	–	3	–	17
Bull, K.A.	12	20	6	31	152	10.85	–	–	–	4
Burgess, M.G.K.	33	47	4	146	1688	39.25	2	10	–	32
Burnham, J.T.A.	39	67	5	135	1616	26.06	1	10	–	13
Burns, J.A.	111	196	14	202*	7365	40.46	17	41	–	102
Burns, R.J.	128	225	14	219*	8918	42.26	17	48	6	112
Buttleman, W.E.L.	1	1	–	0	0	0.00	–	–	–	3
Buttler, J.C.	100	162	13	144	4840	32.48	5	30	–	189/2
Byrom, E.J.	21	40	2	152	1108	29.15	2	4	–	12
Came, H.R.C.	1	1	1	23*	23	–	–	–	–	0
Campbell, J.O.I.	3	4	2	2	2	1.00	–	–	–	0
Cantrell, J.J.	2	3	–	19	46	15.33	–	–	–	0
Cantwell, S.	2	4	3	43	73	73.00	–	–	–	1
Carey, A.T.	31	55	6	139	1538	31.38	2	9	–	113/2
Carey, L.J.	29	39	6	62*	519	15.72	–	3	–	4
Carlson, K.S.	30	52	2	191	1393	27.86	4	3	–	14
Carse, B.A.	21	26	7	77*	513	27.00	–	2	–	3
Carter, M.	14	23	1	33	191	8.68	–	–	–	13
Chapman, L.J.	5	7	–	13	27	3.85	–	–	–	3
Chappell, Z.J.	19	30	5	96	597	23.88	–	2	–	2
Charlesworth, B.G.	11	16	2	77*	339	24.21	–	3	–	5

	M	I	NO	HS	Runs	Avge	100	50	1000	Ct/St
Chopra, V.	190	313	20	233*	10154	34.65	20	50	3	224
Christian, D.T.	83	141	17	131*	3783	30.50	5	16	–	90
Clark, G.	34	63	1	109	1543	24.88	1	10	–	25
Clark, J.	51	74	8	140	1884	28.54	1	10	–	7
Clark, T.G.R.	1	1	–	13	13	13.00	–	–	–	0
Clarke, J.M.	75	130	9	194	4586	37.90	16	15	1	36
Clarke, R.	253	384	46	214	11104	32.85	17	57	1	374
Claughton, T.H.	3	4	–	29	58	14.50	–	–	–	7/1
Claydon, M.E.	108	137	32	77	1611	15.34	–	4	–	11
Coad, B.O.	36	48	16	48	487	15.21	–	–	–	1
Cobb, J.J.	126	216	22	148*	5155	26.57	4	30	–	53
Cockbain, I.A.	51	86	6	151*	2382	29.77	4	13	–	35
Coles, M.T.	116	154	23	103*	2624	20.03	1	12	–	62
Compton, B.G.	2	3	1	16*	43	21.50	–	–	–	1
Conners, S.	3	2	1	14	20	20.00	–	–	–	0
Cook, A.N.	304	538	41	294	23667	47.61	65	114	9+1	323
Cook, S.J.	29	30	14	37*	114	7.12	–	–	–	3
Cooke, C.B.	84	143	18	171	4478	35.82	4	29	–	141/4
Cornall, T.R.	2	4	–	19	43	10.75	–	–	–	2
Cosgrove, M.J.	221	393	22	233	14976	40.36	36	87	4	132
Coughlin, J.	4	6	–	24	66	11.00	–	–	–	1
Coughlin, P.	38	60	8	85	1368	26.30	–	7	–	20
Coulter-Nile, N.M.	37	56	3	64	994	18.75	–	3	–	24
Cox, J.M.	3	4	–	27	71	17.75	–	–	–	1
Cox, O.B.	116	188	24	124	4539	27.67	4	26	–	305/13
Crane, M.S.	38	53	18	29	386	11.02	–	–	–	9
Crawley, Z.	36	61	–	168	1908	31.27	3	11	–	32
Critchley, M.J.J.	48	81	9	137*	2020	28.05	3	9	–	30
Croft, S.J.	176	270	25	156	8263	33.72	13	48	–	176
Cross-Zamirski, J.O.	2	4	2	6*	7	3.50	–	–	–	1
Cullen, T.N.	17	25	3	63	502	22.81	–	4	–	44/1
Cummins, M.L.	79	103	42	29*	408	6.68	–	–	–	31
Cummins, P.J.	37	54	14	82*	864	21.60	–	4	–	15
Curran, B.J.	13	22	3	83*	619	32.57	–	4	–	6
Curran, S.M.	59	93	11	96	2410	29.39	–	18	–	14
Curran, T.K.	59	81	11	60	1241	17.72	–	5	–	20
Dahl, A.E.C.	2	4	–	46	106	26.50	–	–	–	1
Dal, A.K.	15	26	4	92	402	18.27	–	2	–	9
Davey, J.H.	32	52	9	72	725	16.86	–	3	–	12
Davies, A.L.	75	114	5	147	3766	34.55	5	23	1	156/15
Davies, S.M.	225	374	35	200*	13097	38.63	24	61	6	532/33
Davis, W.S.	24	34	12	39*	254	11.54	–	–	–	3
Dawson, L.A.	151	246	26	169	7320	33.27	9	41	1	145
de Lange, M.	82	109	16	90	1450	15.59	–	3	–	34
de Villiers, A.B.	141	238	23	278*	10689	49.71	25	60	0+1	275/6
Dearden, H.E.	37	63	2	87	1269	20.80	–	6	–	27
Dell, J.J.	7	12	–	61	158	13.16	–	1	–	5
Delport, C.S.	61	106	6	163	3206	32.06	3	19	–	36
Denly, J.L.	203	352	25	227	11947	36.53	29	59	4	83
Dent, C.D.J.	143	256	23	268	8981	38.54	18	51	4	156
Dernbach, J.W.	113	139	47	56*	871	9.46	–	1	–	17
Dewes, A.H.J.	2	3	–	11	11	3.66	–	–	–	1
Dewhurst, A.C.H.	3	6	–	91	207	34.50	–	2	–	1
Dexter, N.J.	162	270	30	180	8316	34.65	18	39	–	98
Dickson, S.R.	69	117	9	318	3736	34.59	10	14	–	59
Diwakar, J.	1	2	–	24	45	22.50	–	–	–	0

244

	M	I	NO	HS	Runs	Avge	100	50	1000	Ct/St
D'Oliveira, B.L.	59	101	3	202*	2793	28.50	7	7	–	28
Donald, A.H.T.	48	86	5	234	2610	32.22	3	15	1	35
Douthwaite, D.A.	9	15	1	100*	443	31.64	1	1	–	1
Drissell, G.S.	7	11	–	19	77	7.00	–	–	–	0
du Plessis, F.	139	230	26	176	8243	40.40	17	50	–	132
du Plooy, J.L.	53	84	12	181	3370	46.80	11	18	–	47
Duckett, B.M.	90	156	9	282*	5746	38.56	16	26	2	67/3
Dunn, M.P.	39	43	21	31*	146	6.63	–	–	–	7
Eckersley, E.J.H.	121	215	16	158	6499	32.65	15	23	1	217/3
Edwards, F.H.	138	190	74	40	789	6.80	–	–	–	26
Elgar, D.	198	345	26	268	13464	42.20	40	52	0+2	158
Emanuel, J.F.	1	1	–	20	20	20.00	–	–	–	0
Eskinazi, S.S.	51	89	4	179	2874	33.81	6	12	–	45
Evans, B.N.	4	4	1	3*	3	1.00	–	–	–	0
Evans, H.A.	3	5	3	7*	16	8.00	–	–	–	0
Evans, L.J.	68	116	6	213*	3302	30.01	6	17	–	55
Evans, S.T.	9	13	1	114	249	20.75	1	–	–	2
Evison, J.D.M.	1	2	–	45	57	28.50	–	–	–	1
Faheem Ashraf	40	58	8	116	1478	29.56	2	5	–	18
Fakhar Zaman	40	67	4	205	2581	40.96	6	15	–	34
Fallows, J.B.	2	3	1	19	32	16.00	–	–	–	1
Fanning, M.J.	2	1	–	1	1	1.00	–	–	–	0
Faulkner, J.P.	63	95	12	121	2566	30.91	2	15	–	26
Fell, T.C.	79	134	5	171	3808	29.51	5	16	1	61
Ferguson, C.J.	137	255	21	213	8758	37.42	19	46	–	77
Finch, A.J.	84	140	6	288*	4811	35.90	7	32	–	79
Finch, A.W.	8	10	5	18*	61	12.20	–	–	–	0
Finch, H.Z.	48	79	6	135*	1907	26.12	3	11	–	62
Finn, S.T.	157	191	62	56	1266	9.81	–	2	–	49
Fisher, M.D.	13	17	3	47*	246	17.57	–	–	–	4
Fletcher, L.J.	117	174	28	92	2029	13.89	–	4	–	28
Foakes, B.T.	109	172	28	141*	5474	38.01	9	30	–	225/23
Foster, F.J.H.	1	1	–	1	1	1.00	–	–	–	1
Foster, M.T.	3	3	–	6	13	4.33	–	–	–	0
Fraine, W.A.R.	13	20	1	106	490	25.78	1	–	–	8
Fuller, J.K.	53	69	9	93	1239	20.65	–	6	–	21
Gabriel, S.T.	103	141	56	20*	470	5.52	–	–	–	25
Garrett, G.A.	3	4	2	24	32	16.00	–	–	–	0
Garton, G.H.S.	13	15	5	59*	213	21.30	–	2	–	6
Gay, E.N.	1			–	–	–	–	–	–	1
Gibbs, J.H.	1	1	–	0	0	0.00	–	–	–	0
Gleadall, A.F.	2	4	1	27*	29	9.66	–	–	–	0
Gleeson, R.J.	33	38	16	31	253	11.50	–	–	–	8
Glover, B.D.	9	13	6	12*	38	5.42	–	–	–	1
Godleman, B.A.	157	283	13	227	8754	32.42	21	38	2	97
Graves, B.W.M.	5	4	–	66	106	26.50	–	1	–	1
Greenidge, A.D.	5	7	–	24	84	12.00	–	–	–	3
Greenwell, R.L.	1	2	–	31	35	17.50	–	–	–	0
Gregory, L.	86	127	13	137	2491	21.85	2	8	–	48
Griffiths, G.T.	23	33	11	40	303	13.77	–	–	–	3
Groenewald, T.D.	138	200	66	78	2375	17.72	–	6	–	45
Gubbins, N.R.T.	73	129	2	201*	4184	32.94	7	26	1	28
Guest, B.D.	2	4	–	17	36	9.00	–	–	–	5
Guest, C.J.	5	7	–	34	68	9.71	–	–	–	4
Guptill, M.J.	109	197	13	227	6987	37.97	15	36	–	116
Gurney, H.F.	103	131	63	42*	424	6.23	–	–	–	12

245

	M	I	NO	HS	Runs	Avge	100	50	1000	Ct/St
Hain, S.R.	75	117	12	208	3897	37.11	10	19	–	64
Haines, T.J.	16	25	–	124	583	23.32	1	2	–	5
Hales, A.D.	107	182	6	236	6655	37.81	13	38	3	84
Hameed, H.	63	106	11	122	2907	30.60	5	15	1	35
Hamidullah Qadri	10	20	8	17*	81	6.75	–	–	–	6
Hammond, M.A.H.	25	42	3	123*	928	23.79	2	4	–	21
Hammond, N.A.	4	4	–	28	29	7.25	–	–	–	0
Handscomb, P.S.P.	102	172	12	215	6153	38.45	14	35	–	159/4
Hankins, G.T.	28	45	2	116	961	22.34	1	6	–	29
Hankins, H.J.	1	1	–	9	9	9.00	–	–	–	0
Hannon-Dalby, O.J.	69	83	28	40	396	7.20	–	–	–	7
Harding, G.H.I.	3	4	–	36	43	10.75	–	–	–	0
Hargrave, G.T.	1	2	–	146	151	75.50	1	–	–	0
Harmer, S.R.	145	218	43	102*	4290	24.51	2	22	–	140
Harris, J.A.R.	144	209	49	87*	3734	23.33	–	18	–	42
Harris, M.S.	86	158	9	250*	5575	37.41	12	25	0+1	42
Harrison, C.G.	2	3	1	37	65	32.50	–	–	–	1
Harte, G.J.	20	38	2	114	951	26.41	3	3	–	6
Haynes, J.A.	5	7	–	31	119	17.00	–	–	–	1
Haynes, J.L.	2	4	–	20	38	9.50	–	–	–	1
Haynes, T.S.	1	2	–	13	19	9.50	–	–	–	0
Hazlewood, J.R.	84	99	38	43*	741	12.14	–	–	–	31
Head, T.M.	93	170	9	192	6312	39.20	10	42	0+1	40
Heathfield, T.D.	5	5	2	47	88	29.33	–	–	–	0
Helm, T.G.	29	39	8	52	530	17.09	–	1	–	9
Hemphrey, C.R.	42	79	6	118	2293	31.41	4	14	–	29
Henriques, M.C.	92	149	14	265	4588	33.98	8	21	–	42
Henry, M.J.	62	81	15	81	1415	21.43	–	5	–	26
Higgins, R.F.	33	53	8	199	1613	35.84	5	5	–	10
Hildreth, J.C.	263	435	32	303*	17164	42.59	46	77	7	223
Hill, L.J.	41	71	9	126	1459	23.53	1	5	–	96/3
Hogan, M.G.	155	218	85	57	2170	16.31	–	3	–	78
Holden, M.D.E.	38	68	4	153	1732	27.06	3	7	–	11
Holder, J.O.	69	108	11	202*	2569	26.48	3	10	–	53
Holland, I.G.	26	41	6	143	871	24.88	1	5	–	9
Holland, J.M.	69	85	35	55	738	14.76	–	1	–	23
Holling, J.B.R.	2	4	–	13	16	4.00	–	–	–	0
Hooper, E.O.	1	1	–	20	20	20.00	–	–	–	0
Horton, P.J.	218	373	26	209	12308	35.46	24	67	3	201/1
Hose, A.J.	19	35	1	111	746	21.94	1	4	–	5
Hosein, H.R.	47	80	14	138*	2042	30.93	2	14	–	108/4
Howell, B.A.C.	86	136	13	163	3378	27.46	2	18	–	52
Hudson-Prentice, F.J.	12	20	2	99	426	23.66	–	2	–	1
Hughes, A.L.	71	125	11	142	3277	28.74	6	13	–	53
Hurt, L.J.	1	1	–	38	38	38.00	–	–	–	0
Hutton, B.A.	56	88	12	74	1371	18.03	–	4	–	34
Hyde, E.R.B.	4	7	1	32	80	13.33	–	–	–	9
Imad Wasim	76	114	24	207	3669	40.76	6	20	–	35
Imran Tahir	194	246	62	77*	2617	14.22	–	4	–	81
Ingram, C.A.	111	195	17	190	6641	37.30	14	30	–	75
Ironside, D.A.	2	4	–	24	52	13.00	–	–	–	0
Jacks, W.G.	19	29	2	120	748	27.70	1	5	–	22
James, L.W.	1	2	–	13	14	7.00	–	–	–	0
Javid, A.	43	70	6	143	1503	23.48	3	5	–	18
Jennings, K.K.	132	231	14	221*	7300	33.64	18	27	1	103
Johns, N.R.	1	2	–	14	24	12.00	–	–	–	0

246

	M	I	NO	HS	Runs	Avge	100	50	1000	Ct/St
Jones, M.A.	3	5	–	10	22	4.40	–	–	–	0
Jones, R.P.	27	40	5	122	1098	31.37	2	5	–	24
Jordan, C.J.	114	159	23	166	3443	25.31	3	15	–	137
Kapil, A.	15	26	3	104*	499	21.69	1	1	–	4
Keeping, J.B.R.	2	1	–	10	10	10.00	–	–	–	1
Kendall, J.S.	2	3	1	37*	95	47.50	–	–	–	0
Keogh, R.I.	79	129	8	221	3607	29.80	9	10	–	22/1
Khawaja, U.T.	142	247	22	214	9750	43.33	28	47	0+1	106
Kimber, L.P.J.	2	3	–	62	99	33.00	–	1	–	1
King, A.E.	2	3	–	33	53	17.66	–	–	–	2
Klaassen, F.J.	2	3	1	14*	37	18.50	–	–	–	2
Klein, D.	64	91	18	94	1390	19.04	–	6	–	19
Klinger, M.	182	321	33	255	11320	39.31	30	49	1+2	179
Kohler-Cadmore, T.	61	100	7	176	3332	35.82	9	15	1	85
Kolk, O.M.D.	2	3	–	33	42	14.00	–	–	–	2
Kuhn, H.G.	173	303	27	244*	11240	40.72	23	58	0+1	369/18
Labuschagne, M.	66	121	8	182	4342	38.42	9	26	1	70
Lace, T.C.	16	31	1	143	1084	36.13	3	4	–	12
Lamb, D.J.	5	7	2	49	106	21.20	–	–	–	1
Lamb, M.J.	16	28	2	173	690	26.53	1	3	–	5
Lawlor, J.L.	11	18	2	81	384	24.00	–	3	–	9
Lawrence, D.W.	69	110	12	161	3679	37.54	9	17	1	53
Leach, J.	88	132	16	114	2872	24.75	2	18	–	22
Leach, M.J.	86	118	30	92	1069	12.14	–	3	–	36
Leaning, J.A.	68	108	11	123	2955	30.46	4	16	–	52
Lees, A.Z.	110	190	13	275*	6064	34.25	15	27	2	77
Lehmann, J.S.	50	90	6	205	2999	35.70	7	14	–	31
Lester, T.J.	13	15	9	8	22	3.66	–	–	–	3
Levi, R.E.	105	174	18	168	5703	36.55	10	32	–	88
Libby, J.D.	55	96	6	144	2574	28.60	5	11	–	19
Liddle, C.J.	34	36	18	53	208	11.55	–	1	–	8
Lilley, A.M.	15	18	5	63	426	32.76	–	2	–	4
Livingstone, L.S.	54	85	14	224	2955	41.61	7	15	–	68
Lloyd, D.L.	69	116	12	119	2939	28.25	4	11	–	34
Logan, J.E.G.	2	3	1	20*	33	16.50	–	–	–	1
Loten, T.W.	1	1	–	58	58	58.00	–	1	–	0
Ludlow, J.H.	4	4	–	19	28	7.00	–	–	–	6
Lynn, C.A.	41	71	8	250	2743	43.53	6	12	–	26
Lyon, N.M.	150	192	55	75	1762	12.86	–	2	–	65
Lyth, A.	176	296	14	251	10674	37.85	23	57	3	231
McBride, C.J.	2	3	–	28	35	11.66	–	–	–	0
McBrine, A.R.	18	27	2	77	509	20.36	–	3	–	16
McCollum, J.A.	17	26	2	119*	1087	45.29	2	6	–	3
McDermott, B.R.	25	44	6	104	1090	28.68	1	8	–	15
MacDonagh, N.C.	1	1	–	17	17	17.00	–	–	–	1/1
McKerr, C.J.	14	15	4	29	133	12.09	–	–	–	2
McKiernan, M.H.	1	2	–	7	7	3.50	–	–	–	3
McManus, L.D.	39	56	6	132*	1414	28.28	1	6	–	83/10
Machado, L.	4	4	–	19	32	8.00	–	–	–	1/1
Madsen, W.L.	184	329	23	231*	11964	39.09	30	61	5	188
Maharaj, K.A.	123	175	26	114*	3044	20.42	2	10	–	44
Mahmood, S.	16	18	7	34	154	14.00	–	–	–	1
Malan, D.J.	188	321	21	199	11229	37.43	25	59	3	198
Markram, A.K.	60	102	5	182	4217	43.47	10	22	0+1	57
Marsh, M.R.	101	174	14	211	5116	31.97	11	20	–	52
Marsh, S.E.	158	279	28	182	10174	40.53	26	50	–	137

247

	M	I	NO	HS	Runs	Avge	100	50	1000	Ct/St
Maxwell, G.J.	65	109	10	278	3960	40.00	7	22	–	52
Meaker, S.C.	89	117	24	94	1445	15.53	–	6	–	20
Mellor, A.J.	9	16	1	59	282	18.80	–	1	–	15
Melton, D.R.	3	4	2	1*	1	0.50	–	–	–	1
Meschede, C.A.J.	70	101	13	107	2250	25.56	2	13	–	23
Mike, B.W.M.	11	18	2	72	293	18.31	–	1	–	2
Miles, C.N.	73	102	15	62*	1420	16.32	–	5	–	19
Mills, T.S.	32	38	15	31*	260	11.30	–	–	–	9
Milne, A.F.	30	45	14	97	756	24.38	–	4	–	10
Milnes, M.E.	23	32	11	43	292	13.90	–	–	–	12
Milnes, T.P.	26	36	4	56	638	19.93	–	3	–	6
Milton, A.G.	14	22	2	104*	358	17.90	1	1	–	12/1
Mir Hamza	66	79	34	25	292	6.48	–	–	–	12
Mitchell, D.K.H.	206	371	39	298	13066	39.35	37	50	6	281
Moen, A.J.	1	2	–	6	6	3.00	–	–	–	0
Mohammad Abbas	99	143	51	40	615	6.68	–	–	–	28
Mohammad Amir	67	102	16	66	1366	15.88	–	2	–	15
Mohammad Hafeez	210	364	14	224	12160	34.74	26	56	0+1	182
Mohammad Nabi	34	55	4	117	1276	25.01	2	5	–	20
Mohammed Rizvi	1	1	–	2	2	2.00	–	–	–	1
Moores, T.J.	34	59	1	103	1165	20.08	1	2	–	77/1
Morgan, A.O.	21	37	6	103*	638	20.58	1	1	–	6
Morgan, E.J.G.	102	169	18	209*	5042	33.39	11	24	1	76/1
Morkel, M.	152	190	35	82*	2029	13.09	–	4	–	51
Morris, C.A.J.	60	83	47	53*	454	12.61	–	1	–	12
Morris, C.H.	58	86	10	154	2489	32.75	4	11	–	50
Mousley, D.R.	1	2	–	3	3	1.50	–	–	–	0
Mujeeb Zadran	1	2	–	15	18	9.00	–	–	–	0
Mulder, P.W.A.	25	41	9	146	1220	38.12	3	4	–	12
Mullaney, S.J.	138	234	9	179	7492	33.29	15	40	1	132
Munsey, H.G.	4	5	1	100*	224	56.00	1	1	–	1
Murtagh, T.J.	232	308	88	74*	4171	18.95	–	11	–	64
Muzarabani, B.	9	14	3	23	140	12.72	–	–	–	3
Narine, S.P.	13	18	6	40*	213	17.75	–	–	–	10
Nash, C.D.	206	355	20	184	12474	37.23	24	67	4	122
Neal, A.J.	2	4	–	15	28	7.00	–	–	–	1
Neser, M.G.	47	71	10	77	1604	26.29	–	11	–	22
Newton, R.I.	98	172	13	202*	5675	35.69	15	24	1	28
Nijjar, A.S.S.	13	15	5	53	237	23.70	–	1	–	3
Northeast, S.A.	164	280	21	191	10183	39.31	24	51	4	84
Norwell, L.C.	72	92	36	102	823	14.69	1	2	–	16
O'Brien, K.J.	47	66	11	171*	2039	37.07	2	14	–	37
Odedra, Y.J.	1	2	–	4	4	2.00	–	–	–	0
Olivier, D.	110	142	45	72	1230	12.68	–	3	–	30
Onions, G.	193	248	86	65	2100	12.96	–	1	–	35
Organ, F.S.	7	12	–	100	316	26.33	1	2	–	4
O'Riordan, M.K.	1	2	–	12	21	10.50	–	–	–	0
Overton, C.	88	129	16	138	2388	21.13	1	9	–	58
Overton, J.	64	92	21	56	1245	17.53	–	6	–	29
Owen, X.G.	3	4	3	24	33	33.00	–	–	–	0
Paine, T.D.	124	210	28	215	5253	28.86	1	30	–	387/17
Palladino, A.P.	166	239	50	106	2915	15.42	1	8	–	40
Panayi, G.D.	2	3	–	16	17	5.66	–	–	–	0
Parkinson, C.F.	25	39	7	75	593	18.53	–	1	–	4
Parkinson, M.W.	20	26	9	14	90	5.29	–	–	–	6
Park-Johnson, J.C.H.	2	3	–	12	28	9.33	–	–	–	1

248

	M	I	NO	HS	Runs	Avge	100	50	1000	Ct/St
Parnell, W.D.	75	101	11	111*	2502	27.80	2	15	–	23
Parry, S.D.	28	34	2	44	456	14.25	–	–	–	7
Patel, A.Y.	57	82	22	45	743	12.38	–	–	–	38
Patel, J.S.	293	391	78	120	6695	21.38	3	28	–	155
Patel, R.K.	6	8	–	35	146	18.25	–	–	–	6
Patel, R.S.	23	36	4	100*	848	26.50	1	2	–	9
Patel, S.R.	226	369	20	257*	12482	35.76	26	62	4	138
Patterson, K.R.	67	117	11	157	4327	40.82	8	27	–	52
Patterson, S-A.	155	186	43	63*	2354	16.46	–	4	–	31
Patterson-White, L.A.	5	8	2	58*	91	15.16	–	1	–	3
Pattinson, J.L.	64	81	19	89*	1483	23.91	–	5	–	19
Payne, D.A.	95	117	38	67*	1628	20.60	–	6	–	31
Pearce, S.J.	4	4	–	35	55	13.75	–	–	–	0
Pennington, D.Y.	12	22	3	37	138	7.26	–	–	–	4
Pepper, M.S.	3	6	–	22	61	10.16	–	–	–	6
Pereira, W.J.N.	4	5	1	28*	32	8.00	–	–	–	0
Pettman, T.H.S.	6	6	1	54*	104	20.80	–	1	–	3
Philander, V.D.	161	221	43	168	4679	26.28	3	17	–	41
Pillans, M.W.	42	59	5	56	730	13.51	–	1	–	20
Plunkett, L.E.	158	216	39	126	4378	24.73	3	22	–	86
Podmore, H.W.	42	62	17	66*	773	17.17	–	3	–	10
Pollard, K.A.	27	44	2	174	1584	37.71	4	7	–	42
Pollock, E.J.	5	7	1	52	184	30.66	–	1	–	1
Pooran, N.	3	6	–	55	143	23.83	–	1	–	2/2
Pope, O.J.D.	31	46	7	251	2293	58.79	8	6	1	37
Porter, J.A.	84	97	34	34	357	5.66	–	–	–	24
Porterfield, W.T.S.	136	226	9	207	6867	31.64	11	34	–	146
Potts, M.J.	9	13	4	53*	166	18.44	–	1	–	1
Powe, T.B.	2	3	–	33	74	24.66	–	–	–	0
Poynter, S.W.	39	62	2	170	1379	22.98	2	4	–	117/4
Poysden, J.E.	14	14	4	47	96	9.60	–	–	–	2
Pretorius, D.	51	71	7	177	2502	39.09	5	15	–	16
Pringle, R.D.	40	63	8	99	1336	24.29	–	8	–	24
Procter, L.A.	94	149	15	137	4108	30.65	3	22	–	23
Pucovski, W.J.	14	24	2	243	939	42.68	3	3	–	5
Pujara, C.A.	189	311	37	352	14789	53.97	49	50	0+3	125/1
Punja, Y.	3	4	1	6	12	4.00	–	–	–	0
Qais Ahmad	11	15	2	46*	203	15.61	–	–	–	7
Qayyum, I.	6	9	4	39	55	11.00	–	–	–	3
Quinn, M.R.	34	44	11	50	347	10.51	–	1	–	7
Rackow, A.J.W.	4	5	1	95	218	54.50	–	2	–	2
Rahane, A.M.	134	229	23	265*	10227	49.64	31	45	0+3	140
Raine, B.A.	79	129	11	82	2465	20.88	–	10	–	16
Rampaul, R.	92	135	33	64*	1317	12.91	–	2	–	25
Rankin, W.B.	108	129	52	56*	704	9.14	–	1	–	29
Rashid, A.U.	175	251	41	180	6822	32.48	10	37	–	79
Rashid Khan	6	7	1	52	154	25.66	–	1	–	0
Rawlins, D.M.W.	14	24	1	100	642	27.91	1	5	–	5
Rayner, O.P.	151	201	32	143*	3432	20.30	2	13	–	196
Read, J.	3	5	–	15	48	9.60	–	–	–	9
Reece, L.M.	63	113	7	184	3528	33.28	6	20	–	29
Reingold, S.J.	2	3	–	22	29	9.66	–	–	–	0
Renshaw, M.T.	56	105	6	184	3566	36.02	10	12	–	49
Revis, M.L.	1	2	–	9	9	4.50	–	–	–	1
Rhodes, G.H.	24	45	6	61*	873	22.38	–	5	–	10
Rhodes, W.M.H.	49	77	3	137	2571	34.74	5	13	–	28

	M	I	NO	HS	Runs	Avge	100	50	1000	Ct/St
Richardson, M.J.	103	176	11	148	4828	29.26	6	26	2	186/5
Riley, A.E.N.	61	75	28	34	495	10.53	–	–	–	37
Rimmington, N.J.	53	76	16	102*	1221	20.35	1	4	–	15
Rippington, S.E.	5	7	3	8*	13	3.25	–	–	–	1
Robertson, W.J.R.	3	2	1	8*	8	8.00	–	–	–	0
Robinson, O.E.	55	80	16	110	1369	21.39	1	5	–	19
Robinson, O.G.	18	30	2	143	845	30.17	2	3	–	55
Robson, A.J.	61	111	3	120	3261	30.19	2	29	2	51
Robson, S.D.	157	276	18	231	9750	37.79	23	39	2	144
Roderick, G.H.	96	156	20	171	4801	35.30	6	32	–	265/5
Rogers, O.J.W.	2	2	–	13	13	6.50	–	–	–	2
Roland-Jones, T.S.	114	159	30	103*	2824	21.89	1	11	–	33
Root, J.E.	145	254	23	254	11129	48.17	26	62	3	142
Root, W.T.	28	46	2	229	1465	33.29	4	3	–	7
Rossington, A.M.	77	123	12	138*	3903	35.16	6	28	–	167/11
Rossouw, R.R.	108	190	10	319	7363	40.90	19	33	0+1	118
Rouse, A.P.	36	51	4	95*	1103	23.46	–	5	–	112/4
Roy, J.J.	86	142	11	143	4832	36.88	9	23	1	74
Rushworth, C.	127	179	57	57	1460	11.96	–	1	–	28
Russell, A.D.	17	24	1	128	609	26.47	2	–	–	6
Rutherford, H.D.	98	171	3	239	6065	36.10	14	28	0+1	67
Sakande, A.	18	23	9	33	151	10.78	–	–	–	6
Salisbury, M.E.T.	31	53	11	37	374	8.90	–	–	–	4
Salt, P.D.	34	58	2	148	1677	29.94	4	7	–	27
Salter, A.G.	56	87	17	88	1629	23.27	–	8	–	28
Sanders, C.W.G.	4	5	–	56	80	16.00	–	1	–	0
Sanderson, B.W.	60	77	30	42	421	8.95	–	–	–	9
Santner, M.J.	45	67	4	118	1823	28.93	2	11	–	37
Sayers, C.J.	70	104	22	56	1110	13.53	–	1	–	20
Scott, C.F.B.	2	3	–	32	40	13.33	–	–	–	0
Scott, D.N.C.	3	5	–	18	45	9.00	–	–	–	1
Scott, G.F.B.	12	18	3	55	257	17.13	–	1	–	5
Seabrook, B.M.A.	3	3	1	44*	94	47.00	–	–	–	1
Searle, C.J.	3	3	1	8	14	7.00	–	–	–	0
Selman, N.J.	51	93	6	150	2527	29.04	7	11	–	54
Seward, J.C.	3	3	–	28	50	16.66	–	–	–	2
Shadab Khan	13	18	2	132	504	31.50	1	3	–	8
Shaheen Shah Afridi	6	10	2	14	40	5.00	–	–	–	1
Shamsi, T.	76	91	26	30*	521	8.01	–	–	–	19
Shaw, J.	34	45	9	42	411	11.41	–	–	–	8
Shaw, L.J.P.	2	2	–	11	11	5.50	–	–	–	1
Short, D.J.M.	13	24	1	66	582	25.30	–	3	–	11
Sibley, D.P.	66	112	11	244	4197	41.55	12	20	1	51
Siddle, P.M.	171	229	42	103*	3214	17.18	1	6	–	56
Sidebottom, R.N.	18	28	14	27*	87	6.21	–	–	–	5
Sidwell, B.D.	1	2	1	42*	45	45.00	–	–	–	0
Simpson, J.A.	155	245	37	167*	6680	32.11	7	38	–	467/24
Singh, A.R.	3	4	–	44	77	19.25	–	–	–	4
Sisodiya, P.	4	7	1	38	83	13.83	–	–	–	2
Slater, B.T.	83	154	7	130	4604	31.31	5	25	1	30
Smit, D.	137	208	37	156*	6077	35.53	9	33	0+1	362/22
Smith, J.L.	9	15	1	127	465	33.21	1	2	–	5/2
Smith, M.J.E.	1	2	–	17	17	8.50	–	–	–	0
Smith, R.A.J.	29	42	6	57*	655	18.19	–	2	–	4
Smith, S.P.D.	123	216	26	239	11221	59.05	40	47	–	186
Smith, T.M.J.	48	67	12	84	1316	23.92	–	4	–	15

250

	M	I	NO	HS	Runs	Avge	100	50	1000	Ct/St
Smith, W.R.	183	313	22	210	9541	32.78	18	37	1	115
Snater, S.	3	4	1	50*	73	24.33	–	1	–	1
Soames, O.C.	12	20	–	62	238	11.90	–	1	–	3
Sookias, J.H.	2	2	–	1	1	0.50	–	–	–	6
Sowter, N.A.	8	13	1	57*	221	18.41	–	2	–	4
Starc, M.A.	93	119	32	99	2007	23.06	–	11	–	43
Steel, C.T.	37	65	2	224	1985	31.50	3	11	–	18
Steel, S.	2	4	–	39	48	12.00	–	–	–	1
Stevens, D.I.	303	476	30	237	15633	35.05	34	79	3	197
Stevenson, R.A.	5	6	1	51	124	24.80	–	–	–	1
Stewart, G.	17	26	4	103	542	24.63	1	3	–	3
Stirling, P.R.	70	110	5	146	2932	27.92	6	14	–	40
Stokes, B.A.	132	225	12	258	7383	34.66	16	38	–	100
Stone, O.P.	37	48	10	60	573	15.07	–	1	–	15
Stoneman, M.D.	190	331	8	197	11180	34.61	23	58	5	88
Subramanyan, J.	2	1	–	11	11	11.00	–	–	–	0
Suresh, K.	2	4	–	54	77	19.25	–	1	–	0
Swanson, B.	2	3	1	3	3	1.50	–	–	–	3
Swindells, H.J.	7	10	–	37	168	16.80	–	–	–	12/1
Tattersall, J.A.	22	34	3	135*	1008	32.51	1	5	–	55/4
Taylor, B.J.	6	10	3	36	133	19.00	–	–	–	2
Taylor, J.E.	103	161	25	106	1595	11.72	1	1	–	25
Taylor, J.M.R.	77	118	9	156	3229	29.62	7	9	–	39
Taylor, J.P.A.	2	2	2	11*	11	–	–	–	–	0
Taylor, L.R.P.L.	169	284	22	290	11326	43.22	26	60	–	215
Taylor, M.D.	52	67	28	48	514	13.17	–	–	–	7
Taylor, M.J.	2	3	1	61*	101	50.50	–	1	–	1
Taylor, N.P.	2	4	–	59	65	16.25	–	1	–	1
Taylor, T.A.I.	30	46	7	80	743	19.05	–	3	–	7
ten Doeschate, R.N.	188	275	39	259*	10766	45.61	29	49	1	118
Thomason, A.D.	4	8	–	90	129	16.12	–	1	–	1
Thompson, J.A.	2	3	–	34	36	12.00	–	–	–	0
Thompson, S.R.	19	29	2	148	582	21.55	1	1	–	7
Thomson, A.T.	8	9	–	26	140	15.55	–	–	–	2
Thurston, C.O.	8	10	–	126	236	23.60	1	–	–	2
Tillcock, A.D.	6	7	1	60	139	23.16	–	1	–	3
Tongue, J.C.	31	43	7	41	392	10.88	–	–	–	4
Topley, R.J.W.	36	43	20	16	100	4.34	–	–	–	8
Trego, P.D.	218	324	38	154*	9528	33.31	15	54	1	89
Tremain, C.P.	57	77	12	111	860	13.23	1	–	–	13
Trescothick, M.E.	391	675	36	284	26234	41.05	66	127	8	560
Trevaskis, L.	11	19	1	64	406	22.55	–	2	–	2
Turner, A.J.	39	64	6	110	2105	36.29	3	10	–	40
Turner, S.A.	2	4	–	38	91	22.75	–	–	–	0
Tye, A.J.	9	10	–	10	52	5.20	–	–	–	1
van Beek, L.V.	50	69	15	111*	1339	24.79	1	7	–	34
van Buuren, G.L.	85	132	21	235	4711	42.44	10	28	–	46
van den Bergh, F.O.E.	9	11	1	34	78	7.80	–	–	–	1
van der Gugten, T.	43	62	18	60*	652	14.81	–	3	–	8
van der Merwe, R.E.	67	108	15	205*	3184	34.23	6	19	–	53
van Zyl, S.	175	293	42	228	11132	44.35	27	50	1+1	99
Vasconcelos, R.S.	33	61	5	184	2057	36.73	5	11	–	44/4
Vijay, M.	134	225	7	266	9158	42.00	25	38	0+1	116
Vilas, D.J.	156	239	29	266	8872	42.24	21	41	1	430/20
Viljoen, G.C.	113	160	19	72	2100	14.89	–	7	–	31
Vince, J.M.	162	269	20	240	9692	38.92	25	36	2	137

251

	M	I	NO	HS	Runs	Avge	100	50	1000	Ct/St
Virdi, G.S.	23	27	14	21*	125	9.61	–	–		5
Vitali, J.C.	1	2	1	46*	61	61.00	–	–		0
Wade, M.S.	139	219	37	152	7346	40.36	17	42	0+1	423/21
Wagg, G.G.	161	240	25	200	5804	26.99	5	32		51
Wainman, J.C.	1	–	–	–	–	–	–	–		0
Waite, M.J.	8	11	1	42	160	16.00	–	–		1
Wakely, A.G.	146	233	16	123	6865	31.63	9	37		96
Waller, M.T.C.	9	10	1	28	91	10.11	–	–		5
Walter, P.I.	10	10	3	68*	240	34.28	–	1		0
Warner, D.A.	107	194	7	253	8703	46.54	28	38		76
Warner, J.D.	2	2	2	13*	14	–	–	–		0
Watling, B.T.J.	155	261	32	176	9005	39.32	17	53		370/10
Watt, M.R.J.	4	3	1	81*	128	64.00	–	1		2
Weatherley, J.J.	32	52	3	126*	1158	23.63	1	5		14
Weighell, W.J.	15	25	4	84	506	24.09	–	3		4
Welch, N.R.	5	7	–	83	179	25.57	–	1		1
Wells, J.W.	56	107	6	120	2365	23.41	3	8		36
Wells, L.W.P.	141	237	16	258	7779	35.19	18	33	2	63
Wessels, M.H.	212	351	31	202*	11342	35.44	23	58	2	332/16
Westley, T.	179	297	21	254	9973	36.13	21	47	1	115
Wheal, B.T.J.	25	29	8	25*	157	7.47	–	–		11
Wheater, A.J.A.	138	202	24	204*	6373	35.80	12	35		235/14
White, G.G.	39	55	5	65	659	13.18	–	2		12
White, R.G.	16	23	1	69	274	12.45	–	1		24/2
Whiteley, R.A.	87	142	13	130*	3543	27.46	3	19		59
Wiese, D.	123	192	20	208	5753	33.44	11	31		69
Willey, D.J.	71	100	12	104*	2350	26.70	2	14		17
Williamson, K.S.	141	242	19	284*	10948	49.09	30	57		133
Wilson, G.C.	108	166	22	160*	4834	33.56	3	29		197/5
Woakes, C.R.	145	216	49	152*	5753	34.44	10	23		59
Wood, C.P.	43	62	6	105*	1326	23.67	1	6		14
Wood, L.	40	63	14	100	1211	24.71	1	5		14
Wood, M.A.	51	84	17	72*	1433	21.38	–	5		14
Wood, T.A.	3	5	–	15	47	9.40	–	–		3
Woodland, A.J.	3	3	–	11	12	4.00	–	–		2
Worrall, D.J.	43	65	28	50	430	11.62	–	1		14
Wright, C.J.C.	161	208	45	77	2994	18.36	–	12		28
Wright, L.J.	144	223	23	226*	7622	38.11	17	38	1	58
Yates, R.M.	12	19	–	141	570	30.00	1	2		10
Zaib, S.A.	16	24	3	65*	494	23.52	–	3		3
Zampa, A.	36	59	7	74	1118	21.50	–	6		9

BOWLING

'50wS' denotes instances of taking 50 or more wickets in a season. Where these have been achieved outside the British Isles they are shown after a plus sign.

	Runs	Wkts	Avge	Best	5wI	10wM	50wS
Abbott, K.J.	9256	442	20.94	9- 40	30	4	3+1
Abbott, S.A.	4374	129	33.90	7- 45	3	–	–
Abell, T.B.	934	35	26.68	4- 39	–	–	–
Ackermann, C.N.	2608	60	43.46	5- 69	1	–	–
Adair, M.R.	652	19	34.31	3- 32	–	–	–
Agar, A.C.	5359	137	39.11	6-110	5	2	–
Akhter, Z.	112	0					
Ali, A.M.	86	1	86.00	1- 10	–	–	–
Ali, M.M.	13965	368	37.94	6- 29	12	2	–

252

	Runs	Wkts	Avge	Best	5wI	10wM	50wS
Allen, F.A.	332	10	33.20	4- 47	–	–	–
Allison, B.M.J.	139	4	34.75	3-109	–	–	–
Alsop, T.P.	81	3	27.00	2- 59	–	–	–
Ambrose, T.R.	1	1	1.00	1- 0	–	–	–
Amin, A.R.	82	6	13.66	4- 56	–	–	–
Amla, H.M.	277	1	277.00	1- 10	–	–	–
Anderson, C.J.	1675	40	41.87	5- 22	1	–	–
Anderson, J.M.	23728	950	24.97	7- 42	47	6	4
Andersson, M.K.	239	12	19.91	4- 25	–	–	–
Angus, W.F.	102	2	51.00	2- 71	–	–	–
Archer, J.C.	3517	153	22.98	7- 67	7	1	1
Ashwin, R.	14541	546	26.63	7- 59	43	11	0+1
Azad, M.H.	2	0					
Azhar Ali	1979	46	43.02	4- 34	–	–	–
Azharullah	10765	383	28.10	7- 74	20	3	0+1
Babar Azam	423	5	84.60	1- 13	–	–	–
Bailey, T.E.	4873	193	25.24	5- 12	9	2	1
Bairstow, J.M.	1	0					
Balbirnie, A.	245	13	18.84	4- 23	–	–	–
Balderson, T.W.	156	3	52.00	2- 91	–	–	–
Ball, J.T.	5434	191	28.45	6- 49	6	–	1
Ballance, G.S.	154	0					
Bamber, E.R.	1154	47	24.55	5- 93	1	–	–
Bancroft, C.T.	67	1	67.00	1- 67	–	–	–
Banks, L.	9	0					
Barber, T.E.	131	0					
Barker, K.H.D.	10123	397	25.49	6- 40	15	1	3
Barnard, E.G.	5086	187	27.19	6- 37	5	1	–
Bartlett, G.A.	27	0					
Batty, G.J.	22356	682	32.78	8- 64	27	4	2
Bavuma, T.	313	7	44.71	2- 34	–	–	–
Beard, A.P.	1233	38	32.44	4- 23	–	–	–
Bedingham, D.G.	18	0					
Beer, W.A.T.	1480	40	37.00	6- 29	2	1	–
Behardien, F.	1199	32	37.46	3- 48	–	–	–
Behrendorff, J.P.	3002	126	23.82	9- 37	6	2	–
Bell-Drummond, D.J.	241	10	24.10	2- 6	–	–	–
Berg, G.K.	8575	273	31.41	6- 56	5	–	–
Bess, D.M.	3193	111	28.76	7-117	8	1	–
Bhabra, B.J.	149	1	149.00	1-101	–	–	–
Billings, S.W.	4	0					
Bird, J.M.	8546	348	24.55	7- 45	16	5	0+2
Blake, A.J.	138	3	46.00	2- 9	–	–	–
Blatherwick, J.M.	192	2	96.00	1- 82	–	–	–
Bohannon, J.J.	468	10	46.80	3- 46	–	–	–
Bopara, R.S.	9381	257	36.50	5- 49	3	–	–
Borthwick, S.G.	7940	206	38.54	6- 70	3	–	–
Bracewell, D.A.J.	10125	308	32.87	7- 35	9	–	–
Bracey, J.R.	35	0					
Brathwaite, K.C.	1330	26	51.15	6- 29	1	–	–
Bresnan, T.T.	17092	552	30.96	5- 28	9	–	–
Briggs, D.R.	9390	270	34.77	6- 45	8	–	–
Broad, S.C.J.	20891	759	27.52	8- 15	29	3	–
Brook, H.C.	132	1	132.00	1- 54	–	–	–
Brookes, E.A.	41	0					
Brookes, H.J.H.	1863	53	35.15	4- 54	–	–	–
Brooks, J.A.	12631	462	27.33	6- 65	20	–	4

	Runs	Wkts	Avge	Best	5wI	10wM	50wS
Brown, B.C.	109	1	109.00	1- 48	–	–	–
Brown, P.R.	266	7	38.00	2- 15	–	–	–
Browne, N.L.J.	175	0					
Buck, N.L.	8526	250	34.10	6- 34	8	–	–
Bull, K.A.	861	22	39.13	4- 62	–	–	–
Burgess, M.G.K.	14	0					
Burnham, J.T.A.	17	0					
Burns, J.A.	48	1	48.00	1- 0	–	–	–
Burns, R.J.	127	2	63.50	1- 18	–	–	–
Buttler, J.C.	11	0					
Byrom, E.J.	39	0					
Campbell, J.O.I.	261	1	261.00	1- 43	–	–	–
Cantrell, J.J.	177	2	88.50	1- 40	–	–	–
Cantwell, S.	185	2	92.50	1- 67	–	–	–
Carey, L.J.	2748	80	34.35	4- 54	–	–	–
Carlson, K.S.	293	6	48.83	5- 28	1	–	–
Carse, B.A.	1738	55	31.60	6- 26	3	–	–
Carter, M.	1726	39	44.25	7- 56	2	1	–
Chapman, L.J.	586	13	45.07	6- 78	1	–	–
Chappell, Z.J.	1369	38	36.02	6- 44	1	–	–
Charlesworth, B.G.	131	7	18.71	3- 25	–	–	–
Chopra, V.	128	0					
Christian, D.T.	5679	163	34.84	5- 24	3	–	–
Clark, G.	58	2	29.00	1- 10	–	–	–
Clark, J.	3364	99	33.97	5- 58	2	–	–
Clarke, J.M.	22	0					
Clarke, R.	15524	505	30.74	7- 55	7	–	–
Claughton, T.H.	27	1	27.00	1- 16	–	–	–
Claydon, M.E.	9595	299	32.09	6-104	9	–	2
Coad, B.O.	3043	145	20.98	6- 25	8	2	1
Cobb, J.J.	1607	18	89.27	2- 11	–	–	–
Cockbain, I.A.	44	1	44.00	1- 23	–	–	–
Coles, M.T.	10553	358	29.47	6- 51	12	2	2
Conners, S.	113	5	22.60	2- 13	–	–	–
Cook, A.N.	211	7	30.14	3- 13	–	–	–
Cook, S.J.	2143	87	24.63	7- 23	6	1	–
Cosgrove, M.J.	2393	52	46.01	3- 3	–	–	–
Coughlin, J.	251	7	35.85	2- 31	–	–	–
Coughlin, P.	2826	86	32.86	5- 49	2	1	–
Coulter-Nile, N.M.	3557	124	28.68	6- 84	2	–	–
Crane, M.S.	4144	82	50.53	5- 35	2	–	–
Crawley, Z.	33	0					
Critchley, M.J.J.	3221	65	49.55	6-106	1	1	–
Croft, S.J.	2974	72	41.30	6- 41	1	–	–
Cross-Zamirski, J.O.	171	3	57.00	2- 96	–	–	–
Cummins, M.L.	5672	218	26.01	7- 45	9	1	–
Cummins, P.J.	3734	163	22.90	6- 23	4	1	–
Curran, S.M.	4722	164	28.79	7- 58	7	1	–
Curran, T.K.	5613	195	28.78	7- 20	7	1	1
Dahl, A.E.C.	128	2	64.00	2- 41	–	–	–
Dal, A.K.	181	9	20.11	3- 11	–	–	–
Davey, J.H.	1978	81	24.41	5- 21	2	–	–
Davies, A.L.	6	0					
Davis, W.S.	2217	69	32.13	7-146	1	–	–
Dawson, L.A.	7181	203	35.37	7- 51	3	–	–
Dearden, H.E.	108	2	54.00	1- 0	–	–	–
de Lange, M.	9168	305	30.05	7- 23	11	2	–

	Runs	Wkts	Avge	Best	5wI	10wM	50wS
de Villiers, A.B.	138	2	69.00	2- 49	–	–	–
Delport, C.S.	723	14	51.64	2- 10	–	–	–
Denly, J.L.	2583	66	39.13	4- 36	–	–	–
Dent, C.D.J.	813	9	90.33	2- 21	–	–	–
Dernbach, J.W.	10139	311	32.60	6- 47	10	–	1
Dewes, A.H.J.	75	3	25.00	1- 1	–	–	–
Dexter, N.J.	5813	169	34.39	6- 63	6	–	–
Dickson, S.R.	53	2	26.50	1- 15	–	–	–
D'Oliveira, B.L.	2537	51	49.74	7- 92	2	–	–
Douthwaite, D.A.	902	21	42.95	4- 48	–	–	–
Drissell, G.S.	504	8	63.00	4- 83	–	–	–
du Plessis, F.	1477	41	36.02	4- 39	–	–	–
du Plooy, J.L.	1177	23	51.17	3- 76	–	–	–
Duckett, B.M.	65	1	65.00	1- 21	–	–	–
Dunn, M.P.	3853	112	34.40	5- 43	4	–	–
Eckersley, E.J.H.	67	2	33.50	2- 29	–	–	–
Edwards, F.H.	13751	455	30.22	7- 87	27	2	2
Elgar, D.	2736	55	49.74	4- 22	–	–	–
Emanuel, J.F.	89	2	44.50	2- 81	–	–	–
Eskinazi, S.S.	4	0					
Evans, B.N.	349	8	43.62	4- 53	–	–	–
Evans, H.A.	229	7	32.71	3- 49	–	–	–
Evans, L.J.	270	2	135.00	1- 29	–	–	–
Evans, S.T.	24	0					
Evison, J.D.M.	33	0					
Faheem Ashraf	3172	117	27.11	6- 65	5	–	–
Fakhar Zaman	97	0					
Fallows, J.B.	155	0					
Fanning, M.J.	128	3	42.66	3- 47	–	–	–
Faulkner, J.P.	4759	192	24.78	5- 5	5	–	–
Fell, T.C.	17	0					
Ferguson, C.J.	99	2	49.50	2- 32	–	–	–
Finch, A.J.	318	5	63.60	1- 0	–	–	–
Finch, A.W.	682	12	56.83	2- 23	–	–	–
Finch, H.Z.	118	2	59.00	1- 9	–	–	–
Finn, S.T.	15981	551	29.00	9- 37	14	1	2
Fisher, M.D.	1077	31	34.74	5- 54	1	–	–
Fletcher, L.J.	9654	343	28.14	5- 27	6	–	–
Foakes, B.T.	6	0					
Foster, F.J.H.	80	3	26.66	2- 36	–	–	–
Foster, M.T.	147	5	29.40	2- 38	–	–	–
Fuller, J.K.	4964	150	33.09	6- 24	5	1	–
Gabriel, S.T.	8575	289	29.67	8- 62	8	1	–
Garrett, G.A.	302	8	37.75	2- 53	–	–	–
Garton, G.H.S.	1049	28	37.46	3- 20	–	–	–
Gibbs, J.H.	116	2	58.00	2- 54	–	–	–
Gleadall, A.F.	119	1	119.00	1- 20	–	–	–
Gleeson, R.J.	3001	140	21.43	6- 43	10	1	–
Glover, B.D.	733	20	36.65	4- 83	–	–	–
Godleman, B.A.	35	0					
Graves, B.W.M.	338	4	84.50	2- 56	–	–	–
Gregory, L.	6782	264	25.68	6- 32	13	2	1
Griffiths, G.T.	1755	55	31.90	6- 49	1	1	–
Groenewald, T.D.	11785	401	29.38	6- 50	16	–	–
Gubbins, N.R.T.	52	0					
Guest, C.J.	388	8	48.50	3-100	–	–	–
Guptill, M.J.	670	11	60.90	3- 11	–	–	–

	Runs	Wkts	Avge	Best	5wI	10wM	50wS
Gurney, H.F.	9472	310	30.55	6- 25	8	–	–
Hain, S.R.	31	0					
Haines, T.J.	294	7	42.00	1- 9	–	–	–
Hales, A.D.	173	3	57.66	2- 63	–	–	–
Hameed, H.	21	0					
Hamidullah Qadri	826	23	35.91	5- 60	1	–	–
Hammond, M.A.H.	331	1	331.00	1- 96	–	–	–
Handscomb, P.S.P.	21	0					
Hankins, G.T.	13	0					
Hankins, H.J.	101	0					
Hannon-Dalby, O.J.	5555	168	33.06	5- 18	4	–	–
Harding, G.H.I.	321	6	53.50	4-111	–	–	–
Harmer, S.R.	16903	608	27.80	9- 95	34	6	3+1
Harris, J.A.R.	13910	485	28.68	9- 34	15	2	3
Harris, M.S.	17	0					
Harrison, C.G.	113	3	37.66	1- 30	–	–	–
Harte, G.J.	429	13	33.00	4- 15	–	–	–
Haynes, J.L.	193	4	48.25	3- 37	–	–	–
Hazlewood, J.R.	7854	313	25.09	6- 50	8	–	–
Head, T.M.	2599	41	63.39	3- 42	–	–	–
Heathfield, T.D.	348	5	69.60	2- 57	–	–	–
Helm, T.G.	2293	78	29.39	5- 36	3	–	–
Hemphrey, C.R.	574	8	71.75	2- 56	–	–	–
Henriques, M.C.	3472	112	31.00	5- 17	2	–	–
Henry, M.J.	6587	267	24.67	7- 42	14	3	1
Higgins, R.F.	2355	110	21.40	5- 21	4	–	1
Hildreth, J.C.	492	6	82.00	2- 39	–	–	–
Hill, L.J.	6	0					
Hogan, M.G.	14352	594	24.16	7- 92	23	2	3
Holden, M.D.E.	452	5	90.40	2- 59	–	–	–
Holder, J.O.	4500	176	25.56	6- 59	9	1	–
Holland, I.G.	1196	40	29.90	4- 16	–	–	–
Holland, J.M.	7316	229	31.94	7- 82	10	–	0+1
Holling, J.B.R.	192	4	48.00	3- 56	–	–	–
Hooper, E.O.	65	1	65.00	1- 65	–	–	–
Horton, P.J.	80	2	40.00	2- 6	–	–	–
Howell, B.A.C.	3222	96	33.56	5- 57	1	–	–
Hudson-Prentice, F.J.	516	20	25.80	3- 27	–	–	–
Hughes, A.L.	1735	35	49.57	4- 46	–	–	–
Hurt, L.J.	66	0					
Hutton, B.A.	5045	187	26.97	8- 57	9	2	–
Imad Wasim	4340	140	31.00	8- 81	3	1	–
Imran Tahir	20881	784	26.63	8- 42	53	11	2+2
Ingram, C.A.	2133	50	42.66	4- 16	–	–	–
Ironside, D.A.	40	2	20.00	2- 20	–	–	–
Jacks, W.G.	87	0					
James, L.W.	68	3	22.66	3- 54	–	–	–
Javid, A.	441	5	88.20	1- 1	–	–	–
Jennings, K.K.	960	29	33.10	3- 37	–	–	–
Jones, R.P.	38	1	38.00	1- 18	–	–	–
Jordan, C.J.	10730	335	32.02	7- 43	10	–	1
Kapil, A.	408	14	29.14	3- 17	–	–	–
Keeping, J.B.R.	23	1	23.00	1- 23	–	–	–
Keogh, R.I.	3759	88	42.71	9- 52	1	1	–
Khawaja, U.T.	103	1	103.00	1- 21	–	–	–
Kimber, L.P.J.	86	2	43.00	1- 34	–	–	–
Klaassen, F.J.	170	2	85.00	1- 44	–	–	–

	Runs	Wkts	Avge	Best	5wI	10wM	50wS
Klein, D.	6040	212	28.49	8- 72	10	1	–
Klinger, M.	3	0					
Kuhn, H.G.	12	0					
Labuschagne, M.	2215	52	42.59	3- 45	–	–	–
Lamb, D.J.	235	6	39.16	4- 70	–	–	–
Lamb, M.J.	254	6	42.33	1- 15	–	–	–
Lawlor, J.L.	279	7	39.85	3- 59	–	–	–
Lawrence, D.W.	372	9	41.33	2- 63	–	–	–
Leach, J.	8125	311	26.12	6- 73	13	1	3
Leach, M.J.	7186	287	25.03	8- 85	20	3	3
Leaning, J.A.	455	8	56.87	2- 20	–	–	–
Lees, A.Z.	77	2	38.50	2- 51	–	–	–
Lehmann, J.S.	169	4	42.25	2- 17	–	–	–
Lester, T.J.	1132	17	66.58	4- 41	–	–	–
Libby, J.D.	296	4	74.00	1- 13	–	–	–
Liddle, C.J.	2326	48	48.45	3- 42	–	–	–
Lilley, A.M.	1407	40	35.17	5- 23	2	–	–
Livingstone, L.S.	1212	34	35.64	6- 52	1	–	–
Lloyd, D.L.	2812	61	46.09	3- 36	–	–	–
Logan, J.E.G.	85	4	21.25	4- 22	–	–	–
Lynn, C.A.	64	0					
Lyon, N.M.	18300	530	34.52	8- 50	17	2	–
Lyth, A.	1624	34	47.76	2- 9	–	–	–
McBride, C.J.	15	1	15.00	1- 15	–	–	–
McBrine, A.R.	1019	26	39.19	4- 35	–	–	–
McCollum, J.A.	88	5	17.60	5- 32	1	–	–
McDermott, B.R.	52	0					
McKerr, C.	1054	38	27.73	5- 54	2	1	–
Madsen, W.L.	1708	33	51.75	3- 45	–	–	–
Maharaj, K.A.	12439	465	26.75	9-129	26	6	–
Mahmood, S.	1214	42	28.90	4- 48	–	–	–
Malan, D.J.	2431	59	41.20	5- 61	1	–	–
Markram, A.K.	245	3	81.66	1- 1	–	–	–
Marsh, M.R.	4778	156	30.62	6- 84	2	–	–
Marsh, S.E.	155	2	77.50	2- 20	–	–	–
Maxwell, G.J.	2947	74	39.82	5- 40	1	–	–
Meaker, S.C.	8701	279	31.18	8- 52	11	2	1
Melton, D.R.	149	2	74.50	1- 24	–	–	–
Meschede, C.A.J.	5310	142	37.39	5- 84	1	–	–
Mike, B.W.M.	1034	31	33.35	5- 37	1	–	–
Miles, C.N.	7347	272	27.01	6- 63	14	1	3
Mills, T.S.	2008	55	36.50	4- 25	–	–	–
Milne, A.F.	2872	88	32.63	5- 47	2	–	–
Milnes, M.E.	2113	72	29.34	5- 68	2	–	1
Milnes, T.P.	2036	47	43.31	7- 39	2	–	–
Mir Hamza	5815	306	19.00	7- 59	26	6	0+1
Mitchell, D.K.H.	1295	28	46.25	4- 49	–	–	–
Moen, A.J.	16	0					
Mohammad Abbas	8978	442	20.31	8- 46	34	10	1+2
Mohammad Amir	5850	260	22.50	7- 61	13	2	0+1
Mohammad Hafeez	6764	253	26.73	8- 57	7	2	–
Mohammad Nabi	2083	90	23.14	6- 33	3	–	–
Mohammed Rizvi	46	0					
Morgan, A.O.	1003	15	66.86	2- 37	–	–	–
Morgan, E.J.G.	94	2	47.00	2- 24	–	–	–
Morkel, M.	14388	567	25.37	6- 23	20	2	1
Morris, C.A.J.	5464	183	29.85	7- 45	5	–	2

	Runs	Wkts	Avge	Best	5wI	10wM	50wS
Morris, C.H.	4671	194	24.07	8- 44	4	1	–
Mujeeb Zadran	75	1	75.00	1- 75	–	–	–
Mulder, P.W.A.	1821	76	23.96	7- 25	1	–	–
Mullaney, S.J.	3901	109	35.78	5- 32	1	–	–
Murtagh, T.J.	20518	816	25.14	7- 82	35	4	8
Muzarabani, B.	561	24	23.37	5- 32	1	–	–
Narine, S.P.	1398	65	21.50	8- 17	8	3	–
Nash, C.D.	3271	78	41.93	4- 12	–	–	–
Neal, A.J.	199	4	49.75	3- 77	–	–	–
Neser, M.G.	3933	144	27.31	6- 57	2	–	–
Newton, R.I.	107	1	107.00	1- 82	–	–	–
Nijjar, A.S.S.	785	19	41.31	2- 28	–	–	–
Northeast, S.A.	147	1	147.00	1- 60	–	–	–
Norwell, L.C.	7050	262	26.90	8- 43	11	3	2
O'Brien, K.J.	1304	47	27.74	5- 39	1	–	–
Odedra, Y.J.	95	2	47.50	1- 41	–	–	–
Olivier, D.	10180	446	22.82	6- 37	24	4	0+3
Onions, G.	18583	723	25.70	9- 67	31	3	8
Organ, F.S.	125	8	15.62	5- 25	1	–	–
O'Riordan, M.K.	33	0					
Overton, C.	7358	286	25.72	6- 24	7	–	–
Overton, J.	5063	164	30.87	6- 95	3	–	–
Owen, X.G.	277	7	39.57	3- 55	–	–	–
Paine, T.D.	23	0					
Palladino, A.P.	13255	464	28.56	7- 53	17	1	3
Panayi, G.D.	141	4	35.25	3- 41	–	–	–
Parkinson, C.F.	2148	46	46.69	8-148	1	1	–
Parkinson, M.W.	1564	62	25.22	6- 23	3	1	–
Park-Johnson, J.C.H.	236	1	236.00	1- 69	–	–	–
Parnell, W.D.	6542	220	29.73	7- 51	7	1	–
Parry, S.D.	1926	58	33.20	5- 23	2	–	–
Patel, A.Y.	7115	225	31.62	6- 48	18	3	–
Patel, J.S.	29239	892	32.77	8- 36	38	7	7
Patel, R.S.	701	15	46.73	6- 5	1	–	–
Patel, S.R.	13262	344	38.55	7- 68	5	1	–
Patterson, S.A.	11454	409	28.00	6- 40	8	–	2
Patterson-White, L.A.	420	20	21.00	5- 73	1	–	–
Pattinson, J.L.	5815	266	21.86	6- 32	11	–	–
Payne, D.A.	8214	263	31.23	6- 26	3	–	–
Pearce, S.J.	164	1	164.00	1- 74	–	–	–
Pennington, D.Y.	1079	30	35.96	4- 53	–	–	–
Pereira, W.J.N.	278	5	55.60	3- 61	–	–	–
Pettman, T.H.S.	577	27	21.37	5- 19	2	–	–
Philander, V.D.	12242	569	21.51	7- 61	24	2	0+2
Pillans, M.W.	3710	131	28.32	6- 67	3	1	0+1
Plunkett, L.E.	14433	453	31.86	6- 33	11	1	3
Podmore, H.W.	3449	130	26.53	6- 36	3	–	1
Pollard, W.A.	436	14	31.14	5- 36	1	–	–
Porter, J.A.	8001	329	24.31	7- 41	12	2	5
Porterfield, W.T.S.	138	2	69.00	1- 70	–	–	–
Potts, M.J.	715	17	42.05	3- 48	–	–	–
Powe, T.B.	3	0					
Poysden, J.E.	1084	33	32.84	5- 29	2	–	–
Pretorius, D.	3669	152	24.13	6- 38	6	1	–
Pringle, R.D.	2401	63	38.11	7-107	2	1	–
Procter, L.A.	3819	106	36.02	7- 71	3	–	–
Pujara, C.A.	146	5	29.20	2- 4	–	–	–

	Runs	Wkts	Avge	Best	5wI	10wM	50wS
Punja, Y.	63	1	63.00	1- 19	–	–	–
Qais Ahmad	1367	67	20.40	7- 41	5	3	–
Qayyum, I.	524	12	43.66	3-158	–	–	–
Quinn, M.R.	3559	120	29.65	7- 76	1	1	–
Rahane, A.M.	75	0					
Raine, B.A.	6971	267	26.10	6- 27	8	–	3
Rampaul, R.	8160	274	29.78	7- 51	11	1	–
Rankin, W.B.	9316	352	26.46	6- 55	9	–	1
Rashid, A.U.	17949	512	35.05	7-107	20	1	2
Rashid Khan	783	44	17.79	8- 74	5	1	–
Rawlins, D.M.W.	557	11	50.63	3- 19	–	–	–
Rayner, O.P.	10411	313	33.26	8- 46	10	1	1
Reece, L.M.	2272	88	25.81	7- 20	4	–	1
Reingold, S.J.	256	3	85.33	2- 64	–	–	–
Renshaw, M.T.	174	2	87.00	1- 12	–	–	–
Rhodes, G.H.	631	6	105.16	2- 83	–	–	–
Rhodes, W.M.H.	1500	42	35.71	5- 17	1	–	–
Richardson, M.J.	13	0					
Riley, A.E.N.	4776	128	37.31	7-150	5	–	1
Rimmington, N.J.	4235	134	31.60	5- 27	3	–	–
Rippington, S.E.	603	13	46.38	3- 51	–	–	–
Robertson, W.J.R.	219	6	36.50	3- 32	–	–	–
Robinson, O.E.	5123	229	22.37	8- 34	13	4	2
Robson, A.J.	127	0					
Robson, S.D.	199	4	49.75	2- 4	–	–	–
Rogers, O.J.W.	13	1	13.00	1- 7	–	–	–
Roland-Jones, T.S.	10387	403	25.77	7- 52	19	4	2
Root, J.E.	2120	43	49.30	4- 5	–	–	–
Root, W.T.	176	8	22.00	3- 29	–	–	–
Rossington, A.M.	86	0					
Rossouw, R.R.	70	3	23.33	1- 1	–	–	–
Roy, J.J.	495	14	35.35	3- 9	–	–	–
Rushworth, C.	11276	494	22.82	9- 52	25	4	5
Russell, A.D.	1104	54	20.44	5- 36	3	–	–
Rutherford, H.D.	79	0					
Sakande, A.	1425	40	35.62	5- 43	1	–	–
Salisbury, M.E.T.	2804	90	31.15	6- 37	1	–	–
Salt, P.D.	32	1	32.00	1- 32	–	–	–
Salter, A.G.	4130	86	48.02	4- 80	–	–	–
Sanders, C.W.G.	374	5	74.80	2- 67	–	–	–
Sanderson, B.W.	4676	233	20.06	8- 73	12	2	3
Santner, M.J.	3037	70	43.38	3- 27	–	–	–
Sayers, C.J.	7001	276	25.36	7- 46	14	2	0+1
Scott, D.N.C.	8	0					
Scott, G.F.B.	267	5	53.40	2- 49	–	–	–
Seabrook, B.M.A.	78	0					
Searle, C.J.	302	6	50.33	2- 31	–	–	–
Selman, N.J.	36	1	36.00	1- 22	–	–	–
Shadab Khan	1452	57	25.47	6- 77	2	1	–
Shaheen Shah Afridi	697	30	23.23	8- 39	1	–	–
Shamsi, T.	7923	303	26.14	8- 85	19	5	0+2
Shaw, J.	3157	89	35.47	5- 79	2	–	–
Short, D.J.M.	630	18	35.00	3- 78	–	–	–
Sibley, D.P.	264	4	66.00	2-103	–	–	–
Siddle, P.M.	15937	585	27.24	8- 54	23	–	0+1
Sidebottom, R.N.	1366	51	26.78	6- 35	1	1	–
Sidwell, B.D.	84	1	84.00	1- 58	–	–	–

	Runs	Wkts	Avge	Best	5wI	10wM	50wS
Simpson, J.A.	23	0					
Singh, A.R.	411	8	51.37	3- 79	–	–	–
Sisodiya, P.	369	15	24.60	4- 79	–	–	–
Slater, B.T.	113	0					
Smit, D.	3501	106	33.02	7- 27	3	–	–
Smith, M.J.E.	54	1	54.00	1- 34	–	–	–
Smith, R.A.J.	2288	65	35.20	5- 87	1	–	–
Smith, S.P.D.	3562	67	53.16	7- 64	1	–	–
Smith, T.M.J.	3858	78	49.46	4- 35	–	–	–
Smith, W.R.	1629	32	50.90	3- 34	–	–	–
Snater, S.	324	12	27.00	5- 88	2	–	–
Sowter, N.A.	675	15	45.00	3- 42	–	–	–
Starc, M.A.	9524	358	26.60	8- 73	16	3	–
Steel, C.T.	630	20	31.50	2- 7	–	–	–
Steel, S.	16	0					
Stevens, D.I.	13020	517	25.18	8- 75	26	2	4
Stevenson, R.A.	357	4	89.25	1- 15	–	–	–
Stewart, G.	1108	39	28.41	6- 22	1	–	–
Stirling, P.R.	1118	27	41.40	2- 21	–	–	–
Stokes, B.A.	9081	304	29.87	7- 67	7	1	–
Stone, O.P.	3108	126	24.66	8- 80	6	1	–
Stoneman, M.D.	165	0					
Subramanyan, J.	249	4	62.25	2- 42	–	–	–
Suresh, K.	249	5	49.80	3-172	–	–	–
Swanson, B.	104	2	52.00	1- 26	–	–	–
Taylor, B.J.	544	13	41.84	4- 64	–	–	–
Taylor, J.E.	8401	326	25.76	8- 59	16	2	–
Taylor, J.M.R.	3341	75	44.54	4- 16	–	–	–
Taylor, J.P.A.	151	7	21.57	3- 26	–	–	–
Taylor, L.R.P.L.	378	6	63.00	2- 4	–	–	–
Taylor, M.D.	4734	142	33.33	5- 15	5	–	1
Taylor, T.A.I.	2837	90	31.52	6- 47	3	1	–
ten Doeschate, R.N.	7193	212	33.92	6- 20	7	–	–
Thomason, A.D.	358	4	89.50	2-107	–	–	–
Thompson, J.A.	105	5	21.00	2- 28	–	–	–
Thompson, S.R.	1155	38	30.39	3- 28	–	–	–
Thomson, A.T.	380	10	38.00	6-138	1	–	–
Thurston, C.O.	16	0					
Tillcock, A.D.	401	1	401.00	1- 53	–	–	–
Tongue, J.C.	2674	110	24.30	6- 97	5	–	–
Topley, R.J.W.	3482	133	26.18	6- 29	7	2	–
Trego, P.D.	14017	383	36.59	7- 84	5	1	1
Tremain, C.P.	5281	225	23.47	7- 82	8	1	0+1
Trescothick, M.E.	1551	36	43.08	4- 36	–	–	–
Trevaskis, L.	536	7	76.57	2- 96	–	–	–
Turner, A.J.	507	11	46.09	6-111	1	–	–
Turner, S.A.	50	0					
Tye, A.J.	991	27	36.70	3- 47	–	–	–
van Beek, L.V.	4213	130	32.40	6- 46	6	1	–
van Buuren, G.L.	2812	87	32.32	4- 12	–	–	–
van den Bergh, F.O.E.	896	19	47.15	4- 84	–	–	–
van der Gugten, T.	4104	153	26.82	7- 42	10	1	1
van der Merwe, R.E.	4519	133	33.97	4- 22	–	–	–
van Zyl, S.	2535	68	37.27	5- 32	1	–	–
Vasconcelos, R.S.	9	0					
Vijay, M.	619	11	56.27	3- 46	–	–	–
Vilas, D.J.	3	0					

	Runs	Wkts	Avge	Best	5wI	10wM	50wS
Viljoen, G.C.	11749	438	26.82	8- 90	25	5	0+1
Vince, J.M.	1031	22	46.86	5- 41	1	–	–
Virdi, G.S.	1986	69	28.78	8- 61	3	1	–
Vitali, J.C.	58	2	29.00	2- 50	–	–	–
Wade, M.S.	263	8	32.87	3- 13	–	–	–
Wagg, G.G.	15762	454	34.71	6- 29	12	1	2
Wainman, J.C.	112	3	37.33	3-112	–	–	–
Waite, M.J.	583	23	25.34	5- 16	1	–	–
Wakely, A.G.	426	6	71.00	2- 62	–	–	–
Waller, M.T.C.	493	10	49.30	3- 33	–	–	–
Walter, P.I.	540	13	41.53	3- 44	–	–	–
Warner, D.A.	455	6	75.83	2- 45	–	–	–
Warner, J.D.	141	4	35.25	3- 35	–	–	–
Watling, B.J.	8	0					
Watt, M.R.J.	322	8	40.25	3- 60	–	–	–
Weatherley, J.J.	228	4	57.00	1- 2	–	–	–
Weighell, W.J.	1472	52	28.30	7- 32	2	–	–
Wells, J.W.	203	1	203.00	1- 28	–	–	–
Wells, L.W.P.	3172	69	45.97	5- 63	1	–	–
Wessels, M.H.	130	3	43.33	1- 10	–	–	–
Westley, T.	2693	59	45.64	4- 55	–	–	–
Wheal, B.T.J.	2080	56	37.14	6- 51	1	–	–
Wheater, A.J.A.	86	1	86.00	1- 86	–	–	–
White, G.G.	2730	65	42.00	6- 44	1	–	–
Whiteley, R.A.	2064	40	51.60	2- 6	–	–	–
Wiese, D.	9606	343	28.00	6- 58	10	1	–
Willey, D.J.	5416	178	30.42	5- 29	5	1	–
Williamson, K.S.	3686	85	43.36	5- 75	1	–	–
Wilson, G.C.	89	0					
Woakes, C.R.	12564	490	25.64	9- 36	20	4	3
Wood, C.P.	3174	105	30.22	5- 39	3	–	–
Wood, L.	3208	96	33.41	5- 40	3	–	–
Wood, M.A.	4435	162	27.37	6- 46	9	–	–
Woodland, A.J.	102	0					
Worrall, D.J.	4741	172	27.56	7- 64	6	1	–
Wright, C.J.C.	15109	457	33.06	6- 22	13	–	2
Wright, L.J.	4862	120	40.51	5- 65	3	–	–
Zaib, S.A.	413	13	31.76	6-115	2	–	–
Zampa, A.	4804	102	47.09	6- 62	2	1	–

LIMITED-OVERS CAREER RECORDS

Compiled by Philip Bailey

The following career records, to the end of the 2019 season, include all players currently registered with first-class counties. These records are restricted to performances in limited-overs matches of 'List A' status as defined by the Association of Cricket Statisticians and Historians now incorporated by ICC into their Classification of Cricket. The following matches qualify for List A status and are included in the figures that follow: Limited-Overs Internationals; Other International matches (e.g. Commonwealth Games, 'A' team internationals); Premier domestic limited-overs tournaments in Test status countries; Official tourist matches against the main first-class teams.

The following matches do NOT qualify for inclusion: World Cup warm-up games; Tourist matches against first-class teams outside the major domestic competitions (e.g. Universities, Minor Counties etc.); Festival, pre-season friendly games and Twenty20 Cup matches.

	M	Runs	Avge	HS	100	50	Wkts	Avge	Best	Econ
Abbott, K.J.	104	485	15.64	56	–	1	141	29.06	4-21	5.22
Abbott, S.A.	57	568	17.21	50	–	1	92	24.40	5-43	5.39
Abell, T.B.	25	636	31.80	106	1	1	2	13.00	2-19	4.33
Ackermann, C.N.	83	2260	36.45	152*	2	15	42	39.59	4-48	4.83
Ali, M.M.	218	5061	28.43	158	11	20	159	43.84	4-33	5.38
Allen, F.A.	21	246	20.50	62*	–	2	10	56.30	2-18	5.32
Alsop, T.P.	48	1465	32.55	130*	4	6	–	–	–	33/5
Ambrose, T.R.	182	4145	32.38	135	3	25	–	–	–	172/34
Amla, H.M.	243	9972	45.12	159	30	52	0	–	–	10.50
Anderson, C.J.	85	1988	28.00	131*	1	11	69	24.75	5-26	5.88
Anderson, J.M.	261	378	9.00	28	–	–	358	28.57	5-23	4.82
Archer, J.C.	28	205	17.08	45	–	–	44	27.59	5-42	4.96
Ashwin, R.	167	1304	18.11	79	–	4	226	30.93	4-25	4.63
Babar Azam	135	6123	53.24	142*	20	33	12	46.25	2-20	5.26
Bailey, T.E.	15	81	16.20	33	–	–	20	33.00	3-31	5.83
Ball, J.T.	95	198	8.60	28	–	–	118	33.51	5-51	5.87
Ballance, G.S.	110	4360	49.54	156	8	26	–	–	–	–
Bancroft, C.T.	49	1601	42.13	176	3	9	–	–	–	44/1
Banks, L.	8	250	31.25	61	–	2	–	–	–	–
Banton, T.	18	524	30.82	112	2	3	–	–	–	14/1
Barber, T.E.	7	1	0.16	1	–	–	9	35.77	3-62	6.44
Barker, K.H.D.	62	560	20.00	56	–	1	69	32.79	4-33	5.79
Barnard, E.G.	44	554	29.15	61	–	3	53	35.22	3-26	5.87
Bartlett, G.A.	9	207	34.50	57*	–	1	–	–	–	–
Batty, G.J.	271	2374	15.21	83*	–	5	255	32.48	5-35	4.63
Beard, A.P.	2	24	24.00	22*	–	–	3	32.33	3-51	5.10
Bedingham, D.G.	19	492	30.75	104*	2	2	0	–	–	3.84
Beer, W.A.T.	60	444	15.85	75	–	1	54	41.59	3-27	5.18
Behardien, F.	214	5233	39.34	113*	5	32	35	50.68	3-16	5.59
Bell-Drummond, D.J.	89	3381	42.26	171*	6	22	5	24.20	2-22	4.68
Berg, G.K.	98	1416	23.60	75	–	7	86	35.34	5-26	5.42
Bess, D.M.	15	100	9.09	24*	–	–	11	56.00	3-35	5.70
Billings, S.W.	90	2694	40.81	175	6	18	–	–	–	82/8
Birkhead, B.D.	1						–	–	–	1/0
Blake, A.J.	106	2125	30.35	116	1	12	4	55.75	2-13	6.55
Blatherwick, J.M.	3	6	6.00	3*	–	–	1	72.00	1-55	9.00
Bohannon, J.J.	15	210	26.25	55*	–	1	1	208.00	1-33	8.32
Bopara, R.S.	323	9845	40.18	201*	15	60	248	29.02	5-63	5.33
Borthwick, S.G.	99	1350	22.13	87	–	7	69	40.18	5-38	6.05
Bracey, J.R.	9	487	60.87	113*	1	4	1	23.00	1-23	7.66
Bresnan, T.T.	279	3221	21.61	95*	–	10	315	34.26	5-48	5.24
Briggs, D.R.	107	402	12.56	37*	–	–	112	37.39	4-32	5.11

	M	Runs	Avge	HS	100	50	Wkts	Avge	Best	Econ
Broad, S.C.J.	151	620	11.92	45*	–	–	216	30.51	5-23	5.27
Brook, H.C.	15	343	31.18	103	1	1	0	–	–	6.33
Brookes, H.J.H.	12	13	4.33	12*	–	–	17	35.35	3-50	6.54
Brooks, J.A.	36	49	4.90	10	–	–	37	34.48	3-30	4.83
Brown, B.C.	74	1102	24.48	73*	–	8	–	–	–	67/12
Brown, P.R.	10	3	3.00	3	–	–	12	36.50	3-53	6.28
Browne, N.L.J.	21	557	30.94	99	–	3	–	–	–	–
Buck, N.L.	61	141	7.83	21	–	–	69	38.14	4-39	6.24
Bull, K.A.	2	–	–	–	–	–	1	48.00	1-40	5.53
Burgess, M.G.K.	18	352	22.00	58	–	2	–	–	–	–
Burnham, J.T.A.	13	139	23.16	45	–	–	–	–	–	–
Burns, R.J.	57	1722	35.14	95	–	12	–	–	–	–
Carey, L.J.	18	124	24.80	39	–	–	12	62.91	2-57	5.56
Carlson, K.S.	17	341	22.73	63	–	2	1	47.00	1-30	6.71
Carse, B.A.	7	2	2.00	2	–	–	10	22.30	3-52	5.46
Carter, M.	16	65	7.22	21*	–	–	23	27.17	4-40	5.34
Chappell, Z.J.	17	141	17.62	59*	–	1	17	45.00	3-45	6.27
Charlesworth, B.G.	1	14	14.00	14	–	–	–	–	–	–
Chopra, V.	114	4789	46.04	160	12	28	0	–	–	6.00
Christian, D.T.	119	2844	32.68	117	2	14	107	33.50	6-48	5.52
Clark, G.	32	665	21.45	114	1	2	3	6.00	3-18	4.50
Clark, J.	51	954	30.77	79*	–	5	34	45.17	4-34	6.34
Clarke, J.M.	62	1846	34.18	139	4	9	–	–	–	22/2
Clarke, R.	232	4087	25.22	98*	–	21	154	37.66	5-26	5.42
Claydon, M.E.	110	276	8.36	19	–	–	138	32.61	5-31	5.62
Coad, B.O.	17	15	15.00	9	–	–	20	37.40	4-63	5.87
Cobb, J.J.	99	3330	38.27	146*	7	21	35	48.91	3-34	5.84
Cockbain, I.A.	68.	1633	34.02	108*	2	10	–	–	–	–
Conners, S.	3	4	4.00	4	–	–	2	75.00	1-45	6.52
Cook, A.N.	168	6055	39.06	137	12	35	0	–	–	3.33
Cook, S.J.	12	9	4.50	6	–	–	11	41.54	3-37	4.71
Cooke, C.B.	88	2607	36.20	161	3	14	–	–	–	54/5
Cosgrove, M.J.	160	4821	32.14	121	4	39	18	63.38	2-21	6.41
Coughlin, P.	27	177	12.64	22	–	–	18	50.83	3-36	5.61
Coulter-Nile, N.M.	73	672	19.20	92	–	3	129	25.78	5-26	5.05
Cox, J.M.	1	21	21.00	21	–	–	–	–	–	1/0
Cox, O.B.	74	1371	27.97	122*	1	5	–	–	–	80/9
Crane, M.S.	39	112	28.00	28*	–	–	67	29.98	4-30	6.08
Crawley, Z.	23	743	35.38	120	1	4	0	–	–	8.50
Critchley, M.J.J.	43	685	27.40	64*	–	2	31	54.00	4-48	6.56
Croft, S.J.	157	4252	36.65	127	3	31	62	41.30	4-24	5.51
Cummins, M.L.	29	42	10.50	20	–	–	36	31.02	4-27	5.12
Curran, B.J.	3	102	34.00	69	–	1	–	–	–	–
Curran, S.M.	51	597	20.58	57	–	1	68	31.30	4-32	5.57
Curran, T.K.	75	614	19.80	47*	–	1	119	26.45	5-16	5.61
Dal, A.K.	5	72	36.00	52	–	1	–	–	–	–
Davey, J.H.	84	1184	23.21	91	–	5	103	26.63	6-28	5.37
Davies, A.L.	49	1380	32.09	147	1	7	–	–	–	48/11
Davies, S.M.	184	5645	33.50	127*	9	35	–	–	–	147/42
Davis, W.S.	4	17	17.00	15*	–	–	2	89.00	1-60	7.91
Dawson, L.A.	159	3499	33.00	113*	3	18	161	30.04	6-47	4.72
de Lange, M.	95	750	15.62	58*	–	2	169	25.28	5-49	5.47
Dearden, H.E.	10	341	34.10	91	–	3	–	–	–	–
Dell, J.J.	1	46	46.00	46	–	1	–	–	–	–
Delport, C.S.	107	2765	30.38	169*	3	15	38	42.00	4-42	6.09
Denly, J.L.	156	4749	35.97	150*	8	24	47	24.63	4-35	5.07
Dent, C.D.J.	70	1946	32.43	151*	3	6	12	34.33	4-43	5.64

	M	Runs	Avge	HS	100	50	Wkts	Avge	Best	Econ
Dernbach, J.W.	144	242	7.56	31	–	–	228	27.10	6-35	5.90
Dickson, S.R.	42	992	27.55	99	–	8	0	–	–	10.00
D'Oliveira, B.L.	66	1032	22.93	79	–	6	50	43.32	3-35	5.27
Donald, A.H.T.	30	424	16.30	57	–	2	–	–	–	–
Douthwaite, D.A.	4	99	49.50	52*	–	1	5	25.20	3-43	5.47
Drissell, G.S.	1	0	0.00	0	–	–	0	–	–	6.42
du Plooy, J.L.	45	1865	58.28	155	5	10	11	35.36	3-19	5.84
Duckett, B.M.	73	2341	38.37	220*	3	16	–	–	–	38/3
Dunn, M.P.	1	–	–	–	–	–	2	16.00	2-32	5.33
Eckersley, E.J.H.	44	1041	28.91	108	1	5	–	–	–	27/1
Edwards, F.H.	92	138	8.62	21*	–	–	120	30.04	6-22	5.23
Eskinazi, S.S.	17	496	35.42	107*	1	1	–	–	–	–
Evans, L.J.	63	1735	37.71	134*	3	5	1	82.00	1-29	9.11
Evans, S.T.	1	20	20.00	20	–	–	–	–	–	–
Faheem Ashraf	65	683	16.26	71	–	2	87	27.43	5-22	5.16
Faulkner, J.P.	121	1936	30.25	116	1	10	168	30.37	4-20	5.35
Fell, T.C.	45	1369	35.10	116*	1	11	–	–	–	–
Finch, H.Z.	35	1125	37.50	108	1	8	0	–	–	9.00
Finn, S.T.	143	411	12.08	42*	–	–	199	29.27	5-33	5.14
Fisher, M.D.	34	228	28.50	36*	–	–	32	42.68	3-32	5.92
Fletcher, L.J.	75	495	20.62	53*	–	1	81	36.24	5-56	5.66
Foakes, B.T.	73	1941	37.32	92	–	18	–	–	–	86/11
Fraine, W.A.R.	4	27	13.50	13	–	–	–	–	–	–
Fuller, J.K.	62	759	23.00	55*	–	1	75	32.29	6-35	5.93
Garton, G.H.S.	24	103	11.44	38	–	–	29	34.24	4-43	6.32
Gleeson, R.J.	21	53	6.62	13	–	–	28	29.14	5-47	5.82
Glover, B.D.	6	55	18.33	27	–	–	4	49.50	2-60	5.03
Godleman, B.A.	69	2559	43.37	137	6	12	–	–	–	–
Green, C.J.	8	78	26.00	24	–	–	8	28.75	5-53	4.91
Gregory, L.	76	1206	23.64	105*	1	7	106	27.79	4-23	5.98
Griffiths, G.T.	22	29	14.50	15*	–	–	29	33.72	4-30	6.01
Groenewald, T.D.	109	793	19.82	57	–	2	123	32.93	4-22	5.62
Gubbins, N.R.T.	56	2067	39.00	141	5	12	–	–	–	–
Guest, B.D.	2	41	20.50	36	–	–	–	–	–	0/1
Gurney, H.F.	93	61	5.54	13*	–	–	114	33.94	5-24	5.90
Hain, S.R.	58	2810	59.78	161*	10	15	–	–	–	–
Hales, A.D.	175	6260	38.40	187*	17	32	0	–	–	15.00
Hameed, H.	19	556	34.75	88	–	4	–	–	–	–
Hamidullah Qadri	3	4	4.00	4	–	–	1	61.00	1-31	6.00
Hammond, M.A.H.	8	185	30.83	95	–	1	5	19.40	2-18	5.10
Handscomb, P.S.P.	101	2949	37.32	140	3	18	–	–	–	91/5
Hankins, G.T.	15	535	38.21	92	–	5	–	–	–	–
Hannon-Dalby, O.J.	42	88	14.66	21*	–	–	63	32.41	5-27	6.36
Harmer, S.R.	83	1002	20.44	44*	–	–	78	42.29	4-42	5.13
Harris, J.A.R.	64	417	14.37	117	1	–	88	30.10	4-38	5.82
Harte, G.J.	9	205	41.00	51*	–	1	4	43.00	2-35	5.73
Haynes, J.A.	1	33	33.00	33	–	–	–	–	–	–
Head, T.M.	91	3118	37.11	202	7	16	20	59.75	2- 9	5.94
Helm, T.G.	40	206	12.87	30	–	–	56	31.10	5-33	5.75
Hemphrey, C.R.	21	422	22.21	87	–	2	2	75.50	1-18	5.80
Henriques, M.C.	98	2474	33.43	164*	3	9	77	37.64	4-17	5.15
Henry, M.J.	116	562	12.48	48*	–	1	187	27.38	6-45	5.33
Higgins, R.F.	33	680	28.33	81*	–	3	24	35.20	4-50	5.54
Hildreth, J.C.	212	5781	35.46	159	7	27	6	30.83	2-26	7.40
Hill, L.J.	41	846	24.17	118	1	3	–	–	–	24/2
Hogan, M.G.	69	171	17.10	27	–	–	102	29.57	5-44	5.09
Holden, M.D.E.	11	412	45.77	166	1	2	1	93.00	1-29	4.65

264

	M	Runs	Avge	HS	100	50	Wkts	Avge	Best	Econ
Holland, I.G.	7	38	12.66	11*	–	–	7	47.42	2-38	6.82
Horton, P.J.	121	2953	29.82	111*	3	14	1	8.00	1- 7	3.69
Hose, A.J.	29	761	33.08	101*	1	4	–	–	–	–
Hosein, H.R.	13	139	23.16	41*	–	–	–	–	–	8/3
Howell, B.A.C.	86	2050	35.34	122	1	13	76	34.73	3-37	5.20
Hudson-Prentice, F.J.	3	67	33.50	48	–	–	0	–	–	8.00
Hughes, A.L.	65	852	23.66	96*	–	3	43	44.13	4-44	5.61
Hurt, L.J.	5	34	34.00	15*	–	–	7	27.57	2-24	5.84
Hutton, B.A.	15	173	28.83	34*	–	–	16	48.50	3-72	6.39
Ingram, C.A.	186	7584	47.40	142	18	48	40	33.62	4-39	5.44
Jacks, W.G.	22	506	24.09	121	1	2	11	38.45	2-32	5.26
James, L.W.	1	0	0.00	0	–	–	–	–	–	–
Jennings, K.K.	68	2271	41.29	139	4	17	11	55.81	2-19	6.20
Jones, M.A.	5	194	38.80	87	–	2	–	–	–	–
Jones, R.P.	13	205	25.62	65	–	1	2	61.00	1- 3	6.00
Jordan, C.J.	81	633	15.43	55	–	1	119	29.77	5-28	5.72
Keogh, R.I.	46	1272	32.61	134	2	11	8	115.62	2-26	5.53
Klaassen, F.J.	18	59	11.80	13	–	–	28	25.17	3-30	4.83
Klein, D.	33	206	13.73	46	–	–	49	27.91	5-35	5.20
Kohler-Cadmore, T.	56	1808	34.11	164	3	10	–	–	–	–
Kuhn, H.G.	174	4859	34.46	141*	13	22	–	–	–	179/22
Labuschagne, M.	27	809	32.36	91	–	9	7	51.71	3-46	5.93
Lace, T.C.	9	115	16.42	48	–	–	2	10.00	2-20	10.00
Lamb, D.J.	2	5	–	4*	–	–	4	27.00	2-51	5.40
Lamb, M.J.	3	61	20.33	47	–	–	0	–	–	9.00
Lamichhane, S.	30	79	7.18	15	–	–	62	17.35	5-20	4.02
Lawrence, D.W.	28	670	26.80	115	1	4	11	54.27	3-35	6.25
Leach, J.	38	539	26.95	63	–	1	43	39.97	4-30	6.04
Leach, M.J.	16	22	7.33	18	–	–	21	30.52	3- 7	4.66
Leaning, J.A.	50	1061	29.47	131*	2	5	9	31.77	5-22	5.66
Lees, A.Z.	54	1533	34.84	115	2	12	–	–	–	–
Levi, R.E.	140	4614	36.61	166	8	29	–	–	–	–
Libby, J.D.	7	117	23.40	66	–	1	–	–	–	–
Lilley, A.M.	18	92	10.22	25	–	–	15	34.40	4-30	5.73
Livingstone, L.S.	55	1552	36.09	129	1	10	23	49.30	3-51	5.21
Lloyd, D.L.	46	942	24.78	92	–	5	17	43.58	5-53	5.96
Loten, T.W.	1	–	–	–	–	–	–	–	–	–
Lynn, C.A.	50	1597	36.29	135	2	12	1	45.00	1- 3	3.91
Lyon, N.M.	71	213	14.20	37*	–	–	83	37.72	4-10	4.86
Lyth, A.	122	3765	35.18	144	5	18	6	62.16	2-27	6.21
McDermott, B.R.	14	652	50.15	117	2	3	–	–	–	–
McKerr, C.	6	56	14.00	26*	–	–	8	41.75	3-56	6.44
McManus, L.D.	32	430	21.50	47	–	–	–	–	–	24/8
Madsen, W.L.	105	3323	41.53	138	6	19	16	35.81	3-27	5.14
Maharaj, K.A.	92	593	14.82	43*	–	–	114	30.71	5-34	4.87
Mahmood, S.	27	117	19.50	45	–	–	50	25.32	6-37	5.83
Malan, D.J.	149	5135	41.41	185*	10	25	40	32.75	4-25	5.83
Marsh, M.R.	106	3001	38.97	124	3	21	89	30.03	5-33	5.40
Maxwell, G.J.	177	4665	33.08	146	4	28	91	43.84	4-46	5.44
Meaker, S.C.	73	198	9.90	50	–	1	80	35.52	4-37	6.17
Meschede, C.A.J.	55	472	13.88	45	–	–	52	35.61	4- 5	5.56
Mike, B.W.M.	4	80	20.00	41	–	–	1	145.00	1-47	9.66
Miles, C.N.	37	115	9.58	31	–	–	44	37.09	4-29	6.30
Mills, T.S.	23	7	1.75	3*	–	–	22	35.77	3-23	5.97
Milnes, M.E.	8	77	15.40	26	–	–	16	30.87	5-79	6.87
Milton, A.G.	1	0	0.00	0	–	–	–	–	–	0/0
Mitchell, D.K.H.	135	3466	33.65	107	4	22	81	36.11	4-19	5.51

	M	Runs	Avge	HS	100	50	Wkts	Avge	Best	Econ
Mohammad Abbas	52	136	8.00	15*	–	–	67	30.19	4-31	4.81
Mohammad Nabi	156	3703	28.92	146	3	17	176	30.38	5-12	4.25
Moores, T.J.	21	566	35.37	76	–	5	–	–	–	18/5
Morgan, A.O.	3	32	16.00	29	–	–	2	40.50	2-49	5.78
Morgan, E.J.G.	363	11206	38.90	161	21	66	0	–	–	7.00
Morkel, M.	156	378	9.45	35	–	–	239	25.71	5-21	4.92
Morris, C.A.J.	34	58	9.66	16*	–	–	40	34.47	4-33	5.89
Mujeeb Zadran	44	73	7.30	15	–	–	66	23.13	5-50	3.88
Mullaney, S.J.	123	2611	35.28	124	2	19	100	34.58	4-29	5.21
Munsey, H.G.	36	756	27.00	96	–	3	–	–	–	–
Murtagh, T.J.	211	820	10.00	35*	–	–	275	29.57	5-21	4.99
Muzarabani, B.	24	39	3.90	18	–	–	25	38.28	4-47	5.41
Narine, S.P.	96	606	11.88	51	–	1	160	20.33	6- 9	3.72
Nash, C.D.	129	3548	30.85	124*	2	24	45	32.82	4-40	5.52
Neser, M.G.	48	567	23.62	122	1	1	52	37.94	4-41	5.39
Newton, R.I.	45	1148	29.43	107	1	6	–	–	–	–
Nijjar, A.S.S.	3	21	21.00	21	–	–	1	107.00	1-39	5.09
Northeast, S.A.	106	2986	33.93	132	4	17	–	–	–	–
Norwell, L.C.	17	47	5.87	16	–	–	23	31.13	6-52	5.50
Olivier, D.	49	201	13.40	25*	–	–	63	28.20	4-34	5.29
Onions, G.	99	185	8.04	30*	–	–	113	32.37	4-45	5.20
Organ, F.S.	4	0	0.00	0	–	–	2	16.50	1- 6	3.14
Overton, C.	69	756	22.23	66*	–	2	90	31.33	5-18	5.32
Overton, J.	42	399	17.34	40*	–	–	57	30.54	4-42	6.28
Palladino, A.P.	57	268	10.72	31	–	–	54	37.70	5-49	5.33
Parkinson, C.F.	13	222	27.75	52*	–	1	4	147.25	1-34	6.40
Parkinson, M.W.	25	43	14.33	15*	–	–	42	26.54	5-51	5.13
Parnell, W.D.	165	2088	25.15	129	2	6	233	28.96	6-51	5.45
Parry, S.D.	96	342	12.21	31	–	–	116	30.04	5-17	5.02
Patel, J.S.	226	801	9.88	50	–	1	283	30.09	5-43	4.67
Patel, R.K.	3	65	21.66	35	–	–	–	–	–	–
Patel, R.S.	3	57	28.50	41*	–	–	2	41.00	2-65	6.83
Patel, S.R.	245	6270	35.22	136*	8	33	225	33.29	6-13	5.40
Patterson, S.A.	96	249	13.10	25*	–	–	122	28.88	6-32	5.13
Payne, D.A.	66	171	17.10	36*	–	–	110	24.96	7-29	5.74
Pennington, D.Y.	3	7	7.00	4*	–	–	8	22.25	5-67	6.84
Philander, V.D.	129	1418	23.63	79*	–	5	129	32.61	4-12	4.65
Pillans, M.W.	19	133	16.62	31	–	–	32	21.50	5-29	5.62
Plunkett, L.E.	214	1675	20.42	72	–	3	282	30.29	5-52	5.54
Podmore, H.W.	18	111	18.50	40	–	–	18	50.55	4-57	6.30
Pollard, K.A.	138	3134	26.55	119	3	15	85	28.78	4-32	5.52
Pollock, E.J.	17	362	24.13	57	–	2	–	–	–	–
Pooran, N.	31	931	38.79	118	1	5	–	–	–	–
Pope, O.J.D.	28	751	37.55	93*	–	5	–	–	–	–
Porter, J.A.	31	35	8.75	7*	–	–	33	36.15	4-29	5.19
Potts, M.J.	9	53	17.66	30	–	–	13	24.53	4-62	5.90
Poynter, S.W.	47	581	18.74	109	1	–	–	–	–	42/3
Poysden, J.E.	32	35	3.50	10*	–	–	30	41.60	3-33	5.84
Price, T.J.	1	0	0.00	0	–	–	0	–	–	8.66
Procter, L.A.	45	710	30.86	97	–	5	23	45.30	3-29	5.73
Pujara, C.A.	103	4445	54.20	158*	11	29	0	–	–	8.00
Qais Ahmad	10	107	26.75	66	–	1	13	35.46	3-53	5.17
Qayyum, I.	28	99	8.25	26*	–	–	29	40.17	4-33	5.17
Quinn, M.R.	34	128	16.00	36	–	–	46	36.56	4-71	5.88
Raine, B.A.	26	392	21.77	83	–	1	27	43.00	3-31	5.68
Rampaul, R.	189	637	11.37	86*	–	1	285	24.68	5-48	4.89
Rashid, A.U.	216	1705	19.15	71	–	2	288	31.19	5-27	5.44

	M	Runs	Avge	HS	100	50	Wkts	Avge	Best	Econ
Rashid Khan	70	924	20.53	60*	–	4	135	17.93	7-18	4.16
Rawlins, D.M.W.	6	133	22.16	53	–	1	1	161.00	1-33	5.96
Reece, L.M.	40	908	29.29	128	1	5	19	50.73	4-35	6.16
Rhodes, G.H.	10	228	38.00	106	1	1	5	50.40	2-34	6.30
Rhodes, W.M.H.	31	542	21.68	69	–	2	13	47.07	2-22	5.83
Rimmington, N.J.	56	534	17.80	55	–	1	74	31.58	4-34	4.72
Robinson, O.E.	14	122	17.42	30	–	–	14	40.57	3-31	5.91
Robinson, O.G.	8	132	26.40	49	–	–	–	–		4/0
Robson, S.D.	20	603	33.50	106	1	3	1	43.00	1-27	7.16
Roderick, G.H.	51	1184	33.82	104	2	8	–	–		50/4
Roland-Jones, T.S.	79	684	21.37	65	–	1	126	25.24	4-10	5.19
Root, J.E.	181	7069	48.75	133*	17	41	35	52.60	3-52	5.58
Root, W.T.	24	773	48.31	113*	2	3	6	51.66	2-36	6.36
Rossington, A.M.	49	1381	37.32	97	–	11	–	–		34/5
Rossouw, R.R.	152	5646	40.04	156	12	34	1	44.00	1-17	5.86
Rouse, A.P.	40	682	27.28	75*	–	3	–	–		36/3
Roy, J.J.	179	6362	39.03	180	16	33	0	–		12.00
Rushworth, C.	72	188	12.53	38*	–	–	111	24.90	5-31	5.28
Russell, A.D.	93	1953	32.55	132*	2	8	131	26.09	6-28	5.42
Rutherford, H.D.	86	2927	36.13	154	10	9	1	33.00	1- 4	4.71
Salisbury, M.E.T.	13	8	8.00	5*	–	–	14	35.14	4-55	5.78
Salt, P.D.	16	494	32.93	137*	1	2	–	–		–
Salter, A.G.	36	371	20.61	51	–	1	17	67.94	2-41	5.38
Sanderson, B.W.	33	99	11.00	31	–	–	37	35.29	3-36	5.94
Santner, M.J.	93	1525	28.24	86	–	6	99	33.47	5-50	4.72
Scott, G.F.B.	11	194	27.71	63	–	1	1	239.00	1-65	6.63
Selman, N.J.	9	242	26.88	92	–	1	–	–		–
Shadab Khan	53	525	26.25	56	–	4	73	29.52	4-28	5.14
Shaheen Shah Afridi	24	45	15.00	19*	–	–	45	24.62	6-35	5.59
Shaw, J.	1	–	–	–	–	–	0	–		7.42
Short, D.J.M.	30	922	40.08	257	2	3	17	44.29	3-53	5.89
Sibley, D.P.	22	416	23.11	115	1	–	1	62.00	1-20	6.88
Siddle, P.M.	61	248	11.80	62	–	1	71	33.87	4-27	4.71
Simpson, J.A.	93	1587	26.01	82*	–	8	–	–		81/19
Slater, B.T.	36	1611	55.55	148*	5	9	–	–		–
Smith, J.L.	5	110	22.00	40	–	–	–	–		–
Smith, R.A.J.	18	71	8.87	14	–	–	18	32.83	4- 7	6.19
Smith, S.P.D.	164	5607	44.85	164	10	36	47	38.63	3-16	5.41
Smith, T.M.J.	83	513	22.30	65	–	1	68	40.67	4-26	5.40
Snater, S.	16	68	8.50	23*	–	–	14	40.07	5-60	5.36
Sole, T.B.	15	130	13.00	54	–	1	14	41.35	4-15	4.90
Sowter, N.A.	19	134	14.88	31	–	–	36	25.77	6-62	5.52
Starc, M.A.	113	499	14.25	52*	–	1	243	19.83	6-25	4.95
Steel, C.T.	11	181	20.11	77	–	1	0	–		9.40
Steel, S.	8	227	32.42	68	–	2	1	53.00	1-38	5.88
Stevens, D.I.	314	7612	29.50	147	7	46	160	31.97	6-25	4.80
Stevenson, R.A.	3	0	0.00	0	–	–	2	71.00	1-28	7.10
Stewart, G.	5	69	23.00	44	–	–	8	19.00	3-17	3.76
Stirling, P.R.	199	6745	36.45	177	16	32	70	40.60	6-55	4.99
Stone, O.P.	30	122	24.40	24*	–	–	24	42.62	4-71	5.45
Stoneman, M.D.	82	2763	37.84	144*	6	17	1	8.00	1- 8	12.00
Swindells, H.J.	4	43	21.50	28	–	–	–	–		–
Tattersall, J.A.	15	375	41.66	89	–	4	–	–		16/3
Taylor, B.J.	18	355	35.50	69	–	3	15	44.06	4-26	4.65
Taylor, J.E.	135	518	10.15	43*	–	–	203	26.66	5-40	5.05
Taylor, J.M.R.	51	1100	33.33	75	–	9	29	35.41	4-38	5.20
Taylor, J.P.A.	1	6	–	6*	–	–	2	33.00	2-66	9.42

	M	Runs	Avge	HS	100	50	Wkts	Avge	Best	Econ
Taylor, M.D.	28	41	13.66	16	–	–	20	58.70	3-39	5.63
Taylor, T.A.I.	12	242	48.40	98*	–	2	13	46.30	3-48	6.00
ten Doeschate, R.N.	225	6053	45.17	180	11	31	174	30.21	5-50	5.76
Thomason, A.D.	17	176	25.14	28	–	–	14	32.85	4-45	7.11
Thompson, J.A.	1	–	–	–	–	–	0	–	–	8.60
Thomson, A.T.	9	258	43.00	68*	–	2	13	29.15	3-27	5.05
Thurston, C.O.	4	128	32.00	53	–	1	–	–	–	–
Tongue, J.C.	13	76	19.00	34	–	–	14	42.85	2-35	6.80
Topley, R.J.W.	55	54	9.00	19	–	–	93	25.44	4-16	5.54
Trego, P.D.	198	4962	32.86	147	10	26	171	32.56	5-40	5.56
Trevaskis, L.	8	16	5.33	16	–	–	7	26.71	2-37	4.45
Turner, A.J.	33	867	36.12	84*	–	5	6	57.16	2-26	5.81
van Buuren, G.L.	70	1454	29.08	119*	1	7	52	33.75	5-35	4.76
van der Gugten, T.	58	350	16.66	36	–	–	68	35.01	5-24	5.56
van der Merwe, R.E.	186	2854	26.42	165*	1	11	249	26.63	5-26	4.88
van Zyl, S.	120	3400	34.69	114*	5	18	20	46.35	4-24	5.26
Vasconcelos, R.S.	26	713	29.70	112	1	4	–	–	–	19/2
Vilas, D.J.	172	4888	37.03	166	9	24	–	–	–	172/29
Vince, J.M.	136	4848	40.40	190	9	23	2	62.00	1-18	5.63
Wade, M.S.	173	4536	33.10	155	9	19	–	–	–	191/20
Wagg, G.G.	140	2060	20.39	68	–	5	156	34.47	4-35	5.92
Waite, M.J.	13	278	34.75	71	–	1	16	32.62	4-65	6.44
Wakely, A.G.	90	2532	32.88	109*	2	18	5	26.20	2-14	5.77
Walker, R.I.	1	7	–	7*	–	–	0	–	–	5.25
Waller, M.T.C.	58	109	15.57	25*	–	–	45	37.68	3-37	5.65
Walter, P.I.	10	96	19.20	25	–	–	13	28.84	4-37	6.85
Warner, D.A.	161	6741	44.34	197	22	25	4	39.50	1-11	6.58
Warner, J.D.	1	–	–	–	–	–	0	–	–	6.40
Watling, B.J.	122	3858	37.82	145*	8	25	–	–	–	96/3
Weatherley, J.J.	20	509	31.81	105*	1	3	8	27.62	4-25	4.05
Weighell, W.J.	12	49	9.80	23	–	–	22	28.72	5-57	6.19
Wells, J.W.	32	734	31.91	121*	2	2	1	36.00	1- 6	5.14
Wells, L.W.P.	26	232	11.60	62	–	1	10	38.40	3-19	5.27
Wessels, M.H.	179	4764	30.93	146	5	26	1	48.00	1- 0	5.87
Westley, T.	88	2853	36.57	134	5	22	21	41.00	4-60	4.98
Wheal, B.T.J.	28	63	7.00	18*	–	–	44	26.22	4-38	5.24
Wheater, A.J.A.	80	1713	28.55	135	2	9	–	–	–	41/12
White, G.G.	85	543	15.08	41*	–	–	92	29.44	6-37	5.05
White, R.G.	9	99	19.80	21*	–	–	–	–	–	15/2
Whiteley, R.A.	80	1609	27.27	131	1	9	14	40.21	4-58	6.66
Wiese, D.	148	3580	36.53	171	2	21	133	37.12	5-25	5.37
Willey, D.J.	129	1761	24.45	167	3	6	140	32.36	5-62	5.70
Williamson, K.S.	210	8253	46.62	148	17	51	67	35.56	5-51	5.18
Willows, G.P.	1	10	10.00	10	–	–	–	–	–	–
Woakes, C.R.	181	1927	22.67	95*	–	5	220	33.19	6-45	5.54
Wood, C.P.	79	400	12.90	41	–	–	106	27.96	5-22	5.38
Wood, L.	4	73	73.00	52	–	1	5	25.00	2-36	5.95
Wood, M.A.	85	118	6.55	24	–	–	107	32.94	4-33	5.33
Wood, T.A.	2	44	44.00	44	–	–	–	–	–	–
Wright, C.J.C.	103	263	11.43	42	–	–	102	36.92	4-20	5.61
Wright, L.J.	211	5126	33.07	166	11	19	111	38.11	4-12	5.34
Yates, R.M.	1	66	66.00	66	–	1	–	–	–	–
Zaib, S.A.	10	73	10.42	17	–	–	3	67.33	2-22	6.96
Zampa, A.	82	563	15.63	66	–	3	118	33.64	4-18	5.44

FIRST-CLASS CRICKET RECORDS

To the end of the 2019 season

TEAM RECORDS
HIGHEST INNINGS TOTALS

1107	Victoria v New South Wales	Melbourne	1926-27
1059	Victoria v Tasmania	Melbourne	1922-23
952-6d	Sri Lanka v India	Colombo	1997-98
951-7d	Sind v Baluchistan	Karachi	1973-74
944-6d	Hyderabad v Andhra	Secunderabad	1993-94
918	New South Wales v South Australia	Sydney	1900-01
912-8d	Holkar v Mysore	Indore	1945-46
910-6d	Railways v Dera Ismail Khan	Lahore	1964-65
903-7d	England v Australia	The Oval	1938
900-6d	Queensland v Victoria	Brisbane	2005-06
887	Yorkshire v Warwickshire	Birmingham	1896
863	Lancashire v Surrey	The Oval	1990
860-6d	Tamil Nadu v Goa	Panjim	1988-89
850-7d	Somerset v Middlesex	Taunton	2007

Excluding penalty runs in India, there have been 36 innings totals of 800 runs or more in first-class cricket. Tamil Nadu's total of 860-6d was boosted to 912 by 52 penalty runs.

HIGHEST SECOND INNINGS TOTAL

770	New South Wales v South Australia	Adelaide	1920-21

HIGHEST FOURTH INNINGS TOTAL

654-5	England (set 696 to win) v South Africa	Durban	1938-39

HIGHEST MATCH AGGREGATE

2376-37	Maharashtra v Bombay	Poona	1948-49

RECORD MARGIN OF VICTORY

Innings and 851 runs: Railways v Dera Ismail Khan	Lahore	1964-65

MOST RUNS IN A DAY

721	Australians v Essex	Southend	1948

MOST HUNDREDS IN AN INNINGS

6	Holkar v Mysore	Indore	1945-46

LOWEST INNINGS TOTALS

12	†Oxford University v MCC and Ground	Oxford	1877
12	Northamptonshire v Gloucestershire	Gloucester	1907
13	Auckland v Canterbury	Auckland	1877-78
13	Nottinghamshire v Yorkshire	Nottingham	1901
14	Surrey v Essex	Chelmsford	1983
15	MCC v Surrey	Lord's	1839
15	†Victoria v MCC	Melbourne	1903-04
15	†Northamptonshire v Yorkshire	Northampton	1908
15	Hampshire v Warwickshire	Birmingham	1922

† Batted one man short

There have been 28 instances of a team being dismissed for under 20.

LOWEST MATCH AGGREGATE BY ONE TEAM

34 (16 and 18)	Border v Natal	East London	1959-60

LOWEST COMPLETED MATCH AGGREGATE BY BOTH TEAMS

105	MCC v Australians	Lord's	1878

FEWEST RUNS IN AN UNINTERRUPTED DAY'S PLAY

95	Australia (80) v Pakistan (15-2)	Karachi	1956-57

TIED MATCHES

Before 1949 a match was considered to be tied if the scores were level after the fourth innings, even if the side batting last had wickets in hand when play ended. Law 22 was amended in 1948 and since then a match has been tied only when the scores are level after the fourth innings has been completed. There have been 61 tied first-class matches, five of which would not have qualified under the current law. The most recent is:

Lancashire (99 & 170) v Somerset (192 & 77)   Taunton   2018

BATTING RECORDS
35,000 RUNS IN A CAREER

	Career	I	NO	HS	Runs	Avge	100
J.B.Hobbs	1905-34	1315	106	316*	61237	50.65	197
F.E.Woolley	1906-38	1532	85	305*	58969	40.75	145
E.H.Hendren	1907-38	1300	166	301*	57611	50.80	170
C.P.Mead	1905-36	1340	185	280*	55061	47.67	153
W.G.Grace	1865-1908	1493	105	344	54896	39.55	126
W.R.Hammond	1920-51	1005	104	336*	50551	56.10	167
H.Sutcliffe	1919-45	1088	123	313	50138	51.95	149
G.Boycott	1962-86	1014	162	261*	48426	56.83	151
T.W.Graveney	1948-71/72	1223	159	258	47793	44.91	122
G.A.Gooch	1973-2000	990	75	333	44846	49.01	128
T.W.Hayward	1893-1914	1138	96	315*	43551	41.79	104
D.L.Amiss	1960-87	1139	126	262*	43423	42.86	102
M.C.Cowdrey	1950-76	1130	134	307	42719	42.89	107
A.Sandham	1911-37/38	1000	79	325	41284	44.82	107
G.A.Hick	1983/84-2008	871	84	405*	41112	52.23	136
L.Hutton	1934-60	814	91	364	40140	55.51	129
M.J.K.Smith	1951-75	1091	139	204	39832	41.84	69
W.Rhodes	1898-1930	1528	237	267*	39802	30.83	58
J.H.Edrich	1956-78	979	104	310*	39790	45.47	103
R.E.S.Wyatt	1923-57	1141	157	232	39405	40.04	85
D.C.S.Compton	1936-64	839	88	300	38942	51.85	123
G.E.Tyldesley	1909-36	961	106	256*	38874	45.46	102
J.T.Tyldesley	1895-1923	994	62	295*	37897	40.60	86
K.W.R.Fletcher	1962-88	1167	170	228*	37665	37.77	63
C.G.Greenidge	1970-92	889	75	273*	37354	45.88	92
J.W.Hearne	1909-36	1025	116	285*	37252	40.98	96
L.E.G.Ames	1926-51	951	95	295	37248	43.51	102
D.Kenyon	1946-67	1159	59	259	37002	33.63	74
W.J.Edrich	1934-58	964	92	267*	36965	42.39	86
J.M.Parks	1949-76	1227	172	205*	36673	34.76	51
M.W.Gatting	1975-98	861	123	258	36549	49.52	94
D.Denton	1894-1920	1163	70	221	36479	33.37	69
G.H.Hirst	1891-1929	1215	151	341	36323	34.13	60
I.V.A.Richards	1971/72-93	796	63	322	36212	49.40	114
A.Jones	1957-83	1168	72	204*	36049	32.89	56
W.G.Quaife	1894-1928	1203	185	255*	36012	35.37	72
R.E.Marshall	1945/46-72	1053	59	228*	35725	35.94	68
M.R.Ramprakash	1987-2012	764	93	301*	35659	53.14	114
G.Gunn	1902-32	1061	82	220	35208	35.96	62

HIGHEST INDIVIDUAL INNINGS

501*	B.C.Lara	Warwickshire v Durham	Birmingham	1994
499	Hanif Mohammed	Karachi v Bahawalpur	Karachi	1958-59
452*	D.G.Bradman	New South Wales v Queensland	Sydney	1929-30
443*	B.B.Nimbalkar	Maharashtra v Kathiawar	Poona	1948-49
437	W.H.Ponsford	Victoria v Queensland	Melbourne	1927-28

429		W.H.Ponsford	Victoria v Tasmania	Melbourne	1922-23
428		Aftab Baloch	Sind v Baluchistan	Karachi	1973-74
424		A.C.MacLaren	Lancashire v Somerset	Taunton	1895
405*		G.A.Hick	Worcestershire v Somerset	Taunton	1988
400*		B.C.Lara	West Indies v England	St John's	2003-04
394		Naved Latif	Sargodha v Gujranwala	Gujranwala	2000-01
390		S.C.Cook	Lions v Warriors	East London	2009-10
385		B.Sutcliffe	Otago v Canterbury	Christchurch	1952-53
383		C.W.Gregory	New South Wales v Queensland	Brisbane	1906-07
380		M.L.Hayden	Australia v Zimbabwe	Perth	2003-04
377		S.V.Manjrekar	Bombay v Hyderabad	Bombay	1990-91
375		B.C.Lara	West Indies v England	St John's	1993-94
374		D.P.M.D.Jayawardena	Sri Lanka v South Africa	Colombo	2006
369		D.G.Bradman	South Australia v Tasmania	Adelaide	1935-36
366		N.H.Fairbrother	Lancashire v Surrey	The Oval	1990
366		M.V.Sridhar	Hyderabad v Andhra	Secunderabad	1993-94
365*		C.Hill	South Australia v NSW	Adelaide	1900-01
365*		G.St A.Sobers	West Indies v Pakistan	Kingston	1957-58
364		L.Hutton	England v Australia	The Oval	1938
359*		V.M.Merchant	Bombay v Maharashtra	Bombay	1943-44
359*		S.B.Gohel	Gujarat v Orissa	Jaipur	2016-17
359		R.B.Simpson	New South Wales v Queensland	Brisbane	1963-64
357*		R.Abel	Surrey v Somerset	The Oval	1899
357		D.G.Bradman	South Australia v Victoria	Melbourne	1935-36
356		B.A.Richards	South Australia v W Australia	Perth	1970-71
355*		G.R.Marsh	W Australia v S Australia	Perth	1989-90
355*		K.P.Pietersen	Surrey v Leicestershire	The Oval	2015
355		B.Sutcliffe	Otago v Auckland	Dunedin	1949-50
353		V.V.S.Laxman	Hyderabad v Karnataka	Bangalore	1999-00
352		W.H.Ponsford	Victoria v New South Wales	Melbourne	1926-27
352		C.A.Pujara	Saurashtra v Karnataka	Rajkot	2012-13
351*		S.M.Gugale	Maharashtra v Delhi	Mumbai	2016-17
351		K.D.K.Vithanage	Tamil Union v SL Air	Katunayake	2014-15
350		Rashid Israr	Habib Bank v National Bank	Lahore	1976-77

There have been 220 triple hundreds in first-class cricket, W.V.Raman (313) and Arjan Kripal Singh (302*) for Tamil Nadu v Goa at Panjim in 1988-89 providing the only instance of two batsmen scoring 300 in the same innings.

MOST HUNDREDS IN SUCCESSIVE INNINGS

6	C.B.Fry	Sussex and Rest of England	1901
6	D.G.Bradman	South Australia and D.G.Bradman's XI	1938-39
6	M.J.Procter	Rhodesia	1970-71

TWO DOUBLE HUNDREDS IN A MATCH

244	202*	A.E.Fagg	Kent v Essex	Colchester	1938

TRIPLE HUNDRED AND HUNDRED IN A MATCH

333	123	G.A.Gooch	England v India	Lord's	1990
319	105	K.C.Sangakkara	Sri Lanka v Bangladesh	Chittagong	2013-14

DOUBLE HUNDRED AND HUNDRED IN A MATCH MOST TIMES

4	Zaheer Abbas	Gloucestershire	1976-81

TWO HUNDREDS IN A MATCH MOST TIMES

8	Zaheer Abbas	Gloucestershire and PIA	1976-82
8	R.T.Ponting	Tasmania, Australia and Australians	1992-2006
7	W.R.Hammond	Gloucestershire, England and MCC	1927-45
7	M.R.Ramprakash	Middlesex, Surrey	1990-2010

MOST HUNDREDS IN A SEASON

18	D.C.S.Compton	1947	16	J.B.Hobbs	1925

100 HUNDREDS IN A CAREER

	Total		100th Hundred	
	Hundreds	Inns	Season	Inns
J.B.Hobbs	197	1315	1923	821
E.H.Hendren	170	1300	1928-29	740
W.R.Hammond	167	1005	1935	679
C.P.Mead	153	1340	1927	892
G.Boycott	151	1014	1977	645
H.Sutcliffe	149	1088	1932	700
F.E.Woolley	145	1532	1929	1031
G.A.Hick	136	871	1998	574
L.Hutton	129	814	1951	619
G.A.Gooch	128	990	1992-93	820
W.G.Grace	126	1493	1895	1113
D.C.S.Compton	123	839	1952	552
T.W.Graveney	122	1223	1964	940
D.G.Bradman	117	338	1947-48	295
I.V.A.Richards	114	796	1988-89	658
M.R.Ramprakash	114	764	2008	676
Zaheer Abbas	108	768	1982-83	658
A.Sandham	107	1000	1935	871
M.C.Cowdrey	107	1130	1973	1035
T.W.Hayward	104	1138	1913	1076
G.M.Turner	103	792	1982	779
J.H.Edrich	103	979	1977	945
L.E.G.Ames	102	951	1950	915
G.E.Tyldesley	102	961	1934	919
D.L.Amiss	102	1139	1986	1081

MOST 400s: 2 – B.C.Lara, W.H.Ponsford

MOST 300s or more: 6 – D.G.Bradman; 4 – W.R.Hammond, W.H.Ponsford

MOST 200s or more: 37 – D.G.Bradman; 36 – W.R.Hammond; 22 – E.H.Hendren

MOST RUNS IN A MONTH

1294 (avge 92.42)	L.Hutton	Yorkshire	June 1949

MOST RUNS IN A SEASON

Runs			I	NO	HS	Avge	100	Season
3816	D.C.S.Compton	Middlesex	50	8	246	90.85	18	1947
3539	W.J.Edrich	Middlesex	52	8	267*	80.43	12	1947
3518	T.W.Hayward	Surrey	61	8	219	66.37	13	1906

The feat of scoring 3000 runs in a season has been achieved 28 times, the most recent instance being by W.E.Alley (3019) in 1961. The highest aggregate in a season since 1969 is 2755 by S.J.Cook in 1991.

1000 RUNS IN A SEASON MOST TIMES

28 W.G.Grace (Gloucestershire), F.E.Woolley (Kent)

HIGHEST BATTING AVERAGE IN A SEASON

(Qualification: 12 innings)

Avge			I	NO	HS	Runs	100	Season
115.66	D.G.Bradman	Australians	26	5	278	2429	13	1938
106.50	K.C.Sangakkara	Surrey	16	2	200	1491	8	2017
104.66	D.R.Martyn	Australians	14	5	176*	942	5	2001
103.54	M.R.Ramprakash	Surrey	24	2	301*	2278	8	2006
102.53	G.Boycott	Yorkshire	20	5	175*	1538	6	1979
102.00	W.A.Johnston	Australians	17	16	28*	102	–	1953
101.70	G.A.Gooch	Essex	30	3	333	2746	12	1990

Avge			*I*	*NO*	*HS*	*Runs*	*100*	*Season*
101.30	M.R.Ramprakash	Surrey	25	5	266*	2026	10	2007
100.12	G.Boycott	Yorkshire	30	5	233	2503	13	1971

FASTEST HUNDRED AGAINST AUTHENTIC BOWLING

35 min	P.G.H.Fender	Surrey v Northamptonshire	Northampton	1920

FASTEST DOUBLE HUNDRED

103 min	Shafiqullah Shinwari	Kabul v Boost	Asadabad	2017-18

FASTEST TRIPLE HUNDRED

181 min	D.C.S.Compton	MCC v NE Transvaal	Benoni	1948-49

MOST SIXES IN AN INNINGS

23	C.Munro	Central Districts v Auckland	Napier	2014-15

MOST SIXES IN A MATCH

24	Shafiqullah Shinwari	Kabul v Boost	Asadabad	2017-18

MOST SIXES IN A SEASON

80	I.T.Botham	Somerset and England		1985

MOST BOUNDARIES IN AN INNINGS

72	B.C.Lara	Warwickshire v Durham	Birmingham	1994

MOST RUNS OFF ONE OVER

36	G.St A.Sobers	Nottinghamshire v Glamorgan	Swansea	1968
36	R.J.Shastri	Bombay v Baroda	Bombay	1984-85

Both batsmen hit for six all six balls of overs bowled by M.A.Nash and Tilak Raj respectively.

MOST RUNS IN A DAY

390*	B.C.Lara	Warwickshire v Durham	Birmingham	1994

There have been 19 instances of a batsman scoring 300 or more runs in a day.

LONGEST INNINGS

1015 min	R.Nayyar (271)	Himachal Pradesh v Jammu & Kashmir	Chamba	1999-00

HIGHEST PARTNERSHIPS FOR EACH WICKET

First Wicket

561	Waheed Mirza/Mansoor Akhtar	Karachi W v Quetta	Karachi	1976-77
555	P.Holmes/H.Sutcliffe	Yorkshire v Essex	Leyton	1932
554	J.T.Brown/J.Tunnicliffe	Yorkshire v Derbys	Chesterfield	1898

Second Wicket

580	Rafatullah Mohmand/Aamer Sajjad	WAPDA v SSGC	Sheikhupura	2009-10
576	S.T.Jayasuriya/R.S.Mahanama	Sri Lanka v India	Colombo	1997-98
480	D.Elgar/R.R.Rossouw	Eagles v Titans	Centurion	2009-10
475	Zahir Alam/L.S.Rajput	Assam v Tripura	Gauhati	1991-92
465*	J.A.Jameson/R.B.Kanhai	Warwickshire v Glos	Birmingham	1974

Third Wicket

624	K.C.Sangakkara/D.P.M.D.Jayawardena	Sri Lanka v South Africa	Colombo	2006
594*	S.M.Gugale/A.R.Bawne	Maharashtra v Delhi	Mumbai	2016-17
539	S.D.Jogiyani/R.A.Jadeja	Saurashtra v Gujarat	Surat	2012-13
523	M.A.Carberry/N.D.McKenzie	Hampshire v Yorkshire	Southampton	2011

Fourth Wicket

577	V.S.Hazare/Gul Mahomed	Baroda v Holkar	Baroda	1946-47
574*	C.L.Walcott/F.M.M.Worrell	Barbados v Trinidad	Port-of-Spain	1945-46
502*	F.M.M.Worrell/J.D.C.Goddard	Barbados v Trinidad	Bridgetown	1943-44
470	A.I.Kallicharran/G.W.Humpage	Warwickshire v Lancs	Southport	1982

Fifth Wicket

520*	C.A.Pujara/R.A.Jadeja	Saurashtra v Orissa	Rajkot	2008-09
494	Marchall Ayub/Mehrab Hossain Jr	Central Zone v East Zone	Bogra	2012-13
479	Misbah-ul-Haq/Usman Arshad	Sui NGP v Lahore Shalimar	Lahore	2009-10
464*	M.E.Waugh/S.R.Waugh	NSW v W Australia	Perth	1990-91

428*	B.C.Williams/M.Marais	Border v Eastern Province	East London	2017-18
423	Mosaddek Hossain/Al-Amin	Barisal v Rangpur	Savar	2014-15
420	Mohd. Ashraful/Marshall Ayub	Dhaka v Chittagong	Chittagong	2006-07
410*	A.S.Chopra/S.Badrinath	India A v South Africa A	Delhi	2007-08
405	S.G.Barnes/D.G.Bradman	Australia v England	Sydney	1946-47
401	M.B.Loye/D.Ripley	Northants v Glamorgan	Northampton	1998

Sixth Wicket

487*	G.A.Headley/C.C.Passailaigue	Jamaica v Tennyson's	Kingston	1931-32
428	W.W.Armstrong/M.A.Noble	Australians v Sussex	Hove	1902
417	W.P.Saha/L.R.Shukla	Bengal v Assam	Kolkata	2010-11
411	R.M.Poore/E.G.Wynyard	Hampshire v Somerset	Taunton	1899

Seventh Wicket

460	Bhupinder Singh jr/P.Dharmani	Punjab v Delhi	Delhi	1994-95
371	M.R.Marsh/S.M.Whiteman	Australia A v India A	Brisbane	2014
366*	J.M.Bairstow/T.T.Bresnan	Yorkshire v Durham	Chester-le-Street	2015

Eighth Wicket

433	V.T.Trumper/A.Sims	Australians v C'bury	Christchurch	1913-14
392	A.Mishra/J.Yadav	Haryana v Karnataka	Hubli	2012-13
332	I.J.L.Trott/S.C.J.Broad	England v Pakistan	Lord's	2010

Ninth Wicket

283	J.Chapman/A.Warren	Derbys v Warwicks	Blackwell	1910
268	J.B.Commins/N.Boje	SA 'A' v Mashonaland	Harare	1994-95
261	W.L.Madsen/T.Poynton	Derbys v Northants	Northampton	2012
251	J.W.H.T.Douglas/S.N.Hare	Essex v Derbyshire	Leyton	1921

Tenth Wicket

307	A.F.Kippax/J.E.H.Hooker	NSW v Victoria	Melbourne	1928-29
249	C.T.Sarwate/S.N.Banerjee	Indians v Surrey	The Oval	1946
239	Aqil Arshad/Ali Raza	Lahore Whites v Hyderabad	Lahore	2004-05

BOWLING RECORDS
2000 WICKETS IN A CAREER

	Career	Runs	Wkts	Avge	100w
W.Rhodes	1898-1930	69993	4187	16.71	23
A.P.Freeman	1914-36	69577	3776	18.42	17
C.W.L.Parker	1903-35	63817	3278	19.46	16
J.T.Hearne	1888-1923	54352	3061	17.75	15
T.W.J.Goddard	1922-52	59116	2979	19.84	16
W.G.Grace	1865-1908	51545	2876	17.92	10
A.S.Kennedy	1907-36	61034	2874	21.23	15
D.Shackleton	1948-69	53303	2857	18.65	20
G.A.R.Lock	1946-70/71	54709	2844	19.23	14
F.J.Titmus	1949-82	63313	2830	22.37	16
M.W.Tate	1912-37	50571	2784	18.16	13+1
G.H.Hirst	1891-1929	51282	2739	18.72	15
C.Blythe	1899-1914	42136	2506	16.81	14
D.L.Underwood	1963-87	49993	2465	20.28	10
W.E.Astill	1906-39	57783	2431	23.76	9
J.C.White	1909-37	43759	2356	18.57	14
W.E.Hollies	1932-57	48656	2323	20.94	14
F.S.Trueman	1949-69	42154	2304	18.29	12
J.B.Statham	1950-68	36999	2260	16.37	13
R.T.D.Perks	1930-55	53771	2233	24.07	16
J.Briggs	1879-1900	35431	2221	15.95	12
D.J.Shepherd	1950-72	47302	2218	21.32	12
E.G.Dennett	1903-26	42571	2147	19.82	12
T.Richardson	1892-1905	38794	2104	18.43	10
T.E.Bailey	1945-67	48170	2082	23.13	9

	Career	Runs	Wkts	Avge	100w
R.Illingworth	1951-83	42023	**2072**	20.28	10
F.E.Woolley	1906-38	41066	**2068**	19.85	8
N.Gifford	1960-88	48731	**2068**	23.56	4
G.Geary	1912-38	41339	**2063**	20.03	11
D.V.P.Wright	1932-57	49307	**2056**	23.98	10
J.A.Newman	1906-30	51111	**2032**	25.15	9
A.Shaw	1864-97	24580	**2026+1**	12.12	9
S.Haigh	1895-1913	32091	**2012**	15.94	11

ALL TEN WICKETS IN AN INNINGS

This feat has been achieved 82 times in first-class matches (excluding 12-a-side fixtures).
Three Times: A.P.Freeman (1929, 1930, 1931)
Twice: V.E.Walker (1859, 1865); H.Verity (1931, 1932); J.C.Laker (1956)
Instances since 1945:

W.E.Hollies	Warwickshire v Notts	Birmingham	1946
J.M.Sims	East v West	Kingston on Thames	1948
J.K.R.Graveney	Gloucestershire v Derbyshire	Chesterfield	1949
T.E.Bailey	Essex v Lancashire	Clacton	1949
R.Berry	Lancashire v Worcestershire	Blackpool	1953
S.P.Gupte	President's XI v Combined XI	Bombay	1954-55
J.C.Laker	Surrey v Australians	The Oval	1956
K.Smales	Nottinghamshire v Glos	Stroud	1956
G.A.R.Lock	Surrey v Kent	Blackheath	1956
J.C.Laker	England v Australia	Manchester	1956
P.M.Chatterjee	Bengal v Assam	Jorhat	1956-57
J.D.Bannister	Warwicks v Combined Services	Birmingham (M & B)	1959
A.J.G.Pearson	Cambridge U v Leicestershire	Loughborough	1961
N.I.Thomson	Sussex v Warwickshire	Worthing	1964
P.J.Allan	Queensland v Victoria	Melbourne	1965-66
I.J.Brayshaw	Western Australia v Victoria	Perth	1967-68
Shahid Mahmood	Karachi Whites v Khairpur	Karachi	1969-70
E.E.Hemmings	International XI v W Indians	Kingston	1982-83
P.Sunderam	Rajasthan v Vidarbha	Jodhpur	1985-86
S.T.Jefferies	Western Province v OFS	Cape Town	1987-88
Imran Adil	Bahawalpur v Faisalabad	Faisalabad	1989-90
G.P.Wickremasinghe	Sinhalese v Kalutara	Colombo	1991-92
R.L.Johnson	Middlesex v Derbyshire	Derby	1994
Naeem Akhtar	Rawalpindi B v Peshawar	Peshawar	1995-96
A.Kumble	India v Pakistan	Delhi	1998-99
D.S.Mohanty	East Zone v South Zone	Agartala	2000-01
O.D.Gibson	Durham v Hampshire	Chester-le-Street	2007
M.W.Olivier	Warriors v Eagles	Bloemfontein	2007-08
Zulfiqar Babar	Multan v Islamabad	Multan	2009-10
P.M.Pushpakumara	Colombo v Saracens	Moratuwa	2018-19

MOST WICKETS IN A MATCH

19	J.C.Laker	England v Australia	Manchester	1956

MOST WICKETS IN A SEASON

Wkts		Season	Matches	Overs	Mdns	Runs	Avge
304	A.P.Freeman	1928	37	1976.1	423	5489	18.05
298	A.P.Freeman	1933	33	2039	651	4549	15.26

The feat of taking 250 wickets in a season has been achieved on 12 occasions, the last instance being by A.P.Freeman in 1933. 200 or more wickets in a season have been taken on 59 occasions, the last being by G.A.R.Lock (212 wickets, average 12.02) in 1957.

The highest aggregates of wickets taken in a season since the reduction of County Championship matches in 1969 are as follows:

Wkts		Season	Matches	Overs	Mdns	Runs	Avge
134	M.D.Marshall	1982	22	822	225	2108	15.73
131	L.R.Gibbs	1971	23	1024.1	295	2475	18.89
125	F.D.Stephenson	1988	22	819.1	196	2289	18.31
121	R.D.Jackman	1980	23	746.2	220	1864	15.40

Since 1969 there have been 50 instances of bowlers taking 100 wickets in a season.

MOST HAT-TRICKS IN A CAREER

7	D.V.P.Wright
6	T.W.J.Goddard, C.W.L.Parker
5	S.Haigh, V.W.C.Jupp, A.E.G.Rhodes, F.A.Tarrant

ALL-ROUND RECORDS
THE 'DOUBLE'

3000 runs and 100 wickets: J.H.Parks (1937)
2000 runs and 200 wickets: G.H.Hirst (1906)
2000 runs and 100 wickets: F.E.Woolley (4), J.W.Hearne (3), W.G.Grace (2), G.H.Hirst (2), W.Rhodes (2), T.E.Bailey, D.E.Davies, G.L.Jessop, V.W.C.Jupp, J.Langridge, F.A.Tarrant, C.L.Townsend, L.F.Townsend
1000 runs and 200 wickets: M.W.Tate (3), A.E.Trott (2), A.S.Kennedy
Most Doubles: 16 – W.Rhodes; 14 – G.H.Hirst; 10 – V.W.C.Jupp
Double in Debut Season: D.B.Close (1949) – aged 18, the youngest to achieve this feat.

The feat of scoring 1000 runs and taking 100 wickets in a season has been achieved on 305 occasions. R.J.Hadlee (1984) and F.D.Stephenson (1988) being the only players to complete the 'double' since the reduction of County Championship matches in 1969.

WICKET-KEEPING RECORDS
1000 DISMISSALS IN A CAREER

	Career	Dismissals	Ct	St
R.W.Taylor	1960-88	**1649**	1473	176
J.T.Murray	1952-75	**1527**	1270	257
H.Strudwick	1902-27	**1497**	1242	255
A.P.E.Knott	1964-85	**1344**	1211	133
R.C.Russell	1981-2004	**1320**	1192	128
F.H.Huish	1895-1914	**1310**	933	377
B.Taylor	1949-73	**1294**	1083	211
S.J.Rhodes	1981-2004	**1263**	1139	124
D.Hunter	1889-1909	**1253**	906	347
H.R.Butt	1890-1912	**1228**	953	275
J.H.Board	1891-1914/15	**1207**	852	355
H.Elliott	1920-47	**1206**	904	302
J.M.Parks	1949-76	**1181**	1088	93
R.Booth	1951-70	**1126**	948	178
L.E.G.Ames	1926-51	**1121**	703	418
C.M.W.Read	1997-2017	**1104**	1051	53
D.L.Bairstow	1970-90	**1099**	961	138
G.Duckworth	1923-47	**1096**	753	343
H.W.Stephenson	1948-64	**1082**	748	334
J.G.Binks	1955-75	**1071**	895	176
T.G.Evans	1939-69	**1066**	816	250
A.Long	1960-80	**1046**	922	124
G.O.Dawkes	1937-61	**1043**	895	148
R.W.Tolchard	1965-83	**1037**	912	125
W.L.Cornford	1921-47	**1017**	675	342

MOST DISMISSALS IN AN INNINGS

9	(8ct, 1st)	Tahir Rashid	Habib Bank v PACO	Gujranwala	1992-93
9	(7ct, 2st)	W.R.James	Matabeleland v Mashonaland CD	Bulawayo	1995-96
8	(8ct)	A.T.W.Grout	Queensland v W Australia	Brisbane	1959-60
8	(8ct)	D.E.East	Essex v Somerset	Taunton	1985
8	(8ct)	S.A.Marsh	Kent v Middlesex	Lord's	1991
8	(6ct, 2st)	T.J.Zoehrer	Australians v Surrey	The Oval	1993
8	(7ct, 1st)	D.S.Berry	Victoria v South Australia	Melbourne	1996-97
8	(7ct, 1st)	Y.S.S.Mendis	Bloomfield v Kurunegala Youth	Colombo	2000-01
8	(7ct, 1st)	S.Nath	Assam v Tripura (*on debut*)	Gauhati	2001-02
8	(8ct)	J.N.Batty	Surrey v Kent	The Oval	2004
8	(8ct)	Golam Mabud	Sylhet v Dhaka	Dhaka .	2005-06
8	(8ct)	D.C.de Boorder	Otago v Wellington	Wellington	2009-10
8	(8ct)	R.S.Second	Free State v North West	Bloemfontein	2011-12
8	(8ct)	T.L.Tsolekile	South Africa A v Sri Lanka A	Durban	2012
8	(7ct, 1st)	M.A.R.S.Fernando	Chilaw Marians v Colts	Columbo (SSC)	2017-18

MOST DISMISSALS IN A MATCH

14	(11ct, 3st)	I.Khaleel	Hyderabad v Assam	Guwahati	2011-12
13	(11ct, 2st)	W.R.James	Matabeleland v Mashonaland CD	Bulawayo	1995-96
12	(8ct, 4st)	E.Pooley	Surrey v Sussex	The Oval	1868
12	(9ct, 3st)	D.Tallon	Queensland v NSW	Sydney	1938-39
12	(9ct, 3st)	H.B.Taber	NSW v South Australia	Adelaide	1968-69
12	(12ct)	P.D.McGlashan	Northern Districts v Central Districts	Whangarei	2009-10
12	(11ct, 1st)	T.L.Tsolekile	Lions v Dolphins	Johannesburg	2010-11
12	(12ct)	Kashif Mahmood	Lahore Shalimar v Abbottabad	Abbottabad	2010-11
12	(12ct)	R.S.Second	Free State v North West	Bloemfontein	2011-12

MOST DISMISSALS IN A SEASON

128	(79ct, 49st)	L.E.G.Ames	1929

FIELDING RECORDS
750 CATCHES IN A CAREER

1018	F.E.Woolley	1906-38	784	J.G.Langridge	1928-55
887	W.G.Grace	1865-1908	764	W.Rhodes	· 1898-1930
830	G.A.R.Lock	1946-70/71	758	C.A.Milton	1948-74
819	W.R.Hammond	1920-51	754	E.H.Hendren	1907-38
813	D.B.Close	1949-86			

MOST CATCHES IN AN INNINGS

7	M.J.Stewart	Surrey v Northamptonshire	Northampton	1957
7	A.S.Brown	Gloucestershire v Nottinghamshire	Nottingham	1966
7	R.Clarke	Warwickshire v Lancashire	Liverpool	2011

MOST CATCHES IN A MATCH

10	W.R.Hammond	Gloucestershire v Surrey	Cheltenham	1928
9	R.Clarke	Warwickshire v Lancashire	Liverpool	2011

MOST CATCHES IN A SEASON

78	W.R.Hammond	1928	77	M.J.Stewart	1957

ENGLAND LIMITED-OVERS INTERNATIONALS 2019

WEST INDIES v ENGLAND

LIMITED-OVERS INTERNATIONALS

Kensington Oval, Bridgetown, Barbados, 20 February. Toss: West Indies. **ENGLAND** won by six wickets. West Indies 360-8 (50; C.H.Gayle 135, S.D.Hope 64, B.A.Stokes 3-37, A.U.Rashid 3-74). England 364-4 (48.4; J.J.Roy 123, J.E.Root 102, E.J.G.Morgan 65). Award: J.J.Roy.

Kensington Oval, Bridgetown, Barbados, 22 February. Toss: England. **WEST INDIES** won by 26 runs. West Indies 289-6 (50; S.O.Hetmyer 104*, C.H.Gayle 50). England 263 (47.4; B.A.Stokes 79, E.J.G.Morgan 70, S.S.Cottrell 5-46, J.O.Holder 3-53). Award: S.O.Hetmyer.

The third LOI in St George's, Grenada, on 25 February was abandoned with a toss.

National Cricket Stadium, St George's, Grenada, 27 February. Toss: West Indies. **ENGLAND** won by 29 runs. England 418-6 (50; J.C.Buttler 150, E.J.G.Morgan 103, A.D.Hales 82, J.M.Bairstow 56). West Indies 389 (48; C.H.Gayle 162, D.M.Bravo 61, C.R.Brathwaite 50, A.U.Rashid 5-85, M.A.Wood 4-60). Award: J.C.Buttler.
J.C.Buttler 150 (77b, 13 fours, 12 sixes) went from 50 to 150 in 31 balls, inc 9 fours and 9 sixes; A.U.Rashid took four wickets in his last five balls.

Darren Sammy National Cricket Stadium, Gros Islet, St Lucia, 2 March. Toss: West Indies. **WEST INDIES** won by seven wickets. England 113 (28.1; O.Thomas 5-21). West Indies 115-3 (12.1; C.H.Gayle 77). Award: O.Thomas. Series award: C.H.Gayle.
West Indies won with 227 balls remaining – England's heaviest defeat by balls remaining.

TWENTY20 INTERNATIONALS

Darren Sammy National Cricket Stadium, Gros Islet, St Lucia, 5 March. Toss: England. **ENGLAND** won by four wickets. West Indies 160-8 (20; N.Pooran 58, T.K.Curran 4-36). England 161-6 (18.5; J.M.Bairstow 68, S.S.Cottrell 3-29). Award: J.M.Bairstow.

Warner Park, Basseterre, St Kitts, 8 March. Toss: West Indies. **ENGLAND** won by 137 runs. England 182-6 (20; S.W.Billings 87, J.E.Root 55). West Indies 45 (11.5; C.J.Jordan 4-6). Award: S.W.Billings.
England's largest winning margin by runs; C.J.Jordan's figures of 4-6 are the best for England in IT20s.

Warner Park, Basseterre, St Kitts, 10 March. Toss: West Indies. **ENGLAND** won by eight wickets. West Indies 71 (13; D.J.Willey 4-7, M.A.Wood 3-9). England 72-2 (10.3). Award: D.J.Willey. Series award: C.J.Jordan.
England's largest winning margin by balls remaining (57).

IRELAND v ENGLAND

LIMITED-OVERS INTERNATIONAL

The Village, Malahide, Dublin, 3 May. Toss: England. **ENGLAND** won by four wickets. Ireland 198 (43.1/45; L.E.Plunkett 4-35, T.K.Curran 3-35). England 199-6 (42/45; B.T.Foakes 61*; J.B.Little 4-45). Award: B.T.Foakes. England debuts: J.C.Archer, B.T.Foakes, D.J.Malan.

ENGLAND v PAKISTAN

TWENTY20 INTERNATIONAL

Sophia Gardens, Cardiff, 5 May. Toss: Pakistan. **ENGLAND** won by seven wickets. Pakistan 173-6 (20; Babar Azam 65, Haris Sohail 50). England 175-3 (19.2; E.J.G.Morgan 57*). Award: E.J.G.Morgan. England debuts: J.C.Archer, B.M.Duckett, B.T.Foakes.

LIMITED-OVERS INTERNATIONALS

The Oval, London, 8 May. Toss: England. **NO RESULT**. Pakistan 80-2 (19).

Rose Bowl, Southampton, 11 May. Toss: Pakistan. **ENGLAND** won by 12 runs. England 373-3 (50; J.C.Buttler 110*, J.J.Roy 87, E.J.G.Morgan 71*, J.M.Bairstow 51). Pakistan 361-7 (50; Fakhar Zaman 138, Babar Azam 51, Asif Ali 51). Award: J.C.Buttler.

County Ground, Bristol, 14 May. Toss: England. **ENGLAND** won by six wickets. Pakistan 358-9 (50; Imam-ul-Haq 151, Asif Ali 52, C.R.Woakes 4-67). England 359-4 (44.5; J.M.Bairstow 128, J.J.Roy 76). Award: J.M.Bairstow.

Trent Bridge, Nottingham, 17 May. Toss: England. **ENGLAND** won by three wickets. Pakistan 340-7 (50; Babar Azam 115, Mohammad Hafeez 59, Fakhar Zaman 57, T.K.Curran 4-75). England 341-7 (49.3; J.J.Roy 114, B.A.Stokes 71*). Award: J.J.Roy.

Headingley, Leeds, 19 May. Toss: England. **ENGLAND** won by 54 runs. England 351-9 (50; J.E.Root 84, E.J.G.Morgan 76, Shaheen Shah Afridi 4-82, Imad Wasim 3-53). Pakistan 297 (46.5; Sarfraz Ahmed 97, Babar Azam 80, C.R.Woakes 5-54). Award: C.R.Woakes. Series award: J.J.Roy.

ICC Cricket World Cup – see pages 280-282.

NEW ZEALAND v ENGLAND

TWENTY20 INTERNATIONALS

Hagley Oval, Christchurch, 1 November. Toss: England. **ENGLAND** won by seven wickets. New Zealand 153-5 (20). England 154-3 (18.3; J.M.Vince 59, M.J.Santner 3-23). Award: J.M.Vince. England debuts: P.R.Brown, S.M.Curran, L.Gregory.

Westpac Stadium, Wellington, 3 November. Toss: England. **NEW ZEALAND** won by 21 runs. New Zealand 176-8 (20; C.J.Jordan 3-23). England 155 (19.5; M.J.Santner 3-25). Award: M.J.Santner. England debut: S.Mahmood.

Saxton Oval, Nelson, 5 November. Toss: New Zealand. **NEW ZEALAND** won by 14 runs. New Zealand 180-7 (20; C.de Grandhomme 55). England 166-7 (20; D.J.Malan 55). Award: C.de Grandhomme. England debuts: T.Banton, M.W.Parkinson.

McLean Park, Napier, 8 November. Toss: England. **ENGLAND** won by 76 runs. England 241-3 (20; D.J.Malan 103*, E.J.G.Morgan 91). New Zealand 165 (16.5; M.W.Parkinson 4-47). Award: D.J.Malan.

Eden Park, Auckland, 10 November. Toss: England. **MATCH TIED**. New Zealand 146-5 (11/11; M.J.Guptill 50). England 146-7 (11/11). Award: J.M.Bairstow (47 in 18b). Series award: M.J.Santner. England won the one-over eliminator.

ENGLAND RESULTS IN 2019

	P	W	L	T	NR
Limited Overs	22	14	5	1	2
Twenty20	9	6	2	1	–
Overall	31	20	7	2	2

700 RUNS IN LIMITED-OVERS INTERNATIONALS IN 2019

	P	I	NO	HS	Runs	Ave	100	50	S/Rate
J.E.Root	22	20	2	107	910	50.55	3	4	92.85
J.J.Roy	14	12	–	153	845	70.41	3	6	118.18
J.M.Bairstow	20	18	–	128	844	46.88	3	4	102.92
E.J.G.Morgan	21	18	3	148	791	52.73	2	5	112.19
B.A.Stokes	20	17	5	89	719	59.91	–	7	92.53

20 WICKETS IN LIMITED-OVERS INTERNATIONALS IN 2019

	P	O	M	Runs	W	Ave	Best	4wI	Econ
C.R.Woakes	19	145.0	8	864	29	29.79	5-54	2	5.95
M.A.Wood	16	132.4	2	736	27	27.25	4-60	1	5.54
A.U.Rashid	21	151.5	–	927	24	38.62	5-85	1	6.10
J.C.Archer	14	122.5	10	569	23	24.73	3-27	–	4.63
L.E.Plunkett	15	106.0	–	586	20	29.30	4-35	1	5.52

ICC CRICKET WORLD CUP 2019

The 12th ICC Cricket World Cup was held in England between 30 May and 14 July.

Team	P	W	L	T	NR	Pts	Net RR
1 India	9	7	1	–	1	15	+0.80
2 Australia	9	7	2	–	–	14	+0.86
3 England	9	6	3	–	–	12	+1.15
4 New Zealand	9	5	3	–	1	11	+0.17
5 Pakistan	9	5	3	–	1	11	–0.43
6 Sri Lanka	9	3	4	–	2	8	–0.91
7 South Africa	9	3	5	–	1	7	–0.03
8 Bangladesh	9	3	5	–	1	7	–0.41
9 West Indies	9	2	6	–	1	5	–0.22
10 Afghanistan	9	–	9	–	–	0	–1.32

England's Group Stage games:

The Oval, London, 30 May. Toss: South Africa. **ENGLAND** won by 104 runs. England 311-8 (50; B.A.Stokes 89, E.J.G.Morgan 57, J.J.Roy 54, J.E.Root 51, L.T.Ngidi 3-66). South Africa 207 (39.5; Q.de Kock 68, H.E.van der Dussen 50, J.C.Archer 3-27). Award: B.A.Stokes.

Trent Bridge, Nottingham, 3 June. Toss: England. **PAKISTAN** won by 14 runs. Pakistan 348-8 (50; Mohammad Hafeez 84, Babar Azam 63, Sarfraz Ahmed 55, M.M.Ali 3-50, C.R.Woakes 3-71). England 334-9 (50; J.E.Root 107, J.C.Buttler 103, Wahab Riaz 3-82). Award: Mohammad Hafeez.

Sophia Gardens, Cardiff, 8 June. Toss: Bangladesh. **ENGLAND** won by 106 runs. England 386-6 (50; J.J.Roy 153, J.C.Buttler 64, J.M.Bairstow 51). Bangladesh 280 (48.5; Shakib Al Hasan 121, B.A.Stokes 3-23, J.C.Archer 3-29). Award: J.J.Roy.

Rose Bowl, Southampton, 14 June. Toss: England. **ENGLAND** won by eight wickets. West Indies 212 (44.4; N.Pooran 63, M.A.Wood 3-18, J.C.Archer 3-30). England 213-2 (33.1; J.E.Root 100*). Award: J.E.Root.

Old Trafford, Manchester, 18 June. Toss: England. **ENGLAND** won by 150 runs. England 397-6 (50; E.J.G.Morgan 148, J.M.Bairstow 90, J.E.Root 88, Gulbadin Naib 3-68, Dawlat Zadran 3-85). Afghanistan 247-8 (50; Hashmatullah Shahidi 76, J.C.Archer 3-52, A.U.Rashid 3-66). Award: E.J.G.Morgan.
England's highest score in World Cup games; E.J.G.Morgan hit an LOI world record 17 sixes in his innings of 148.

Headingley, Leeds, 21 June. Toss: Sri Lanka. **SRI LANKA** won by 20 runs. Sri Lanka 232-9 (50; A.D.Mathews 85*, M.A.Wood 3-40, J.C.Archer 3-52). England 212 (47; B.A.Stokes 82*, J.E.Root 57, S.L.Malinga 4-43, D.M.de Silva 3-32). Award: S.L.Malinga.

Lord's, London, 25 June. Toss: England. **AUSTRALIA** won by 64 runs. Australia 285-7 (50; A.J.Finch 100, D.A.Warner 53). England 221 (44.4; B.A.Stokes 89, J.P.Behrendorff 5-44, M.A.Starc 4-43). Award: A.J.Finch.

Edgbaston, Birmingham, 30 June. Toss: England. **ENGLAND** won by 31 runs. England 337-7 (50; J.M.Bairstow 111, B.A.Stokes 79, J.J.Roy 66, Mohammed Shami 5-69). India 306-5 (50; R.G.Sharma 102, V.Kohli 66, L.E.Plunkett 3-55). Award: J.M.Bairstow.

Riverside Ground, Chester-le-Street, 3 July. Toss: England. **ENGLAND** won by 119 runs. England 305-8 (50; J.M.Bairstow 106, J.J.Roy 60). New Zealand 186 (45; T.W.M.Latham 57, M.A.Wood 3-34). Award: J.M.Bairstow.

Semi-finals

Old Trafford, Manchester, 9-10 July. Toss: New Zealand. **NEW ZEALAND** won by 18 runs. New Zealand 239-8 (50; L.R.P.L.Taylor 74, K.S.Williamson 67, B.Kumar 3-43). India 221 (49.3; R.A.Jadeja 77, M.S.Dhoni 50, M.J.Henry 3-37). Award: M.J.Henry.

Edgbaston, Birmingham, 11 July. Toss: Australia. **ENGLAND** won by eight wickets. Australia 223 (49; S.P.D.Smith 85, C.R.Woakes 3-20, A.U.Rashid 3-54). England 226-2 (32.1; J.J.Roy 85). Award: C.R.Woakes.

Statistical Highlights in ICC Cricket World Cup 2019

Highest total	397-5		England v Afghanistan	Manchester
Biggest victory (runs)	150		England v Afghanistan	Manchester
Biggest victory (wkts)	10		New Zealand beat Sri Lanka	Cardiff
Biggest victory (balls)	218		West Indies beat Pakistan	Nottingham
Most runs	648 (ave 81.00)		R.G.Sharma (India)	
	647 (ave 71.88)		D.A.Warner (Australia)	
	606 (ave 86.57)		Shakib Al Hasan (Bangladesh)	
Highest innings	166	D.A.Warner	Australia v Bangladesh	Nottingham
Most sixes (inns)	17	E.J.G.Morgan	England v Afghanistan	Manchester
Highest partnership	192	D.A.Warner/U.T.Khawaja	Australia v Bangladesh	Nottingham
Most wickets	27 (ave 18.59)		M.A.Starc (Australia)	
	21 (ave 19.47)		L.H.Ferguson (New Zealand)	
	20 (ave 23.05)		J.C.Archer (England)	
	20 (ave 24.20)		Mustafizur Rahman (Bangladesh)	
Best bowling	6-35	Shaheen Shah Afridi	Pakistan v Bangladesh	Lord's
Most economical	10-0-23-2	Mohammad Nabi	Afghanistan v Pakistan	Leeds
Most expensive	9-0-110-0	Rashid Khan	Afghanistan v England	Manchester
Most w/k dismissals	21	T.W.M.Latham (New Zealand)		
	20	A.T.Carey (Australia)		
Most w/k dismissals (inns)	5	A.T.Carey	Australia v Afghanistan	Bristol
	5	T.W.M.Latham	New Zealand v Afghanistan	Taunton
Most catches	13	J.E.Root (England)		
	10	F.du Plessis (South Africa)		
Most catches (inns)	4	C.R.Woakes	England v Pakistan	Nottingham

2019 ICC CRICKET WORLD CUP FINAL

ENGLAND v NEW ZEALAND

At Lord's, London, on 14 July.
Result: **MATCH TIED (ENGLAND** won on boundary countback after Super Over).
Toss: New Zealand. Award: B.A.Stokes. Series Award: KC.Williamson.

NEW ZEALAND		Runs	Balls	4/6	Fall
M.J.Guptill	lbw b Woakes	19	18	2/1	1- 29
H.M.Nicholls	b Plunkett	55	77	4	3-118
* K.S.Williamson	c Buttler b Plunkett	30	53	2	2-103
L.R.P.L.Taylor	lbw b Wood	15	31	–	4-141
† T.W.M.Latham	c sub (J.M.Vince) b Woakes	47	56	2/1	7-232
J.D.S.Neesham	c Root b Plunkett	19	25	3	5-173
C.de Grandhomme	c sub (J.M.Vince) b Woakes	16	28	–	6-219
M.J.Santner	not out	5	9	–	
M.J.Henry	b Archer	4	2	1	8-240
T.A.Boult	not out	1	2	–	
L.H.Ferguson					
Extras	(LB 12, NB 1, W 17)	30			
Total	**(8 wkts; 50 overs)**	**241**			

ENGLAND		Runs	Balls	4/6	Fall
J.J.Roy	c Latham b Henry	17	20	3	1- 28
J.M.Bairstow	b Ferguson	36	55	7	3- 71
J.E.Root	c Latham b de Grandhomme	7	30	–	2- 59
* E.J.G.Morgan	c Ferguson b Neesham	9	22	–	4- 86
B.A.Stokes	not out	84	98	5/2	
† J.C.Buttler	c sub (T.G.Southee) b Ferguson	59	60	6	5-196
C.R.Woakes	c Latham b Ferguson	2	4	–	6-203
L.E.Plunkett	c Boult b Neesham	10	10	1	7-220
J.C.Archer	b Neesham	0	1	–	8-227
A.U.Rashid	run out	0	0	–	9-240
M.A.Wood	run out	0	0	–	10-241
Extras	(B 2, LB 3, W 12)	17			
Total	**(50 overs)**	**241**			

ENGLAND	O	M	R	W	NEW ZEALAND	O	M	R	W
Woakes	9	0	37	3	Boult	10	0	67	0
Archer	10	0	42	1	Henry	10	2	40	1
Plunkett	10	0	42	3	De Grandhomme	10	2	25	1
Wood	10	1	49	1	Ferguson	10	0	50	3
Rashid	8	0	39	0	Neesham	7	0	43	3
Stokes	3	0	20	0	Santner	3	0	11	0

Umpires: H.D.P.K.Dharmasena (Sri Lanka) and M.Erasmus (South Africa)

SUPER OVER

England 15-0: bowler T.A.Boult – 3 to B.A.Stokes; 1 to J.C.Buttler; 4 to Stokes; 1 to Stokes; 2 to Buttler; 4 to Buttler.
New Zealand 15-1: bowler J.C.Archer – wide; 2 to J.D.S.Neesham; 6 to Neesham; 2 to Neesham; 2 to Neesham; 1 to Neesham; 1 to M.J.Guptill, run out coming for second run. Scores level in Super Over, so England win on boundary countback 26-17.

LIMITED-OVERS INTERNATIONALS
CAREER RECORDS

These records, complete to 11 March 2020, include all players registered for county cricket and The Hundred for the 2020 season at the time of going to press, plus those who have appeared in LOI matches for ICC full member countries since 8 December 2018.

ENGLAND – BATTING AND FIELDING

	M	I	NO	HS	Runs	Avge	100	50	Ct/St
M.M.Ali	102	83	14	128	1783	25.84	3	5	32
T.R.Ambrose	5	5	1	6	10	2.50	–	–	3
J.M.Anderson	194	79	43	28	273	7.58	–	–	53
J.C.Archer	14	7	3	7*	13	3.25	–	–	4
J.M.Bairstow	77	70	8	141*	2923	47.14	9	11	35/2
J.T.Ball	18	6	2	28	38	9.50	–	–	5
G.S.Ballance	16	15	1	79	279	21.21	–	2	8
T.Banton	3	2	–	32	50	25.00	–	–	–
G.J.Batty	10	8	2	17	30	5.00	–	–	4
I.R.Bell	161	157	14	141	5416	37.87	4	35	54
S.W.Billings	15	12	–	62	271	22.58	–	2	13
R.S.Bopara	120	109	21	101*	2695	30.62	1	14	35
S.G.Borthwick	2	2	–	15	18	9.00	–	–	–
T.T.Bresnan	85	64	20	80	871	19.79	–	1	20
D.R.Briggs	1	–	–	–	–	–	–	–	–
S.C.J.Broad	121	68	25	45*	529	12.30	–	–	27
J.C.Buttler	142	117	23	150	3843	40.88	9	20	171/31
R.Clarke	20	13	–	39	144	11.07	–	–	11
A.N.Cook	92	92	4	137	3204	36.40	5	19	36
S.M.Curran	4	3	–	15	24	8.00	–	–	–
T.K.Curran	20	13	8	47*	198	39.60	–	–	4
S.M.Davies	8	8	–	87	244	30.50	–	1	8
L.A.Dawson	3	2	–	10	14	7.00	–	–	–
J.L.Denly	16	13	–	87	446	34.30	–	4	7
J.W.Dernbach	24	8	1	5	19	2.71	–	–	5
B.M.Duckett	3	3	–	63	123	41.00	–	2	–
S.T.Finn	69	30	13	35	136	8.00	–	–	15
B.T.Foakes	1	1	1	61*	61	–	–	–	2/1
H.F.Gurney	10	6	4	6*	15	7.50	–	–	1
A.D.Hales	70	67	3	171	2419	37.79	6	14	27
C.J.Jordan	34	23	9	38*	170	12.14	–	–	19
S.Mahmood	1	–	–	–	–	–	–	–	–
D.J.Malan	1	1	–	24	24	24.00	–	–	–
S.C.Meaker	2	2	–	1	2	1.00	–	–	–
E.J.G.Morgan †	213	196	30	148	6624	39.90	12	41	74
G.Onions	4	1	–	1	1	1.00	–	–	–
C.Overton	1	–	–	–	–	–	–	–	2
M.W.Parkinson	2	–	–	–	–	–	–	–	–
S.D.Parry	2	–	–	–	–	–	–	–	–
S.R.Patel	36	22	7	70*	482	32.13	–	1	7
L.E.Plunkett	89	50	19	56	646	20.83	–	1	26
A.U.Rashid	100	44	12	69	590	18.43	–	1	30
T.S.Roland-Jones	1	1	1	37*	37	–	–	–	–
J.E.Root	146	137	21	133*	5922	51.05	16	33	74
J.J.Roy	87	83	2	180	3434	42.39	9	18	31
B.A.Stokes	95	81	15	102*	2682	40.63	3	20	45
O.P.Stone	4	1	1	9*	9	–	–	–	–
J.M.Vince	13	11	–	51	265	24.09	–	1	4
D.J.Willey	46	27	12	50	279	18.60	–	1	21

	M	I	NO	HS	Runs	Avge	100	50	Ct/St
C.R.Woakes	101	69	20	95*	1226	25.02	–	4	44
M.A.Wood	51	17	10	13	56	8.00	–	–	11
L.J.Wright	50	39	4	52	707	20.20	–	2	18

ENGLAND – BOWLING

	O	M	R	W	Avge	Best	4wI	R/Over
M.M.Ali	785.4	10	4131	85	48.60	4-46	1	5.25
J.M.Anderson	1597.2	125	7861	269	29.22	5-23	13	4.92
J.C.Archer	122.5	10	569	23	24.73	3-27	–	4.63
J.T.Ball	157.5	5	980	21	46.66	5-51	1	6.20
G.J.Batty	73.2	1	366	5	73.20	2-40	–	4.99
I.R.Bell	14.4	0	88	6	14.66	3- 9	–	6.00
R.S.Bopara	310	11	1523	40	38.07	4-38	1	4.91
S.G.Borthwick	9	0	72	0	–	–	–	8.00
T.T.Bresnan	703.3	35	3813	109	34.98	5-48	4	5.42
D.R.Briggs	10	0	39	2	19.50	2-39	–	3.90
S.C.J.Broad	1018.1	56	5364	178	30.13	5-23	10	5.26
R.Clarke	78.1	3	415	11	37.72	2-28	–	5.30
S.M.Curran	19	0	134	2	67.00	2-44	–	7.05
T.K.Curran	145	5	894	27	33.11	5-35	2	6.16
L.A.Dawson	14	0	96	3	32.00	2-70	–	6.85
J.L.Denly	17	0	101	1	101.00	1-24	–	5.94
J.W.Dernbach	205.4	6	1308	31	42.19	4-45	1	6.35
S.T.Finn	591.4	38	2996	102	29.37	5-33	6	5.06
H.F.Gurney	75.5	4	432	11	39.27	4-55	1	5.69
C.J.Jordan	269.4	5	1611	45	35.80	5-29	1	5.97
S.Mahmood	5	1	17	1	17.00	1-17	–	3.40
S.C.Meaker	19	1	110	2	55.00	1-45	–	5.78
G.Onions	34	1	185	4	46.25	2-58	–	5.44
C.Overton	7	0	55	0	–	–	–	7.85
M.W.Parkinson	10.4	0	63	0	–	–	–	5.90
S.D.Parry	19	2	92	4	23.00	3-32	–	4.84
S.R.Patel	197.5	4	1091	24	45.45	5-41	1	5.51
L.E.Plunkett	689.3	14	4010	135	29.70	5-52	7	5.81
A.U.Rashid	818.3	6	4598	146	31.49	5-27	9	5.61
T.S.Roland-Jones	7	2	34	1	34.00	1-34	–	4.85
J.E.Root	250.4	2	1445	24	60.20	3-52	–	5.76
B.A.Stokes	485.2	7	2920	70	41.71	5-61	2	6.01
O.P.Stone	16	0	97	1	97.00	1-23	–	6.06
D.J.Willey	328.3	17	1889	52	36.32	4-34	2	5.75
C.R.Woakes	786	40	4384	143	30.65	6-45	12	5.57
M.A.Wood	430.5	13	2385	61	39.09	4-33	2	5.53
L.J.Wright	173	2	884	15	58.93	2-34	–	5.10

† E.J.G.Morgan has also made 23 appearances for Ireland (see below).

AUSTRALIA – BATTING AND FIELDING

	M	I	NO	HS	Runs	Avge	100	50	Ct/St
S.A.Abbott	1	1	–	3	3	3.00	–	–	–
A.C.Agar	13	11	2	46	189	21.00	–	–	6
J.P.Behrendorff	11	5	3	11*	19	9.50	–	–	3
A.T.Carey	35	31	6	85	883	35.32	–	4	40/5
D.T.Christian	19	18	5	39	273	21.00	–	–	10
M.J.Cosgrove	3	3	–	74	112	37.33	–	1	–
N.M.Coulter-Nile	32	21	6	92	252	16.80	–	1	7
P.J.Cummins	63	39	12	36	246	9.11	–	–	14

	M	I	NO	HS	Runs	Avge	100	50	Ct/St
J.P.Faulkner	69	52	22	116	1032	34.40	1	4	21
A.J.Finch	125	121	3	153*	4822	40.86	16	25	60
P.S.P.Handscomb	22	20	1	117	632	33.26	1	4	14
J.R.Hazlewood	47	15	12	11*	39	13.00	–	–	13
T.M.Head	42	39	2	128	1273	34.40	1	10	12
M.C.Henriques	11	10	1	18	81	9.00	–	–	4
U.T.Khawaja	40	39	2	104	1554	42.00	2	12	13
M.Labuschagne	6	5	–	108	249	49.80	1	1	1
C.A.Lynn	4	4	–	44	75	18.75	–	–	3
N.M.Lyon	29	14	10	30	77	19.25	–	–	7
M.R.Marsh	56	52	9	102*	1512	35.16	1	11	27
S.E.Marsh	73	72	4	151	2773	40.77	7	15	22
G.J.Maxwell	110	100	11	102	2877	32.32	1	19	65
M.G.Neser	2	2	–	6	8	4.00	–	–	–
J.A.Richardson	13	8	3	29	92	18.40	–	–	4
K.W.Richardson	25	12	7	24*	75	15.00	–	–	7
D.J.M.Short	7	7	1	69	206	34.33	–	1	1
P.M.Siddle	20	6	3	10*	31	10.33	–	–	1
S.P.D.Smith	124	109	12	164	4148	42.76	9	25	66
B.Stanlake	7	5	2	2	4	1.33	–	–	1
M.A.Starc	90	50	18	52*	362	11.31	–	1	25
M.P.Stoinis	41	38	7	146*	1050	33.87	1	6	12
A.J.Turner	6	5	1	84*	142	35.50	–	1	2
M.S.Wade	94	80	11	100*	1777	25.75	1	10	108/9
D.A.Warner	122	120	4	179	5200	45.61	18	20	55
A.Zampa	54	24	7	22	117	6.88	–	–	11

AUSTRALIA – BOWLING

	O	M	R	W	Avge	Best	4wI	R/Over
S.A.Abbott	5	0	25	1	25.00	1-25	–	5.00
A.C.Agar	109	3	619	10	61.90	2-48	–	5.67
J.P.Behrendorff	98.3	7	517	16	32.31	5-44	1	5.24
D.T.Christian	121.1	4	595	20	29.75	5-31	1	4.91
M.J.Cosgrove	5	0	13	1	13.00	1- 1	–	2.60
N.M.Coulter-Nile	279.4	10	1555	52	29.90	4-48	1	5.56
P.J.Cummins	552.3	33	2868	102	28.11	5-70	6	5.19
J.P.Faulkner	535.1	12	2962	96	30.85	4-32	4	5.53
A.J.Finch	47.2	0	259	4	64.75	1- 2	–	5.47
J.R.Hazlewood	411.5	27	1966	76	25.86	6-52	4	4.77
T.M.Head	127.3	0	737	12	61.41	2-22	–	5.78
M.C.Henriques	59	1	306	7	43.71	3-32	–	5.18
M.Labuschagne	4	0	36	0	–	–	–	9.00
N.M.Lyon	271	11	1334	29	46.00	4-44	1	4.92
M.R.Marsh	298.5	6	1671	44	37.97	5-33	2	5.59
G.J.Maxwell	449.4	9	2525	50	50.50	4-46	2	5.61
M.G.Neser	16.4	1	120	2	60.00	2-46	–	7.20
J.A.Richardson	118	11	690	24	28.75	4-26	1	5.84
K.W.Richardson	218.4	11	1240	39	31.79	5-68	1	5.67
D.J.M.Short	15	0	114	0	–	–	–	7.60
P.M.Siddle	150.1	10	743	17	43.70	3-55	–	4.94
S.P.D.Smith	178.2	1	963	28	34.39	3-16	–	5.40
B.Stanlake	59	3	324	7	46.28	3-35	–	5.49
M.A.Starc	767.4	39	3923	178	22.03	6-28	18	5.11
M.P.Stoinis	235.4	2	1446	33	43.81	3-16	–	6.13
D.A.Warner	1	0	8	0	–	–	–	8.00
A.Zampa	473.2	5	2651	73	36.31	4-43	1	5.60

SOUTH AFRICA – BATTING AND FIELDING

	M	I	NO	HS	Runs	Avge	100	50	Ct/St
K.J.Abbott	28	13	4	23	76	8.44	–	–	7
H.M.Amla	181	178	14	159	8113	49.46	27	39	87
T.Bavuma	6	6	–	113	335	55.83	1	1	4
F.Behardien	59	49	14	70	1074	30.68	–	6	27
Q.de Kock	121	121	6	178	5135	44.65	15	25	164/9
M.de Lange	4	–	–	–	–	–	–	–	–
F.du Plessis	143	136	20	185	5507	47.47	12	35	81
J.P.Duminy	199	179	40	150*	5117	36.81	4	27	82
D.M.Dupavillon	1	–	–	–	–	–	–	–	–
B.C.Fortuin	1	–	–	–	–	–	–	–	–
B.E.Hendricks	7	2	1	3	5	5.00	–	–	2
R.R.Hendricks	21	21	2	102	507	26.68	1	2	13
Imran Tahir	107	36	16	29	157	7.85	–	–	25
C.A.Ingram	31	29	3	124	843	32.42	3	5	12
H.Klaasen	17	16	4	123*	493	41.08	1	3	17/3
K.A.Maharaj	7	3	–	17	27	9.00	–	–	1
J.N.Malan	3	3	1	129*	152	76.00	1	–	3
A.K.Markram	26	24	1	67*	643	27.95	–	2	12
D.A.Miller	132	114	34	139	3231	40.38	5	14	61
M.Morkel	114	45	17	32*	239	8.53	–	–	29
C.H.Morris	42	27	4	62	467	20.30	–	1	9
P.W.A.Mulder	10	8	3	19*	74	14.80	–	–	4
L.T.Ngidi	26	9	6	19*	47	15.66	–	–	8
A.A.Nortje	7	2	1	8	9	9.00	–	–	2
D.Olivier	2	–	–	–	–	–	–	–	–
W.D.Parnell	65	38	14	56	508	21.16	–	1	12
D.Paterson	4	–	–	–	–	–	–	–	2
A.L.Phehlukwayo	58	34	15	69*	563	29.63	–	1	13
V.D.Philander	30	19	7	30*	151	12.58	–	–	6
D.Pretorius	22	10	1	50	135	15.00	–	1	6
K.Rabada	75	28	12	31*	259	16.18	–	–	22
R.R.Rossouw	36	35	3	132	1239	38.71	3	5	22
T.Shamsi	22	3	2	0*	0	0.00	–	–	5
L.L.Sipamla	4	1	1	10*	10	–	–	–	1
J.T.Smuts	5	4	1	84	163	54.33	–	1	2
D.W.Steyn †	123	49	12	60	361	9.75	–	1	28
H.E.van der Dussen	21	16	6	95	707	70.70	–	7	9
R.E.van der Merwe ‡	13	7	3	12	39	9.75	–	–	3
D.Wiese	6	6	1	41*	102	20.40	–	–	–
K.Verreynne	3	3	–	50	101	33.66	–	1	3

SOUTH AFRICA – BOWLING

	O	M	R	W	Avge	Best	4wI	R/Over
K.J.Abbott	217.1	13	1051	34	30.91	4-21	1	4.83
F.Behardien	124.4	2	719	14	51.35	3-19	–	5.76
M.de Lange	34.5	1	198	10	19.80	4-46	1	5.68
F.du Plessis	32	0	189	2	94.50	1- 8	–	5.90
J.P.Duminy	585.3	9	3143	69	45.55	4-16	1	5.36
D.M.Dupavillon	6	0	21	1	21.00	1-21	–	3.50
B.E.Hendricks	39	1	211	5	42.20	3-59	–	5.41
R.R.Hendricks	7	0	47	1	47.00	1-13	–	6.71
Imran Tahir	923.3	38	4297	173	24.83	7-45	10	4.65
C.A.Ingram	1	0	17	0	–	–	–	17.00
H.Klaasen	3	0	19	0	–	–	–	6.33
K.A.Maharaj	61.1	0	312	7	44.57	3-25	–	5.10
A.K.Markram	20	0	132	3	44.00	2-18	–	6.60
M.Morkel	930	45	4595	180	25.52	5-21	9	4.94

	O	M	R	W	Avge	Best	4wI	R/Over
C.H.Morris	315.4	10	1756	48	36.58	4-31	2	5.56
P.W.A.Mulder	53	0	308	8	38.50	2-59	–	5.81
L.T.Ngidi	205	15	1140	53	21.50	6-58	3	5.56
A.A.Nortje	55.4	1	283	14	20.21	3-57	–	5.08
D.Olivier	19	0	124	3	41.33	2-73	–	6.52
W.D.Parnell	485.1	20	2738	94	29.12	5-48	5	5.64
D.Paterson	34.5	0	217	4	54.25	3-44	–	6.22
A.L.Phehlukwayo	383.1	15	2151	69	31.17	4-22	3	5.61
V.D.Philander	213.1	20	986	41	24.04	4-12	2	4.62
D.Pretorius	170.2	9	813	29	28.03	3- 5	–	4.77
K.Rabada	640.2	42	3199	117	27.34	6-16	7	4.99
R.R.Rossouw	7.3	0	44	1	44.00	1-17	–	5.86
T.Shamsi	186.3	4	993	26	38.19	4-33	1	5.32
L.L.Sipamla	24.2	1	122	2	61.00	1-40	–	5.01
J.T.Smuts	22	1	97	3	32,33	2-42	–	4.40
D.W.Steyn	1032.3	69	5045	194	26.00	6-39	7	4.88
R.E.van der Merwe	117.3	2	561	17	33.00	3-27	–	4.77
D.Wiese	49	0	316	9	35.11	3-50	–	6.44

† D.W.Steyn has also made 2 appearances for an Africa XI.
‡ R.E.van der Merwe has also made 2 appearances for Netherlands (see below).

WEST INDIES – BATTING AND FIELDING

	M	I	NO	HS	Runs	Avge	100	50	Ct/St
F.A.Allen	14	12	3	51	143	15.88	–	1	6
S.W.Ambris	13	12	2	148	447	44.70	1	2	2
D.Bishoo	42	25	10	29*	164	10.93	–	–	7
C.R.Brathwaite	44	37	3	101	559	16.44	1	1	11
D.M.Bravo	113	108	13	124	2902	30.54	3	18	34
J.D.Campbell	6	5	–	179	248	49.60	1	–	–
J.L.Carter	33	28	3	54	581	23.24	–	3	7
R.L.Chase	30	23	3	94	520	26.00	–	2	11
S.S.Cottrell	35	17	10	17	84	12.00	–	–	19
M.L.Cummins	11	3	1	5	10	5.00	–	–	4
S.O.Dowrich	1	1	–	6	6	6.00	–	–	–
F.H.Edwards	50	22	14	13	73	9.12	–	–	4
S.T.Gabriel	25	16	9	12*	24	3.42	–	–	1
C.H.Gayle †	298	291	17	215	10425	38.04	25	53	123
C.Hemraj	6	6	–	32	82	13.66	–	–	2
S.O.Hetmyer	45	42	3	139	1430	36.66	5	4	18
J.O.Holder	115	92	19	99*	1821	24.94	–	9	50
S.D.Hope	78	73	10	170	3289	52.20	9	17	83/10
A.S.Joseph	28	13	7	29*	121	20.16	–	–	9
B.A.King	4	4	–	39	97	24.25	–	–	3
E.Lewis	51	48	3	176*	1610	35.77	3	8	17
S.P.Narine	65	45	12	36	363	11.00	–	–	14
A.R.Nurse	54	40	14	44	502	19.30	–	–	15
K.M.A.Paul	19	13	4	46	214	23.77	–	–	10
K.Pierre	3	2	–	21	39	19.50	–	–	–
K.A.Pollard	113	104	8	119	2496	26.00	3	10	61
N.Pooran	25	23	4	118	932	49.05	1	7	8/1
K.O.A.Powell	46	44	–	83	1005	22.84	–	9	14
R.Powell	34	31	3	101	670	23.92	1	2	14
R.Rampaul	92	40	11	86*	362	12.48	–	1	14
R.A.Reifer	2	1	–	7	7	7.00	–	–	–
K.A.J.Roach	92	57	34	34	308	13.39	–	–	21

	M	I	NO	HS	Runs	Avge	100	50	Ct/St
A.D.Russell	56	47	9	92*	1034	27.21	–	4	11
M.N.Samuels	207	196	26	133*	5606	32.97	10	30	50
R.Shepherd	5	3	–	8	15	5.00	–	–	2
J.E.Taylor	90	42	9	43*	278	8.42	–	–	20
O.R.Thomas	20	10	5	6*	13	2.60	–	–	–
H.R.Walsh ‡	9	4	2	46*	72	36.00	–	–	2
K.O.K.Williams	8	5	4	16*	19	19.00	–	–	–

WEST INDIES – BOWLING

	O	M	R	W	Avge	Best	4wI	R/Over
F.A.Allen	66	0	397	4	99.25	2-40	–	6.01
D.Bishoo	337	8	1668	38	43.89	3-30	–	4.94
C.R.Brathwaite	304.1	11	1766	43	41.06	5-27	3	5.80
J.D.Campbell	1	0	13	0	–	–	–	13.00
R.L.Chase	148.5	3	719	15	47.93	3-30	–	4.83
J.L.Carter	22.4	0	160	4	40.00	2-14	–	7.05
S.S.Cottrell	268	10	1577	49	32.18	5-46	3	5.88
M.L.Cummins	75	3	474	9	52.66	3-82	–	6.32
F.H.Edwards	356.2	23	1812	60	30.20	6-22	2	5.08
S.T.Gabriel	191.2	6	1134	33	34.36	3-17	–	5.92
C.H.Gayle	1229.3	38	5868	167	35.13	5-46	4	4.77
C.Hemraj	1.1	0	9	0	–	–	–	7.71
J.O.Holder	891.1	48	4948	136	36.38	5-27	6	5.55
A.S.Joseph	232.1	8	1372	48	28.58	5-56	5	5.90
S.P.Narine	590	35	2435	92	26.46	6-27	6	4.12
A.R.Nurse	397.2	6	2125	49	43.36	4-51	2	5.34
K.M.A.Paul	145.4	3	881	23	38.30	3-44	–	6.04
K.Pierre	26	0	158	1	158.00	1-50	–	6.07
K.A.Pollard	364.4	4	2105	53	39.71	3-27	–	5.77
R.Powell	40.5	0	243	3	81.00	1- 7	–	5.95
R.Rampaul	672.1	33	3434	117	29.35	5-49	10	5.10
R.A.Reifer	8.5	0	54	2	27.00	2-23	–	6.11
K.A.J.Roach	743.1	53	3763	124	30.34	6-27	6	5.06
A.D.Russell	381.4	14	2229	70	31.84	4-35	5	5.84
M.N.Samuels	848.3	23	4127	89	46.37	3-12	–	4.86
R.Shepherd	38.2	3	174	4	43.50	2-32	–	4.53
J.E.Taylor	723.3	35	3780	128	29.53	5-48	4	5.22
O.R.Thomas	128.3	1	866	27	32.07	5-21	2	6.73
H.R.Walsh	61.4	0	322	12	26.83	4-36	1	5.22
K.O.K.Williams	55	0	293	9	32.55	4-43	1	5.32

† C.H.Gayle has also made 3 appearances for an ICC World XI.
‡ H.R.Walsh has also made 1 appearance for the USA v PNG.

NEW ZEALAND – BATTING AND FIELDING

	M	I	NO	HS	Runs	Avge	100	50	Ct/St
C.J.Anderson	49	45	5	131*	1109	27.72	1	4	11
T.D.Astle	9	5	2	49	79	26.33	–	–	2
H.K.Bennett	19	7	5	4*	10	5.00	–	–	3
T.A.Blundell	2	2	–	22	31	15.50	–	–	1
T.A.Boult	89	39	23	21*	154	9.62	–	–	30
D.A.J.Bracewell	19	12	2	57	158	15.80	–	1	3
M.S.Chapman	6	6	1	124*	161	32.20	1	–	1
C.de Grandhomme	41	32	7	74*	697	27.88	–	4	14
L.H.Ferguson	36	15	7	19	62	7.75	–	–	10
M.J.Guptill	182	179	19	237*	6803	42.51	16	37	90

	M	I	NO	HS	Runs	Avge	100	50	Ct/St
M.J.Henry	52	21	7	48*	211	15.07	–	–	17
K.A.Jamieson	2	1	1	25*	25	–	–	–	2
T.W.M.Latham	98	91	10	137	2658	32.81	4	16	81/7
C.Munro	57	53	2	87	1271	24.92	–	8	22
J.D.S.Neesham	62	53	10	97*	1278	29.72	–	6	23
H.M.Nicholls	48	46	10	124*	1319	36.63	1	11	17
J.S.Patel	43	15	8	34	95	13.57	–	–	13
H.D.Rutherford	4	4	–	11	15	3.75	–	–	2
M.J.Santner	71	55	22	67	910	27.57	–	2	27
T.L.Seifert	3	2	–	22	33	16.50	–	–	7/1
I.S.Sodhi	32	13	2	24	67	6.09	–	–	7
T.G.Southee	143	86	32	55	679	12.57	–	1	39
L.R.P.L.Taylor	231	215	39	181*	8570	48.69	21	51	138
B.J.Watling	28	25	2	96*	573	24.91	–	5	20
K.S.Williamson	150	143	14	148	6154	47.70	13	39	60

NEW ZEALAND – BOWLING

	O	M	R	W	Avge	Best	4wI	R/Over
C.J.Anderson	247.3	10	1502	60	25.03	5-63	3	6.06
T.D.Astle	45	1	246	10	24.60	3-33	–	5.46
H.K.Bennett	148.4	5	820	33	24.84	4-16	3	5.51
T.A.Boult	814	58	4111	164	25.06	7-34	12	5.05
D.A.J.Bracewell	155.2	15	798	23	34.69	4-55	1	5.13
C.de Grandhomme	237	9	1151	27	42.62	3-26	–	4.85
L.H.Ferguson	317	6	1719	67	25.65	5-45	3	5.42
M.J.Guptill	18.1	0	98	4	24.50	2- 6	–	5.39
M.J.Henry	450.3	27	2437	92	26.48	5-30	9	5.40
K.A.Jamieson	20	1	95	3	31.66	2-42	–	4.75
C.Munro	92	1	481	7	68.71	2-10	–	5.22
J.D.S.Neesham	320.5	4	1968	61	32.26	5-31	3	6.13
J.S.Patel	335.4	9	1691	49	34.51	3-11	–	5.03
M.J.Santner	533.1	12	2627	69	38.07	5-50	1	4.92
I.S.Sodhi	262	9	1457	40	36.42	4-58	1	5.56
T.G.Southee	1199.1	74	6558	190	34.51	7-33	7	5.46
L.R.P.L.Taylor	7	0	35	0	–	–	–	5.00
K.S.Williamson	244.3	2	1310	37	35.40	4-22	1	5.35

INDIA – BATTING AND FIELDING

	M	I	NO	HS	Runs	Avge	100	50	Ct/St
M.A.Agarwal	3	3	–	32	36	12.00	–	–	7
K.K.Ahmed	11	3	1	5	9	4.50	–	–	1
J.J.Bumrah	64	15	10	10*	19	3.80	–	–	17
Y.S.Chahal	52	9	3	18*	49	8.16	–	–	15
D.L.Chahar	3	2	1	12	18	18.00	–	–	–
S.Dhawan	136	133	7	143	5688	45.14	17	29	62
M.S.Dhoni †	347	294	83	183*	10599	50.23	9	73	318/120
S.Dube	1	1	–	9	9	9.00	–	–	–
S.S.Iyer	18	16	1	103	748	49.86	1	8	8
R.A.Jadeja	165	110	38	87	2296	31.88	–	12	58
K.M.Jadhav	73	52	19	120	1389	42.09	2	6	33
K.D.Karthik	94	79	21	79	1752	30.20	–	9	64/7
V.Kohli	248	239	39	183	11867	59.33	43	58	128
Kuldeep Yadav	60	21	12	19	118	13.11	–	–	7
B.Kumar	114	52	15	53*	126	14.21	–	1	27
Mohammed Shami	77	36	17	25	147	7.73	–	–	27
Mohammed Siraj	1	–	–	–	–	–	–	–	–

289

	M	I	NO	HS	Runs	Avge	100	50	Ct/St
M.K.Pandey	26	21	7	104*	492	35.14	1	2	7
H.H.Pandya	54	38	6	83	957	29.90	–	4	22
R.R.Pant	16	14	–	71	374	26.71	–	1	8/1
K.L.Rahul	32	31	5	112	1239	47.65	4	7	13/2
A.T.Rayudu	55	50	14	124*	1694	47.05	3	10	17
N.A.Saini	5	2	1	45	53	53.00	–	–	3
V.Shankar	12	8	1	46	223	31.85	–	–	7
R.G.Sharma	224	217	32	264	9115	49.27	29	43	77
P.P.Shaw	3	3	–	40	84	28.00	–	–	–
Shubman Gill	2	2	–	9	16	8.00	–	–	–
S.N.Thakur	11	6	2	22*	77	19.25	–	–	3

INDIA – BOWLING

	O	M	R	W	Avge	Best	4wI	R/Over
K.K.Ahmed	80	2	465	15	31.00	3-13	–	5.81
J.J.Bumrah	557.4	38	2541	104	24.43	5-27	6	4.55
Y.S.Chahal	463.1	13	2351	91	25.83	6-42	4	5.07
D.L.Chahar	21	0	129	2	64.50	1-37	–	6.14
M.S.Dhoni	6	0	31	1	31.00	1-14	–	5.16
S.Dube	7.5	0	68	0	–	–	–	8.68
S.S.Iyer	2	0	15	0	–	–	–	7.50
R.A.Jadeja	1396.1	50	6839	187	36.57	5-36	8	4.89
K.M.Jadhav	197.5	1	1020	27	37.77	3-23	–	5.15
V.Kohli	106.5	1	665	4	166.25	1-15	–	6.22
Kuldeep Yadav	532	12	2721	104	26.16	6-25	5	5.11
B.Kumar	908.3	68	4568	132	34.60	5-42	5	5.02
Mohammed Shami	655	39	3661	144	25.42	5-69	10	5.58
Mohammed Siraj	10	0	76	0	–	–	–	7.60
H.H.Pandya	394.4	5	2195	54	40.64	3-31	–	5.56
A.T.Rayudu	20.1	1	124	3	41.33	1-5	–	6.14
N.A.Saini	48	0	301	5	60.20	2-58	–	6.27
V.Shankar	38.5	0	210	4	52.50	2-15	–	5.40
R.G.Sharma	98.5	2	515	8	64.37	2-27	–	5.21
S.N.Thakur	87	1	609	12	50.75	4-52	1	7.00

† *M.S.Dhoni also made 3 appearances for an Asia XI.*

PAKISTAN – BATTING AND FIELDING

	M	I	NO	HS	Runs	Avge	100	50	Ct/St
Abid Ali	4	4	–	112	191	47.75	1	1	3
Asif Ali	18	14	1	52	361	27.76	–	3	5
Babar Azam	74	72	10	125*	3359	54.17	11	15	36
Faheem Ashraf	23	15	2	28	162	12.46	–	–	5
Fakhar Zaman	46	46	4	210*	1958	46.61	4	13	21
Haris Sohail	41	40	5	130	1614	46.11	2	13	17
Hasan Ali	53	29	9	59	280	14.00	–	2	12
Hussain Talat	1	1	–	2	2	2.00	–	–	–
Iftikhar Ahmed	4	4	2	32*	68	34.00	–	–	3
Imad Wasim	53	39	16	63*	952	41.39	–	5	12
Imam-ul-Haq	37	37	5	151	1723	53.84	7	6	7
Junaid Khan	76	31	17	25	68	4.85	–	–	8
Mohammad Abbas	3	–	–	–	–	–	–	–	–
Mohammad Amir	61	30	10	73*	363	18.15	–	2	8
Mohammad Hafeez	218	216	15	140*	6614	32.90	11	38	85
Mohammad Hasnain	5	2	–	28	28	14.00	–	–	1
Mohammad Nawaz	15	12	3	53	199	22.11	–	–	5

	M	I	NO	HS	Runs	Avge	100	50	Ct/St
Mohammad Rizwan	32	28	7	115	705	33.57	2	3	29/1
Saad Ali	2	2	–	7	11	5.50	–	–	
Sarfraz Ahmed	116	90	22	105	2302	33.85	2	11	116/24
Shadab Khan	43	22	9	54	337	25.92	–	3	8
Shaheen Shah Afridi	19	8	6	19*	42	21.00	–	–	2
Shan Masood	5	5	–	50	111	22.20	–	1	1
Shoaib Malik	287	258	40	143	7534	34.55	9	44	98
Umar Akmal	121	110	17	102*	3194	34.34	2	20	77/13
Usman Khan	17	4	1	6	6	2.00	–	–	3
Wahab Riaz	89	64	15	54*	680	13.87	–	2	27
Yasir Shah	25	13	6	32*	127	13.59	–	–	6

PAKISTAN – BOWLING

	O	M	R	W	Avge	Best	4wI	R/Over
Asif Ali	0.5	0	9	0	–	–	–	10.80
Faheem Ashraf	150.2	6	744	20	37.20	5-22	1	4.94
Fakhar Zaman	22.3	0	111	1	111.00	1-19	–	4.93
Haris Sohail	107	0	613	11	55.72	3-45	–	5.72
Hasan Ali	424.4	14	2381	82	29.03	5-34	4	5.60
Hussain Talat	2	0	16	0	–	–	–	8.00
Iftikhar Ahmed	23	2	101	1	101.00	1-31	–	4.39
Imad Wasim	385.3	8	1865	42	44.40	5-14	1	4.83
Junaid Khan	600.1	33	3216	110	29.23	4-12	4	5.35
Mohammad Abbas	27	0	153	1	153.00	1-44	–	5.66
Mohammad Amir	502.1	34	2400	81	29.62	5-30	2	4.77
Mohammad Hafeez	1288.5	48	5400	139	38.84	4-41	1	4.18
Mohammad Hasnain	41	0	303	5	60.60	2-52	–	7.39
Mohammad Nawaz	116.3	2	607	17	35.70	4-42	1	5.21
Sarfraz Ahmed	2	0	15	0	–	–	–	7.50
Shadab Khan	348	7	1750	59	29.66	4-28	3	5.02
Shaheen Shah Afridi	154	7	847	40	21.17	6-35	5	5.50
Shoaib Malik	1326.2	38	6192	158	39.18	4-19	1	4.66
Usman Khan	128	8	633	34	18.61	5-34	5	4.94
Wahab Riaz	701.3	20	4011	115	34.87	5-46	5	5.71
Yasir Shah	215.3	4	1150	24	47.91	6-26	2	5.33

SRI LANKA – BATTING AND FIELDING

	M	I	NO	HS	Runs	Avge	100	50	Ct/St
P.V.D.Chameera	23	14	7	19*	93	13.28	–	–	4
L.D.Chandimal	146	132	21	111	3599	32.42	4	22	59/7
D.M.de Silva	45	42	7	84	895	25.57	–	5	20
P.W.H.de Silva	15	13	3	42*	190	19.00	–	–	5
D.P.D.N.Dickwella	52	49	1	116	1571	32.72	2	9	38/9
A.N.P.R.Fernando	45	23	16	7	29	4.14	–	–	6
B.O.P.Fernando	6	6	–	49	128	21.33	–	–	1
W.I.A.Fernando	18	18	–	127	653	36.27	2	3	6
D.A.S.Gunaratne	31	25	4	114*	575	27.38	1	1	10
M.D.Gunathilleke	38	37	3	133	1249	34.69	2	8	12
G.S.N.F.G.Jayasuriya	12	10	1	96	195	21.66	–	1	1
F.D.M.Karunaratne	31	27	2	97	683	27.32	–	5	10
C.B.R.L.S.Kumara	13	6	3	7*	17	5.66	–	–	3
R.A.S.Lakmal	85	48	22	26	244	9.38	–	–	19
S.L.Malinga	226	119	36	56	567	6.83	–	1	31
A.D.Mathews	217	187	48	139*	5830	41.94	3	40	53
B.K.G.Mendis	76	74	3	119	2167	30.52	2	17	39
B.M.A.J.Mendis	58	44	10	72	636	18.70	–	1	13

	M	I	NO	HS	Runs	Avge	100	50	Ct/St
P.H.K.D.Mendis	2	2	1	9	17	17.00	–	–	–
A.K.Perera	6	4	1	31	52	13.00	–	–	1
M.D.K.J.Perera	101	96	5	135	2825	31.04	5	14	43/3
M.K.P.A.D.Perera	36	27	5	50*	283	12.86	–	1	14
N.L.T.C.Perera	164	131	16	140	2316	20.13	1	10	62
P.A.R.P.Perera	2	2	–	33	33	16.50	–	–	1
S.Prasanna	40	37	3	95	421	12.38	–	2	7
C.A.K.Rajitha	9	3	2	0*	0	0.00	–	–	1
M.B.Ranasinghe	1	1	–	36	36	36.00	–	–	–
W.S.R.Samarawickrama	7	7	–	54	138	19.71	–	1	1
P.A.D.L.R.Sandakan	24	14	4	6	34	3.40	–	–	3
M.D.Shanaka	22	19	1	68	468	26.00	–	3	3
T.A.M.Siriwardana	27	24	1	66	516	22.43	–	3	6
W.U.Tharanga †	234	222	17	174*	6941	33.85	15	37	50
H.D.R.L.Thirimanne	127	106	14	139*	3194	34.71	4	21	38
I.Udana	18	15	3	78	190	15.83	–	1	5
J.D.F.Vandersay	12	7	1	25	71	11.83	–	–	2

SRI LANKA – BOWLING

	O	M	R	W	Avge	Best	4wI	R/Over
P.V.D.Chameera	149.1	7	796	19	41.89	3-20	–	5.33
D.M.de Silva	179.2	1	928	22	42.18	3-32	–	5.17
P.W.H.de Silva	97.1	3	547	17	32.17	3-15	–	5.62
A.N.P.R.Fernando	353.1	18	2099	57	36.82	4-31	2	5.94
B.O.P.Fernando	2	0	16	0	–	–	–	8.00
D.A.S.Gunaratne	139	3	723	22	32.86	3-10	–	5.20
M.D.Gunathilleke	51	1	296	6	49.33	3-48	–	5.80
G.S.N.F.G.Jayasuriya	52	1	277	3	92.33	1-15	–	5.32
F.D.M.Karunaratne	2.4	0	18	0	–	–	–	6.75
C.B.R.L.S.Kumara	90.4	0	623	13	47.92	2-26	–	6.87
R.A.S.Lakmal	637.2	35	3478	107	32.50	4-13	3	5.45
S.L.Malinga	1822.4	103	9760	338	28.87	6-38	19	5.35
A.D.Mathews	865.1	54	4003	120	33.35	6-20	3	4.62
B.K.G.Mendis	3.2	0	28	0	–	–	–	8.40
B.M.A.J.Mendis	234	2	1204	28	43.00	3-15	–	5.14
P.H.K.D.Mendis	14	0	79	1	79.00	1-45	–	5.64
A.K.Perera	6	0	33	0	–	–	–	5.50
M.K.P.A.D.Perera	295.3	5	1506	51	29.52	6-29	4	5.09
N.L.T.C.Perera	971.2	28	5668	172	32.95	6-44	9	5.83
S.Prasanna	324.1	9	1767	32	55.21	3-32	–	5.45
C.A.K.Rajitha	58.5	0	379	9	42.11	2-17	–	6.44
P.A.D.L.R.Sandakan	179.2	0	1161	20	58.05	4-52	1	6.47
M.D.Shanaka	47	0	274	10	27.40	5-43	1	5.82
T.A.M.Siriwardana	100.1	2	547	9	60.77	2-27	–	5.46
H.D.R.L.Thirimanne	17.2	0	94	3	31.33	2-36	–	5.42
I.Udana	130.3	1	810	16	50.62	3-82	–	6.20
J.D.F.Vandersay	81.5	2	480	11	43.63	3-50	–	5.86

† W.U.Tharanga also made 1 appearance for an Asia XI.

A.N.P.R.Fernando is also known as N.Pradeep; D.S.M.Kumara is also known as D.S.K.Madushanka; M.K.P.A.D.Perera is also known as A.Dananjaya; M.B.Ranasinghe is also known as M.Bhanuka.

ZIMBABWE – BATTING AND FIELDING

	M	I	NO	HS	Runs	Avge	100	50	Ct/St
R.P.Burl	18	15	3	53	243	20.25	–	1	8
R.W.Chakabva	41	38	2	78*	646	17.94	–	1	29/4
B.B.Chari	11	11	–	39	150	13.63	–	–	3/1
T.L.Chatara	70	45	20	23	165	6.60	–	–	6
C.J.Chibhabha	104	104	2	99	2399	23.51	–	16	33
C.R.Ervine	93	90	11	130*	2571	32.54	3	15	42
K.M.Jarvis	49	33	10	37	222	9.65	–	–	11
T.S.Kamunhukamwe	6	6	–	51	93	15.50	–	1	1
W.N.Madhevere	3	3	–	52	129	43.00	–	1	1
T.Maruma	21	18	1	35	196	11.52	–	–	12
H.Masakadza	209	208	4	178*	5658	27.73	5	34	71
B.A.Mavuta	7	5	1	20	52	13.00	–	–	2
S.F.Mire	47	47	–	112	955	20.31	1	3	12
P.J.Moor	49	45	5	58*	827	20.67	–	4	22/1
C.B.Mpofu	84	41	21	9*	57	2.85	–	–	11
C.T.Mumba	5	5	3	13	20	10.00	–	–	1
C.T.Mutombodzi	14	13	1	34	177	14.75	–	–	7
R.Mutumbami	36	34	2	74	618	19.31	–	3	24/5
B.Muzarabani	18	15	7	7	16	2.00	–	–	7
A.Ndlovu	2	–	–	–	–	–	–	–	–
Sikandar Raza	100	96	15	141	2801	34.58	3	16	40
B.R.M.Taylor	196	195	15	145*	6326	35.14	10	38	125/29
D.T.Tiripano	34	25	7	55*	343	19.05	–	1	4
C.K.Tshuma	2	1	–	0	0	0.00	–	–	–
S.C.Williams	133	129	18	129*	3761	33.88	3	31	50

ZIMBABWE – BOWLING

	O	M	R	W	Avge	Best	4wI	R/Over
R.P.Burl	35	1	207	7	29.57	4-32	1	5.91
T.L.Chatara	571.5	45	2905	95	30.57	4-33	1	5.08
C.J.Chibhabha	277.5	12	1615	35	46.14	4-25	1	5.81
K.M.Jarvis	393.4	23	2088	58	36.00	4-17	2	5.30
W.N.Madhevere	20	0	115	2	57.50	1-38	–	5.75
T.Maruma	37.3	1	230	4	57.50	2-50	–	6.13
H.Masakadza	307.2	5	1636	39	41.94	3-39	–	5.32
B.A.Mavuta	46	0	266	7	38.00	2-30	–	5.78
S.F.Mire	84.3	1	515	12	42.91	4-43	1	6.09
C.B.Mpofu	660	41	3581	93	38.50	6-52	3	5.42
C.T.Mumba	36.2	0	245	6	40.83	3-69	–	6.74
C.T.Mutombodzi	61.5	0	359	7	51.28	2-33	–	5.80
B.Muzarabani	131	4	733	18	40.72	4-47	1	5.59
A.Ndlovu	17	0	80	1	80.00	1-29	–	4.70
Sikandar Raza	501.2	20	2448	59	41.49	3-21	–	4.88
B.R.M.Taylor	66	0	406	9	45.11	3-54	–	6.15
D.T.Tiripano	226.2	12	1298	31	41.87	5-63	1	5.73
C.K.Tshuma	11	1	83	1	83.00	1-35	–	7.54
S.C.Williams	696	31	3381	71	47.61	4-43	1	4.85

BANGLADESH – BATTING AND FIELDING

	M	I	NO	HS	Runs	Avge	100	50	Ct/St
Abu Jayed	2	–	–	–	–	–	–	–	–
Afif Hossain	1	1	–	7	7	7.00	–	–	–
Al-Amin Hossain	15	7	5	2*	4	2.00	–	–	1
Anumul Haque	38	35	–	120	1052	30.05	3	3	10
Imrul Kayes	78	78	2	144	2434	32.02	4	16	21
Liton Das	36	36	3	176	1079	32.69	3	3	24/3

	M	I	NO	HS	Runs	Avge	100	50	Ct/St
Mahmudullah	188	163	42	128*	4070	33.63	3	21	64
Mashrafe Mortaza †	218	156	28	51*	1773	13.85	–	1	61
Mehedi Hasan	41	26	4	51	393	17.86	–	1	13
Mithun Ali	27	23	3	63	575	28.75	–	5	7
Mohammad Naim	1	–	–	–	–	–	–	–	2
Mohammad Saifuddin	22	13	4	51*	290	32.22	–	2	3
Mosaddek Hossain	35	30	10	52*	549	27.45	–	2	13
Mushfiqur Rahim	218	204	34	144	6174	36.31	7	38	181/44
Mustafizur Rahman	58	27	17	18*	78	7.80	–	–	12
Nazmul Hossain	5	5	–	29	55	11.00	–	–	2
Rubel Hossain	101	52	24	17	140	5.00	–	–	20
Sabbir Rahman	66	59	7	102	1333	26.34	1	6	37
Shafiul Islam	60	34	12	24*	134	6.09	–	–	8
Shakib Al Hasan	206	~194	29	134*	6323	37.86	9	47	50
Soumya Sarkar	55	54	3	127*	1728	33.88	2	11	33
Taijul Islam	9	5	1	39*	63	15.75	–	–	1
Tamim Iqbal	207	205	9	158	7202	36.74	13	47	54

BANGLADESH – BOWLING

	O	M	R	W	Avge	Best	4wI	R/Over
Abu Jayed	18	0	114	5	22.80	5-58	1	6.33
Afif Hossain	2	0	12	1	12.00	1-12	–	6.00
Al-Amin Hossain	110.3	7	608	22	27.63	4-51	2	5.50
Mahmudullah	688.4	14	3561	76	46.85	3- 4	–	5.17
Mashrafe Mortaza	1804.3	122	8785	269	32.65	6-26	8	4.86
Mehedi Hasan	349.1	10	1625	40	40.62	4-29	1	4.65
Mohammad Saifuddin	165.3	7	972	31	31.35	4-41	1	5.87
Mosaddek Hossain	150.2	1	787	14	56.21	3-13	–	5.23
Mustafizur Rahman	480.5	22	2512	109	23.04	6-43	8	5.22
Rubel Hossain	756.4	28	4300	126	34.12	6-26	8	5.68
Sabbir Rahman	51	0	345	3	115.00	1-12	–	6.76
Shafiul Islam	423.2	26	2529	70	36.12	4-21	4	5.97
Shakib Al Hasan	1752.5	83	7857	260	30.21	5-29	10	4.48
Soumya Sarkar	54	0	318	9	35.33	3-56	–	5.88
Taijul Islam	85	7	337	12	28.08	4-11	1	3.96
Tamim Iqbal	1	0	13	0	–	–	–	13.00

† *Mashrafe Mortaza also made 2 appearances for an Asia XI.*

IRELAND – BATTING AND FIELDING

	M	I	NO	HS	Runs	Avge	100	50	Ct/St
M.R.Adair	12	11	2	32	162	18.00	–	–	3
A.Balbirnie	67	64	4	145*	1910	31.83	5	9	20
J.Cameron-Dow	4	1	1	7*	7	–	–	–	2
G.J.Delany	2	2	–	19	33	16.50	–	–	–
G.H.Dockrell	87	57	22	62*	579	16.54	–	2	36
S.C.Getkate	3	2	1	16*	23	23.00	–	–	1
J.B.Little	4	2	–	9	9	4.50	–	–	–
A.R.McBrine	45	28	10	79	296	16.44	–	1	19
B.J.McCarthy	30	21	5	18	148	9.25	–	–	10
J.A.McCollum	9	9	–	73	185	20.55	–	2	1
E.J.G.Morgan	23	23	2	115	744	35.42	1	5	9
T.J.Murtagh	58	36	12	23*	188	7.83	–	–	16
K.J.O'Brien	145	133	17	142	3546	30.56	2	18	64
W.T.S.Porterfield	139	136	3	139	4091	30.75	11	17	64
S.W.Poynter	21	19	5	36	185	13.21	–	–	22/1

	M	I	NO	HS	Runs	Avge	100	50	Ct/St
W.B.Rankin †	68	32	20	18*	95	7.91	–	–	17
Simi Singh	18	17	1	45	242	15.12	–	–	10
P.R.Stirling	117	114	2	177	4121	36.79	8	24	45
L.J.Tucker	8	8	1	56	142	20.28	–	1	13/1
G.C.Wilson	105	99	12	113	2072	23.81	1	12	73/10
C.A.Young	14	7	2	11*	29	5.80	–	–	2

IRELAND – BOWLING

	O	M	R	W	Avge	Best	4wI	R/Over
M.R.Adair	92.3	3	598	16	37.37	4-19	1	6.46
A.Balbirnie	10	0	68	2	34.00	1-26	–	6.80
J.Cameron-Dow	31	0	151	5	30.20	3-32	–	4.87
G.J.Delany	2	0	33	0	–	–	–	16.50
G.H.Dockrell	705.2	31	3327	89	37.38	4-24	4	4.71
S.C.Getkate	27	2	120	6	20.00	2-30	–	4.44
J.B.Little	36	0	262	5	52.40	4-45	1	7.27
A.R.McBrine	367.5	20	1616	47	34.38	3-38	–	4.39
B.J.McCarthy	254.1	9	1483	55	26.96	5-46	3	5.83
T.J.Murtagh	503.2	45	2290	74	30.94	5-21	5	4.54
K.J.O'Brien	704	29	3672	113	32.49	4-13	5	5.21
W.B.Rankin	617	42	2955	106	27.87	4-15	4	4.78
Simi Singh	125	4	499	18	27.72	3-15	–	3.99
P.R.Stirling	398.4	8	1902	43	44.23	6-55	2	4.77
C.A.Young	118.3	1	620	28	22.14	5-46	1	5.23

† *W.B.Rankin also made 7 appearances for England.*

AFGHANISTAN – BATTING AND FIELDING

	M	I	NO	HS	Runs	Avge	100	50	Ct/St
Aftab Alam	27	17	10	16*	80	11.42	–	–	6
Asghar Stanikzai	111	105	9	101	2356	24.54	1	12	24
Dawlat Zadran	82	56	27	47*	513	17.68	–	–	16
Gulbadin Naib	65	56	8	82*	1041	21.68	–	5	12
Hamid Hassan	38	22	6	17	107	6.68	–	–	9
Hashmatullah Shahidi	39	39	6	97*	1062	32.18	–	9	9
Hazratullah Zazai	16	16	–	67	361	22.56	–	2	3
Ibrahim Zadran	1	1	–	2	2	2.00	–	–	1
Ikram Ali Khil	12	12	3	86	234	26.00	–	2	3/3
Javed Ahmadi	44	41	–	81	976	23.80	–	7	11
Mohammad Nabi	124	112	12	116	2782	27.82	1	15	55
Mohammad Shahzad	84	84	3	131*	2727	33.66	6	14	64/25
Mujeeb Zadran	40	21	10	15	69	6.27	–	–	6
Najibullah Zadran	67	62	9	104*	1586	29.92	1	11	37
Naveen-ul-Haq	4	3	2	8*	9	9.00	–	–	2
Noor Ali Zadran	51	50	1	114	1216	24.81	1	7	15
Rahmat Shah	73	69	2	114	2359	35.20	4	16	19
Rashid Khan	71	56	9	60*	905	19.25	–	4	22
Samiullah Shinwari	84	74	12	96	1811	29.20	–	11	21
Sayed Shirzad	2	1	–	25	25	25.00	–	–	–
Shapoor Zadran	44	27	17	17	67	6.70	–	–	5
Sharafuddin Ashraf	17	10	3	21	66	9.42	–	–	5
Yamin Ahmadzai	4	2	1	3*	3	3.00	–	–	2
Zahir Khan	1								

AFGHANISTAN – BOWLING

	O	M	R	W	Avge	Best	4wI	R/Over
Aftab Alam	209.3	14	1033	41	25.19	4-25	1	4.93
Asghar Stanikzai	23.1	1	91	3	30.33	1- 1	–	3.92
Dawlat Zadran	628.1	42	3423	115	29.76	4-22	3	5.44
Gulbadin Naib	365.4	11	1968	59	33.35	6-43	3	5.38
Hamid Hassan	289	24	1330	59	22.54	5-45	3	4.60
Hashmatullah Shahidi	3	0	25	0	–	–	–	8.33
Javed Ahmadi	66.2	0	319	9	35.44	4-37	1	4.80
Mohammad Nabi	986.3	39	4231	130	32.54	4-30	3	4.28
Mujeeb Zadran	358.5	29	1414	63	22.44	5-50	3	3.94
Najibullah Zadran	5	0	30	0	–	–	–	6.00
Naveen-ul-Haq	35.2	1	201	6	33.50	3-60	–	5.68
Rahmat Shah	87.2	2	504	14	36.00	5-32	1	5.77
Rashid Khan	593	26	2467	133	18.54	7-18	8	4.16
Samiullah Shinwari	351.5	10	1729	46	37.58	4-31	–	4.91
Sayed Shirzad	8	0	56	1	56.00	1-56	–	7.00
Shapoor Zadran	330.3	34	1589	43	36.95	4-24	2	4.80
Sharafuddin Ashraf	127.2	3	559	13	43.00	3-29	–	4.39
Yamin Ahmadzai	26.4	3	139	2	69.50	1-23	–	5.21
Zahir Khan	10	0	55	2	27.50	2-55	–	5.50

ASSOCIATES – BATTING AND FIELDING

	M	I	NO	HS	Runs	Avge	100	50	Ct/St
J.H.Davey (Scot)	31	28	6	64	497	22.59	–	2	10
B.D.Glover (Neth)	1	–	–	–	–	–	–	–	1
M.A.Jones (Scot)	8	8	–	87	281	35.12	–	3	3
F.J.Klaassen (Neth)	4	3	1	13	30	15.00	–	–	2
S.Lamichhane (Nepal)	10	8	2	28	78	13.00	–	–	2
H.G.Munsey (Scot)	25	25	3	61	562	25.54	–	2	11
R.A.J.Smith (Scot)	2	1	–	10	10	10.00	–	–	–
S.Snater (Neth)	2	2	–	12	12	6.00	–	–	3
T.B.Sole (Scot)	10	7	1	20	46	7.66	–	–	4
R.N.ten Doeschate (Neth)	33	32	9	119	1541	67.00	5	9	13
T.van der Gugten (Neth)	4	2	–	2	4	2.00	–	–	–
R.E.van der Merwe (Neth)	2	1	–	57	57	57.00	–	1	1
B.T.J.Wheal (Scot)	13	7	3	14	16	4.00	–	–	3
S.G.Whittingham (Scot)	5	4	2	3*	7	3.50	–	–	3

ASSOCIATES – BOWLING

	O	M	R	W	Avge	Best	4wI	R/Over
J.H.Davey	216.5	18	1082	49	22.08	3-8	3	4.99
B.D.Glover	10	0	37	1	37.00	1-37	–	3.70
F.J.Klaassen	40	3	150	10	15.00	3-30	–	3.75
S.Lamichhane	89.1	8	375	23	16.30	6-16	3	4.20
R.A.J.Smith	15	0	97	1	97.00	1-34	–	6.46
S.Snater	11.5	1	63	1	63.00	1-41	–	5.32
T.B.Sole	84	7	387	10	38.70	4-15	1	4.60
R.N.ten Doeschate	263.2	18	1327	55	24.12	4-31	3	5.03
T.van der Gugten	21	3	85	8	10.62	5-24	1	4.04
R.E.van der Merwe	14	0	97	1	97.00	1-57	–	6.92
B.T.J.Wheal	114.3	9	508	23	22.08	3-34	–	4.43
S.G.Whittingham	41.5	2	224	8	28.00	3-58	–	5.35

LIMITED-OVERS INTERNATIONALS RESULTS

1970-71 to 11 March 2020

This chart excludes all matches involving multinational teams.

	Opponents	Matches	Won													Tied	NR
			E	A	SA	WI	NZ	I	P	SL	Z	B	Ire	Afg	Ass		
England	Australia	149	62	82	–	–	–	–	–	–	–	–	–	–	–	2	3
	South Africa	63	28	–	30	–	–	–	–	–	–	–	–	–	–	1	4
	West Indies	102	52	–	–	44	–	–	–	–	–	–	–	–	–	–	6
	New Zealand	91	41	–	–	–	43	–	–	–	–	–	–	–	–	3	4
	India	100	42	–	–	–	–	53	–	–	–	–	–	–	–	2	3
	Pakistan	88	53	–	–	–	–	–	32	–	–	–	–	–	–	–	3
	Sri Lanka	75	36	–	–	–	–	–	–	36	–	–	–	–	–	1	2
	Zimbabwe	30	21	–	–	–	–	–	–	–	8	–	–	–	–	–	1
	Bangladesh	21	17	–	–	–	–	–	–	–	–	4	–	–	–	–	1
	Ireland	10	8	–	–	–	–	–	–	–	–	–	1	–	–	–	1
	Afghanistan	2	2	–	–	–	–	–	–	–	–	–	–	0	–	–	–
	Associates	15	13	–	–	–	–	–	–	–	–	–	–	–	1	–	1
Australia	South Africa	103	–	48	51	–	–	–	–	–	–	–	–	–	–	3	1
	West Indies	140	–	74	–	60	–	–	–	–	–	–	–	–	–	3	3
	New Zealand	137	–	91	–	–	39	–	–	–	–	–	–	–	–	–	7
	India	140	–	78	–	–	–	52	–	–	–	–	–	–	–	–	10
	Pakistan	104	–	68	–	–	–	–	32	–	–	–	–	–	–	1	3
	Sri Lanka	97	–	61	–	–	–	–	–	32	–	–	–	–	–	–	4
	Zimbabwe	30	–	27	–	–	–	–	–	–	2	–	–	–	–	–	1
	Bangladesh	21	–	19	–	–	–	–	–	–	–	1	–	–	–	–	1
	Ireland	5	–	4	–	–	–	–	–	–	–	–	0	–	–	–	1
	Afghanistan	3	–	3	–	–	–	–	–	–	–	–	–	0	–	–	–
	Associates	16	–	16	–	–	–	–	–	–	–	–	–	–	0	–	–
S Africa	West Indies	62	–	–	44	15	–	–	–	–	–	–	–	–	–	1	2
	New Zealand	71	–	–	41	–	25	–	–	–	–	–	–	–	–	–	5
	India	84	–	–	46	–	–	35	–	–	–	–	–	–	–	–	3
	Pakistan	79	–	–	50	–	–	–	28	–	–	–	–	–	–	–	1
	Sri Lanka	77	–	–	44	–	–	–	–	31	–	–	–	–	–	1	1
	Zimbabwe	41	–	–	38	–	–	–	–	–	2	–	–	–	–	–	1
	Bangladesh	21	–	–	17	–	–	–	–	–	–	4	–	–	–	–	–
	Ireland	5	–	–	5	–	–	–	–	–	–	–	0	–	–	–	–
	Afghanistan	1	–	–	1	–	–	–	–	–	–	–	–	0	–	–	–
	Associates	18	–	–	18	–	–	–	–	–	–	–	–	–	0	–	–
W Indies	New Zealand	65	–	–	–	30	28	–	–	–	–	–	–	–	–	–	7
	India	133	–	–	–	63	–	64	–	–	–	–	–	–	–	2	4
	Pakistan	134	–	–	–	71	–	–	60	–	–	–	–	–	–	3	–
	Sri Lanka	60	–	–	–	28	–	–	–	29	–	–	–	–	–	–	3
	Zimbabwe	48	–	–	–	36	–	–	–	–	10	–	–	–	–	1	1
	Bangladesh	38	–	–	–	21	–	–	–	–	–	15	–	–	–	–	2
	Ireland	12	–	–	–	10	–	–	–	–	–	–	1	–	–	–	1
	Afghanistan	9	–	–	–	5	–	–	–	–	–	–	–	3	–	–	1
	Associates	19	–	–	–	18	–	–	–	–	–	–	–	–	1	–	–
N Zealand	India	110	–	–	–	–	49	55	–	–	–	–	–	–	–	1	5
	Pakistan	107	–	–	–	–	48	–	55	–	–	–	–	–	–	1	3
	Sri Lanka	99	–	–	–	–	49	–	–	41	–	–	–	–	–	1	8
	Zimbabwe	38	–	–	–	–	27	–	–	–	9	–	–	–	–	1	1
	Bangladesh	35	–	–	–	–	25	–	–	–	–	10	–	–	–	–	–
	Ireland	4	–	–	–	–	3	–	–	–	–	–	0	–	–	–	1
	Afghanistan	2	–	–	–	–	2	–	–	–	–	–	–	0	–	–	–
	Associates	12	–	–	–	–	12	–	–	–	–	–	–	–	0	–	–
India	Pakistan	132	–	–	–	–	–	55	73	–	–	–	–	–	–	–	4
	Sri Lanka	159	–	–	–	–	–	91	–	56	–	–	–	–	–	1	11
	Zimbabwe	63	–	–	–	–	–	51	–	–	10	–	–	–	–	2	–
	Bangladesh	36	–	–	–	–	–	30	–	–	–	5	–	–	–	–	1
	Ireland	3	–	–	–	–	–	3	–	–	–	–	0	–	–	–	–
	Afghanistan	3	–	–	–	–	–	2	–	–	–	–	–	1	–	–	–
	Associates	24	–	–	–	–	–	22	–	–	–	–	–	–	2	–	–
Pakistan	Sri Lanka	155	–	–	–	–	–	–	92	58	–	–	–	–	–	1	4
	Zimbabwe	59	–	–	–	–	–	–	52	–	4	–	–	–	–	1	2

	Opponents	Matches	E	A	SA	WI	NZ	I	P (Won)	SL	Z	B	Ire	Afg	Ass	Tied	NR
	Bangladesh	37	–	–	–	–	–	–	32	–	–	5	–	–	–	–	–
	Ireland	7	–	–	–	–	–	–	5	–	–	–	1	–	–	1	–
	Afghanistan	4	–	–	–	–	–	–	4	–	–	–	–	0	–	–	–
	Associates	21	–	–	–	–	–	–	21	–	–	–	–	–	0	–	–
Sri Lanka	Zimbabwe	57	–	–	–	–	–	–	–	44	11	–	–	–	–	–	2
	Bangladesh	48	–	–	–	–	–	–	–	39	–	7	–	–	–	–	2
	Ireland	4	–	–	–	–	–	–	–	2	–	–	0	–	–	–	2
	Afghanistan	4	–	–	–	–	–	–	–	3	–	–	–	1	–	–	–
	Associates	17	–	–	–	–	–	–	–	16	–	–	–	–	1	–	–
Zimbabwe	Bangladesh	75	–	–	–	–	–	–	–	–	28	47	–	–	–	–	–
	Ireland	13	–	–	–	–	–	–	–	–	6	–	6	–	–	1	–
	Afghanistan	25	–	–	–	–	–	–	–	–	10	–	–	15	–	–	–
	Associates	50	–	–	–	–	–	–	–	–	38	–	–	–	9	1	2
Bangladesh	Ireland	10	–	–	–	–	–	–	–	–	–	7	2	–	–	–	1
	Afghanistan	8	–	–	–	–	–	–	–	–	–	5	–	3	–	–	–
	Associates	26	–	–	–	–	–	–	–	–	–	18	–	–	8	–	–
Ireland	Afghanistan	27	–	–	–	–	–	–	–	–	–	–	13	13	–	–	1
	Associates	56	–	–	–	–	–	–	–	–	–	–	43	–	9	2	2
Afghanistan	Associates	38	–	–	–	–	–	–	–	–	–	–	–	24	13	–	1
Associates	Associates	157	–	–	–	–	–	–	–	–	–	–	–	–	152	–	5
		4244	375	571	385	401	351	513	486	389	138	128	67	59	196	38	148

MERIT TABLE OF ALL L-O INTERNATIONALS

	Matches	Won	Lost	Tied	No Result	% Won (exc NR)
South Africa	625	385	216	6	18	63.42
Australia	945	571	331	9	34	62.67
India	987	513	424	9	41	54.22
Pakistan	927	486	413	8	20	53.58
England	746	375	334	9	28	52.22
West Indies	822	401	381	10	30	50.63
New Zealand	771	351	373	7	40	48.01
Afghanistan	126	59	63	1	3	47.96
Sri Lanka	852	389	421	5	37	47.73
Ireland	156	67	78	3	8	45.27
Bangladesh	376	128	241	–	7	34.68
Zimbabwe	529	138	373	7	11	26.64
Associate Members (v Full*)	312	44	259	3	6	14.37

* Results of games between two Associate Members and those involving multi-national sides are excluded from this list; Associate Members have participated in 469 LOIs, 157 LOIs being between Associate Members.

TEAM RECORDS

HIGHEST TOTALS

† Batting Second

481-6	(50 overs)	England v Australia	Nottingham	2018
444-3	(50 overs)	England v Pakistan	Nottingham	2016
443-9	(50 overs)	Sri Lanka v Netherlands	Amstelveen	2006
439-2	(50 overs)	South Africa v West Indies	Johannesburg	2014-15
438-9†	(49.5 overs)	South Africa v Australia	Johannesburg	2005-06
438-4	(50 overs)	South Africa v India	Mumbai	2015-16
434-4	(50 overs)	Australia v South Africa	Johannesburg	2005-06
418-5	(50 overs)	South Africa v Zimbabwe	Potchefstroom	2006-07
418-5	(50 overs)	India v West Indies	Indore	2011-12
418-6	(50 overs)	England v West Indies	St George's	2018-19

417-6	(50 overs)	Australia v Afghanistan	Perth	2014-15
414-7	(50 overs)	India v Sri Lanka	Rajkot	2009-10
413-5	(50 overs)	India v Bermuda	Port of Spain	2006-07
411-8†	(50 overs)	Sri Lanka v India	Rajkot	2009-10
411-4	(50 overs)	South Africa v Ireland	Canberra	2014-15
408-5	(50 overs)	South Africa v West Indies	Sydney	2014-15
408-9	(50 overs)	England v New Zealand	Birmingham	2015
404-5	(50 overs)	India v Sri Lanka	Kolkata	2014-15
402-2	(50 overs)	New Zealand v Ireland	Aberdeen	2008
401-3	(50 overs)	India v South Africa	Gwalior	2009-10
399-6	(50 overs)	South Africa v Zimbabwe	Benoni	2010-11
399-9	(50 overs)	England v South Africa	Bloemfontein	2015-16
399-1	(50 overs)	Pakistan v Zimbabwe	Bulawayo	2018
398-5	(50 overs)	Sri Lanka v Kenya	Kandy	1995-96
398-5	(50 overs)	New Zealand v England	The Oval	2015
397-5	(44 overs)	New Zealand v Zimbabwe	Bulawayo	2005
397-6	(50 overs)	England v Afghanistan	Manchester	2019
393-6	(50 overs)	New Zealand v West Indies	Wellington	2014-15
392-6	(50 overs)	South Africa v Pakistan	Pretoria	2006-07
392-4	(50 overs)	India v New Zealand	Christchurch	2008-09
392-4	(50 overs)	India v Sri Lanka	Mohali	2017-18
391-4	(50 overs)	England v Bangladesh	Nottingham	2005
389	(48 overs)	West Indies v England	St George's	2018-19
387-5	(50 overs)	India v England	Rajkot	2008-09
387-5	(50 overs)	India v West Indies	Visakhapatnam	2019-20
386-6	(50 overs)	England v Bangladesh	Cardiff	2019
385-7	(50 overs)	Pakistan v Bangladesh	Dambulla	2010
384-6	(50 overs)	South Africa v Sri Lanka	Centurion	2016-17
383-6	(50 overs)	India v Australia	Bangalore	2013-14
381-6	(50 overs)	India v England	Cuttack	2016-17
381-3	(50 overs)	West Indies v Ireland	Dublin	2019
381-5	(50 overs)	Australia v Bangladesh	Nottingham	2019
378-5	(50 overs)	Australia v New Zealand	Canberra	2016-17
377-6	(50 overs)	Australia v South Africa	Basseterre	2006-07
377-8	(50 overs)	Sri Lanka v Ireland	Dublin	2016
377-5	(50 overs)	India v West Indies	Mumbai (BS)	2018-19
376-2	(50 overs)	India v New Zealand	Hyderabad, India	1999-00
376-9	(50 overs)	Australia v Sri Lanka	Sydney	2014-15
375-3	(50 overs)	Pakistan v Zimbabwe	Lahore	2015
375-5	(50 overs)	India v Sri Lanka	Colombo (RPS)	2017

The highest score for Zimbabwe is 351-7 (v Kenya, Mombasa, 2008-09), for Afghanistan is 338 (v Ire, Greater Noida, 2016-17), for Bangladesh is 333 (v A, Nottingham, 2019) and for Ireland is 331-8 (v Z, Hobart, 2014-15) and 331-6 (v Scotland, Dubai, 2017-18).

HIGHEST MATCH AGGREGATES

872-13	(99.5 overs)	South Africa v Australia	Johannesburg	2005-06
825-15	(100 overs)	India v Sri Lanka	Rajkot	2009-10
807-16	(98 overs)	West Indies v England	St George's	2018-19

LARGEST RUNS MARGINS OF VICTORY

290 runs	New Zealand beat Ireland	Aberdeen	2008
275 runs	Australia beat Afghanistan	Perth	2014-15
272 runs	South Africa beat Zimbabwe	Benoni	2010-11
258 runs	South Africa beat Sri Lanka	Paarl	2011-12
257 runs	India beat Bermuda	Port of Spain	2006-07
257 runs	South Africa beat West Indies	Sydney	2014-15
256 runs	Australia beat Namibia	Potschefstroom	2002-03
256 runs	India beat Hong Kong	Karachi	2008
255 runs	Pakistan beat Ireland	Dublin	2016
245 runs	Sri Lanka beat India	Sharjah	2000-01
244 runs	Pakistan beat Zimbabwe	Bulawayo	2018

243 runs	Sri Lanka beat Bermuda	Port of Spain	2006-07
242 runs	England beat Australia	Nottingham	2018
234 runs	Sri Lanka beat Pakistan	Lahore	2008-09
233 runs	Pakistan beat Bangladesh	Dhaka	1999-00
232 runs	Australia beat Sri Lanka	Adelaide	1984-85
231 runs	South Africa beat Netherlands	Mohali	2010-11
229 runs	Australia beat Netherlands	Basseterre	2006-07
226 runs	Ireland beat UAE	Harare	2017-18
224 runs	Australia beat Pakistan	Nairobi	2002
224 runs	India beat West Indies	Mumbai (BS)	2018-19
221 runs	South Africa beat Netherlands	Basseterre	2006-07

LOWEST TOTALS (Excluding reduced innings)

35	(18.0 overs)	Zimbabwe v Sri Lanka	Harare	2003-04
35	(12.0 overs)	USA v Nepal	Kirtipur	2019-20
36	(18.4 overs)	Canada v Sri Lanka	Paarl	2002-03
38	(15.4 overs)	Zimbabwe v Sri Lanka	Colombo (SSC)	2001-02
43	(19.5 overs)	Pakistan v West Indies	Cape Town	1992-93
43	(20.1 overs)	Sri Lanka v South Africa	Paarl	2011-12
44	(24.5 overs)	Zimbabwe v Bangladesh	Chittagong	2009-10
45	(40.3 overs)	Canada v England	Manchester	1979
45	(14.0 overs)	Namibia v Australia	Potchefstroom	2002-03
54	(26.3 overs)	India v Sri Lanka	Sharjah	2000-01
54	(23.2 overs)	West Indies v South Africa	Cape Town	2003-04
54	(13.5 overs)	Zimbabwe v Afghanistan	Harare	2016-17
55	(28.3 overs)	Sri Lanka v West Indies	Sharjah	1986-87
58	(18.5 overs)	Bangladesh v West Indies	Dhaka	2010-11
58	(17.4 overs)	Bangladesh v India	Dhaka	2014
58	(16.1 overs)	Afghanistan v Zimbabwe	Sharjah	2015-16
61	(22.0 overs)	West Indies v Bangladesh	Chittagong	2011-12
63	(25.5 overs)	India v Australia	Sydney	1980-81
63	(18.3 overs)	Afghanistan v Scotland	Abu Dhabi	2014-15
64	(35.5 overs)	New Zealand v Pakistan	Sharjah	1985-86
65	(24.0 overs)	USA v Australia	Southampton	2004
65	(24.3 overs)	Zimbabwe v India	Harare	2005
67	(31.0 overs)	Zimbabwe v Sri Lanka	Harare	2008-09
67	(24.4 overs)	Canada v Netherlands	King City	2013
67	(24.0 overs)	Sri Lanka v England	Manchester	2014
67	(25.1 overs)	Zimbabwe v Pakistan	Bulawayo	2018
68	(31.3 overs)	Scotland v West Indies	Leicester	1999
69	(28.0 overs)	South Africa v Australia	Sydney	1993-94
69	(22.5 overs)	Zimbabwe v Kenya	Harare	2005-06
69	(23.5 overs)	Kenya v New Zealand	Chennai	2010-11
70	(25.2 overs)	Australia v England	Birmingham	1977
70	(26.3 overs)	Australia v New Zealand	Adelaide	1985-86
70	(23.5 overs)	West Indies v Australia	Perth	2012-13
70	(24.4 overs)	Bangladesh v West Indies	St George's	2014

The lowest for England is 86 (v A, Manchester, 2001) and for Ireland is 77 (v SL, St George's, 2007).

LOWEST MATCH AGGREGATES

71-12	(17.2 overs)	USA (35) v Nepal (36-2)	Kirtipur	2019-20
73-11	(23.2 overs)	Canada (36) v Sri Lanka (37-1)	Paarl	2002-03
75-11	(27.2 overs)	Zimbabwe (35) v Sri Lanka (40-1)	Harare	2003-04
78-11	(20.0 overs)	Zimbabwe (38) v Sri Lanka (40-1)	Colombo (SSC)	2001-02

BATTING RECORDS
6000 RUNS IN A CAREER

		LOI	I	NO	HS	Runs	Avge	100	50
S.R.Tendulkar	I	463	452	41	200*	18426	44.83	49	96
K.C.Sangakkara	SL/Asia/ICC	404	380	41	169	14234	41.98	25	93
R.T.Ponting	A/ICC	375	365	39	164	13704	42.03	30	82
S.T.Jayasuriya	SL/Asia	445	433	18	189	13430	32.36	28	68
D.P.M.D.Jayawardena	SL/Asia	448	418	39	144	12650	33.37	19	77
V.Kohli	I	248	239	39	183	11867	59.33	43	58
Inzamam-ul-Haq	P/Asia	378	350	53	137*	11739	39.52	10	83
J.H.Kallis	SA/Afr/ICC	328	314	53	139	11579	44.36	17	86
S.C.Ganguly	I/Asia	311	300	23	183	11363	41.02	22	72
R.S.Dravid	I/Asia/ICC	344	318	40	153	10889	39.16	12	83
M.S.Dhoni	I/Asia	350	297	84	183*	10773	50.57	10	73
C.H.Gayle	WI/ICC	301	294	17	215	10480	37.83	25	54
B.C.Lara	WI/ICC	299	289	32	169	10405	40.48	19	63
T.M.Dilshan	SL	330	303	41	161*	10290	39.27	22	47
Mohammad Yousuf	P/Asia	288	272	40	141*	9720	41.71	15	64
A.C.Gilchrist	A/ICC	287	279	11	172	9619	35.89	16	55
A.B.de Villiers	SA/Afr	228	218	39	176	9577	53.50	25	53
M.Azharuddin	I	334	308	54	153*	9378	36.92	7	58
P.A.de Silva	SL	308	296	30	145	9284	34.90	11	64
R.G.Sharma	I	224	217	32	264	9115	49.27	29	43
Saeed Anwar	P	247	244	19	194	8824	39.21	20	43
S.Chanderpaul	WI	268	251	40	150	8778	41.60	11	59
Yuvraj Singh	I/Asia	304	278	40	150	8701	36.55	14	52
D.L.Haynes	WI	238	237	28	152*	8648	41.37	17	57
L.R.P.L.Taylor	NZ	231	215	39	181*	8570	48.69	21	51
M.S.Atapattu	SL	268	259	32	132*	8529	37.57	11	59
M.E.Waugh	A	244	236	20	173	8500	39.35	18	50
V.Sehwag	I/Asia/ICC	251	245	9	219	8273	35.05	15	38
H.M.Amla	SA	181	178	14	159	8113	49.46	27	39
H.H.Gibbs	SA	248	240	16	175	8094	36.13	21	37
Shahid Afridi	P/Asia/ICC	398	369	27	124	8064	23.57	6	39
S.P.Fleming	NZ/ICC	280	269	21	134*	8037	32.40	8	49
M.J.Clarke	A	245	223	44	130	7981	44.58	8	58
S.R.Waugh	A	325	288	58	120*	7569	32.90	3	45
Shoaib Malik	P	287	258	40	143	7534	34.55	9	44
A.Ranatunga	SL	269	255	47	131*	7456	35.84	4	49
Javed Miandad	P	233	218	41	119*	7381	41.70	8	50
E.J.G.Morgan	E/Ire	236	219	32	148	7368	39.40	13	46
Younus Khan	P	265	255	23	144	7249	31.24	7	48
Tamim Iqbal	B	207	205	9	158	7202	36.74	13	47
Salim Malik	P	283	256	38	102	7170	32.88	5	47
N.J.Astle	NZ	223	217	14	145*	7090	34.92	16	41
G.C.Smith	SA/Afr	197	194	10	141	6989	37.98	10	47
W.U.Tharanga	SL/Asia	235	223	17	174*	6951	33.74	15	37
M.G.Bevan	A	232	196	67	108*	6912	53.58	6	46
M.J.Guptill	NZ	182	179	19	237*	6803	42.51	16	37
G.Kirsten	SA	185	185	19	188*	6798	40.95	13	45
A.Flower	Z	213	208	16	145	6786	35.34	4	55
I.V.A.Richards	WI	187	167	24	189*	6721	47.00	11	45
Mohammad Hafeez	P	218	216	15	140*	6614	32.90	11	38
G.W.Flower	Z	221	214	18	142*	6571	33.52	6	40
Ijaz Ahmed	P	250	232	29	139*	6564	32.33	10	37
A.R.Border	A	273	252	39	127*	6524	30.62	3	39
B.R.M.Taylor	Z	196	195	15	145*	6326	35.14	10	38
Shakib Al Hasan	B	206	194	27	134*	6323	37.86	9	47
R.B.Richardson	WI	224	217	30	122	6248	33.41	5	44
Mushfiqur Rahim	B	218	204	34	144	6174	36.31	7	38
K.S.Williamson	NZ	150	143	14	148	6154	47.70	13	39

		LOI	I	NO	HS	Runs	Avge	100	50
M.L.Hayden	A/ICC	161	155	15	181*	**6133**	43.80	10	36
B.B.McCullum	NZ	260	228	28	166	**6083**	30.41	5	32
D.M.Jones	A	164	161	25	145	**6068**	44.61	7	46

The most runs for Ireland is 4121 by P.R.Stirling (114 innings) and for Afghanistan 2782 by Mohammad Nabi (112 innings).

HIGHEST INDIVIDUAL INNINGS

264	R.G.Sharma	India v Sri Lanka	Kolkata	2014-15
237*	M.J.Guptill	New Zealand v West Indies	Wellington	2014-15
219	V.Sehwag	India v West Indies	Indore	2011-12
215	C.H.Gayle	West Indies v Zimbabwe	Canberra	2014-15
210*	Fakhar Zaman	Pakistan v Zimbabwe	Bulawayo	2018
209	R.G.Sharma	India v Australia	Bangalore	2013-14
208*	R.G.Sharma	India v Sri Lanka	Mohali	2017-18
200*	S.R.Tendulkar	India v South Africa	Gwalior	2009-10
194*	C.K.Coventry	Zimbabwe v Bangladesh	Bulawayo	2009
194	Saeed Anwar	Pakistan v India	Madras	1996-97
189*	I.V.A.Richards	West Indies v England	Manchester	1984
189*	M.J.Guptill	New Zealand v England	Southampton	2013
189	S.T.Jayasuriya	Sri Lanka v India	Sharjah	2000-01
188*	G.Kirsten	South Africa v UAE	Rawalpindi	1995-96
186*	S.R.Tendulkar	India v New Zealand	Hyderabad	1999-00
185*	S.R.Watson	Australia v Bangladesh	Dhaka	2010-11
185	F.du Plessis	South Africa v Sri Lanka	Cape Town	2016-17
183*	M.S.Dhoni	India v Sri Lanka	Jaipur	2005-06
183	S.C.Ganguly	India v Sri Lanka	Taunton	1999
183	V.Kohli	India v Pakistan	Dhaka	2011-12
181*	M.L.Hayden	Australia v New Zealand	Hamilton	2006-07
181*	L.R.P.L.Taylor	New Zealand v England	Dunedin	2017-18
181	I.V.A.Richards	West Indies v Sri Lanka	Karachi	1987-88
180*	M.J.Guptill	New Zealand v South Africa	Hamilton	2016-17
180	J.J.Roy	England v Australia	Melbourne	2017-18
179	D.A.Warner	Australia v Pakistan	Adelaide	2016-17
179	J.D.Campbell	West Indies v Ireland	Dublin	2019
178*	H.Masakadza	Zimbabwe v Kenya	Harare	2009-10
178	D.A.Warner	Australia v Afghanistan	Perth	2014-15
178	Q.de Kock	South Africa v Australia	Centurion	2016-17
177	P.R.Stirling	Ireland v Canada	Toronto	2010
176*	E.Lewis	West Indies v England	The Oval	2017
176	A.B.de Villiers	South Africa v Bangladesh	Paarl	2017-18
176	Liton Das	Bangladesh v Zimbabwe	Sylhet	2019-20
175*	Kapil Dev	India v Zimbabwe	Tunbridge Wells	1983
175	H.H.Gibbs	South Africa v Australia	Johannesburg	2005-06
175	S.R.Tendulkar	India v Australia	Hyderabad, India	2009-10
175	V.Sehwag	India v Bangladesh	Dhaka	2010-11
175	C.S.MacLeod	Scotland v Canada	Christchurch	2013-14
174*	W.U.Tharanga	Sri Lanka v India	Kingston	2013
173	M.E.Waugh	Australia v West Indies	Melbourne	2000-01
173	D.A.Warner	Australia v South Africa	Cape Town	2016-17
172*	C.B.Wishart	Zimbabwe v Namibia	Harare	2002-03
172	A.C.Gilchrist	Australia v Zimbabwe	Hobart	2003-04
172	L.Vincent	New Zealand v Zimbabwe	Bulawayo	2005
171*	G.M.Turner	New Zealand v East Africa	Birmingham	1975
171*	R.G.Sharma	India v Australia	Perth	2015-16
171	A.D.Hales	England v Pakistan	Nottingham	2016
170*	L.Ronchi	New Zealand v Sri Lanka	Dunedin	2014-15
170	S.D.Hope	West Indies v Ireland	Dublin	2019

The highest for Afghanistan is 131* by Mohammad Shahzad (v Z, Sharjah, 2015-16).

HUNDRED ON DEBUT

D.L.Amiss	103	England v Australia	Manchester	1972
D.L.Haynes	148	West Indies v Australia	St John's	1977-78
A.Flower	115*	Zimbabwe v Sri Lanka	New Plymouth	1991-92
Salim Elahi	102*	Pakistan v Sri Lanka	Gujranwala	1995-96
M.J.Guptill	122*	New Zealand v West Indies	Auckland	2008-09
C.A.Ingram	124	South Africa v Zimbabwe	Bloemfontein	2010-11
R.J.Nicol	108*	New Zealand v Zimbabwe	Harare	2011-12
P.J.Hughes	112	Australia v Sri Lanka	Melbourne	2012-13
M.J.Lumb	106	England v West Indies	North Sound	2013-14
M.S.Chapman	124*	Hong Kong v UAE	Dubai	2015-16
K.L.Rahul	100*	India v Zimbabwe	Harare	2016
T.Bavuma	113	South Africa v Ireland	Benoni	2016-17
Imam-ul-Haq	100	Pakistan v Sri Lanka	Abu Dhabi	2017-18
R.R.Hendricks	102	South Africa v Sri Lanka	Pallekele	2018
Abid Ali	112	Pakistan v Australia	Dubai, DSC	2018-19

Shahid Afridi scored 102 for P v SL, Nairobi, 1996-97, in his second match having not batted in his first.

Fastest 100	31 balls	A.B.de Villiers (149)	SA v WI	Johannesburg	2014-15
Fastest 50	16 balls	A.B.de Villiers (149)	SA v WI	Johannesburg	2014-15

16 HUNDREDS

		Inns	100	E	A	SA	WI	NZ	I	P	SL	Z	B	Ire	Afg	Ass
S.R.Tendulkar	I	452	49	2	9	5	4	5	–	5	8	5	1	–		5
V.Kohli	I	239	43	3	8	4	9	5	–	2	8	1	3	–	–	
R.T.Ponting	A	365	30*	5	–	2	2	6	6	1	4	1	1	–		1
R.G.Sharma	I	217	29	2	8	3	3	1	–	2	6	1	3	–	–	
S.T.Jayasuriya	SL	433	28	4	2	–	1	5	7	3	–	1	4	–		1
H.M.Amla	SA	178	27	2	1	–	5	2	2	3	5	3	2	1	–	1
A.B.de Villiers	SA	218	25	2	1	–	5	1	6	3	2	3	1	–		1
C.H.Gayle	WI	294	25	4	–	3	–	2	4	3	1	3	1	–		4
K.C.Sangakkara	SL	380	25	4	2	–	2	2	6	2	–	–	5	–		2
S.C.Ganguly	I	300	22	1	1	3	–	3	–	2	4	3	1	–		4
T.M.Dilshan	SL	303	22	1	2	–	3	4	2	–	2	4	–			2
L.R.P.L.Taylor	NZ	215	21	5	2	1	1	–	3	3	2	2	2	–		1
H.H.Gibbs	SA	240	21	2	3	–	5	2	2	2	1	2	1	–		1
Saeed Anwar	P	244	20	–	1	–	2	4	4	–	7	2	–	–		
B.C.Lara	WI	289	19	1	3	3	–	2	–	5	2	1	1	–		1
D.P.M.D.Jayawardena	SL	418	19*	5	–	1	3	4	2	–	1	1	–			1
D.A.Warner	A	120	18	1	–	4	–	2	3	3	3	–	1	–		1
M.E.Waugh	A	236	18	1	–	2	3	3	3	1	1	3	–	–		1
S.Dhawan	I	133	17	–	4	3	2	–	–	1	4	1	–	1		1
D.L.Haynes	WI	237	17	2	6	–	–	2	2	4	1	–	–			1
J.H.Kallis	SA	314	17	1	1	–	4	3	3	1	1	–	–			1
A.J.Finch	A	121	16	7	–	2	–	–	3	2	1	–	–			1
J.E.Root	E	137	16	–	–	2	4	3	3	1	2	–	1			–
M.J.Guptill	NZ	179	16	2	1	2	–	–	2	1	2	2	3	–		
N.J.Astle	NZ	217	16	2	1	1	1	–	5	2	–	3	–	–		1
A.C.Gilchrist	A	279	16*	2	–	2	–	2	1	1	6	1	–	–		1

* = Includes hundred scored against multi-national side.

The most for Zimbabwe is 10 by B.R.M.Taylor (195 innings), for Bangladesh 13 by Tamim Iqbal (205), for Ireland 11 by W.T.S.Porterfield (136), and for Afghanistan 6 by Mohammad Shahzad (84).

HIGHEST PARTNERSHIP FOR EACH WICKET

1st	365	J.D.Campbell/S.D.Hope	West Indies v Ireland	Dublin	2019
2nd	372	C.H.Gayle/M.N.Samuels	West Indies v Zimbabwe	Canberra	2014-15
3rd	258	D.M.Bravo/D.Ramdin	West Indies v Bangladesh	Basseterre	2014
4th	275*	M.Azharuddin/A.Jadeja	India v Zimbabwe	Cuttack	1997-98
5th	256*	D.A.Miller/J.P.Duminy	South Africa v Zimbabwe	Hamilton	2014-15

6th	267*	G.D.Elliott/L.Ronchi	New Zealand v Sri Lanka	Dunedin	2014-15
7th	177	J.C.Buttler/A.U.Rashid	England v New Zealand	Birmingham	2015
8th	138*	J.M.Kemp/A.J.Hall	South Africa v India	Cape Town	2006-07
9th	132	A.D.Mathews/S.L.Malinga	Sri Lanka v Australia	Melbourne	2010-11
10th	106*	I.V.A.Richards/M.A.Holding	West Indies v England	Manchester	1984

BOWLING RECORDS
200 WICKETS IN A CAREER

		LOI	Balls	R	W	Avge	Best	5w	R/Over
M.Muralitharan	SL/Asia/ICC	350	18811	12326	534	23.08	7-30	10	3.93
Wasim Akram	P	356	18186	11812	502	23.52	5-15	6	3.89
Waqar Younis	P	262	12698	9919	416	23.84	7-36	13	4.68
W.P.J.U.C.Vaas	SL/Asia	322	15775	11014	400	27.53	8-19	4	4.18
Shahid Afridi	P/Asia/ICC	398	17620	13632	395	34.51	7-12	9	4.62
S.M.Pollock	SA/Afr/ICC	303	15712	9631	393	24.50	6-35	5	3.67
G.D.McGrath	A/ICC	250	12970	8391	381	22.02	7-15	7	3.88
B.Lee	A	221	11185	8877	380	23.36	5-22	9	4.76
S.L.Malinga	SL	226	10936	9760	338	28.87	6-38	8	5.35
A.Kumble	I/Asia	271	14496	10412	337	30.89	6-12	2	4.30
S.T.Jayasuriya	SL	445	14874	11871	323	36.75	6-29	4	4.78
J.Srinath	I	229	11935	8847	315	28.08	5-23	3	4.44
D.L.Vettori	NZ/ICC	295	14060	9674	305	31.71	5- 7	2	4.12
S.K.Warne	A/ICC	194	10642	7541	293	25.73	5-33	1	4.25
Saqlain Mushtaq	P	169	8770	6275	288	21.78	5-20	6	4.29
A.B.Agarkar	I	191	9484	8021	288	27.85	6-42	2	5.07
Z.Khan	I/Asia	200	10097	8301	282	29.43	5-42	1	4.93
J.H.Kallis	SA/Afr/ICC	328	10750	8680	273	31.79	5-30	2	4.84
A.A.Donald	SA	164	8561	5926	272	21.78	6-23	2	4.15
Mashrafe Mortaza	B/Asia	210	10922	8893	270	32.93	6-26	1	4.88
J.M.Anderson	E	194	9584	7861	269	29.22	5-23	2	4.92
Abdul Razzaq	P/Asia	265	10941	8564	269	31.83	6-35	3	4.69
Harbhajan Singh	I/Asia	236	12479	8973	269	33.35	5-31	3	4.31
M.Ntini	SA/ICC	173	8687	6559	266	24.65	6-22	4	4.53
Shakib Al Hasan	B	206	10517	7857	260	30.21	5-29	2	4.48
Kapil Dev	I	225	11202	6945	253	27.45	5-43	1	3.72
Shoaib Akhtar	P/Asia/ICC	163	7764	6169	247	24.97	6-16	4	4.76
K.D.Mills	NZ	170	8230	6485	240	27.02	5-25	1	4.72
M.G.Johnson	A	153	7489	6038	239	25.26	6-31	3	4.83
H.H.Streak	Z/Afr	189	9468	7129	239	29.82	5-32	1	4.51
D.Gough	E/ICC	159	8470	6209	235	26.42	5-44	2	4.39
C.A.Walsh	WI	205	10822	6918	227	30.47	5- 1	1	3.83
C.E.L.Ambrose	WI	176	9353	5429	225	24.12	5-17	4	3.48
Abdur Razzak	B	153	7965	6065	207	29.29	5-29	4	4.56
C.J.McDermott	A	138	7460	5018	203	24.71	5-44	1	4.03
C.Z.Harris	NZ	250	10667	7613	203	37.50	5-42	1	4.28
C.L.Cairns	NZ/ICC	215	8168	6594	201	32.80	5-42	1	4.84

The most wickets for Ireland is 113 by K.J.O'Brien (145 matches) and for Afghanistan 133 by Rashid Khan (71).

BEST FIGURES IN AN INNINGS

8-19	W.P.J.U.C.Vaas	Sri Lanka v Zimbabwe	Colombo (SSC)	2001-02
7-12	Shahid Afridi	Pakistan v West Indies	Providence	2013
7-15	G.D.McGrath	Australia v Namibia	Potchefstroom	2002-03
7-18	Rashid Khan	Afghanistan v West Indies	Gros Islet	2017
7-20	A.J.Bichel	Australia v England	Port Elizabeth	2002-03
7-30	M.Muralitharan	Sri Lanka v India	Sharjah	2000-01
7-33	T.G.Southee	New Zealand v England	Wellington	2014-15
7-34	T.A.Boult	New Zealand v West Indies	Christchurch	2017-18
7-36	Waqar Younis	Pakistan v England	Leeds	2001
7-37	Aqib Javed	Pakistan v India	Sharjah	1991-92
7-45	Imran Tahir	South Africa v West Indies	Basseterre	2016
7-51	W.W.Davis	West Indies v Australia	Leeds	1983
6- 4	S.T.R.Binny	India v Bangladesh	Dhaka	2014

6-12	A.Kumble	India v West Indies	Calcutta	1993-94
6-13	B.A.W.Mendis	Sri Lanka v India	Karachi	2008
6-14	G.J.Gilmour	Australia v England	Leeds	1975
6-14	Imran Khan	Pakistan v India	Sharjah	1984-85
6-14	M.F.Maharoof	Sri Lanka v West Indies	Mumbai	2006-07
6-15	C.E.H.Croft	West Indies v England	Kingstown	1980-81
6-16	Shoaib Akhtar	Pakistan v New Zealand	Karachi	2001-02
6-16	K.Rabada	South Africa v Bangladesh	Dhaka	2015
6-16	S.Lamichhane	Nepal v USA	Kirtipur	2019-20
6-18	Azhar Mahmood	Pakistan v West Indies	Sharjah	1999-00
6-19	H.K.Olonga	Zimbabwe v England	Cape Town	1999-00
6-19	S.E.Bond	New Zealand v Zimbabwe	Harare	2005
6-20	B.C.Strang	Zimbabwe v Bangladesh	Nairobi	1997-98
6-20	A.D.Mathews	Sri Lanka v India	Colombo (RPS)	2009-10
6-22	F.H.Edwards	West Indies v Zimbabwe	Harare	2003-04
6-22	M.Ntini	South Africa v Australia	Cape Town	2005-06
6-23	A.A.Donald	South Africa v Kenya	Nairobi	1996-97
6-23	A.Nehra	India v England	Durban	2002-03
6-23	S.E.Bond	New Zealand v Australia	Port Elizabeth	2002-03
6-24	Imran Tahir	South Africa v Zimbabwe	Bloemfontein	2018-19
6-25	B.B.Styris	New Zealand v West Indies	Port of Spain	2002
6-25	W.P.J.U.C.Vaas	Sri Lanka v Bangladesh	Pietermaritzburg	2002-03
6-25	Kuldeep Yadav	India v England	Nottingham	2018
6-26	Waqar Younis	Pakistan v Sri Lanka	Sharjah	1989-90
6-26	Mashrafe Mortaza	Bangladesh v Kenya	Nairobi	2006
6-26	Rubel Hossain	Bangladesh v New Zealand	Dhaka	2013-14
6-26	Yasir Shah	Pakistan v Zimbabwe	Harare	2015-16
6-27	Naved-ul-Hasan	Pakistan v India	Jamshedpur	2004-05
6-27	C.R.D.Fernando	Sri Lanka v England	Colombo (RPS)	2007-08
6-27	M.Kartik	India v Australia	Mumbai	2007-08
6-27	K.A.J.Roach	West Indies v Netherlands	Delhi	2010-11
6-27	S.P.Narine	West Indies v South Africa	Providence	2016
6-28	H.K.Olonga	Zimbabwe v Kenya	Bulawayo	2002-03
6-28	J.H.Davey	Scotland v Afghanistan	Abu Dhabi	2014-15
6-28	M.A.Starc	Australia v New Zealand	Auckland	2014-15
6-29	B.P.Patterson	West Indies v India	Nagpur	1987-88
6-29	S.T.Jayasuriya	Sri Lanka v England	Moratuwa	1992-93
6-29	B.A.W.Mendis	Sri Lanka v Zimbabwe	Harare	2008-09
6-29	M.K.P.A.D.Perera	Sri Lanka v South Africa	Colombo (RPS)	2018
6-30	Waqar Younis	Pakistan v New Zealand	Auckland	1993-94
6-31	P.D.Collingwood	England v Bangladesh	Nottingham	2005
6-31	M.G.Johnson	Australia v Sri Lanka	Pallekele	2011
6-33	T.A.Boult	New Zealand v Australia	Hamilton	2016-17
6-34	Zahoor Khan	UAE v Ireland	Dubai (ICCA)	2016-17
6-35	S.M.Pollock	South Africa v West Indies	East London	1998-99
6-35	Abdul Razzaq	Pakistan v Bangladesh	Dhaka	2001-02
6-35	Shaheen Shah Afridi	Pakistan v Bangladesh	Lord's	2019

The best figures for Ireland are 6-55 by P.R.Stirling (v Afg, Greater Noida, 2016-17).

HAT-TRICKS

Jalaluddin	Pakistan v Australia	Hyderabad	1982-83
B.A.Reid	Australia v New Zealand	Sydney	1985-86
C.Sharma	India v New Zealand	Nagpur	1987-88
Wasim Akram	Pakistan v West Indies	Sharjah	1989-90
Wasim Akram	Pakistan v Australia	Sharjah	1989-90
Kapil Dev	India v Sri Lanka	Calcutta	1990-91
Aqib Javed	Pakistan v India	Sharjah	1991-92
D.K.Morrison	New Zealand v India	Napier	1993-94
Waqar Younis	Pakistan v New Zealand	East London	1994-95
Saqlain Mushtaq	Pakistan v Zimbabwe	Peshawar	1996-97
E.A.Brandes	Zimbabwe v England	Harare	1996-97
A.M.Stuart	Australia v Pakistan	Melbourne	1996-97
Saqlain Mushtaq	Pakistan v Zimbabwe	The Oval	1999

305

W.P.J.U.C.Vaas	Sri Lanka v Zimbabwe	Colombo (SSC)	2001-02
Mohammad Sami	Pakistan v West Indies	Sharjah	2001-02
W.P.J.U.C.Vaas[1]	Sri Lanka v Bangladesh	Pietermaritzburg	2002-03
B.Lee	Australia v Kenya	Durban	2002-03
J.M.Anderson	England v Pakistan	The Oval	2003
S.J.Harmison	England v India	Nottingham	2004
C.K.Langeveldt	South Africa v West Indies	Bridgetown	2004-05
Shahadat Hossain	Bangladesh v Zimbabwe	Harare	2006
J.E.Taylor	West Indies v Australia	Mumbai	2006-07
S.E.Bond	New Zealand v Australia	Hobart	2006-07
S.L.Malinga[2]	Sri Lanka v South Africa	Providence	2006-07
A.Flintoff	England v West Indies	St Lucia	2008-09
M.F.Maharoof	Sri Lanka v India	Dambulla	2010
Abdur Razzak	Bangladesh v Zimbabwe	Dhaka	2010-11
K.A.J.Roach	West Indies v Netherlands	Delhi	2010-11
S.L.Malinga	Sri Lanka v Kenya	Colombo (RPS)	2010-11
S.L.Malinga	Sri Lanka v Australia	Colombo (RPS)	2011
D.T.Christian	Australia v Sri Lanka	Melbourne	2011-12
N.L.T.C.Perera	Sri Lanka v Pakistan	Colombo (RPS)	2012
C.J.McKay	Australia v England	Cardiff	2013
Rubel Hossain	Bangladesh v New Zealand	Dhaka	2013-14
P.Utseya	Zimbabwe v South Africa	Harare	2014
Taijul Islam	Bangladesh v Zimbabwe	Dhaka	2014-15
S.T.Finn	England v Australia	Melbourne	2014-15
J.P.Duminy	South Africa v Sri Lanka	Sydney	2014-15
K.Rabada	South Africa v Bangladesh	Mirpur	2015
J.P.Faulkner	Australia v Sri Lanka	Colombo (RPS)	2016
Taskin Ahmed	Bangladesh v Sri Lanka	Dambulla	2016-17
P.W.H.de Silva	Sri Lanka v Zimbabwe	Galle	2017
Kuldeep Yadav	India v Australia	Kolkata	2017-18
D.S.K.Madushanka	Sri Lanka v Bangladesh	Dhaka	2017-18
Imran Tahir	South Africa v Zimbabwe	Bloemfontein	2018-19
T.A.Boult	New Zealand v Pakistan	Abu Dhabi	2018-19
Mohammed Shami	India v Afghanistan	Southampton	2019
T.A.Boult	New Zealand v Australia	Lord's	2019
Kuldeep Yadav	India v West Indies	Visakhapatnam	2019-20

[1] The first three balls of the match. Took four wickets in opening over (W W W 4 wide W 0).
[2] Four wickets in four balls.

WICKET-KEEPING RECORDS

150 DISMISSALS IN A CAREER

Total			LOI	Ct	St
482†‡	K.C.Sangakkara	Sri Lanka/Asia/ICC	360	384	98
472‡	A.C.Gilchrist	Australia/ICC	287	417	55
444	M.S.Dhoni	India/Asia	350	321	123
424	M.V.Boucher	South Africa/Africa	295	402	22
287‡	Moin Khan	Pakistan	219	214	73
242†‡	B.B.McCullum	New Zealand	185	227	15
233	I.A.Healy	Australia	168	194	39
223	Mushfiqur Rahim	Bangladesh	218	179	44
220‡	Rashid Latif	Pakistan	166	182	38
206‡	R.S.Kaluwitharana	Sri Lanka	187	131	75
204‡	P.J.L.Dujon	West Indies	169	183	21
202	J.C.Buttler	England	142	171	31
189	R.D.Jacobs	West Indies	147	160	29
188	D.Ramdin	West Indies	139	181	7
187	Kamran Akmal	Pakistan	154	156	31
181	B.J.Haddin	Australia	126	170	11
173	Q.de Kock	South Africa	121	164	9

Total			*LOI*	*Ct*	*St*
165	D.J.Richardson	South Africa	122	148	17
165†‡	A.Flower	Zimbabwe	213	133	32
163†‡	A.J.Stewart	England	170	148	15
154‡	N.R.Mongia	India	140	110	44

† *Excluding catches taken in the field.* ‡ *Excluding matches when not wicket-keeper.*

The most for Ireland is 96 by N.J.O'Brien (103 matches) and for Afghanistan 88 by Mohammad Shahzad (84).

SIX DISMISSALS IN AN INNINGS

6	(6ct)	A.C.Gilchrist	Australia v South Africa	Cape Town	1999-00
6	(6ct)	A.J.Stewart	England v Zimbabwe	Manchester	2000
6	(5ct/1st)	R.D.Jacobs	West Indies v Sri Lanka	Colombo (RPS)	2001-02
6	(5ct/1st)	A.C.Gilchrist	Australia v England	Sydney	2002-03
6	(6ct)	A.C.Gilchrist	Australia v Namibia	Potchefstroom	2002-03
6	(6ct)	A.C.Gilchrist	Australia v Sri Lanka	Colombo (RPS)	2003-04
6	(6ct)	M.V.Boucher	South Africa v Pakistan	Cape Town	2006-07
6	(5ct/1st)	M.S.Dhoni	India v England	Leeds	2007
6	(6ct)	A.C.Gilchrist	Australia v India	Baroda	2007-08
6	(5ct/1st)	A.C.Gilchrist	Australia v India	Sydney	2007-08
6	(6ct)	M.J.Prior	England v South Africa	Nottingham	2008
6	(6ct)	J.C.Buttler	England v South Africa	The Oval	2013
6	(6ct)	M.H.Cross	Scotland v Canada	Christchurch	2013-14
6	(5ct/1st)	Q.de Kock	South Africa v New Zealand	Mt Maunganui	2014-15
6	(6ct)	Sarfraz Ahmed	Pakistan v South Africa	Auckland	2014-15

FIELDING RECORDS

100 CATCHES IN A CAREER

Total			*LOI*		*Total*			*LOI*
218	D.P.M.D.Jayawardena	Sri Lanka/Asia	448		120	B.C.Lara	West Indies/ICC	299
160	R.T.Ponting	Australia/ICC	375		118	T.M.Dilshan	Sri Lanka	330
156	M.Azharuddin	India	334		113	Inzamam-ul-Haq	Pakistan/Asia	378
140	S.R.Tendulkar	India	463		111	S.R.Waugh	Australia	325
138	L.R.P.L.Taylor	New Zealand	231		109	R.S.Mahanama	Sri Lanka	213
133	S.P.Fleming	New Zealand/ICC	280		108	P.D.Collingwood	England	197
131	J.H.Kallis	South Africa/Africa/ICC	328		108	M.E.Waugh	Australia	244
130	Younus Khan	Pakistan	265		108	H.H.Gibbs	South Africa	248
130	M.Muralitharan	Sri Lanka/Asia/ICC	350		108	S.M.Pollock	South Africa/Africa/ICC	303
128	V.Kohli	India	248		106	M.J.Clarke	Australia	245
127	A.R.Border	Australia	273		105	M.E.K.Hussey	Australia	185
127	Shahid Afridi	Pakistan/Asia/ICC	398		105	G.C.Smith	South Africa/Africa	197
124	C.H.Gayle	West Indies/ICC	301		105	J.N.Rhodes	South Africa	245
124	R.S.Dravid	India/Asia/ICC	344		102	S.K.Raina	India	226
123	S.T.Jayasuriya	Sri Lanka/Asia	445		100	I.V.A.Richards	West Indies	187
120	C.L.Hooper	West Indies	227		100	S.C.Ganguly	India/Asia	311

The most for Zimbabwe is 86 by G.W.Flower (221), for Bangladesh 64 by Mahmudullah (188), for Ireland 64 by W.T.S.Porterfield (139) and by K.J.O'Brien (145), and for Afghanistan 55 by Mohammad Nabi (124).

FIVE CATCHES IN AN INNINGS

5	J.N.Rhodes	South Africa v West Indies	Bombay (BS)	1993-94

APPEARANCE RECORDS – 250 MATCHES

463	S.R.Tendulkar	India		299	B.C.Lara	West Indies/ICC
448	D.P.M.D.Jayawardena	Sri Lanka/Asia		295	M.V.Boucher	South Africa/Africa
445	S.T.Jayasuriya	Sri Lanka/Asia		295	D.L.Vettori	New Zealand/ICC
404	K.C.Sangakkara	Sri Lanka/Asia/ICC		288	Mohammad Yousuf	Pakistan/Asia
398	Shahid Afridi	Pakistan/Asia/ICC		287	A.C.Gilchrist	Australia/ICC
378	Inzamam-ul-Haq	Pakistan/Asia		287	Shoaib Malik	Pakistan
375	R.T.Ponting	Australia/ICC		283	Salim Malik	Pakistan
356	Wasim Akram	Pakistan		280	S.P.Fleming	New Zealand/ICC
350	M.S.Dhoni	India/Asia		273	A.R.Border	Australia
350	M.Muralitharan	Sri Lanka/ICC		271	A.Kumble	India/Asia
344	R.S.Dravid	India/Asia/ICC		269	A.Ranatunga	Sri Lanka
334	M.Azharuddin	India		268	M.S.Atapattu	Sri Lanka
330	T.M.Dilshan	Sri Lanka		268	S.Chanderpaul	West Indies
328	J.H.Kallis	South Africa/Africa/ICC		265	Abdul Razzaq	Pakistan/Asia
325	S.R.Waugh	Australia		265	Younus Khan	Pakistan
322	W.P.J.U.C.Vaas	Sri Lanka/Asia		262	Waqar Younis	Pakistan
311	S.C.Ganguly	India/Asia		260	B.B.McCullum	New Zealand
308	P.A.de Silva	Sri Lanka		251	V.Sehwag	India/Asia/ICC
304	Yuvraj Singh	India/Asia		250	C.Z.Harris	New Zealand
303	S.M.Pollock	South Africa/Africa/ICC		250	Ijaz Ahmed	Pakistan
301	C.H.Gayle	West Indies/ICC		250	G.D.McGrath	Australia/ICC

The most for England is 213 by E.J.G.Morgan, for Zimbabwe 221 by G.W.Flower, for Bangladesh 218 by Mashrafe Mortaza and Mushfiqur Rahim, for Ireland 145 by K.J.O'Brien, and for Afghanistan 124 by Mohammad Nabi.

The most consecutive appearances is 185 by S.R.Tendulkar for India (Apr 1990-Apr 1998).

100 MATCHES AS CAPTAIN

LOI			W	L	T	NR	% Won (exc NR)
230	R.T.Ponting	Australia/ICC	165	51	2	12	75.68
218	S.P.Fleming	New Zealand	98	106	1	13	47.80
200	M.S.Dhoni	India	110	74	5	11	58.20
193	A.Ranatunga	Sri Lanka	89	95	1	8	48.10
178	A.R.Border	Australia	107	67	1	3	61.14
174	M.Azharuddin	India	90	76	2	6	53.57
150	G.C.Smith	South Africa/Africa	92	51	1	6	63.88
147	S.C.Ganguly	India/Asia	76	66	–	5	53.52
139	Imran Khan	Pakistan	75	59	1	4	55.55
138	W.J.Cronje	South Africa	99	35	1	3	73.33
129	D.P.M.D.Jayawardena	Sri Lanka	71	49	1	8	58.67
125	B.C.Lara	West Indies	59	59	–	7	50.42
118	S.T.Jayasuriya	Sri Lanka	66	47	2	3	57.39
114	E.J.G.Morgan	England	69	36	2	7	64.48
113	W.T.S.Porterfield	Ireland	50	55	2	6	46.72
109	Wasim Akram	Pakistan	66	41	2	–	60.55
106	A.D.Mathews	Sri Lanka	49	51	1	5	48.51
106	S.R.Waugh	Australia	67	35	3	1	63.80
105	I.V.A.Richards	West Indies	67	36	–	2	65.04
103	A.B.de Villers	South Africa	59	39	1	4	59.59

The most for Zimbabwe is 86 by A.D.R.Campbell, for Bangladesh 88 by Mashrafe Mortaza, and for Afghanistan 56 by Asghar Afghan.

150 LOI UMPIRING APPEARANCES

209	R.E.Koertzen	South Africa	09.12.1992	to	09.06.2010
208	Alim Dar	Pakistan	16.02.2000	to	07.02.2020
200	B.F.Bowden	New Zealand	23.03.1995	to	06.02.2016
181	S.A.Bucknor	West Indies	18.03.1989	to	29.03.2009
174	D.J.Harper	Australia	14.01.1994	to	19.03.2011
174	S.J.A.Taufel	Australia	13.01.1999	to	02.09.2012
172	D.R.Shepherd	England	09.06.1983	to	12.07.2005
154	R.B.Tiffin	Zimbabwe	25.10.1992	to	22.07.2018

ENGLAND TWENTY20 INTERNATIONALS CAREER RECORDS

These records, complete to 2 April 2020, include all players registered for county cricket for the 2020 season at the time of going to press.

BATTING AND FIELDING

	M	I	NO	HS	Runs	Avge	100	50	Ct/St
M.M.Ali	28	25	7	72*	235	15.77	–	1	8
T.R.Ambrose	1	–	–	–	–	–	–	–	1/1
J.M.Anderson	19	4	3	1*	1	1.00	–	–	3
J.C.Archer	1	–	–	–	–	–	–	–	–
J.M.Bairstow	37	32	6	68	725	27.88	–	4	32
J.T.Ball	2	–	–	–	–	–	–	–	1
T.Banton	3	3	–	31	56	18.66	–	–	4
G.J.Batty	1	1	–	4	4	4.00	–	–	–
I.R.Bell	8	8	1	60*	188	26.85	–	1	4
S.W.Billings†	25	22	3	87	344	18.10	–	2	15/1
R.S.Bopara	38	35	10	65*	711	28.44	–	3	7
S.G.Borthwick	1	1	–	14	14	14.00	–	–	1
T.T.Bresnan	34	22	9	47*	216	16.61	–	–	10
D.R.Briggs	7	1	1	0*	0	–	–	–	1
S.C.J.Broad	56	26	10	18*	118	7.37	–	–	21
P.R.Brown	4	1	1	4*	4	–	–	–	2
J.C.Buttler	69	61	11	73*	1334	26.68	–	8	25/4
A.N.Cook	4	4	–	26	61	15.25	–	–	1
M.S.Crane	2	–	–	–	–	–	–	–	–
S.M.Curran	5	3	–	24	35	11.66	–	–	–
T.K.Curran	18	8	5	14*	38	12.66	–	–	41
S.M.Davies	5	5	–	33	102	20.40	–	–	2/1
L.A.Dawson	6	2	1	10	17	17.00	–	–	2
J.L.Denly	12	11	1	30	96	9.60	–	–	4
J.W.Dernbach	34	7	2	12	24	4.80	–	–	8
B.M.Duckett	1	1	–	9	9	9.00	–	–	–
S.T.Finn	21	3	3	8*	14	–	–	–	6
B.T.Foakes	1	–	–	–	–	–	–	–	1
L.Gregory	5	3	–	15	21	7.00	–	–	–
H.F.Gurney	2	–	–	–	–	–	–	–	–
A.D.Hales	60	60	7	116*	1664	31.01	1	8	32
C.J.Jordan	46	27	12	36	223	14.86	–	–	25
L.S.Livingstone	2	2	–	16	16	8.00	–	–	1
S.Mahmood	3	2	1	4	7	7.00	–	–	1
D.J.Malan	10	10	1	103*	469	52.11	1	5	2
S.C.Meaker	2	–	–	–	–	–	–	–	1
T.S.Mills†	4	1	–	0	0	0.00	–	–	1
E.J.G.Morgan	89	87	18	91	2138	30.98	–	13	37
M.W.Parkinson	2	–	–	–	–	–	–	–	–
S.D.Parry	5	1	1	1	1	1.00	–	–	2
S.R.Patel	18	14	2	67	189	15.75	–	1	3
L.E.Plunkett	22	11	4	18	42	6.00	–	–	7
A.U.Rashid	43	16	8	9*	52	6.50	–	–	11
J.E.Root	32	30	5	90*	893	35.72	–	5	18
J.J.Roy	35	35	–	78	860	24.57	–	5	5
B.A.Stokes	26	23	6	47*	305	17.94	–	–	13
J.M.Vince	12	12	–	59	340	28.33	–	1	5
D.J.Willey	28	19	7	29*	166	13.83	–	–	12
C.R.Woakes	8	7	4	37	91	30.33	–	–	1
M.A.Wood	8	2	2	5*	10	–	–	–	–
L.J.Wright	51	45	5	99*	759	18.97	–	4	14

BOWLING

	O	M	R	W	Avge	Best	4wI	R/Over
M.M.Ali	68.2	0	588	16	36.75	2-21	–	8.60
J.M.Anderson	70.2	1	552	18	30.66	3-23	–	7.84
J.C.Archer	4	0	29	2	14.50	2-29	–	7.25
J.T.Ball	7	0	83	2	41.50	1-39	–	11.85
G.J.Batty	3	0	17	0	–	–	–	5.66
R.S.Bopara	53.4	1	387	16	24.18	4-10	1	7.21
S.G.Borthwick	4	0	15	1	15.00	1-15	–	3.75
T.T.Bresnan	110.3	1	887	24	36.95	3-10	–	8.02
D.R.Briggs	18	0	199	5	39.80	2-25	–	11.05
S.C.J.Broad	195.3	2	1491	65	22.93	4-24	1	7.62
P.R.Brown	13	0	128	3	42.66	1-29	–	9.84
M.S.Crane	8	0	62	1	62.00	1-38	–	7.75
S.M.Curran	18	0	153	6	25.50	2-22	–	8.50
T.K.Curran	59	1	537	21	25.57	4-36	1	9.10
L.A.Dawson	20	0	152	5	30.40	3-27	–	7.60
J.L.Denly	11	0	85	7	12.14	4-19	1	7.72
J.W.Dernbach	117	1	1020	39	26.15	4-22	1	8.71
S.T.Finn	80	0	583	27	21.59	3-16	–	7.28
L.Gregory	4	0	29	1	29.00	1-10	–	7.25
H.F.Gurney	8	0	55	3	18.33	2-26	–	6.87
C.J.Jordan	162.3	0	1408	58	24.27	4- 6	2	8.66
S.Mahmood	10	0	115	3	38.33	1-20	–	11.50
D.J.Malan	2	0	27	1	27.00	1-27	–	13.50
S.C.Meaker	7.5	0	70	2	35.00	1-28	–	8.93
T.S.Mills	16	0	116	3	38.66	1-27	–	7.25
M.W.Parkinson	6	0	61	5	12.20	4-47	1	10.16
S.D.Parry	16	0	138	3	46.00	2-33	–	8.62
S.R.Patel	42	0	321	7	45.85	2- 6	–	7.64
L.E.Plunkett	79.2	1	627	25	25.08	3-21	–	7.90
A.U.Rashid	144	1	1099	41	26.80	3-11	–	7.63
J.E.Root	14	0	139	6	23.16	2- 9	–	9.92
B.A.Stokes	64.4	1	571	14	40.78	3-26	–	8.82
D.J.Willey	92.5	0	761	34	22.38	4- 7	1	8.19
C.R.Woakes	27	0	253	7	36.14	2-40	–	9.37
M.A.Wood	27.3	0	266	15	17.73	3- 9	–	9.67
L.J.Wright	55	0	465	18	25.83	2-24	–	8.45

† S.W.Billings and T.S.Mills also played one game for an ICC World XI v West Indies at Lord's in 2018.

INTERNATIONAL TWENTY20 RECORDS

From 1 January 2019, the ICC granted official IT20 status to all 20-over matches between its 105 members. As a result, 318 IT20 matches have been played since the last edition of *Playfair* was published, many featuring very minor nations. In the records that follow, except for the first-ranked record, only those games featuring a nation that has also played a full LOI are listed.

MATCH RESULTS

2004-05 to 28 February 2020

Opponents		Matches	Won													Tied	NR
			E	A	SA	WI	NZ	I	P	SL	Z	B	Ire	Afg	Ass		
England	Australia	16	6	9	–	–	–	–	–	–	–	–	–	–	–	–	1
	South Africa	18	8	–	9	–	–	–	–	–	–	–	–	–	–	–	1
	West Indies	18	7	–	–	11	–	–	–	–	–	–	–	–	–	–	–
	New Zealand	21	12	–	–	–	7	–	–	–	–	–	–	–	–	1	1
	India	14	7	–	–	–	–	7	–	–	–	–	–	–	–	–	–
	Pakistan	15	10	–	–	–	–	–	4	–	–	–	–	–	–	1	–
	Sri Lanka	9	5	–	–	–	–	–	–	4	–	–	–	–	–	–	–
	Zimbabwe	1	1	–	–	–	–	–	–	–	0	–	–	–	–	–	–
	Bangladesh	0	0	–	–	–	–	–	–	–	–	0	✓	–	–	–	–
	Ireland	1	0	–	–	–	–	–	–	–	–	–	0	–	–	–	1
	Afghanistan	2	2	–	–	–	–	–	–	–	–	–	–	0	–	–	–
	Associates	2	0	–	–	–	–	–	–	–	–	–	–	–	2	–	–
Australia	South Africa	21	–	13	8	–	–	–	–	–	–	–	–	–	–	–	–
	West Indies	11	–	5	–	6	–	–	–	–	–	–	–	–	–	–	–
	New Zealand	9	–	7	–	–	1	–	–	–	–	–	–	–	–	1	–
	India	20	–	8	–	–	–	11	–	–	–	–	–	–	–	–	1
	Pakistan	23	–	9	–	–	–	–	12	–	–	–	–	–	–	1	1
	Sri Lanka	16	–	8	–	–	–	–	–	8	–	–	–	–	–	–	–
	Zimbabwe	3	–	2	–	–	–	–	–	–	1	–	–	–	–	–	–
	Bangladesh	4	–	4	–	–	–	–	–	–	–	0	–	–	–	–	–
	Ireland	1	–	1	–	–	–	–	–	–	–	–	0	–	–	–	–
	Afghanistan	0	–	0	–	–	–	–	–	–	–	–	–	0	–	–	–
	Associates	1	–	1	–	–	–	–	–	–	–	–	–	–	0	–	–
S Africa	West Indies	10	–	–	6	4	–	–	–	–	–	–	–	–	–	–	–
	New Zealand	15	–	–	11	–	4	–	–	–	–	–	–	–	–	–	–
	India	15	–	–	6	–	–	9	–	–	–	–	–	–	–	–	–
	Pakistan	14	–	–	8	–	–	–	6	–	–	–	–	–	–	–	–
	Sri Lanka	13	–	–	7	–	–	–	–	5	–	–	–	–	–	1	–
	Zimbabwe	5	–	–	5	–	–	–	–	–	0	–	–	–	–	–	–
	Bangladesh	6	–	–	6	–	–	–	–	–	–	0	–	–	–	–	–
	Ireland	0	–	–	0	–	–	–	–	–	–	–	0	–	–	–	–
	Afghanistan	2	–	–	2	–	–	–	–	–	–	–	–	0	–	–	–
	Associates	2	–	–	2	–	–	–	–	–	–	–	–	–	0	–	–
W Indies	New Zealand	13	–	–	–	3	6	–	–	–	–	–	–	–	–	3	1
	India	17	–	–	–	6	–	10	–	–	–	–	–	–	–	–	1
	Pakistan	14	–	–	–	3	–	–	11	–	–	–	–	–	–	–	–
	Sri Lanka	9	–	–	–	3	–	–	–	6	–	–	–	–	–	–	–
	Zimbabwe	3	–	–	–	2	–	–	–	–	1	–	–	–	–	–	–
	Bangladesh	12	–	–	–	6	–	–	–	–	–	5	–	–	–	–	1
	Ireland	7	–	–	–	3	–	–	–	–	–	–	2	–	–	–	2
	Afghanistan	7	–	–	–	4	–	–	–	–	–	–	–	3	–	–	–
	Associates	0	–	–	–	0	–	–	–	–	–	–	–	–	0	–	–
N Zealand	India	16	–	–	–	–	8	6	–	–	–	–	–	–	–	2	–
	Pakistan	21	–	–	–	–	8	–	13	–	–	–	–	–	–	–	–
	Sri Lanka	19	–	–	–	–	10	–	–	7	–	–	–	–	–	1	1
	Zimbabwe	6	–	–	–	–	6	–	–	–	0	–	–	–	–	–	–
	Bangladesh	7	–	–	–	–	7	–	–	–	–	0	–	–	–	–	–
	Ireland	1	–	–	–	–	1	–	–	–	–	–	0	–	–	–	–
	Afghanistan	0	–	–	–	–	0	–	–	–	–	–	–	0	–	–	–
	Associates	3	–	–	–	–	3	–	–	–	–	–	–	–	0	–	–

	Opponents	Matches	E	A	SA	WI	NZ	I	P	SL	Z	B	Ire	Afg	Ass	Tied	NR
										Won								
India	Pakistan	8	–	–	–	–	–	6	1	–	–	–	–	–	–	1	–
	Sri Lanka	19	–	–	–	–	–	13	–	5	–	–	–	–	–	–	1
	Zimbabwe	7	–	–	–	–	–	5	–	2	–	–	–	–	–	–	–
	Bangladesh	11	–	–	–	–	–	10	–	–	–	1	–	–	–	–	–
	Ireland	3	–	–	–	–	–	3	–	–	–	–	0	–	–	–	–
	Afghanistan	2	–	–	–	–	–	2	–	–	–	–	–	0	–	–	–
	Associates	2	–	–	–	–	–	1	–	–	–	–	–	–	0	–	1
Pakistan	Sri Lanka	21	–	–	–	–	–	–	13	8	–	–	–	–	–	–	–
	Zimbabwe	11	–	–	–	–	–	–	11	–	0	–	–	–	–	–	–
	Bangladesh	12	–	–	–	–	–	–	10	–	–	2	–	–	–	–	–
	Ireland	1	–	–	–	–	–	–	1	–	–	–	0	–	–	–	–
	Afghanistan	1	–	–	–	–	–	–	1	–	–	–	–	0	–	–	–
	Associates	7	–	–	–	–	–	–	7	–	–	–	–	–	0	–	–
Sri Lanka	Zimbabwe	3	–	–	–	–	–	–	–	3	0	–	–	–	–	–	–
	Bangladesh	11	–	–	–	–	–	–	–	7	–	4	–	–	–	–	–
	Ireland	1	–	–	–	–	–	–	–	1	–	–	0	–	–	–	–
	Afghanistan	1	–	–	–	–	–	–	–	1	–	–	–	0	–	–	–
	Associates	4	–	–	–	–	–	–	–	4	–	–	–	–	0	–	–
Zimbabwe	Bangladesh	11	–	–	–	–	–	–	–	–	4	7	–	–	–	–	–
	Ireland	3	–	–	–	–	–	–	–	–	1	–	2	–	–	–	–
	Afghanistan	9	–	–	–	–	–	–	–	–	1	–	–	8	–	–	–
	Associates	12	–	–	–	–	–	–	–	–	8	–	–	–	2	2	–
Bangladesh	Ireland	5	–	–	–	–	–	–	–	–	–	3	1	–	–	–	1
	Afghanistan	6	–	–	–	–	–	–	–	–	–	2	–	4	–	–	–
	Associates	9	–	–	–	–	–	–	–	–	–	6	–	–	3	–	–
Ireland	Afghanistan	15	–	–	–	–	–	–	–	–	–	–	3	12	–	–	–
	Associates	57	–	–	–	–	–	–	–	–	–	–	33	–	20	1	3
Afghanistan	Associates	33	–	–	–	–	–	–	–	–	–	–	–	26	7	–	–
Associates	Associates	314	–	–	–	–	–	–	–	–	–	–	–	–	302	3	9
		1062	58	67	70	51	61	83	90	59	18	30	41	53	336	18	27

MATCH RESULTS SUMMARY

	Matches	Won	Lost	Tied	NR	% Won (ex NR)
Afghanistan	78	53	25	0	0	67.94
India	134	83	44	3	4	63.84
Pakistan	148	90	54	3	1	61.22
South Africa	121	70	49	1	1	58.33
Australia	125	67	53	2	3	54.91
England	117	58	53	2	4	51.32
New Zealand	131	61	59	8	3	47.65
Sri Lanka	126	59	63	2	2	47.58
Ireland	95	41	46	1	7	46.59
West Indies	121	51	62	3	5	43.96
Bangladesh	94	30	62	0	2	32.60
Associates (v Full)	132	34	91	3	4	26.56
Zimbabwe	74	18	54	2	0	24.32

Results of games between two Associate Members and Pakistan's three IT20s v a World XI in 2017 (W2, L1) and West Indies' IT20 v an ICC World XI in 2018 (W1) are excluded from these figures.

INTERNATIONAL TWENTY20 RECORDS

(To 28 February 2020)

TEAM RECORDS

HIGHEST INNINGS TOTALS † Batting Second

278-3	Afghanistan v Ireland	Dehradun	2018-19
263-3	Australia v Sri Lanka	Pallekele	2016
260-6	Sri Lanka v Kenya	Johannesburg	2007-08

260-5	India v Sri Lanka	Indore	2017-18
252-3	Scotland v Netherlands	Dublin	2019
248-6	Australia v England	Southampton	2013
245-6	West Indies v India	Lauderhill	2016
245-5†	Australia v New Zealand	Auckland	2017-18
244-4†	India v West Indies	Lauderhill	2016
243-5	New Zealand v West Indies	Mt Maunganui	2017-18
243-6	New Zealand v Australia	Auckland	2017-18
241-6	South Africa v England	Centurion	2009-10
241-3	England v New Zealand	Napier	2019-20
240-3	Namibia v Botswana	Windhoek	2019
240-3	India v West Indies	Mumbai	2019-20
236-6†	West Indies v South Africa	Johannesburg	2014-15
236-3	Nepal v Bhutan	Kirtipur	2019-20
233-8	Afghanistan v Ireland	Greater Noida	2016-17
233-2	Australia v Sri Lanka	Adelaide	2019-20
231-7	South Africa v West Indies	Johannesburg	2014-15
230-8†	England v South Africa	Mumbai	2015-16
229-4	South Africa v England	Mumbai	2015-16
229-2	Australia v Zimbabwe	Harare	2018
226-5†	England v South Africa	Centurion	2019-20
225-7	Ireland v Afghanistan	Abu Dhabi	2013-14

The highest total for Pakistan is 205-3 (v West Indies, Karachi, 2017-18), for Zimbabwe 200-2 (v New Zealand, Hamilton, 2011-12) and for Bangladesh is 215-5 (v Sri Lanka, Colombo (RPS), 2017-18).

LOWEST COMPLETED INNINGS TOTALS † Batting Second

21† (8.3)	Turkey v Czech Republic	Ilfov County	2019
39 (10.3)	Netherlands v Sri Lanka	Chittagong	2013-14
45† (11.5)	West Indies v England	Basseterre	2018-19
46 (12.1)	Botswana v Namibia	Kampala	2019
53 (14.3)	Nepal v Ireland	Belfast	2015
56† (18.4)	Kenya v Afghanistan	Sharjah	2013-14
60† (15.3)	New Zealand v Sri Lanka	Chittagong	2013-14
60† (13.4)	West Indies v Pakistan	Karachi	2017-18
61-8	Iran v UAE	Al Amerat	2019-20
64 (11.0)	Nepal v Oman	Al Amerat	2019-20
66-9	Cayman Islands v USA	Sandys Parish	2019
66-9	Nigeria v Ireland	Abu Dhabi	2019-20
67 (17.2)	Kenya v Ireland	Belfast	2008
68† (16.4)	Ireland v West Indies	Providence	2009-10
68-8	Cayman Islands v USA	Hamilton, Ber	2019
69† (17.0)	Hong Kong v Nepal	Chittagong	2013-14
69† (17.4)	Nepal v Netherlands	Amstelveen	2015
70	Bermuda v Canada	Belfast	2008
70† (15.4)	Bangladesh v New Zealand	Kolkata	2015-16
70† (12.3)	Ireland v India	Dublin	2018

The lowest total for England is 80 (v India, Colombo (RPS), 2012-13).

LARGEST RUNS MARGIN OF VICTORY

257 runs	Czech Republic beat Turkey	Ilfov County	2019
172 runs	Sri Lanka beat Kenya	Johannesburg	2007
143 runs	Pakistan beat West Indies	Karachi	2017-18
143 runs	India beat Ireland	Dublin	2018
141 runs	Nepal beat Bhutan	Kirtipur	2019-20
137 runs	England beat West Indies	Basseterre	2018-19

There have been 22 victories by ten wickets, with Austria beating Turkey by a record margin of 104 balls remaining (Ilfov County, 2019).

BATTING RECORDS
1600 RUNS IN A CAREER

Runs			M	I	NO	HS	Avge	50	R/100B
2794	V.Kohli	I	82	76	21	94*	50.80	24	138.2
2773	R.G.Sharma	I	108	100	15	118	32.62	25	138.7
2536	M.J.Guptill	NZ	88	85	7	105	32.51	17	134.6
2321	Shoaib Malik	P/ICC	113	105	31	75	31.36	8	124.1
2207	D.A.Warner	A	79	79	9	100*	31.52	18	140.4
2140	B.B.McCullum	NZ	71	70	10	123	35.66	15	136.2
2138	E.J.G.Morgan	E	89	87	18	91	30.98	13	137.4
2052	P.R.Stirling	Ire	75	74	6	95	30.17	17	139.5
1992	Mohammad Hafeez	P	91	88	9	86	25.21	11	116.6
1989	A.J.Finch	A	61	61	9	172	38.25	14	155.8
1936	Mohammad Shahzad	Afg	65	65	3	118*	31.22	13	134.8
1934	J.P.Duminy	SA	81	75	25	96*	38.68	11	126.2
1909	L.R.P.L.Taylor	NZ	100	92	20	63	26.51	7	122.6
1889	T.M.Dilshan	SL	80	79	12	104*	28.19	14	120.5
1724	C.Munro	NZ	65	62	7	109*	31.34	14	156.4
1717	Tamim Iqbal	B/Wd	77	77	5	103*	23.84	8	116.8
1690	Umar Akmal	P	84	79	14	94	26.00	8	122.7
1672	A.B.de Villiers	SA	78	75	11	79*	26.12	10	135.1
1665	K.S.Williamson	NZ	60	58	7	95	32.64	11	125.1
1662	H.Masakadza	Z	66	66	2	93*	25.96	11	117.2
1644	A.D.Hales	E	60	60	7	116*	31.01	9	136.6
1627	C.H.Gayle	WI	58	54	4	117	32.54	15	142.8
1617	M.S.Dhoni	I	98	85	42	56	37.60	2	126.1
1611	M.N.Samuels	WI	67	65	10	89*	29.29	10	116.2
1605	S.K.Raina	I	78	66	11	101	29.18	5	134.8

HIGHEST INDIVIDUAL INNINGS

Score	Balls				
172	76	A.J.Finch	A v Z	Harare	2018
162*	62	Hazratullah Zazai	Afg v Ire	Dehradun	2018-19
156	63	A.J.Finch	A v E	Southampton	2013
145*	65	G.J.Maxwell	A v SL	Pallekele	2016
127*	56	H.G.Munsey	Scot v Neth	Dublin	2019
125*	62	E.Lewis	WI v I	Kingston	2017
124*	71	S.R.Watson	A v I	Sydney	2015-16
124	62	K.J.O'Brien	Ire v HK	Al Amerat	2019-20
123	58	B.B.McCullum	NZ v B	Pallekele	2012-13
122	60	Babar Hayat	HK v Oman	Fatullah	2015-16
119	56	F.du Plessis	SA v WI	Johannesburg	2014-15
118*	67	Mohammad Shahzad	Afg v Z	Sharjah	2015-16
118	43	R.G.Sharma	I v SL	Indore	2017-18
117*	51	R.E.Levi	SA v NZ	Hamilton	2011-12
117*	68	Shaiman Anwar	UAE v PNG	Abu Dhabi	2017
117	57	C.H.Gayle	WI v SA	Johannesburg	2007-08
116*	56	B.B.McCullum	NZ v A	Christchurch	2009-10
116*	64	A.D.Hales	E v SL	Chittagong	2013-14
114*	70	M.N.van Wyk	SA v WI	Durban	2014-15
113*	55	G.J.Maxwell	A v I	Bengaluru	2018-19
111*	62	Ahmed Shehzad	P v B	Dhaka	2013-14
111*	61	R.G.Sharma	I v WI	Lucknow	2018-19
110*	51	K.L.Rahul	I v WI	Lauderhill	2016
109*	58	C.Munro	NZ v I	Rajkot	2017-18
107*	60	T.P.Ura	PNG v Phil	Port Moresby	2018-19
107	55	G.Malla	Nep v Bhut	Kirtipur	2019-20

106*	52	P.Khadka	Nep v Sing	Singapore	2019-20
106	66	R.G.Sharma	I v SA	Dharamsala	2015-16
105	54	M.J.Guptill	NZ v A	Auckland	2017-18
104*	57	T.M.Dilshan	SL v A	Pallekele	2011
104	53	C.Munro	NZ v WI	Mt Maunganui	2017-18
103*	63	Tamim Iqbal	B v Oman	Dharmasala	2015-16
103*	58	G.J.Maxwell	A v E	Hobart	2017-18
103*	51	D.J.Malan	E v NZ	Napier	2019-20
103	59	R.Sandaruwan	Kuw v Bah	Al Amerat	2018-19

The highest score for Zimbabwe is 94 by S.F.Mire (v P, Harare, 2018).

MOST SIXES IN AN INNINGS

16	Hazratullah Zazai (162*)	Afg v Ire	Dehradun	2018-19
14	A.J.Finch (156)	A v E	Southampton	2013
14	H.G.Munsey (127*)	Scot v Neth	Dublin	2019
13	R.E.Levi (117*)	SA v NZ	Hamilton	2011-12
12	E.Lewis (125*)	WI v I	Kingston	2017

HIGHEST PARTNERSHIP FOR EACH WICKET

1st	236	Hazratullah Zazai/Usmann Ghani	Afg v Ire	Dehradun	2018-19
2nd	166	D.P.M.D.Jayawardena/K.C.Sangakkara	SL v WI	Bridgetown	2009-10
3rd	182	D.J.Malan/E.J.G.Morgan	E v NZ	Napier	2019-20
4th	161	D.A.Warner/G.J.Maxwell	A v SA	Johannesburg	2015-16
5th	119*	Shoaib Malik/Misbah-ul-Haq	P v A	Johannesburg	2007-08
6th	101*	C.L.White/M.E.K.Hussey	A v SL	Bridgetown	2009-10
7th	91	P.D.Collingwood/M.H.Yardy	E v WI	The Oval	2007
8th	80	P.L.Mommsen/S.M.Sharif	Sc v Ne	Edinburgh	2015
9th	66	D.J.Bravo/J.E.Taylor	WI v P	Dubai	2016-17
10th	38	Mohammad Adnan/Usman Ali	Saud v Qat	Al Amerat	2018-19

BOWLING RECORDS
55 WICKETS IN A CAREER

Wkts			Matches	Overs	Mdns	Runs	Avge	Best	R/Over
106	S.L.Malinga	SL	82	292.5	1	2142	20.20	5- 6	7.31
98	Shahid Afridi	P/Wd	99	361.2	4	2396	24.44	4-11	6.63
92	Shakib Al Hasan	B	76	277.5	2	1894	20.58	5-20	6.81
85	Umar Gul	P	60	200.3	2	1443	16.97	5- 6	7.19
85	Saeed Ajmal	P	64	238.2	2	1516	17.83	4-19	6.36
84	Rashid Khan	Afg/IC	45	171.0	1	1052	12.52	5- 3	6.15
78	T.G.Southee	NZ	71	253.0	2	2141	27.44	5-18	8.46
76	G.H.Dockrell	Ire	75	225.2	1	1590	20.92	4-20	7.05
69	Mohammad Nabi	Afg	75	256.4	5	1839	26.65	4-10	7.16
66	B.A.W.Mendis	SL	39	147.3	5	952	14.42	6- 8	6.45
66	K.M.D.N.Kulasekara	SL	58	205.1	6	1530	23.18	4-31	7.45
65	S.C.J.Broad	E	56	195.3	2	1491	22.93	4-24	7.62
64	D.W.Steyn	SA	47	169.1	3	1175	18.35	4- 9	6.94
63	Imran Tahir	SA/Wd	38	140.5	–	948	15.04	5-23	6.73
59	J.J.Bumrah	I	50	179.1	7	1195	20.25	3-11	6.66
59	Mohammad Amir	P	48	175.4	5	1224	20.74	4-13	6.96
58	K.J.O'Brien	Ire	93	150.3	–	1134	19.55	4-45	7.53
58	N.L.McCullum	NZ	63	187.1	–	1278	22.03	4-16	6.82
58	C.J.Jordan	E	46	162.3	–	1408	24.27	4- 6	8.66
57	D.J.Bravo	WI	69	183.5	–	1535	26.92	4-28	8.34
56	S.Badree	WI/Wd	52	191.0	4	1180	21.07	4-15	6.17
55	Y.S.Chahal	I	42	163.3	1	1339	24.34	6-25	8.18

The most wickets for Australia is 48 by S.R.Watson (58 matches) and for Zimbabwe 35 by A.G.Cremer (29 matches).

BEST FIGURES IN AN INNINGS

6- 7	D.L.Chahar	I v B	Nagpur	2019-20
6- 8	B.A.W.Mendis	SL v Z	Hambantota	2012-13
6-16	B.A.W.Mendis	SL v A	Pallekele	2011
6-25	Y.S.Chahal	I v E	Bangalore	2016-17
5- 3	H.M.R.K.B.Herath	SL v NZ	Chittagong	2013-14
5- 3	Rashid Khan	Afg v Ire	Greater Noida	2016-17
5- 4	Khizar Hayat	Malay v HK	Kuala Lumpur	2019-20
5- 6	Umar Gul	P v NZ	The Oval	2009
5- 6	Umar Gul	P v SA	Centurion	2012-13
5- 6	S.L.Malinga	SL v NZ	Pallekele	2019
5- 9	C.Viljoen	Nam v Bots	Kampala	2019
5-11	Karim Janat	Afg v WI	Lucknow	2019-20
5-13	Elias Sunny	B v Ire	Belfast	2012
5-13	Samiullah Shenwari	Afg v Ken	Sharjah	2013-14
5-14	Imad Wasim	P v WI	Dubai	2016-17
5-15	K.M.A.Paul	WI v B	Dhaka	2018-19
5-15	D.Ravu	PNG v Vanu	Apia	2019
5-15	Aamir Kaleem	Oman v Nep	Al Amerat	2019-20
5-17	N.Vanua	PNG v Vanu	Apia	2019
5-18	T.G.Southee	NZ v P	Auckland	2010-11
5-18	A.C.Douglas	Ber v Cay Is	Sandys Parish	2019
5-19	R.McLaren	SA v WI	North Sound	2009-10
5-19	Ahsan Malik	Neth v SA	Chittagong	2013-14
5-19	N.Nipiko	Vanu v PNG	Apia	2019
5-20	N.Odhiambo	Ken v Sc	Nairobi (Gym)	2009-10
5-20	Shakib Al Hasan	B v WI	Dhaka	2018-19

The best figures for England are 4-6 by C.J.Jordan (v WI, Basseterre, 2018-19), for Australia 5-24 by A.C.Agar (v SA, Johannesburg, 2019-20), for Zimbabwe 4-28 by W.P.Masakadza (v Sc, Nagpur, 2015-16), and for Ireland 4-11 by A.R.Cusack (v WI, Kingston, 2013-14).

HAT-TRICKS

B.Lee	Australia v Bangladesh	Melbourne	2007-08
J.D.P.Oram	New Zealand v Sri Lanka	Colombo (RPS)	2009
T.G.Southee	New Zealand v Pakistan	Auckland	2010-11
N.L.T.C.Perera	Sri Lanka v India	Ranchi	2015-16
S.L.Malinga	Sri Lanka v Bangladesh	Colombo (RPS)	2016-17
Faheem Ashraf	Pakistan v Sri Lanka	Abu Dhabi	2017-18
Rashid Khan†	Afghanistan v Ireland	Dehradun	2018-19
S.L.Malinga†	Sri Lanka v New Zealand	Pallekele	2019
Mohammad Hasnain	Pakistan v Sri Lanka	Lahore	2019-20
Khawar Ali	Oman v Netherlands	Al Amerat	2019-20
N.Vanua	PNG v Bermuda	Dubai	2019-20
D.L.Chahar	India v Bangladesh	Nagpur	2019-20
A.C.Agar	Australia v South Africa	Johannesburg	2019-20

† Four wickets in four balls.

WICKET-KEEPING RECORDS – 30 DISMISSALS IN A CAREER

Dis			Matches	Ct	St
91	M.S.Dhoni	India	98	57	34
63	D.Ramdin	West Indies	71	43	20
60	Kamran Akmal	Pakistan	58	28	32
58	Mushfiqur Rahim	Bangladesh	84	30	28
54	Mohammad Shahzad	Afghanistan	65	26	28
50	Q.de Kock	South Africa	44	39	11
45	K.C.Sangakkara	Sri Lanka	56	25	20
45	Sarfraz Ahmed	Pakistan	58	35	10

Dis†			Matches	Ct	St
36†	G.C.Wilson	Ireland	81	29	7
33	M.H.Cross	Scotland	43	22	11
32†	B.B.McCullum	New Zealand	71	24	8
30‡	L.Ronchi	Aus/ICC/N Zealand	33	24	6

† Excluding catches taken in the field. ‡ L.Ronchi played 3 matches for Australia.

MOST DISMISSALS IN AN INNINGS

5 (3 ct, 2 st)	Mohammad Shahzad	Afghanistan v Oman	Abu Dhabi	2015-16
5 (5 ct)	M.S.Dhoni	India v England	Bristol	2018
5 (2 ct, 3 st)	I.A.Karim	Kenya v Ghana	Kampala	2019
5 (5 ct)	K.Doriga	PNG v Vanuatu	Apia	2019

FIELDING RECORDS – 25 CATCHES IN A CAREER

Total			Matches	Total			Matches
57	D.A.Miller	South Africa	78	40	R.G.Sharma	India	108
50	Shoaib Malik	Pakistan/ICC	113	39	G.H.Dockrell	Ireland	75
46	M.J.Guptill	New Zealand	88	39	Umar Akmal	Pakistan	84
46	L.R.P.L.Taylor	New Zealand	100	37	E.J.G.Morgan	England	89
44†	A.B.de Villiers	South Africa	78	36	D.J.Bravo	West Indies	69
44	D.A.Warner	Australia	79	35	T.G.Southee	New Zealand	71
42	S.K.Raina	India	78	35	K.A.Pollard	West Indies	71
41	Mohammad Nabi	Afghanistan	75	35	J.P.Duminy	South Africa	81
41	V.Kohli	India	82				

† Excluding catches taken as a wicket-keeper.

MOST CATCHES IN AN INNINGS

4	D.J.G.Sammy	West Indies v Ireland	Providence	2009-10
4	P.W.Borren	Netherlands v Bangladesh	The Hague	2012
4	C.J.Anderson	New Zealand v South Africa	Port Elizabeth	2012-13
4	L.D.Chandimal	Sri Lanka v Bangladesh	Chittagong	2013-14
4	A.M.Rahane	India v England	Birmingham	2014
4	Babar Hayat	Hong Kong v Afghanistan	Dhaka	2015-16
4	D.A.Miller	South Africa v Pakistan	Cape Town	2018-19
4	L.Siaka	PNG v Vanuatu	Apia	2019
4	C.S.MacLeod	Scotland v Ireland	Dublin	2019
4	T.H.David	Singapore v Scotland	Dubai	2019-20
4	C.de Grandhomme	New Zealand v England	Wellington	2019-20

APPEARANCE RECORDS – 80 APPEARANCES

113	Shoaib Malik	Pakistan/ICC		85	Mahmudullah	Bangladesh
108	R.G.Sharma	India		84	Mushfiqur Rahim	Bangladesh
100	L.R.P.L.Taylor	New Zealand		84	Umar Akmal	Pakistan
99	Shahid Afridi	Pakistan/ICC		82	V.Kohli	India
98	M.S.Dhoni	India		82	S.L.Malinga	Sri Lanka
93	K.J.O'Brien	Ireland		81	J.P.Duminy	South Africa
91	Mohammad Hafeez	Pakistan		81	G.C.Wilson	Ireland
89	E.J.G.Morgan	England		80	T.M.Dilshan	Sri Lanka
88	M.J.Guptill	New Zealand				

The most for West Indies is 71 by K.A.Pollard and D.Ramdin, for Zimbabwe 66 by H.Masakadza, and for Afghanistan 75 by Mohammad Nabi.

45 MATCHES AS CAPTAIN

			W	L	T	NR	%age wins
72	M.S.Dhoni	India	41	28	1	2	58.57
56	W.T.S.Porterfield	Ireland	26	26	–	4	50.00
47	D.J.G.Sammy	West Indies	27	17	1	2	60.00
46	Asghar Stanikzai	Afghanistan	37	9	–	–	80.43
46	E.J.G.Morgan	England	25	19	2	–	54.34

INDIAN PREMIER LEAGUE 2019

The 12th IPL tournament was held in India between 23 March and 12 May

Team	P	W	L	T	NR	Pts	Net RR
1 Mumbai Indians (5)	14	9	5	–	–	18	+0.42
2 Chennai Super Kings (2)	14	9	5	–	–	18	+0.13
3 Delhi Capitals (8)	14	9	5	–	–	18	+0.04
4 Sunrisers Hyderabad (1)	14	6	8	–	–	12	+0.57
5 Kolkata Knight Riders (3)	14	6	8	–	–	12	+0.02
6 Kings XI Punjab (7)	14	6	8	–	–	12	–0.25
7 Rajasthan Royals (4)	14	5	8	–	1	11	–0.44
8 Royal Challengers Bangalore (6)	14	5	8	–	1	11	–0.60

1st Qualifying Match: At M.A.Chidambaram Stadium, Chennai, 7 May (floodlit). Toss: Chennai Super Kings. **MUMBAI INDIANS** won by six wickets. Chennai Super Kings 131-4 (20). Mumbai Indians 132-4 (18.3; S.A.Yadav 71*). Award: S.A.Yadav.

Eliminator: At Dr Y.S.Rajasekhara Reddy ACA-VDCA Cricket Stadium, Visakhapatnam, 8 May (floodlit). Toss: Delhi Capitals. **DELHI CAPITALS** won by two wickets. Sunrisers Hyderabad 162-8 (20; K.M.A.Paul 3-32). Delhi Capitals 165-8 (19.5; P.P.Shaw 56). Award: R.R.Pant (DC, 49 in 21b).

2nd Qualifying Match: At Dr Y.S.Rajasekhara Reddy ACA-VDCA Cricket Stadium, Visakhapatnam, 10 May (floodlit). Toss: Chennai Super Kings. **CHENNAI SUPER KINGS** won by six wickets. Delhi Capitals 147-9 (20). Chennai Super Kings 151-4 (19; F.du Plessis 50, S.R.Watson 50). Award: F.du Plessis.

FINAL: At Rajiv Gandhi International Stadium, Hyderabad, 12 May (floodlit). Toss: Mumbai Indians. **MUMBAI INDIANS** won by 1 run. Mumbai Indians 149-8 (20; D.L.Chahar 3-26). Chennai Super Kings 148-7 (20; S.R.Watson 80). Award: J.J.Bumrah (MI, 2-14). Series award: A.D.Russell (KKR).

IPL winners:	2008	Rajasthan Royals	2009	Deccan Chargers
	2010	Chennai Super Kings	2011	Chennai Super Kings
	2012	Kolkata Knight Riders	2013	Mumbai Indians
	2014	Kolkata Knight Riders	2015	Mumbai Indians
	2016	Sunrisers Hyderabad	2017	Mumbai Indians
	2018	Chennai Super Kings		

TEAM RECORDS
HIGHEST TOTALS

263-5 (20)	Bangalore v Pune	Bangalore	2013
248-3 (20)	Bangalore v Gujarat	Bangalore	2016

LOWEST TOTALS

49 (9.4)	Bangalore v Kolkata	Kolkata	2017
58 (15.1)	Rajasthan v Bangalore	Cape Town	2009

LARGEST MARGINS OF VICTORY

146 runs	Mumbai (212-3) v Delhi (66)	Delhi	2017

There have been 11 victories in IPL history by ten wickets, the most recent being:

10 wickets	Bangalore (92-0) v Punjab (88)	Indore	2018

BATTING RECORDS
MOST RUNS IN IPL

5412	V.Kohli	Bangalore	2008-19
5368	S.K.Raina	Chennai, Gujarat	2008-19

800 RUNS IN A SEASON

Runs			Year	M	I	NO	HS	Ave	100	50	6s	4s	R/100B
973	V.Kohli	Bangalore	2016	16	16	4	113	81.08	4	7	38	83	152.0
848	D.A.Warner	Hyderabad	2016	17	17	3	93*	60.57	–	9	31	88	151.4

HIGHEST SCORES

Score	Balls				
*175**	66	C.H.Gayle	Bangalore v Pune	Bangalore	2013
158*	73	B.B.McCullum	Kolkata v Bangalore	Bangalore	2008
133*	59	A.B.de Villiers	Bangalore v Mumbai	Mumbai	2015
129*	52	A.B.de Villiers	Bangalore v Mumbai	Bangalore	2016
128*	62	C.H.Gayle	Bangalore v Delhi	Delhi	2012
128*	63	R.R.Pant	Delhi v Hyderabad	Delhi	2018

K.P.Pietersen 103* (Delhi v Deccan at Delhi, 2012), B.A.Stokes 103* (Pune v Gujarat at Pune, 2017) and J.M.Bairstow 114 (Hyderabad v Bangalore at Hyderabad, 2019) are the only England-qualified centurions in the IPL.

FASTEST HUNDRED

30 balls	C.H.Gayle (175*)	Bangalore v Pune	Bangalore	2013

MOST SIXES IN AN INNINGS

17	C.H.Gayle	Bangalore v Pune	Bangalore	2013

HIGHEST STRIKE RATE IN A SEASON (Qualification: 100 runs or more)

R/100B	Runs	Balls			
204.81	510	249	A.D.Russell	Kolkata	2019

HIGHEST STRIKE RATE IN AN INNINGS (Qualification: 25 runs, 350+ strike rate)

R/100B	Runs	Balls			
422.2	38*	9	C.H.Morris	Delhi v Pune	Pune	2017
400.0	28	7	J.A.Morkel	Chennai v Bangalore	Chennai	2012
387.5	31	8	A.B.de Villiers	Bangalore v Pune	Bangalore	2013
385.7	27*	7	B.Akhil	Bangalore v Deccan	Hyderabad	2008
372.7	41	11	A.B.de Villiers	Bangalore v Mumbai	Bangalore	2015
369.2	48*	13	A.D.Russell	Kolkata v Bangalore	Bangalore	2019
350.0	35	10	C.H.Gayle	Bangalore v Hyderabad	Hyderabad	2015
350.0	35*	10	S.N.Khan	Bangalore v Hyderabad	Bangalore	2016

BOWLING RECORDS
MOST WICKETS IN IPL

170	S.L.Malinga	Mumbai	2009-19
157	A.Mishra	Deccan, Delhi, Hyderabad	2008-19

26 WICKETS IN A SEASON

Wkts			Year	P	O	M	Runs	Avge	Best	4w	R/Over
32	D.J.Bravo	Chennai	2013	18	62.3	–	497	15.53	4-42	1	7.95
28	S.L.Malinga	Mumbai	2011	16	63.0	2	375	13.39	5-13	1	5.95
28	J.P.Faulkner	Rajasthan	2013	16	63.1	2	427	15.25	5-16	2	6.75
26	D.J.Bravo	Chennai	2015	17	52.2	–	426	16.38	3-22	–	8.14
26	B.Kumar	Hyderabad	2017	14	52.2	–	369	14.19	5-19	1	7.05
26	Imran Tahir	Chennai	2019	17	64.2	1	431	16.57	4-12	2	6.69

BEST BOWLING FIGURES IN AN INNINGS

6-12	A.S.Joseph	Mumbai v Hyderabad	Hyderabad	2109
6-14	Sohail Tanvir	Rajasthan v Chennai	Jaipur	2008
6-19	A.Zampa	Pune v Hyderabad	Visakhapatnam	2016
5- 5	A.Kumble	Bangalore v Rajasthan	Cape Town	2009

MOST ECONOMICAL BOWLING ANALYSIS

O	M	R	W				
4	1	6	0	F.H.Edwards	Deccan v Kolkata	Cape Town	2009
4	1	6	0	A.Nehra	Delhi v Punjab	Bloemfontein	2009
4	1	6	1	Y.S.Chahal	Bangalore v Chennai	Chennai	2019

MOST EXPENSIVE BOWLING ANALYSIS

O	M	R	W				
4	0	70	0	Basil Thampi	Hyderabad v Bangalore	Bangalore	2018
4	0	66	0	I.Sharma	Hyderabad v Chennai	Hyderabad	2013
4	0	66	0	Mujeeb Zadran	Punjab v Hyerabad	Hyderabad	2019

BIG BASH 2019-20

The ninth Big Bash tournament was held in Australia between 17 December and 8 February.

Team	P	W	L	T	NR	Pts	Net RR
1 Melbourne Stars (4)	14	10	4	–	–	20	+0.52
2 Sydney Sixers (3)	14	9	4	–	1	19	+0.26
3 Adelaide Strikers (7)	14	8	5	–	1	17	+0.56
4 Hobart Hurricanes (1)	14	6	7	–	1	13	–0.35
5 Sydney Thunder (6)	14	6	7	–	1	13	–0.44
6 Perth Scorchers (8)	14	6	8	–	–	12	–0.02
7 Brisbane Heat (5)	14	6	8	–	–	12	–0.23
8 Melbourne Renegades (2)	14	3	11	–	–	6	–0.34

Knockout: At Adelaide Oval, 1 February (floodlit). Toss: Adelaide Strikers. **SYDNEY THUNDER** won by 8 runs. Sydney Thunder 151-7 (20); A.D.Hales 59). Adelaide Strikers 143-9 (20; D.R.Sams 3-26). Award: A.D.Hales.

Challenger: At Melbourne Cricket Ground, 6 February (floodlit). Toss: Melbourne Stars. **MELBOURNE STARS** won by 28 runs. Melbourne Stars 194-2 (20; N.C.R.Larkin 83*, M.P.Stoinis 83). Sydney Thunder 166-8 (20; A.I.Ross 58, Haris Rauf 3-17). Award: N.C.R.Larkin.

FINAL: At Sydney Cricket Ground, 8 February. Toss: Melbourne Stars. **SYDNEY SIXERS** won by 19 runs. Sydney Sixers 116-5 (12; J.R.Philippe 52). Melbourne Stars 97-6 (12). Award: J.R.Philippe.

Big Bash winners:

2011-12	Sydney Sixers	2012-13	Brisbane Heat
2013-14	Perth Scorchers	2014-15	Perth Scorchers
2015-16	Sydney Thunder	2016-17	Perth Scorchers
2017-18	Adelaide Strikers	2018-19	Melbourne Renegades

TEAM RECORDS
HIGHEST TOTALS

223-8 (20)	Hurricanes v Renegades	Melbourne (Dock)	2016-17
222-4 (20)	Renegades v Hurricanes	Melbourne (Dock)	2016-17

LOWEST TOTALS

57 (12.4)	Renegades v Stars	Melbourne (Dock)	2014-15
69 (15.2)	Scorchers v Stars	Perth	2012-13

LARGEST MARGINS OF VICTORY

112 runs	Renegades (57) v Stars (169-6)	Melbourne (Dock)	2014-15
10 wickets	Scorchers (171-0) v Renegades (170-4)	Melbourne (Dock)	2015-16
10 wickets	Strikers (154-5) v Hurricanes (158-0)	Adelaide	2018-19
10 wickets	Stars (156-8) v Heat (158-0)	Brisbane	2018-19
10 wickets	Heat (100) v Strikers (104-0)	Adelaide	2019-20

BATTING RECORDS
MOST RUNS IN BIG BASH

2332 (av 37.61)	C.A.Lynn	Heat	2011-20
2252 (av 38.82)	A.J.Finch	Renegades	2011-20

MOST RUNS IN A SEASON

Runs			Year	M	I	NO	HS	Ave	100	50	6s	4s	R/100B
705	M.P.Stoinis	Stars	2019-20	17	17	4	147*	54.23	1	6	28	62	136.6

HIGHEST SCORES

Score	Balls				
147*	79	M.P.Stoinis	Stars v Sixers	Melbourne	2019-20
130*	61	M.S.Wade	Hurricanes v Strikers	Adelaide	2019-20
122*	69	D.J.M.Short	Hurricanes v Heat	Brisbane	2017-18

FASTEST HUNDRED

39 balls	C.J.Simmons (102)	Scorchers v Strikers	Perth	2013-14

MOST SIXES IN AN INNINGS

11	C.H.Gayle (100*)	Thunder v Strikers	Sydney (SA)	2011-12
11	C.J.Simmons (112)	Scorchers v Sixers	Sydney	2013-14
11	C.A.Lynn (98*)	Heat v Scorchers	Perth	2016-17
11	C.A.Lynn (94)	Heat v Sixers	Sydney	2019-20

HIGHEST STRIKE RATE IN AN INNINGS (Qualification: 25 runs, 325+ strike rate)

R/100B	Score	Balls				
377.7	34	9	D.T.Christian	Heat v Hurricanes	Hobart	2014-15
329.4	56	17	C.H.Gayle	Renegades v Strikers	Melbourne (Dk)	2015-16
327.2	36*	11	B.J.Rohrer	Renegades v Heat	Melbourne (Dk)	2013-14

HIGHEST PARTNERSHIPS

207	M.P.Stoinis/H.W.R.Cartwright	Stars v Sixers	Melbourne	2019-20
203	M.S.Wade/D.J.M.Short	Hurricanes v Strikers	Adelaide	2019-20

BOWLING RECORDS
MOST WICKETS IN BIG BASH

110	B.Laughlin	Strikers, Heat, Hurricanes		2011-20
99	S.A.Abbott	Sixers, Thunder		2011-20

MOST WICKETS IN A SEASON

Wkts			Year	P	O	M	Runs	Avge	Best	4w	R/Over
30	D.R.Sams	Thunder	2019-20	17	58.5	2	461	15.36	4-34	1	7.83

BEST BOWLING FIGURES IN AN INNINGS

6- 7	S.L.Malinga	Stars v Scorchers	Perth	2012-13
6-11	I.S.Sodhi	Strikers v Thunder	Sydney (Show)	2016-17
5-14	D.T.Christian	Hurricanes v Strikers	Hobart	2016-17

MOST ECONOMICAL BOWLING ANALYSIS

O	M	R	W				
4	2	3	3	M.G.Johnson	Scorchers v Stars	Perth	2016-17
4	1	7	6	S.L.Malinga	Stars v Scorchers	Perth	2012-13
4	1	7	1	Fawad Ahmed	Renegades v Heat	Melbourne (Dk)	2014-15
4	0	7	3	B.J.Dwarshuis	Sixers v Strikers	Sydney	2018-19

MOST EXPENSIVE BOWLING ANALYSIS

O	M	R	W				
4	0	61	0	B.J.Dwarshuis	Sixers v Stars	Melbourne	2019-20
4	0	60	0	D.J.Worrall	Stars v Hurricanes	Melbourne	2014-15
4	0	60	1	B.Laughlin	Heat v Scorchers	Perth	2019-20

WICKET-KEEPING RECORDS
MOST DISMISSALS IN BIG BASH

39	J.J.Peirson	Heat		2014-20

MOST DISMISSALS IN A SERIES

14	A.T.Carey	Strikers		2017-18
14	J.J.Peirson	Heat		2019-20

MOST DISMISSALS IN AN INNINGS

5 (5ct)	T.I.F.Triffitt	Scorchers v Renegades	Perth	2012-13
5 (4ct, 1st)	J.J.Peirson	Heat v Strikers	Brisbane	2019-20

IRELAND INTERNATIONALS

The following players have played for Ireland in any format of international cricket since 1 December 2018. Details correct to 18 March 2020.

ADAIR, Mark Richard (Sullivan Upper S, Holywood), b Belfast 27 Mar 1996. 6'2''. RHB, RFM. Warwickshire 2015-16. Northern debut 2018. Ireland Wolves 2018-19. **Tests**: 1 (2019); HS 8 and BB 3-32 v E (Lord's) 2019. **LOI**: 12 (2019 to 2019-20); HS 32 v E (Dublin) 2019; BB 4-19 v Afg (Belfast) 2019. **IT20**: 18 (2019 to 2019-20); HS 34 v Z (Bready) 2019; BB 4-40 v Z (Bready) 2019 – on debut, different matches. HS 91 Northern v Leinster (Dublin, Sandymount) 2018. BB 3-32 (*see LOI*). LO HS 44 Northern v NW (La Manga) 2019. LO BB 4-19 (*see LOI*). T20 HS 38. T20 BB 4-22.

BALBIRNIE, Andrew (St Andrew's C, Dublin; UWIC), b Dublin 28 Dec 1990. 6'2''. RHB, OB. Cardiff MCCU 2012-13. Ireland debut 2012. Middlesex 2012-15. Leinster debut 2017. Ireland Wolves 2017-18. **Tests**: 3 (2018 to 2019); HS 82 v Afg (Dehradun) 2018-19. **LOI**: 67 (2010 to 2019-20, 3 as captain); HS 145* v Afg (Dehradun) 2018-19; BB 1-26 v Afg (Dubai, DSC) 2014-15. **IT20**: 40 (2015 to 2019-20, 3 as captain); HS 83 v Neth (Al Amerat) 2018-19. HS 205* Ire v Neth (Dublin) 2017. BB 4-23 Lein v NW (Bready) 2017. LO HS 160* Ire W v Bangladesh A (Dublin, CA) 2018. LO BB 1-26 (*see LOI*). T20 HS 83.

CAMERON-DOW, James, b Cape Town, South Africa 18 May 1990. LHB, SLA. Northern debut 2018. Ireland Wolves 2018-19. Sussex 2nd XI 2009. **Tests**: 1 (2018-19); HS 32* and BB 2-94 v Afg (Dehradun) 2018-19. **LOI**: 4 (2018-19); HS 7* and BB 3-32 (Dehradun) 2018-19. HS 76* Ire W v SL A (Hambantota) 2018-19. BB 7-77 Ire W v Sri Lanka A (Colombo, SSC) 2018-19. LO HS 34* Ire A v Z (Eglinton) 2019. LO BB 3-32 (*see LOI*). T20 HS 8*. T20 BB 3-12.

CHASE, Peter Karl David (Malahide Community S), b Dublin 9 Oct 1993. 6'4''. RHB, RMF. Durham 2014, taking 5-64 v Notts (Chester-le-St) on debut. Ireland debut 2016. Leinster debut 2017. **LOI**: 25 (2014-15 to 2018); HS 14 v NZ (Dublin) 2017; BB 3-33 v B (Dublin) 2017. **IT20**: 12 (2018 to 2018-19); HS 4 v Afg (Bready) 2018; BB 4-35 v I (Dublin) 2018. HS 24 and BB 5-24 Leinster v NW (Bready) 2018. LO HS 22* Ire v Sri Lanka A (Belfast) 2014. LO BB 5-42 Ire W v Bangladesh A (Dublin, CA) 2018. T20 HS 9*. T20 BB 4-11.

DELANY, David Colin Alex, b Dublin 28 Dec 1997. Cousin of G.J.Delany. LHB, RMF. Leinster 2017-18. Northern debut 2019. **IT20**: 8 (2019 to 2019-20); HS 7 v Scot (Dublin) 2019; BB 2-12 v Jersey (Abu Dhabi, TO) 2019-20. HS 17 Northern v Leinster (Dublin) 2019. BB 4-31 Leinster v Northern (Dublin, CA) 2017. LO HS 11* and LO BB 1-27 Leinster v Northern (Dublin, OL) 2017. T20 HS 25. T20 BB 2-12.

DELANY, Gareth James, b Dublin 28 Apr 1997. Cousin of D.C.A.Delany. RHB, LBG. Leinster debut 2017. Ireland Wolves 2018-19. **LOI**: 2 (2019-20); HS 19 v WI (Bridgetown) 2019-20; BB – . **IT20**: 20 (2019 to 2019-20); HS 89* v Oman (Abu Dhabi, TO) 2019-20; BB 2-23 v Namibia (Dubai, DSC) 2019-20. HS 22 Ire W v SL A (Colombo, SSC) 2018-19. BB 3-48 Leinster v Northern (Belfast) 2017. LO HS 67 Leinster v NW (Dublin, OL) 2018. LO BB 3-47 Leinster v NW (Bready) 2019. T20 HS 89*. T20 BB 3-25.

DOCKRELL, George Henry (Gonzaga C, Dublin), b Dublin 22 Jul 1992. 6'3''. RHB, SLA. Ireland 2010 to date. Somerset 2011-14. Sussex 2015. Leinster debut 2017. Ireland Wolves 2017-18. **Tests**: 1 (2018-19); HS 39 and BB 2-63 v Afg (Dehradun) 2018-19. **LOI**: 87 (2009-10 to 2019); HS 62* v Afg (Sharjah) 2017-18; BB 4-24 v Scot (Belfast) 2013. **IT20**: 75 (2009-10 to 2019-20); HS 34* v Afg (Dehradun) 2018-19; BB 4-20 v Neth (Dubai) 2009-10. HS 92 Leinster v NW (Bready) 2018. BB 6-27 Sm v Middx (Taunton) 2012. LO HS 98* and LO BB 5-21 Leinster v Northern (Dublin, V) 2018. T20 HS 40*. T20 BB 4-20.

GETKATE, Shane Charles, b Durban, South Africa 2 Oct 1991. Grandson of R.S.Getkate (Natal 1936-37). RHB, RMF. Northern debut 2017. Ireland Wolves 2017-18. Warwickshire 2nd XI 2011. MCC YC 2013-14. Northamptonshire 2nd XI 2014. **LOI**: 3 (2019); HS 16* v Z (Bready) 2019; BB 2-30 v Z (Belfast) 2019. **IT20**: 14 (2018-19 to 2019-20); HS 24 v Afg (Dehradun) 2018-19; BB 2-15 v Scotland (Al Amerat) 2018-19. HS 70 Northern v Leinster (Comber) 2018. BB 4-62 Northern v Leinster (Dublin, CA) 2017. LO HS 86 Ire W v Sri Lanka A (Colombo, SSC) 2018-19. LO BB 5-44 Northern v Leinster (Downpatrick) 2017. T20 HS 49. T20 BB 5-8.

KANE, Tyrone Edward (Catholic Uni S, Dublin; University C, Dublin), b Dublin 8 Jul 1994. RHB, RMF. Leinster debut 2017. Nottinghamshire 2nd XI 2016. **Tests**: 1 (2018); HS 14 v P (Dublin) 2018; BB – . **IT20**: 7 (2015 to 2019); HS 26* v Scot (Bready) 2015; BB 3-19 v PNG (Belfast) 2015. HS 75 and BB 3-45 Leinster v Northern (Dublin, CA) 2017. LO HS 57 Leinster v NW (Dublin, OL) 2018. LO BB 6-42 Leinster v Northern (Belfast) 2019. T20 HS 26*. T20 BB 5-22.

LITTLE, Joshua Brian, b Dublin 1 Nov 1999. RHB, LFM. Leinster debut 2018. Ireland Wolves 2018-19. **LOI**: 4 (2019); HS 9 and BB 4-45 v E (Dublin) 2019. **IT20**: 14 (2016 to 2019-20); HS 7 v Neth (Al Amerat) 2018-19; BB 3-29 v WI (St George's) 2019-20. HS 27 Leinster v NW (Bready) 2018. BB 3-95 Leinster v Northern (Dublin) 2018. LO HS 9 (see LOI). LO BB 4-45 (see LOI). T20 HS 7. T20 BB 3-29.

McBRINE, Andrew Robert, b Londonderry 30 Apr 1993. Son of A.McBrine (Ireland 1985-92), nephew of J.McBrine (Ireland 1986). LHB, OB. Ireland debut 2013. North-West debut 2017. Ireland Wolves 2017-18. **Tests**: 2 (2018-19 to 2019); HS 11 v E (Lord's) 2019; BB 2-77 v Afg (Dehradun) 2018-19. **LOI**: 45 (2014 to 2019-20); HS 79 v SL (Dublin) 2016; BB 3-38 v PNG (Harare) 2017-18. **IT20**: 19 (2013-14 to 2016-17); HS 14* v UAE (Dubai, DSC) 2016-17; BB 2-7 v PNG (Townsville) 2015-16. HS 77 NW v Northern (Comber) 2018. BB 4-35 NW v Northern (Bready) 2018. LO HS 89 Ire W v Bangladesh A (Dublin, CA) 2018. LO BB 3-32 NW v Northern (Waringstown) 2017. T20 HS 52*. T20 BB 3-19.

McCARTHY, Barry John (St Michael's C, Dublin; University C, Dublin), b Dublin 13 Sep 1992. 5'11". RHB, RMF. Durham 2015-18. Leinster debut 2019. **LOI** (Ire): 30 (2016 to 2019-20); HS 18 v Afg (Belfast) 2019; BB 5-46 v Afg (Sharjah) 2017-18. **IT20** (Ire): 9 (2016-17 to 2019-20); HS 18* v WI (Basseterre) 2019-20; BB 4-33 v Afg (Greater Noida) 2016-17. HS 51* Du v Hants (Chester-le-St) 2016. BB 6-63 Du v Kent (Canterbury) 2017. LO HS 43 Du v Leics (Leicester) 2018 (RLC). LO BB 5-46 (see LOI). T20 HS 18*. T20 BB 4-31.

McCOLLUM, James Alexander (Methodist C, Belfast; Durham U), b Craigavon 1 Aug 1995. RHB, RM. Durham MCCU 2017. Northern debut 2017. Ireland Wolves 2018-19. **Tests**: 2 (2018-19 to 2019); HS 39 v Afg (Dehradun) 2018-19. **LOI**: 9 (2018-19 to 2019-20); HS 73 v Z (Belfast) 2019. HS 119* Northern v Leinster (Belfast) 2017. BB 5-32 Northern v NW (Bready) 2018. LO HS 102 Ire W v Sri Lanka A (Colombo, RPS) 2018-19. LO BB 1-14 Northern v NW (Eglinton) 2018. T20 HS 42*.

MURTAGH, T.J. – see MIDDLESEX.

O'BRIEN, Kevin Joseph (Marian C, Dublin; Tallaght I of Tech), b Dublin 4 Mar 1984. RHB, RM. Son of B.A.O'Brien (Ireland 1966-81) and younger brother of N.J.O'Brien (Kent, Northamptonshire, Leicestershire, North-West and Ireland 2004-18). Ireland debut 2006-07. Nottinghamshire 2009. Surrey 2014. Leicestershire 2015-16 (l-o and T20 only). Leinster debut 2017. **Tests**: 3 (2018 to 2019); HS 118 v P (Dublin) 2018 – on debut and Ire record; BB – . **LOI**: 145 (2006 to 2019-20, 4 as captain); HS 142 v Kenya (Nairobi) 2006-07; BB 4-13 v Neth (Amstelveen) 2013. **IT20**: 93 (2008 to 2019-20, 4 as captain); HS 124 v Hong Kong (Al Amerat) 2019-20 – Ire record; BB 4-45 v Afg (Greater Noida) 2016-17. HS 171* Ire v Kenya (Nairobi) 2008-09. BB 5-39 Ire v Canada (Toronto) 2010. LO HS 142 (see LOI). LO BB 4-13 (see LOI). T20 HS 124. T20 BB 4-22.

PORTERFIELD, William Thomas Stuart (Strabane GS; Leeds Met U), b Londonderry 6 Sep 1984. 5'11". LHB, OB. Ireland 2006-07 to date. Gloucestershire 2008-10; cap 2008. Warwickshire 2011-17; cap 2014. North West debut 2018. MCC 2007. **Tests**: 3 (2018 to 2019, 3 as captain); HS 32 v P (Dublin) 2018. **LOI**: 139 (2006 to 2019-20, 113 as captain); HS 139 v UAE (Dubai, ICCA) 2017-18. **IT20**: 61 (2008 to 2018, 56 as captain); HS 72 v UAE (Abu Dhabi) 2015-16. HS 207 NW v Leinster (Bready) 2018. BB 1-29 Ire v Jamaica (Spanish Town) 2009-10. LO HS 139 (*see LOI*). T20 HS 127*.

POYNTER, S.W. – *see DURHAM*.

RANKIN, William Boyd (Strabane GS; Harper Adams UC), b Londonderry, Co Derry 5 Jul 1984. Brother of R.J.Rankin (Ireland U19 2003-04). 6'8". LHB, RFM. Ireland 2006-07 to date. Derbyshire 2007. Warwickshire 2008-17; cap 2013. Became available for England in 2012, before rejoining Ireland in 2015-16. North West debut 2018. **Tests** (E/Ire): 3 (1 for E 2013-14, 2 for Ire 2018 to 2019); HS 17 Ire v P (Dublin) 2018; BB 2-5 Ire v E (Lord's) 2019. **LOI** (E/Ire): 75 (68 for Ire 2006-07 to 2019-20, 7 for E 2013 to 2013-14); HS 18* Ire v SL (Dublin) 2016; BB 4-15 Ire v UAE (Harare) 2017-18. **IT20** (E/Ire): 48 (46 for Ire 2009 to 2019-20, 2 for E 2013); HS 16* Ire v UAE (Abu Dhabi) 2015-16; BB 3-16 Ire v UAE (Dubai, DSC) 2016-17. F-c Tour: a 2013-14. HS 56* Wa v Worcs (Birmingham) 2015. 50 wkts (1): 55 (2011). BB 6-55 Wa v Yorks (Leeds) 2015. LO HS 18* v Northants (Northampton) 2013 (Y40) and *see LOI*. LO BB 4-15 (*see LOI*). T20 HS 16*. T20 BB 4-9.

SINGH, Simranjit ('Simi'), b Bathlana, Punjab, India 4 Feb 1987. RHB, OB. Leinster debut 2017. Ireland debut 2017. Ireland Wolves 2017-18. **LOI**: 18 (2017 to 2019-20); HS 45 v Scot (Dubai, ICCA) 2017-18; BB 3-15 v UAE (Harare) 2017-18. **IT20**: 21 (2018 to 2019-20); HS 57* v Neth (Rotterdam) 2018; BB 3-15 v Oman (Al Amerat) 2018-19. HS 121 Ire W v Bangladesh A (Sylhet) 2017-18. BB 5-38 Leinster v Northern (Dublin) 2019. LO HS 121* Leinster v Northern (Dublin, V) 2018. LO BB 4-51 Ire W v Bangladesh (Dublin, V) 2019. T20 HS 109. T20 BB 3-15.

STIRLING, P.R. – *see NORTHAMPTONSHIRE*.

TECTOR, Harry Tom, b Dublin 6 Nov 1999. Younger brother of J.B.Tector (Leinster 2017 to date). RHB, OB. Northern debut 2018. Ireland Wolves 2018-19. **IT20**: 17 (2019 to 2019-20); HS 60 v Neth (Dublin) 2019. HS 146 Northern v Leinster (Dublin) 2019. BB 4-70 Northern v NW (Bready) 2018. LO HS 103 Ire W v Sri Lanka A (Colombo, SSC) 2018-19. LO BB 5-36 Northern v NW (La Manga) 2019. T20 HS 60. T20 BB 4-21.

THOMPSON, Greg James (Friends S; Durham U), b Lisburn 17 Sep 1987. 6'0". RHB, LB. Ireland 2004-08. Durham UCCE 2007-08. Northern 2017. **LOI**: 3 (2007-08); HS 1 (twice); BB 1-35 v B (Dhaka) 2007-08. **IT20**: 10 (2016 to 2019); HS 44 v Hong Kong (Bready) 2016. HS 38 Durham UCCE v Durham (Durham) 2007. BB 3-76 Ire v Scot (Belfast) 2007. LO HS 23 Northern v NW (Waringstown) 2017. LO BB 1-2 Lancs v Bangladesh A (Liverpool) 2005. T20 HS 80.

THOMPSON, Stuart Robert (Limavady GS; U of Northumbria), b Eglinton, Londonderry 15 Aug 1991. LHB, RM. Ireland debut 2012. North-West debut 2017. Ireland Wolves 2017-18. Played county 2nd XI cricket for four counties 2012-15. **Tests**: 3 (2018 to 2019); HS 53 v P (Dublin) 2018; BB 3-28 v Afg (Dehradun) 2018-19. **LOI**: 20 (2013 to 2017); HS 39 v Scot (Dublin) 2014; BB 2-17 v WI (Kingston) 2013-14. **IT20**: 41 (2013-14 to 2019-20); HS 56 v Afg (Greater Noida) 2016-17; BB 4-18 v Neth (Al Amerat) 2018-19. HS 148 NW v Leinster (Dublin, SP) 2018. BB 3-28 (*see Tests*). LO HS 68 Ire W v Bangladesh A (Oak Hill) 2018. LO BB 4-55 NW v Northern (La Manga) 2019. T20 HS 56. T20 BB 4-18.

TUCKER, Lorcan John, b Dublin 10 Sep 1996. RHB, WK. Leinster debut 2017. Ireland Wolves 2018-19. **LOI**: 8 (2019 to 2019-20); HS 54 v Z (Belfast) 2019. **IT20**: 16 (2018 to 2019-20); HS 22* v Oman (Al Amerat) 2018-19; HS 80 Ire W v Sri Lanka A (Hambantota) 2018-19. LO HS 109 Ire W v Sri Lanka A (Hambantota) 2018-19. T20 HS 51.

WILSON, Gary Craig (Methodist C, Belfast; Manchester Met U), b Dundonald 5 Feb 1986. 5'10". RHB, WK. Ireland 2005 to date. Surrey 2010-16; cap 2014. Derbyshire 2017-18; T20 captain 2018. **Tests** (Ire): 2 (2018 to 2019); HS 33* v P (Dublin) 2018. **LOI** (Ire): 105 (2007 to 2019); HS 113 v Neth (Dublin) 2010. **IT20** (Ire): 81 (2008 to 2019-20, 26 as captain); HS 65* v Scot (Dubai, DSC) 2016-17. HS 160* Sy v Leics (Oval) 2014. BB – . LO HS 113 (*see LOI*). T20 HS 80.

YOUNG, Craig Alexander (Strabane HS; North West IHE, Belfast), b Londonderry 4 Apr 1990. RHB, RM. Ireland debut 2013. North-West debut 2017. Ireland Wolves 2018-19. Sussex 2nd XI 2010-13. Hampshire 2nd XI 2016. **LOI**: 14 (2014 to 2019-20); HS 11* v Scot (Dublin) 2014; BB 5-46 v Scot (Dublin) 2014 – different matches. **IT20**: 29 (2015 to 2019-20); HS 8 v WI (Basseterre) 2019-20; BB 4-13 v Nigeria (Abu Dhabi) 2019-20. HS 23 and BB 5-37 NW v Northern (Eglinton) 2017. LO HS 27 NW v Northern (La Manga) 2019. LO BB 5-46 (*see LOI*). T20 HS 8. T20 BB 5-15.

PRINCIPAL FIXTURES

Thu 14 May		
LOI	Belfast	Ireland v Bangladesh
Sat 16 May		
LOI	Belfast	Ireland v Bangladesh
Tue 19 May		
LOI	Belfast	Ireland v Bangladesh
Fri 22 May		
IT20	Oval	Ireland v Bangladesh
Sun 24 May		
IT20	Chelmsford	Ireland v Bangladesh
Wed 27 May		
IT20	Bristol	Ireland v Bangladesh
Fri 19 June		
IT20	Bready	Ireland v New Zealand
Sun 21 June		
IT20	Bready	Ireland v New Zealand
Tue 23 June		
IT20	Bready	Ireland v New Zealand
Sat 27 June		
LOI	Belfast	Ireland v New Zealand
Tue 30 June		
LOI	Belfast	Ireland v New Zealand
Thu 2 July		
LOI	Belfast	Ireland v New Zealand
Sun 12 July		
IT20	Dublin, Mal	Ireland v Pakistan
Tue 14 July		
IT20	Dublin, Mal	Ireland v Pakistan
Thu 10 September		
LOI	Nottingham	England v Ireland
Sat 12 September		
LOI	Birmingham	England v Ireland
Tue 15 September		
LOI	The Oval	England v Ireland

ENGLAND WOMEN INTERNATIONALS

The following players have played for England since 1 December 2018. Details correct to 2 April 2020.

BEAUMONT, Tamsin (**'Tammy'**) Tilley, b Dover, Kent 11 Mar 1991. RHB, WK. MBE 2018. Kent 2007 to date. Diamonds 2007-12. Sapphires 2008. Emeralds 2011-13. Surrey Stars 2016-17. Adelaide Strikers 2016-17 to 2017-18. Southern Vipers 2018-19. Melbourne Renegades 2019-20. *Wisden* 2018. **Tests**: 4 (2013 to 2019); HS 70 v A (Sydney) 2017-18. **LOI**: 71 (2009-10 to 2019-20); HS 168* v P (Taunton) 2016. **IT20**: 83 (2009-10 to 2019-20); HS 116 v SA (Taunton) 2018.

BRUNT, Katherine Helen, b Barnsley, Yorks 2 Jul 1985. RHB, RMF. Yorkshire 2004 to date. Sapphires 2006-08. Diamonds 2011-12. Perth Scorchers 2015-16 to 2017-18. Yorkshire Diamonds 2016-18. **Tests**: 12 (2004 to 2019); HS 52 v A (Worcester) 2005; BB 6-69 v A (Worcester) 2009. **LOI**: 123 (2004-05 to 2019-20); HS 72* v SA (Worcester) 2018; BB 5-18 v A (Wormsley) 2011. **IT20**: 82 (2005 to 2019-20); HS 42* v SA (Taunton) 2018; BB 3-6 v NZ (Lord's) 2009.

CROSS, Kathryn (**'Kate'**) Laura, b Manchester, Lancs 3 Oct 1991. RHB, RMF. Lancashire 2005 to date. Sapphires 2007-08. Emeralds 2012. W Australia 2017-18 to 2018-19. Brisbane Heat 2015-16. Lancashire Thunder 2016-19. Perth Scorchers 2018-19. **Tests**: 3 (2013-14 to 2015); HS 4* v A (Canterbury) 2015; BB 3-29 v I (Wormsley) 2014. **LOI**: 26 (2013-14 to 2019-20); HS 8* v A (Canterbury) 2019; BB 5-24 v NZ (Lincoln) 2014-15. **IT20**: 13 (2013-14 to 2019-20); HS 0*; BB 2-18 v I (Guwahati) 2018-19.

DAVIES, Freya Ruth, b Chichester, Sussex 27 Oct 1995. RHB, RMF. Sussex 2012 to date. Western Storm 2016-19. **LOI**: 1 (2019-20); HS – ; BB – . **IT20**: 7 (2018-19 to 2019-20); HS – ; BB 2-18 v P (Kuala Lumpur) 2019-20.

DUNKLEY, Sophia Ivy Rose, b Lambeth, Surrey 16 Jul 1998. RHB, LB. Middlesex 2013 to date. Surrey Stars 2016-18. Lancashire Thunder 2019. **IT20**: 10 (2018-19); HS 35 v WI (Gros Islet) 2018-19; BB 1-6 v SL (Colombo, PSS) 2018-19.

ECCLESTONE, Sophie (Helsby HS), b Chester 6 May 1999. RHB, SLA. Cheshire 2013-14. Lancashire 2015 to date. Lancashire Thunder 2016-19. **Tests**: 2 (2017-18 to 2019); HS 9* v A (Taunton) 2019; BB 3-107 v A (Sydney) 2017-18. **LOI**: 24 (2016-17 to 2019-20); HS 27 v A (Leicester) 2019; BB 4-14 v I (Nagpur) 2017-18. **IT20**: 34 (2016 to 2019-20); HS 17* v A (Hove) 2019; BB 4-18 v NZ (Taunton) 2018.

ELWISS, Georgia Amanda, b Wolverhampton, Staffs 31 May 1991. RHB, RMF. Staffordshire 2004-10. Sapphires 2006-12. Diamonds 2008. Australia CT 2009-10 to 2010-11. Emeralds 2011. Sussex 2011 to date. Rubies 2013. Loughborough Lightning 2016-19. Melbourne Stars 2017-18 to 2018-19. **Tests**: 3 (2015 to 2019); HS 46 v A (Canterbury) 2015; BB 1-40 v A (Sydney) 2017-18. **LOI**: 36 (2011-12 to 2018-19); HS 77 v P (Taunton) 2016; BB 3-17 v I (Wormsley) 2012. **IT20**: 14 (2011-12 to 2019); HS 18 v SA (Paarl) 2015-16; BB 2-9 v P (Chennai) 2015-16.

GLENN, Sarah, b Derby 27 Feb 1999. RHB, LB. Derbyshire 2013-18. Worcestershire 2019. Loughborough Lightning 2017-19. **LOI**: 3 (2019-20); HS – ; BB 4-18 v P (Kuala Lumpur) 2019-20. **IT20**: 10 (2019-20); HS – ; BB 3-15 v P (Canberra) 2019-20.

GORDON, Kirstie Louise, b Huntly, Aberdeenshire 20 Oct 1997. RHB, SLA. Nottinghamshire 2016 to date. Loughborough Lightning 2018-19. **Tests**: 1 (2019); HS – ; BB 2-50 v A (Taunton) 2019. **IT20**: 5 (2018-19); HS 1* v A (North Sound) 2018-19; BB 3-16 v B (Gros Islet) 2018-19.

GUNN, Jennifer ('Jenny') Louise, b Nottingham 9 May 1986. MBE 2014. RHB, RMF. Nottinghamshire 2001 to date. Emeralds 2006-08. S Australia 2006-07 to 2007-08. Diamonds 2007. W Australia 2008-09. Yorkshire 2011. Rubies 2012-13. Warwickshire 2016-18. Yorkshire Diamonds 2016-17. Loughborough Lightning 2018-19. **Tests**: 11 (2004 to 2014); HS 62* and BB 5-19 v I (Wormsley) 2014. **LOI**: 144 (2003-04 to 2019); HS 73 v NZ (Taunton) 2007; BB 5-22 v P (Louth) 2013. **IT20**: 104 (2004 to 2018, 3 as captain); HS 69 v SL (Colombo, NCC) 2010-11; BB 5-18 v NZ (Bridgetown) 2013-14. Retired from international cricket in October 2019.

HARTLEY, Alexandra, b Blackburn, Lancs 26 Sep 1993. RHB, SLA. Lancashire 2008 to date. Emeralds 2011-13. Rubies 2012. Middlesex 2013-16. Tasmania 2018-19. Surrey Stars 2016-17. Lancashire Thunder 2018-19. Hobart Hurricanes 2018-19. **LOI**: 28 (2016 to 2018-19); HS 3* v I (Nagpur) 2017-18; BB 4-24 v WI (Kingston) 2016-17. **IT20**: 4 (2016 to 2018-19); HS 2* v I (Mumbai, BS) 2017-18; BB 2-19 v P (Chelmsford) 2016.

JONES, Amy Ellen, b Solihull, Warwicks 13 Jun 1993. RHB, WK. Warwickshire 2008 to date. Diamonds 2011. Emeralds 2012. Rubies 2013. W Australia 2017-18. Loughborough Lightning 2016-19. Sydney Sixers 2016-17 to 2017-18. Perth Scorchers 2018-19 to date. **Tests**: 1 (2019); HS 64 v A (Taunton) 2019. **LOI**: 44 (2012-13 to 2019-20); HS 94 v I (Nagpur) 2017-18. **IT20**: 49 (2013 to 2019-20); HS 89 v P (Kuala Lumpur) 2019-20.

KNIGHT, Heather Clare, b Rochdale, Lancs 26 Dec 1990. RHB, OB. OBE 2018. Devon 2008-09. Emeralds 2008-13. Berkshire 2010 to date. Sapphires 2011-12. Tasmania 2014-15 to 2015-16. Hobart Hurricanes 2015-16 to date. Western Storm 2016-19. *Wisden* 2017. **Tests**: 6 (2010-11 to 2017-18, 2 as captain); HS 157 v A (Wormsley) 2013; BB 2-25 v A (Taunton) 2019. **LOI**: 101 (2009-10 to 2019-20, 46 as captain); HS 106 v P (Leicester) 2017; BB 5-26 v P (Leicester) 2016. **IT20**: 74 (2010-11 to 2019-20, 41 as captain); HS 108* v Thai (Canberra) 2019-20; BB 3-9 v I (North Sound) 2018-19.

MARSH, Laura Alexandra, b Pembury, Kent 5 Dec 1986. RHB, RMF/OB. Sussex 2003-10. Rubies 2006-07. Emeralds 2008. Sapphires 2011. Kent 2011 to date. New South Wales 2015-16. Otago 2015-16. Sydney Sixers 2015-16. Surrey Stars 2016-17. **Tests**: 9 (2006 to 2019); HS 55 v A (Wormsley) 2013; BB 3-44 v I (Leicester) 2006. **LOI**: 103 (2006 to 2019); HS 67 v Ire (Kibworth) 2010; BB 5-15 v P (Sydney) 2008-09. **IT20**: 67 (2007 to 2019); HS 54 v P (Galle) 2012-13; BB 3-12 v P (Chennai) 2015-16. Retired from international cricket in December 2019.

SCIVER, Natalie Ruth (Epsom C), b Tokyo, Japan 20 Aug 1992. RHB, RM. Surrey 2010 to date. Rubies 2011. Emeralds 2012-13. Melbourne Stars 2015-16 to 2016-17. Surrey Stars 2016-19. Perth Scorchers 2017-18 to date. *Wisden* 2017. **Tests**: 5 (2013-14 to 2019); HS 88 v A (Taunton) 2019; BB 1-30 v A (Perth) 2013-14. **LOI**: 67 (2013 to 2019-20); HS 137 v P (Leicester) 2017; BB 3-3 v WI (Bristol) 2017. **IT20**: 75 (2013 to 2019-20); HS 68* v A (Mumbai, BS) 2017-18. BB 4-15 v A (Cardiff) 2015.

SHRUBSOLE, Anya, b Bath, Somerset 7 Dec 1991. RHB, RMF. MBE 2018. Somerset 2004-18. Rubies 2006-12. Emeralds 2006-13. Berkshire 2019. Western Storm 2016-19. Perth Scorchers 2016-17. *Wisden* 2017. **Tests**: 6 (2013 to 2019); HS 20 v A (Sydney) 2017-18; BB 4-51 v A (Perth) 2013-14. **LOI**: 70 (2008 to 2019-20, 1 as captain); HS 32* v WI (Worcester) 2019; BB 6-46 v I (Lord's) 2017, in World Cup final. **IT20**: 75 (2008 to 2019-20); HS 29 v WI (Gros Islet) 2018-19; BB 5-11 v NZ (Wellington) 2011-12.

SMITH, Bryony Frances, b Sutton, Surrey 12 Dec 1997. RHB, OB. Surrey 2014 to date. Surrey Stars 2016-19. **LOI**: 1 (2019); HS – ; BB 1-20 v WI (Chelmsford) 2019. **IT20**: 3 (2017-18); HS 15 v I (Mumbai, BS) 2017-18.

SMITH, Linsey Claire Neale, b Hillingdon, Middx 10 Mar 1995. LHB, SLA. Berkshire 2011-16. Rubies 2011-12. Sussex 2017 to date. Southern Vipers 2016-17. Loughborough Lightning 2018. Yorkshire Diamonds 2019. **IT20:** 9 (2018-19 to 2019); HS – ; BB 3-18 v SL (Colombo, PSS) 2018-19.

TAYLOR, Sarah Jane (Bede's S, Upper Dicker), b Whitechapel, London 20 May 1989. RHB, WK. Sussex 2004 to date. Rubies 2006-12. Emeralds 2008-13. Wellington 2010-11 to 2011-12. S Australia 2014-15 to 2015-16. Adelaide Strikers 2015-16. Lancashire Thunder 2017. Surrey Stars 2018-19. **Tests:** 10 (2006 to 2019); HS 40 v I (Wormsley) 2014. **LOI:** 126 (2006 to 2019); HS 147 v SA (Bristol) 2017. **IT20:** 90 (2006 to 2019); HS 77 v A (Chelmsford) 2013. Retired from international cricket in September 2019.

VILLIERS, Mady Kate, b Havering, Essex 26 Aug 1998. RHB, OB. Essex 2013 to date. Surrey Stars 2018-19. **IT20:** 4 (2019 to 2019-20); HS – ; BB 2-20 v A (Bristol) 2019.

WILSON, Frances Claire, b Aldershot, Hants 7 Nov 1991. RHB, OB. Somerset 2006-14. Diamonds 2011. Emeralds 2012. Rubies 2013. Middlesex 2015-18. Wellington 2016-17 to 2017-18. Kent 2019. Western Storm 2016-19. Sydney Thunder 2017-18. Hobart Hurricanes 2019-20. **Tests:** 1 (2017-18); HS 13 v A (Sydney) 2017-18. **LOI:** 30 (2010-11 to 2019-20); HS 85* v P (Kuala Lumpur) 2019-20. **IT20:** 25 (2010-11 to 2019-20); HS 43* v P (Southampton) 2016.

WINFIELD, Lauren, b York 16 Aug 1990. RHB, WK. Yorkshire 2007 to date. Diamonds 2011. Sapphires 2012. Rubies 2013. Brisbane Heat 2015-16 to 2016-17. Yorkshire Diamonds 2016-19. Hobart Hurricanes 2017-18. Adelaide Strikers 2019-20. **Tests:** 3 (2014 to 2017-18); HS 35 v I (Wormsley) 2014. **LOI:** 42 (2013 to 2018-19); HS 123 v P (Worcester) 2016. **IT20:** 40 (2013 to 2019-20); HS 74 v SA (Birmingham) 2014 and 74 v P (Bristol) 2016.

WYATT, Danielle ('**Danni**') Nicole, b Stoke-on-Trent, Staffs 22 Apr 1991. RHB, OB/RM. Staffordshire 2005-12. Emeralds 2006-08. Sapphires 2011-13. Victoria 2011-12 to 2015-16. Nottinghamshire 2013-15. Sussex 2016 to date. Melbourne Renegades 2015-16 to date. Lancashire Thunder 2016. Southern Vipers 2017-19. **LOI:** 74 (2009-10 to 2019-20); HS 110 v P (Kuala Lumpur) 2019-20; BB 3-7 v SA (Cuttack) 2012-13. **IT20:** 109 (2009-10 to 2019-20); HS 124 v I (Mumbai, BS) 2017-18; BB 4-11 v SA (Basseterre) 2010.

WOMEN'S TEST CRICKET RECORDS

1934-35 to 2 April 2020

RESULTS SUMMARY

| | Opponents | Tests | Won by | | | | | | | | | | Drawn |
			E	A	NZ	SA	WI	I	P	SL	Ire	H	
England	Australia	50	9	12	–	–	–	–	–	–	–	–	29
	New Zealand	23	6	–	0	–	–	–	–	–	–	–	17
	South Africa	6	2	–	–	0	–	–	–	–	–	–	4
	West Indies	3	2	–	–	–	0	–	–	–	–	–	1
	India	13	1	–	–	–	–	2	–	–	–	–	10
Australia	New Zealand	13	–	4	1	–	–	–	–	–	–	–	8
	West Indies	2	–	0	–	–	0	–	–	–	–	–	2
	India	9	–	4	–	–	–	0	–	–	–	–	5
New Zealand	South Africa	3	–	–	1	0	–	–	–	–	–	–	2
	India	6	–	–	0	–	–	0	–	–	–	–	6
South Africa	India	2	–	–	–	0	–	2	–	–	–	–	–
	Netherlands	1	–	–	–	1	–	–	–	–	–	0	–
West Indies	India	6	–	–	–	–	1	1	–	–	–	–	4
	Pakistan	1	–	–	–	–	0	–	0	–	–	–	1
Pakistan	Sri Lanka	1	–	–	–	–	–	–	0	1	–	–	–
	Ireland	1	–	–	–	–	–	–	0	–	1	–	–
		140	20	20	2	1	1	5	0	1	1	0	89

	Tests	Won	Lost	Drawn	Toss Won
England	95	20	14	61	55
Australia	74	20	10	44	26
New Zealand	45	2	10	33	21
South Africa	12	1	5	6	6
West Indies	12	1	3	8	6†
India	36	5	6	25	18†
Pakistan	3	–	2	1	1
Sri Lanka	1	1	–	–	1
Ireland	1	1	–	–	1
Netherlands	1	–	1	–	–

† *Results of tosses in five of the six India v West Indies Tests in 1976-77 are not known*

TEAM RECORDS
HIGHEST INNINGS TOTALS

569-6d	Australia v England	Guildford	1998
525	Australia v India	Ahmedabad	1983-84
517-8	New Zealand v England	Scarborough	1996
503-5d	England v New Zealand	Christchurch	1934-35
497	England v South Africa	Shenley	2003
467	India v England	Taunton	2002
455	England v South Africa	Taunton	2003
448-9d	Australia v England	Sydney	2017-18
440	West Indies v Pakistan	Karachi	2003-04
427-4d	Australia v England	Worcester	1998
426-7d	Pakistan v West Indies	Karachi	2003-04
426-9d	India v England	Blackpool	1986
420-8d	Australia v England	Taunton	2019
414	England v New Zealand	Scarborough	1996
414	England v Australia	Guildford	1998
404-9d	India v South Africa	Paarl	2001-02

| 403-8d | New Zealand v India | Nelson | 1994-95 |
| 400-6d | India v South Africa | Mysore | 2014-15 |

The highest totals for countries not included above are:

316	South Africa v England	Shenley	2003
193-3d	Ireland v Pakistan	Dublin	2000
108	Netherlands v South Africa	Rotterdam	2007

LOWEST INNINGS TOTALS

35	England v Australia	Melbourne	1957-58
38	Australia v England	Melbourne	1957-58
44	New Zealand v England	Christchurch	1934-35
47	Australia v England	Brisbane	1934-35
50	Netherlands v South Africa	Rotterdam	2007
53	Pakistan v Ireland	Dublin	2000

The lowest innings totals for countries not included above are:

65	India v West Indies	Jammu	1976-77
67	West Indies v England	Canterbury	1979
89	South Africa v New Zealand	Durban	1971-72

BATTING RECORDS
1000 RUNS IN TESTS

		Career	M	I	NO	HS	Avge	100	50
1935	J.A.Brittin (E)	1979-98	27	44	5	167	49.61	5	11
1645	C.M.Edwards (E)	1996-2014	22	41	5	117	45.69	4	9
1594	R.Heyhoe-Flint (E)	1960-79	22	38	3	179	45.54	3	10
1301	D.A.Hockley (NZ)	1979-96	19	29	4	126*	52.04	4	7
1164	C.A.Hodges (E)	1984-92	18	31	2	158*	40.13	2	6
1110	S.Agarwal (I)	1984-95	13	23	1	190	50.45	4	4
1078	E.Bakewell (E)	1968-79	12	22	4	124	59.88	4	7
1030	S.C.Taylor (E)	1999-2009	15	27	2	177	41.20	4	2
1007	M.E.Maclagan (E)	1934-51	14	25	1	119	41.95	2	6
1002	K.L.Rolton (A)	1995-2009	14	22	4	209*	55.66	2	5

HIGHEST INDIVIDUAL INNINGS

242	Kiran Baluch	P v WI	Karachi	2003-04
214	M.Raj	I v E	Taunton	2002
213*	E.A.Perry	A v E	Sydney	2017-18
209*	K.L.Rolton	A v E	Leeds	2001
204	K.E.Flavell	NZ v E	Scarborough	1996
204‡	M.A.J.Goszko	A v E	Shenley	2001
200	J.Broadbent	A v E	Guildford	1998
193	D.A.Annetts	A v E	Collingham	1987
192	M.D.T.Kamini	I v SA	Mysore	2014-15
190	S.Agarwal	I v E	Worcester	1986
189	E.A.Snowball	E v NZ	Christchurch	1934-35
179	R.Heyhoe-Flint	E v A	The Oval	1976
177	S.C.Taylor	E v SA	Shenley	2003
176*	K.L.Rolton	A v E	Worcester	1998
167	J.A.Brittin	E v A	Harrogate	1998
161*	E.C.Drumm	E v A	Christchurch	1994-95
160	B.A.Daniels	E v NZ	Scarborough	1996
158*	C.A.Hodges	E v NZ	Canterbury	1984
157	H.C.Knight	E v A	Wormsley	2013
155*	P.F.McKelvey	NZ v E	Wellington	1968-69

‡ *On debut*

330

FIVE HUNDREDS

			M	I	E	A	NZ	SA	WI	IND	P	SL	IRE
							Opponents						
5	J.A.Brittin (E)		27	44	–	3	1	–	1	–	–	–	–

HIGHEST PARTNERSHIP FOR EACH WICKET

1st	241	Kiran Baluch/Sajjida Shah	P v WI	Karachi	2003-04
2nd	275	M.D.T.Kamini/P.G.Raut	I v SA	Mysore	2014-15
3rd	309	L.A.Reeler/D.A.Annetts	A v E	Collingham	1987
4th	253	K.L.Rolton/L.C.Broadfoot	A v E	Leeds	2001
5th	138	J.Logtenberg/C.van der Westhuizen	SA v E	Shenley	2003
6th	229	J.M.Fields/R.L.Haynes	A v E	Worcester	2009
7th	157	M.Raj/J.Goswami	I v E	Taunton	2002
8th	181	S.J.Griffiths/D.L.Wilson	A v NZ	Auckland	1989-90
9th	107	B.Botha/M.Payne	SA v NZ	Cape Town	1971-72
10th	119	S.Nitschke/C.R.Smith	A v E	Hove	2005

BOWLING RECORDS

50 WICKETS IN TESTS

Wkts		Career	M	Balls	Runs	Avge	Best	5wI	10wM
77	M.B.Duggan (E)	1949-63	17	3734	1039	13.49	7- 6	5	–
68	E.R.Wilson (A)	1948-58	11	2885	803	11.80	7- 7	4	2
63	D.F.Edulji (I)	1976-91	20	5098†	1624	25.77	6- 64	1	–
60	M.E.Maclagan (E)	1934-51	14	3432	935	15.58	7- 10	3	–
60	C.L.Fitzpatrick (A)	1991-2006	13	3603	1147	19.11	5- 29	2	–
60	S.Kulkarni (I)	1976-91	19	3320†	1647	27.45	6- 99	5	–
57	R.H.Thompson (A)	1972-85	16	4304	1040	18.24	5- 33	1	–
55	J.Lord (NZ)	1966-79	15	3108	1049	19.07	6-119	4	1
50	E.Bakewell (E)	1968-79	12	2697	831	16.62	7- 61	3	1

† *Excludes balls bowled in Sixth Test v West Indies 1976-77*

TEN WICKETS IN A TEST

13-226	Shaiza Khan	P v WI	Karachi	2003-04
11- 16	E.R.Wilson	A v E	Melbourne	1957-58
11- 63	J.M.Greenwood	E v WI	Canterbury	1979
11-107	L.C.Pearson	E v A	Sydney	2002-03
10- 65	E.R.Wilson	A v NZ	Wellington	1947-48
10- 75	E.Bakewell	E v WI	Birmingham	1979
10- 78	J.Goswami	I v E	Taunton	2006
10-107	K.Price	A v I	Lucknow	1983-84
10-118	D.A.Gordon	A v E	Melbourne	1968-69
10-137	J.Lord	NZ v A	Melbourne	1978-79

SEVEN WICKETS IN AN INNINGS

8-53	N.David	I v E	Jamshedpur	1995-96
7- 6	M.B.Duggan	E v A	Melbourne	1957-58
7- 7	E.R.Wilson	A v E	Melbourne	1957-58
7-10	M.E.Maclagan	E v A	Brisbane	1934-35
7-18	A.Palmer	A v E	Brisbane	1934-35
7-24	L.Johnston	A v NZ	Melbourne	1971-72
7-34	G.E.McConway	E v I	Worcester	1986
7-41	J.A.Burley	NZ v E	The Oval	1966
7-51	L.C.Pearson	E v A	Sydney	2002-03
7-59	Shaiza Khan	P v WI	Karachi	2003-04
7-61	E.Bakewell	E v WI	Birmingham	1979

HAT-TRICKS

E.R.Wilson	Australia v England	Melbourne	1957-58
Shaiza Khan	Pakistan v West Indies	Karachi	2003-04
R.M.Farrell	Australia v England	Sydney	2010-11

WICKET-KEEPING AND FIELDING RECORDS
25 DISMISSALS IN TESTS

Total			Tests	Ct	St	
58	C.Matthews	Australia	20	46	12	1984-95
43	J.Smit	England	21	39	4	1992-2006
36	S.A.Hodges	England	11	19	17	1969-79
28	B.A.Brentnall	New Zealand	10	16	12	1966-72

EIGHT DISMISSALS IN A TEST

9 (8ct, 1st)	C.Matthews	A v I	Adelaide	1990-91
8 (6ct, 2st)	L.Nye	E v NZ	New Plymouth	1991-92

SIX DISMISSALS IN AN INNINGS

8 (6ct, 2st)	L.Nye	E v NZ	New Plymouth	1991-92
6 (2ct, 4st)	B.A.Brentnall	NZ v SA	Johannesburg	1971-72

20 CATCHES IN THE FIELD IN TESTS

Total			Tests	
25	C.A.Hodges	England	18	1984-92
21	S.Shah	India	20	1976-91
20	L.A.Fullston	Australia	12	1984-87

APPEARANCE RECORDS
25 TEST MATCH APPEARANCES

27	J.A.Brittin	England	1979-98

12 MATCHES AS CAPTAIN

			Won	Lost	Drawn	
14	P.F.McKelvey	New Zealand	2	3	9	1966-79
12	R.Heyhoe-Flint	England	2	–	10	1966-76
12	S.Rangaswamy	India	1	2	9	1976-84

ENGLAND TEST RESULT IN 2019

At County Ground, Taunton, on 18, 19, 20, 21 July. Toss: Australia. Result: **MATCH DRAWN**. Australia 420-8d (E.A.Perry 116, R.L.Haynes 87, A.J.Healy 58, M.M.Lanning 57, B.L.Mooney 51) and 230-7 (E.A.Perry 76*). England 275-9d (N.R.Sciver 88, A.E.Jones 64, S.Molineux 4-95). Award: E.A.Perry. England debuts: K.L.Gordon and A.E.Jones.

WOMEN'S LIMITED-OVERS RECORDS

1973 to 21 March 2020
RESULTS SUMMARY

	Matches	Won	Lost	Tied	No Result	% Won (exc NR)
Australia	329	258	63	2	6	79.87
England	348	204	131	2	11	60.53
India	272	151	116	1	4	56.34
South Africa	196	97	88	3	8	51.59
New Zealand	338	170	160	2	6	51.20
West Indies	177	80	91	1	5	46.51
Sri Lanka	167	56	106	–	5	34.56
Trinidad & Tobago	6	2	4	–	–	33.33
Pakistan	165	48	113	1	3	29.62
Ireland	148	39	103	–	6	27.64
Bangladesh	38	9	27	–	2	25.00
Jamaica	5	1	4	–	–	20.00
Netherlands	101	19	81	–	1	19.00
Denmark	33	6	27	–	–	18.18
International XI	18	3	14	–	1	17.64
Young England	6	1	5	–	–	16.66
Scotland	8	1	7	–	–	12.50
Japan	5	–	5	–	–	0.00

TEAM RECORDS – HIGHEST INNINGS TOTALS

491-4 (50 overs)	New Zealand v Ireland	Dublin	2018
455-5 (50 overs)	New Zealand v Pakistan	Christchurch	1996-97
440-3 (50 overs)	New Zealand v Ireland	Dublin	2018
418 (49.5 overs)	New Zealand v Ireland	Dublin	2018
412-3 (50 overs)	Australia v Denmark	Mumbai	1997-98
397-4 (50 overs)	Australia v Pakistan	Melbourne	1996-97
378-5 (50 overs)	England v Pakistan	Worcester	2016

LARGEST RUNS MARGIN OF VICTORY

408 runs	New Zealand beat Pakistan	Christchurch	1996-97
374 runs	Australia beat Pakistan	Melbourne	1996-97

LOWEST INNINGS TOTALS

22 (23.4 overs)	Netherlands v West Indies	Deventer	2008
23 (24.1 overs)	Pakistan v Australia	Melbourne	1996-97
24 (21.3 overs)	Scotland v England	Reading	2001

BATTING RECORDS – 2650 RUNS IN A CAREER

Runs		Career	M	I	NO	HS	Avge	100	50
6888	M.Raj (I)	1999-2019	209	189	53	125*	50.64	7	53
5992	C.M.Edwards (E)	1997-2016	191	180	23	173*	38.16	9	46
4844	B.J.Clark (A)	1991-2005	118	114	12	229*	47.49	5	30
4814	K.L.Rolton (A)	1995-2009	141	132	32	154*	48.14	8	33
4754	S.R.Taylor (WI)	2008-2019	126	123	15	171	44.01	5	36
4534	S.W.Bates (NZ)	2006-2020	124	118	12	168	42.77	10	27
4101	S.C.Taylor (E)	1998-2011	126	120	18	156*	40.20	8	23
4064	D.A.Hockley (NZ)	1982-2000	118	115	18	117	41.89	4	34
4056	S.J.Taylor (E)	2006-2019	126	119	13	147	38.26	7	20
3821	A.E.Satterthwaite (NZ)	2007-2019	119	113	15	147	38.98	6	21
3693	M.M.Lanning (A)	2011-2019	80	80	10	152*	52.75	13	14
3492	A.J.Blackwell (A)	2003-2017	144	124	27	114	36.00	3	25
3239	M.du Preez (SA)	2007-2020	130	121	22	116*	32.71	2	14
3022	E.A.Perry (A)	2007-2019	112	89	31	112*	52.10	2	27
2919	H.M.Tiffen (NZ)	1999-2009	117	111	16	100	30.72	1	18
2856	A.Chopra (I)	1995-2012	127	112	21	100	31.38	1	18
2844	E.C.Drumm (NZ)	1992-2006	101	94	13	116	35.11	2	19
2833	D.J.S.Dottin (WI)	2008-2019	117	111	11	104*	28.33	1	19

Runs		Career	M	I	NO	HS	Avge	100	50
2800	H.C.Knight (E)	2010-2019	101	96	22	106	37.83	1	19
2728	L.C.Sthalekar (A)	2001-2013	125	111	22	104*	30.65	2	16
2693	Javeria Khan (P)	2008-2019	103	100	12	133*	30.60	2	15

HIGHEST INDIVIDUAL INNINGS

232*	A.C.Kerr	New Zealand v Ireland	Dublin	2018
229*	B.J.Clark	Australia v Denmark	Mumbai	1997-98
188	D.B.Sharma	India v Ireland	Potchefstroom	2017
178*	A.C.Jayangani	Sri Lanka v Australia	Bristol	2017
173*	C.M.Edwards	England v Ireland	Pune	1997-98
171*	H.Kaur	India v Australia	Derby	2017
171	S.R.Taylor	West Indies v Sri Lanka	Mumbai	2012-13
168*	T.T.Beaumont	England v Pakistan	Taunton	2016
168	S.W.Bates	New Zealand v Pakistan	Sydney	2008-09
157	R.H.Priest	New Zealand v Sri Lanka	Lincoln	2015-16
156*	L.M.Keightley	Australia v Pakistan	Melbourne	1996-97
156*	S.C.Taylor	England v India	Lord's	2006
154*	K.L.Rolton	Australia v Sri Lanka	Christchurch	2000-01
153*	J.Logtenberg	South Africa v Netherlands	Deventer	2007
152*	M.M.Lanning	Australia v Sri Lanka	Bristol	2017
151	K.L.Rolton	Australia v Ireland	Dublin	2005
151	S.W.Bates	New Zealand v Ireland	Dublin	2018

HIGHEST PARTNERSHIP FOR EACH WICKET

1st	320	D.B.Sharma/P.G.Raut	India v Ireland	Potchefstroom	2017
2nd	295	A.C.Kerr/L.M.Kasperek	New Zealand v Ireland	Dublin	2018
3rd	244	K.L.Rolton/L.C.Sthalekar	Australia v Ireland	Dublin	2005
4th	224*	J.Logtenberg/M.du Preez	South Africa v Netherlands	Deventer	2007
5th	188*	S.C.Taylor/J.Cassar	England v Sri Lanka	Lincoln	2000-01
6th	142	S.Luus/C.L.Tryon	South Africa v Ireland	Dublin	2016
7th	104*	S.J.Tsukigawa/N.J.Browne	New Zealand v England	Chennai	2006-07
8th	88	N.N.D.de Silva/O.U.Ranasinghe	Sri Lanka v England	Hambantota	2018-19
9th	73	L.R.F.Askew/I.T.Guha	England v New Zealand	Chennai	2006-07
10th	76	A.J.Blackwell/K.M.Beams	Australia v India	Derby	2017

BOWLING RECORDS – 100 WICKETS IN A CAREER

		LOI	Balls	Runs	W	Avge	Best	4w	R/Over
J.Goswami (I)	2002-2019	182	8835	4835	225	21.48	6-31	8	3.28
C.L.Fitzpatrick (A)	1993-2007	109	6017	3023	180	16.79	5-14	11	3.01
E.A.Perry (A)	2007-2019	112	5110	3693	152	24.29	7-22	4	4.33
A.Mohammed (WI)	2003-2019	122	5368	3098	151	20.51	7-14	12	3.46
Sana Mir (P)	2005-2019	120	5942	3665	151	24.27	5-32	8	3.70
K.H.Brunt (E)	2005-2019	123	5976	3480	150	23.20	5-18	7	3.49
L.C.Sthalekar (A)	2001-2013	125	5964	3646	146	24.97	5-35	2	3.66
S.R.Taylor (WI)	2008-2019	126	5309	3032	142	21.35	4-17	5	3.42
N.David (I)	1995-2008	97	4892	2305	141	16.34	5-20	6	2.82
S.Ismail (SA)	2007-2020	98	4736	2841	136	20.88	6-10	5	3.59
J.L.Gunn (E)	2004-2019	144	5906	3822	136	28.10	5-22	6	3.88
D.van Niekerk (SA)	2009-2020	102	4344	2549	130	19.60	5-17	8	3.52
L.A.Marsh (E)	2006-2019	103	5328	3463	129	26.84	5-15	4	3.89
H.A.S.D.Siriwardene (SL)	2003-2019	118	5449	3577	124	28.84	4-11	6	3.93
M.Kapp (SA)	2009-2019	108	4695	2879	123	23.40	4-14	4	3.67
C.E.Taylor (E)	1988-2005	105	5140	2443	102	23.95	4-13	2	2.85
J.L.Jonassen (A)	2012-2019	68	3149	2099	101	20.78	5-27	7	3.99
I.T.Guha (E)	2001-2011	83	3767	2345	101	23.21	5-14	4	3.73
N.Al Khadeer (I)	2002-2012	78	4036	2402	100	24.02	5-14	5	3.57

SIX OR MORE WICKETS IN AN INNINGS

7- 4	Sajjida Shah	Pakistan v Japan	Amsterdam	2003
7- 8	J.M.Chamberlain	England v Denmark	Haarlem	1991
7-14	A.Mohammed	West Indies v Pakistan	Dhaka	2011-12

7-22	E.A.Perry	Australia v England	Canterbury	2019
7-24	S.Nitschke	Australia v England	Kidderminster	2005
6-10	J.Lord	New Zealand v India	Auckland	1981-82
6-10	M.Maben	India v Sri Lanka	Kandy	2003-04
6-10	S.Ismail	South Africa v Netherlands	Savar	2011-12
6-20	G.L.Page	New Zealand v Trinidad & T	St Albans	1973
6-20	D.B.Sharma	India v Sri Lanka	Ranchi	2015-16
6-20	Khadija Tul Kubra	Bangladesh v Pakistan	Cox's Bazar	2018-19
6-31	J.Goswami	India v New Zealand	Southgate	2011
6-32	B.H.McNeill	New Zealand v England	Lincoln, NZ	2007-08
6-36	S.Luus	South Africa v Ireland	Dublin	2016
6-45	S.Luus	South Africa v New Zealand	Hamilton	2019-20
6-46	A.Shrubsole	England v India	Lord's	2017

WICKET-KEEPING AND FIELDING RECORDS – 100 DISMISSALS IN A CAREER

Total			LOI	Ct	St
157	T.Chetty	South Africa	111	109	48
136	S.J.Taylor	England	126	85	51
133	R.J.Rolls	New Zealand	104	89	44
114	J.Smit	England	109	69	45
102	M.R.Aguillera	West Indies	112	76	26

SIX DISMISSALS IN AN INNINGS

6 (4ct, 2st)	S.L.Illingworth	New Zealand v Australia	Beckenham	1993
6 (1ct, 5st)	V.Kalpana	India v Denmark	Slough	1993
6 (2ct, 4st)	Batool Fatima	Pakistan v West Indies	Karachi	2003-04
6 (4ct, 2st)	Batool Fatima	Pakistan v Sri Lanka	Colombo (PSS)	2011

50 CATCHES IN THE FIELD IN A CAREER

Total			LOI	Career
66	S.W.Bates	New Zealand	124	2006-2020
64	J.Goswami	India	182	2002-2019
58	S.R.Taylor	West Indies	126	2008-2019
55	A.J.Blackwell	Australia	144	2003-2017
53	M.Raj	India	209	1999-2019
52	D.van Niekerk	South Africa	102	2009-2020
52	L.S.Greenway	England	126	2003-2016
52	C.M.Edwards	England	191	1997-2016

FOUR CATCHES IN THE FIELD IN AN INNINGS

4	Z.J.Goss	Australia v New Zealand	Adelaide	1995-96
4	J.L.Gunn	England v New Zealand	Lincoln, NZ	2014-15
4	Nahida Khan	Pakistan v Sri Lanka	Dambulla	2017-18

APPEARANCE RECORDS – 130 APPEARANCES

209	M.Raj	India	1999-2019
191	C.M.Edwards	England	1997-2016
182	J.Goswami	India	2002-2019
144	A.J.Blackwell	Australia	2003-2017
144	J.L.Gunn	England	2004-2019
141	K.L.Rolton	Australia	1995-2009
134	S.J.McGlashan	New Zealand	2002-2016
130	M.du Preez	South Africa	2007-2020

100 CONSECUTIVE APPEARANCES

109	M.Raj	India	17.04.2004 to 07.02.2013
101	M.du Preez	South Africa	08.03.2009 to 05.02.2018

100 MATCHES AS CAPTAIN

			Won	Lost	No Result	
132	M.Raj	India	82	47	3	2004-2019
117	C.M.Edwards	England	72	38	7	2005-2016
101	B.J.Clark	Australia	83	17	1	1994-2005

WOMEN'S INTERNATIONAL TWENTY20 RECORDS

2004 to 30 March 2020

As for the men's IT20 records, in the section that follows, except for the first-ranked record and the highest partnerships, only those games featuring a nation that has also played a full LOI are listed.

MATCH RESULTS SUMMARY

	Matches	Won	Lost	Tied	NR	Win %
Zimbabwe	14	14	–	–	–	100.0
England	141	99	38	3	1	70.71
Australia	138	91	44	3	–	65.94
New Zealand	124	74	47	2	1	60.16
India	123	67	54	–	2	55.37
West Indies	130	70	53	5	2	54.68
South Africa	111	49	60	–	2	44.95
Pakistan	117	47	65	3	2	40.86
Bangladesh	75	27	48	–	–	36.00
Ireland	71	20	50	–	1	28.57
Sri Lanka	100	24	72	–	4	25.00

WOMEN'S INTERNATIONAL TWENTY20 RECORDS
TEAM RECORDS – HIGHEST INNINGS TOTALS † Batting Second

314-2	Uganda v Mali	Rwanda	2019
255-2	Bangladesh v Maldives	Pokhara	2019-20
250-3	England v South Africa	Taunton	2018
226-3	Australia v England	Chelmsford	2019
226-2	Australia v Sri Lanka	Sydney (NS)	2019-20
217-4	Australia v Sri Lanka	Sydney (NS)	2019-20
216-1	New Zealand v South Africa	Taunton	2018
213-4	Ireland v Netherlands	Deventer	2019
209-4	Australia v England	Mumbai (BS)	2017-18
204-2	England v Sri Lanka	Colombo (PSS)	2018-19
205-1	South Africa v Netherlands	Potchefstroom	2010-11
199-3†	England v India	Mumbai (BS)	2017-18

LOWEST COMPLETED INNINGS TOTALS † Batting Second

6† (12.1)	Maldives v Bangladesh	Pokhara	2019-20
6 (9.0)	Mali v Rwanda	Rwanda	2019
27† (13.4)	Malaysia v India	Kuala Lumpur	2018
30† (18.4)	Malaysia v Pakistan	Kuala Lumpur	2018
30† (12.5)	Bangladesh v Pakistan	Cox's Bazar	2018-19
35† (19.2)	Mozambique v Zimbabwe	Harare	2019
35 (12.1)	Nigeria v Zimbabwe	Harare	2019

The lowest score for England is 87 (v Australia, Hove, 2015).

BATTING RECORDS – 2000 RUNS IN A CAREER

Runs			M	I	NO	HS	Avge	50	R/100B
3243	S.W.Bates	NZ	119	116	9	124*	30.30	22	111.4
2984	S.R.Taylor	WI	103	101	19	90	36.39	21	101.6†
2788	M.M.Lanning	A	104	98	21	133*	36.20	15	117.0
2605	C.M.Edwards	E	95	93	14	92*	32.97	12	106.9
2384	S.F.M.Devine	NZ	91	88	12	105	31.36	15	126.4
2380	D.J.S.Dottin	WI	113	111	19	112*	25.86	12	124.5†

Runs			M	I	NO	HS	Avge	50	R/100B
2364	M.Raj	I	89	84	21	97*	37.52	17	96.3†
2225	Bismah Maroof	P	108	102	21	70*	27.46	11	92.8
2186	H.Kaur	I	114	102	21	103	26.98	7	102.0†
2177	S.J.Taylor	E	90	87	12	77	29.02	16	110.6
2060	A.J.Healy	A	112	97	16	148*	25.43	13	132.0

† No information on balls faced for games at Roseau on 22 and 23 February 2012.

HIGHEST INDIVIDUAL INNINGS

Score	Balls			
148*	61	A.J.Healy	A v E	Sydney (NS)	2019-20
133*	63	M.M.Lanning	A v E	Chelmsford	2019
126*	76	S.L.Kalis	Neth v Ger	Cartagena	2019
126	65	M.M.Lanning	A v Ire	Sylhet	2013-14
124*	66	S.W.Bates	NZ v SA	Taunton	2018
124	64	D.N.Wyatt	E v I	Mumbai (BS)	2017-18
117*	70	B.L.Mooney	A v E	Canberra	2017-18
116*	71	S.A.Fritz	SA v Neth	Potchefstroom	2010-11
116	52	T.T.Beaumont	E v SA	Taunton	2018

HIGHEST PARTNERSHIP FOR EACH WICKET

Wkt					
1st	182	S.W.Bates/S.F.M.Devine	NZ v SA	Taunton	2018
2nd	162*	H.K.Matthews/C.N.Nation	WI v Ire	Dublin	2019
3rd	236*	Nigar Sultana/Fargana Hoque	B v Mald	Pokhara	2019-20
4th	147*	K.L.Rolton/K.A.Blackwell	A v E	Taunton	2005
5th	119*	M.M.Lanning/R.L.Haynes	A v NZ	Sydney	2018-19
6th	84	M.A.A.Sanjeewani/N.N.D.de Silva	SL v P	Colombo (SSC)	2017-18
7th	60	Bismah Maroof/Sidra Nawaz	P v E	Kuala Lumpur	2019-20
8th	39	L.E.Kaushalya/K.A.D.A.Kanchana	SL v I	Ranchi	2015-16
9th	33*	D.Hazell/H.L.Colvin	E v WI	Bridgetown	2013-14
10th	23*	L.N.McCarthy/E.J.Tice	Ire v SL	Dublin	2013

BOWLING RECORDS – 85 WICKETS IN A CAREER

Wkts			Matches	Overs	Mdns	Runs	Avge	Best	R/Over
120	A.Mohammed	WI	111	373.3	6	2077	17.30	5-10	5.56
114	E.A.Perry	A	120	376.5	6	2209	19.37	4-12	5.86
101	A.Shrubsole	E	75	251.2	10	1483	14.68	5-11	5.90
99	S.Ismail	SA	92	321.5	14	1847	18.65	5-30	5.73
98	Nida Dar	P	102	326.1	8	1756	17.91	5-21	5.38
95	Poonam Yadav	I	67	242.0	5	1367	14.38	4- 9	5.64
89	M.Schutt	A	67	226.0	6	1351	15.17	4-18	5.97
89	S.R.Taylor	WI	103	266.5	4	1493	16.77	4-12	5.59
89	Sana Mir	P	105	378.2	9	2085	23.42	4-13	5.51
87	S.F.M.Devine	NZ	91	238.0	6	1488	17.10	4-22	6.25
85	D.Hazell	E	85	317.3	6	1764	20.75	4-12	5.55

BEST FIGURES IN AN INNINGS

6- 0	Anjali Chand	Nep v Mald	Pokhara	2019-20
6-17	A.E.Satterthwaite	NZ v E	Taunton	2007
5- 5	D.J.S.Dottin	WI v B	Providence	2018-19
5- 8	S.Luus	SA v Ire	Chennai	2015-16
5-10	A.Mohammed	WI v SA	Cape Town	2009-10
5-10	M.Strano	A v NZ	Geelong	2016-17
5-11	A.Shrubsole	E v NZ	Wellington	2011-12
5-11	J.Goswami	I v A	Visakhapatnam	2011-12
5-12	A.Mohammed	WI v NZ	Bridgetown	2013-14
5-12	W.Liengprasert	Thai v SL	Kuala Lumpur	2018
5-12	J.L.Jonassen	A v I	Melbourne (JO)	2019-20

HAT-TRICKS

Asmavia Iqbal	Pakistan v England	Loughborough	2012
Ekta Bisht	Sri Lanka v India	Colombo (NCC)	2012-13
M.Kapp	South Africa v Bangladesh	Potchefstroom	2013-14
N.R.Sciver	England v New Zealand	Bridgetown	2013-14
Sana Mir	Pakistan v Sri Lanka	Sharjah	2014-15
A.M.Peterson	New Zealand v Australia	Geelong	2016-17
M.Schutt	Australia v India	Mumbai (BS)	2017-18
Fahima Khatun	Bangladesh v UAE	Utrecht	2018
A.Mohammed	West Indies v South Africa	Tarouba	2018-19
A.Shrubsole	England v South Africa	Gros Islet	2018-19
O.Kamchomphu	Thailand v Ireland	Deventer	2019

WICKET-KEEPING RECORDS – 50 DISMISSALS IN A CAREER

Dis			Matches	Ct	St
88	A.J.Healy	Australia	112	40	48
74	S.J.Taylor	England	90	23	51
72	R.H.Priest	New Zealand	75	41	31
70	M.R.Aguilleira	West Indies	95	36	34
67	T.Bhatia	India	50	23	44
64	T.Chetty	South Africa	76	37	27
50	Batool Fatima	Pakistan	45	11	39

FIVE DISMISSALS IN AN INNINGS

5 (1ct, 4st) Kycia A.Knight	West Indies v Sri Lanka	Colombo (RPS)	2012-13
5 (1ct, 4st) Batool Fatima	Pakistan v Ireland	Dublin	2013
5 (1ct, 4st) Batool Fatima	Pakistan v Ireland	Dublin	2013
5 (3ct, 2st) B.Bezuidenhout	New Zealand v Ireland	Dublin	2018
5 (1ct, 4st) S.J.Bryce	Scotland v Netherlands	Arbroath	2019

FIELDING RECORDS – 35 CATCHES IN A CAREER

Total			Matches	Total			Matches
60	S.W.Bates	New Zealand	119	40	N.R.Sciver	England	75
58	J.L.Gunn	England	104	38	V.Krishnamurthy	India	76
54	L.S.Greenway	England	85	36	M.M.Lanning	Australia	104
43	H.Kaur	India	114	36	E.A.Perry	Australia	120

FOUR CATCHES IN AN INNINGS

4	L.S.Greenway	England v New Zealand	Chelmsford	2010
4	V.Krishnamurthy	India v Australia	Providence	2018-19

APPEARANCE RECORDS – 108 APPEARANCES

120	E.A.Perry	Australia	112	A.J.Healy	Australia
119	S.W.Bates	New Zealand	111	A.Mohammed	West Indies
114	H.Kaur	India	109	D.N.Wyatt	England
113	D.J.S.Dottin	West Indies	108	Bismah Maroof	Pakistan

60 MATCHES AS CAPTAIN

			W	L	T	NR	%age wins
93	C.M.Edwards	England	68	23	1	1	73.91
73	M.R.Aguilleira	West Indies	39	29	3	2	54.92
72	M.M.Lanning	Australia	55	16	1	–	76.38
65	Sana Mir	Pakistan	26	36	2	1	40.62
65	Salma Khatun	Bangladesh	27	38	–	–	41.53
64	S.W.Bates	New Zealand	39	24	1	–	60.93

KIA SUPER LEAGUE 2019

The fourth Kia Super League tournament was held between 6 August and 1 September.

Team	P	W	L	T	NR	Pts	Net RR
1 Western Storm (2)	10	9	1	–	–	39	+1.10
2 Loughborough Lightning (1)	10	7	3	–	–	32	+0.79
3 Southern Vipers (6)	10	4	4	1	1	22	+0.42
4 Yorkshire Diamonds (5)	10	5	5	–	–	20	–0.45
5 Surrey Stars (3)	10	3	6	–	1	16	–0.85
6 Lancashire Thunder (4)	10	–	9	1	–	2	–1.19

4 points for a win, with a bonus point if the winning side has a run rate 1.25 times greater than the opposition. 2 points for no result/tie.

Semi-final: At County Ground, Hove, 1 September. Toss: Loughborough Lightning. **SOUTHERN VIPERS** won by five wickets. Loughborough Lightning 143 (19.5; S.W.Bates 3-22). Southern Vipers 145-5 (19; S.W.Bates 37). Award: S.W.Bates.

FINAL: At County Ground, Hove, 1 September. Toss: Southern Vipers. **WESTERN STORM** won by six wickets. Southern Vipers 172-7 (20; D.N.Wyatt 73). Western Storm 174-4 (19; H.C.Knight 78*). Award: H.C.Knight.

Previous winners:　　2016　　Southern Vipers　　　2017　　Western Storm
　　　　　　　　　　　　2018　　Surrey Stars

TEAM RECORDS – HIGHEST TOTALS

185-4 (20)	Storm v Thunder	Taunton	2018
185-6 (20)	Diamonds v Vipers	York	2019
184-4 (20)	Vipers v Diamonds	York	2019

LOWEST TOTALS

64 (16.3)	Diamonds v Vipers	Southampton	2016
66 (16.4)	Stars v Diamonds	York	2018

LARGEST MARGINS OF VICTORY

95 runs	Diamonds (166-6) v Thunder (71)	Manchester	2016
10 wickets	Diamonds (160-7) v Storm (161-0)	York	2017

BATTING RECORDS – MOST RUNS IN A SEASON

466 (ave 42.36)	D.N.Wyatt	Southern Vipers	2019
421 (ave 60.14)	S.Mandhana	Western Storm	2018
401 (ave 57.28)	J.I.Rodrigues	Yorkshire Diamonds	2019

Score	Balls	HIGHEST SCORES			
119*	72	S.W.Bates	Vipers v Lightning	Derby	2017
112*	58	J.I.Rodrigues	Diamonds v Vipers	York	2019
110	60	D.N.Wyatt	Vipers v Stars	Arundel	2019

HIGHEST STRIKE RATE IN AN INNINGS (Qualification: 30 runs, 250+ strike rate)

R/100B	Score	Balls				
275.0	44	16	R.H.Priest	Storm v Stars	Taunton	2019
273.6	52*	19	S.Mandhana	Storm v Lightning	Taunton	2018
267.8	75	28	L.Lee	Stars v Thunder	Blackpool	2019

BOWLING RECORDS – 16 WICKETS IN A SEASON

Wkts			Year	P	O	M	Runs	Avge	Best	4w	R/Over
19	F.R.Davies	Storm	2019	11	39.0	1	251	13.21	4-18	2	6.43
17	K.L.Gordon	Lightning	2018	11	35.0	–	212	12.47	3-13	–	6.05
16	S.F.M.Devine	Lightning	2018	11	35.5	1	259	16.18	3-15	–	7.22

BEST BOWLING FIGURES IN AN INNINGS

5-23	A.Shrubsole	Storm v Diamonds	Leeds	2016
5-26	R.M.Farrell	Stars v Thunder	Manchester	2017
5-26	K.H.Brunt	Diamonds v Vipers	York	2018

PRINCIPAL WOMEN'S FIXTURES 2020

F	Floodlit match	
100	The Hundred	

LOI	Royal London Limited-overs International
IT20	Vitality Women's IT20

Thu 25 June
IT20[F] Taunton **England v India**

Sat 27 June
IT20[F] Bristol **England v India**

Wed 1 July
LOI Worcester **England v India**

Sat 4 July
LOI Chelmsford **England v India**

Mon 6 July
LOI[F] Canterbury **England v India**

Thu 9 July
LOI[F] Hove **England v India**

Wed 22 July
100 Worcester Phoenix v Originals

Thu 23 July
100 Lord's Spirit v Superchargers

Fri 24 July
100 Sedbergh S Originals v Invincibles
100 Birmingham Phoenix v Brave

Sat 25 July
100 Nottingham Rockets v Fire

Sun 26 July
100 Chelmsford Spirit v Brave
100 S Northumberland Superchargers v Invincibles

Mon 27 July
100 Manchester Originals v Rockets

Tue 28 July
100 Cardiff Fire v Phoenix

Wed 29 July
100 The Oval Invincibles v Spirit

Thu 30 July
100 Bristol Fire v Superchargers
100 Leicester Rockets v Phoenix

Fri 31 July
100 Hove Brave v Invincibles
100 Manchester Originals v Spirit

Sat 1 August
100 Derby Rockets v Superchargers

Sun 2 August
100 Taunton Fire v Brave
100 Beckenham Invincibles v Phoenix

Tue 4 August
100 Southampton Brave v Rockets

Wed 5 August
100 Leeds Superchargers v Originals

Thu 6 August
100 Northampton Spirit v Fire

Fri 7 August
100 Derby Rockets v Invincibles

Sat 8 August
100 Bristol Fire v Originals

Sun 9 August
100 Worcester Phoenix v Spirit
100 York Superchargers v Brave

Tue 11 August
100 Chelmsford Spirit v Rockets
100 York Superchargers v Phoenix

Wed 12 August
100 Hove Brave v Originals
100 Beckenham Invincibles v Fire

Fri 14 August
100 tbc FINALS DAY

Tue 1 September
IT20[F] Hove **England v South Africa**

Fri 4 September
IT20[F] Chelmsford **England v South Africa**

Tue 8 September
LOI[F] Canterbury **England v South Africa**

Fri 11 September
LOI[F] Derby **England v South Africa**

Sun 13 September
LOI Leeds **England v South Africa**

Wed 16 September
LOI[F] Leicester **England v South Africa**

THE HUNDRED FIXTURES 2020

Fri 17 July
The Oval   Invincibles v Welsh Fire

Sat 18 July
Birmingham   Phoenix v London Spirit
Manchester   Originals v Superchargers

Sun 19 July
Nottingham   Trent Rockets v Phoenix
Cardiff   Welsh Fire v Southern Brave

Mon 20 July
Leeds   Superchargers v Invincibles

Tue 21 July
Lord's   London Spirit v Trent Rockets

Wed 22 July
Southampton   Southern Brave v Originals

Thu 23 July
Lord's   London Spirit v Superchargers

Fri 24 July
Birmingham   Phoenix v Southern Brave

Sat 25 July
The Oval   Invincibles v Originals
Nottingham   Trent Rockets v Welsh Fire

Sun 26 July
Southampton   Southern Brave v Invincibles
Leeds   Superchargers v Phoenix

Mon 27 July
Manchester   Originals v Trent Rockets

Tue 28 July
Cardiff   Welsh Fire v Phoenix

Wed 29 July
The Oval   Invincibles v London Spirit

Thu 30 July
Leeds   Superchargers v Southern Brave

Fri 31 July
Manchester   Originals v London Spirit

Sat 1 August
Cardiff   Welsh Fire v Superchargers

Sun 2 August
Nottingham   Trent Rockets v Invincibles

Mon 3 August
Birmingham   Phoenix v Originals

Tue 4 August
Southampton   Southern Brave v Trent Rockets

Wed 5 August
Leeds   Superchargers v Originals

Thu 6 August
Lord's   London Spirit v Invincibles

Fri 7 August
Southampton   Southern Brave v Welsh Fire

Sat 8 August
Birmingham   Phoenix v Trent Rockets

Sun 9 August
Cardiff   Welsh Fire v London Spirit

Mon 10 August
Nottingham   Trent Rockets v Superchargers

Tue 11 August
The Oval   Invincibles v Phoenix

Wed 12 August
Lord's   London Spirit v Southern Brave

Thu 13 August
Manchester   Originals v Welsh Fire

Sat 15 August
                  FINALS DAY

NCCA FIXTURES 2020

Sun 26 April

Peterborough	**TWENTY20 COMPETITION**
Peterborough	Cambridgeshire v Northumberland (1)
New Brighton	Cheshire v Cumberland (1)
Werrington	Cornwall v Dorset (2)
Exeter	Devon v Herefordshire (2)
Welwyn Garden C	Hertfordshire v Bedfordshire (3)
Manor Park	Norfolk v Lincolnshire (3)
High Wycombe	Buckinghamshire v Shropshire (4)
Usk	Wales v Berkshire (4)

Sun 3 May

	TWENTY20 COMPETITION
Carlisle	Cumberland v Staffordshire (1)
S Northumberland	Northumberland v Cheshire (1)
North Perrott	Dorset v Wiltshire (2)
Colwall	Herefordshire v Cornwall (2)
Luton T & I	Bedfordshire v Suffolk (3)
Bourne	Lincolnshire v Hertfordshire (3)
N Maidenhead	Berkshire v Oxfordshire (4)
Wellington	Shropshire v Wales (4)

Sun 17 May

	TWENTY20 COMPETITION
Bowdon	Cheshire v Cambridgeshire (1)
Rolleston	Staffordshire v Northumberland (1)
Wadebridge	Cornwall v Devon (2)
South Wilts	Wiltshire v Herefordshire (2)
Harpenden	Hertfordshire v Norfolk (3)
Ipswich Sch	Suffolk v Lincolnshire (3)
Magdalen C Sch	Oxfordshire v Shropshire (4)
Lisvane	Wales v Buckinghamshire (4)

Mon 18 May

	TWENTY20 COMPETITION
Barrow	Cumberland v Cambridgeshire (1)

Sun 24 May

	TWENTY20 COMPETITION
Sawston	Cambridgeshire v Staffordshire (1)
Almnouth & L	Northumberland v Cumberland (1)
Bovey Tracey	Devon v Wiltshire (2)
Brockhampton	Herefordshire v Dorset (2)
Scunthorpe	Lincolnshire v Bedfordshire (3)
Manor Park	Norfolk v Suffolk (3)
High Wycombe	Buckinghamshire v Oxfordshire (4)
Oswestry	Shropshire v Berkshire (4)

Mon 25 May

	TWENTY20 COMPETITION
Denstone Coll	Staffordshire v Cheshire (1)
North Perrott	Dorset v Devon (2)
Marlborough Coll	Wiltshire v Cornwall (2)
Ampthill	Bedfordshire v Norfolk (3)
Ipswich Sch	Suffolk v Hertfordshire (3)
Wargrave	Berkshire v Buckinghamshire (4)
Banbury (EW)	Oxfordshire v Wales (4)

Sun 7 June

	NCCA TROPHY
Eastnor	Herefordshire v Northumberland (1)
Thame	Oxfordshire v Cumberland (1)
Redruth	Cornwall v Berkshire (2)
Sidmouth	Devon v Bedfordshire (2)
March	Cambridgeshire v Cheshire (3)
Manor Park	Norfolk v Shropshire (3)
Bashley	Dorset v Buckinghamshire (4)
Newbridge	Wales v Staffordshire (4)

Sun 14 June	**NCCA TROPHY**
Bracebridge H	Lincolnshire v Herefordshire (1)
Jesmond	Northumberland v Oxfordshire (1)
Bedford Mod Sch	Bedfordshire v Cornwall (2)
Welwyn Garden C	Hertfordshire v Devon (2)
Wem	Shropshire v Cambridgeshire (3)
Mildenhall	Suffolk v Norfolk (3)
Gerrards Cross	Buckinghamshire v Wales (4)
Warminster	Wiltshire v Dorset (4)
Sun 21 June	**NCCA TROPHY**
Cockermouth	Cumberland v Northumberland (1)
Oxford Downs	Oxfordshire v Lincolnshire (1)
Wargrave	Berkshire v Bedfordshire (2)
Penzance	Cornwall v Hertfordshire (2)
Exning	Cambridgeshire v Suffolk (3)
Nantwich	Cheshire v Shropshire (3)
Himley	Staffordshire v Buckinghamshire (4)
Pembroke Dock	Wales v Wiltshire (4)
Wed 24 June	**TWENTY20 COMPETITION**
	FINALS DAY
Sun 28 June	**NCCA TROPHY**
Brockhampton	Herefordshire v Oxfordshire (1)
Grantham	Lincolnshire v Cumberland (1)
North Devon	Devon v Cornwall (2)
Bishop's Stortford	Hertfordshire v Berkshire (2)
Manor Park	Norfolk v Cambridgeshire (3)
Woolpit	Suffolk v Cheshire (3)
Dorchester	Dorset v Wales (4)
Warminster	Wiltshire v Staffordshire (4)
Sun 5 July	**NCCA TROPHY**
Furness	Cumberland v Herefordshire (1)
S Northumberland	Northumberland v Lincolnshire (1)
Dunstable	Bedfordshire v Hertfordshire (2)
Falkland	Berkshire v Devon (2)
Toft	Cheshire v Norfolk (3)
Whitchurch	Shropshire v Suffolk (3)
High Wycombe	Buckinghamshire v Wiltshire (4)
Checkley	Staffordshire v Dorset (4)
Sun 12 – Tue 14 July	**NCCA CHAMPIONSHIP**
Cleethorpes	Lincolnshire v Norfolk (E1)
Copdock	Suffolk v Cambridgeshire (E1)
Bedford Sch	Bedfordshire v Buckinghamshire (E2)
Tynemouth	Northumberland v Hertfordshire (E2)
Oxton	Cheshire v Dorset (W1)
Corsham	Wiltshire v Berkshire (W1)
Colwall	Herefordshire v Devon (W2)
Abergavenny	Wales v Cornwall (W2)
Wed 15 July	**NATIONAL COUNTY**
Falkland	Berkshire v Middlesex
Truro	Cornwall v Somerset
Thu 16 July	**NATIONAL COUNTY**
Radlett	Hertfordshire v Middlesex
Fri 17 July	**NATIONAL COUNTY**
Bedford Sch	Bedfordshire v Northamptonshire
High Wycombe	Buckinghamshire v Surrey
Saffron Walden	Cambridgeshire v Essex
Chester BH	Cheshire v Warwickshire
Sedbergh Sch	Cumberland v Lancashire
Exmouth	Devon v Somerset

343

North Perrott	Dorset v Hampshire
Eastnor	Herefordshire v Worcestershire
Grantham	Lincolnshire v Durham
Manor Park	Norfolk v Nottinghamshire
Jesmond	Northumberland v Yorkshire
The Parks	Oxfordshire v Sussex
Shifnal	Shropshire v Derbyshire
Knypersley	Staffordshire v Leicestershire
Copdock	Suffolk v Kent
Newport	Wales v Glamorgan
South Wilts	Wiltshire v Gloucestershire

Sun 19 July — **NCCA TROPHY – Quarter-finals**

Match A	Winner Gp 1 v Runner-up Gp 3
Match B	Winner Gp 3 v Runner-up Gp 1
Match C	Winner Gp 2 v Runner-up Gp 4
Match D	Winner Gp 4 v Runner-up Gp 2

Sun 26 – Tue 28 July — **NCCA CHAMPIONSHIP**

Manor Park	Norfolk v Suffolk (E1)
West Brom Dart	Staffordshire v Lincolnshire (E1)
Furness	Cumberland v Northumberland (E2)
Bishop's Stortford	Hertfordshire v Bedfordshire (E2)
Wimborne	Dorset v Wiltshire (W1)
Banbury (White P)	Oxfordshire v Cheshire (W1)
Sandford	Devon v Wales (W2)
Shrewsbury	Shropshire v Herefordshire (W2)

Sun 2 – Tue 4 August — **NCCA CHAMPIONSHIP**

March	Cambridgeshire v Lincolnshire (E1)
Manor Park	Norfolk v Staffordshire (E1)
Flitwick	Bedfordshire v Cumberland (E2)
Tring Park	Buckinghamshire v Hertfordshire (E2)
Finchampstead	Berkshire v Dorset (W1)
South Wilts	Wiltshire v Oxfordshire (W1)
Truro	Cornwall v Devon (W2)
Bangor	Wales v Shropshire (W2)

Sun 9 August — **NCCA TROPHY – Semi-finals**

tbc	Winner Match A v Winner Match B
tbc	Winner Match D v Winner Match C

Sun 16 – Tue 18 August — **NCCA CHAMPIONSHIP**

Sleaford	Lincolnshire v Suffolk (E1)
Longton	Staffordshire v Cambridgeshire (E1)
Barrow	Cumberland v Buckinghamshire (E2)
Jesmond	Northumberland v Bedfordshire (E2)
Alderley Edge	Cheshire v Wiltshire (W1)
Challow & Ch	Oxfordshire v Berkshire (W1)
Eastnor	Herefordshire v Wales (W2)
Bridgnorth	Shropshire v Cornwall (W2)

Sun 23 – Tue 25 August — **NCCA CHAMPIONSHIP**

Wisbech	Cambridgeshire v Norfolk (E1)
Ipswich Sch	Suffolk v Staffordshire (E1)
Chesham	Buckinghamshire v Northumberland (E2)
Hertford	Hertfordshire v Cumberland (E2)
Falkland	Berkshire v Cheshire (W1)
Bournemouth	Dorset v Oxfordshire (W1)
St Austell	Cornwall v Herefordshire (W2)
Sidmouth	Devon v Shropshire (W2)

Wed 2 September — **NCCA TROPHY** FINAL

Sun 6 – Thu 10 September — **NCCA CHAMPIONSHIP** FINAL

SECOND XI CHAMPIONSHIP FIXTURES 2020

FOUR-DAY MATCHES

APRIL

Mon 13	Preston Nom	Sussex v Durham
	Canterbury	Kent v MCC YC
Tue 14	Bristol	Glos v Yorkshire
	Taunton Vale	Somerset v Essex
	Kidderminster	Worcs v Northants
Mon 20	Darlington	Durham v Yorkshire
	Newport	Glamorgan v Somerset
	Rockhampton	Glos v MCC YC
	Manchester	Lancashire v Notts
	Kibworth	Leics v Essex
	Radlett	Middlesex v Surrey
	Hove	Sussex/Kent v Hampshire
	Barnt Green	Warwicks v Worcs
Mon 27	Southampton	Hampshire v Surrey
	Polo Farm Cant	Kent v Middlesex
	H Wycombe	MCC YC v Leics
	Birm EFSG	Warwicks v Notts
Tue 28	Crosby	Lancashire v Derbyshire
	Blackstone	Sussex/Nhants v Essex

MAY

Mon 4	Belper Mead	Derbyshire v Warwicks
	Chester-le-St	Durham v Northants
	Rockhampton	Glos v Essex
	Taunton Vale	Somerset v Middlesex
	New Malden	Surrey v Glamorgan
	Worcester	Worcs v Leics
	Leeds	Yorkshire v Lancashire
Tue 5	Southampton	Hampshire v Kent
Mon 11	Uxbridge	Middlesex v Yorkshire
	Northampton	Northants v Leics
	Notts SC	Notts v Derbyshire
	New Malden	Surrey v MCC YC

JUNE

Mon 8	Billericay	Essex v Glamorgan
	Beckenham	Kent/Sussex v Worcs
	Southgate	Middlesex v Glos
	Desborough	Northants v Lancashire
	Notts SC	Notts v Durham
	Birm EFSG	Warwicks v Yorkshire
Tue 9	Repton S	Derbyshire v Leics
	Finchley	MCC YC v Hampshire
	Taunton Vale	Somerset v Surrey
Mon 22	tbc	Glamorgan v Middlesex
	Southampton	Hampshire v Glos
	Loughboro	Leics v Derbyshire
	Notts SC	Notts v Yorkshire
	New Malden	Surrey v Sussex
	Birm EFSG	Warwicks v Somerset
Mon 29	Richmondshire	Durham v Essex
	Rockhampton	Glos v Sussex
	Polo Farm Cant	Kent/Nhants v Lancashire
	Barnt Green	Worcs v Middlesex
	Leeds Wwood	Yorkshire v Leics
Tue 30	H Wycombe	MCC YC v Glamorgan

JULY

Mon 6	Belper Mead	Derbyshire v Notts
	Cardiff	Glamorgan v Warwicks
	Southport	Lancashire v Durham
	Witham Hall	Leics v Worcs
	Finchley	MCC YC v Essex
Mon 27	Hem H, Stoke	Derbys/Nhants v Essex

AUGUST

Mon 3	Newclose IoW	Hampshire v Lancashire
	Harrogate	Yorkshire v Northants
Mon 10	Neath	Glamorgan v Yorkshire
Mon 17	Derby	Derbyshire v Yorkshire
	Rockhampton	Glos v Surrey
	Kibworth	Leics v Durham
	Radlett	Middlesex v Hampshire
	Horsham	Sussex v Kent
	Stourbridge	Worcs v Glamorgan
Tue 18	Northampton	Northants v Warwicks
Mon 24	S North'land	Durham v Derbyshire
	Coggeshall	Essex v Kent
	Monmouth S	Glamorgan v Northants
	Chester BH	Lancashire v Glos
	Radlett	Middlesex v MCC YC
	Taunton Vale	Somerset v Hampshire
	New Malden	Surrey v Warwicks
	Kidderminster	Worcs v Notts
Mon 31	Rockhampton	Glos v Glamorgan
	Crosby	Lancashire v Leics
	Finchley	MCC YC v Somerset
	Birm EFSG	Warwicks v Durham

SEPTEMBER

Tue 1	Denby	Derbyshire v Middlesex
	Polo Farm Cant	Kent v Notts
	Milton Keynes	Northants v Hampshire
	Blackstone	Sussex v Essex
	Leeds	Yorkshire v Notts
Mon 7	Newport	Glamorgan v Sussex
	Kibworth	Leics v Warwicks
	Taunton Vale	Somerset v Glos
	Kidderminster	Worcs v Lancashire
	York	Yorkshire v Surrey
Tue 8	Billericay	Essex v Hampshire
Mon 14	Billericay	Essex v Middlesex
	Southampton	Hampshire v Glamorgan
	Beckenham	Kent v Somerset
	Notts SC	Notts v Leics
	Scarborough	Yorkshire v Lancashire

SECOND XI TWENTY20 CUP FIXTURES 2020

MAY

Mon 18	Derby	Derbyshire v Notts
	Southend	Essex v Hampshire
	Sudbrook	Glamorgan v MCC YC
	Taunton Vale	Somerset v Surrey
	Doncaster	Yorkshire v Northants
Tue 19	Burnopfield	Durham v Northants
	Bristol	Glos v Kent
	Manchester	Lancashire v Notts
	Uxbridge	Middlesex v Hampshire
	Moseley	Warwicks v Derbyshire
	Stourport	Worcs v Leics
Wed 20	Southend	Essex v Glamorgan
	Rockhampton	Glos v Surrey
	Leicester	Leics v Warwicks
	Finchley	MCC YC v Somerset
	Blackstone	Sussex v Middlesex
	Kidderminster	Worcs v Yorkshire
Thu 21	Southampton	Hampshire v Surrey
	Folkestone	Kent v Glamorgan
	Leicester	Leics v Lancashire
	Finchley	MCC YC v Essex
	Uxbridge	Middlesex v Glos
	Blackstone	Sussex v Somerset
	Birm EFSG	Warwicks v Yorkshire
	Barnt Green	Worcs v Durham
Fri 22	Oundle S	Northants v Lancashire
	New Malden	Surrey v Kent
	Hove	Sussex v Essex
Mon 25	Denby	Derbyshire v Lancashire
	St Fagans	Glamorgan v Hampshire
	Beckenham	Kent v Essex
	Leicester	Leics v Durham
	Uxbridge	Middlesex v MCC YC
	Notts SC	Notts v Yorkshire
	Taunton Vale	Somerset v Glos
	New Malden	Surrey v Sussex
	Birm EFSG	Warwicks v Worcs
Tue 26	Glossop	Derbyshire v Durham
	Cheltenham	Glos v Glamorgan
	Uxbridge	MCC YC v Middlesex
	Taunton Vale	Somerset v Hampshire
	New Malden	Surrey v Essex

	Leeds W'wood	Yorkshire v Lancashire
Wed 27	Jesmond	Durham v Notts
	Chelmsford	Essex v Middlesex
	Blackpool	Lancashire v Warwicks
	Northampton	Northants v Leics
	Hove	Sussex v MCC YC
	Barnsley	Yorkshire v Derbyshire
Thu 28	Sunderland	Durham v Warwicks
	Southampton	Hampshire v Kent
	Finchley	MCC YC v Glos
	Uxbridge	Middlesex v Surrey
	Taunton Vale	Somerset v Glamorgan
	Stourport	Worcs v Northants
Fri 29	tbc	Northants v Derbyshire
	Worksop C	Notts v Leics
	Horsham	Sussex v Kent
JUNE		
Mon 1	Cardiff	Glamorgan v Surrey
	Rockhampton	Glos v Sussex
	Liverpool	Lancashire v Durham
	Leicester	Leics v Derbyshire
	Uxbridge	Middlesex v Somerset
	Welbeck	Notts v Northants
Tue 2	Billericay	Essex v Somerset
	Monmouth S	Glamorgan v Sussex
	Southampton	Hampshire v MCC YC
	Folkestone	Kent v Middlesex
	Liverpool	Lancashire v Worcs
	Moseley	Warwicks v Notts
	Middlesbrough	Yorkshire v Leics
Wed 3	Derby	Derbyshire v Worcs
	Chelmsford	Essex v Glos
	Beckenham	Kent v Somerset
	New Malden	Surrey v MCC YC
Thu 4	S North'land	Durham v Yorkshire
	Newport	Glamorgan v Middlesex
	Southampton	Hampshire v Glos
	Finchley	MCC YC v Kent
	Milton Keynes	Northants v Warwicks
	Trent Coll	Notts v Worcs
Fri 5	Southampton	Hampshire v Sussex
Thu 18	Arundel	Semi-finals and FINAL

PRINCIPAL FIXTURES 2020

CC1	County Championship Division 1
CC2	County Championship Division 2
F	Floodlit
FCF	First-Class Friendly
LOI	Royal London Limited-Overs International
50L	Royal London One-Day Cup

T20	Vitality Blast
IT20	Vitality Twenty20 International
TM	Test Match
MCCU	MCC University
Uni	University match
Var	Varsity match

Thu 2 – Sat 4 April

Uni	Chester-le-St	Durham v Durham MCCU
Uni	Bristol	Glos v Cardiff MCCU
Uni	Canterbury	Kent v Oxford MCCU
Uni	Leicester	Leics v Loughboro MCCU
Uni	Northwood	Middlesex v Cambridge MCCU
Uni	Leeds	Yorkshire v Leeds/Brad MCCU

Tue 7 – Thu 9 April

Uni	Cambridge	Cambridge MCCU v Notts
Uni	Manchester	Lancashire v Durham MCCU
Uni	Leeds W'Wood	Leeds/Brad MCCU v Warwicks
Uni	Loughborough	Loughboro MCCU v Worcs
Uni	Taunton	Somerset v Cardiff MCCU
Uni	Hove	Sussex v Oxford MCCU

Sun 12 – Wed 15 April

CC1	Manchester	Lancashire v Kent
CC1	Taunton	Somerset v Warwicks
CC1	Leeds	Yorkshire v Glos
CC2	Lord's	Middlesex v Worcs
CC2	Nottingham	Notts v Leics
CC2	Hove	Sussex v Durham

Mon 13 – Wed 15 April

Uni	Cambridge	Cambridge MCCU v Essex
Uni	Cardiff	Glamorgan v Cardiff MCCU
Uni	Southampton	Hampshire v Loughboro MCCU
Uni	Northampton	Northants v Leeds/Brad MCCU
Uni	Oxford	Oxford MCCU v Surrey

Tue 14 – Thu 16 April

Uni	Derby	Derbyshire v Durham MCCU

Sun 19 – Wed 22 April

CC1	Chelmsford	Essex v Yorkshire
CC1	Bristol	Glos v Lancashire
CC1	Southampton	Hampshire v Kent
CC1	The Oval	Surrey v Somerset
CC1	Birmingham	Warwicks v Northants
CC2	Derby	Derbyshire v Leics
CC2	Chester-le-St	Durham v Notts
CC2	Cardiff	Glamorgan v Middlesex

Sat 25 – Tue 28 April

CC1	Canterbury	Kent v Glos
CC1	Northampton	Northants v Essex

CC1	Taunton	Somerset v Hampshire
CC1	Birmingham	Warwicks v Lancashire
CC1	Leeds	Yorkshire v Surrey
CC2	Leicester	Leics v Glamorgan
CC2	Lord's	Middlesex v Derbyshire
CC2	Worcester	Worcs v Sussex

Fri 1 – Mon 4 May

CC1	Bristol	Glos v Somerset
CC1	Southampton	Hampshire v Yorkshire
CC1	Manchester	Lancashire v Essex
CC1	Northampton	Northants v Kent
CC1	The Oval	Surrey v Warwicks
CC2	Chester-le-St	Durham v Middlesex
CC2	Cardiff	Glamorgan v Worcs
CC2	Nottingham	Notts v Derbyshire
CC2	Hove	Sussex v Leics

Fri 8 – Mon 11 May

CC1	Chelmsford	Essex v Glos
CC1	Beckenham	Kent v Surrey
CC1	Taunton	Somerset v Northants
CC1	Birmingham	Warwicks v Hampshire
CC2	Derby	Derbyshire v Durham
CC2	Leicester	Leics v Worcs
CC2	Lord's	Middlesex v Notts
CC2	Hove	Sussex v Glamorgan

Fri 15 – Mon 18 May

CC1	Chelmsford	Essex v Hampshire
CC1	Manchester	Lancashire v Somerset
CC1	Guildford	Surrey v Northants
CC1	Leeds	Yorkshire v Kent
CC2	Cardiff	Glamorgan v Derbyshire
CC2	Leicester	Leics v Durham
CC2	Nottingham	Notts v Sussex
CC2	Worcester	Worcs v Middlesex

Fri 22 – Mon 25 May

CC1	Bristol	Glos v Surrey
CC1	Southampton	Hampshire v Lancashire
CC1	Canterbury	Kent v Essex
CC1	Northampton	Northants v Yorkshire
CC1	Birmingham	Warwicks v Somerset
CC2	Derby	Derbyshire v Sussex
CC2	Chester-le-St	Durham v Glamorgan

CC2	Lord's	Middlesex v Leics
CC2	Worcester	Worcs v Notts
FCF	Taunton	Eng Lions v W Indians

Thu 28 – Sun 31 May
| FCF | Worcester | Worcs v W Indians |

Thu 28 May
| T20^F | The Oval | Surrey v Middlesex |
| T20^F | Hove | Sussex v Kent |

Fri 29 May
T20^F	Derby	Derbyshire v Leics
T20^F	Chelmsford	Essex v Glamorgan
T20^F	Southampton	Hampshire v Sussex
T20^F	Canterbury	Kent v Surrey
T20	Liverpool	Lancashire v Northants
T20^F	Nottingham	Notts v Warwicks
T20^F	Taunton	Somerset v Glos
T20^F	Leeds	Yorkshire v Durham

Sat 30 May
| T20 | Leicester | Leics v Northants |

Sun 31 May
T20	Derby	Derbyshire v Lancashire
T20	Chelmsford	Essex v Somerset
T20	Cardiff	Glamorgan v Surrey
T20	Canterbury	Kent v Hampshire
T20	Lord's	Middlesex v Glos
T20	Nottingham	Notts v Yorkshire
T20	Birmingham	Warwicks v Durham

Tue 2 June
| T20 | Worcester | Worcs v Northants |

Wed 3 June
T20^F	Chester-le-St	Durham v Leics
T20^F	Bristol	Glos v Glamorgan
T20^F	Hove	Sussex v Somerset
T20^F	Birmingham	Warwicks v Yorkshire

Thu 4 – Mon 8 June
| TM1 | The Oval | ENGLAND v W INDIES |

Thu 4 June
T20^F	Lord's	Middlesex v Hampshire
T20^F	Nottingham	Notts v Worcs
T20^F	Leeds	Yorkshire v Lancashire

Fri 5 June
T20^F	Derby	Derbyshire v Notts
T20^F	Chelmsford	Essex v Kent
T20^F	Leicester	Leics v Worcs
T20^F	Northampton	Northants v Durham
T20^F	Taunton	Somerset v Surrey
T20^F	Hove	Sussex v Glamorgan
T20^F	Birmingham	Warwicks v Lancashire

Sat 6 June
| T20 | Canterbury | Kent v Glos |

Sun 7 June
T20	Southampton	Hampshire v Glos
T20	Manchester	Lancashire v Durham
T20	Leicester	Leics v Warwicks
T20	Richmond	Middlesex v Glamorgan
T20	Northampton	Northants v Derbyshire
T20	Taunton	Somerset v Essex
T20	Worcester	Worcs v Yorkshire
Var	Lord's	Cambridge U v Oxford U

Wed 10 June
T20^F	Chester-le-St	Durham v Notts
T20^F	Cardiff	Glamorgan v Kent
T20^F	Bristol	Glos v Surrey
T20^F	Southampton	Hampshire v Essex
T20^F	Manchester	Lancashire v Leics
T20^F	Leeds	Yorkshire v Derbyshire

Thu 11 June
| T20^F | Lord's | Middlesex v Sussex |
| T20^F | Northampton | Northants v Worcs |

Fri 12 – Tue 16 June
| TM2 | Birmingham | ENGLAND v W INDIES |

Fri 12 June
T20^F	Chester-le-St	Durham v Warwicks
T20^F	Cardiff	Glamorgan v Somerset
T20^F	Bristol	Glos v Middlesex
T20^F	Manchester	Lancashire v Derbyshire
T20^F	The Oval	Surrey v Essex
T20^F	Hove	Sussex v Hampshire
T20	Worcester	Worcs v Notts
T20^F	Leeds	Yorkshire v Northants

Sat 13 June
| T20^F | Nottingham | Notts v Leics |

Sun 14 – Wed 17 June
CC1	Chelmsford	Essex v Northants
CC1	Southampton	Hampshire v Warwicks
CC1	Taunton	Somerset v Glos
CC1	The Oval	Surrey v Kent
CC1	Scarborough	Yorkshire v Lancashire
CC2	Chesterfield	Derbyshire v Worcs
CC2	Chester-le-St	Durham v Leics
CC2	Hove	Sussex v Middlesex

Mon 15 – Thu 18 June
| CC2 | Nottingham | Notts v Glamorgan |

Thu 18 June
T20^F	Southampton	Hampshire v Somerset
T20^F	Lord's	Middlesex v Kent
T20^F	Hove	Sussex v Surrey

Fri 19 – Sun 21 June

FCF	Northampton	Northants v W Indians

Fri 19 June

T20^F	Chester-le-St	Durham v Yorkshire
T20^F	Chelmsford	Essex v Middlesex
T20 ^{F}	Cardiff	Glamorgan v Glos
T20^F	Canterbury	Kent v Sussex
T20^F	Leicester	Leics v Notts
T20^F	The Oval	Surrey v Somerset
T20	Worcester	Worcs v Warwicks

Sat 20 June

T20	Chesterfield	Derbyshire v Yorkshire
T20	Bristol	Glos v Hampshire

Sun 21 June

T20	Chester-le-St	Durham v Derbyshire
T20	Southampton	Hampshire v Glamorgan
T20	Canterbury	Kent v Essex
T20	Manchester	Lancashire v Notts
T20	Taunton	Somerset v Middlesex
T20	Worcester	Worcs v Leics

Tue 23 June

T20	Taunton	Somerset v Hampshire
T20^F	Birmingham	Warwicks v Northants

Wed 24 June

T20^F	Chelmsford	Essex v Sussex
T20^F	Northampton	Northants v Lancashire
T20^F	Nottingham	Notts v Durham

Thu 25 – Mon 29 June

TM3	Lord's	ENGLAND v W INDIES

Thu 25 June

T20^F	Derby	Derbyshire v Worcs
T20^F	Leicester	Leics v Yorkshire
T20^F	The Oval	Surrey v Glamorgan
T20^F	Hove	Sussex v Glos

Fri 26 June

T20^F	Chester-le-St	Durham v Lancashire
T20^F	Chelmsford	Essex v Glos
T20^F	Cardiff	Glamorgan v Middlesex
T20^F	Southampton	Hampshire v Surrey
T20^F	Northampton	Northants v Notts
T20^F	Taunton	Somerset v Kent
T20^F	Birmingham	Warwicks v Derbyshire
T20^F	Leeds	Yorkshire v Worcs

Sun 28 June – Wed 1 July

CC1	Canterbury	Kent v Somerset
CC1	Manchester	Lancashire v Warwicks
CC1	Northampton	Northants v Surrey
CC1	Leeds	Yorkshire v Essex
CC2	Swansea	Glamorgan v Durham
CC2	Leicester	Leics v Middlesex

CC2	Nottingham	Notts v Worcs
CC2	Arundel	Sussex v Derbyshire

Mon 29 June – Thu 2 July

CC1	Cheltenham	Glos v Hampshire

Thu 2 July

T20^F	Manchester	Lancashire v Worcs
T20^F	Lord's	Middlesex v Surrey
T20^F	Leeds	Yorkshire v Warwicks

Fri 3 July

IT20^F	Chester-le-St	England v Australia
T20^F	Derby	Derbyshire v Warwicks
T20^F	Cardiff	Glamorgan v Essex
T20	Cheltenham	Glos v Sussex
T20^F	Canterbury	Kent v Somerset
T20^F	Northampton	Northants v Leics
T20^F	Nottingham	Notts v Lancashire
T20^F	The Oval	Surrey v Hampshire
T20	Worcester	Worcs v Durham

Sat 4 July

T20	Leicester	Leics v Derbyshire

Sun 5 – Wed 8 July

CC1	Chelmsford	Essex v Somerset
CC1	Cheltenham	Glos v Yorkshire
CC1	Northampton	Northants v Lancashire
CC1	The Oval	Surrey v Hampshire
CC1	Birmingham	Warwicks v Kent
CC2	Derby	Derbyshire v Notts
CC2	Leicester	Leics v Sussex
CC2	Northwood	Middlesex v Glamorgan
CC2	Worcester	Worcs v Durham

Sun 5 July

IT20	Manchester	England v Australia

Mon 6 – Thu 9 July

Var	Oxford	Oxford U v Cambridge U

Tue 7 July

IT20^F	Leeds	England v Australia

Thu 9 July

T20	Cheltenham	Glos v Kent
T20	Northwood	Middlesex v Essex
T20^F	Northampton	Northants v Warwicks
T20^F	The Oval	Surrey v Sussex

Fri 10 July

T20^F	Southampton	Hampshire v Middlesex
T20^F	Manchester	Lancashire v Yorkshire
T20^F	Leicester	Leics v Durham
T20^F	Nottingham	Notts v Derbyshire
T20^F	Taunton	Somerset v Glamorgan
T20^F	The Oval	Surrey v Kent

T20[F]	Hove	Sussex v Essex
T20[F]	Birmingham	Warwicks v Worcs

Sat 11 July

LOI[F]	Lord's	**England v Australia**
T20	Derby	Derbyshire v Northants

Sun 12 July

T20	Chester-le-St	Durham v Northants
T20	Chelmsford	Essex v Hampshire
T20	Cardiff	Glamorgan v Sussex
T20	Bristol	Glos v Somerset
T20	Canterbury	Kent v Middlesex
T20	Birmingham	Warwicks v Notts
T20	Worcester	Worcs v Lancashire
T20	Leeds	Yorkshire v Leics

Tue 14 July

LOI[F]	Southampton	**England v Australia**

Thu 16 July

LOI[F]	Bristol	**England v Australia**

Sun 19 July

50L	Chelmsford	Essex v Kent
50L	Southampton	Hampshire v Worcs
50L	Sedbergh	Lancashire v Middlesex
50L	The Oval	Surrey v Northants
50L	Hove	Sussex v Durham
50L	Scarborough	Yorkshire v Notts

Mon 20 July

50L	Birmingham	Warwicks v Somerset

Tue 21 July

50L	Scarborough	Durham v Glos

Wed 22 July

50L	Derby	Derbyshire v Glamorgan
50L[F]	Chelmsford	Essex v Worcs
50L	tbc	Leics v Surrey
50L	Ladywood	Warwicks v Northants

Thu 23 – Sun 26 July

FCF	Northampton	F-C Cos v Pakistanis

Fri 24 July

50L	Newcastle	Durham v Lancashire
50L	Cardiff	Glamorgan v Surrey
50L	Bristol	Glos v Essex
50L	Radlett	Middlesex v Hampshire
50L	Grantham	Notts v Derbyshire
50L	Eastbourne	Sussex v Kent
50L	Scarborough	Yorkshire v Warwicks

Sun 26 July

50L	Chesterfield	Derbyshire v Yorkshire
50L	Bristol	Glos v Lancashire
50L	Tunbridge W	Kent v Hampshire

50L	tbc	Leics v Glamorgan
50L	Radlett	Middlesex v Durham
50L	Grantham	Notts v Northants
50L	Guildford	Surrey v Somerset
50L	Worcester	Worcs v Sussex

Tue 28 July

50L	Northampton	Northants v Derbyshire
50L	Hove	Sussex v Middlesex
50L	Ladywood	Warwicks v Leics

Wed 29 July

50L	Southampton	Hampshire v Essex
50L	Tunbridge W	Kent v Glos
50L	Blackpool	Lancashire v Worcs
50L	Taunton	Somerset v Glamorgan

Thu 30 July – Mon 3 August

TM1	Lord's	**ENGLAND v PAKISTAN**

Fri 31 July

50L	Newport	Glamorgan v Yorkshire
50L	Southampton	Hampshire v Sussex
50L	Tunbridge W	Kent v Durham
50L	Northampton	Northants v Leics
50L[F]	Taunton	Somerset v Derbyshire
50L	Birmingham	Warwicks v Notts
50L	Worcester	Worcs v Middlesex

Sun 2 August

50L	Chelmsford	Essex v Middlesex
50L	Newport	Glamorgan v Notts
50L	Bristol	Glos v Hampshire
50L	Manchester	Lancashire v Sussex
50L	Leicester	Leics v Yorkshire
50L	Northampton	Northants v Somerset
50L	The Oval	Surrey v Warwicks
50L	Worcester	Worcs v Kent

Tue 4 August

50L	Derby	Derbyshire v Warwicks
50L	Darlington	Durham v Hampshire
50L	Bristol	Glos v Worcs
50L	Liverpool	Lancashire v Essex
50L[F]	Taunton	Somerset v Leics
50L	The Oval	Surrey v Notts
50L	York	Yorkshire v Northants

Thu 6 August

50L	Cardiff	Glamorgan v Warwicks
50L	Canterbury	Kent v Lancashire
50L	Worcester	Worcs v Durham
50L	York	Yorkshire v Surrey

Fri 7 – Tue 11 August

TM2	Manchester	**ENGLAND v PAKISTAN**

Fri 7 August

50L	Chelmsford	Essex v Sussex
50L	Leicester	Leics v Derbyshire
50L	Radlett	Middlesex v Glos
50L	Nottingham	Notts v Somerset

Sun 9 August

50L	Derby	Derbyshire v Surrey
50L	Chester-le-St	Durham v Essex
50L	Newclose IoW	Hampshire v Lancashire
50L	Radlett	Middlesex v Kent
50L	Northampton	Northants v Glamorgan
50L	Mansfield	Notts v Leics
50L	Taunton	Somerset v Yorkshire
50L	Horsham	Sussex v Glos

Thu 13 August

50L^F	tbc	Quarter-finals 1 and 2

Sun 16 August

50L	tbc	Semi-finals 1 and 2

Tue 18 August

T20^F	tbc	Quarter-final 1

Wed 19 August

T20^F	tbc	Quarter-final 2

Thu 20 – Mon 24 August

TM3	Nottingham	ENGLAND v PAKISTAN

Thu 20 August

T20^F	tbc	Quarter-final 3

Fri 21 August

T20^F	tbc	Quarter-final 4

Sun 23 – Wed 26 August

CC1	Southampton	Hampshire v Glos
CC1	Canterbury	Kent v Northants
CC1	Manchester	Lancashire v Surrey
CC1	Taunton	Somerset v Essex
CC1	Scarborough	Yorkshire v Warwicks
CC2	Chester-le-St	Durham v Derbyshire
CC2	Colwyn Bay	Glamorgan v Notts
CC2	Hove	Sussex v Worcs

Wed 26 August
F

	Leicester	Leics v Pakistanis

Sat 29 August – Tue 1 September

CC1	Chelmsford	Essex v Lancashire
CC1	Canterbury	Kent v Hampshire
CC1	Taunton	Somerset v Yorkshire
CC1	Birmingham	Warwicks v Surrey
CC2	Derby	Derbyshire v Glamorgan
CC2	Chester-le-St	Durham v Sussex
CC2	Nottingham	Notts v Middlesex

CC2	Worcester	Worcs v Leics

Sat 29 August

IT20^F	Leeds	England v Pakistan

Sun 30 August – Wed 2 September

CC1	Northampton	Northants v Glos

Mon 31 August

IT20	Cardiff	England v Pakistan

Wed 2 September

IT20^F	Southampton	England v Pakistan

Sat 5 September

T20^F	Birmingham	Semi-finals and FINAL

Tue 8 – Fri 11 September

CC1	Bristol	Glos v Warwicks
CC1	Southampton	Hampshire v Northants
CC1	Manchester	Lancashire v Yorkshire
CC1	The Oval	Surrey v Essex
CC2	Cardiff	Glamorgan v Sussex
CC2	Leicester	Leics v Notts
CC2	Lord's	Middlesex v Durham
CC2	Worcester	Worcs v Derbyshire

Thu 10 September

LOI^F	Nottingham	England v Ireland

Sat 12 September

LOI^F	Birmingham	England v Ireland

Mon 14 – Thu 17 September

CC1	Chelmsford	Essex v Kent
CC1	Manchester	Lancashire v Glos
CC1	Northampton	Northants v Warwicks
CC1	Taunton	Somerset v Surrey
CC1	Leeds	Yorkshire v Hampshire
CC2	Derby	Derbyshire v Middlesex
CC2	Chester-le-St	Durham v Worcs
CC2	Cardiff	Glamorgan v Leics
CC2	Hove	Sussex v Notts

Tue 15 September

LOI^F	The Oval	England v Ireland

Sat 19 September

50L^F	Nottingham	FINAL

Tue 22 – Fri 25 September

CC1	Bristol	Glos v Northants
CC1	Southampton	Hampshire v Somerset
CC1	Canterbury	Kent v Lancashire
CC1	The Oval	Surrey v Yorkshire
CC1	Birmingham	Warwicks v Essex
CC2	Leicester	Leics v Derbyshire
CC2	Lord's	Middlesex v Sussex
CC2	Nottingham	Notts v Durham
CC2	Worcester	Worcs v Glamorgan

First published in 2020

by HEADLINE PUBLISHING GROUP

Front cover photograph
Jofra Archer (Sussex and England)

Back cover photograph
Eoin Morgan (Middlesex and England)

1

Cataloguing in Publication Data is available from the British Library

ISBN: 978 1 4722 6756 6

Typeset in Times by
Letterpart Limited, Caterham on the Hill, Surrey

Printed and bound in Great Britain by
Clays Ltd, Elcograf S.p.A.

Headline's policy is to use papers that are natural, renewable and
recyclable products and made from wood grown in sustainable forests.
The logging and manufacturing processes are expected to conform
to the environmental regulations of the country of origin.

HEADLINE PUBLISHING GROUP

An Hachette UK Company
Carmelite House
50 Victoria Embankment
London EC4Y 0DZ

www.headline.co.uk
www.hachette.co.uk